KB054950

걸프 사태

전망 및 분석, 안보협력 문제, 언론 자료 2

걸프 사태

전망 및 분석, 안보협력 문제, 언론 자료 2

한국학술정보

| 머리말

걸프 전쟁은 미국의 주도하에 34개국 연합군 병력이 수행한 전쟁으로, 1990년 8월 이라크의 쿠웨이트 침공 및 합병에 반대하며 발발했다. 미국은 초기부터 파병 외교에 나섰고, 1990년 9월 서울 등에 고위 관리를 파견하며 한국의 동참을 요청했다. 88올림픽 이후 동구권 국교 수립과 유엔 가입 추진 등 적극적인 외교 활동을 펼치는 당시 한국에 있어 이는 미국과 국제 사회의 지지를 얻기 위해서라도 피할 수 없는 일이었다. 결국 정부는 91년 1월부터 약 3개월에 걸쳐 국군의료지원단과 공군수송단을 사우디아라비아 및 아랍 에미리트 연합 등에 파병하였고, 군 · 민간 의료 활동, 병력 수송 임무를 수행했다. 동시에 당시 걸프 지역 8개국에 살던 5천여 명의 교민에게 방독면 등 물자를 제공하고, 특별기 파견 등으로 비상시 대피할 수 있도록 지원했다. 비록 전쟁 부담금과 유가 상승 등 어려움도 있었지만, 걸프전 파병과 군사 외교를 통해 한국은 유엔 가입에 박차를 가할 수 있었고 미국 등 선진 우방국, 아랍권 국가 등과 밀접한 외교 관계를 유지하며 여러 국익을 창출할 수 있었다.

본 총서는 외교부에서 작성하여 30여 년간 유지한 걸프 사태 관련 자료를 담고 있다. 미국을 비롯한 여러 국가와의 군사 외교 과정, 일일 보고 자료와 기타 정부의 대응 및 조치, 재외동포 철수와 보호, 의료지원단과 수송단 파견 및 지원 과정, 유엔을 포함해 세계 각국에서 수집한 관련 동향 자료, 주변국 지원과 전후복구사업 참여 등 총 48권으로 구성되었다. 전체 분량은 약 2만 4천여 쪽에 이른다.

2024년 3월

한국학술정보(주)

| 일러두기

· 본 총서에 실린 자료는 2022년 4월과 2023년 4월에 각각 공개한 외교문서 4,827권, 76만 여 쪽 가운데 일부를 발췌한 것이다.

· 각 권의 제목과 순서는 공개된 원본을 최대한 반영하였으나, 주제에 따라 일부는 적절히 변경하였다.

· 원본 자료는 A4 판형에 맞게 축소하거나 원본 비율을 유지한 채 A4 페이지 안에 삽입하였다. 또한 현재 시점에선 공개되지 않아 '공란'이란 표기만 있는 페이지 역시 그대로 실었다.

· 외교부가 공개한 문서 각 권의 첫 페이지에는 '정리 보존 문서 목록'이란 이름으로 기록물 종류, 일자, 명칭, 간단한 내용 등의 정보가 수록되어 있으며, 이를 기준으로 0001번부터 번호가 매겨져 있다. 이는 삭제하지 않고 총서에 그대로 수록하였다.

· 보고서 내용에 관한 더 자세한 정보가 필요하다면, 외교부가 온라인상에 제공하는 『대한민국 외교사료요약집』 1991년과 1992년 자료를 참조할 수 있다.

차례

정 리 보 존 문 서 목 록					
기록물종류	일반공문서철	등록번호	2020120217	등록일자	2020-12-28
분류번호	772	국가코드	XF	보존기간	영구
명 칭	걸프사태, 1990-91. 전12권				
생 산 과	북미1과/중동1과	생산년도	1990~1991	담당그룹	
권 차 명	V.10 걸프지역 안보협력체제 문제 II, 1991.6-11월				
내용목차	* 6.17 다마스커스 선언 실무회의 개최(Doha, 카타르) 7.8-9 유엔 안보리 상임이사국(5개) 중동 군축회담 개최 (Paris) - 중동의 비 대량 파괴무기 지대화 합의 9.19 미국.쿠웨이트 방위조약 체결				

0001

관리번호	91/1108

원 본

외 무 부

종 별 :

번 호 : SBW-1059 일 시 : 91 0602 1400

수 신 : 장 관(중일,정일,기정,국방부)

발 신 : 주 사우디 대사

제 목 : 걸프지역안보협력 체제(자응 18호)

1. 주재국 SULTAN 국방장관은 5.29 기자회견에서 이집트군의 걸프지역 철수등에 대해 아래와 같이 언급하였음

가. 이집트와 GCC 회원국사이에 이견은 없음

나. 걸프사태시 걸프지역에 군대를 파견한 국가는 소기의 임무가 끝났으므로 자국군대의 철수를 결정하는것임

다. 외국군대의 걸프지역 주둔은 해당국의 요청에 근거를 두게 될것이며, 지난 3월 시리아, 이집트 및 GCC 회원국 사이에 이루어진 다마스커스 선언은 GCC각국에 대해 아랍 및 이스람국가 특히 쿠웨이트 해방에 참여한 국가로부터 군대 파견을 요청할 권리를 부여했음

2. 주재국은 현재 외국군대의 주재국내 주둔을 다음과 같은 이유로 희망하지 않고 있는것으로 관측되고있음

가. 외국군대의 주재국 주둔에 따른 경비부담으로 인한 재정압박 예상

나. 중동지역의 군사강대국가인 이라크는 걸프전 패배로 세력이 약화되고, 이란과는 국교를 재개하는등 주변환경의 변화로 앞으로 몇년간은 안보위협이 없을것으로 전망하고, 동전망하에서 앞으로 수년간 국방력 강화를 기해 자국안보를이룩한다는 목표

다. 외국군 특히 비아랍권 국가의 군대가 주재국에 주둔하는 경우 국내외 회교정통 주의자로 부터의 반발예상

3. 다마스커스 선언중 이집트 및 시리아군의 걸프지역 주둔관련 부분은 다음과 같음

THEY CONSIDER THE PRESENCE OF THE EGHYPTIAN AND SYRIAN FORCES IN THE TERRITORY OF THE KINGDOM OF SAUDI ARABIA AND OTHER ARAB STATES IN THE GULF

중아국	장관	차관	1차보	2차보	외연원	외정실	청와대	안기부
국방부								

PAGE 1

91.06.02 22:01 0002

외신 2과 통제관 BS

REGION TO BE IN RESPONSE TO THE DESIRE OF THESE STATES GOVERNMENTS AND TO BEWITHE THE OBJECTIVE OF DEFNDING THEIR TERRITORIES AND AS CONSTITUTING A NUCLEUS FOR AN ARAB PEACE FORCE TO BE PREPARED TO GUARANTEE THE SECURITY AND SAFETY OF THE ARAB STATES IN THE GULF REGION, AND ANEXAMPLE THAT WOULD GUARANTEE THE EFFECTIVENESS OF THE COMPRENENSIVE ARABDEFENSE ORDER. 끝

(대사주병국-국장)

예고:91.12.31 까지

주 사우디 아라비아 대사관

주사우디(정)20231- 266 　　　　　　1991. 6. 2

수 신 : 장 관

참 조 : 중동아프리카국장

제 목 : 자료 송부

연 : SBW-1044

연호 다마스커스 선언 전문(영문)을 별첨 송부합니다.

첨 부 : 동전문 1부. 끝.

주 사우디 아라비아 대 사

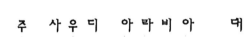

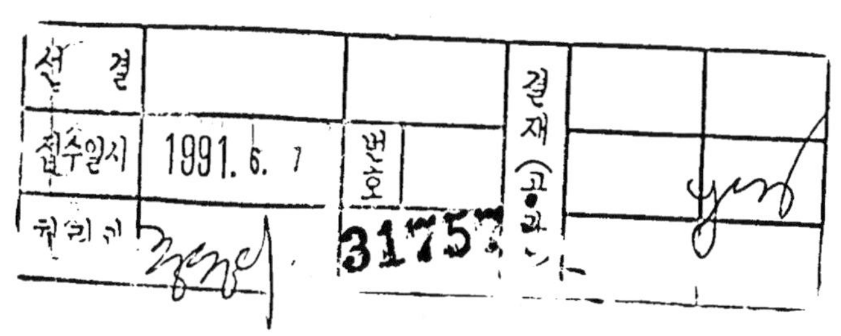

선결			결재 (공람)		
접수일시	1991. 6. 7	번호			
처리과		31757			

0004

COUNTRY: INTER-ARAB AFFAIRS
SUBJ: TAKE 1 OF 3--'TEXT' OF DAMASCUS DECLARATION

REF: NC0603112391 DAMASCUS DOMESTIC ARABIC 061015--RADIO REPORTS 'DAMASCUS DECLARATION'; CLOSED SESSION HELD

SOURCE: DAMASCUS DOMESTIC SERVICE IN ARABIC 1231 GMT 6 MAR 91
TEXT:

(("TEXT" OF "DAMASCUS DECLARATION" SIGNED BY THE FOREIGN MINISTERS OF THE GCC, SYRIA, AND EGYPT IN DAMASCUS ON 6 MARCH--READ BY GCC SECRETARY GENERAL 'ABDALLAH YA'QUB BISHARAH--RECORDED))

((TEXT)) IN THE NAME OF GOD THE COMPASSIONATE, THE MERCIFUL: THE DAMASCUS DECLARATION FOR COORDINATION AND COOPERATION AMONG THE ARAB STATES:

THE GULF COOPERATION COUNCIL ((GCC)) ARAB MEMBER STATES, THE ARAB REPUBLIC OF EGYPT, AND THE SYRIAN ARAB REPUBLIC WHICH PARTICIPATED IN THE MEETINGS IN DAMASCUS ON 19 AND 20 SHA'BAN 1411 HEGIRA, CORRESPONDING TO 5 AND 6 MARCH 1991, PROCEEDING FROM THE FEELINGS OF FRATERNITY AND SOLIDARITY LINKING THEM, WHICH ARE THE PRODUCT OF A GENUINE HERITAGE OF DEDICATION, COHESIVENESS, COMMON STRUGGLE, AND A DEEP AWARENESS OF THE UNITY OF HOPES AND CHALLENGES, THE IDENTITY OF AIMS, AND THE UNITY OF DESTINY;

IN ORDER TO FURTHER THEIR CAPABILITIES FOR ASSUMING THEIR PAN-ARAB RESPONSIBLITIES IN UPGRADING THE STANDING OF THE ARAB NATION, SERVING ITS CAUSES, SAFEGUARDING ITS SECURITY, AND ACHIEVING ITS COMMON INTERESTS;

WITHIN A FRAMEWORK OF A STRICT ADHERENCE TO THE OBJECTIVES AND PRINCIPLES ESTABLISHED BY THE CHARTERS AND RESOLUTIONS OF THE ARAB LEAGUE, THE ISLAMIC CONFERENCE ORGANIZATION, AND THE UN; OUT OF AWARENESS OF THE DEEP CHANGES TAKING PLACE IN THE INTERNATIONAL ARENA AND THE SERIOUS CHALLENGES THEY PLACE BEFORE THE ARAB NATION AND BECAUSE THE CONFRONTATION OF THESE CHALLENGES REQUIRES THE MAXIMUM DEGREE OF COORDINATION AND COOPERATION AMONG THE ARAB STATES;

WHILE THEY ONCE AGAIN REITERATE THEIR POSITION IN REJECTING AND REFUSING TO SIDE WITH THE POLICY OF AGGRESSION, AS WAS THE CASE DURING THE AGGRESSION BY THE IRAQI REGIME'S TROOPS AND THEIR OCCUPATION OF THE STATE OF KUWAIT, WITH THIS OCCUPATION CONSTITUTING A FLAGRANT VIOLATION OF ALL THE ARAB, ISLAMIC, AND INTERNATIONAL NORMS AND RULES AND SWEEPING AWAY MANY OF THE CONCEPTS AND ACHIEVEMENTS OF THE COMMON ARAB ACTION AT A TIME WHEN THE ARAB NATION WAS MORE THAN ANY TIME BEFORE IN NEED OF CLOSING ITS RANKS AND MOBILIZING ITS RESOURCES TO CONFRONT SEVERAL UNPRECEDENTED DANGERS;

THEY DECLARE THEIR WELCOME OF THE LIBERATION OF THE STATE OF KUWAIT AND THE RESTORATION OF LEGITIMACY THEREIN, EXPRESS THEIR DEEP PAIN AND EXTREME SORROW FOR WHAT THE FRATERNAL KUWAITI PEOPLE HAVE SUFFERED AS A RESULT OF THE AGGRESSION OF THE IRAQI REGIME, AND EXPRESS THEIR DEEP REGRET FOR WHAT THE IRAQI PEOPLE ARE BEING SUBJECTED TO IN TERMS OF THE MOST ABOMINABLE FORMS OF SUFFERING AS A RESULT OF THE IRAQI LEADERSHIP'S DISREGARD FOR THEIR INTERESTS. IN THIS RESPECT, THEY AFFIRM THAT THEY STAND ALONGSIDE THE IRAQI PEOPLE IN THEIR ORDEAL AND STRESS THEIR FULL EAGERNESS TO PRESERVE THE IRAQI LANDS' UNITY AND TERRITORIAL INTEGRITY.

0005

THE PARTICIPANTS EMPHASIZE THEIR DETERMINATION TO ENDEAVOR TO INSTILL A NEW SPIRIT TO THE COMMON ARAB ACTION AND TO ESTABLISH FRATERNAL COOPERATION AMONG THE MEMBERS OF THE ARAB FAMILY ON SOLID BASES THAT REST ON THE FOLLOWING PRINCIPLES:

FIRST. THE PRINCIPLES OF COORDINATION AND COOPERATION. COORDINATION AND COOPERATION WILL BE ON THE FOLLOWING BASES:

1. WORKING IN ACCORDANCE WITH THE CHARTERS OF THE ARAB LEAGUE, THE UN, AND THE OTHER ARAB AND INTERNATIONAL CHARTERS; RESPECTING AND PROMOTING THE HISTORICAL AND FRATERNAL TIES AND THE RELATIONS OF NEIGHBORLINESS; AND COMMITMENT TO RESPECT THE UNITY AND TERRITORIAL INTEGRITY, THE EQUALITY OF SOVEREIGNTY, THE INADMISSIBILITY OF GAINING SEIZING TERRITORIES BY FORCE, NONINTERVENTION IN DOMESTIC AFFAIRS, AND COMMITMENT TO SETTLE DISPUTES BY PEACEFUL MEANS.
(MORE) 061231 AA/DUSKA/SE 06/1431Z MAR
BT
#0455

NNNN

COUNTRY: INTER-ARAB AFFAIRS
SUBJ: TAKE 2 OF 3--'TEXT' OF DAMASCUS DECLARATION

REF: NC0603143091 DAMASCUS DOMESTIC ARABIC 061231///BY PEACEFUL MEANS.

TEXT:

((TEXT)) 2. TO BUILD A NEW ARAB ORDER TO BOLSTER JOINT ARAB ACTION. THE AGREED-UPON ARRANGEMENTS AMONG THE PARTIES CONCERNED SHALL BE CONSIDERED A BASIS FOR ACHIEVING THIS. THE DOOR WILL BE LEFT OPEN BEFORE THE OTHER ARAB STATES TO CONTRIBUTE TO THIS DECLARATION IN LIGHT OF THE AGREEMENT OF INTERESTS AND OBJECTIVES.

3. TO ENABLE THE ARAB NATION TO DIRECT ALL ITS RESOURCES TO CONFRONT THE CHALLENGES THREATENING SECURITY AND STABILITY IN THE REGION, AND TO ACHIEVE A JUST AND COMPREHENSIVE SOLUTION TO THE ARAB-ISRAELI CONFLICT AND THE PALESTINE QUESTION BASED ON THE UN CHARTER AND ITS PERTINENT RESOLUTIONS.

4. TO BOLSTER ECONOMIC COOPERATION AMONG THE PARTIES CONCERNED IN ORDER TO ESTABLISH AN ECONOMIC GROUP AMONG THEM WITH THE OBJECTIVE OF ACHIEVING ECONOMIC AND SOCIAL DEVELOPMENT.

5. TO RESPECT THE PRINCIPLE OF EACH ARAB STATE'S SOVEREIGNTY OVER ITS NATURAL AND ECONOMIC RESOURCES.

SECOND: THE OBJECTIVES OF COORDINATION AND COOPERATION:

1. IN THE POLITICAL AND SECURITY FIELDS:

A. THE PARTIES CONCERNED CONSIDER THE CURRENT STAGE THAT FOLLOWED THE LIBERATION OF KUWAIT FROM THE OCCUPATION OF THE IRAQI REGIME'S FORCES TO PROVIDE THE BEST CIRCUMSTANCES TO CONFRONT THE OTHER CHALLENGES AND THREATS THE REGION IS BEING EXPOSED TO, IN THE FOREFRONT OF WHICH ARE THE CHALLENGES RESULTING FROM THE CONTINUED ISRAELI OCCUPATION OF THE ARAB TERRITORIES AND THE SETTLEMENT OF JEWS IN THEM. THE PARTIES CONCERNED BELIEVE THAT HOLDING AN INTERNATIONAL CONFERENCE FOR PEACE UNDER UN AUSPICES IS AN APPROPRIATE FRAMEWORK TO END THE ISRAELI OCCUPATION OF ARAB TERRITORIES AND TO GUARANTEE THE PALESTINIAN PEOPLE'S NATIONAL RIGHTS BASED ON THE PERTINENT UN RESOLUTIONS.

B. THE PARTIES CONCERNED STRESS THEIR RESPECT FOR THE PRINCIPLES OF THE ARAB LEAGUE CHARTER, THEIR COMMITMENT TO THE COLLECTIVE ARAB DEFENSE PACT AND ECONOMIC COOPERATION AMONG THE ARAB LEAGUE MEMBER STATES, AND THEIR DETERMINATION TO ACT JOINTLY TO GUARANTEE THE SECURITY AND SAFETY OF THE ARAB STATES. WHILE REFERRING IN PARTICULAR TO ARTICLE 9 OF THE ARAB LEAGUE CHARTER, THEY CONSIDER THE PRESENCE OF THE EGYPTIAN AND SYRIAN FORCES IN THE TERRITORY OF THE KINGDOM OF SAUDI ARABIA AND OTHER ARAB STATES IN THE GULF REGION TO BE IN RESPONSE TO THE DESIRE OF THESE STATES' GOVERNMENTS AND TO BE WITH THE OBJECTIVE OF DEFENDING THEIR TERRITORIES AND AS CONSTITUTING A NUCLEUS FOR AN ARAB PEACE FORCE TO BE PREPARED TO GUARANTEE THE SECURITY AND SAFETY OF THE ARAB STATES IN THE GULF REGION, AND AN EXAMPLE THAT WOULD GUARANTEE THE EFFECTIVENESS OF THE COMPREHENSIVE ARAB DEFENSE ORDER. THE PARTIES CONCERNED ALSO STRESS THAT COORDINATION AND COOPERATION AMONG THEM WILL NOT BE DIRECTED AGAINST ANY OTHER PARTY, BUT THAT IT CAN BE AN INTRODUCTION FOR OPENING DIALOGUE WITH THE ISLAMIC AND INTERNATIONAL PARTIES WHO RESPECT THE HIGHER INTERESTS OF THE ARAB NATION AND ABIDE BY THE PRINCIPLES OF THE INTERNATIONAL LEGITIMACY, PARTICULARLY THOSE RELATED TO RESPECTING THE STATES' SOVEREIGNTY, NONINTERFERENCE IN DOMESTIC AFFAIRS, AND SETTLING CONFLICTS THROUGH PEACEFUL MEANS. 0008

UNCLASSIFIED FBIS NICOSIA CY 061442Z MAR 91

COUNTRY: INTER-ARAB AFFAIRS
SUBJ: TAKE 3 OF 3--'TEXT' OF DAMASCUS DECLARATION

REF: NC0603143091 DAMASCUS DOMESTIC ARABIC 061231///THROUGH PEACEFUL MEANS.

TEXT:

((TEXT)) C. THE PARTICIPATING PARTIES WILL SEEK TO DECLARE THE MIDDLE EAST A ZONE FREE OF ALL WEAPONS OF MASS DESTRUCTION, ESPECIALLY NUCLEAR WEAPONS, AND WILL WORK TO ACHIEVE THIS THROUGH THE CONCERNED INTERNATIONAL DEPARTMENTS.

2. IN THE ECONOMIC AND CULTURAL FIELDS: IN HARMONY WITH THE ARAB LEAGUE CHARTER, THE JOINT DEFENSE AND ECONOMIC COOPERATION PACT BETWEEN THE ARAB LEAGUE STATES, AND OTHER AGREEMENTS ON JOINT ARAB ACTION, THE PARTICIPATING PARTIES WILL SEEK TO:

A. DEFINE THE RULES OF ECONOMIC COOPERATION AMONG THE FOUNDING PARTIES AS A FIRST STEP WHICH CAN BE BUILT UPON WITH THE OTHER ARAB STATES WITH THE AIM OF EXPANDING THE SCOPES OF COOPERATION.

B. ADOPT ECONOMIC POLICIES WHOSE PURPOSE IS TO ACHIEVE BALANCED ECONOMIC AND SOCIAL DEVELOPMENT AS A PRELUDE TO THE ESTABLISHMENT OF AN ARAB ECONOMIC GROUPING TO CONFRONT THE CHALLENGES AND TO KEEP PACE WITH THE DEVELOPMENTS RESULTING FROM THE ESTABLISHMENT OF MAJOR ECONOMIC GROUPINGS IN THE WORLD.

C. ENCOURAGE THE PRIVATE SECTOR IN THE ARAB STATES TO PARTICIPATE IN THE ECONOMIC AND SOCIAL DEVELOPMENT PROCESSES, INCLUDING SUPPORTING THE TIES BETWEEN THE ARAB CHAMBERS OF COMMERCE, INDUSTRY, AND AGRICULTURE AND OPENING THE DOORS FOR SMALL AND MID-SIZED ESTABLISHMENTS TO BENEFIT FROM THE FRUITS OF JOINT COOPERATION IN AN EASY AND TANGIBLE WAY.

D. SUPPORT THE ROLE OF THE SCIENTIFIC RESEARCH CENTERS AND FACILITATE CONTACTS AMONG THEM TO ENABLE THEM TO PREPARE JOINT RESEARCH TO ACHIEVE INTEGRATION IN VARIOUS FIELDS.

E. BENEFIT FROM SKILLS AND HUMAN RESOURCES IN THE FIELD OF CULTURAL AND INFORMATION EXCHANGE WHILE RESPECTING THE IDEALS OF THE PARTICIPATING STATES AND THEIR TRADITIONS AND NOT INTERFERING IN THEIR INTERNAL AFFAIRS.

3. IN THE FIELD OF THE JOINT ARAB ACTION ESTABLISHMENTS: SUPPORTING THE ARAB LEAGUE, CONFRONTING ALL THE ATTEMPTS TO WEAKEN OR DISINTEGRATE IT, AND REAFFIRMING ADHERENCE AND COMMITMENT TO THE GOALS AND PRINCIPLES INCORPORATED IN THE ARAB LEAGUE CHARTER. THIS CHARTER CAN BE DEVELOPED BY ADDING APPENDICES TO IT AND BY BENEFITING FROM THE RESULTS OF THE WORK OF THE COMMITTEE CHARGED WITH AMENDING THE CHARTER, INCLUDING THE INTRODUCTION OF A MECHANISM FOR SETTLING DISPUTES.

3. ((NUMBER AS HEARD)) THE ORGANIZATIONAL FRAMEWORK FOR COORDINATION AND COOPERATION: COORDINATION AND COOPERATION AMONG THE FOUNDING STATES OCCURS TO ACHIEVE THE REFERENT OBJECTIVES THROUGH MEETINGS HOSTED IN TURN BY EACH OF THE PARTICIPATING STATES AT THE FOREIGN MINISTERIAL LEVEL. THE ASSISTANCE OF EXPERTS AND SPECIALISTS WILL BE SOUGHT TO STUDY THE ASPECTS OF COOPERATION TO ARRIVE AT A NEW CONTRACTUAL FORMULA FOR ARAB COOPERATION AMONG THE PARTICIPATING STATES. THIS FORMULA WILL BE OPEN FOR ALL ARAB STATES.

4. GENERAL RULES. THIS DECLARATION HAS BEEN INITIALED IN DAMASCUS IN EIGHT ORGINIAL COPIES IN ARABIC, EACH OF THEM WITH THE 0009

SAME VALIDITY, ON 2 SHA'BAN 1411 HEGIRA, CORRESPONDING TO 6 MARCH 1991. THIS DECLARATION SHALL BECOME EFFECTIVE AFTER ITS OFFICIAL RATIFICATION AND THE RATIFICATION DOCUMENTS SHALL BE DEPOSITED AT THE MINISTRY OF FOREIGN AFFAIRS OF THE SYRIAN ARAB REPUBLIC.
(ENDALL) 061231 SH/DUSKA/SE 06/1445Z MAR
BT
#0457

NNNN

분류기호 문서번호	중동일 720-	기 안 용 지 (720-2327)	시 행 상 특별취급	
보존기간	영구.준영구 10. 5. 3. 1	장 관		
수 신 처 보존기간		검		
시행일자	1991. 6. 3.			

보조기관	국 장	전결	협조기관		문 서 통 제
	심의관				
	과 장	진개			
기안책임자		조 태 용			발 송 인

경 유 수 신 참 조	수신처 참조	발신명의		
제 목	걸프지역 안보 협력			

표제관련 주이란 대사관 보고를 별첨 송부하니 참고하시기 바랍니다.

첨 부 : 상기 전문(IRW-0447) 1부. 끝.

수신처 : 주 미, 영, 불, 사우디 대사, 주 카이로 총영사.

예 고 : 1991.12.31. 일반

0011

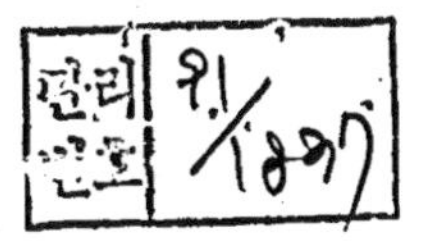

EMBASSY OF THE REPUBLIC OF KOREA

OUTGOING

IRW : 0447

TO : 장관(중동일)

FM : 주이란대사

걸프지역 안보협력

10+23 0900

CLASSIFICATION

	분류번호	보존기간

대 : WIR-0409

연 : IRW-0406

당관이 수집한 정보를 중심으로 분석한 표제동향을 아래 보고함.

가. 6(GCC)+2(시리아, 이집트) 와해

-이라크 패전직후 걸프국가들의 기본 안보개념은 PAN ARABISM의 부활을 통한 안보체제의 구축이었으며, 이는 6+2의 구상으로 나타났음.

-그러나 기본적으로 아랍권은 사우디, 쿠웨이트 등 부유한 걸프국가와 시리아, 레바논, 이집트 등 빈곤한 지중해국가로 구분, 이들국가간 계속되는 이해의 대립(예로서 GCC와 시리아, 이집트는 대 이스라엘 문제에 있어 상치되는 입장을 보이고 있음)은 '6+2'가 구체화 되는 경우에도 상호 역할 및 경비분담(대 이집트 경협등 보상문제 포함)또는 기능의 조정을 둘러싸고 더욱 고조될 것으로 예상된 바 있음. 이러한 배경하에서 당초 공동적으로 가상되었던 이라크에 대한 불안해소는 상황적으로 군사동맹성격의 SECURITY 수립문제를 재고하도록 하였음.

-또한 이라크의 쿠웨이트 침공이라는 과거 아랍형제국의 배신에 대한 불만은 대 시리아, 이집트 불만으로도 이어져 쿠웨이트 등 GCC소국은 오히려 미국의 주둔을 은밀히 선호하고 있으며 사우디도 비록 표면상으로는 외국군 철수를 표방하였지만 사실은 미군의 역할을 어느정도

TOT:

0012

EMBASSY OF THE REPUBLIC OF KOREA

TEHRAN

IRW:

TO :

FM :

OUTGOING

CLASSIFICATION

	분류번호	보존기간

인정하고 있는바, 이러한 속에서 이집트군 등 아랍군의 사우디, 쿠웨이트 주둔은 의미가 희석될수 밖에 없었던 것으로 보임.

나. '6+I(이란)' 개념의 부상

- 상기 상황변화에 맞추어 GCC는 이란의 역할의 중요성을 재평가하게 되었으며 나아가 군사동맹적 성격의 SECURITY ARRANGEMENT가 아닌 새로운 협력의 틀을 모색하게 되었는바, GCC측의 새로운 협력의 개념은 현재 이란측 구상 COMPREHENSIVE SECURITY ARRANGEMENT와 일치, 적극 검토되고 있는 것으로 보임.(그러나 아직 구체적 청사진은 어느 쪽에서도 표면화된 바 없는바, 아직은 구상단계로 추정됨)

- 물론 이들 GCC의 대이란 우려가 완전히 불식된 것은 아니나 이란의 대 GCC 관계는 점진적으로 발전하고 있으며 특히 이.사우디관계 개선으로 더욱 공고해지고 있는 것으로 보임.(지난 4월 VELAYATI외무장관의 사우디 방문시 양측은 역내 안보수립을 위해 공동 노력할 것을 확인한바 있음)

다. 전망 및 평가

- 당관 김서기관이 접촉한 주재국 외무부 관계자는 '6+I'이 분명 거론되고 있으며, 동 전망도 낙관적으로 보고있다고 설명하였음. 한편 당지 유력언론인은 현재 이란과 GCC국가간 경제협력(이란측 자원제공 및 GCC측 투자)이 일부 분야에서 가시화되고 있으며, 앞으로 이란을 통해

0013

EMBASSY OF THE REPUBLIC OF KOREA

TEHRAN

IRW :

TO :

FM :

CLASSIFICATION

OUTGOING

	분류번호	보존기간

ECO(이란, 파키스탄, 터어키 경제협력 위원회)가 GCC와 협력하는 방안 (파키스탄은 노동력, 터어키는 기술 제공등)도 검토 될 것이라고 언급 하였음.

-즉 6+I은 6+2에 대체한 종합적 협력체제로서 이에 대신하는 새로운 개념이 나오지 않는 한 당분간 차선책으로서 계속 협의될 것으로 보임.

~~(참고로 당지 5.19자 RESALAT지는 6+I에 이락크까지 포함시키는 새로운 형태의 6+2을 제의하였음을 주목할 가치가 있는 것으로 보임)~~

(대사 정 경일 - 국장)

예고 : 91.12.31. 일반

1991.12.31에 예고문에 의거 일반문서로 재 분류됨.

0014

원 본

외 무 부

종 별 :

번 호 : CAW-0683 일 시 : 91 0603 1525

수 신 : 장관(중동이, 정일)

발 신 : 주 카이로총영사

제 목 : 걸프전관련 아랍연합국 협의회 개최

(자료응신 제 129호)

1. 6.1 정책 협의차 당지를 방문한 MOHAMED ALMANSOURI 사우디 외무차관은 MOUSSA 주재국 외무장관과 면담후 DAMASCUS 선언 이행을위한 관계국(이집트,시리아 및 GCC 제국)전문가회의가 7.2 리야드에서 개최될 것이라함.

2. 한편 AMR MOUSSA 외무장관은 중동 평화문제를 포함하는 역내 제반문제 협의차 금주내로 시리아를 방문할 것이라함.끝.

(총영사 박동순-국장)

중아국 1차보 외정실 청와대 안기부

0015

PAGE 1 91.06.04 00:21 BU

외신 1과 통제관

원 본

외 무 부

종 별 :

번 호 : SBW-1069 일 시 : 91 0604 1500

수 신 : 장관(중일,정일,기정,국방)

발 신 : 주 사우디대사

제 목 : 제 39차 GCC 외무장관 회담 (자응 19호)

주재국 AL-KHOBAR에서 개최된 제 39차 GCC 외무장관 회의가 2일간의 일정을 마치고 6.3 폐막 되었는바, 동폐막후 발표된 성명서 주요 내용 아래 보고함

1.중동문제

-중동 평화회담 개최에 대한 지지를 재확인하고 동회의에 GCC 옵서버를 파견하는데 동의

-아랍-이스라엘 분쟁이 해결에 도달할 상황이 도래하였고, 지금이 팔레스타인문제의 정당한 해결책을 추구하는 시기라는데 의견일치

-미국의 중동문제 해결시도를 환영하고 부시대통령이 중동지역내의 대량 살상무기 제거노력에 특별언급

-이스라엘 점령지역 거주 팔레스타인인이 처한 곤경에 깊은 우려를 표명하고 이스라엘군에 의한 팔인의 살상및 대량체포와 점령지역내 정착촌 건설을 비난하고 국제사회가 이스라엘의 이와같은 행동을 중지하도록 압력을 가할것을 촉구

2.이라크문제

-TAHA RAMADAN 이라크 부통령이 쿠웨이트에 대한 권리를 주장한것을 비난하고 이와같은 무책임한 발언은 사태를 악화시킴

-아라크의 쿠에 대한 보상지연과 유엔 결의안이 요구하고 있는 쿠인과 기타국 포로석방 촉구

-이라크 정권이 국제사회의 인질석방 요구를 무시하고 있는것을 비난하고, 국제사회가 인질석방을 위해 이라크에 대해 정치적 압력을 가할것을 촉구

3.평화군 배치

-이라크와 쿠웨이트간 비군사 지대를 설치하고 유엔 평화군을 동지역에 배치한것을 환영

중아국 1차보 안기부 국방부

0016

PAGE 1 91.06.04 21:53 DA

외신 1과 통제관

4.GCC와 이란관계

-GCC와 이란과의 관계증진을 위한 대화계속을 환영

-GCC와 이란과의 새로운 협력시대 기대

5.레바논 문제

-레바논의 사태진전을 환영하고, 최근 시리아와 레바논간에 합의된 사항에 대한 지지표명.

끝

(대사 주병국-국장)

PAGE 2

0017

원 본

외 무 부

종 별 :

번 호 : CAW-0695 일 시 : 91 0606 1330

수 신 : 장 관(중동이,정보)

발 신 : 주 카이로 총영사

제 목 : AL ASSAD 시리아대통령 전격 방애

1. 6.5. AL-ASSAD 시리아 대통령은 당지를 전격방문, MUBARAK 대통령과 중동평화모색문제, 중동정세 역내 군축문제및 양국간공통 관심사에 관해 협의한후 (5시간 체류), 귀국 하였음.

이와관련 정상회담에 배석했던 AMR MOUSSA 주재국 외무장관은 동일 기자회견에서 요지하기와 같이 언급함.

1) 쿠웨이트 파견 이집트군과 시리아군의 귀국문제는 내무 DAMASCUS 선언국 실무자모임에서 토의를 거쳐, 추후 각료급 회의에서 논의하게 될것임.

2) 이집트는 시리아와 이스라엘간의 간격을 좁히기위해 중재역을 하는것이 아니며,평화모색활동(PEACE PROCESS)이 조속히 추진되어야 한다는입장임. 이를 위해 자신이 내주에 DAMASCUS 를방문할 것임.

3) 금일 양 대통령간의 회담에 새로운 것은없었으나 제반 문제점에 관해 의견을같이하였음.

4) 군비통제 문제를 토의하였으며, 역내 군축노력은 예외없이 모든 나라에 적용되어야 함.

5) 시간이 소진되고 있기 때문에 평화모색활동이 조속 추진되어야 한다는데 합의가 되어있으며, 이를 위해 우리는 UN 의 제결의 사항과 UN 헌장에 따라 동평화모색활동을 추진해야함.

6) BAKER 의 중동순방 일정은 잡혀진바 없음.

7) 제3세계가 UN 을 주도하고 있다는 구실로 이스라엘은 UN 역할을 축소 시키고자 하나 UN은 전세계와 국제사회를 대표하는기구이며, 동 헌장의 제원칙과 함께 평화회담 기초가 되는 결의사항(242 및 338)을 발표한바 이를 외면할수 없음.

2. 상기 AL ASSAD 의 돌연한 방애는 최근중동평화 모색활성화를 위한 AL ASSAD

중아국 외정실 안기부 1차보 분석관 차관 청와대

0018

PAGE 1 91.06.06 20:05 FO

외신 1과 통제관

시리아 대통령을 포함 역내 관계 제국 지도자앞 BUSH 대통령의 친서내용과 무관치 않는 것으로보이며, 애 - 시 양국 지도자가 조속한 중동평화 모색활동을 추진해야 하는데 인식을 같이 한다고하는 것으로 봐서 동회담 추진을 위해 BAKER 장관의 중동순방가능성을 한층 밝게하는것으로 관측됨. 끝.

(총영사 박동순-국장)

원 본

외 무 부

종 별 :

번 호 : ECW-0488 일 시 : 91 0606 1630

수 신 : 장관 (중동일,구일,정보)

발 신 : 주 EC 대사

제 목 : EC-이스라엘 외무장관 회담(자료응신 제 91-75호)

1. DAVID LEVY 이스라엘 외무장관은 작 6.5.파리에서 EC TROIKA 외무장관과 회담을 갖고,장차 개최될 중동평화 국제회의 및 실무회의에서 미.소와 함께 EC 의장국이 참석하는데 원칙적인 합의 (전제조건:이스라엘과 인근 아랍국간의 직접 평화협상에 EC 불개입) 를 표시하였음. 또한 이스라엘측은 팔레스타인에 대한 EC 측 경제원조를 관리하기 위한 피점령지역에서의 EC 집행위 대표단에 외교관 지위를 부여하는데 동의함.

2. 상기 합의는 중동평화문제 관련 EC 측 역할에 대한 이스라엘측의 기존입장 전환을 시사하는 것으로서 커다란 의미가 있음. 그간 이스라엘측은 아랍입장에 동조적인 EC 가 중동평화협상에 개입할 경우, PLO 의 동회의 참석및 궁극적인 팔레스타인 국가 창설을 지지할 것으로 우려하여 EC 측의 참여에 부정적 견해를 보여왔음.그러나 EC 측이 중동평화협상에 참여할 경우 시리아등 아랍강경국들이 주장하는 UN주관하 국제회의개최 압력을 완화시킬 수 있으며, 또한 이스라엘의 최대 수출 시장인 EC 로 부터 상당한 경제지원과 무역상 특혜를 얻기위한 실리적 차원에서 이스라엘이 상기와 같이 기존 입장을 변경한 것으로 보여짐. 끝

(대사 권동만-국장)

중아국 1차보 구주국 외정실

0020

PAGE 1 91.06.07 07:43 DF

외신 1과 통제관

美의 中東정책은 "야누스"

"무기감축" 외치며 「판매」 앞장

"友邦 방위능력 높인다" 변명…설득력 없어

中東지역의 무기제한협정을 제안한 美國이 다른 나라에 앞서 이 지역에 무기를 계속 팔고 있어 중동평화에 대한 美國의 의지가 의심받고 있다.

부시대통령은 지난주 중동지역의 평화정착 일환으로 야심적인 이 지역 무기감축계획안을 발표했다.

부시는 이 지역에 핵무기·화학무기등 대량살상무기와 다탄두 미사일의 반입을 금지하는 것은 물론 재래식 무기의 증강조차 동결하자고 제안했다.

그는 이를 위해 美·英·佛·蘇·中國 5대무기수출국이 이번달 파리에 모여 구체적인 절차등을 협의하자고 제의해놓고 있다.

美國은 부시의 이러한 발표가 있은지 일주일도 못되어 이스라엘과 걸프국가에대한 무기수출계획을 발표했다.

체니美국방장관은 이스라엘을 방문한 자리에서 이스라엘에 최신 F15 10대와 2억달러 상당의 방어용 애로미사일을 제공하겠다고 발표했다.

뒤이어 이번주초 美국방부는 최신예 공격용 아파치헬기를 아랍에미리트연합에 20대 바레인에 6대를 팔기로 했음을 밝혔다.

이와함께 백악관은 21억달러에 상당하는 3백37대의 M1A1 에이브럼스 탱크와 1백60대의 장갑차를 아랍에미리트연합에 파는등 사우디아라비아를 포함, 이 지역국가에 무기수출계획을 검토하고 있는 것으로 알려지고 있다.

美國은 이러한 모순적인 행위에 대해 나름으로의 변명을 하고 있다.

체니국방장관은 이들 나라에 무기를 공급하는 것은 우방의 방위능력을 높이기위한 조치이며 이것이 중동에서 무기를 감축하자는 부시의 제안과는 상반되지 않는다고 선명하고 있다.

체니국방장관은 『중동지역의 무기감축이란 것이 이 지역에 무기를 제공하지 않는다는 의미는 아니다』면서 『중동에 무기판매를 중단한다는 것은 현명한 조치가 아니다』고 밝혔다.

이러한 미국의 상반된 태도는 앞으로 파리에서 있게될 중동무기감축 회의의 전망을 어둡게 만들고 있다.

즉 미국 스스로는 무기판매에 열을 올리면서 다른국가들에는 자제를 권유한다면 설득력이 없기 때문이다.

美의회는 행정부의 이러한 모순을 지적하며 이 지역에 어떤 종류의 무기수출도 당분간 유예하자는 주장이 나오고 있다. 그 내막 역시 복잡하다.

즉 아랍국가에 무기판매를 반대해온 의회내의 유대계 의원들은 현재 이스라엘이 아랍국가와 비교할때 힘의 우위를 갖고 있으므로 현순간에서 무기판매를 동결한다는 것이 이스라엘에 유리하다는 판단때문에 이같은 무기수출 유예를 주장하고있는 것이다.

일부에서는 부시의 제안 자체가 현실성이 없는 말잔치에 불과하다고 혹평하고 있다.

이들의 비판은 부시의 제안이 종전과 더불어 쉽게 점화될줄 알았던 중동평화의 실마리가 풀리지 않자 분위기 조성용으로 던진 것에 불과하다는 것이다.

역사적인 반목의 뿌리를 갖고 있는 이스라엘·아랍 양진영간에 진정한 화해가 선행되지 않고 무기감축을 시행한다는 것이 우선 불가능하며 현수준에서 무기를 동결시키자는 案도 이를 검증할 방법면에서 불가능한 발상이라는 것이다.

또 비록 5대 무기수출강국간에는 합의를 이룰지 몰라도 광범한 군소무기수출국을 일률적으로 규제하기 힘들다.

그러나 이보다 더 힘든 것은 미국경제의 근간이 되는 방위산업계의 압력을 미국 스스로가 감당할 수 있겠느냐는 점이다.

특히 美蘇가 유럽배치 재래식 무기감축협상에 성공할 경우 이지역에 공급되던 재래식 무기가 갈수 있는 곳이란 아랍지역 뿐이라는 것이다.

美國은 세계를 통틀어 제1의 무기수출국 위치를 고수하고 있다.

스톡홀름의 국제평화연구소의 집계에 따르면 지난해 전세계 무기수출의 40%는 美國이 차지했으며 그 금액은 87억달러에 달했다.

또 美국방예산의 감축에 따른 방위산업의 위축을 보충해줄수 있는 곳은 오일머니를 갖고 있는 아랍국가 뿐이라는 것을 미국 자신이 잘 알고 있다.

결국 부시의 中東무기감축안은 미국은 이러한 형편때문에 무기를 계속 팔수 밖에 없으나 다른 나라는 아랍평화를 위해 무기수출을 자제하라는 주문일뿐이라는 비아냥이 나올수 밖에 없게 되어있다.

【워싱턴=文昌克특파원】

(중앙 4 면)

美國은 「正義」인가

美國이 입으로는 中東의 평화와 군비축소를 외치면서도 행동으로는 이 지역에 대한 무기판매에 열을 올리는 이율배반적인 행태를 서슴없이 자행하고 있다.

지난달29일 조지 부시美대통령이 포괄적인 中東군축안을 발표한지 하루만에 더 체니 국방장관은 이스라엘에 F15전투기 10대를 제공하겠다고 밝혔다. 이를 필두로 對이스라엘 방공망 구축지원, UAE(아랍에미리트연합)와 바레인에 대한 공격용 헬기판매, 이스라엘에 美國의 무기비축계획 등이 잇따라 발표돼 아랍국가 등 다른 나라는 물론 미국내의 의회와 전문가들을 당혹시켰다.

이처럼 모순된 행동에 대한 美국방부의 해명은 단순하다. 中東에서의 무기증강경쟁을 억제하려는 부시의 계획은 「평화를 지키려는 나라들이 방어능력을 갖추는 노력마저 저지하기 위한 것은 아니므로 무기판매는 군축안과 모순되지 않는다는 것이다. 펜터건은 이 같은 논리에 따라 곧 2백40억달러규모로 알려진 對中東무기판매안을 의회에 제출할 계획이라고 6일 발표하기에 이르렀다. 부시의 5대 군비수출국에 대한 對中東무기수출자제 제안은 미국의 기존무기판매계획을 정당화시키기 위한 들러리로 나온 셈이다.

美국방부가 무기를 건네주려는 이른바 「평화적인 국가」의 목록에는 이스라엘이 맨위에 있고 이집트 사우디아라비아 UAE및 터키등이 올라있다. 펜터건은 전쟁후 약화된 이라크軍만해도 아직 일부 이웃국가보다 더 강하므로 이불균형을 해소하기 위해서도 무기판매는 필요하다는 궤변을 늘어놓고 있다. 그렇다면 재래식 무기만으로도 이미 中東최강이라는 이스라엘에는 왜 첨단무기를 제공하는가. F15기와 아파치헬기가 과연 방어용무기인가. 또 과연 영원한 「평화적 국가」와 「우방」이 어디 있으며 무엇이 「정당한」무기판매냐는 관점은 누가 내릴 것인가.

自國의 판단만이 평화를 위한 선택이라는 미국의 이같은 독단이 계속되는 한 미국은 최신무기의 판촉시범을 위해 걸프전쟁을 일으켰다는 비난마저 불러 일으킬 것이며 언제 또 제2의 이라크를 만들지도 모른다. 현단계에서 미국은 中東평화에 보탬이 된다기보다는 저해요인이 되고 있는 것같다.

<林恒기자>

(국민 5 면)

日本人 "본받을것 없는 부도덕한 生物"

美연구소 보고서 「2000년의 日本」

"세계지배획책"…양국 감정싸움 飛火조짐

日本이 막강한 경제력과 교묘한 선전술을 이용, 세계지배를 획책하고 있다고 비난하는 한 비밀보고서가 최근 美國언론에 공개돼 논란이 되고있다.

日本기업들로부터 상당한 재정적 지원을 받고있는 뉴욕州소재 로체스터기술연구소(RIT)가 美중앙정보국(CIA)을 위해 마련한 「2000년의 日本」이라는 제목의 이 비밀보고서는 『日本의 근간을 이루는 계층은 나이값도 못하고 부도덕하며 뒷전에서 음모를 꾸미는가하면 문화를 조작·통제하려드는 그야말로 하나도 본받을게 없는 생물들』이라고까지 극단적 용어들로 日本人들을 혹평, 美日간의 감정싸움으로 번질 소지를 안고있다.

더구나 이 보고서가 최근 점증하는 日本의 영향력과 경쟁적 우위를 우려한 나머지 美학계및 언론계에서도 對日비난 분위기가 높아지고 있는 가운데 나온 것이라는 점에서 관심을 끌고 있다.

RIT는 이 보고서에서 日本이 자신의 막강한 경제력을 십분 이용, 전세계에 日本의 문화와 가치를 강요하려 드는가하면 日本내에서 그릇된 정보를 의도적으로 유포, 美國人들을 對日本 비난자들로 비치게 하거나 美國이 日本의 문화를 바꾸려하고 있다는 그릇된 인식을 심어줌으로써 美日간의 감정적 대립을 불러일으키고 있다고 주장했다.

그러나 RIT관계자들은 이 보고서가 『연구소내부의 의견수렴용으로 배포된 초안이 언론쪽에 잘못 흘러들어간 것』이라고 해명했다.

RIT의 홍보담당 부소장인 잭 스미스는 『보고서 초안의 어조나 용어, 註釋부분들은 마지막 손질을 거치지 않은것으로 日本과 일본문화, 그리고 RIT를 지원하는 많은 日本기업들에 대한 RIT의 입장과 분위기를 전혀 반영하지 않고 있다』고 강조했다.

그는 또 『이 보고서의 원래 취지는 日本기업들이 매우 경쟁력이 있으며 우리도 하나의 국가로서 이와 동등한 경쟁력을 확보해야 한다는 점을 강조하기 위한 것』이라고 설명했다.

CIA가 전략기획연구의 일환으로 RIT에 연구를 의뢰한 「2000년의 日本」 보고서 초안은 로즈소장의 고위 보좌관인 앤드루 더허티가 작성한 것으로 전해졌다. 또 駐美日本대사관측은 신중한 입장을 견지, 아무런 논평도 할수 없다는 입장을 나타냈다. 【워싱턴 AFP=聯合】

0021

(중앙 5 면)

1991. 6. 7

외 무 부

종 별 :

번 호 : CAW-0700 일 시 : 91 0608 1300

수 신 : 장관(중동이,정보)

발 신 : 주 카이로총영사

제 목 : 중동평화 추진

연:CAW-0695

6.7 총근 중동평화 추진을 위한 관계국(이집트, 시리아, 요르단, 레바논, 이스라엘)지도자앞 BUSH 대통령의 친서 관련, 이스라엘측은 UN 역할 거부입장을 재천명한것으로 보도되고 있는 가운데,동일 주재국 AMR MOUSSA 외무장관은 SHAMIR 수상이 언급한 WEST BANK 와 GAZA 지구 협상가능성이사실이라면 이는 동평화 추진에 진일보로박차를 가 하게 될것이라고 논급함. 또한 동외무장관은 시리아없는 중동평화는 불가하다고 언급(6.6)하면서 시리아와 협의를 위해 6.11 PQDAMASCUS 로 향발할것이라고한바 있 음.끝.

(총영사 박동순-국장)

중아국 1차보 외정실 청와대 안기부

0022

PAGE 1 91.06.08 22:34 BX

외신 1과 통제관

외 무 부

암호수신

종 별 :

번 호 : CPW-1193　　　　일 시 : 91 0609 1700

수 신 : 장관(미일,아이,정안,중동)

발 신 : 주 북경 대표

제 목 : 중국, 중동군비 통제회의 찬성

1. 주재국 외교부 대변인은 6.8 최근 부시미대통령이 제안한 미.쏘.중.영. 불 5 국간 중동군비통제 회의에 중국도 찬성하며 이미 양상곤 국가주석 명의의 서한을 부시 대통령에게 보냈다고 발표함.

2. 또한 동 대변인은 중국이 전면적이고 균형된 원칙하에 국제군비통제 및감축 실현을 위하여 적절하고도 공정한 조치를 취하는 것을 일관되게 주장해왔음을 상기시키면서 중국은 평등한 기초위에서 관련국가들과 이러한 중대한 문제를 깊이 토의할것을 희망한다고 밝히었음.

(대사 노재원-국장)

미주국	장관	차관	1차보	2차보	아주국	중아국	외정실	분석관
청와대	안기부							

0023

PAGE 1　　　　91.06.09　18:53

외신 2과　통제관 FE

연합 H1-464 S06 외신(782)

中國,서방의 對중동 무기통제노력 균형촉구

(北京 UPI.AFP.로이터=聯合) 미사일의 해외 판매 중단 압력을 받고 있는 中國은 13일 중동지역에서의 '균형된' 무기 감축 노력을 촉구하면서 중동에 무기를 판매하고 있는 다른 국가들이 먼저 무기 선적을 자제해야 할 것이라고 주장했다.

殷律 中國 외교부 대변인은 이날 주례 뉴스 브리핑에서 中國 정부는 무기 통제 노력에 지지를 보낸다고 밝히고 그러나 다량의 무기를 이 지역에 판매한 국가들이 맨먼저 책임성있는 태도를 취하고 아울러 극도의 자제심을 보여야 하며 무기 공급 국가들이 공정하고도 합리적인 조치 및 균등한 토론과정을 거쳐 포괄적이고 균형된 접근법을 채택해야 할 것이라고 강조했다.

殷律 대변인은 또 중동은 긴장이 계속되고 있는 최대 분쟁지역이라고 지적하고 中國은 핵무기나 생화학 무기와 같이 대량파괴 무기를 전면 폐기하는데 대해 항상 지지해 왔으며 저차원의 무장에 기반을 둔 중동 안전을 지지한다고 말했다.

그는 중동에서 무기 증강을 성공적으로 중단시키기 위해서는 우선 중동지역 內外 국가들이 대량의 무기 유입을 중단시키려는 공동 노력을 기울여야 할 것이라고 역설하고 스스로 무기선적을 통제해야 할 것이라는 주장의 대상국가와 관련, 美國이라는 국명을 구체적으로 거명하지는 않았으나 관영 요망誌는 최신호 사설을 통해 미국이 이스라엘에 전투기를 판매하고 다른 중동지역에 무기를 비축하기로 한 것에대해 불만을 토로한 바 있다.

한편 서방 국가들은 중국 정부가 中國製 M-11 미사일을 파키스탄에 선적하고 있으며 조만간 시리아에도 中國製 M-9 미사일을 판매할 지도 모른다고 우려를 표명해왔다.

앞서 中國은 지난주 잠재적인 위험을 항상 간직하고 있는 중동에서의 무기 확산을 통제하기 위해 파리에서 개최되는 美國주도의 유엔 安保理 5개 상임이사국 회의에 참석키로 동의했었다.(끝)

(YONHAP) 910613 2134 KST

0024

13

관리 번호 91/1168

원 본

외 무 부

종 별 :

번 호 : QTW-0153 일 시 : 91 0618 1315

수 신 : 장 관(중동일, 정보)

발 신 : 주 카타르 대사

제 목 : 다마스커스 선언 실무회의 개최

1. 91.3.6 다마스커스에서 GCC6 개국, 이집트, 시리아의 8 개국 외상회담후채택된 ''다마스커스 선언''실천방안 협의를 위한 실무회의가 6.17 당지에서 개최되었음.

2. 동회의는 AHMED BIN ABDULLAH AL-MAHMOUD 카타르 외무차관이 주재하였는바 동차관은 회의 결과에 대해 다음과 같이 언급하였음.

- 범아랍안보문제는 정치, 경제 안정없이는 이루어질수없는바 다마스커스 선언은 안보, 정치, 경제문제를 집중적으로 다루었음.

- 금번회의의 목적은 다마스커스 선언의 세부사항에대한 합의와 의견교환의폭을 넓히는데 있음.

- 금번회의의 토의사항은 7.9 쿠웨이트에서 열릴 8 개국 외상회의에 제출될것임.

3. 동회의 참가자는 아래와 같음.

-카타르: 외무차관, 외무성 GCC 국장

-사우디:정무담당외무차관, 외무성 GCC 국장

-UAE: 외무성 GCC 부국장

-바레인:외무성법률담당차관보, 주 사우디 바레인 대사

-쿠웨이트: 외무성 GCC 국장

-오만: 외무성법률담당 차관보

-이집트: 외무성차관보, 외무성법률담당공사, 주카타르 이집트대사

-시리아: 외뭉성 법규국장, 주 이집트 시리아대사, 외무장관 비서실장

4. 동회의 상세내용은 밝혀지지않았으나 파악되는대로 추보예정임.

끝

(대사 유내형-국장)

예고:91.9.30 일반

1991. 9.30. 에 예고문에 의거 일반문서로 재 분류됨.

중아국	장관	차관	1차보	2차보	외정실	분석관	청와대	안기부

0025

PAGE 1

91.06.18 21:55

외신 2과 통제관 BS

원 본

외 무 부

종 별 :

번 호 : CAW-0730 일 시 : 91 0619 1510

수 신 : 장관(중동이,정보)

발 신 : 주 카이로총영사

제 목 : 무바락 대통령의 쿠웨이트및 바레인 전격방문 (자료응신 제 137호)

1. 6.18 무바락대통령은 쿠웨이트와 바레인을방문코 당일 귀국 하였음.

2. 동 대통령의 전격방문 이면에는 간 이집트군주도외 아랍인에 의한 걸프지역 전후 안보체제 구축문제, 쿠웨이트 전후 복구사업에 이집트 참여문제, 이락점령군 치하 쿠웨이트내에 이집트인 잔류자들에 대한 학대문제등으로 이집트와 GCC국 특히 쿠웨이트 와의 관계가 불편스럽게 전개되고 있었으나,이의 해소를 위한 일연의노력 즉최근 GCC 의장국인 오만의 QABOOS국왕의 방애에 이어 ALI SABAH AL-SALEM 쿠웨이트국방장관과 IBN ABDEL AZIZ 사우디 국방장관의 방애와 이집트 경제각료들의 잦은 쿠웨이트 방문, MEGUID AL 사무총장의 GCC 국순방 등으로 모종의 타협안 이 마련된 결과 풀이됨.(당초 보다 축소된 규모의 이집트군 주둔,전후 복구사업에 이집트 건설업체참여,이집트인에 대한 박해중지).끝.

(총영사 박동순-국장)

중아국 1차보 외정실 청와대 안기부 문서관

0026

PAGE 1 91.06.19 23:40 FN

외신 1과 통제관

원 본

외 무 부

종 별 :

번 호 : CAW-0733 일 시 : 91 0620 1510

수 신 : 장관(중동이,정보)

발 신 : 주 카이로총영사

제 목 : 걸프지역 안보군구성 보도

(자료응신 제 138호)

연:CAW-0730

6.20. 당지 언론은 연호 무바락 대통령의 쿠웨이트및 바레인 전격 방문으로 타결된 걸프지역 안보군창설 구도는 하기와 같은 것이라 보도하면서, 이의 후속조치를 위해 7 월초 MOUSSA 외무장관이 쿠웨이트와 바레인을 방문한다함.

1. 쿠웨이트주둔 안보군 구성: 총규모 26,000명

(사우디 10,000 , 기존 쿠웨이트군 5,000을 포함한 여타 GCC 국으로부터 10000, 이집트와 시리아 각 3000명)

2. 미.영군 주둔문제

3500명의 미군은 잠정주둔

1500명의 영군은 91.7월말 철수

3. 이란군의 참여는 배제하되 외교적 관계를 강화함.

4. 연내에 걸프지역 안보군은 창설토록 함(91.12.GCC 정상회담 전까지).

끝.

(총영사 박동순-국장)

중아국 1차보 외정실 분석관 안기부 국방부

0027

PAGE 1

91.06.20 22:54 DA

외신 1과 통제관

관리 번호	91/1916

외 무 부

원 본

종 별 :

번 호 : QTW-0157 일 시 : 91 0621 1620

수 신 : 장관(중동일,정보,사본:주사우디,바레인,쿠웨이트,오만,UAE 대사,카이로 총영사)

발 신 : 주 카탈 대사

제 목 : GCC 실무회담 결과 파악보고(자료응신제4호)

연:QTW-153

1. 본직은 6.20 20:00-22:30 간 주재국 외무성의 HUSSAIN ALI AL-DOOSARI GCC 국장을 대사 관저에 초청하여 만찬을 같이하면서 연호 GCC 실무회담내용에 관하여 탐문한바 요지 다음과 같이 보고함.

2. 면담요지

0 동 GCC 실무회담에서는 오는 7.9-10 간 쿠웨이트에서 개최예정인 다마스커스 선언 서명국 (GCC6 개국과 이집트 및 시리아)외상회담에서 토의될 다음의제를 선정하였음.

. 다마스커스 선언 이행을 위한 정치, 안보, 경제협력

. 지역정세의 검토와 국제신질서의 관한 의견교환

. 중동평화 국제회의에 대한 GCC 참가와 대이스라엘공동대응

. 핵, 화학무기를 포함한 무기통제 문제

. 아랍민족 국가간 관계의 재조정

0 금후의 지역내 안보정세에 관하여는 이스라엘과 이란에 대응하는 문제를 중시

0 다국적군을 대체할 전후 안보체제에 관하여는 이집트 및 시리아군을 주축으로 하여 GCC6 개국군 병력으로 구성하는 아랍 평화 유지군(55000 명 규모)의 설치에 합의하고 있으나 주둔지역 , 사령부 구성, 경비의 SHARING PERCENTAGE 등에 관해 이견이 있어 계속조정이 필요함

. 주둔지역에 관해 사우디측은 국내주둔에 반대하고 있으며 쿠웨이트에 주둔하게될 공산이 큼. 다만 쿠웨이트는 상금 미군병력의 계속주둔을 희망하고 있으나 미국측은 명확히 지상군 병력주둔에 반대하고 GULF 해역 배치의 해병대잔류를 검토하고 있음.

. 지휘권을 위요하고 이집트, 시리아, 사우디간에 이견이 있으나 조정가능할

중아국	장관	차관	1차보	2차보	외정실	분석관	청와대	안기부

0028

PAGE 1

91.06.21 23:56

외신 2과 통제관 CA

것으로 봄.

. 경비의 SHARING PERCENTAGE 에관하여는 이집트 및 시리아측의 요구와 GCC6개국의 분담비율문제가 얽혀있으나 GCC6 개국간에 협의 결정될것임

0 GCC6 개국간의 의견조정관 BURDEN SHARING 문제협의를 위하여 오는 7.1 사우디의 리야드에서 GCC 외무차관 회담과 GCC 재무차관회담이 각각 개최될예정임.

0 작년 12 월 당시 DOHA 에서 개최된 GCC 정상회담에서 아랍회교국가에 대한 100 억 내지 150 억불 규모의 원조기금 계획결정시 논의된 GCC6 개국간 BURDEB SHARING 안 (사우디측제안으로사우디 25%, 쿠웨이트 25%, UAE 25%, 여타 3 개국 25%)은 사우디 및 쿠웨이트를 제외한 4 개국이 찬동치 않음으로 7.1 개최예정인 GCC 재무차관회담에서 재검토된후 아마도 금년 12 월 쿠웨이트에서 개최될 GCC정상회담에서 확정될 것으로 예상됨.

0 이집트와 시리아는 거반 걸프전쟁에 있어서의 군사적 공헌과 금후의 평화유지군 참가를 이유로 군사비부담은 물론 GCC 의 대아랍회교국 원조에 있어서도 최우선적 배려를 강력히 요구할 뿐만 아니라 GCC 와 군사협력과 경제 지원을 상호 보완하는 공동체 구성의 필요성을 강조하고 있음.

끝

(대사 유내형-국장)

예고:91.12.31 일반

1991. 12. 31. 에 예고문에 의거 일반문서로 재 분류됨. ㊞

PAGE 2

0029

관리번호 91/1200

외 무 부

원 본

종 별 :

번 호 : IRW-0507 일 시 : 91 0626 1200

수 신 : 장관(중동일,정일,기정)

발 신 : 주 이란 대사

제 목 : 걸프안보협력체제

1. 6 프러스 2 의 변홍된형태로 ARAB DEFENSE FORCE(사우디 1 만명, 시리아, 이집트각 3 천명, 여타 GCC 국가 1 만명제공)의 쿠웨이트, 이락국경배치 가능성이 보도되고있는 가운데 BESHARATI 주재국 외무부 수석차관은 6.24 당지언론 인터뷰를통해 6 프러스 2 구상자체가 애초잘못된것이었다고 설명하며 (시리아, 이집트는 걸프만 국가가 아니며, 이들국가는 기본적으로 이해를 달리하고있음. 시리아는 특히 레바논 문제에 관심이있으며, 이집트는 내부경제문제로 안보협력면에서 적극적역할수행이 어려움)오히려 이.사우디관계를 비롯한 전반적인 이.GCC 협력증진방안협의를위해 VELAYATI 외무장관이 최근 HAJJ 성지순례계기 사우디 방문한바 있으며 이란-UAE 간 대사급 외교관계가 조만간 재개예정으로 알려짐)

2. 이와관련 당관 김서기관이 접촉한 당지 GCC 국 대사관 관계자들 언급요지 아래와같음.

-역내 안보체제수립관련 사우디.구웨이트등 GCC 국가간 근본적의견대립은 없으나, 지리적으로 사우디와 이란사이에 위치한 쿠웨이트의 대이란입장이 사우디의 입장과 반드시 같지는 않음을 시인함.(GCC 국가들간에는 대이란 불신감이 아직 상존하고있으나, 적어도 경제적으로 이란이 시리아, 이집트보다 중요한 파트너이며, 지정학적으로도 이란이 페만국가라는 점에 인식을 같이하고있음)

-6 프러스 2 는 당초 장식적개념이었으며, 따라서 처음부터 실현가능성이 회의적이었음.

-그러나 6 프러스 2 가 완전히 포기된것은 아님. 이의 대안으로 6 프러스 1의 개념이 현재 적절히 논의되고있는것도 사실이나, 6 프러스 1 이 성공하기위해서는 미.이란관계가 변수로 작용할것임.

-앞으로 추구되어야할 안보개념은 COMPRESENSIVE(ECONOMIC)SECURITY 가되어야

중아국	장관	차관	1차보	2차보	외정실	분석관	청와대	안기부

PAGE 1 91.06.26 20:16

외신 2과 통제관 DO

0030

할것임.

3. 한편 LARIJANI 주재국 외무부및 국가최고안보회의 고문은 당지일간지 기고를 통해 사담대통령이 정권유지를위한 제반여건의 제약으로 4 개월이내에 몰락될 것으로 전망한바있음. 끝

(대사정경일-국장)

예고:91.12.31 까지

19 . . . 에 예고문에 의거 일반문서로 재 분류됨.

PAGE 2

0031

원 본

외 무 부

종 별 :

번 호 : CAW-0740　　　　일 시 : 91 0627 1700

수 신 : 장관(중동이,정보)

발 신 : 주 카이로총영사

제 목 : 걸프지역 안보구도관련 이란 외무차관 논평에관한 주재국반응(자료응신139)

6.26. AMRO MOUSSA 주재국 외무장관은 BESHARATI이란 외무차관이 걸프지역 안보체제 구축관련 이집트 경제사정 악화로 이집트의 역할기대는 어렵다고 논평(6.25)한 데 대해 이란은 이집트가역내 대국으로 국제적으로나 지역적으로 군사.정치적인 최대영향력 보유국이며,중동지역에서 이집트 역할없이 안보질서논의를 할수 없다는 것을이해 해야 하며, 과거 걸프지역에서의 이란 역할이라는 것은 비판(LEVELOF CRITICISM)내지 의심 수준(LEVEL OF SUSPICION)에불과하다' 고 동 논평을 반박하고 최근 주요정세에 관해 요지 하기와 같이 언급함.

1. 걸프지역 안보체제 구축문제는 DAMASCUSDECLARATION 서명국의 주관심사로 완전한 협력과 이해하에 추진되고 있음.

2. 중동평화 모색활동은 이스라엘측의 거부조건을 극복키 위해 계속 노력 하고있으며,점령지내에 이스라엘 정착촌 건립은평화모색에 엄청난 도전이 되고 있음.

3. UN은 UNSC 결의 제242호 및 338호를 만든기구로, 변죽 역할만 담당해야 한다는 것은 아무도수락하지 않을것임.

4. 이디오피아 사태를 예의 주시하고 있으며,이디오피아내에 범민족회의 개최를촉구함.

5. 이집트는 소마리아의분렬을 반대함.

6. 이집트는 NAM 주도 우방국인 유고사태를 예의주시하고 있으며,동국의 단합 강화를 지지함.끝.

(총영사 박동순-국장)

중아국　1차보　외정실　분석관　안기부

0032

PAGE 1　　　　91.06.28　07:50 DN

외신 1과 통제관

관리번호 91/1212

외 무 부

종 별 :

번 호 : PAW-0700 일 시 : 91 0630 1500

수 신 : 장관(아서,중동)

발 신 : 주 파 대사

제 목 : 주재국 대사우디 파견군 철수

1. 주재국은 걸프전 개전직전 약 11,000 명 규모의 육군을 사우디에 파견한바 있는바, 동사우디 주둔군 전원이 불원철수 할것으로 최근 당지에 알려지고있음.

2. 동파견군은 걸프전 전부에 참가치 않고 주로 사우디 후방경계를 담당하였으며, 동 보수도 주재국정부측에서 지급하고 사우디정부에서는 소액의 수당을 지급해온것으로 알려지고있음. 끝.

(대사 전순규-국장)

예고 91.12.31 일반

1991 12 31 에 예고문에 의거 일반문서로 재 분류됨.

아주국	차관	1차보	2차보	중아국	분석관	청와대	안기부

PAGE 1 91.06.30 21:42

외신 2과 통제관 DO

0033

관리번호	91/1215

원 본

외 무 부

종 별 :

번 호 : QTW-0161 일 시 : 91 0701 1230

수 신 : 장관(중동일,정보)

발 신 : 주 카타르 대사

제 목 : GCC외무차관 및 재무차관회담연기

연:QTW-157

연호로 기보고한바 있는 GCC 실무회담관련,7.1 사우디 리야드에서 개최예정이었던 GCC 외무차관 및 재무차관 회담은 7.9-10 간 쿠웨이트에서 개최되는 상기8 개국 외상회담이후로 연기되었다는바, 상세한 일자는 미정임.

끝

(대사 유내형-국장)

예고:91.12.31 일반

1991. 12. 31. 에 예고문에 의거 일반문서로 재 분류됨.

중아국	장관	차관	1차보	2차보	외정실	외정실	분석관	청와대
안기부								

PAGE 1 91.07.01 22:16 0034

외신 2과 통제관 CA

원 본

외 무 부

종 별 :

번 호 : JOW-0516 일 시 : 91 0701 1600

수 신 : 장 관(중동이,구일,정일,기정)

발 신 : 주 요르단 대사

제 목 : 프랑스 외상 요르단 방문

1. 6.29. 주재국을 방문한 프랑스의 DUMAS 외상은 후세인 국왕, MASRI 수상및 ENSOUR 외상등과 회담후 중동 평화문제등에 관해 요지 다음과 같이 언급함

가.중동 PEACE PROCESS 에 관한 미국의 노력을 지지하며, 미국과 소련 후원하의S 지역 평화회담 개최를 촉구하나 성공여부가 확실치 않음. 성공하더라도 유엔의 역할을 배제해서는 안됨

나.아랍.이스라엘간 대화 추진에의 미국 참여는 절대적으로 필요함

다.요르단과 프랑스는 미국의 노력이 실패하면 다른방법의 PEACE PROCESS 강구 필요성에 대해 합의 하였는바, 프랑스는 유엔 주도하의 중동평화회담 개최를 추진할 준비가 되어있음

라.프랑스는 유엔안보리 상임이사국의 지위를 이용, 실질적인 아랍.이스라엘 평화 회담 개최를 위해 미테랑 대통령의 안보리 이사국 회의소집 제안을 부활시킬것임

마.PEACE PROCESS 를 위해 한시가 급한 차제에 일부에서는 이를 지연시키고 있으며 PEACE PROCESS의 교착상태는 매우 위험한바, 중동문제 해결에는 시간이 가장중요한 요소임을 인식해야 함

(이스라엘이 점령지내의 정착촌 건설에 박차를 가하고 있음을 환기시킴)

바.프랑스는 아랍.이스라엘 분쟁을 평화적인 방법으로 해결코자 하는 요르단의노력을 높이 평가하며 요르단이 여하한 형태로든 분쟁 해결에있어 중요한 역할을담당하고 있음

사.대 이라크 경제제제, AQABA 항 봉쇄등으로 인해 발생한 요르단의 경제난은프랑스에 의해 검토되어 대요르단 보상 방안을 강구중임

2.걸프사태를 전후해서 요르단과 프랑스는 타 서방제국에 비해 우호적인 관계를유지하여 왔는바, 특히 미.소 주도하 PEACE PROCESS 의 성공 가능성이 희박한

중아국 1차보 구주국 문협국 외정실 분석관 안기부

0035

PAGE 1 91.07.01 23:00 DA

외신 1과 통제관

것으로 보이는 지금 동계획이 실패할 경우 유엔 참여하 프랑스 주도의 새로운 PEACE PROCESS 에 대해 주재국은 기대를 걸고 상호 추진방안을 모색할 것으로 보임. 그러나 이스라엘이나 시리아등 강경 아랍제국들의 종전 입장의 변화가 없는한 가까운시일내 중동평화회담 개최 가능성은 희박한 것으로 판단됨

(대사 박태진-국장)

0036

05/07 '91 09:36 ☎5053067 KOREA BEIJING ∅001

장관실	차관실	一차보	二차보	기획실	외정실	분석관	의전장	아주국	미주국	구주국	중아국	국기국	경제국	통상국	문협국	영교국	총무과	감사관	공보관	외연원	청와대
/	/	/	/	/	/	/		0		/											/

駐北京代表部

CPW(F)- 022 日時 : 10705 0940 (PAGE 2-2)

受信 : 長官 (아이. 중동)

發信 : 駐北京代表

題目 : 이붕총리, 중동순방 (중국, 중동평화에 관한 입장)

보안 통제	

Li stresses Arab unity for Middle East peace

by our staff reporter
Wang Ximin

CAIRO — Visiting Chinese Premier Li Peng stressed the importance for Arab countries to coordinate their positions and speak with one voice in their quest for a settlement of the Middle East question.

Li made the remarks at a banquet given Wednesday by Egyptian President Mohammed Hosni Mubarak.

During talks held yesterday with Egyptian Prime Minister Atef Mohammed Naguib Sedki, Li also reiterated China's support for an important role by the United Nations in the Middle East peace process and for all forms of dialogue and consultations conducive to the peace in the region.

The talks between Li and the Egyptian leaders did not touch upon the issue of arms sales, according to a Chinese Foreign Ministry official.

Answering questions by foreign reporters in Beijing, Wu Jianmin, director of the Information Department of the ministry, also stressed that China has not sold missiles to Syria.

At Wednesday's banquet, the Chinese Premier said that the Middle East issue has lasted for more than 40 years, with its resolution having become all the more urgent in the wake of the Gulf crisis.

In this connection, he said, China appreciated the positive efforts made by President Mubarak and the Egyptian Government.

The Chinese Premier reiterated China's support for the Palestinian and other Arab peoples in their just cause of recovering lost territories and regaining their national rights.

He said that UN Security Council resolutions 242 and 338 and other relevant resolutions are the basis for a just and reasonable settlement of the Middle East question.

2-1

0037

"The occupied Arab territories should be returned; the legitimate national rights of the Palestinian people should be restored and meanwhile the sovereignty and security of the State of Israel should also be respected and guaranteed," he pointed out.

In his talks with Sedki, Li said that to have a final solution to the Middle East issue, an international peace conference under the auspices of the UN and with the participation of the five permanent members of the Security Council should be convened.

China, a permanent member of the UN Security Council, cannot be ignored for its influence in the international affairs, Sedki said.

The Egyptian Prime Minister said he hoped that China would play an important role in pushing forward the peace process in the region.

Premier Li said China appreciated the efforts made by the Egyptian Government for a political settlement to the Middle East issue.

"The stability and peace of the region is not only an issue in the region itself but also can have influence on other regions and even on world peace and security," Li noted.

He pledged China's willingness to make efforts together with Egypt and other countries to realize stability and peace in the Middle East.

Li, on behalf of the Chinese Government and in his own name, extended an invitation to Prime Minister Sedki and his wife for a visit to China at an appropriate time, and Sedki accepted the invitation.

2-2

0038

번호 : USW(F) - 2611
수신 : 장 관 (아이, 미일, 중동일, 정일선) 발신 : 주미대사
제목 : 중국 무기수출 및 MFN 문제 (3 매)

On MFN, Chinese Send Mixed Signals

Beijing Issues Barrage of Harsh Rhetoric While Making Some Conciliatory Moves

By Lena H. Sun
Washington Post Foreign Service

BEIJING, July 6—As the debate in Congress on China's trade status heats up, Beijing seems to be trying to take steps to keep its U.S. trade privileges while not giving the appearance that it has caved in to foreign pressure to change its policies, according to Chinese and Western analysts.

As a result, China often appears to be sending mixed signals: it issues a barrage of harsh rhetoric denouncing U.S. interference in China's national affairs, while at the same time it seeks to be seen as conciliatory and takes measures to address some of Washington's human rights, trade imbalance and missile proliferation concerns.

NEWS ANALYSIS

"They have made certain efforts, but from the U.S. point of view, the other rhetoric that is coming out sounds antagonistic about MFN," said John Frisbie, director of the Beijing office of the U.S.-China Business Council, which supports unconditional most-favored-nation status renewal. "That rhetoric is due to their own political considerations and pressures." MFN is a standard international trade convention in which one country grants another the lowest possible tariffs available.

Analysts say the anti-U.S. rhetoric in public speeches and state-controlled press here results from China's view that the MFN debate strikes at the heart of its national sovereignty.

"As a country with a long history of 5,000 years and a population of more than 1.1 billion, any of the major changes are the historical choice of the Chinese people. . . . This cannot be changed by any outside pressure or 'peaceful evolution,'" an article in the People's Daily, the Communist Party's official mouthpiece, said in a recent bristling broadside.

To many of the conservative elders who dominate the senior leadership, "peaceful evolution" means an attempt by the United States to undermine China's political system through Western political and social thought, analysts said.

Some of these leaders believe "the United States is out to get them," said one U.S. official in Washington, and this affects their decisions on key issues, even in the face of sophisticated analyses from the Chinese Embassy in Washington.

In addition, conservative Chinese elders are believed to be reluctant to agree to make too many concessions to the United States for fear of opening the door to an endless series of demands, according to U.S. officials in Washington. However, China has taken some steps it considers conciliatory in an effort to retain its most-favored-nation status.

Although President Bush has said he wants to extend the status without conditions for another year, many members of Congress are seeking to deny the status or impose conditions that would require Beijing to modify human rights, trade and arms proliferation policies.

The House is expected to debate and vote on the issue next week, and the Senate is likely to follow soon after that. A joint bill on MFN probably will be voted on by both houses before Congress's August recess.

> *Chinese policies "cannot be changed by any outside pressure or 'peaceful evolution.'"*
>
> — People's Daily newspaper

China has sent two state-backed buying delegations to the United States as a sign of its effort to offset Beijing's growing trade surplus. The most recent delegation signed contracts totaling $1.2 billion in U.S. goods, much of it for agricultural products.

In the view of some Western analysts, China appears to be concentrating its conciliatory efforts on missile proliferation issues because those concerns have drawn great attention in Congress.

Chinese officials have confirmed the sale of "short-range tactical missiles" to Pakistan, but have said the missile, known in the West as the M-11, would have a range of less than 180 miles. That is below the special limitations agreed to by the United States and other nations—but not China—in the Missile Technology Control Regime, an international agreement intended to slow the spread of missiles capable of carrying nuclear warheads.

China is also believed to be on the verge of selling M-9 missiles, with a probable range of about 375 miles, to Syria. But Beijing has agreed to participate in a U.S.-sponsored international conference in Paris starting Sunday on limiting arms sales to the Middle East. Chinese Premier Li Peng, who is now visiting six Mideast nations, is also expected

W.P. July 7. '91

2684-1

0039

to discuss arms control with regional political leaders.

Still, one congressional source said that unless China signs the nuclear Non-Proliferation Treaty or joins the Missile Technology Control Regime, anything else that it might do to appease U.S. concerns will only be regarded in Congress as "getting that 34th vote in the Senate," the congressional source said, referring to the number of votes needed to prevent an override if the president should veto a bill blocking or tying conditions to MFN status for China.

Chinese officials have also hinted that there may be some additional conciliatory gestures, one Western diplomat said. Rumors about a possible release on parole of some of the pro-democracy activists jailed since the 1989 army crackdown have been circulating in Beijing for the last month. Prior to last year's debate on MFN, the government released hundreds of jailed dissidents.

In addition, the tone of Chinese officials in their recent discussions with Reginald Bartholemew, undersecretary of state for international security affairs, was also more encouraging than in the past, one Western diplomat said. Beijing informed Bartholomew that it is actively considering signing the Non-Proliferation Treaty and may join the Missile Technology Control Regime, which restricts sales of missiles capable of delivering warheads with a range of more than 180 miles.

These steps have been accompanied by strong language about the importance of Chinese sovereignty and noninterference in Beijing's internal affairs, and on what the leadership sees as the arrogant behavior of the United States. Even in the academic community, "there is unbelievable America-bashing," said David Shambaugh, a professor of Chinese politics at the University of London who is conducting research here.

For example, a television documentary on June 30 about the United States and capitalist nations showed pictures of starving children in Africa and blamed their misery on U.S. oppression.

Another attack came in the recent People's Daily article, which said, "The Chinese people have experienced how foreign powers 'guaranteed' China's 'human rights' with aggression, interference and blockades," a reference to the siege of Beijing by foreign countries during the Boxer Rebellion of 1900, and an alleged sinister U.S. cooperation with Nationalist Chinese against the Chinese Communists in the wartime capital of Chongqing in the 1940s.

Appeals to nationalism strike a chord among many Chinese, particularly older Chinese who remember the Sino-Japanese War, and the Korean and Vietnam wars, where China and the United States were on opposing sides.

"China has been a feudal society for thousands of years, and most Chinese don't understand human rights and at least some believe that the American Congress is trying to interfere in our internal affairs," said one intellectual.

W.P
July 7. '91

2684-2

0040

번호 : USW(F) -

수신 : 장 관 발신 : 주미대사 (통제)

제목 : (매)

To Curb China's Arms Trade

Despite pledges to curb sales of advanced arms, China now confirms it has begun delivering new missiles to Pakistan. And it's about to ship others to Syria. Understandably, the news fuels Congressional fervor to deny China trade privileges. A Democratic-sponsored bill would cancel China's most-favored-nation trade status for making such sales.

But economic sanctions have failed to restrain Chinese arms merchants in the past. A new strategy combining carrot and stick might be worth a try — provided the Bush Administration is willing to curb its own arms sales.

In a depressing ritual, the U.S. gets assurances from China that it won't sell advanced arms and then learns that it has. The gap between word and deed stems from internal divisions in China. The assurances that arms won't be sold come from the Foreign and Defense Ministries, as a timely article in International Security by John W. Lewis, Hua Di and Xue Litai at Stanford's Center for International Security and Arms Control explains. But the sales are made by an army commission that has considerable autonomy and substantial inducement to sell as much as it can.

As China's leader, Deng Xiaoping, accelerated modernization in the 1980's, the commission became China's engine for technological development. It's as if the U.S. Army Corps of Engineers ran the Manhattan Project, NASA, the National Science Foundation and Silicon Valley combined.

At the same time Mr. Deng slashed the military budget. That led the commission to promote sales in order to raise revenues and import advanced technology. Administrators of its two main arms export firms, who stand to profit personally from sales, have family ties to China's leaders.

One of those firms signed a contract in 1988 to sell medium-range M-9 missiles to Syria and has received some proceeds, but has yet to deliver any missiles. And it sent "a very small number" of shorter-range M-11 missiles to Pakistan.

The deals can still be killed. But discriminating against China's trade with the U.S. might spur its arms sales. And sanctions, by denying contact and technology, come down hardest on the modernizers who back liberalization and opposed the Tiananmen crackdown. A threat of sanctions may be more effective than their actual imposition.

A different strategy is worth a try — cooperating with China in arms suppliers' groups while holding out a threat of trade sanctions by the U.S., Japan and other nations that want the missile sales curbed. Beijing has now told Washington it may join the 16-nation Missile Technology Control Regime, which seeks to halt the spread of medium-range missiles. And the world's five leading arms suppliers, China included, will meet soon in Paris to draw up guidelines for Mideast arms sales. China can be pressed in these forums to curb its sales — but is not likely to comply unless the Bush Administration shows some sales restraint of its own.

Congress could facilitate that by renewing most-favored-nation status for one year, requiring Mr. Bush to report within the year on China's arms sales practices and imposing its own temporary moratorium on U.S. sales by year's end if Mr. Bush fails to exercise restraint.

NYT July 6, '91

2614 -3 (END)

0041

원 본

외 무 부

종 별 :

번 호 : CAW-0782 일 시 : 91 0707 1540

수 신 : 장관(중동이,정보)

발 신 : 주 카이로총영사대리

제 목 : DAMASCUS 선언 서명국 외무장관회의

연: CAW-0740

쿠웨이트 DAMASCUS 선언 서명국 외무장관회의(7.8) 참석에 앞선 기자회견(7.6)에서 AMRO MOUSSA 주재국 외무장관은 종래의 주재국 입장을 재천명하고 동회담은걸프지역 안보문제만을 다루어야 한다고 언급함.

1. 이집트의 참여내지 이집트와 협의없는 역내 안보체제는 있을수 없음.

2. 미대통령이 제의한 중동평화안은 여전히 유효하며, 다른 대안 논의는 불요함.

3. ISRAEL 의 점령지내에 정착촌 건립 계속추진을 평화추진 장애물임.

4. 평화회담 개최 적기 결정을 위해 무바락 대통령은 일면 BUSH 대통령과 계속접촉하고 있을뿐 아니라 타면 아랍권과 파레스타인 측과도 접촉을 계속하고 있음.

5. 중동문제에 아랍권내에 다양한 견해 노출은 건전 징후임.

6. 아랍권내의 이견은 LEGITIMACY 와 INTERESTS 입각 해소되어야 함.

7. 금차 KUWAIT 회담은 걸프지역 안보문제만 다루어야함.

끝.

(총영사대리 공선섭-국장)

중아국 1차보 외정실 분석관 안기부

0042

PAGE 1 91.07.08 06:20 FL

외신 1과 통제관

원 본

외 무 부

종 별 :

번 호 : CAW-0784 일 시 : 91 0708 1420

수 신 : 장 관(중동이,정보)

발 신 : 주 카이로총영사대리

제 목 : DAMASCUS 선언 서명국 외무장관회의 연기

(자료응신 제 140호)

연: CAW-0782,0740

1. 7.7 AMRO MOUSSA 주재국 외무장관은 표제회의가 일부 관계국들 외무장관의 바쁜 일정관계로 부득 3-4일간 연기되었다고 함.

2. 동연기 이면에는 안보군의 구성, 규모 및 경비 문제뿐 아니라 대이란 관계설정에 관한이견이 아직 완전해소에 이르지 못한것으로 풀이됨.끝.

(총영사대리 공선섭-국장)

중아국 1차보 외정실

PAGE 1 91.07.08 21:35 CT 0043

외신 1과 통제관

원 본

외 무 부

종 별 :

번 호 : CAW-0789 일 시 : 91 0708 2220

수 신 : 장관(중동이,정보)

발 신 : 주 카이로총영사대리

제 목 : 중동지역 군비통제를 위한 PARIS 회담에 즈음한 주재국 입장

1. 7.8부터 PARIS 에서 이틀간 개최되는 중동지역 군비통제를 위한 UNSC 상임이사국의 전문가회의 개최관련, 이집트정부는 UNSC 5대 상임이사국 주요 산업선진국및 기타관계 제국에 하기 요지의 이집트 입장을 전달하였음.

' 중동지역에서의 군비 통제는 90.4 MUBARAK 대통령이 천명한 중동지역을 비 대량 살상 무기지대화 방안에 기초해야 되며, 이스라엘은 핵비확산조약(NPT)에 가입해야 함'

2. 90.4.8. 무바락대통령의 중도지역의 비대량살상무기 지대화 제의 이면에는 이스라엘도 여타아랍 제국과 같이 동일한 통제하에 두어야 한다는것에 주안점을 둔것이었음.끝.

(총영사대리 공선섭-국장)

중아국 1차보 외정실 안기부

0044

PAGE 1 91.07.09 15:20 DF

외신 1과 통제관

외 무 부

종 별 :

번 호 : CPW-1598 일 시 : 91 0709 1130

수 신 : 장 관(아이,정안,중동일)

발 신 : 주 북경 대표

제 목 : 중국 무기 수출 3원칙

주재국 외교부 대변인은 7.6 요르단에서 가진 기자회견에서 (이붕 총리 수행중), 다음과 같은 중국의 무기수출 3원칙을 발표하였음.

1. 무기 수출의 목적은 무기수입국의 방어력을 증진시키는데 있음.
2. 무기수출시 지역내 세력균형을 깨지 않아야한다는 것을 고려하고 있음.
3. 무기수출을 통해서 타국 내정에 간섭을 시도하지않음.끝.

(대사 노재원-국장)

이주국 중아국 외정실

0045

PAGE 1

91.07.09 13:48 WG

외신 1과 통제관

외 무 부

종 별 :

번 호 : UNW-1771　　　　일 시 : 91 0709 1830

수 신 : 장 관 (국연,중동일,정안)

발 신 : 주 유엔 대사

제 목 : 안보리 상임이사국 동향

안보리 상임이사국 5개국은 대중동 무기판매 규제문제 토의를 위해 7.8-7.9 파리에서 회동한 바, 금 7.9자 NYT 지 관련기사를 별첨 송부함.

첨부:상기 기사: UNW(F)-314

끝

(대사 노창희-국장)

국기국　1차보　중아국　외정실　안기부

0046

PAGE 1　　　　91.07.10　09:15 WI

외신 1과　통제관

UNW(F)-314 10709 1830
(국연. 중동일. 정안) 총1매

Talks Begin on Arms Sales to 3d World

By ALAN RIDING

Special to The New York Times

PARIS, July 8 — Fearful that the end of the Persian Gulf war may set off a new arms race in the Middle East, the United States, the Soviet Union, China, Britain and France today began their first effort to negotiate limits on weapons sales to volatile regions of the world.

The talks, described by a French official as "the beginning of a long, complex and subtle process," followed an American call for a ban on weapons of mass destruction in the Mideast, France's proposal for arms control worldwide, and Britain's idea of an international arms-sales register.

No concrete agreement was expected from the two-day closed-door session, but French officials said the negotiators hoped to offer some specific ideas for debate at the meeting of the Group of Seven industrial democracies in London next week.

Senior officials from the five permanent members of the United Nations Security Council are focusing first on the situation in the Mideast, where there is said to be broad agreement on the need to destroy and ban production of chemical and biological weapons.

Comparison of Proposals

The American plan for the region contemplates a freeze and eventual ban on ballistic missiles, a ban on biological weapons, an end to production of matériel that could be used in nuclear weapons, and guidelines on the sale of conventional weapons.

France's plan, by contrast, calls for the elimination of chemical weapons, a ban on biological armaments, reduction of nuclear arsenals, and negotiations to achieve a balance of forces in all regions. It also supports the establishment of a conventional arms-sales register at the United Nations.

With all five countries scrambling to resupply their Mideast allies after the gulf war, however, political experts believe it has become difficult to reach an accord on limiting the sales of conventional weapons. Together, the five have provided 85 percent of the weapons arsenals in the region.

Further, the United States, France and Britain are expected to face resistance to such an accord from domestic arms contractors who, feeling the squeeze of military budget cutbacks with the end of the cold war, have been seeking new opportunities in the third world.

American and French officials argue that Mideast countries have a legitimate right to defend themselves. Since the end of the gulf war, the United States has promised to sell more F-15 combat aircraft to Israel and strike helicopters to some gulf nations.

Last week, France disclosed that orders for its weapons rose 70 percent, from $3.2 billion in 1989 to $5.4 billion in 1990, largely as a result of the gulf war. It said more than half of these orders came from the Mideast and North Africa, compared with one-third in 1989.

1-1

UNW-1771
첨부물

0047

그니까

무기거래통제회담 전망

중동 세력판도에 결정적 영향

수출국 이중성으로 성공 여부 불투명
미국주도 거래질서 확립 첫걸음될 듯

세계 5대 무기수출국인 미국·소련·프랑스·영국·중국이 2차대전 이후 처음으로 중동지역 군비확산 방지를 위한 회담을 갖기 위해 파리에 모였다.

8~9일 이틀에 걸쳐 대량파괴무기 제거 등 군비축소와 중동에 대한 무기거래의 통제방안을 논의하게 될 이번 회의는 참가국들이 중동지역에 공급되는 무기의 85%를 수출하고 있다는 점에서 앞으로 이 지역의 세력판도 변화에 있어서도 중대한 영향을 끼칠 것으로 보인다.

이번 회담은 걸프전 이후 전쟁 도발의 잠재적 가능성을 가진 국가에 대한 무기판매가 국제평화를 위협할 수 있다는 여론을 배경으로 지난 5월말 조지 부시 미 대통령이 지대지미사일의 제거 등 포괄적인 중동지역 군비확산 방지안을 제시하면서 구체화됐다.

부시 대통령은 당시 △중동지역 국가들의 지대지미사일 구입·생산·시험의 동결 및 이의 궁극적 제거 △모든 중동국가들간에 조속한 화학무기 금지조약 체결 △72년 체결된 세균무기 금지에 대한 조약의 강화 등을 제안했었다.

과거 대부분의 군비축소회담들이 강대국간의 군비축소를 논의했던 데 비해 이번 회담은 강대국들이 제3세계의 무분별한 국제무기거래 통제를 위해 자신들의 기준과 그 감시방안을 마련하는 데 초점이 있다.

레지널드 바돌로뮤 국무부 국제안보담당차관이 이끄는 미 대표단 가운데 한명인 리처드 클라크는 "이라크의 경우 6천여대의 탱크를 생산, 보유했으며 이는 분명히 자기나라 방위의 수준을 넘어서는 것이었다. 우리는 그것이 잘못됐다고 말할 수 있는 합의된 기준을 마련하고자 하는 것이다"라고 회담의 의의를 설명했다.

이러한 미국의 입장은 냉전종식과 함께 미-소 협력 아래 국제적 지역분쟁에 대처한다는 미국의 정책변화와 일맥상통하는 것으로 미국이 주도하는 5대 무기수출국의 기준 아래 제3세계에 대한 국제무기거래를 통제한다는 뜻을 담고 있다. 그러나 미국 등의 이러한 노력에도 불구하고 회담의 성공 전망은 그다지 밝지 않다. 이들 5개국은 중동지역의 군축과 평화를 주장하면서도 한편으론 막대한 외화수입이 보장되는 무기수출을 쉽게 포기하지 않으려 하기 때문이다.

미국의 경우 부시 대통령이 중동 군축방안을 발표한 바로 다음날 리처드 체니 국방장관은 F-15 전투기 10대를 포함, 이스라엘에 대한 대규모 군사지원방안을 발표했다. 나아가 미국은 이집트·사우디·아랍에미리트연합 등 중동국가들에 대해 2백40억달러의 무기판매계획을 갖고 있는 것으로 알려졌다.

프랑스 역시 지난해 무기판매액이 전해에 비해 70% 증가했으며 총액 가운데 61%가 중동지역을 대상으로 하고 있다.

무기수출국들의 이러한 이중성 외에 또다른 장애요인은 중동국가들의 끊임없는 무기 수입 욕구다.

회담을 며칠 앞두고 이집트는 중동군비통제안이 모든 국가들에 공평하게 적용돼야 한다고 주장한 반면 모세 아렌스 이스라엘 국방장관은 아랍국가들에 대한 군사적 우위를 유지할 수 있도록 미국의 군사원조를 연 18억달러에서 25억달러로 40% 증액해줄 것을 요구했었다.

일부 전문가들은 아랍-이스라엘간 분쟁이 계속되는 한 중동지역 군비통제 구상은 결코 성공할 수 없을 것이라고 지적하고 있다. 그런 의미에서 이번 파리회담은 평화를 위한 회담이라기보다는 미국이 주도하는 강대국 위주의 새로운 국제무기거래질서를 확립하기 위한 첫걸음이라고 보는 것이 옳을 듯하다.

〈정남기 기자〉

1991. 7. 9
한겨레 신문

0048

관리번호	91/1967

외 무 부

종 별 :

번 호 : CPW-1613 일 시 : 91 0710 1100

수 신 : 장 관(아이,아서,중동일,정보,기정) 사본:주몽고대사-중계필

발 신 : 주 북경대표

제 목 : 중.이스라엘 및 중.몽고 관계

당관 윤해중 참사관이 7.9 당지 인도대사관 RANADE 참사관으로 부터 청문한중국.이스라엘 관계 및 중국.몽고 관계 다음 보고함.

1. 중국.이스라엘 관계

가. 중국 외교부 관계관은 이붕 총리의 중동순방 출발 직전 당지 이스라엘 대표처에 이붕의 중동순방 내용을 사전 설명

나. 당지 인도대사관측은 상기 중국측 조치가 대 이스라엘 자극을 회피하기위한 조치로 평가

다. 중국은 대중동 무기수출 통제회의(파리)에 대표단을 파견하는 한편, 향후 중동 평화 회의에 적극 참여할 뜻을 밝힌바 있는바 향후 중동정세의 추이를 보아가며 대 이스라엘 정식 외교관계 수립 방향으로 나아가고 있음.

2. 중.몽고 관계

가. 중국은 최근 대몽고 협력사업을 적극 추진하고 있는바 이는 중국이 몽고와의 협력에서 어떤 경제적 이득을 기대하는것 보다는 인접국으로서 몽고의 중국에 대한 안보상의 이익을 고려하고 있기 때문으로 봄.

나. 중국이 몽고에 대해 특히 관심을 가지기 시작한 것은 소련국의 몽고로 부터 철수에 따른 소위 힘의 공백을 미국이 메꾸게 되지 않을까 하는 우려와 경계 때문인것으로 관측됨.끝.

(대사 노재원-국장)

예고: 91.12.31. 일반

1991.12.31. 에 예고문에 의거 일반문서로 재 분류됨.

아주국	장관	차관	1차보	2차보	아주국	중아국	외연원	외정실
분석관	청와대	안기부						

0049

PAGE 1 91.07.10 12:28

외신 2과 통제관 BS

報告畢

報 告 事 項

1991. 7.10.
外交政策企劃室
安保政策課(4)

題 目 : 유엔 安保理 5개 常任理事國의 中東 軍縮 會談

유엔 安保理 5개 常任理事國은 7.8-9간 파리에서 中東 軍縮會談을 開催, 中東의 非 大量破壞 武器 地帶化에 合意하였는 바, 同 要旨를 아래와 같이 報告 드립니다.

1. 開催 背景

   o 美.蘇間 軍縮 協商 急進展, 부쉬 大統領의 5.29. 中東 軍縮提案, 프랑스 미테랑 大統領의 6.3. 軍縮案 提議등이 同 會談 背景으로서, 美國의 提議에 의해 開催

2. 主要 合意 內容

   o 核武器

     - 核施設에 대한 國際 査察 許容과 核武器 製造에 사용 가능한 物質의 輸入 禁止

   o 在來式 武器

     - 中東地域으로의 在來式 武器 販賣 抑制와 武器 移轉에 관한 情報交換을 容易하게 하기 위한 指針 樹立

   o 미사일

     - 地對地 미사일을 現 水準에서 凍結하되 궁극적으로는 完全 禁止

0050

o 化學武器

- 모든 中東國家가 明年 成立될 化學武器 協定에 加入

3. 次期 會議

o 7.15-17간 런던 開催 豫定인 G-7 西方 先進國 頂上 會談에서 同 合意 事項 論議 豫定

o 同 合意 事項 履行을 위한 具體的 措置 마련을 위해 今年 10月中 런던에서 次期 會議 開催

4. 評價 및 分析

o 걸프전 이후 武器 擴散 危險이 가장 큰 中東 地域에서의 大量破壞 武器 擴散防止가 美國이 구상중인 新 國際秩序 構築에 긴요하다는 美國의 視角과 立場이 反映

o 금번 會談 合意內容의 實效性은 未知數.

- 이스라엘 支持 與否 不透明

- 尖端 技術이나 部品 密賣등 loophole의 效果的 防止 與否 不確實

o 금번 會談은 紛爭地域에서 大量破壞 武器 擴散 防止를 위해 5强에 의해 시도된 最初의 共同 軍縮努力으로, 그 成果에 따라서는 향후 韓半島를 포함한 餘他 紛爭 地域에서도 시도 가능.

o 大量破壞 武器 擴散防止 體制가 確立되면 北韓의 對中東 미사일 輸出 抑制 豫想

- 다만, 그때까지는 不足分을 메꾸기 위한 北韓 미사일 需要增加 可能性 不排除

(別添 : 北韓의 對中東 地域 미사일 輸出現況 參照)

예 고 : 1991.12.31. 일반

91. 12. 31. 일반 재 고

北韓의 對 中東地域 미사일 輸出 現況

對象國	內譯	金額	備考
시리아	- 91年 Scud-C 150基 契約 (91.3.月末 100基 引渡)	$ 5억	Scud-C 는 Scud-B改良型 (在來式, 化學武器 裝着 可能)
이 란	- 88年, Scud-B 40基 販賣	$ 30억	미사일외 탱크, 야포 販賣
	- 90年, 20基 追加 契約	(原油로 償還)	
	- 91年, Scud-C 미사일 部品販賣 및 組立支援		
리비아	- 86-91年間 Scud-B,C 販賣	$ 10억	在來式 武器도 販賣
	- 最新 Scud-D형 生産 設備 建設契約		
이 락	- 90年, Scud-B,C 販賣 契約 締結		代金 償還 問題로 契約 未履行
애 급	- 90年, Scud-C 生産 設備 建設 支援		

o 出 處 : Wall Street Journal (1991. 7. 10.字)

0052

외 무 부

종 별 :

번 호 : UNW-1789 일 시 : 91 0710 2120

수 신 : 장 관(국연,중동일,정일)

발 신 : 주 유엔 대사

제 목 : 안보리 상임이사국동향(대중동무기 판매규제토의)

연: UNW-1771

표제 파리회담 (7.8-9)결과에 관한 금 7.10 자 NYT,WP 지 기사를 별첨송부합니다

첨부: 상기기사: UNW(F)-316

끝

(대사 노창희-국장)

국기국 1차보 중아국 외정실 분석관 안기부

0053

PAGE 1

91.07.11 10:12 WG

외신 1과 통제관

JUL 10 '91 19:49 KOREAN MISSION

5 Powers Will Seek Ban On Major Mideast Arms

By ALAN RIDING

Special to The New York Times

PARIS, July 9 — The United States, the Soviet Union, China, Britain and France committed themselves today to the goal of eliminating all weapons of mass destruction from the Middle East.

The five permanent members of the United Nations Security Council, who are themselves the main arms suppliers to the Middle East, also pledged to observe "rules of restraint" when transferring conventional weapons to their allies in the region.

After a two-day negotiating session called as a direct result of the Persian Gulf war, the five countries further agreed to develop more specific guidelines and mechanisms aimed at restricting arms sales to the Middle East, which they described as "a primary area of tension."

Experts from the five countries are to meet in September to prepare concrete proposals before another negotiating session of senior officials in London in October. "There's agreement to take the fast track," Reginald Bartholomew, the American representative, said.

Proposed by Bush

The talks were proposed by President Bush in May when, focusing on the Middle East, he called for a freeze and eventual ban on ballistic missiles, a ban on biological weapons, an end to production of matériel that could be used in nuclear weapons and guidelines on sales of conventional weapons.

President François Mitterrand of France later suggested a global approach to control of weapons sales and production as well as negotiations to achieve "a balance of forces" in all regions. Prime Minister John Major of Britain in turn promoted establishment of a conventional arms sales register at the United Nations.

Mr. Bartholomew, who is Under Secretary of State for International Security Affairs, said this week's meeting concentrated on Mr. Bush's proposals for the Middle East because all five governments recognized the region to be a priority for arms control.

"We're not speaking of achieving a full treaty with legally binding commitments," he said. "What we're trying to do is to create rules, mechanisms, patterns of consultation, all of which can have the effect of encouraging care and prudence to avoid arms sales that can destabilize."

'Harmonized Controls' Sought

In a final statement, the five countries agreed to develop and maintain "stringent national and, as far as possible, harmonized controls" on transfers of nuclear, chemical and biological weapons or technology that could be used to develop them with the aim of achieving a "weapons of mass destruction-free zone."

They also called on countries of the Middle East to negotiate their own regional arms agreements including a freeze and eventual elimination of ground-to-ground missiles, acceptance of international safeguards on nuclear activities and eventual adherence to agreements banning chemical and biological weapons.

They recognized that countries have a legitimate right to self-defense, but warned that "indiscriminate transfers of military weapons and technology contribute to regional instability."

5 on Security Council Would Bar A-Weapons

By Sharon Waxman

Special to The Washington Post

PARIS, July 9—The five permanent members of the U.N. Security Council agreed today to seek exclusion of weapons of mass destruction from the Middle East, to develop "rules of restraint" on conventional arms sales and to achieve the sharing of information about weapons transfers to the region.

At their first meeting on limiting global arms proliferation, representatives of the United States, Soviet Union, China, France and Britain laid the groundwork for mechanisms to control the spread of conventional weapons, missile systems and nuclear-related materials in the Middle East, according to a communique.

After two days of talks, the five agreed specifically to support a zone free of "weapons of mass destruction . . . in the Middle East" and advocated a missile freeze, the statement said. All nuclear activities there would be put under international safeguards.

The meeting grew out of an initiative by President Bush in May to limit weapons sales to the Middle East. It was expanded to address global weapons sales.

Undersecretary of State for International Security Affairs Reginald Bartholomew, the U.S. delegate, said, "We already put quite a bit of meat on the bones of what a restraint regime would look like," adding that it was too early to tell if the five could agree on ceilings or bans on the sales of certain weapons.

"It is a considerable achievement to get this group to adopt the guidelines that it has. What the ultimate shape will be we have some idea of, based on the discussions we had today," Bartholomew said.

Bartholomew said any measures adopted regarding the Middle East could be extended to the rest of the world, but in the wake of the Persian Gulf war that region had a particularly urgent need for arms control. He said Security Council members would consult with countries in the Middle East on the proposals.

The five also agreed to support a British initiative to create an international arms registry at the United Nations. The representatives are to meet in Britain in October to work on details of the guidelines.

#UNW-1789

첨부물

0054

원 본

외 무 부

종 별 :

번 호 : CAW-0799 일 시 : 91 0711 1400

수 신 : 장관(중동이,정보)

발 신 : 주 카이로총영사대리

제 목 : 중동지역 군비통제를 위한 PARIS 회담

연:CAW-0789

7.10 주재국 AMR MOUSSA 외무장관은 표제회담에서 UNSC 5개 상임 이사국 대표의 중동지역 비대량 살상무기 지대화 촉구를 환영하면서 ' 우리는 회의결과 성명서에서 중동지역의 비대량 살상무기 지대화에 여러가지 긍정요인을 찾아볼수 있으며,이는 또한 무차별 원칙에 입각한 역내 모든 나라에 대한 군비 통제노력의 진일보'라고 논평함.

끝.

(총영사대리 공선섭-국장)

중아국 1차보 외정실 분석관 안기부 국방부

0055

PAGE 1

91.07.11 21:09 DA

외신 1과 통제관

원 본

외 무 부

종 별 :

번 호 : KUW-0356 일 시 : 91 0715 1400

수 신 : 장관(중일)

발 신 : 주 쿠에이트대사

제 목 : 6+2 외상회의 개최

GCC 회원국및 애급,시리아 (이른바 육 플러스이) 외상회의가 7.15 부터 2일간개최될 예정인바, 동외상회의 결과를 파악, 보고 예정임. (이회의는 당초 7.9개최 예정이었음.).

끝

(대사-국장)

중아국 1차보 외정실 분석관 안기부

0056

PAGE 1

91.07.15 22:14 DA

외신 1과 통제관

원 본

외 무 부

종 별 :

번 호 : CAW-0819 일 시 : 91 0716 1755

수 신 : 장관(중동이,정보)

발 신 : 주 카이로총영사

제 목 : 주요 중동문제에 관한 MUBARAK 대통령 논급

(자료응신 제 143호)

1. 7.15 무바락대통령은 런던소재 아랍어지 AL-HAYAT지와의 회견에서 역내 주요현안에 대해 요지하기와 같이 논급함.

1) BUSH 대통령의 중동평화 제안에 대한 시리아측 회신은 융통성이 있는바, 이의 성공여부는 이스라엘측 SHAMIR 내각에달려있음.

2) GULF 안보는 역내 국가 필요에 의거해야 하며, DAMASCUS 선언의 요체는 공동경제협력과 아랍방어조약에 구체화되어 있음.

- 선언문 내용중 다소의 자구(A FEW WORDS)가 첨가될수 있을것임.

3) 이락 SADDAM 에게 UN 의 핵사찰에 협조할것을 촉구하였음.

4) 대이란 협력 형태는 ARAB 제국들이 결정할수 있을것임. 안보문제에 반드시 병력을수반할 필요는 없는바, 다른 협력형태로도 가능할것임.

5) 대 SUDAN 관계에 있어 문제가 AL-BASHIR에 있다기 보다 위험천만한 무슬림 원리주의자HASSAN AL-TORABI 에 있음. 이집트는 테러주의원천이 어디에 있는지 알고 있으며, ISLAM 은폭력과 테러주의 종교가 아니라 우정의 종교임.

6) 사우디와의 협조관계는 EXCELLENT 함.

7) ACC 는 완전 폐지된 것이 아니라 아직도 박물관에 있음.

2. 최근 중동평화 관련 시리아측 긍정회신이면에는 그간 이집트측이 이를 위해 시리아와 팔레스타인측과 부단히 접촉해온 것과 무관치않은것으로 풀이되며, 또한 이스 라엘 역시 그간이집트와의 관계 증진을 바라온 점에 비춰 중동평화 회담 추진을 위해 주재국은 향후 ISRAEL 과도 모종의 막후 접촉을 추진할가능성이 높음. DAMASCUS선언 이행을 위요하고그간 난항을 거듭해오던 걸프지역 안보문제에 이란측의 참여는군사형태가 아닌 다른 형태로 그해결책을 모색하고 있는것으로

중아국 1차보 외정실 분석관 안기부

0057

PAGE 1 91.07.17 07:47 DN

외신 1과 통제관

풀이되며,수단과의 관계정상화는 걸프전관련 휴유증보다는 국내치안상 (회교 과격 원리주의자준동) 어려움이 있는 것으로 관측됨.끝.

(총영사 박동순-국장)

안보정책과

주 불 대 사 관

불정 760 - 631
수신 장 관
참조 외정실장
제목 중동군축회의

대 : WFR - 1445

대호, 5개국 최종 선언문(Communique Final) 전문을 별첨 송부합니다.

첨부 : 최종 선언문 1부 (4 Page, 5 개조). 끝.

공람	안보정책과	년월일	담당	과장	심의관	실장	차관보	차관	장관

주 불 대

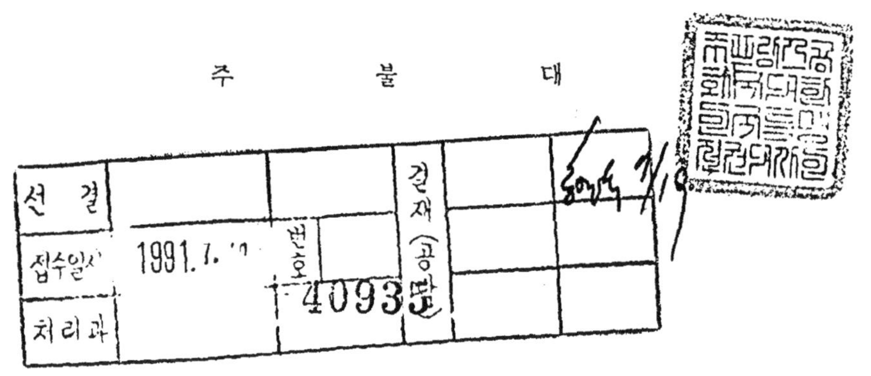

선결			결재(공람)	
접수일시	1991.7.17	번호	40935	
처리과				

0059

REUNION DES CINQ
SUR LES TRANSFERTS D'ARMES ET LA NON-PROLIFERATION

(Paris, 8 et 9 juillet 1991)

de la France

1. Des représentants des Etats-Unis d'Amérique, de la République Populaire de Chine, du Royaume-Uni et de l'Union des Républiques Socialistes Soviétiques se sont réunis à Paris les 8 et 9 juillet afin d'examiner les questions posées par les transferts d'armements conventionnels et la non-prolifération des armes de destruction massive.

Ils ont noté avec préoccupation les dangers liés à l'accumulation excessive de potentiels militaires, et ils ont confirmé qu'ils ne transféreraient pas d'armes conventionnelles lorsque ces transferts, compte-tenu des circonstances, seraient de nature à porter atteinte à la stabilité. Ils ont également noté les menaces à la paix et à la stabilité que constitue la prolifération des armes nucléaires, des armes chimiques et biologiques ainsi que des missiles, et ils ont entrepris d'élaborer de façon juste, raisonnable, complète et équilibrée, des mesures concrètes de non-prolifération et de contrôle des armements sur le plan mondial aussi bien que régional.

.../...

0060

2. Ils ont eu un échange de vues approfondi et de caractère positif sur la base des propositions de maîtrise des armements présentées en particulier par le Président Bush, le Président Mitterrand et le Premier Ministre Major, ainsi que sur la base d'autres propositions dans lesquelles ces problèmes sont évoqués sur un plan global et, à titre d'urgence, pour le Moyen-Orient. Ils sont également convenus d'appuyer la poursuite des travaux visant à mettre en place, sous l'égide du Secrétaire Général des Nations-Unies, un registre des transferts d'armements établi sur une base non- discriminatoire, en tant qu'étape vers une plus grande transparence dans le domaine des transferts d'armes et plus généralement, dans les affaires militaires.

Ils ont souligné que la véritable réponse à la menace de la prolifération consiste en des accords vérifiables de désarmement et de maîtrise des armements entre les parties concernées. Ils ont exprimé leur ferme soutien à la mise en oeuvre intégrale des régimes existants de maîtrise des armements. Pour leur part, ils contribueront à cet objectif en développant et en maintenant des contrôles nationaux stricts et, dans la mesure du possible, harmonisés, afin d'assurer que les équipements et matières relevant des armes de destruction massive ne sont transférés qu'à des fins autorisées et ne sont pas détournés.

Ils se sont également prononcés fermement en faveur de l'objectif qui vise à établir une zone libre d'armes de destruction massive au Moyen-Orient. Ils ont exprimé l'opinion que les étapes essentielles pour atteindre cet objectif comprennent la mise en oeuvre intégrale de la résolution 687 du Conseil de Sécurité et l'adoption par les pays de la région d'un programme global de contrôle des armements pour la région incluant :

- le gel et, et à titre d'objectif final, l'élimination des missiles sol-sol dans la région ;

- la soumission par tous les pays de la région de l'ensemble de leurs activités nucléaires aux contrôles de l'AIEA ;

0061

- l'interdiction d'importation et de production de matières utilisables à des fins de fabrication d'armes nucléaires ;

- l'engagement de tous les Etats de la région à devenir parties à la convention sur les armes chimiques dès que celle-ci sera conclue en 1992.

3. Ils ont rappelé que l'article 51 de la Charte des Nations-Unies garantit à chaque Etat le droit à la légitime défense. Ce droit implique que les Etats ont également le droit d'acquérir les moyens de leur défense. A ce titre, les transferts d'armes conventionnelles, conduits de façon responsable, doivent contribuer à mettre les Etats en mesure d'assumer leurs obligations de sécurité et de souveraineté nationale, et à participer de manière active aux mesures collectives requises par les Nations-Unies dans le but de maintenir ou restaurer la paix et la sécurité internationales.

Ils ont reconnu que des transferts d'armes et de technologies militaires faits sans discernement contribuent à l'instabilité régionale. Ils sont pleinement conscients des responsabilités particulières qui leur incombent de faire en sorte que de tels risques soient évités. Ils sont également conscients du rôle particulier qu'ils doivent exercer pour promouvoir une plus grande responsabilité, une plus grande confiance et une plus grande transparence en ce domaine. Ils reconnaissent également qu'une solution durable de ce problème devrait être recherchée en étroite consultation avec les pays acquéreurs d'armes.

4. Ils ont exprimé l'intention :

- d'observer des règles de retenue lorsqu'ils se prononceront, dans le cadre de leurs procédures nationales de contrôle, sur des transferts d'armements. Sur cette base, ils chercheront à s'entendre pour mettre au point des principes directeurs;

- d'entreprendre de mettre au point, en prenant en considération la situation particulière du Moyen-Orient, en tant que zone première de tension, et s'agissant en priorité de cette région du monde, des modalités de consultation et d'échange d'informations concernant les transferts d'armes ;

- de réunir un groupe d'experts au mois de septembre en vue de rechercher un accord sur cette approche ;

- de tenir une nouvelle réunion plénière au mois d'octobre à Londres ;

- d'organiser périodiquement de nouvelles rencontres afin d'examiner ces questions.

5. Ils expriment la conviction que ce processus de coopération continue contribuera à créer dans le monde, en ce domaine, un climat de vigilance que les autres pays sauront partager./.

0063

외 무 부

암호수신

종 별 : 지 급

번 호 : FRW-1648 일 시 : 91 0717 1710

수 신 : 장 관(구일,외정,정일,경일)

발 신 : 주 불 대사

제 목 : G-7 정상회담

7.16 발표된 " 국제 질서 강화" 제하의 G-7 정치 선언 관련, 당지 반응 및 평가를 하기 보고함.

1. 경제 선진 7 개국이 동 정치 선언에서 유엔 역할 강화, 이라크, 중동평화 , 유고사태 및 소련 개혁 문제등 현금의 국제 정세에 대한 협력 방안을 광범위하게 포괄함으로써 G-7 이 세계 경제 협의를 위한 본래의 기능에서 점차 냉전 시대이후 " 세계 지도부(DIRECTOIRE MONDIAL) 역할을 담당하게되는 새로운 계기를 마련한것으로 풀이됨.

2. 주재국으로서는 국제 정치 문제가 경제 선진 7 개국에 의해 주도 되는것을 피하기 위해 불란서가 안보리 상임 이사국인 유엔 차원에서의 협의 필요성을 강조하였으나, G-7 을 중심으로한 독일, 일본등 경제 강국의 점증하는 국제정치역향력을 견제하기에는 어려울것으로 보임.

3. 한편 G-7 정상은 정치 선언과는 별도로 무기 판매 제한 및 핵 비확산선언을 채택하였으며, 특히 걸프 사태 이후 수차 논의되어 왔던" 무기 이전에 관한유엔 등록제" 합의는 무기 통제를 위한 새로운 국제 협력 방안으로 긍정적으로평가되고 있으나 동 선언에 언급된 " 무기 수출국간 구체적 판매 통제를 위한 지속적 협의" 가 소기의 성과를 보기에는 상당 기간이 소요될것으로 전망됨.

4. 상기 3 항 관련, 불란서는 영국이 제의한 G-7 내 무기 교역통제 실무작업단 설치등 G-7 의 제도화에 적극 반대, 이를 저지하는 한편, 불란서 주창에 의해 관례화 되고 있는 긴급 조력권(DROIT D'ASSISTANCE)을 뒷받침하게될 유엔 긴급 구호 전담 사무차장급에 주재국 KOUCHNER 구호 담당 국무상이 우선적으로 검토되는것을 비롯, 국제평화 유지, 인권, 긴급구호등 인도적인 차원에 있어서의 유엔 기능강화에 합의를 도출한것으로 금번회담의 외교적 성과로 평가함. 끝.

(대사 노영찬 - 국장)

구주국	장관	차관	1차보	2차보	경제국	~~문협국~~	외정실	분석관
청와대	안기부	아주국	미주국	중아국	국기국			

PAGE 1

91.07.18 06:37

외신 2과 통제관 FI

0064

관리번호	91/1270

외 무 부

종 별 : 지 급

번 호 : UKW-1467 일 시 : 91 0717 2140

수 신 : 장 관(경일,구일,아일,미일,국연)

발 신 : 주 영 대사

제 목 : G-7 정상회담(평가)

연: UKW-1465

G-7 정상회담에 관한 당관의 평가를 아래와 같이 보고함

1. 금번 회담은 정치적 측면에서는 " 국제질서의 강화", 그리고 경제적 측면에서는 "세계적인 동반자 관계의 구축" 이라는 기치하에 소련 및 동구사태와 걸프전 이후 국제관계의 재정립을 모색하여 안정과 번영을 위한 국제체제의 마련을 목표로 했으며, 특히 소련의 시장경제에로의 전환을 위한 G-7 과의 협조관계가 개시되고, 유엔의 기능강화와 무기확산규제 체제를 공고히 하는 성과를 거둠

2. 회의전체가 대소지원 문제에 의해 압도된(HIJACKED)측면이 있었으며, 소련이 시장경제에로 동화되기 위해 불가결한 서방측과의 유기적 연계가 본격적으로 출범되는 계기가됨. G-7 의 고르바쵸프에 대한 적극적 지원 방침 결정은 소련의 중앙정부와 공화국간의 정치적 갈등과 심각한 경제적 난관을 극복해 나가는데있어 현 고르바쵸프 체제를 지속적으로 강화해 나감이 유익하다는 판단에 기초한 것으로 분석됨.

3. 우루과이라운드를 금년말까지 타결시킨다는 강한 결의를 분명히 했으며 세계경제의 불원간 회복전망에 비추어 경제정책에 관한 회원국간의 협조 증진의 분위기가 강조되었음. 다만 작년도 휴스톤 회담에서도 우루과이라운드에 관해 조기종결의 확고한 입장을 분명히 했으나 실패한 전례가 있으며, 농산물, 써비스등주요 현안에 관한 배후의 어떤 합의를 전제로한 것인지 불분명한 점이 주목됨

4. 미국은 당초 고르바쵸프 초청에 소극적이었던 것으로 알려졌으나, 미.소간 전략무기감축 조약에 대한 합의를 유도하는데 금번 계기를 충분히 활용했으며, 중동문제 협상과 관련 이스라엘에 대한 압력을 위해 G-7 총체의 영향력을 이용함

5. 영국은 주최국으로서 유엔무기등록안, 최빈국 부채 감면안등 실질적 문제에 자국의 입장을 반영시켰으며, 총선을 앞둔 메이저 수상은 자신의 국내 정치적 위상을

경제국	장관	차관	1차보	2차보	아주국	미주국	구주국	국기국
외정실	분석관	청와대	안기부	청와대(경제)	중아국	통상국	상공부	경기원

PAGE 1 91.07.18 06:48 0065

외신 2과 통제관 FI

제고시키는데 성과를 거둠

6. 일본은 대소 지원문제에 수동적 자세를 견지하면서 소련의 신 외교정책이 구주뿐만 아니고 아세아에도 적용되어야 하고특히 북방영토 문제도 이러한 관점에서 해결되어야 한다는 점을 강조하였으며, 이러한 입장을 회담선언에 반영시킴. 일본은 또한 한. 중. 아세안등 아세아 문제를 대변하여, 반영시킨 점을 스스로 평가하고 있음

7. 독.불.이등 대륙의 제국은 소련의 시장경제에로의 전환문제에 가장 큰 관심을 경주하는 반면 유엔 기능 강화나 무기규제등 새로운 국제질서 구축문제에관해서는 전체적인 분위기에 추종하는 태도를 보임

8. 한반도 문제와 관련, 작년도 휴스톤 회담에 이어 금년에도 북한의 핵안전조치 협정의 서명 및 시행 지연에 대해 강한 우려가 표명된 바, 이 문제에 관한 국제여론의 환기는 물론 대북한 압력행사에 효과적이었던 것으로 관찰됨. 끝

(대사 이홍구-장관)

91.12.31. 까지

원 본

외 무 부

종 별 :

번 호 : CAW-0823 일 시 : 91 0718 1610

수 신 : 장관(중동이,정보)

발 신 : 주 카이로총영사

제 목 : 무바락대통령 시리아 방문

연:CAW-0820

1. 무바락 대통령은 7.17. 시리아를 전격방문, 역내 주요문제들에 관해 협의후 귀국하였는바, 동방문 이면에는 7.14 시리아측의 중동평화 추진관련 대미긍정회신에 따른 BAKER 미국무장관의 제 5차 중동순방 대비를 위한것으로 풀이됨.

2. 이와관련 연호 당초 예상과는 달리 7.19 BAKER 장관이 당지를 방문할 가능성이 높은 것으로 관측됨.

끝.

(총영사 박동순-국장)

중아국 1차보 외정실 분석관 안기부

PAGE 1 91.07.18 23:17 DA 0067

외신 1과 통제관

원 본

외 무 부

종 별 :

번 호 : SBW-1176 일 시 : 91 0722 1410

수 신 : 장관(중일,정보,국방,기정)

발 신 : 주사우디대사

제 목 : 미국무장관 중동 순방(자응23호)

연:SBW-1173

1.7.21 SAUD 주재국 외무장관은 베이커 미국무장관 공항 영송시 기자회견을 통해 연호 성명(점령지역 이주 동결시 대이스라엘 경제 보이콧 중단에 관한 이집트제의지지)에 이어 중동평화의 성사를 위한 미국의 노력에 전폭적인 지지를 표시하는 주재국의 입장을 아래와 같이 밝힘.

-사우디정부는 이랍,이스라엘 분쟁을 종식시키려는 베이커장관의 노력에 지지와사의를 표함

-사우디정부는 중동에서 평화를 달성하기 위한 아사드대통령 및 무바락대통령의노력을 치하하며,조속한 평화정착을 위해 협력을 아끼지 않을것임

-중동의 여러나라들도 사우디,시리아,이집트의 입장을 따라 주기를 바람

-평화노력의 성사를 위해서 이스라엘도 점령지역에 대한 이주를 즉각 중지해야함

2.이집트 및 사우디의 점령지역 이주 동결과 대이스라엘 경제보이콧의 상호 교환제의는 베이커장관이 무바락대통령에게 요청하여 나온것으로 당지 외교가에서는 알려지고 있는바,이는 미국이 중동평화회의 개최안에 대한 시리아의 동의를 받은후,보다광범위하고 적극적인 아랍권의 지지를 받아 이스라엘에 대한 수락압력을 가중시키려는 노력의 일환으로 분석됨

3.한편 파드국왕은 작 7.21 부시대통령 및 무바락대통령과 통화,중동평화 문제를협의하였다고 하며,사우디의 주도로 대이스라엘 보이콧 중단제의에 대한 GCC 전회원국의 지지를 받아낸것으로 알려지고 있음

(대사주병국-국장)

중아국 1차보 외정실 분석관 안기부 국방부

PAGE 1 0068

91.07.22 22:49 DQ

외신 1과 통제관

원 본

외 무 부

종 별 :

번 호 : IRW-0582 일 시 : 91 0729 1200

수 신 : 장 관(중동일)

발 신 : 주 이란 대사대리

제 목 : 벨지움외상 주재국방문

1. 벨지움 MARK EYESKENS 외상이 7.25-28간 이란을 공식방문, 주재국 대통령, 외상, 국회의장등과 양국간 경제협력, 이란-EC 간 경제관계확대, 지역안보및 이라크 난민문제등을 협의함.

2. 당지 일간지 보도에 의하면 RAFSANJANI 대통령은 미국의 대중동정책이 친이스라엘적으로 지역내안정을 가져올수없는 것이라고 주장한데 대해, 벨지움 외상은 세계안보에 긴요한 페만지역안보를 위한 각종제안 내용에 확실치않은점이 많다고 지적함. 또한 이란-벨지움 경제공동위원회 제 1차회의를 91.12월 에부르셀에서 개최하기로 협의 함.

3. 방문결과 관련 파악되는 내용이 있을시 추보하겠음. 끝

(대사대리-국장)

중아국 1차보 외정실 안기부

0069

PAGE 1 91.07.29 17:30 WG

외신 1과 통제관

관리 번호	91/752

원 본

외 무 부

종 별 :

번 호 : AGW-0413 일 시 : 91 0805 1420

수 신 : 장관(중동이,중동일,기정)

발 신 : 주 알제리 대사

제 목 : 미국무장관 알제 방문

1. BAKER 미국무장관은 모로코, 튀니지 방문에 이어 금 8.5(월) 알제 도착예정이며 CHADLI 대통령, GHOZALI 수상 및 BRAHIMI 외무장관과 일련의 회담을 가질 예정임.

2. 이에앞서 8.4(일) ARAFAT PLO 의장은 주재국에 내방, CHADLI 대통령과 회담을 가진바 있으며 내달 9 월 알제에서 PNC(팔레스타인민족 평의회)를 개최할예정임을 발표하였음. 동 PNC 는 88.11 월에 당지에서 개최된바 있으며 오는 10월 개최예정인 팔레스타인문제 해결을 위한 국제회의에 대비, PLO 의 입장을 천명하기 위한것으로 분석됨.

3. 걸프전중 이락지지 이유로 PLO 의 현지도부는 아랍세계에서 완전 고립되어 있는바, PLO 와 함께 이락입장을 적극 지지한바 있는 주재국으로서는 PLO 가 당면하고 있는 현재의 어려운 입장을 지원하기 위해 최대한의 노력을 경주할것으로 예측됨. 끝.

(대사 한석진-국장)

예고:1991.12.31. 일반

중아국	장관	차관	1차보	2차보	중아국	분석관	안기부

PAGE 1 91.08.05 23:51 0070

외신 2과 통제관 CA

원 본

외 무 부

종 별 :

번 호 : TNW-0330 일 시 : 91 0805 1200

수 신 : 장 관(중동이,정보)

발 신 : 주 튀니지 대사

제 목 : BAKER 미 국무장관 튀니지 방문

1. 마그레브 3개국을 순방중인 BAKER 장관은 8.4 BEN ALI 대통령과 3시간동안 회담을 가진후 기자회견을 한바, 그 내용은 다음과 같음.

0 양국관계를 걸프전쟁 이전의 최상의 상태로 조기회복시키로 합의

0 튀니지는 팔레스타인 문제의 정당한 해결을 보장하는 모든 협상개시를 적극 지지함.

0 미국은 마그레브제국이 중동평화회담에 참여하며모든 협상에 기여해주기를 환영함.

2.한편 아라파트 PLO 의장은 7.31 라바트를 방문 HASSAN 국왕을 면담한데 이어 8.3 BEN ALI 대통령과 면담, 미국이 주선하고 있는중동평화회담에 대한 PLO 입장등을 설명한바 있음.

3. 중동평화회담에 대한 튀니지측의 기본태도는아래와 같음.

가.유엔결의안 242,338호와 동부예루살렘에 관한결의안을 기초로 해야 한다.

나.PALESTINE 의 정식대표 참가

다.UMA 의 회담 참석 문제

당지 관측은 상기사항에 대하여 미국측이 그간접촉해 온 내용을 밝힌바 없으나 아랍측으로서는 상기와같은 기본적인 문제에 미국측과 사전합의한것으로 보이며,다만평화회담 개최 성공을위하여 마지막 단계까지 비밀을 유지할것으로 보고있음.

특히 시리아와 애급이 미국측과 충분한 협의를가졌으므로 금번 회담에서 이스라엘측이 상당한수용태도를 보여야 될것으로 기대하고 있음.끝.

(대사 변정현-실장)

중아국 1차보 2차보 미주국 외정실 청와대 안기부

PAGE 1 91.08.06 09:59 DU 0071

외신 1과 통제관

관리번호	91/760

외 무 부

종 별 :

번 호 : AGW-0414 일 시 : 91 0806 1135

수 신 : 장관(중동이,중동일,기정)

발 신 : 주 알제리 대사

제 목 : 미국무장관 알제리 방문

연:AGW-0413

1. 8.5(월) 오전 주재국에 도착한 BAKER 미국무장관은 바로 대통령궁으로 향발, CHADLI 대통령과 면담하였으며 이어 BRAHIMI 외무장관과 별도 회담을 가진후 GHOZALI 수상과 오찬을 같이 하였으며, 동일 오후 주재국 외무장관과 함께 공동 기자회견을 가진후 당지를 출발하였음.

2. 동 기자회견에서 BAKER 국무장관은 중동문제의 포괄적 해결을 위해 알제리아의 역할이 중요함을 강조하고 알제리아가 중동평화 모색을 위해 미국이 주도하는 국제회의 개최노력을 지지함에 만족을 표하고, 일부 중동국가는 매우 어려운 상황에도 과감하게 결정을 하였음을 상기하면서, 여타 국가들도 대의를 위해 평화모색에 동참해줄것을 희망하였음. 동장관은 국제회의에 팔레스타인대표 참가여부 질문에 대하여 중동평화 협상은 이스라엘과 아랍제국간의 관계 및 이스라엘과 팔레스타인과의 관계를 별개로 추진해야 할것이라고 대답하였음.

3. 주재국 BRAHIMI 외무장관은 미국의 평화제의 내용을 검토하기 위하여 마그레브통합기구(UMA) 5 개국의 외상회의 개최를 요청하겠다고 말하고 향후 팔레스타인측과 여타 아랍제국과도 협의를 계속하겠다고 말하므로써 전적인 지지 언질은 유보하였음. 끝.

(대사 한석진-국장)

예고:1991.12.31. 일반

19 91 12 31. 에 예고문에 의거 일반문서로 재 분류됨

중아국	장관	차관	1차보	2차보	중아국	분석관	청와대	안기부

PAGE 1 91.08.06 20:51 0072

외신 2과 통제관 CE

원 본

외 무 부

종 별 :

번 호 : SBW-1213 일 시 : 91 0806 1400

수 신 : 장 관(중일,국방,기정)

발 신 : 주 사우디대사

제 목 : 주재국 외무장관 OIC 연설

8.5 SAUD 주재국 외무장관의 이스탄불 OIC외상회의 기조연설중 지역문제에 관한 주요 언급 내용을 하기 보고함.

1.이락

0 이슬람의 결속을 무너뜨린 당사국을 적절히 응징하지 않고는 이슬람의 결속은회복될수 없음

0 따라서 금번 OIC회의는 이락의 침략을 규탄하고, 이락으로 하여금 유엔결의들을이행시키도록 해야함

0 이락에 대한 경제 재제는 유엔안보리 결의이행시까지 계속 되어야 하며, 이락국민들에 대한 인도적 고려는 유엔특별위원회의 조치를 따라야 함

0 사우디는 이락의 주권, 영토 및 UNITY를 존중함

2.중동평화회의

0 팔레스타인 문제에 대한 근본적 해결이 없는 한 평화를 기대할수 없으며, 사우디는 안보리결의 242 및 338에 입각한 안전 및 안정구축을 지지함

0 동부예루사렘은 분리할수없는 아랍영토임

3.레바논

0 이스VEEONKFKHKGM부 레바논으로 부터의 철수를 요구한 안보리결의 425의 이행을 촉구함

4.아프카니스탄

0 정치적 해결을 촉구하며,아프칸 인민의 정당한 부쟁 및 아프칸난민에 대한 인도적 지원을 계속 지지함.끝

(대사주병국-국장)

중아국 1차보 외정실 안기부 국방부

PAGE 1 91.08.07 07:49 WH

외신 1과 통제관 0073

외 무 부

종 별 :

번 호 : JOW-0565 일 시 : 91 0806 1600

수 신 : 장 관(중동일,중동이,기정)

발 신 : 주 요르단 대사

제 목 : 걸프사태 관련 백서발표

1. 8.4. 주재국 외무성 정무국장은 본직은 초치, 걸프사태 발생 1주년을 맞아 걸프사 태 해결을 위한 주재국의 입장, 조치 및 노력등에 관해 기술한 주재국의 백서 전달에 관한 후세인국왕의 노대통령각하앞 친서와 백서를 본직에게 수교하면서 요르단 입장등을 상세하게 설명함

(한.요 의원친선 협회 사절단의 HASSAN 왕세자 예방시에도 동백서를 전달한바 있음)

2.동백서 발행 이유등에 관해 밝힌 주재국의 발표요지는 다음과 같음

가.요르단의 지정학적인 위치와 이라크, 쿠웨이트등 걸프국가들과의 관계에 비추어 요르단 정부는 걸프사태 전단계에 걸쳐 요르단이 관여한 기록, 사건 및 결의안들을 분석, 발표하여야 할 필요성을 느꼈음

나.백서는 유엔헌장에 부응하여 걸프사태에 대한 아랍해결책을 평화적으로 확보하고자 노력하였던 후세인 주재국 국왕과 고위관리들의 활동사항들을 구체적으로 제시함

다.90.8.2. 걸프사태의 발생과 함께 중동전체에 세계의 관심이 집중되었으며 특히 걸프사태에 대한 요르단의 입장에 관심이 집중되었으며 요르단에 대한 다수의 '평결'은 요르단에 '징계'를가 하기 위한 압력으로 작용하여 이와같은 제반오해를 분석하고 요르단의 입장을 분명히 하기 위해 발간하였음.

라.백서는 90년 여름에서 91년초까지의 걸프사태전 단계에 걸쳐 요르단이 취한 정책들을 포함하고 있음

마.90.8.2. 이라크의 쿠웨이트 침공이후의 사건들과이에 관련된 요르단의 반응들을 제시하고 있으며, 특히 유엔 안보리 결의안 존중과 외교적 해결책 필요성과 관련중립적인 입장을 고수하고자 했던 요르단의 노력이 강조되고 있음

3.동친서 및 백서 파견 송부 위계임

(대사-국장)

중아국 1차보 중아국 외정실 안기부

PAGE 1 91.08.07 07:49 WH

외신 1과 통제관 0074

원 본

외 무 부

암호수신

종 별 :

번 호 : CAW-0872 일 시 : 91 0807 1650

수 신 : 장관(중동이,정보)

발 신 : 주 카이로 총영사

제 목 : 이집트의 대리비아 국경개방 상응조치

연:CAW-0868

1. 주재국 내각은 91.8.6 부터 이집트-리비아 국경을 양국민에게 개방(국경지역 세관 및 이민초소 철폐와 입국자들의 경찰서 등록신고제 해제) 키로 결정함.

동 조치는 8.5. 리비아에서 귀국한 무바락대통령의 지시에 따른 것이나 이는 91.3.29 GADDAFY 대통령이 내린 양국국경 인위장벽 제거 조치를 이집트측이 뒤 늦게 수용한 것으로, 이로인해 향후 양국간 각종 경제통합 조치가 빠른 속도로 추진될 가능성이 높음.

2. 당초 영군의 철수 21 주년 기념식에 즈음 GADDAFY 가 양국국경 초소는 식민주의자들이 인위적으로 만들은 장벽임을 지적, 이를 동일 후에인 양국민을 위해 철폐한다고 했을때만 해도 주재국 조야에서는 GADDAFY 의 변덕스런 성격 소치로 간주, 탐탐치않게 여겼던 것임.

그러나 중동평화 추진관련 반미주의자인 GADDAFY 의 협력 획득을 위해 MUBARAK 대통령이 리비아를 방문한 후에 이루어진 점을 감안하며, 이집트측이 GADDAFY 의 오랜 꿈인 이집트. 리비아 및 수단통합을 위한 호의적인 제스츄어를 취하는 댓가로 중동평화 추진에대한 리비아측의 협력을 얻어냈을 가능성이 높은것으로 관측됨. 끝.

(총영사 박동순-국장)

중아국 차관 1차보 2차보 외정실 분석관 청와대 안기부

PAGE 1 91.08.07 23:07

외신 2과 통제관 CF

0075

외 무 부

종 별 :

번 호 : NJW-0572 일 시 : 91 0813 1030

수 신 : 장관(아프일,중이,정보,기정)사본:국방부장관

발 신 : 주나이지리아

제 목 : 미국부통령 주재국방문(자료응신38호)

연: NJW-0564

DAN QUAYLE 미부통령이 9.9.-11기간 주재국을 공식방문,바방기다 대통령과 10월로 예정된 중동평화회담을 나이지리아에서 개최하는 문제와 남아공에 대한 제재해제 문제에 관하여 협의할 것으로 알려짐

(대사조명행-국장)

중아국 중아국 외정실 안기부 국방부

PAGE 1

91.08.13 20:56 DF

외신 1과 통제관

0076

주 국 련 대 표 부

주국련20313- **657** 91. 8. 21.

수신 : 장관

참조 : 국제기구조약국장, 중동아프리카국장

제목 : 중동군축안(이집트)(안보리)

표제관련 안보리 문서를 별첨과 같이 송부합니다.

첨 부 : 상기 문서. 끝.

주 국 련 대 사

선 결			결재(공람)		
접수일시	1991.8.26				
처리과		47641			

0077

UNITED
NATIONS

A S

General Assembly Security Council

Distr.
GENERAL

A/46/329
S/22855
30 July 1991
ENGLISH
ORIGINAL: ARABIC AND ENGLISH

GENERAL ASSEMBLY
Forty-sixth session
Items 35, 54, 59, 60, 61, 62, 63, 67 and 68 of the provisional agenda*
THE SITUATION IN THE MIDDLE EAST
ESTABLISHMENT OF A NUCLEAR-WEAPON-FREE ZONE IN THE REGION OF THE MIDDLE EAST
CHEMICAL AND BACTERIOLOGICAL (BIOLOGICAL) WEAPONS
GENERAL AND COMPLETE DISARMAMENT
REVIEW AND IMPLEMENTATION OF THE CONCLUDING DOCUMENT OF THE TWELFTH SPECIAL SESSION OF THE GENERAL ASSEMBLY
REVIEW OF THE IMPLEMENTATION OF THE RECOMMENDATIONS AND DECISIONS ADOPTED BY THE GENERAL ASSEMBLY AT ITS TENTH SPECIAL SESSION
ISRAELI NUCLEAR ARMAMENT
STRENGTHENING OF SECURITY AND COOPERATION IN THE MEDITERRANEAN REGION
REVIEW OF THE IMPLEMENTATION OF THE DECLARATION ON THE STRENGTHENING OF INTERNATIONAL SECURITY

SECURITY COUNCIL
Forty-sixth year

Letter dated 29 July 1991 from the Chargé d'affaires a.i. of the Permanent Mission of Egypt to the United Nations addressed to the Secretary-General

On instructions from my Government, I have the honour to transmit herewith a letter from His Excellency Mr. Amre Moussa, Minister for Foreign Affairs of the Arab Republic of Egypt, dated 21 July 1991, concerning the initiatives of arms limitation and disarmament in the Middle East.

---

* A/46/150.

91-24365 2489f (E) /...

0078

I should be grateful if you would have the present letter and its annex circulated as an official document of the General Assembly, under items 35, 54, 59, 60, 61, 62, 63, 67 and 68 of the provisional agenda, and of the Security Council.

(Signed) Mohamed Noman GALAL
Chargé d'affaires, a.i.

0079

/...

ANNEX

Letter dated 21 July 1991 from the Minister for Foreign Affairs of Egypt addressed to the Secretary-General

The world has in recent years been the scene of momentous and historic developments which have radically changed the climate of international relations. This change has been accompanied by progress whose significance resides in agreement on concrete measures for arms reduction and disarmament. These are all developments which will, we hope, have a positive impact at the international level and direct results at the regional level, particularly in areas of tension and conflict.

In this connection, Egypt has consistently affirmed that the Middle East region requires intensive efforts on the part of all nations of the region to initiate a peace process which will lead to a just solution of its unresolved problems - first and foremost being the question of Palestine - in such a way as to ensure peaceful coexistence between the various parties in an atmosphere of peace, stability and justice. This process may be accompanied by activity in the sphere of arms reduction and disarmament, the objective being to spare the region from superfluous threats. It is our conviction that the arms race in the region - including nuclear weapons and weapons of mass destruction - impedes and threatens peace efforts, besides constituting a serious threat to the region's future.

Accordingly, Egypt has since 1974 - in the context of the United Nations - called for the establishment of a nuclear-weapon-free zone in the Middle East. This call has been the object of a consensus in the General Assembly for over 10 years in succession. In addition, President Hosni Mubarak proposed in April 1990 that the Middle East should be declared a region free of all weapons of mass destruction, because it is Egypt's perception that threats to the region have continued to grow, particularly in the course of recent years, as a result of the accumulation of arms. This proposal was designed to reaffirm Egypt's role in evaluating the situation in the region and in contributing to the suggestion of practical and constructive solutions to counter any danger to which the region may be subjected.

The recent events in the Middle East induced many States to endorse our latest initiative, which was also endorsed by the Security Council in the context of its resolution 687 (1991). These developments also prompted a number of countries to make their own proposals on arms limitation, particularly in the Middle East. Egypt welcomed all initiatives and ideas designed to contribute to the promotion of international and regional stability and security and promised to engage in a constructive dialogue concerning such initiatives.

As a first step, and with a view to demonstrating the extent of Egypt's commitment and determination to take part in these discussions in a constructive manner, President Hosni Mubarak addressed letters to the Heads of State and Government of the five permanent members of the Security Council and

0080 /...

the major industrialized countries engaged in consultations on these matters, in order to acquaint them both with Egypt's position on the subjects of arms reduction and with its recent proposals.

In this connection, I should like to note that Egypt regards positively all disarmament proposals which ensure the following:

(a) Increased security for the nations of our region while maintaining lower quantities of armaments, bearing in mind that security can be achieved only through peaceful relations, dialogue and political arrangements, eschewing the logic of force;

(b) A qualitative and quantitative balance between the military capabilities of all States in the region, because a continuation of the current imbalance is unacceptable in a region which is striving for a just and comprehensive peace;

(c) The conclusion of agreements on arms reduction and disarmament which may be applied to all States of the region and be complemented by effective monitoring measures and at the same time secure equal rights and responsibilities for those nations, while allowing the nations of the region to cooperate with the international community in establishing arrangements for arms reduction and disarmament so that the problem may be addressed in an integrated and comprehensive manner in accordance with those nations' real security requirements;

(d) The accordance of priority to ridding the region of weapons of mass destruction - particularly nuclear, chemical and biological weapons - together with consideration of measures for conventional arms reduction when political circumstances permit, following the achievement of peace in the region or, at least, once the peace process has made substantial progress towards the attainment of its goal.

I am pleased to inform you that, on 5 July 1991, Egypt announced a series of additional ideas and proposals designed to contribute to the ongoing dialogue on efforts to reduce armaments in our region and, in particular, to accelerate the establishment of the Middle East as a zone free of weapons of mass destruction.

These proposals are as follows:

(a) Egypt calls on the major arms-producing States - and particularly the permanent members of the Security Council - as well as Israel, Iran and the Arab States to deposit undertakings with the Security Council in which they clearly and unconditionally endorse the declaration of the Middle East as a region free of weapons of mass destruction and commit themselves not to take any steps or measures which would run counter to or impede the attainment of that objective.

(b) Egypt calls on the arms-producing States and the parties to the Treaty on the Non-Proliferation of Nuclear Weapons to step up their efforts to

/...

ensure that all Middle East nations which have not yet done so adhere to the Treaty, in recognition of the fact that this is a step of the utmost importance and urgency.

(c) Egypt calls on nations of the Middle East region which have not yet done so to declare their commitment:

(i) Not to use nuclear, chemical or biological weapons;

(ii) Not to produce or acquire any nuclear weapons;

(iii) Not to produce or acquire any nuclear materials susceptible to military use and to dispose of any existing stocks of such materials;

(iv) To accept the International Atomic Energy Agency safeguards regime whereby all their nuclear facilities become subject to international inspection.

(d) Egypt calls on those nations of the region which have not yet done so to declare their commitment to adhere to the Treaty on the Non-Proliferation of Nuclear Weapons, as well as to the Convention concerning the prohibition of biological weapons of 1972, no later than the conclusion of the negotiations on the prohibition of chemical weapons being conducted by the Conference on Disarmament in Geneva.

(e) Egypt calls on Middle East States to declare their commitment actively and fairly to address measures relating to all forms of delivery systems for weapons of mass destruction.

(f) Egypt calls on nations of the region to approve the assignment to an organ of the United Nations or another international organization of a role, to be agreed upon at a future date, in the verification of those nations' compliance with such agreements on arms reduction and disarmament as may be concluded between them.

In order to give added impetus to the negotiations between all the parties concerned with these matters, Egypt intends to make direct contact with the major parties concerned - both internationally and in the Middle East region - by dispatching envoys and through the use of conventional diplomatic channels, with a view to discussing these various ideas and means for their implementation in both the bilateral and multilateral contexts at the regional and international levels.

(Signed) Amre MOUSSA
Minister for Foreign Affairs
of the Arab Republic of Egypt

0082

원 본

외 무 부

암호수신

종 별 : 지 급

번 호 : KUW-0479 일 시 : 91 0825 1300

수 신 : 장관(중동이)

발 신 : 주 쿠웨이트 대사

제 목 : 소련사태보고

연:KUW-0470

1. 쿠웨이트 왕은 8.22 고르바쵸프와 옐친에게 각각 사태진압을 축하하고 소련의 합법정부가 수복된것을 지지하며, 이라크의 쿠웨이트 침공때 보여준 소련의 태도에 대하여 감사를 표시하는 내용의 전문을 타전하였음.

2. 쿠웨이트 외무부의 구주국장 (미주국장 임시겸임) AL-MUTAWA 대사는 고르바쵸프 체재 수복과 안정이 쿠웨이트의 안전과 중동지역 안정에 긴요하다고 본직과의 대담에서 강조하였음. 끝

(대사-국장)

중아국	장관	차관	1차보	2차보	외정실	분석관	청와대	안기부

PAGE 1 91.08.26 14:50 0083

외신 2과 통제관 BN

외 무 부

종 별 : 긴 급

번 호 : USW-4460 일 시 : 91 0906 1750

수 신 : 장 관 (미일,미남,동구일,중동이)

발 신 : 주 미 대사

제 목 : BAKER 장관 동정

금 9.6 국무성 정례 브리핑시 TUTWILER 대변인은 BAKER 장관의 소련및 중동 순방일정 을 하기와 같이 발표함. (발표문 별첨 USW(F)-3628)

일시, 장소, 면담 예정자(순)

9.8, 멕시코, -

9.10-13, 모스크바, 고르바쵸프, 옐친대통령, 소연방외무, 러시아공 외무장관등

9.13, 레닌그라드, 레닌그라드 시장

9.14, 에스토니아, 라트비아, 리투아니아, -

9.15, 카작스탄, 카작스탄 대통령

9.16, 이스라엘, -

9.17-20 경, 이집트, 요르단, 시리아, -.끝.

(대사 현홍주-국장)

미주국 1차보 미주국 구주국 중아국 외정실 안기부

PAGE 1 91.09.07 07:20 FO

외신 1과 통제관 0084

원 본

외 무 부

종 별 :

번 호 : AEW-0381 일 시 : 91 0908 1430

수 신 : 장 관(중동일)

발 신 : 주 UAE 대사

제 목 : 쿠웨이트국왕 주재국 방문(자료응신32호)

1. SABAH 쿠웨이트 국왕이 금 9.8.오전에 주재국을 방문, 오후에 출국함.

2. 동 방문은 명일 ZAYED 대통령의 불란서 방문에 앞서 갑작스레 이루어 진것임.

3. 동건관련 특이사항있을시 추보위계임. 끝.

(대사 홍순용-국장)

중아국 1차보 외정실 안기부

PAGE 1

91.09.08 21:33 FO

외신 1과 통제관

0085

관리 번호	91/1577

	분류번호	보존기간

발 신 전 보

번 호 : WKU-0340 910909 1359 FN 종별 :

~~WUS~~ -4100

수 신 : 주 주쿠웨이트, 미대사 ~~//총영사/~~

발 신 : 장 관 (중동일)

제 목 : 미.쿠웨이트 방위조약

대 : KUW-0504

대호 3항 미.쿠웨이트 방위조약관련, 최근 외신보도는 미국방부 대변인 말을인용, 미.쿠웨이트간에 9월중 합동 군사훈련과 쿠웨이트내의 미군 장비배치등을 내용으로 하는 유효기간 10년의 방위조약에 가조인 했다하는바, 동사실 확인및 자베르국왕 방미(9.20)등 미.쿠관계 정세파악 보고바람. 끝.

(중동아국장 이 해 순)

예 고 : 91.12.31.까지

1991 12.31 에 예고문에 의거 일반문서로 재 분류됨.

보안 통제	

앙 고 재	91년 9월 9일	중동일과	기안자 성명		과 장	심의관	국 장		차 관	장 관
							전결			

외신과통제

0086

관리번호	91/1576

분류번호	보존기간

발 신 전 보

번 호 : WUK-1652 외 별지참조 종별 :

수 신 : 주 수신처 참조 ///대사//총영사

발 신 : 장 관 (중동일)

제 목 : 미.쿠웨이트 방위조약

1. 최근 외신보도는 9.5. 미 국방부 대변인말을 인용, 미.쿠웨이트간에 9월중 합동 군사훈련과 쿠웨이트내의 미국 장비배치등을 내용으로하는 유효기간 10년의 방위 조약에 가조인 했다하는바, 이에대한 귀주재국 정부입장및 언론의 반응을 조사 보고바람. 끝.

(중동아국장 이 해 순)

수신처 : 주 영, 불, 독, 이태리, 사우디, 이란, 요르단, 바레인, 카타르, UAE, 오만대사, 주 카이로총영사

예 고 : 91.12.31. 까지

1991. 12.31. 에 예고문에 의거 일반문서로 재 분류됨.

2. 걸프전 직후 걸프6개국과 애굽, 시리아는 다마스커스에서 소위 6 프러스 2의 ~~중동군~~ 아랍평화유지군 창설에 합의한 것으로 보도되었으나 그후 이란의 이의제기 및 소위 6 프러스 1 으로의 대체논의, 애굽및 시리아군의 철수, 일부 걸프국가의 미군 계속주둔 희망보도등 상기 다마스커스 선언이 당초합의대로 추진되지 못하고 있는듯한 인상인바, 금번 미.쿠 협정체결도 이런 맥락에서 파악해야할 것인지 주재국측 입장도 파악에 참고바람.

보안통제	

앙고재	91년 9월 9일	중동일과	기안자 성명		과 장	심의관	국 장	차 관	장 관
							전결		

외신과통제

0087

WUK-1652 910909 1357 FN

WFR -1865 WGE -1431 WIT -1000 WIR -0627 WJO -0537

WBH -0338 WQT -0212 WAE -0399 WOM -0201 WCA -0611

WSB -0949

0088

美-쿠웨이트, 10개년 방위조약 서[illegible] 예정

(워싱턴 로이터=聯合) 美國과 쿠웨이트는 9월 합동 군사훈련과 쿠웨이트내의 美軍장비 배치등을 내용으로 하는 유효기간 10년의 방위조약에 서명할 것이라고 美국방부가 5일 밝혔다.

피트 윌리엄스 美국방부 대변인은 양국관리들이 이 조약에 가조인했다는 쿠웨이트 정부의 발표를 확인했다.

쿠웨이트는 지난 4일 이 방위조약이 걸프戰이후에도 계속되는 이라크의 위협에 대응하기 위한 것이라고 말했다.

윌리엄스 대변인은 쿠웨이트와의 이번 조약으로 美軍은 쿠웨이트의 불특정 항구들을 이용할 수 있으며 쿠웨이트軍과 군사훈련도 가능하며 또한 美軍장비를 쿠웨이트내 미리 배치할 수 있게 되었다고 설명하고 이같은 사실은 美軍이 쿠웨이트내 영구히 주둔하는 것을 의미하지는 않는다고 말했다.

그는 이어 "우리는 쿠웨이트내 영구기지를 갖거나 페르시아만내의 어느 지역에 지상군을 영구주둔시킬 생각은 없다"고 말했다.

그는 또 걸프戰이후 해군함정을 비롯한 약 4만명의 美軍이 아직 이 지역에 주둔하고 있으며 이들의 대부분은 올해말까지 철수할 것이라고 덧붙였다.(끝)

Carter backs White House delay on loan guarantee for Israel

WASHINGTON, Sept 5 (AFP) - Former President Jimmy Carter Thursday backed a White House decision to delay 10 billion dollars in housing loan guarantees for Israel, saying that Israeli settlements in the occupied territories were an obstacle to peace in the Middle East.

"President (George) Bush is correct in wanting to delay approval of these loan guarantees for three or four months to see what happens in the Soviet Union," Carter said after meeting with the president.

The Soviet Union and the United States are organizing a Middle East Peace conference tentatively scheduled for late October.

"I would like to see the peace process have a chance now that there's no more Soviet Union," added Carter, who presented Bush with a report on future U.S.-Japanese relations which he had formulated with former Japanese Prime-Minister Yasuhiro Nakasone.

Carter said he was concerned with the continued influx of Israeli settlers into the Israeli occupied territories of the West Bank and Gaza. "I always thought it was a major obstacle to peace," he added.

U.S. Secretary of State James Baker said Wednesday he wanted to put off considering a credit guarantee for the construction in Israel of housing for Jewish immigrants from the Soviet Union so as not to jeopardize a proposed Mideast peace conference.

Informed sources said the U.S. administration sought the delay because of continued concern in Arab countries that the aid would be used by the Shamir government to tighten Israel's grip on occupied Palestinian territories.

Israeli Prime Minster Yitzhak Shamir Thursday rejected any link between the settlements and the Middle East peace process, but ruled out a freeze in new settlements in the occupied territories in lieu of regional peace negotiations.

112

0089

원 본

외 무 부

종 별 :

번 호 : AEW-0383 일 시 : 91 0909

수 신 : 장 관 (중동일)

발 신 : 주 UAE 대사

제 목 : 쿠웨이트 국왕 주재국 방문(자료응신 34호)

연:AEW-0381

1. 연호, SABAH 쿠웨이트국왕은 주재국 ZAYED대통령에게 걸프전시 쿠웨이트를 신실하고 확고하게 도와준데 대하여 사의를 표명함.

2. ZAYED 대통령은 쿠웨이트가 재건되어 역내번영과 발전에 기여할수 있도록 가능한 모든 지원을 아끼지 않을 것을 확언하였음을 보고함.끝.

(대사 홍순용-국장)

중아국 1차보 외정실 안기부

PAGE 1

91.09.09 17:45 WG

외신 1과 통제관

0090

관리번호	91/1583

원 본

외 무 부

종 별 : 지 급

번 호 : KUW-0520 일 시 : 91 0910 1200

수 신 : 장관(중동일)

발 신 : 주 쿠 대사

제 목 : 쿠웨이트.미 방위조약

대:WKU-340

연:KUW-504

1. 쿠웨이트와 미국은 10 년 유효한 상호방위조약 문안에 합의하고 9.8 쿠웨이트에서 양국대사(주미 쿠웨이트대사 일시귀국)가 가서명 하였음. 아직 협정문안은 공표되지 않았지만 연호보고대로 지역평화와 미.쿠웨이트의 방위를 위한 군사협력, 합동군사 훈련실시및 미국무기, 장비의 쿠웨이트내 배치, 미해. 공군의쿠웨이트기지.시설이용등을 주내용으로 하고있는것으로 알려지고있으며, 문안이입수되는대로 보고하겠음.

2. 쿠의 국민감정은 미국의 지상전부병력 주둔을 강력하게 희망하고 있는데미국으로서는 해외지상군을 감축한다는 일반원칙과 중동지역의 가변적 정치조건및 국제관계, 영토가 작고 자연적 방어은페물이 없는 사막의 특수조건등으로 인하여 지상군주둔을 고려하고 있지않으며, 쿠 정부당국자들도 이점에 관해 미측의 입장을 양해하고, 한편 미국주둔에 따른 정치적 부담도 고려하여 미지상전부병력은 주둔치않기로 양측간에 합의된것으로 보임.

3.9.8 주쿠 미국대사를 방문, 위내용을 확인하였는바, 방위조약서명은 쿠웨이트왕의 워싱턴 방문기간에 국방장관이 수행하거나, 또는 국방장관이 별도로 가서 서명할 예정이라함. 미대사는 미국은 걸프지역 군사안보를 위해 GCC 6 개국과양자협정을 체결할 방침이며, 사우디, 바레인, 오만과는 이미 체결되어있고, 카탈, UAE 와의 교섭도 순조롭게 진행되고있다함. 또한 쿠와의 합동군사훈련은 이집트와의 BRIGHT STAR 와 같은 대규모의 연습보다는 작은 규모로 자주실시하는방식으로대처할것이며, 특히 이락이 계속해서 쿠와의 국경지역 침투를 도발하고있고, 최근 부비얀섬 사건은 민간인으로 위장, 부비얀섬에 서서히 조금씩

중아국 장관 차관 1차보 2차보 외정실 분석관 청와대 안기부

PAGE 1 91.09.10 19:23 0091

외신 2과 통제관 BW

침부시켜 종국에는 이락영토임을 기정사실화하려는 기도가 드러난것으로 해석되므로 이락에 대한 강력한 대처가 필요하다고 언급하였음.(외교단과 민간일부에서는쿠정부가 쿠 피납자 석방부진, 물가등귀, 써비스 불만등 국민불만을 겨냥하여 부비얀사건을 과장했다는 관측과 함께 미국과의 안보조약체결 분위기조성을 위해서 그랬다는 관측도있음)

4. 관찰

가. 미국은 지상전투병력의 항시적 주둔대신 소규모 군사연습을 자주함으로써 지상전투부대 주둔없이 사실상 지상군의 상주와 다름없는 효과를 내는방식을 택했다고 생각되며, 금번 방위조약에 SOFA 규정이 포함된것도 이러한 이유때문일것으로 생각됨.

나.8 월말까지 걸프전 참가미군병력은 일단 철수하였으나, 서독주둔 병력이3 개월간 주둔을 위하여 교체병력으로 와있으며, 미국측은 "아직 쿠의 안보태세가 되어있지 않아 9.1 까지의 철수계획을 수정, 당분간 더 주둔할 계획이다"라고 말했음.

다. 쿠는 영, 불등과도 쌍무적으로 안보조약체결 교섭을 하고있음. 소위 다마스커스 선언에의한 아랍연합군 주둔문제는 아직도 관련아랍국가들간에 합의를 못보고있고,9.10 카이로 개최예정인 외상회의에서 좀 자세한 윤곽이 드러날것같음. 기보한대로 쿠정부는 이집트와 시리아군대의 주둔을 원하지않고 "필요한때 즉각와서 돕는다"는 방식을 원하고 있는것같음. 쿠 외무차관이 벨지움대사에게 말한내용을 보면 이집트, 시리아의 주둔 가능성은 없고 10 만명의 걸프연합군을 조직하여 5 만을 사우디에 2.5 만을 UAE 에,2.5 만을 쿠웨이트에 주둔시키는 쪽으로 GCC 국가사이에 협의를 진행하고있으나, 이것도 현재로서는 큰진전이 없다함.

라. 쿠는 기본적으로 인구기반이 적어서 병력을 늘리더라도 전전수준인 2 만이상을 가질수는 없고, 지난해 이라크의 침공을 포함한 과거 경험으로 보아 아랍 "형제국가"들을 믿을수도 없는 사정이므로 자국방위와 걸프지역안보를 미국에의존할수 밖에 없는실정이며, 쿠정부와 국민도 이를인식, 공언하고 있음. 끝.

(대사-국장)

예고:91.12.31. 까지

원 본

암호수신

외 무 부

종 별 :

번 호 : CAW-0968 일 시 : 91 0910 1215

수 신 : 장관(중동이,정보)

발 신 : 주 카이로 총영사

제 목 : 미-쿠웨이트 방위조약

대:WCA-0611

최근 향후 10 년간 쿠웨이트 영내에 미군주둔 미구기저장 및 육해공군의 정기합동 군사훈련등을 골자로 하는 쿠-미 안보구도 양해설(미서명)에 관해 AMR MOUSSA 주재국 외무장관은 9.3.NAM 외상회의 참석길에 당지를 방문한 SHEKH SALEM AL-SABAH 쿠웨이트 부수상겸 외무장관과의 기자회견에서 아래와 같이 각국의 입장을 천명한바있음.

1. 이집트 외무장관

1)이집트는 쿠웨이트정부가 체결한 어떤 협정도 쿠웨이트 이해에 관한 사항으로 이를 존중할 것이며

2)쿠웨이트가 추진하는 개별 협정과는 관계없이 범아랍 안보 필요에 따라 마련된 DAMASCUS 선언에 따른 평화유지 임무는 계속할 것임.

2. 쿠웨이트 외무장관

1)이집트와 시리아는 쿠웨이트의 가까운 우호국이므로 쿠-미 협정이 결코 DAMASCUS 선언에 부정적인 영향을 주지 않을것이며

2)DAMASCUS 선언 이행문제들에 관해 선언 서명국대표가 불원(9-10 월중)카이로에 모여 재협의 확정지을 예정임.끝.

(총영사 박동순-국장)

중아국	장관	차관	1차보	외정실	분석관	청와대	안기부

PAGE 1 91.09.10 21:12 0093

외신 2과 통제관 DO

관리번호	91/1584

원 본

외 무 부

종 별 :

번 호 : QTW-0204 일 시 : 91 0910 1230

수 신 : 장 관(중동일)

발 신 : 주 카타르 대사

제 목 : 미.쿠 웨이트 방위조약

대:WQT-0212

1. 표제 조약 초안이 쿠웨이트 각의에서 승인(9.4)된데 대하여 주재국의 영자 일간지 GULF TIMES(9.5)는 관련기사를 일면 톱으로 보도하고 "UP TO THE KUWAITIS" 제목의 다음요지 사설을 게재함.

"..... 다마스커스선언과 관련하여 의문이 제기될수 있으나 쿠웨이트는 독립국가로서 자국의 영토와국민을 수호하기 위한 수단을 선택할 권리가 있다 ... 연합군의참전없이 이라크군을 축출할수 있었을것이라고 생각하는 쿠웨이트군이나걸프지역 사람은 하나도 없다. 솔직히말해서, 아랍군 힘만으로 쿠웨이트를 수복할수 없었을것이다. ... 따라서 쿠웨이트는 과거의 허구적인 슬로건(아랍국가간의 해결 추구)에 개의함이 없이 스스로의 장래를 결정할수있도록 맡겨져야한다."

2. 이에대한 주재국 정부의 입장은 공표된바 없으나 대체로 상기 사설 내용과 같은 입장으로 추정되며 외무성 HUSSAIN ALI AL-DOOSARI GCC 국장에의하면(개인적인 견해라고전제) 다마스커스 선언은 쿠웨이트 수복직후인 3 월초에 당시 애급및 시리아의영향하에 군사적지원과 경제협력을 결부한 내용을 졸속으로 채택되었으나, 이란으로부터의 제동과 애급및 시리아로부터의 과도한 반대급부요구와 아울러 쿠웨이트뿐만아니라 사우디를 비롯한 GCC 각국의 지역안전 보장에 실효성이 없는 애급및 시리아 양국의 상시주둔을 원치 않는 분위기하에서, 당초부터 미군주둔을 희망해온 쿠웨이트선택에 귀결하게 된것으로 본다고함.

3. 한편 GCC6 개국은 지난 8.27-28 간 오만에서 국군 총참모장회의를 갖고 걸프지역 6 개국 공동방위군의 설립을 독자적으로 추진키로 합의한바 있음. 끝

(대사 유내형-국장)

중아국	장관	차관	1차보	2차보	외정실	분석관	청와대	안기부

PAGE 1 91.09.10 22:08 0094

외신 2과 통제관 FK

예고:91.12.31 까지

1991 12.31. 에 예고문에
의거 일반문서로 재 분류됨.

PAGE 2

0095

원 본

외 무 부

종 별 :

번 호 : AEW-0385 일 시 : 91 0910 1300

수 신 : 장 관(중동일,서구일)

발 신 : 주 UAE 대사

제 목 : ZAYED 대통령 방불(2)

연:AEW-0380

대:WAE-0399

1.주재국 언론은 표제관련, ZAYED 대통령의 기자회견 내용을 보도하였는바, 주요내용 아래와 같음을 보고함.

가.전후 역내 안보문제

-역내 외군기지및 주둔을 반대함

-단, 쿠웨이트는 국가방위상 외국과 방위조약이 절실히 필요함

-UAE는 걸프전후 최신에 무기도입및 고도의 군사훈련으로 안보문제를 스스로 해결하기 위하여 노력하고 있음(필요시 우방의 도움요청)

나.중동평화문제-미국과 국제사회는 중동평화문제를 공평하고 포괄적으로 다루어야함

-중동평화가 정착되기 위해서는 이스라엘이 탐욕을 버리고 아랍의 권리가 회복되어야함

-팔레스타인 대표권 문제는 팔레스타인인 스스로가 해결해야 함(PLO가 상금 팔레스타인 합법대표기구임을 인정하는 기본입장은 불변)

2.불.UAE는 항공.사법.투자등 3개의 상무협정을 금번에 맺었음을 참고로 첨언보고 함.끝.

(대사 홍순용-국장)

중아국 구주국 분석관

PAGE 1 91.09.10 22:29 FG

외신 1과 통제관

0096

관리번호	91/1582

원 본

외 무 부

종 별 :

번 호 : GEW-1840 일 시 : 91 0910 1730

수 신 : 장 관(중동일)

발 신 : 주 독 대사

제 목 : 미.쿠웨이트 방위조약

대:WGE-1431

1. 대호 관련, 주재국 정부는 입장을 밝힌바 없으며, 언론도 간략히 사실 보도하고 있음

2. 동건 관련 권세영 서기관이 외무부 쿠웨이트 담당관을 접촉, 문의한바 동담당관은 쿠웨이트로서는 최근 아랍평화유지군 창설이 이란의 중근동 평화질서의 참여 주장등으로 인하여 당초 다마스커스 합의대로 진전되기는 어렵다는 판단하에 자국의 안보를 모색하기 위해 미국과의 방위조약을 체결하게 된것으로 본다고 말함. 끝

(대사-국장)

예고:91.12.31. 까지

1991. 12. 31. 에 예고문에 의거 일반문서로 재 분류됨.

중아국 장관 차관 분석관 청와대 안기부

PAGE 1

91.09.11 07:33

외신 2과 통제관 BS

0097

관리 번호	

원 본

외 무 부

종 별 :

번 호 : IRW-0687 일 시 : 91 0911 1500

수 신 : 장관(중동일,정일,기정)

발 신 : 주 이란 대사

제 목 : 미.쿠웨이트 방위조약

대:WIR-0637

대호관련 HABIBI 주재국 부통령은 9.9 주례 기자회견을통해 표제 조약체결을강력비난하며, 역내문제의 역내국가간 해결 필요성을 강조하였음. 주재국 언론반을 종합한 당관 관찰을 아래요약 보고함.

-이란은 걸프전 종료이래 계속 기회있을때마다 걸프지역내 안보는 역내국가간 협력에의해 이루어져야 한다고 강조하며, 외국군의 주둔에 강력반대하는 한편, 6 프러스 2 에 대해서도 시리아, 이집트, 가 걸프국가가 아니라는 이유로 반대하는 입장을 보여왔음.

-이란은 걸프지역 안보협력체제로서 6 프러스 1 구상을 실현 시키기위해 노력하여왔으며, 여기서 발전시킨 개념으로 새로운 형태의 6 프러스 2 (이락포함)을 제시하기도 하였음에 비추어 이란이 걸프지역내 외국군의 주둔을 내용으로 하는 표제 조약체결에 반발하는것은 충분히 예상되어왔음.(참고로 최근 당지를 방문한바있는 AL-KHUWAITER 사우디 특사는 걸프지역내 외국군의 장기주둔에 반대한다는 입장을 보임으로서 사실상 표제 조약체결에 대한 사우디측 불만을 간접 표명한바있으며, 이란 언론은 이를 적극 평가함으로써 상기 이란 정부의 입장을 재확인한바있음)

-그러나 표제협약 체결로 현재까지 논의되어온 6 프러스 2 나 6 프러스 1 가 포기될것으로 보는것은 무리이며 향후 걸프안보체제는 6 프러스 2 와 6 프러스 1 이 조화를 이루는 COMPREENSIVE SECURITY 을 모색하는 방향으로 협의가 진행될것으로 전망됨.

-현재 이란은 자신의 입장강화를 위해 GCC 국가와 관계강화를 도모하고있으며, 그일환으로 상기 사우디특사의 방이 외에 오만 외무장관, 카타르왕자, 바레인 에너지장관의 방이가 가까운 장래에 예정되어 있는것으로 알려짐.끝

중아국 장관 차관 1차보 2차보 외정실 분석관 청와대 안기부

PAGE 1 91.09.11 22:32

외신 2과 통제관 BW

0098

(대사 정경일-국장)

예고:91.12.31 까지

1991. 12. 31. 에 예고문에
의거 일반문서로 재 분류됨.
㊞

PAGE 2

0099

관리번호	

원 본

외 무 부

종 별 :

번 호 : SBW-1293 일 시 : 91 0911 1530

수 신 : 장관(중일)

발 신 : 주 사우디 대사

제 목 : 미.쿠웨이트 군사협약

대:WSB-949

1. 표제협약관련 주재국정부가 공식적인 논평등을 발표한바 없으나, 주재국정부의 입장은 동협약 체결의 필요성을 전폭적으로 이해하는것으로 알려지고 있음

당지 언론들은 특별한 논평없이 동협약에 관한 외신보도를 비교적 상세히 게재하고 있음

2. 대호 2 항관련, 당관 정우성 참사관이 접촉한 미, 불등 주요대사관 관계관들의 언급요지는 아래와같음

가. 미.쿠간 협약과 비슷한 성격의 군사협력을 위한 협의가 미국과 사우디간 진행중임. 특히 쿠의 지리적 특성상 미군 군사장비의 대규모 비축은 바람직 스럽지 않다고 보고있는 미국으로서는 사우디에 군사장비를 비축하는 방안에 큰역점을 두고있음, 한편 추후 미.사우디간 군사협력관련 합의사항은 대외적으로 발표되지 않을 가능성이 큼

나. 사우디는 가까운 장래에 이락으로부터 군사적 위협이 없을것으로 보고있으며, 따라서 자국에게 상당한 경제적 부담이 예상되는 다마스커스선언에 의한아랍평화군 창설에 소극적 태도를 보이고있음, 더욱 사우디는 자국영토내에 일체의 외국군주둔을 원치않은 입장이며, 쿠웨이트 또한 이집트, 시리아군의 자국주둔에 난색을 표하고있어 아랍평화군 창설은 현실적으로 쉽지않을것으로 보여짐(만약 창설되는 경우에도 상징적인 소규모병력의 쿠웨이트에 주둔케 될것으로 예상)

다. 현재 1 만명으로 되어있는 "PENINSULA SHIELD"군 (GCC 회원국간 연합군)의 규모확대 문제가 최근 거론되고 있으나, 회원국간 이견이 커서 단시일내에 파견될것으로는 보이지않음.(사우디는 병력규모 확대에 반대하는 입장)

라. 이란의 걸프안보체제 참여문제도 오만등이 적극적인 태도를 보이고 있으나

중아국	장관	차관	1차보	2차보	외정실	분석관	청와대	안기부

PAGE 1 91.09.11 22:57

외신 2과 통제관 BW

0100

사우디등은 반대로 실질적인 진전이 예상되지 않음

(대사 주병국-국장)

예고:91.12.31 까지

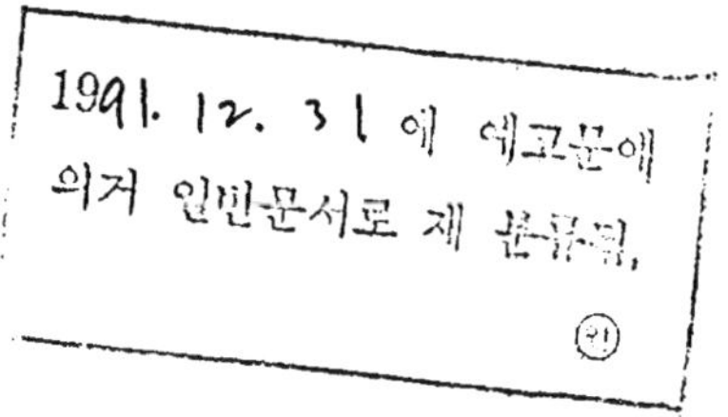
1991. 12. 31 에 예고문에
의거 일반문서로 재 분류됨.

PAGE 2

0101

관리 번호	91/1623

원 본

외 무 부

종 별 :

번 호 : QTW-0208 일 시 : 91 0912 1230

수 신 : 장관(중동일,정보)

발 신 : 주 카타르 대사

제 목 : 쿠웨이트국왕 카타르 방문(자료응신제9호)

1.SH.JABER 쿠웨이트국왕은 GCC 각국 순방계획의 일환으로 9.11 정오 당지 방문후 오후 3 시경 바레인으로 향발한바, KHALIFA 카타르 국왕이 공항에서 영접하고 공식환영행사를 가짐.

2. 당지 GULF TIMES 지는 "TALKS FOCUS ON SECURITY, STABILITY" 제하에 양국 원수는 GULF 지역의 안보와 안정을 위한 GCC 국가간 단결강화 취지에서 다각적인 협력방안을 논의하고 중동평화 문제와 최근의 걸프및 아랍. 이슬람 국가간의 정세에 관한 의견교환이 있었다고 보도함.

3. 한편 당지 외교가에서는 쿠웨이트와 미국간의 방위조약가조인 문제를 비롯한 GCC 각국간의 안보협력 방안과 관련하여 카타르도 미국과 지상군 병력 주둔을 제외한 모종의 안보협약 체결을 협의중인 것으로 알려짐.끝

(대사 유내형 -국장)

예고:91.12.31 까지.

1991. 12. 31.에 예고문에 의거 일반문서로 재 분류됨.

중아국	장관	차관	1차보	2차보	외정실	분석관	청와대	안기부

PAGE 1

91.09.13 00:09

외신 2과 통제관 FM

0102

관리번호	91/1604

원 본

외 무 부

종 별 :

번 호 : JOW-0643 일 시 : 91 0912 1300

수 신 : 장 관(중동일,중동이)

발 신 : 주 요르단 대사

제 목 : 미.쿠웨이트 방위조약

대:WJO-0537

1. 대호관련, 9.12. 외무성 AL-GHAZAWI 정무국장은 중동국가 방위문제는 ARAB CONTEXT 내에서 아랍국가간 집단 방위조약에 의거 해결됨이 바람직할 것이라는 견해를 피력함

2. 주재국은 여타 다수 아랍국가들과 같이 아랍연맹의 집단 방위조약에 가입되어 있음

3. 주재국 언론에는 현재까지 논평이나 반응이 나오고 있지 않음

(대사 이한춘-국장)

예고:91.12.31 까지

1991.12.31 에 예고문에 의거 일반문서로 재 분류됨.

중아국 장관 차관 1차보 2차보 중아국 분석관 청와대 안기부

PAGE 1 91.09.13 00:15

외신 2과 통제관 FM

0103

관리번호	91/1606

원 본

외 무 부

종 별 :

번 호 : OMW-0190 일 시 : 91 0912 1440

수 신 : 장관(중동일)

발 신 : 주 오만 대사

제 목 : 미.쿠웨이트 방위조약(자응 91-5)

대:WOM-0201

표제조약 가서명과 관련, 주재국 정부나 언론은 일체공식 반응을 표명한바 없는바, 당관이 그간 주재국 외무부및 외교단 인사와 접촉 탐문한바를 기초로 아래와 같이 보고함.

1. 다마스커스 선언에 의한 62 아랍평화 유지군 창설논의는 초기에 약간의 진전을 보였고 당시 GCC 제국은 그들의 방위를 위해 이집트와 시리아로부터 그들의 우월하고 배타적인 역활을 수용하도록 유인, 고무되었었음. 그러나 GCC 제국은 각회원국이 필요하다면 이집트와 시리아군을 개별적으로 영입할 수있도록 수정을 가하자는 의견의 대두와 함께 동방안이 당장에는 사실상 실행 불가능한 것으로 인식하게 되었음.

2. 차선책으로 GCC 제국과 이란까지 포함하는 친근 아랍제국으로 구성하는 합동군 설치 방안이 검토되었으나 이방안 역시 쿠웨이트, 바레인및 사우디아라비아 등의 이란을 포함시키는데 대한 우려에 봉착, 별로 진지하게 추진되지 못하고 있음.

3. 결국 다음 방안으로는 미국및 영국등의 안보우산을 제공받는 서구제국으로부터의 군사지원을 추구하는 방안이 있는바, 현재 동방안이 다수국의 지지를 획득하고 있다고 할수있으며 이에따라 각국은 미.영. 불등과 개별적인 방위협약을 체결하게 된것으로 보임.(최근 이라크의"부비안"도 습격은 GCC 제국의 취약성에 대한 우려를 재점화함으로써 서구제국의 개입에 좋은 근거를 제공함.)

4. 따라서 금번의 미.쿠방위조약의 가서명및 불란서, UAE 군사협약체결등은 전항과 같은 맥락에서 파악되어야 할것으로 봄.

주재국은 1980.6.4. 주재국 군사기지에 미군의 필요시 이용을 허용하는 협정을 체결한바 있으며 당시 이에 대해 가장 비판적이었던 쿠웨이트가 10 년후 오늘에는 미국의 군사지원을 가장 앞장서 추구하게 된것은 좋은 대조가 되고있음.

중아국 장관 차관 1차보 2차보 외정실 분석관 청와대 안기부

PAGE 1

91.09.13 00:13

외신 2과 통제관 DO

0104

5. GCC 제국은 작년말 도하정상회의시 장기적 안보체제 구축을 위해 HIGH COMMITTEE ON SECURITY 를 설치하고 가능한 모든 방안을 검토, 금년 12 월 쿠웨이트 정상회의시 건의안을 제출토록하여 지난 5 월 당지에서 10 만명의 GCC 합동군 설치안을 검토키위해 각료회의가 개최됨.(동 위원회 의장은 주재국 국왕인바 이는 동국왕이 영국사관학교 출신의 군사전문가라는 개인적 자격에서 옹립된것임)

또한 지난 8.27.-28 간 당지에서 GCC 참모총장 회의를 개최, 동방안의 기술적 측면을 검토하였으나 결론을 보지못하고 9 월말경 당지에서 회의를 재개, 건의안 채택을 위해 노력할것으로 알려지고 있음.

6. 이러한 노력에도 불구하고 궁극적인 GCC 통합군 설치목적 달성 가능성은 다음과 같은점에서 가시적인 장래에는 희박한 것으로 전망됨.

가. 회원국 상호간의 위협에 대한 인식의 상이및 상호간의 의구심작용으로 합의 도출의 곤란성.

나. 각국의 군사장비의 다양성, 인력충원상의 부적절성, 국민의 군대복무에 대한 적성미흡및 통합군 지휘, 훈련체제의 기본적 요건 결여.

7. 이상과 같이 GCC 통합군 설치, 나아가 범아랍합동군 설치에 의한 지역안보체제 구축 노력은 계속해나갈것이지만 가까운 장래에 이룩되기 어려운 난제로 평가되고, 이를위한 여건과 시기가 성숙될때까지는 각지역국가는 각기 개별적으로 군사력증강 노력을 추진해 나가면서 한편으로 점진적 장기적 입장에서 지역안보체제 구축을 위해 노력해 나갈것으로 보는것이 지배적 의견임.끝

(대사 강종원-국장)

예고:91.12.31. 일반

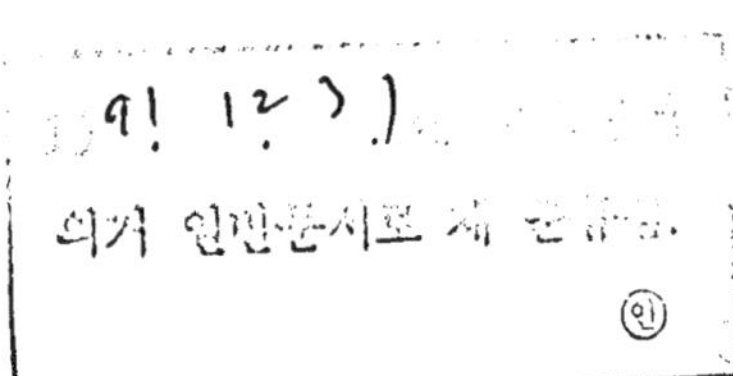

PAGE 2

0105

원 본

외 무 부

암호수신

종 별 :

번 호 : CAW-0981　　　　일 시 : 91 0912 1700

수 신 : 장관(중동이,정보)

발 신 : 주 카이로 총영사

제 목 : PRIMAKOV 쏘련 대통령특사 방애

(자료응신 제 152 호)

1. 중동순방(수우디, UAE, 쿠웨이트, 이란, 터키)일환으로 당지를 방문(9.10)한 소련대통령특사 YEVGENY PRIMAKOV 는 9.11. 주재국 무바락대통령에게 GORBACHEV 친서를 전달한후 기자회견에서 요지 하기와 같이 말함.

1) 방애목적은 양국관계 증진을 위함이지 중동평화나 여타문제를 협의하기 위한 것은 아님.

2) 중동문제와 애-쏘 양국관계들을 협의키 위해 불원(일정미정) 무바락대통령이 방소(WORKING VISIT)할 것임.

3) 소련은 대이스라엘 외교관계 재개에 어떠한 외압도 느끼지 않고 있으며,또한 국내정치 소용돌이를 겪고 있으나 중동평화회의 개최에 능동적 역할을 수행코자 함.

2. 상기 특사 방애가 시기상 10 월 중동평화회담 개최 성사를 위해 당지 방문 예정(9.17)인 BAKER 장관에 앞서기는 하나, 소련이 미국과 함께 10 월 평화회의 개최에 공동초청국이 된것은 어디까지나 모양새 갖추기에 불과한점, 최근 소련은 국내경제난국으로 애-쏘 간 청산거래 협정 이행관련 쏘련측의 대이집트 석탄, 철, 지류, 냉동어류등 공급 약속품들이 공급차질을 빚고 있다는점, 순방대상국이 주로 GCC 의 석유수출국(기존 쏘련 원유공급 약속국에 대한 공급 차질관련)이란 점외에도, PRIMAKOV 가 경제전문가인 점을 감안할때에, 동인의 방애는 단순한 최근 쏘련국내 정치정세 설명과 동정치 소용돌이와는 무관히 10 월 중동평화 회의 개최 지지 입장 재천명외에도 소련측의 어려운 경제사정에 대한 주재국측의양해를 구하기 위함일 가능성이 높음. 끝.

(총영사 박동순-국장)

중아국	장관	차관	1차보	2차보	외정실	분석관	청와대	안기부

PAGE 1　　　　91.09.13　06:29

외신 2과 통제관 FM

0106

관리번호	91/

원 본

외 무 부

종 별 :

번 호 : ITW-1330 일 시 : 91 0913 1810

수 신 : 장 관(중동일)

발 신 : 주 이태리 대사

제 목 : 미.쿠웨이트 방위조약

대:WIT-1000

당관 문병록 참사관은 금 9.13. 외무성 중동국장 SCARPA 공사와 면담, 미.쿠웨이트 방위조약 및 중동평화회의 추진관련 내용을 청문한 바 동인의 발언 내용을 아래 보고함.

1. 미.쿠웨이트 방위조약

0 이태리는 미.쿠 방위조약 가조인 및 양국간의 군사협력관계를 지지함.

0 쿠웨이트는 자국방위를 위해 한편으론 서방국가와 군사협력관계를 발전시키고 있으며, 또 한편으로는 GCC 6 개국과의 자주국방강화를 기하고 있음.

0 EC 국가도 개별국가자격 내지 WEU 범주내에서 쿠웨이트와의 군사협력이 가능한 바, 특히 영. 불등은 미.쿠와 유사한 군사협력관계를 모색할 가능성이 있음.

0 다마스커스 선언은 당초 선언정신이 다소 변화되었으나 계속 추진되고 있음. 걸프지역 국가는 자국의 방위를 스스로 해결하겠다는 의지하에 시리아, 이집트군의 걸프주둔대신 GCC 6 개국간의 자주국방을 강화하는 방향으로 추진되고 있음.

GCC 공동군 창설등 지역안보 협의를 위해 아랍 관계국간 회의가 조만간 카이로에서 개최될 예정임.

2. 중동평화회의 추진

0 베이커 국무장관이 9.16. 걸프전후 7 번째로 중동을 방문 이스라엘, 시리아, 이집트등과 중동평화회의 개최를 협의할 예정인 바 금번 방문이 동회의 개최여부를 결정하는 중요한 회담이 될것임.

0 금번 중동방문에 있어서는 두가지의 중요한 협의사항이 있는 바 첫째는 미국의 이스라엘과 팔레스타인및 아랍국가에 대한 MECHANISM OF ASSURANCE 문제이며 둘째는 팔레스타인 대표권 문제임.

중아국	장관	차관	1차보	2차보	외정실	분석관	청와대	안기부

PAGE 1

91.09.14 06:26

외신 2과 통제관 FK

0107

0 미국은 이미 쌍방에 대해 상호 보장책을 제시하고 있으므로 이는 별 어려움이 없을 것이나 팔레스타인 대표권 문제에 있어 이스라엘은 PLO, 해외거주 팔레스타인인, 동부 요르단 대표등의 회의 참석을 거부하고 있는 반면 PLO 등은 대표단 파견권을 주장하고 있어 상호간 타협, 해결해야하는 문제가 남아 있음.

0 PLO 는 9.23. 튜니스에서 회의를 개최 자체 대표권 문제를 협의할 예정임.

3. 데미켈리스 외상의 이스라엘 방문

0 데 미켈리스 이태리 외상은 9.4.-5 간 이스라엘을 방문, 정부지도자와 면담하고 이스라엘과 EC 와의 협력관계를 위한 아래 요지의 멧세지를 전달하였음.

- 이스라엘이 시장경제국이며 민주국가로서 EC 의 경제권에 통합되기를 희망하고 EC/EFTA 경제협력형태와 마찬가지로 이스라엘도 EUROPEAN ECONOMIC SPACE에 참여할 것을 권유한 바 이스라엘측은 기본적으로 이에 동의하였음.

- 소련 쿠테타 이후 세계질서가 변화되고 있음을 감안 모든 나라가 세계평화를 위해 기여해야 할것임을 지적하고 유럽과 이스라엘은 평화창출을 위해 경제적인 면뿐만 아니라 안보면에서도 유럽과 밀접히 연계되어야 함을 강조함. 이는 유럽의 이스라엘에 대한 새로운 정치적인 접근임.- 세계평화 구축을 위해서는 유엔의 권능과 역할 그리고 민족자결이라는 2 개의 PILLAR가 있음을 지적하고 이스라엘이 유엔의 권능을 수락할것과 민족자결원칙이 중동에서도 적용되어야 함을 주장함.

0 동외상은 또한 금번 방문시 현재 미국이 이스라엘/ 아랍, 이스라엘/ 팔레스타인간의 DUAL TRACK 을 통한 평화해결 방안추구외에 THIRD TRACK 으로서 중동지역에서의 군축, 안보, 환경 문제등 해결위한 다자간 협상을 추진하고 있음과 관련 이러한 미국측 구상이 추진된다면 이는 이태리가 추진하고 있는 CSCM 과 유사할 것임을 설명함. 끝

(대사 김석규-국장)

예고:91.12.31. 까지

1991.12.31. 에 예고문에 의거 일반문서로 재 분류됨

PAGE 2

0108

원 본

외 무 부

종 별 :

번 호 : OMW-0191 일 시 : 91 0914 1420

수 신 : 장관(중동일,정일)

발 신 : 주오만대사

제 목 : 주재국외상 이란 방문

주재국 외상 이란 방문(자료응신 91-6)

주재국 YOUSUF BIN ALAWI 외무장관은 9.13. 2일간 이란방문후 귀임한바, 금9.14.자 당지 OBSERVER지는 귀국직전 기자회견 내용을 아래요지 보도함.

1. 동외상은 금번 방문시 양국간 협력의 중요성및 회교국간의 협조 필요성을 강조하는 주재국 국왕의 멧세지를 이란 대통령에게 전달했으며, 이란 대통령은 이란 주변아랍 국과의 결속증진에 깊은 관심을 표명함과 동시 지역정세에 관해 의견을 같이했다고 말함.

2. 안보체제 구축문제 관련, 지역국가간의 상호신뢰와 이해 기반 위에서 장래를위한 안보체제구축 필요성에 상당한 이해가 이루어졌다고 역설함.

3. 이란.이락 전쟁관련, 유엔결의 598호 제8항 이행을 위해 유엔사무총장이 수행할수 있는 역활에 대하여 이란과 GULF 제국간에 완전한 이해에 도달했다고 말함.

4. GULF 제국과 이란간의 안보문제관련, 양측간의 협력을 위한 견실한 기반이없는한 달성될수 없다고 말함.

5. 이란과 이집트관계와 관련, 이란은 이집트와의 관계정상화를 희망하고 있다고말함.끝

(대사 강종원-국장)

중아국 1차보 외정실 분석관 청와대 안기부

PAGE 1 91.09.15 00:48 DW

외신 1과 통제관

0109

원 본

외 무 부

종 별 :
번 호 : SBW-1312 일 시 : 91 0916 1400
수 신 : 장관(중일,정보,기정)
발 신 : 주사우디대사
제 목 : GCC 외무장관회의

연:SBW-1308

1. 연호 제40차 GCC 외무장관회의는 9.15 하기요지의 코뮤니케를 발표하고 폐회됨

0 이락의 유엔안보리결의 불이행,쿠웨이트 포로석방 지연,쿠웨이트와의 국경확정지연등을 비난하고,유엔안보리의 대이락 압력 강화를 촉구

0 다마스커스선언의 제반원칙을 재확인하고,11월 카이로에서 개최예정인 동선언참가국 회의에서 세부사항 협의 의사표명

0 최근 이란과의 관계개선에 만족을 표시하고,걸프지역 안보를 위한 이란과의 협력방안 모색 용의 표명

0 아프카니탄문제 해결을 위한 최근의 국제적 노력환영

0 아랍-이스라엘문제 해결을 위한 부시대통령의 노력에 지지를 표명하는 한편,중동평화회의의 조속한 개최 희망

0 이스라엘의 점령지 이주정책 규탄

0 레바논정부의 국민화합 노력을 치하하고,레바논 복구계획에 대한 지지 재확인

0 소련의 합법정부 복귀 및 개방정책의 지속에 만족을 표시하고,세계평화를 위한소련의 기여 희망

2. 한편 9.16자 당지 일간지들은 금번회의 결과를 보도하며,GCC의 이란과의 관계강화 용의표명을 크게 취급하였으며,9월말 GCC외무장관과 이란외무장관과의 회동이ㅇ 유엔에서 있게될것이라고 보도함.끝

(대사주병국-국장)

중아국 1차보 외정실 분석관 안기부

PAGE 1

91.09.16 21:23 DQ

외신 1과 통제관

0110

원 본

외 무 부

종 별 :

번 호 : SBW-1314 일 시 : 91 0916 1420

수 신 : 장관(중일,기정)

발 신 : 주사우디대사

제 목 : 주재국 외무장관 영국 방문

1.SAUD외무장관은 9.16-17간 영국을 공식방문하여 사우디대사관 신축청사 개관식에 참석하고,MAJOR 수상,HURD 외무장관등과 회담할 예정임

2.9.15 SAUD 장관은 이락의 유엔안보리 결의 불이행문제,이스라엘의 점령지 이주정책문제등을 동회담에서 거론하겠다고 말하였으며,그밖에도 중동평화회의,걸프지역안보문제등이 논의될것으로 보임.끝

(대사주병국-국장)

중아국 1차보 외정실 분석관 안기부

PAGE 1 91.09.16 21:25 DQ

외신 1과 통제관

0111

報告畢

長官報告事項

1991. 9.16.
中東1課(41)

題 目 : 美.쿠웨이트 防衛條約

9.8. 美國과 쿠웨이트間 有效期間 10년의 防衛條約이 假調印 되었는바, 關聯 事項을 아래와 같이 報告 드립니다.

~~1. 防衛條約 槪要~~

~~o 條約締結 : 9.20. 쿠웨이트 國王 訪美期間中 正式署名 豫定~~

o 主要內容 :

- o 地域 平和와 美.쿠웨이트 防衛를 위한 軍事協力
- o 美 地上軍은 駐屯치 않고 合同 軍事訓鍊 實施 (今年 9월중)
- o 美國 武器, 裝備의 쿠웨이트內 配置및 쿠웨이트 基地 施設 利用

2. 背 景

o 걸프地域의 各國別 安保威脅에 대한 認識 相異로 쿠웨이트는 隣近 아랍兄弟 國과의 集團防衛 能力 및 實效性등에 懷疑的

o 다마스커스 宣言이 이란의 制動과 이집트, 시리아의 過度한 反對給付 要求로 ~~現在 事實上~~ 아랍 平和維持軍 창설 不可能

o 쿠웨이트의 王政에 대한 國民不滿으로 現 政府 不安感 作用

3. 各國反應

o 사우디, 카타르, 오만, UAE등 GCC 會員國과 EC 國家들은 同 協定이 필요한 것으로 理解, 肯定的 反應

o 이란및 요르단 등은 域內 安保는 域內 國家間 協力에의해 이루어져야 한다는 立場으로 否定的 反應

4. 分析 및 評價

o 쿠웨이트는 GCC 會員國과 이집트, 시리아 또는 이란을 包含한 地域 安保體制 構築을 위한 協商은 계속할 것으로 豫想

o 美國의 지나친 域內 影響力을 牽制하기 위해 英, 佛등과도 協力 體制를 多邊化할 展望

5. 言論對策 및 關聯措置 : 없음.

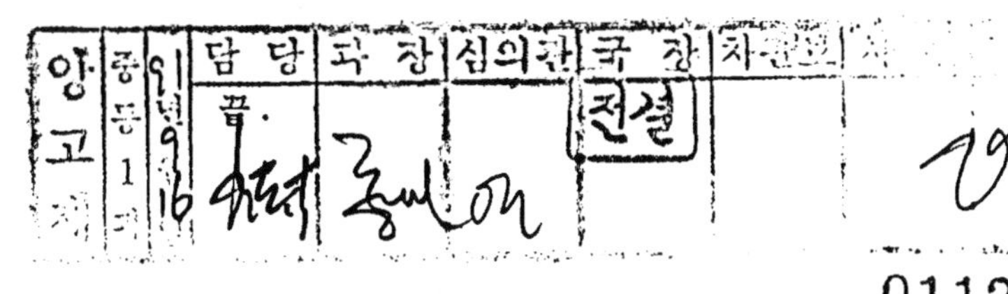

0112

報 告 畢

長 官 報 告 事 項

1991. 9.16.
中東1課(41)

題 目 : 美.쿠웨이트 防衛條約

9.8. 美國과 쿠웨이트間 有效期間 10년의 防衛條約이 假調印 되었는바, 關聯 事項을 아래와 같이 報告 드립니다.

1. 主要內容

   o 地域 平和와 美.쿠웨이트 防衛를 위한 軍事協力

   o 美 地上軍은 駐屯치 않고 合同 軍事訓鍊 實施 (今年 9월중)

   o 美國 武器, 裝備의 쿠웨이트內 配置및 쿠웨이트 基地 施設 利用

2. 背 景

   o 걸프地域의 各國別 安保威脅에 대한 認識 相異로 쿠웨이트는 隣近 아랍兄弟國과의 集團防衛 能力 및 實效性등에 懷疑的

   o 다마스커스 宣言이 이란의 制動과 이집트, 시리아의 過度한 反對給付 要求로 아랍 平和維持軍 창설 不可能

   o 쿠웨이트의 王政에 대한 國民不滿으로 現 政府 不安感 作用

3. 各國反應

   o 사우디, 카타르, 오만, UAE등 GCC 會員國과 EC 國家들은 同 協定이 필요한 것으로 理解 肯定的 反應

   o 이란및 요르단 등은 域內 安保는 域內 國家間 協力에의해 이루어져야 한다는 立場으로 否定的 反應

4. 分析 및 評價

   o 쿠웨이트는 GCC 會員國과 이집트, 시리아 또는 이란을 包含한 地域 安保體制 構築을 위한 協商은 계속할 것으로 豫想

   o 美國의 지나친 域內 影響力을 牽制하기 위해 英, 佛등과도 協力 體制를 多邊化할 展望

5. 言論對策 및 關聯措置 : 없음. 끝.

0113

원 본

외 무 부

종 별 :

번 호 : OMW-0198 일 시 : 91 0917 1410

수 신 : 장관(중동일,정보)

발 신 : 주 오만 대사

제 목 : GCC 외상회의(자응91-8)

연: OMW-0193

연호 제40차 표제회의 참석후 9.16.귀국한 주재국 외무 장관은 공항도착 성명에서 아래 요지 언급함.(OBSERVER 지 9.17.1면 보도)

1.금번 회의는 GCC 제국과 이란과의 관계 문제를 논의, 금추 유엔 총회시 뉴욕에서 GCC 외상과 이란 외상간의 회담을 갖기로 했으며 그 결과를 토대로 GCC 제국과 이란간의 통일된 관계를 갖을 수 있도록 12월 GCC 정상 회의에 건의키로 함.

2.동 회의는 또한 유엔 안보리가 이라크에 대해 전쟁포로 석방 및 쿠웨이트와의국경 확정을 촉구 하도록 요청함과 동시에 지역 안보를 위해 이락크와 협조 하는데관한 GCC의 공동 의견을 유엔 사무총장에게 서면 제출키로함.

3.동 회의는 발틱 3국의 독립을 환영하고 이들 3국의 독립을 승인하는 성명을 각각 발표키로 합의함.

4.12월 정상회의 준비를 위해 11.25.쿠웨이트에서 외상 회의를 개최키로함.끝

(대사 강종원-국장)

91.09.21 金

중아국 1차보 외정실 분석관 안기부

PAGE 1

91.09.18 02:01 FH

외신 1과 통제관

0114

0 미국은 이미 쌍방에 대해 상호 보장책을 제시하고 있으므로 이는 별 어려움이 없을 것이나 팔레스타인 대표권 문제에 있어 이스라엘은 PLO, 해외거주 팔레스타인인, 동부 요르단 대표등의 회의 참석을 거부하고 있는 반면 PLO 등은 대표단 파견권을 주장하고 있어 상호간 타협, 해결해야하는 문제가 남아 있음.

0 PLO 는 9.23. 튜니스에서 회의를 개최 자체 대표권 문제를 협의할 예정임.

3. 데미켈리스 외상의 이스라엘 방문

0 데 미켈리스 이태리 외상은 9.4.-5 간 이스라엘을 방문, 정부지도자와 면담하고 이스라엘과 EC 와의 협력관계를 위한 아래 요지의 멧세지를 전달하였음.

- 이스라엘이 시장경제국이며 민주국가로서 EC 의 경제권에 통합되기를 희망하고 EC/EFTA 경제협력형태와 마찬가지로 이스라엘도 EUROPEAN ECONOMIC SPACE에 참여할 것을 권유한 바 이스라엘측은 기본적으로 이에 동의하였음.

- 소련 쿠테타 이후 세계질서가 변화되고 있음을 감안 모든 나라가 세계평화를 위해 기여해야 할것임을 지적하고 유럽과 이스라엘은 평화창출을 위해 경제적인 면뿐만 아니라 안보면에서도 유럽과 밀접히 연계되어야 함을 강조함. 이는 유럽의 이스라엘에 대한 새로운 정치적인 접근임.- 세계평화 구축을 위해서는 유엔의 권능과 역할 그리고 민족자결이라는 2 개의 PILLAR 있음을 지적하고 이스라엘이 유엔의 권을 수락할것과 민족자결원칙이 중동에서도 적용되어야 함을 주장함.

0 동외상은 또한 금번 방문시 현재 미국이 이스라엘/ 아랍, 이스라엘/ 팔레스타인간의 DUAL TRACK 을 통한 평화해결 방한추구외에 THIRD TRACK 으로서 중동지역에서의 군축, 안보, 환경 문제등 해결위한 다자간 협상을 추진하고 있음과 관련 이러한 미국측 구상이 추진된다면 이는 이태리가 추진하고 있는 CSCM 과 유사할 것임을 설명함. 끝

(대사 김석규-국장)

예고:91.12.31. 까지

1991. 12.31. 에 예고문에 의거 일반문서로 재 분류됨.

PAGE 2

0115

원 본

외 무 부

종 별 :

번 호 : KUW-0539 일 시 : 91 0917 1800

수 신 : 장 관(중동일)

발 신 : 주 쿠웨이트 대사

제 목 : 쿠웨이트 피납인 석방요청

1.걸프전 당시 이락크군에 의해 납치된후 아직도 송환되지 않고있는 쿠웨이트인들의 가족대표 3인이 9.12 당관을 방문, 조속한 석방실현에 우리정부가 협조하여 줄것을 요청하는 호소문을 피납인가족 대표 20여명과 쿠웨이트 언론등의 참석하에 당관에 전달하기 위해 이들의 당관내방 (9.24,09:00)을 허용하여 줄것을 요청하였음으로 당관은 본건의 인도주의적측면을 고려하여 이들의 래방을 허용하였음.

2.이들은 상기협조 요청 호소문을 미.영.불등 쿠웨이트 우방국대사관에 이와같은 방식으로 이미 전달하였음.

3.이락크군에 의해 납치되어 현재까지도 송환되지않고있는 쿠웨이트인은 약 2천명인 것으로 알려지고 있는데 (피납총인원은 5-6천명) 간헐적으로 이락크측이 수십명단위로 사우디국경의 교환소에 '쿠웨이트인들'을 데려오며 쿠웨이트인측은 이들을 심사하여 일부는 인수하고 나머지는 이라크측이 불순분자, 쿠웨이트인이 아닌 3국인등을 쿠웨이트인으로 가장시켜 송환하고있다는 이유로 동접수를 거절하고 있고, 이에대하여 이라크측은 쿠웨이트측의 접수거절로 송환이 이루어지지않고 있다고 비난하는등 피납인 송환을 문제 해결이 지연되고있음.

4.POW (쿠웨이트는 민간인 피납자 포함 POW 로분류) 송환이 유정화재 진화와 함께 정부의 최우선 과제이며, 쿠웨이트는 동피납인 조기석방 운동일환으로 가구마다 황색기를 게양하는 주간을 설정하고 있음.끝

(대사-국장)

중아국 1차보 외정실 분석관 안기부 청와대

PAGE 1 91.09.18 13:59 WG

외신 1과 통제관 0116

원 본

외 무 부

종 별 :

번 호 : CAW-1007 일 시 : 91 0919 1040

수 신 : 장 관(중동이,정보)

발 신 : 주 카이로 총영사

제 목 : BAKER 장관 방애

연:CAW-0994

9.17 당지를 방문 BAKER 미국무장관은 MUBARAK대통령과 면담후 동대통령과 가진 기자회견에서 요지 하기와 같이 말하므로 10월 중동평화회담 개최 가능성은 아직 미정인 것으로 사료되는바, 이는 팔레스타인대표 문제와 이스라엘의 점령지내에 정착촌건립 중지문제들에 대해 양해가 이루어 지지않고 있는데 기인한 것으로 보임.

1. 대통령

1) 역내 모든 관계당사자가 모여 모든 문제들을 협상할 회의 시기가 다가오고 있으며, 역내 모든 나라가 평화 수익자가 될것이므로 관계 당사자의 합의가 필요함.

2) 그중 이스라엘은 최대 수혜자가 될것이므로 10월회담이 개최되기를 희망함.

3) 팔레스타인대표 문제는 평화 실현과 회의 개최를 위한 HELPING FACTOR 임.

4) 회담 개최지는 아직 결정되지 않았음.

2. 국무장관

1) 점령지내에 정착촌건립 문제를 SHAMIR수상과 토의하였으나 아직 합의를 보지 못했음. 본건 협의를 계속할 것이며, 이스라엘측이 이해하기를 희망함.

2) 팔레스타인 인민들의 자결권과 LAND-FOR-PEACE원칙에 관해 상세한 양해각서를 이스라엘과 팔레스타인측에 주었으며, 유사 각서를 요르단, 시리아및 레바논에도 줄것임. 또한 이는 비밀일수 없으며 합의후 모든 관계국에 줄것임.

3) 회담참석 여부에 관해 팔레스타인측의 회신을 기다리고 있으며, 평화모색으로 최대수혜측은 팔레스타인 인민들일 것이며, 실패시 최대 손해를 입는측도 팔레스타인 인민들일 것임.

4) 정착촌 건립문제는 중요한 것이므로 회담개최전이 아니라, 회담과정에서 토의되어야함.

중아국 1차보 외정실 분석관 청와대 안기부

PAGE 1 91.09.19 17:13 WG

외신 1과 통제관 0117

3. BAKER 장관 수행 고위보좌관

미측은 하기 6개 대이스라엘 약속으로 이스라엘측이 미측의 정착촌 건립차관 (100억불)토의 연기요청에 동의토록 설득중이라함.

1) 미행정부는 91.1. 대이스라엘 차관보증에 관한 적절한 법안 마련에 미의회와 협력함

2) ~~91~~ 92.1. 다시 연기요청을 하지 않을것임.

3) 이스라엘측의 이민자 수용을 지지

4) 미납세자들이 반대하지 않게 재무당국과 절차비용 (THE COST OF THE PROCESS)을 계산할것임.

5) 4개월 지연에 따른 이자보전 방안 강구

6) 제3국으로 하여금 이스라엘측의 쏘련 유태인 유입사업을 돕도록 노력함.끝

(총영사 박동순-국장)

상기 non-paper에 있음.

PAGE 2

0118

관리 번호	91/1629

원 본

외 무 부

종 별 :

번 호 : FRW-2056 일 시 : 91 0919 1200

수 신 : 장관(중동일)

발 신 : 주 불 대사

제 목 : 걸프 안보협력 추진 동향

대:WFR-1865

표제건 관련,9.18 당관 손세주서기관이 주재국 외무성 M.FRAYSSE GCC 담당관과 면담한 바, 동인의 언급요지 하기 보고함.

1.GCC 제국은 각국이 이질적인 요소를 가진 국가로서 전통적으로 상호 협력보다는 경쟁관계를 의식해 왔으며, 또한 대국 사우디에 대한 의존이 불가피한 점등 문제점을 안고 있어, 걸프이사국 자체방위 노력이 결실을 거두지 못하고 있긴하나, 그 전망이 비관적이라고는 생각치 않음. 오는 12 월 GCC 정상회의 결과를 주시할 것임.

2. 걸프전에 참가한 이집트 및 시리아와 걸프전중 우호적인 입장을 보여 GCC 국가와의 관계가 개선되고 있는 이란등의 경우, 걸프 자체방위체계와는 다른 성격의 군사협정 또는 상호불가침 조약을 추진하는 것이 바람직할 것으로 봄.

3. 미.쿠웨이트 방위협정에 미군상주를 포함하지 않고 있는 점에 비추어, 동 협정이 상기 GCC 자체방위 노력과 배치되는 것이 아니라, 상호 보완적인 성격으로 볼수 있음.

4. 불란서도, 최근 UAE 대통령 방불을 계기로, 일반적인 정보교환 협정(산업, 기술, 법률등), 항공협정 및 부자협정외에 공동군사 훈련을 주내용으로 하는군사협정을 체결하였는 바, 이는 UAE 가 GCC 방위와 병행, 자국안보를 위한 추가보장을 확보한데 의미가 있음.

5. 또한 불란서는, 역사적 연고가 있는 영국 및 이스라엘과 특수 유대를 가지고 있는 미국에 비해, 보다 중립적인 차원에서 동 지역과 협력할수 있다고 봄.

6. 상기 동인의 발언에 비추어, 불란서가 UAE (군사장비중 불장비가 80 프로), 카타르(90 프로)와의 협력을 증대하여 미국의 주도적 영향력을 견제하면서,동 지역에 대한 진출 발판을 계속 강화할 것으로 전망됨. 끝.

중아국 장관 차관 1차보 2차보 분석관 청와대 안기부

PAGE 1

1991.12.31.에 예고문에 의거 일반문서로 재 분류

91.09.19 21:25 0119

외신 2과 통제관 CE

(대사 노영찬-국장)
예고:91.12.31. 까지

PAGE 2

0120

관리번호	91/1636

원 본

외 무 부

종 별 :

번 호 : QTW-0211 일 시 : 91 0919 1200

수 신 : 장관(중동일)

발 신 : 주 카타르 대사

제 목 : 미.쿠웨이트 방위조약

1. 9.17 본직 관저를 방문한 외무성 AL-DOOSARI GCC 국장에의하면 금년 3 월초 채택된바있는 다마스커스 선언은 현재 참가국간에 일부 수정이 검토되고있는바, 특히 애급및 시리아군이 역내에 주둔하게되면 걸프지역을 제 2 의 레바논화하는 결과를 초래할것이라는 우려에서, 양국군의 파견은 "필요시 요청에 의하여"라는 수정 합의 조인될 전망이라고함.

2. 미.쿠웨이트간 조인될 방위조약의 체결은 예상되었던 바이며, 수복직후부터 쿠웨이트는 미군기지의 주둔을 희망하였으나 미국이 이에 불응하였으며, 따라서 그내용도 미해군의 계속배치, 중장비 비축, 군사훈련 지원및 합동연습 실시등이 될것으로 추정된다고함.

2. 주재국도 미국과의 방의협력에 있어서 걸프전쟁 당시와같은 미공군에대한기지 사용 허용정도의 공조를 할것으로 예상된다고 하는바, 걸프전당시 주재국은 미국, 카나다 및 프랑스 공군 전부기부대의 기지사용을 허용한바있으나 3 개국으로부터 기지사용료및 연료대금을 징수 한바있다고 함. 끝

(대사-유내형-국장)

예고:91.12.31 까지

1991. 12.31. 에 예고문에 의거 일반문서로 재 분류됨.

중아국	장관	차관	1차보	2차보	분석관	청와대	안기부

PAGE 1 91.09.20 22:22 0121

외신 2과 통제관 BW

원 본

암호수신

외 무 부

종 별 : 지 급

번 호 : KUW-0550 　　　　일 시 : 91 0920 1800

수 신 : 장관(중동일)

발 신 : 주 쿠웨이트 대사

제 목 : 쿠웨이트.미국 안보조약

연:KUW-0520

연호 쿠웨이트. 미국 안보조약이 9.19(목) 워싱턴에서 양국국방장관이 서명,정식체결되었음. 끝

(대사-국장)

예고:91.12.13. 까지

1991.12.31 에 예고문에 의거 일반문서로 재 분류됨

중아국 장관 차관 1차보 외정실 분석관 청와대 안기부

PAGE 1

91.09.21 22:07 0122

외신 2과 통제관 CH

관리 번호 91/1637

원 본

외 무 부

종 별 :

번 호 : USW-4726 일 시 : 91 0920 1830

수 신 : 장 관 (중동일,미일,미이) 사본:주시애틀총영사경유 주미대사(직송필)

발 신 : 주 미 대사

제 목 : 미.쿠웨이트 군사협력 조약

대: WKU-0340

금 9.20(금) 당관 노광일 서기관은 국무부 정보조사국 STEPHEN GRUMMON 중동담당관을 접촉, 미.쿠웨이크 군사협력 조약에 대해 탐문한바, 동 내용 하기 보고함.

1. 주요내용

0 향후 10 년간을 대상으로 미국은 쿠웨이트내 주요 군장비의 비축, 합동군사훈련 실시및 향후 비상사태를 대비한 미군의 공항및 항구 사용 방안을 규정함.

0 군장비 비축규모및 장소, 합동군사훈련 실시회수등 구체적, 기술적 사항은 양국 군당사자간의 합의를 통해 확정함.

0 쿠웨이트내 미군의 자동적 배치 또는 주둔을 규정하고 있지 않음.

2. 미측입장

0 동 조약은 행정협정 형식(상원 비준 불요)으로 작 9.19. 체니 국방장관과방미중인 AL-SABAH 쿠웨이트 국방장관간 체결됨.

0 동 조약은 향후 걸프지역에 비상사태 발생시 미군의 개입을 원활히 하기 위한 군사물자의 사전배치등 주목적으로 한 군사협력에 대한 합의이지 쿠웨이트에 대한 안보공약(SECURITY GURANTEE)를 한 것은 아님.

- 다만, 쿠웨이트내 비상사태시 미군의 개입을 상정함으로써 향후 쿠웨이트안보 위협국에 대한 억지효과는 있음.

0 미국은 이와같은 군사협력 조약을 모든 GCC 국가와 체결할 예정이며, 가장 중요한 사우디와의 합의도 현재 잘 진행되고 있음.

0 지난 걸프전 종전직후에 발표된 다마스커스 선언은 미국이 추구하는 GCC 국가와의 군사협력 조약으로 인해 의미가 없어졌다고 보지 않음.

중아국 장관 차관 1차보 2차보 미주국 미주국 외정실 분석관
청와대 안기부

19 91 12 31 에 예고문에 의거 일반문서로 재 분류됨.

PAGE 1 91.09.21 08:47 0123

외신 2과 통제관 BW

- 미국과 GCC 역내 국가와의 군사협력조약은 군사적 성격이 강한 반면, 다마스커스 선언은 걸프지역내 안전보장에 대한 아랍국(이집트및 시리아)내부의 정치적 지지효과가 있음. 끝.

(대사대리-국장)

예고:91.12.31. 일반

1991. 12. 31. 에 예고문에 의거 일반문서로 재 분류됨.

PAGE 2

0124

관리 번호	91/1640

원 본

외 무 부

종 별 :

번 호 : UKW-1925 일 시 : 91 0920 1900

수 신 : 장관(중동일)

발 신 : 주 영 대사

제 목 : 미.쿠웨이트 방위조약

2011.12.31 金

대: WUK-1652

1. 당관 최참사관은 9.20 외무성 ELDON 중동담당관을 면담, 대호관련 주재국 입장을 타진한 바, 동인은 걸프지역의 집단안보를 위한 다마스커스 선언이 이란의 이의제기등으로 진전을 보지 못하고 있는 상황하에서 미.쿠웨이트의 방위조약 체결은 안전보장을 위하여 바람직한 것으로 본다 하고, 영국도 한시적이기는 하나 함대주둔, 군사교육실시, 장비제공등을 내용으로 하는 군사협력 방안을 쿠웨이트측과 협의중에 있다고 부연하였음

2. 당지 언론은 본건관련 별다른 반응을 보이지 않고 있음을 첨언함. 끝

(대사 이홍구-국장)

91.12.31. 까지

1991.12.31.에 예고문에 의거 일반문서로 재분류됨.

중아국 차관 1차보 외정실 청와대 안기부

91.09.21 10:35 0125

외신 2과 통제관 CD

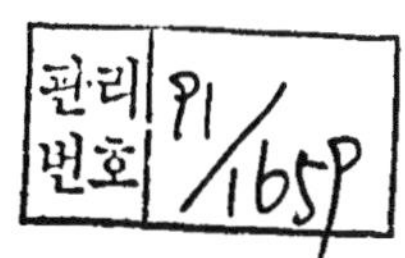

관리번호 91/1659

주 오 만 대 사 관

문서번호 : 오 만 720 - 172 1991. 9. 20.

수 신 : 장 관

참 조 : 중동아국장 (외교정책기획실장)

제 목 : 오만.미국 군사기지 협정 (자료송신 91-92)

연 : OMW-190

연호 4항에 언급한 주재국과 미국간의 미군의 기지 이용을 허용하는 군사 협정 (1980.6.4.체결) 내용 및 관련자료를 별첨과 같이 송부합니다.

1991. 12. 31 에 예고문에 의거 일반문서로 재 분류됨.

첨 부 : 전기협정자료 사본 1부. 끝.

전 결			결재(공람)		
접수일시	1991. 9	번호 46645			
처리과					

주 오 만 대 사

0126

Annex II

The Omani-American agreement of 1980

97th Congress
1st Session

COMMITTEE PRINT

U.S. SECURITY INTERESTS IN THE PERSIAN GULF

REPORT

OF A

STAFF STUDY MISSION TO THE PERSIAN GULF,
MIDDLE EAST, AND HORN OF AFRICA
OCTOBER 21–NOVEMBER 13, 1980

TO THE

COMMITTEE ON FOREIGN AFFAIRS
U.S. HOUSE OF REPRESENTATIVES

MARCH 16, 1981

Printed for the use of the Committee on Foreign Affairs

U.S. GOVERNMENT PRINTING OFFICE
73-3540 WASHINGTON: 1981

0127

Oman

The study mission was in Oman from October 23 to October 27 1980. It met with Omani defense and foreign military officials and with British officers seconded to the Sultan of Oman's Armed Forces. The group visited Omani military facilities on Masirah Island, Ghanam Island and at Khasab, overflew the Musandam Peninsula, and entered the Strait of Hormuz in an Omani Navy frigate. U.S. Embassy personnel, including the U.S. Ambassador, briefed the study mission.

UNITED STATES-OMANI RELATIONS

—On 4 June 1980, after 7 months of negotiations, the United States and Oman signed an agreement to permit U.S. access to Omani military bases. The United States sought this agreement in order to enhance its ability to assure U.S. interests in the Persian Gulf.

—Omani facilities were attractive to the United States because of Oman's strategic location on the Strait of Hormuz and the friendly orientation of the Government. Under the leadership of Sultan Qaboos, in power since 1970, Oman has supported U.S. policies in the Middle East. For example, Oman welcomed the Egyptian-Israeli Peace Treaty even though this has placed it at odds with its Arab neighbours. The willingness to act independently within the Arab world stems from Oman's geography and history and allows Oman to permit U.S. access to its bases even while other Gulf States do not.

UNITED STATES INTERESTS IN OMAN

—Oman's security is essential to the United States and to the West. If a hostile power with Soviet support controlled Oman, it could close the Strait of Hormuz by artillery fire from Omani islands in the gulf. It could, thus, block the supply to the West of the 40 per cent of its oil which flows through the strait.[1] Moreover, an unfriendly regime in Oman could not only deprive U.S. military forces in the region of support, it could prevent the U.S. Navy from operating in the gulf without exposing itself to land-based attack.

---

1 By virtue of Musandam, a peninsula which is noncontinuous to the body of Oman, shipping lanes in and out of the Persian Gulf lie almost totally within Omani territorial waters. These lanes transit international waters only briefly and do not fall within Iranian territorial waters at any point. It is important to note, however, that Oman ships its own oil from ports outside the Strait of Hormuz.

0128

—Responsibility for keeping open the Strait of Hormuz in the event of a serious regional conflict ultimately must be with the United States and the West. The Omani Navy is, however, now doing a valuable and effective job of patrolling the shipping lanes in the strait. Oman has, undoubtedly, contributed to the continued free and safe passage of international shipping through its territorial waters during the Iranian-Iraqi war. This is a responsibility which it has assumed and which it takes seriously. But Oman's Navy is small, aging, and slow. Its patrol boats, for example, lack the requisite speed to remain apace of large tankers violating the shipping lanes. Moreover, the outbreak of the Iran-Iraq war forced Oman to shift 60 per cent of its naval forces to the strait, thereby depleting its naval assets along its southern coast and increasing its military vulnerability to the People's Democratic Republic of Yemen. The West, therefore, cannot rely on Oman to continue its heightened level of naval activity in the strait over a long period of time.

[Security deletion.]

THE UNITED STATES-OMANI FACILITIES ACCESS AGREEMENT

—The agreement with Oman will enhance the United States military capability to protect its interests in the Persian Gulf by permitting the following:

[Security deletion.]

—The agreement provides for United States access to Omani military bases in circumstances where both countries would benefit from this use. The United States clearly could use Omani bases to respond to a Soviet attack on the region. It is not certain, however, whether the United States would be able to use Omani facilities to intervene in an intra-Arab conflict were American interests threatened.

[Security deletion.]

—The government of Sultan Qaboos is anxious to keep United States military visibility in Oman to a minimum. [Security deletion.]

Oman defines a low profile to mean little publicity about U.S. military activities, military personnel wearing civilian apparel rather than uniforms, maximum use of civilian contractors rather than military personnel, and U.S. military exercises conducted away from populated areas. United States diplomatic and some military personnel appear to be sensitive to Omani concerns about United States military visibility. Bilateral discussions will have to continue in order to explore what can be done to meet Omani concerns while, at the same time, not unnecessarily restricting the United States.

[Security deletion.] A facility to which the United States has access is the Omani airbase on Masirah Island which is, however, 400 miles from the Strait of Hormuz. Masirah has certain drawbacks which have not yet been fully explored by the United States: Monsoons make Masirah unreachable by ship 4 months a year so that petroleum, oil, lubricants (POL) and water storage to handle United States aircraft, crews, and ground support as well as local Omani forces must be sufficient to cover that lengthy period; strong crosswinds during monsoons make takeoffs and landing difficult though not impossible. In addition, as an island, Masirah is extremely vulnerable to air attack. The cost of improving the airbase at Masirah to make it suitable for U.S. needs could be extremely high.

[Security deletion.]

—The total cost to the United States of improving Omani military facilities to make them suitable for United States needs is now estimated to be [security deletion]. This will provide for certain improvements. [Security deletion.]

[Security deletion.]

—The Government of Oman is frustrated by the United States delay in implementing the agreement. At the end of 1980, Oman was still awaiting the arrival of an Army Corps of Engineers survey team, originally promised in September, charged with identifying specific construction needs and projects. Continued delay in United States implementation of the agreement could reinforce the Omani perception that the United States does not live up to security commitments.

—Oman regards this agreement as tantamount to a U.S. commitment to its security. [Security deletion.] Oman is prepared to defend itself with U.S. military assistance should it be attacked by a state in the region such as the People's Democratic Republic of Yemen. However, in the event of a Soviet attack on Oman or clear Soviet involvement in a People's Democratic Republic of Yemen attack, Oman would expect direct United States military intervention and assistance. [Security deletion.]

—While some states in the Persian Gulf which are friendly to the United States have publicly criticized Oman for signing the agreement; privately some officials will state that they see the agreement as a welcome sign of United States commitment to the security of the region.

INTERNAL SITUATION

—Oman, like other states in the region, faces threats to its internal stability. Although the prognosis for stability in the coming years appears good, over a longer period there are some negative factors, which, if worsened, could attempt to provoke turmoil in Oman and, as a consequence, uncertainty in United States-Omani relations and United States access to Omani facilities:

—An increase in externally supported terrorist groups such as the Popular Front for the Liberation of Oman which may change their focus from rural to urban areas;

—The lack of an heir to succeed the present Sultan, Qaboos Bin Said;

—The future absence of increased opportunities for political participation for a population which is increasingly educated. Those who return from higher education abroad may be among those who most want to contribute to the political process.

—The frustration of rising economic expectations should oil resources become depleted over the next 30 years, revenues dwindle and other income sources not be generated. In recent years, there has been rapid growth, significantly higher public spending, and development to which Omanis have become accustomed.

—Poor income distribution; and

—Allegations of corruption.

On the other hand, there are factors which help stabilize the country:

—A new Omani 5-year plan to develop the country's agricultural and fishing sectors;

—The possibility that Oman might have more untapped oil resources than originally thought as well as rising oil prices which increase Government revenues;

—Effective security forces to control terrorism;

—The lack of widespread opposition based on politically active religious elements of the foreign population and the absence of large numbers of Palestinians;

—A strong Government initiative to provide roads, schools, and services to populations in areas that have opposed or have been alienated from the regime in Muscat such as Dhofar and Musandam and a successful effort to bring former Dhofari opposition leaders into Government positions.

BRITISH-OMANI TIES AND UNITED STATES INTERESTS

—The United States recognizes the importance of coordinating its military assistance effort in Oman with Great Britian whose own security relationship with Oman has been deep and longstanding. It is in United States interests that Great Britain remain committed to Omani security and assist in assuring that security. British involvement removes the possibility that the United States presence in the region will be unique and, thereby, more easily criticized by unfriendly forces.

—The British presence in Oman has, however, inhibited the "Omanization" of Oman's Armed Forces. Each military service has many British seconded or contract officers. The three service chiefs and many of the Sultan's closest military advisers are British citizens.

For the past few years, Omanis have been rising through the ranks to assume officer rank in all three services. The pace of this Omanization is reasonably rapid in the army but less so in the air force. The process is the slowest and least complete in the navy, arguably because of the greater complexity of naval weaponry and the machinery.

The slow pace of the Omanization of the armed forces can be explained in part by Oman's population of less than 1 million people and competition for manpower with the private sector and even foreign armies such as the United Arab Emirates which pay better salaries than Oman's. [Security deletion.]

There is a general consensus, however, that potential Omani dissatisfaction with the foreign control of their armed forces and the lack of opportunity for their own advancement may pose a greater threat to stability than Omanization. The Omani Government is, therefore, committed to moving British officers out of the chain of command in all three services and into advisory positions over a period of years.

THE U.S. MILITARY ASSISTANCE PROGRAM

—As part of the agreement with Oman, the United States is committed to responding quickly to Omani requests for information on any items recommended by the 1980 U.S. Defense Requirements Survey. The United States is providing $25 million in FMS financing in fiscal year 1980 and again in fiscal year 1981. Congress can expect requests for continued FMS programs in future years. [Security deletion.]

—In 1980 the United States sold Oman six M–60 tanks and may sell additional tanks in the future. It has also sold TOW missiles and launchers and Sidewinder missiles for Oman's Jaguar (British built) fighter aircraft. US training advisory field teams are now in Oman to train Omanis on these weapons systems. Oman seems satisfied with the efforts and programs of these TAFT's. The United States has also agreed to sell Oman C–130 aircraft while Oman has expressed an additional interest in K–130 tanker refueling aircraft. The United States will probably not expand its sales of military equipment to Oman in the future significantly beyond what it has already agreed to sell. Britain will most likely remain Oman's principal arms supplier.

—It is in United States interests to help Oman to develop the conventional war fighting capability it needs to deter the People's Democratic Republic of Yemen threat. At the same time, it is important that United States military assistance not detract from Oman's developed ability to combat internal subversion which remains a real threat to Omani security.

THE U.S. ECONOMIC ASSISTANCE PROGRAM

—It is extremely important to the Government of Oman that it demonstrate economic benefits resulting from the agreement. It, therefore, regards as essential the Joint United States-Omani Commission provided for in the agreement which is to fund and promote economic development in Oman. The Government of Oman stresses the urgency of the commission's initiating and completing projects which are highly visible to the public in the very near future. Projects which depend on lengthy AID planning and study will not satisfy the Omani Government's needs.

—While a small portion of the fiscal year 1981 funding may finance technical education for Omanis in U.S. institutions most of the funding will be used to develop indigenous water resources for agricultural irrigation. However, there are indications that U.S. officials see the need for lengthy study of specific projects despite the fact that many studies are already available. This could delay project implementation, thus frustrating United States and Omani political needs.

—Economic diversification and projects to remedy the poor income distribution in Oman may improve the prospects for stability there and work to our mutual interests. Despite a relatively high per capita income of $4000, Oman remains a developing country in need of U.S. financial and technical aid. Moreover, it spends 34 per cent of its gross domestic product on defense despite pressing economic development needs. While the level of economic assistance the United States is providing to Oman through the Joint Commission is low – $5 million in grant aid in fiscal year 1980 and an anticipated $5 million grant and $10 million loan in fiscal year 1982 – the Commission could fulfill its purpose of establishing model development projects and stimulating efficient and effective spinoff development efforts by Oman if it could quickly initiate projects. The fact that the Government of Oman has committed to matching the $10 million fiscal year 1981 loan should help insure Omani interest in the feasibility and relevance of the projects.

Oman
Economic and Military Assistance
(Fiscal years: in millions of dollars)

Type of assistance	*1977*	*1978*	*1979*	*1980*	*1981*	*1962–81*	*1946–81*
Total economic assistance (includes Peace Corps)	0.4	0.3	0.5	5.6	1.2	9.0	9.0
Total military assistance (includes foreign military sales financing and grant military training)				25.2	25.1	50.3	50.3

Arms Sales
(Fiscal years: in millions of dollars)

Type of arms sale	*1971*	*1972*	*1973*	*1974*	*1975*	*1976*	*1977*	*1978*	*1979*	*1980*	*1971–80*
Foreign military sales agreements					1.610	0.223	0.754		0.059	23.71	26.366
Commercial sales	0.013	0.174	0.065	0.4	0.531	0.821	1.146	1.405	0.639	0.186	5.380

U.S. INTERESTS IN, AND POLICIES TOWARD, THE PERSIAN GULF, 1980

HEARINGS

BEFORE THE

SUBCOMMITTEE ON

EUROPE AND THE MIDDLE EAST

OF THE

COMMITTEE ON FOREIGN AFFAIRS

HOUSE OF REPRESENTATIVES

NINETY-SIXTH CONGRESS

SECOND SESSION

MARCH 24; APRIL 2; MAY 5; JULY 1, 28; AND SEPTEMBER 3, 1980

Printed for the use of the Committee on Foreign Affairs

Let me direct your attention to the United States–Omani relationship for just a moment. We concluded an agreement which gives us access to certain facilities in Oman. How long does that agreement run?

Mr O'DONOHUE. The access agreement with Oman was concluded on June 4, 1980. It entered into force on that date and has an initial term of 10 years.

Mr HAMILTON. Does that agreement express the total agreement?

Mr O'DONOHUE. The access agreement expresses the total agreement as it applies to the use of Omani facilities. It was reached in the context of establishing a framework for bilateral cooperation relating to economic development and trade, and to defense equipment, training and development. At that time we informed the Omanis of our intentions in regard to security and economic assistance, and expressed our interest in the security and independence of Oman. Since then, we have signed agreements relating to the formation of a Joint Economic Commission. The Congress has been kept informed of these actions.

Mr HAMILTON. Is there a Presidential letter relating to the agreement? I don't know anything about the contents of that letter.

Mr O'DONOHUE. I will have to check on that.[1]

Mr HAMILTON. So far as I know, no members have been briefed on that Presidential letter.

Under that agreement does our access differ in peace or war, or do we have the same access under both circumstances?

Mr O'DONOHUE. The access agreement does not differentiate between situations of peace or war. As a practical matter, the kinds of use we might make will probably vary according to the situation.

Mr HAMILTON. Will Oman own all improvements at the facilities where U.S. construction takes place?

Mr O'DONOHUE. The facilities to which we will have access will remain the property of the host government. Under the provisions of the access agreement, we will, in coordination with them, be able to make improvements to those facilities. The host government will, however, own all such improvements to real property.

Mr SAUNDERS. The problem is most of the attachments are classified, and I think Mr Bartholomew went over that in closed session, but when you have the package of agreements, all of this will be answered by the documents themselves.

Mr HAMILTON. Let me be specific about some of the questions we are interested in. I want to know whether the United States will have

---

1 The subcommittee pursued the matter privately with the executive branch.

priority use of any of the facilities. I want to know if our access will differ in peace or in war. I want to know what happens if the facilities come under internal or external attack. And I want you to describe for us what approval by, or consultation with, the Omanis is required in the case of planned visits or exercises in peacetime and staging for combat use.

My request is very modest, as you can see.

Mr O'DONOHUE. The facilities will remain under host government control, and we will share their use. If the facilities come under attack, we would consult with the Omanis on an appropriate response, and we would, of course, comply with any applicable requirements of the War Powers Resolution. No approval or consultation is required for routine use, which is subject only to advance notification. As is the case elsewhere, we consult on other uses.

Mr SAUNDERS. I think all that is in the documents themselves.

AID TO OMAN

Mr HAMILTON. Is there any relationship between the facilities access agreement and the aid that we are going to give Oman?

Mr O'DONOHUE. In the context of the broader relationship that was established, which is one that includes economic and security assistance, this is part of that general package.

Mr HAMILTON. So if the U.S. Congress says we are going to cut it or deny the aid, what happens to the agreement?

Mr O'DONOHUE. From our point of view we stated very clearly our intention is to seek the congressional authority.

Mr HAMILTON. So, in your view, then, if we were to do that, we would still have the access to the facilities?

Mr O'DONOHUE. I think that the Omanis would view the establishing of this broader relationship involves not simply the use of the facilities but——

Mr HAMILTON. So would we, or would we not, have access to the facilities? Suppose the U.S. Congress said, no, we are not going to give you that.

Mr O'DONOHUE. That would be a matter we would have to discuss with them, but as far as the agreement, itself, they have signed.

Mr HAMILTON. And the expectation of the Omanis is they will receive the amount of money specified?

Mr O'DONOHUE. Yes. However, the need for appropriate congressional action was quite clear.

Mr HAMILTON. Our new security relationship with Oman involves an assistance package for that country that apparently includes $25 million in FMS credits in both fiscal year 1980 and fiscal year 1981: $5 million in ESF grant funding in fiscal year 1980; $90 million in Eximbank financing in fiscal year 1982 and fiscal year 1983, and access to certain military equipment. ESF will also be provided in 1981.

Mr O'DONOHUE. However, the $5 million ESF is the total for the 1980–81 period, not individual amounts for each year.

Mr HAMILTON. You have a specific provision in the Foreign Assistance Act which prohibits granting assistance to economically developed countries. Oman has a per capita income of $4,000. Have you made a determination that Oman can receive grant aid consistent with the terms of section 620(m)?

Mr TWINAM. We considered that question.

Mr HAMILTON. I am glad you did.

Mr TWINAM. We concluded that Oman has the characteristics of a developing country despite a higher per capita income.

Mr HAMILTON. So you are going to say they are entitled to the assistance despite section 620(m)?

Mr TWINAM. At this stage.

Mr HAMILTON. And you do that on the basis that they are not an economically developed country, even though they have a very high per capita income.

Mr TWINAM. That is correct.

Mr HAMILTON. Have you made that determination to us in writing at this point?

Mr TWINAM. No: we have not.

Mr HAMILTON. Will you do so?

[The information requested follows:]

APPLICATION OF SECTION 620(m) OF THE FOREIGN ASSISTANCE ACT TO OMAN

Section 620(m) of the Foreign Assistance Act of 1961, as amended, with certain limited exceptions, prohibits the furnishing of assistance on a grant basis under the Act to "any economically developed nation capable of sustaining its own defense burden and economic growth. * * *" This statutory prohibition is not a legal bar to the proposed grant assistance to Oman, even though that country has a high per capita income.

The legislative history of section 620(m) shows that the Congress did not intend to require the application of any single test or rigid set of tests to determine the meaning of the term "economically developed nation capable of sustaining its own defense burden and economic growth." To the contrary, a definition of this term proposed by the Senate was specifically rejected by the Committee of Conference in favor of leaving the statute's application as a "matter of reasonable judgment." See H.R. Rep. No. 1006, 88th Cong., 1st Sess. 30 (1963).

In applying the statute since its enactment in 1963 the Executive Branch has looked to a number of factors in attempting to formulate reasonable judgments. In particular, evaluations by the OECD and the World Bank have provided useful data in assessing the capabilities of particular countries.

With respect to Oman, while oil exports have substantially increased per capita GNP since 1967 (when its per capita GNP was less than $100), this recent income has not been sufficient to overcome Oman's substantial development needs. The World Bank Development Report for 1979, for example, cites serious deficiencies in Oman's education and health care systems and in the production of food through the subsistence agriculture by which the vast majority of the population attempts to earn a livelihood. Living conditions are primitive, and there is a high rate of infant mortality. The OECD publication *Development Cooperation* for 1979 describes Oman as a "higher income developing country."

Consideration has also been given to the fact that Oman continues to receive assistance from neighboring countries to help it sustain the burdens of defense and economic development. It is evident that the donors do not regard Oman as capable of meeting these burdens on its own.

In conclusion, Oman's recently increased income from oil exports has improved the prospects for development but has not yet transformed Oman into an economically developed nation. The other relevant factors described above provide an ample basis for a reasonable judgment that Oman's economy remains under-developed and that Oman is not yet capable of sustaining its own defense burden and economic growth.

Mr HAMILTON. Mrs Fenwick.

Mrs FENWICK. You said something about priority use or would it be exclusive use?

Mr O'DONOHUE. There has never been any discussion of exclusive use. The facilities are Omani and will remain under Omani control.

Mr HAMILTON. Does the United States now plan in excess of $200 million in military construction in Oman over the next 3 years?

Mr SAUNDERS. We prefer actually taking all this up in the briefing.

원 본

외 무 부

종 별 :

번 호 : JOW-0666 일 시 : 91 0921 0900

수 신 : 장 관(중동일,중동이,기정)

발 신 : 주 요르단 대사

제 목 : 미국무장관 요르단 방문

1. 9.19. BAKER 미국무장관은 요르단을 방문,후세인 국왕과 중동평화회의 문제등과관련 회담한후 기자회견에서 밝힌 요지는 다음과같음

가. 후세인 국왕 발언 요지

-PEACE PROCESS 에 있어서 팔레스타인 문제가 가장 중요한 요소이며 금번 회담의 주 의제였음

-중동문제관련 전국가들이 평화회의가 지연됨이 없이 재회될것이라는 희망을 갖고 있음

-팔레스타인 문제 해결을 위해 팔레스타인 대표단이 참석할것이며, 팔레스타인측이 원할경우 합동대표단의 참석도 가능할것임

-BAKER 미국무장관은 부시 미대통령을 대신하여 중동문제를 진실과 성의를 가지고 균형있게 모든것을 분명히 처리하려는 미국의 책임을 시현하고 있음

나. BAKER 미국무장관의 발언요지

-해당 당사국들에게 제시된 GUARANTEE LETTERS내용은 유엔결의안 242호및 338호에 의거'평화를 위한 영토'의 원칙을 근거로한 중동평화의 포괄적인 해결책의 의사를확인할것임

-예루살렘문제는 협상석상에서 해결될것이며,참가준비가 되어있는 모든 관련 당사자들과 함께 회의를 주관할것임

-중동지역에서 공평되고, 포괄적인 평화 정착을 위해 노력하고 행동하는 지도자로서 후세인 국왕보다 더 진지하고, 용감한 분은 없을것임

2.BAKER 장관은 9.20. 시리아를 재차 방문,시리아측에 제시한 미국의 보장문서 내용을 분명히 설명할 것으로 알려짐

(대사 이한춘-국장)

중아국 1차보 중아국 외정실 분석관 안기부

PAGE 1 91.09.21 21:00 DQ

외신 1과 통제관

0140

원 본

외 무 부

암 호 수 신

종 별 :

번 호 : IRW-0714 일 시 : 91 0923 1100

수 신 : 장관(중동일,정일,기정)

발 신 : 주 이란 대사

제 목 : 걸프안보 협력체제

연:IRW-0687

1. 주재국 국가최고 안보회의(대통령주재)는 9.21 연호 이.쿠웨이 방위협정에대한 반대입장을 공식 표명한것으로 알려짐.

2. 이와관련 동 국가최고 안보회의 구성원 15 인중 1 인인 LARIJANI 외무장관 고문은 지난주 N.Y 지와의 회견에서 이란으로서는 걸프지역내 안보를위해 걸프국가들이 미국과 방위협정을 체결하는것에 반대하지 않는다고 언급한것으로 보도된바 있으나 동인은 9.20 당지 언론인터뷰를 통해 동기사가 왜곡되었다고 설명하며 자신의 의도는 UN 보장하의 집단 안보체제 구상이었다고 설명하였음을 참고바람. 끝

(대사정경일-국장)

중아국	장관	차관	1차보	2차보	문협국	외정실	분석관	청와대
안기부								

0141

PAGE 1

91.09.23 18:27

외신 2과 통제관 DG

관리 번호	91/1641

원 본

외 무 부

종 별 :

번 호 : BHW-0423 일 시 : 91 0923 1310

수 신 : 장관(중동일)

발 신 : 주 바레인 대사

제 목 : 걸프안보 체제

연:BHW-417

당관 김종용 참사관은 작 9.21 SHAIKH ISA BIN MUBARAK 수상 대외관계담당비서관(현 MOHAMED 외무장관의 실제)의 HASSAN 보좌관과 접촉한바, 표제건 관련동인의 언급 요지 아래 보고함.

1. 그간 62 내지 61 체제에 대한 GCC 회원국들간의 이해와 의견이 계속 상충되는데 대해 오만의 QABOOS 국왕이 GCC 국적민들로만 구성된 10 만 규모의 합동군을 창설, 이를 근간으로 걸프전 당시의 연합국들과 방위협력을 확대해 나가는 일방, 이란과의 관계 정상화를 도모함으로서 걸프지역 안보 확립방안을 모색하자고 제의함으로서 동 합동군 창설문제와 관련 지난 8 월말 오만에서 GCC 참모총장회의가 개최된바 있었음.

2. 그러나 지난 쿠웨이트 사태시 "반도의 방패(PENINSULA SHIELD)"라는 GCC합동군이 전혀 유명무실했던 선례등으로 쿠웨이트를 위시한 일부 회원국들이 동합동군 창설에 소극적 입장을 보이고 있어, 동 합동군의 사령부 설치, 군대의구성 비율, 주둔 위치및 형식, 예산 분담등의 문제와 관련 별다른 진전이 이루어 지지 않고 있음.

3. 동인의 판단으로는, 동 합동군 창설이 설령 이루어 진다고 해도 단지 상징적 의미일뿐 실질적 역할 수행은 매우 의문시된다고 언급하였는바, 주재국, 쿠웨이트등 걸프 소국들의 방위 문제에 있어서는 지난 9.9 미.쿠 방위조약등과 같은 대미 의존이외의 현실적 대안이 없음을 시사하고 있는 것으로 사료됨. 끝.

(대사 곽회정-국장)

예고:91.12.31 일반

1991. 12. 31. 에 예고문에 의거 일반문서로 재 분류됨.

중아국	차관	1차보	2차보	외정실	분석관	청와대	안기부

PAGE 1 91.09.23 22:40

외신 2과 통제관 DG

0142

원 본

외 무 부

암호수신

종 별 :

번 호 : BHW-0424 일 시 : 91 0923 1330

수 신 : 장관(중동일)

발 신 : 주 바레인 대사

제 목 : 미.쿠 방위조약

연:BHW-423

당지 아랍어 일간지 AKHBAR AL-KHALEEJ 는 9.22 표제 협정관계 아래 요지의사설을 게재함.

1. 쿠웨이트가 외국의 우호국가와 안보협정을 체결한 것은 이라크 침공 이후의 당연한 귀결임.

2. 과거 쿠웨이트를 위시한 걸프국가들은 아랍. 비아랍권을 망라한 전세계국가들과 상호 비적대.불가침 원칙의 평화 우호관계를 유지하여 왔으며, 이러한정책에 따라 아랍민족 안보의 개념인 아랍공동 방위협정 이외의 어떠한 방위협정 체결 필요성도 느끼지 못하였고, 또한 실제에 있어 과거 많은 외국국가들의이지역내 군사기지 설치 제의도 거부하여 왔었던 것임.

3. 그러나, 무자비한 이라크의 침공은 그러한 평화정책만으로는 국민들의안녕과 안전을 확실히 보장해줄 수 없다는 점을 여실히 보여 주었음.

4. 국민이 안전하게 살 수 있는 환경을 제공해주는 것은 국가의 의무이며,국익에 도움이 된다는 판단에 의해서 외국의 우호국과 안보협력을 강화하는 것도 국제법 상에 보장된 주권국가의 권리임.끝.

(대사 곽회정)

중아국 차관 1차보 2차보 외정실 분석관 청와대 안기부

PAGE 1 91.09.23 22:41 0143

외신 2과 통제관 DG

관리번호 91/1646

원 본

외 무 부

종 별 : 지 급

번 호 : KUW-0559 일 시 : 91 0924 1800

수 신 : 장관(중동일)

발 신 : 주 쿠웨이트 대사

제 목 : 쿠웨이트.영국 방위협정 추진

연:KUW-520,530

1. 쿠웨이트 정부는 영국과도 방위협력 협정체결을 추진중인데, 쿠웨이트측요청으로 지난 7 월 영국이 동협정초안을 쿠웨이트측에 제안하였고, 쿠웨이트측이 이를 검토중인것으로 알려지고 있음.

2. 영국측이 제안한 협정초안은 쿠웨이트 방위에 관한 영국의 자문, 쿠웨이트군의 영국기지내 군사훈련, 양측의 합동훈련과 위기사태 발생시 양측의 협의가주요내용으로 되어있다고 함. 장부의 사전배치 (PREPOSITION) 는 동조항에 포함되어 있지않다고 하는데, 이는 1961 년 이라크의 침공직후 체결된 영. 쿠 방위협정에 PREPOSITION 조항이 포함되어 있었으나, 그후 경비부담, 장비종류등에 관해 양측간에 심한분규가 있었던 경험때문이라고 함.

3. 영국측의 초안내용이 쿠웨이트측 입장에서 볼때 미흡하고, 이미 미국과 방위협정을 체결하여 안보기반을 마련하고 있는 터에 이를 서둘러 수락하면 아랍제국으로부터 "아랍형제국"을 견제하기 위하여 서방에 너무 밀착하고 있다는 정치적 비난을 받게 될것을 우려하여 시간을 끌고 있는것으로 당지 영국대사관은 풀이하고 있음. 끝

(대사-국장)

예고:92.6.30. 까지

검 토 필 (1991 . 12 . 31 .)

중아국 장관 차관 1차보 2차보 외정실 분석관 청와대 안기부

PAGE 1

91.09.25 14:25 0144

외신 2과 통제관 BN

OPEC 각료 회의 결과

1991.9.26.
자원협력과

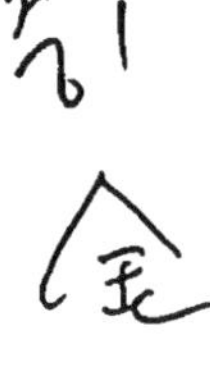

1. 개최시기 및 장소 : 1991.9.24-25, 제네바

2. 참가국 : 13개 전 회원국

3. 회의 결과

o 4/4분기 OPEC 생산량 상한선을 2,365만B/D로 합의
(이라크, 쿠웨이트 생산량 포함)

o 90.7 합의된 OPEC 기준 유가목표 21$/B를 재확인

4. 평가 및 분석

o 금번 합의된 2,365만 B/D은 3/4분기 생산량 상한선(2230만 B/D)보다 약 130만 배럴 상회하는 것이나, 실제 3/4분기 생산량 2,350만 배럴과 비슷한 수준이어서 국제유가에 영향은 미치지 않을 것임

o 유가가 배럴당 21$이 유지되지 않을 경우, 시장감시위원회 회의를 소집키로 하였으며, 국가별 생산쿼타는 논의되지 않았음.

o 쏘련의 정정불안으로 인한 산유량 감소, 세계 경제의 회복, 북반구의 한파 예상등으로 수급상의 불균형 요인이 상존하나, OPEC내 최대 산유국인 사우디 (현재 850만B/D 생산하고 있으며 금번 회의에서도 동일 수준으로 합의)와 비 걸프 산유국들의 생산확대 움직임으로 당분간 유가는 안정세를 유지할 것으로 보임

o 금번 회의는 생산량 보다는 유가에 우선권을 둠

※ 현재 OPEC 국가생산 유가는 목표 유가보다 약 2달러 낮은 19배럴임.

0145

원 본

외 무 부

암호수신

종 별 :

번 호 : BHW-0428 일 시 : 91 0928 1240

수 신 : 장관(중동일,통일)

발 신 : 주 바레인 대사

제 목 : GCC 수입 관세율 통일(자료응신 제33호)

1. 당지 AL-AYAM 아랍어 일간지는 9.26, GCC 는 오는 93.3 월까지 역내 수입관세율을 통일할 예정이라고 보도하였음.

2. 동 관세율 통일은 GCC-EC 간 자유무역협정 체결 교섭과 관련 EC 측의 주요 요구조건중의 하나였음.

3. 현재 GCC 의 수입관세율은 동일 품목에 대해서도 각 회원국에 따라 최고20%에서 최저 2%까지 서로 상이한 실정임.끝.

(대사 곽희정-국장)

중아국 차관 1차보 2차보 통상국 외정실 청와대 안기부

PAGE 1 91.09.28 19:10 0146

외신 2과 통제관 CD

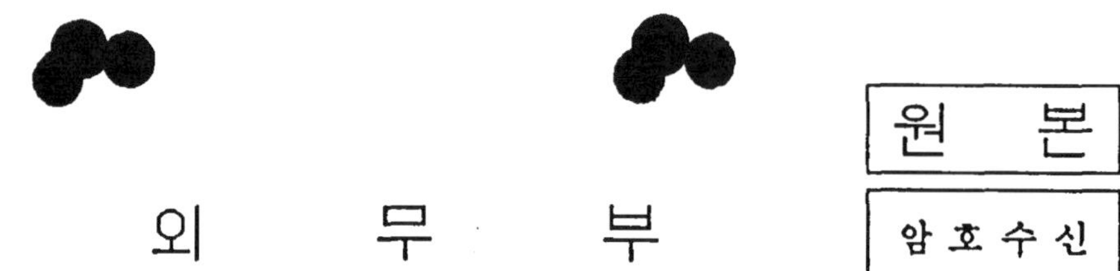

원 본

외 무 부

암 호 수 신

종 별 :

번 호 : CAW-1040　　　　일 시 : 91 0930 1810

수 신 : 장관(중동이,정보)

발 신 : 주 카이로 총영사

제 목 : 무바락대통령 방쏘　　　(재수신분)

(자료응신 제 156 호)

연:CAW-0995

1. 무바락대통령은 9.27 소련을 방문, GORBACHEV 등 소련지도자들과 양국관계 및 지역정세등에 관해 회담후 9.28 귀국함.

2. 방소의 구체적 목적이 밝혀지지 않고있으나, 하기 몇가지 점들을 감안하면 무바락대통령은 양국간 청산거래 무역이행에 있어 소측에 CREDIT 제공 약속으로 GORBACHEV 의 국제외적 정치 경제적 입지 강화를 돕는한편, 소련으로부터 이스라엘 점령지내로의 유태인 정착촌건립 계속화에 대한 제동강구 약속을 얻어냈을 가능성이 높음.

1) 지난 9.10 GORBACHEV 의 경제특사로 PRIMAKOV 가 당지를 방문하는 데서 갑작스럽게 이루어진점.

2) 시기상 GORBACHEV 가 비록 수구파 쿠데타 기도에서 살아 났으나 경제적으로 대단히 어려운 상황에 처해 있다는점.

3) 아랍권과 제 3 세계의 주도국의 일환인 이집트는 50 년대와 60 년대에 소련 원조의 주요 수원국이었다는점.

4) 현재 청산거래 협정에 의한 양국간 부역(91 년도 4 억파운드) 에 있어 이집트의 대소 수출은 순조로운데 반해 소측의 대애수출은 국내사정으로 인해 부진할 뿐 아니라 이집트의 대소 CREDIT 이 2 억 5 천만파운드로 증가하고 있다는점.

5) 이스라엘 정부의 소련거주 유태인 유입을 위한 점령지내 정착촌 건립계속화가 미.소 후원하에 추진중인 중동평화 개최에 하나의 걸림돌로 작용하고 있다는점.끝.

(총영사 박동순-국장)

중아국	장관	차관	1차보	2차보	구주국	외정실	분석관	청와대
안기부								

PAGE 1　　　　91.10.01　16:14　0147

외신 2과　통제관 CD

관리번호	91/1678

원 본

외 무 부

종 별 :

번 호 : OMW-0222 일 시 : 91 ~~0101~~ 1001 1305

수 신 : 장관(중동일,정보)

발 신 : 주 오만 대사

제 목 : GCC 참모총장회의 무기연기(자응91-12)

연:OMW-0190,0209

1.GCC 합동군 설립을 위한 GCC 참모총장회의가 10.1-2 간 당지에서 개최될 예정이었으나 무기연기된바 이유는 상금 미상임.

2. 한편 9.28. 미국의 지역 CENTRAL COMMAND 사령관 JOSEPH B. HAWR 장군및9.29. 영국의 국방부 중동지역 ADVISOR 인 SIR PETER DE BILLIERE 장군이 각각주재국을 방문, 각각 주재국 국왕을 살랄라에서 알현한바, 이들의 방문이 전항참모총장회의와 관련성이 있는것으로 추측되기도 하였으나 당관이 미.영 대사관측에 개별적으로 탐문한바 이는 우연한 시기적 일치라고함. 끝

(대사 강종원-국장)

예고:91.12.31. 일반

1991. 12. 31. 에 예고문에 의거 일반문서로 재 분류됨.

중아국 차관 1차보 외정실 분석관 청와대 안기부

PAGE 1 91.10.01 20:56 0148

외신 2과 통제관 CE

분류번호	보존기간

발 신 전 보

번 호 : WTN-0251 911001 1504 FO 종별 :

수 신 : 주 튀니지 대사. 총영사 WSV -3192 (사본—주소대사)

발 신 : 장 관 (중동이)

제 목 : 소련 외무차관 튀니지 방문

벨로노고프 소련 외무차관이 중동평화회의 촉진을 위해 PLO 본부가 있는 귀지를 방문할 것이라는 소련 외무부의 발표가 9.17 있었는바, 동 외무차관의 귀주재국 방문(여부 및 방문시) 결과를 보고바람. 끝.

(중동아국장 이 해 순)

보안통제	

앙고재	91년 10월 1일	중동2과	기안자 성명		과장	심의관	국장		차관	장관
			이승열				전결			

외신과통제

0149

관리 번호	91/2254

원 본

외 무 부

종 별 :

번 호 : IRW-0739　　　　　일 시 : 91 1006 1200

수 신 : 장관(중동일,정일)

발 신 : 주 이란 대사

제 목 : 걸프안보협력체제

연:IRW-0714

1. 표제관련 당관 김서기관이 접촉한 일본대사관 OKU 1 등서기관은 일본경단련의 최근 당지방문기간중 있었던 브리핑 SESSION 시 연호 LARIJANI 국가최고안보회의 위원(대통령및 외무장관고문)이 참석 역내안보체제에 대한 주재국의 입장을 설명하였다고 말하였음.

2. 동고문은 이란으로서는 걸프국가들이 자신의 안보를 위해 미국과 방위협정을 체결하는데 기본적으로 반대하지는 않으나 그것보다는 역내 안보를 총체적으로 보장할수있는 집단안보체제의 구성이 더욱 바람직한것으로 본다고 언급한것으로 알려짐(이는 지난번 동인의 NY 지 회견내용및 반박내용을 모두포함하는것임)

3.OKU 서기관은 동고문의 상기 발언은 걸프안보문제에대한 미국의 영향력을인정하지 않을수없는 현실하에서 국내 강경파를 의식 이들의 반응을 사전탐지하기위해 상기 발언을 한것으로 보인다고 설명하였음을 참고바람. 끝

(대사정경일-국장)

예고:91.12.31 일반

중아국	장관	차관	1차보	2차보	외정실	분석관	청와대	안기부

PAGE 1　　　　　91.10.06 20:37 0150

외신 2과 통제관 CE

원 본

외 무 부

암호수신

종 별 :

번 호 : FRW-2200 일 시 : 91 1008 1630

수 신 : 장관(중동일)

발 신 : 주 불 대사

제 목 : 불.쿠웨이트 군사협력협정 체결 추진

1.CHEIK JABER 쿠웨이트 국왕의 미국 및 영국 방문후 지난 10.4 주재국 방문시, MITTERRAND 대통령은 쿠웨이트가 공식 제의한 양국간 군사협정 체결을 원칙적으로 수락하고 세부사항은 양국 외상간 협의토록 한것으로 알려짐.

2. 동 협정은 미.쿠 군사협정 및 협의중인 영. 쿠 군사협정과 같이, 유사시쿠웨이트 기지 이용, 쿠웨이트내 불란서 군사장비 저장, 공동 군사훈련 및 쿠웨이트군 현지 교육 또는 불 군사학교 연수등을 주내용으로 할것이라는 당지 언론보도에 대해, 주재국 외무성 및 국방성은 불.쿠 양국간 협의는, 상당히 진전되고 있는 영. 쿠 협정추진에 비해, 시작에 불과하다는 신중한 반응을 보이고 있음.

3. 이러한 신중한 반응은 주재국이, 쿠웨이트에 대해 발언권을 지니고 있는미국을 의식한 동시에, 불 군사장비의 대쿠 진출(현재로서는 극소수의 MIRAGE F1 전투기 뿐임) 나아가서는, 미국에 대거할당된 쿠웨이트 전후 복구사업에 대한 불란서의 참여노력을 반영하고 있는 것으로 관측됨. 끝.

(대사 노영찬-국장)

중아국 차관 1차보 구주국 외정실 분석관 안기부

PAGE 1 91.10.09 07:52 0151

외신 2과 통제관 BD

원 본

외 무 부

종 별 :

번 호 : JOW-0719 일 시 : 91 1012 2300

수 신 : 장 관(중동이,중동일,기정)

발 신 : 주 요르단 대사

제 목 : 요르단 국민회의개최

1.10.12. 주재국 각계 2,500 명의 대표들의 참석하후세인 국왕 주재로 개막된 국민회의에서후세인 국왕은 중동평화회의 관련 주요회의 진행 개요, 주재국의 방침및 대국민 요망사항등을 발표하고 국민들의 지원을 요청한바요지 다음과 같음

가. 평화회의 개괄적인 FRAMEWORK

1)평화협상은 2개 방도로 진행될것임

-팔레스타인. 이스라엘

-아랍. 이스라엘, BILATERAL COMITTEE 에 의해진행됨

(예:시리아. 이스라엘 위원회, 레바논. 이스라엘위원, 요르단. 팔레스타인. 이스라엘 위원회)

2)중동지역 전국가와 관련된 지역적문제는 제3위원회에 의해 논의될것이며 GCC국가들이 참석할것임

(수자원,환경,군축,사회문제,경제균형을 위한 합동개발사업 실시등)

3)유엔안보리 결의안 242호와 338호가 회의근거가되고 협상의 기초가 될것이. 미국과 소련의 후원하에 EC 대표,유엔사무총장 대표가 참석할것이며 미국과 소련이 유엔사무총장에게 협상진전사항을 통보할것임

4)협상대표단에 의해 합의된 사항들은 유엔에등록될것임

5)요르단이 요르단. 팔레스타인 합동대표단을 주관할것이나 요르단 대표단은 요르단 문제, 팔레스타인 대표단은 팔레스타인 문제를 협의할것임

6)평화회의는 요르단과 팔레스타인을 포함한 전관련국가가 자국의 입장과 견해를 완전하게 표명할수 있는 기회를 부여하게 될것임

7)회의 참석대표는 유익하다고 판단한 안건을 제안할수 있으며 그어느 누구도 이를 거부할 권한이없음

중아국 1차보 중아국 외정실 분석관 청와대 안기부

0152

PAGE 1 91.10.13 06:57 FL

외신 1과 통제관

8)팔레스타인문제는 2단계로 협의될것임

-첫단계는 과도기와 관련된 문제

-둘째단계는 FINAL STATUS 에 대한 합의

-양단계는 연관되어 있으며 2년간의 과도기가 종료되는 3년째초에 아랍예루살렘을 포함하는 WEST BANK 문제등을 2단계에서 협상할것임

9)중요한 원칙은 협상 제1단계에서 합의된사항이 다음단계에서 협의될 사항에 영향을 미치지 않는다는 것임

10)유엔 안보리 결의안 242호는 아랍예루살렘을 포함 67년 전쟁에 점령된 전아랍영토에 적용되어야 할것임

11)미국은 요르단에게 팔레스타인의 과도기가 1년에 종결될수 있도록 협상시 최선을 다하겠다고 보장한바 있음

나.문제해결을 위한 요르단 국민들의 협조사항

1)전수준에서의 강화된 책임

2)용기

3)규율과 조직화

4)애국심

5)경각심과 이해

2.표제회의관련, 주재국 각계반응등 상세추보위계임

(대사 이한춘-국장)

외 무 부

종 별 :

번 호 : JOW-0726 일 시 : 91 1014 1400

수 신 : 장관(중동이,중동일,기정)

발 신 : 주 요르단대사

제 목 : 요르단 국민회의

사본→중2

연:JOW-0719

1. 연호 10.12. 국민회의에서 행한 후세인 국왕연 설에 대한 반응

가.PETRA 통신 언론조사

-팔인들에 대한 요르단의 책임을 재확인 한것으로 환영함.

-요르단이 요르단인과팔인들에 대한 현재와 장래의 보장과 국력의 계속적인 낭비를 막고,팔인들에 대한 지지를 부여하기 위해 미국 주도하의 PEACE PROCESS에의 동참을 수락한다는 국왕의 제안을 전폭 지지함.

나. 언론계

-국왕의 결의에찬 호소는 중동지역인들의 안정과 평화를 위한 노력에 새로운 전기 마련을 위해 이루어 졌으며, 동지역 인민들도 선택의 여지없이 수용해야만 하는새로운 현실들을 지적함

-역사상 가장 중대한 시기에 지도자가 국민들에게 현실적으로 사리를 판단하고발전을 위해 호소한 담대하고 용기있는 대국민메시지 였으며 평화를 위한 양심의 외침임

-평화회의의 수용은 이성적인 국민적 토론과형평 적, 객관적 전망을 근거로 민주적으로 결정된 냉정한 정책의 채택을 의미함

다. 정계

-TALHOUNI 상원부의장(전수상) 국왕의 연설은 공명정대한 평화구현과 유엔안보리 결의안 242호 의 수행을 위해 67년부터 계속해온 요르단의 노력을 요약한 것이며,평화추구 및 팔인들의 권리회복을 갈망하는 요르단 국민들의 내심을 반영한것임

-HINDAWI 하원의원(CONSTITUTION BLOC 지도자)

중아국 1차보 중아국 외정실 분석관 정와대 안기부

PAGE 1 91.10.14 22:09 BX

외신 1과 통제관

0154

국왕의 연설은 유엔안보리 결의안 242호및338호에 기초한 해결책을 통해 아랍점령지가 원주민들에게 반환되는것을 강조하였음

- ALIM 하원의원

아랍국가들 특히 요르단은 유엔결의안의 이행을 위해 이스라엘에 압력을 가할수있는 기회를 포착 하여야 할것이며,평화회의에의 참석거부는 이스라엘에 더많은 이주민을 흡수, 아랍영토를 추가로 병탄할수 있는 기회를 부여하는것임

라.종교계

-국왕의 노력은 팔인들을 지원하기 위한것이 확실하며 PEACE PROCESS는 그들의 권리회복을 목표로 하고있음

-요르단내의 기독교 지도자들은 대화와 이성을지지하고 무력사용을 반대하므로 평화적 방법으로 아랍의 권리회복을 추구하고있는 국왕의 로력을 지지함

마.경제계

-국왕의 연설은 이성, 객관성 및 현실주의의 구체적 표현임

-요르단은 새로운 현실과 상황에 접하고 있으므로 평화를 성취하기 위해 제반변화에 적응하고 노력하는 길 외에는 선택의 여지가 없음

2.하원에서 최다 의석(23석)을 차지하고 있는 MUSLIM BROTHERHOOD 계열 인사들은 요르단의 평화회의 참여를 반대하는 입장이므로 동국민회의에 불참한바 있음. 그러나 동 MB의 지도자인 ARABIYAT하원의장은 의장자격으로 참석함 (대사 이한춘-국장)

원 본

외 무 부

종 별 :

번 호 : BHW-0445 일 시 : 91 1014 1500

수 신 : 장관(중동일)

발 신 : 주바레인 대사

제 목 : 이스라엘 이라크 영공 침범 비난(자료응신 제36호)

주재국 정부는 작10.13 KHALIFA 수상 주재하의 각의에서, 최근 이스라엘 전투기의 이라크영공에의 도발적 비행은 아랍영공 침범행위라고 비난하였음.끝.

(대사 곽희정-국장)

중아국 1차보 외정실 분석관 청와대 안기부

PAGE 1

91.10.14 21:39 BX

외신 1과 통제관

0156

원 본

외 무 부

종 별 :

번 호 : JOW-0732　　　　　　일 시 : 91 1015 1400

수 신 : 장 관(중동이,중동일,미북,기정)

발 신 : 주 요르단 대사

제 목 : 미국무장관 요르단 방문

1. 10.14. 후세인 국왕은 주재국을 방문한 베커 미국무장관과 중동평화 회의관련회담을 갖고요지 다음과 같이 발언함

가. 미국이 요르단에 제시한 보장문서의 최종안에 만족함

나. 중동평화회의가 곧있게 될것이 만족스럽고, 희망적이며 성공할 것으로 확신함

다. 양자간에 현재까지의 진전사항에 관해 논의했는바, 이는 매우 성공 가능성이높고 매우 긍정적이었음

라. 공명정대하고 항구적인 역내 평화회복을 위해 추진해온 미국무장관의 PEACE PROCESS 를 요르단이 지지하고 뒤따라 왔으며 동인의 진지한 노력에 대해 감동과 존경을 표함

마. 금번 국무장관의 요르단 방문은 매우 중요한 방문이며 우리가 오랫동안 가져왔던공포, 의혹, 의심등의 장애를 제거할 새로운시대로의 진입을 대비하는 시기에 이루어진것으로 봄

바. 요르단은 팔레스타인과 합동 대표단 구성을 제의하고 점령지내 및 해외거주 팔인들과의 접촉과 대화를 계속하고 있으며 조만간 결과가 나올것으로 기대함

사. 요르단은 이스라엘과의 양자회의에서 수자원, 환경문제등 지역적 안건등도 논의할것임

2. 베커 미국무장관의 발언내용

가. 팔인들이 평화회의에의 참석을 거부하면 자신들의 장래를 결정할수 있는 역사적 기회를 일실할것임. 이번 평화회의는 팔레스타인 으로서는 최대의 이득을 볼수 있는기회가 되거나 그렇지 않으면 최대의 손실을 보게될것임

나. 10월말까지 평화회의 개최를 추진하는 자신의 목표가 실현될것으로 확신함

다. 요르단은 지역 평화를 위한 미국측의 노력에 가장 긍정적이었으며 진지했던

중아국	장관	차관	1차보	미주국	중아국	외정실	분석관	청와대
안기부								

PAGE 1　　　　91.10.15　22:01 FN

외신 1과 통제관 0157

국가임

라.PEACE PROCESS 추진에 있어 후세인 국왕보다 더용감하고 적극적이며 더 지원적 자세를 보인 지도자는 없었음. 국왕의 적극적이고 강력한 지지와 참여없이 아랍.이스라엘간 포괄적인 해결책 모색을 위한 능동적이고 실현가능한 PEACE PROCESS 의 추진이 이루어질수 없었을 것임

3.베커 장관은 10.15. 당지를 출발 시리아를 방문,ASSAD 대통령과 회담예정으로알려짐

(대사 이한춘-국장

PAGE 2

0158

원 본

외 무 부

종 별 :

번 호 : CAW-1092 일 시 : 91 1016 1550

수 신 : 장 관(중동이)

발 신 : 주 카이로총영사

제 목 : BAKER 국무장관 방애

연:CAW-1086

연호 BAKER 장관은 10.13. 당지를 방문, 무바락 대통령과 MOUSSA 외무장관을 면담한후 14. 요르단 향발에 앞서 주재국 대통령과 가진공동 기자회견에서 요지 하기와 같이 언급함.

1. MUBARAK 대통령

1) 이집트는 중동평화 회담개최를 위해 모든 관계 당사국들과 긴밀 협의하고있으며, 시리아 ASSAD 대통령도 일정이 확정되는대로 참석을 바라고 있음.

2) 지금은 큰 장애물은 없으나 제거해야할 몇가지 작은 문제(ONLY SMALL ONES)들이 있을뿐임.

3) 시리아측이 구상하는 회담 개최전 아랍관계국(이집트,시리아,요르단,PLO)소정상회담은 관계국 상호간 협의가 계속되고있기 때문에 불필요함.

4) 필요한 경우 회담전 PLO 의 ARAFAT과 면담할 것임.

5) 회담개최 일시와 장소는 아직 결정되지않았으나 BAKER 장관이 이번 중동순방끝에 발표할 것임.

2. BAKER 장관

1) 팔레스타인 대표권문제가 아직 미결로 남아있으며

2) LEBANON 측도 회담참석에 동의했음.

3) 시리아대통령도 회담참석을 열망(EAGER ANDKEEN) 하고 있음.

3. 제거해야할 미진부분(ONLY SMALL ONES)을 구체적으로 말하지 않았으나, 그 가운데에는 팔레스타인 대표단구성 문제가 핵을 이루고 있은것으로 보이며, 이와 관련 무바락대통령이 90.8.이락의 쿠웨이트 침공이래 직접 면담을 거부해온 PLO ARAFAT와의

중아국 1차보 외정실 분석관 청와대 안기부

PAGE 1 91.10.16 23:55 FL

외신 1과 통제관 0159

면담용의 표명과 10.14 PLO의 강경파인 인민전선(PFLP)측이 PLO의 회담참석 결정(10.12) 비난하고 나온것으로 미루어봐서 10월말 회담개최 가능성을 한층 밝게하는것으로 관측됨.끝.

(총영사 박동순-국장)

PAGE 2

0160

원 본

외 무 부

종 별 :

번 호 : FRW-2318 일 시 : 91 1023 1640

수 신 : 장 관 (중동이)

발 신 : 주 불 대사

제 목 : 레바논 대통령 방불

표제 관련, 당지 반응 하기 보고함.

1. 10.21-22간 GRAOUI 레바논 대통령이 주재국을 방문, MITTERRAND 대통령과 정상회담을 가졌는 바, 레바논 군인훈련(불란서 ECOLE MILITAIRE 연수 확대), 불 장비 지원, 병원지원 문제 및 급수, 전기, 전화, 수송, 베이루트항구 복원등INFRASTRUCTURE협력문제에 관해 협의하였으며, 마드리드 중동평화 회의에 대해서도 논의한 것으로관측됨.

2. 또한 HRAOUI 대통령은 당지 언론과의 인터뷰에서 , TAEF 협정에 따라 92.9. 시리아의 BEKKA 철수가 이루어질 것이며, 이어서 92년말 또는 93년초에 레바논 총선을실시 할 것이라고 밝혔음. 끝.

(대사 노영찬-국장)

중아국 1차보 외정실 분석관 청와대 안기부

91.10.24 07:56 WH

외신 1과 통제관 0161

관리 번호	91 -693

분류번호	보존기간

발 신 전 보

번 호 : WUS-4833 911024 1552 ED 종별 :

수 신 : 주 미 대사. 총영사 (안호영 서기관)

발 신 : 장 관 (북미2 유재현)

제 목 : 무기 수출

대 : USW(F)-4440

1. 미국등 5대국이 재래식 무기 수출 관련 지침 작성에 합의 하였다는 대호 관련 기사 내용의 사실 여부를 국무부에 확인하여 사실일 경우 동 합의 배경, 합의 내용을 파악 공전으로 보고해 주시기 바라며 가능한 관련 지침 문안을 입수 송부해 주시기 바랍니다.

2. 건승 기원합니다. 끝.

1991.12.31.에 예고문에 의거 일반문서로 재분류됨

보 안 통 제	

앙 고 재	91년 10월 24일	북미2과	기안자 성명		과 장		국 장		차 관	장 관

외신과통제

0162

10/21/91 13:59 ☎202 797 0595 EMBASSY OF KOREA --- WOI ☎010

번호 : USW(F) - 4456

수신 : 장 관 (미안, 기정)

발신 : 주미대사

제목 : 武器 輸出

U.S. and 4 Other Big Arms Makers Adopt Guidelines on Sales

By CRAIG R. WHITNEY
Special to The New York Times

LONDON, Oct. 19 — The United States, the Soviet Union, China, Britain and France have agreed to share information with one another about their sales of tanks, artillery, military aircraft, ships and some missile systems to countries in the Middle East.

The United States Assistant Secretary of State for Politico-Military Affairs, Richard A. Clarke, said on Friday that the five countries had also agreed on guidelines for the export of conventional weapons anywhere in the world.

"This is a major breakthrough, the first time in history that five great powers have agreed on rules governing their export of arms," Mr. Clarke said at the end of a two-day meeting at Lancaster House.

The guidelines are the result of an agreement among most of the five countries that the uncontrolled race to sell arms to Iraq had backfired on them when the Persian Gulf war began last winter.

The United States hopes the agreement will bring a reduction in arms transfers to the Middle East, Mr. Clarke said. The arrangements for sharing information about sales of the major categories of conventional weapons to the region will not come into effect until next year.

The five countries which account for about 85 percent of all arms exports, said in a statement that they would continue their talks in the hope of regulating exports of all ground-to-ground missiles as well as nuclear, chemical and biological weapons and other arms of mass destruction.

Major reservations about missiles were apparently expressed by China, which made the Silkworm missiles that Iraq used against ships in the gulf last winter.

"This is a voluntary agreement among the five, but we are all agreed that these guidelines ought to be applied beyond the five," Mr. Clarke said. "There are no sanctions."

He said the five nations would continue talks on such issues as extending the accord on information-sharing to include other areas of the world and other arms exporters like South Africa and Brazil.

President Bush called on May 29 for a set of rules among the five countries, who held preliminary talks in Paris in July. The guidelines they agreed to on Friday commit them to do jointly what all of them swear they have been doing separately for years.

END

Oct. 20, 1991
NYT

0163

9

관리 번호	91-610

원 본

외 무 부

종 별 :

번 호 : USW-5338 일 시 : 91 1030 1813

수 신 : 장 관 (미안,정안)

발 신 : 주 미국 대사

제 목 : 재래식 무기 공급에 대한 정보교환

1. NYT 지는 10.20. 미,영,불,중,소 5 개국이 중동에 대한 재래식 무기공급에 대한 정보를 교환하기로 합의하였다고 보도한바 있음.

2. 동건관련, 당관 안호영 서기관이 국무부 정치.군사국 PETRIOUS 보좌관(동 문제와 관련 CLARK 차관보 특별 보좌)으로 부터 탐문한 내용을 하기 보고함.

가. 경과

- 5.29 BUSH 대통령 제의에 따라 동건에 대한 5 개국간 협의가 시작된바, 7 월 파리회의에 이어 9 월에 런던에서 전문가 회의가 있었고, 10.17-18 간 런던에서 CLARK 차관보 주재하에 본회의가 개최되었음.

- 금번 런던회의에서 논의된 것은 주로 중동에 대한 무기 공급에 적용될 일반원칙과 상호 정보를 교환한다는 원칙에 관한 것이었으며, 상세한 절차등은 추후 협의를 통하여 결정될 것임.

- 런던 회의에서는 차기 본회의를 내년중 미국에서 개최하기로 하였는바, 그 이전에라도 필요성이 인정되면 전문가 회의를 소집할 가능성도 있음.

나. 실시방식

- (5 개국이 서로 정보를 교환하는 것인지 아니면 별도의 중앙 사무국을 설치할 것인지 문의한데 대하여), 별도의 사무국을 설치하지 않고, 외교 경로를 통하여 상호 교환하기로 함.

- (각국마다 어떤 정부부서가 정보교환의 주된 임무를 수행할 것인지 ?)

아직 구체적인 협의는 없었으나, 미국 경우에는 국무부가 될 것으로 봄.

- (언제부터 정보교환이 개시될 수 있을 것으로 보는지 ?)

5 개국간 회의의 진전속도에 연계된 문제이나, 1 년 이내에 실시하기는 어렵지 않을까 하는 개인적인 의견임.(BEYOND MY IMAGINATION)

미주국 장관 차관 1차보 2차보 외정실 분석관 청와대 안기부

PAGE 1 91.10.31 09:54 0164

외신 2과 통제관 BS

- (가령, 중국 경우에는 중동에 대한 무기수출이 전체 무기 수출의 80%를 능가하는데, 자발적 통보에 의한 정보교환이 얼마나 효과적일 것인지, 검증의 필요성은 논의되지 않았는지 ?)

금번 조치를 가능하게 한 것은 5 개국간의 신의(GOOD FAITH)이므로, 검증문제는 제기될 수가 없었는바, 미국이 보기로는 신의를 지키지 않는 대가가 가장 큰 담보라고 생각함(THE COST OF OPERATING IN BAD FAITH WILL HAVE THE GREATEST DETERRENCE EFFECT.)

다. 개념 정의

- 런던 회의에서는 7 개 무기 카테고리가 제시된바, 특히 미사일등과 관련 구체적으로 어떤 무기가 이 카테고리에 속하느냐 하는 문제도 금후 협의되어야 함.

- '중동'에 대한 개념 정의와 관련, 중국은 터키도 이에 포함되어야 한다는 입장이나, 미국으로서는 터키는 NATO 회원국이고 중동문제에 깊이 관여된 국가가 아니므로 터키는 중동에 포함될 수 없다는 입장임.

3. 국무부로 부터 입수한 런던회의 발표문을 별도 FAX 송부함(USW(F)-4665).끝.

(대사 현홍주-국장)

예고: ~~92-6-30. 까지~~

19 . . .에 예고문에 의거 일반문서로 재분류됨

PAGE 2

0165

10/30/91 19:32 ☎202 7 0595 EMBASSY OF KOR → WOI 001

번 : USW(F) - 4665
수 신 : 장 관 (미안, 기사) 발신 : 주미대사
제 목 : 재래식 무기 수출 guideline (첨부물) (5 매)

보안 통제

USW(F) -4665

MEETING OF THE FIVE ON ARMS TRANSFERS AND NON-PROLIFERATION: LONDON 17/18 OCTOBER 1991

1. In accordance with their agreement in Paris on 8 and 9 July 1991, representatives of the United States of America, the People's Republic of China, France, the United Kingdom of Great Britain and Northern Ireland, and the Union of Soviet Socialist Republics met in London on 17 and 18 October to take forward their discussions on issues related to conventional arms transfers and to the non-proliferation of weapons of mass destruction.

2. Recalling the statement which was issued in Paris on 9 July, they;

- agreed common guidelines for the export of conventional weapons (annexed). They expressed the hope that other arms exporting countries will adopt similar guidelines of restraint;

- agreed to inform each other about transfers to the region of the Middle East, as a matter of priority, of tanks, armoured combat vehicles, artillery, military aircraft and helicopters, naval vessels, and certain missile systems, without prejudice to existing commitments to other governments;

- agreed to make arrangements to exchange information for the purpose of meaningful consultation, bearing in mind their shared concern to ensure the proper application of the agreed guidelines, and to continue discussions on how best to develop these arrangements on a global and regional basis in order to achieve this objective;

4665-1

0166

- welcomed work at the United Nations General Assembly on the early establishment of a UN register of conventional arms transfers, and supported the current consultations on this issue between a wide range of UN members in which they are actively participating. They called for universal support for this work;

- noted the threats to peace and stability posed by the proliferation of nuclear weapons, chemical and biological weapons, missiles etc, and undertook to seek effective measures of non-proliferation and arms control in a fair, reasonable, comprehensive and balanced manner on a global as well as on a regional basis. They reaffirmed the importance of maintaining stringent and, so far as possible, harmonised guidelines for exports in this area. They embarked on a comparison of their national export controls on equipment related to weapons of mass destruction and agreed to examine the scope for further harmonisation of those controls. They agreed to pursue discussions at their next meeting on these subjects;

- agreed to continue discussing the possibilities for lowering tension and arms levels, including the development of further measures of restraint concerning arms transfers and ways of encouraging regional and global efforts towards arms control and disarmament;

- agreed to continue to give these efforts high priority and meet again in the new year in the United States to take forward their discussions, and to meet regularly thereafter at least once a year.

4665-2

0167

GUIDELINES FOR CONVENTIONAL ARMS TRANSFERS

The People's Republic of China, the French Republic, the Union of Soviet Socialist Republics, the United Kingdom of Great Britain and Northern Ireland, and the United States of America,

recalling and reaffirming the principles which they stated as a result of their meeting in Paris on 8 and 9 July 1991,

mindful of the dangers to peace and stability posed by the transfer of conventional weapons beyond levels needed for defensive purposes,

reaffirming the inherent right to individual or collective self-defence recognised in Article 51 of the Charter of the United Nations, which implies that states have the right to acquire means of legitimate self-defence,

recalling that in accordance with the Charter of the United Nations, UN Member States have undertaken to promote the establishment and maintenance of international peace and security with the least diversion for armaments of the world's human and economic resources,

seeking to ensure that arms transferred are not used in violation of the purposes and principles of the UN Charter,

mindful of their special responsibilities for the maintenance of international peace and security,

reaffirming their commitment to seek effective measures to promote peace, security, stability and arms control on a global and regional basis in a fair reasonable,

44665-3 0168

comprehensive and balanced manner,

noting the importance of encouraging international commerce for peaceful purposes,

determined to adopt a serious, responsible and prudent attitude of restraint regarding arms transfers,

declare that, when considering under their national control procedures conventional arms transfers, they intend to observe rules of restraint, and to act in accordance with the following guidelines:

1. They will consider carefully whether proposed transfers will:

   a) promote the capabilities of the recipient to meet needs for legitimate self-defence;

   b) serve as an appropriate and proportionate response to the security and military threats confronting the recipient country;

   c) enhance the capability of the recipient to participate in regional or other collective arrangements or other measures consistent with the Charter of the United Nations or requested by the United Nations;

2. They will avoid transfers which would be likely to

   a) prolong or aggravate an existing armed conflict;

   b) increase tension in a region or contribute to regional instability;

4665-4

0169

c) introduce destabilising military capabilities in a region;

d) contravene embargoes or other relevant internationally agreed restraints to which they are parties;

e) be used other than for the legitimate defence and security needs of the recipient state;

f) support or encourage international terrorism;

g) be used to interfere with the internal affairs of sovereign states;

h) seriously undermine the recipient state's economy.

4665-5 (END)

0170

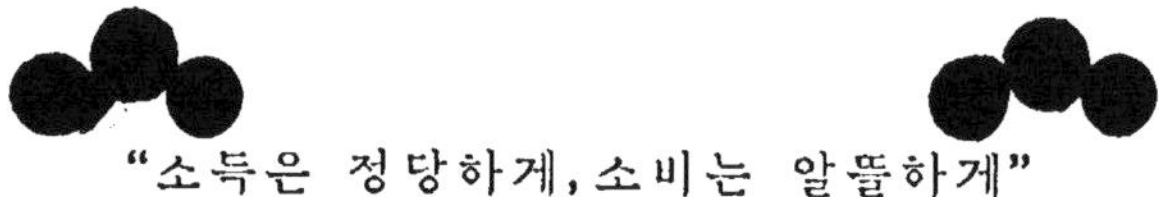

"소득은 정당하게, 소비는 알뜰하게"

주 카 이 로 총 영 사 관

문서번호 : 주카(정)20405-356　　　　1991.10.29

경　　유 :

수　　신 : 장관

참　　조 : 중동아국장, 외정실장, 외교안보연구원장

제　　목 : 중동지역 수자원문제의 심각성

그간 중동지역 문제에 관한 많은 전문가들은 역내 화전 요인이었던 이스라엘 생존권 허용문제, 석유자원 확보문제가 진화되면 다음으로 수자원 문제가 화전 요인으로 부상하게 될 가능성이 가장 높은 것으로 주시해 오고 있읍니다.

이 역내 수자원 문제에 관해 11월 터키 Istanbul에서 개최 예정이었던 Mideast Water Summit이 Madrid 중동평화 개최(10.30)에 악영향을 줄 우려(10.5.시리아측은 이스라엘 참여시 첨석거부 표명) 관계로 명춘으로 연기되었을 뿐 아니라, 10월 6일 Tantawi 이집트 국방장관은 Nile강물 확보를 위해서는 향후 무력사용도 불사하겠다(10.6)고 함으로 전기전문가들의 우려를 충분히 뒷받침한 것으로 사료됩니다.

이와관련 지난 10월 1일에서 3일까지 Cyprus의 Nicosia에서 개최된 "Middle East Strategy to the Year 2004"제하 제5차 연례 Arab Press Service회의에서 Jordan대학교 Elias Salameh교수는 역내의 이용 수자원이 아래와 같이 그 발원국과 이용국이 상이한 가운데 인구증가, 수자원의 퇴화 및 주민들의 생활향상에 따른 수요증대등으로 고갈화 되어가고 있음에 우려를 표하고 그 대책으로 공유의식 도출, 새로운 수자원 개발, 수자원(인력자원 및 석유자원포함) 이용에 관한 합의사항 준수 및 분쟁해결 기구 설치를 제의하였읍니다.

상기 Elias Salameh교수의 발표문 요지를 별첨으로 송부하오니 참고하시기 바랍니다.

발송 1991.10.31

0171

각국 물이용 현황

지 역	1일 1인당 사용량(Litre)
1. 사막지역 Bedouin	4-5
2. 요르단인	85
3. 일반 아랍인(평균)	125
4. 이스라엘인	275
5. 유럽인	250-350
6. 북미인	500-600

각국 용수의 수원지

국 명	타국 수원의존도
1. 이락	66%(자급도 34%)
2. 이집트	98%(자급도 2%)
3. 시리아	34%(" 66%0
4. 요르단	36%(" 64%)
5. 수단	77%(" 23%)
6. 모리타니아	77%(" 23%)
7. 이스라엘	80%(점령지인 West Bank 와 Gaza Strip과 요르단 강에서 각각 40%)

첨 부 : 상기자료

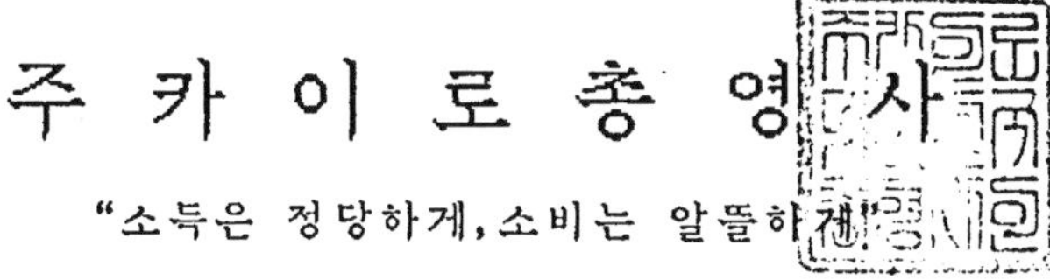

0172

the aps diplomat 

Editor
Pierre W. Shammas

news service

Monday 7/14 October 1991 - 19th Year, Vol. 35, No. 15 SP 175

Middle East Business & Political Prospects To Year 2004 Assessed: 0173

NICOSIA - Middle East business opportunities and political superstructures will improve considerably during the second half of the 1990s. Apart from some mega-projects to be implemented in the next five years, however, the first half of the 1990s will be a period of turbulence both in the Middle East and the new Soviet Union. This is one of the conclusions reached at the 5th Annual APS Conference, 'Middle East Strategy To The Year 2004', held in Nicosia on Oct. 1-3. The following are the main points and recommendations of the conference.

Comparison in risks and opportunities was drawn between the Middle East and the Soviet Union. It was concluded that the two have become closely related, perhaps more than ever before, mainly because emerging issues in both areas have a similar pre-World War I set of motivations, such as national/ethnic and sectarian currents trying to fill the vacuum left by the demise of Communism as well as bipolarism.

Pierre Shammas, head of the APS Group who chaired the conference, said people in the Middle East as well as companies dealing with this region should "simplify strategic objectives while making their means of implementation as flexible and as diverse as they can". This is because in the next 12 years a strategy based on inflexible factors, such as a rigid forecast for oil prices or government spending, "will be exposed dangerously to elements of uncertainty which are already obvious to all concerned... Resultant risks can be fatal. Even those powers depending on a unipolar order in world politics, trade or finance could be fatally exposed... For corporate strategists the price of oil no longer matters as much as simple objectives like profitability, expansion through diversified operations, or contraction for optimum benefits to shareholders". The same would apply to rulers in the Middle East who "no longer have a viable insurance policy" (see overleaf).

Prof. Alexander Arbatov, of the Soviet Academy of Sciences, proposed that aid to and oil/gas imports from the Soviet Union be tied to reducing the energy intensiveness of this region, mainly Russia. "Energy saving in the Soviet Union can thus be conceived as a global program that will open up an important energy source for many countries" and could eventually become a crucial factor to "a cleaner environment worldwide". Prof. Ivan Nesterov, President of the West Siberian Oil & Gas Research Institute, offered a new technology to clean up the Gulf area from oil pollution.

Dr. Peter Oppenheimer, of Oxford University, said multinational oil companies "must consider the management of their basic factors of production - people and capital. The cessation of growth twenty years ago, combined with high upstream profitability and continued technical progress, led both to lower personnel requirements and to cash mountains". In the 1990s this situation will be different and challenges will be quite serious. Anthony Scanlan, Chairman of BIEE, stressed that loyalties or moral commitments in market economies are being focused on share holders rather than governments, company management or customers - one consequence of trends in the past decade which, according to Shammas, will generate "a number of negative social factors arising from the demise of Communism". In a debate with Scanlan and other speakers, Shammas added that "the challenge of this demise to capitalism is likely to be greater than the challenge of Communism itself".

Published by the Arab Press Service Organisation, Lebanon. APS is an independent centre for Middle East information and research, founded in Beirut in 1972. Ask for APS brochure outlining its publications, consultancy and other services, and for APS "Who's Who".

Annual Subscription to Diplomat Package: US$ 800. Annual Subscription to Full Diplomat & Review Package: US$ 1,200. All APS publications are posted from Cyprus. Apply to: APS, P.O.Box 3898, Nicosia, Cyprus. Fax No. 357-2-350265.

Middle East Risks & Opportunities: In his opening address, Shammas again spoke of a balance of wisdom, as he did last year, for a world based on "a functional equilibrium between law and justice...and of fairness among both rich and poor (see his October 1990 proposals in Vol. 33, SP 149-150). He also said, among other things, that oil can be an element of risk. "In 1980 the Gulf states earned $180 billion from oil, which was a record. But two wars since 1980 have cost the region about $800 billion...while the total oil revenues of these states from 1984 to 1990 have reached a mere $390 billion. Within less than four decades oil has made major producers of food hungry to the extent that a country like Algeria - not to mention Iraq - now spends much of its export earnings on food imports. Oil has done a lot of other things..."

Risks and opportunities in the Middle East were weighed on a multi-disciplinary basis. Dr. Elias Salameh, of Jordan University, discussed the water problem (see FAP of next week's Diplomat). Christian Doumit dealt with the demographic problem. Faris Glubb reviewed Arab political issues since August 1990 and outlined the prospects for political structures and decision making. Daniel Champion of Institut Francais du Petrole and Robert Robinson of KPMG gave a presentation on the latest trends in information technology for the petroleum industry and the way benefits can be maximised. Sylvie Cornot covered the oil and gas sectors. The petrochemical sector was covered by Hans Wallrabenstein of BASF and Shoji Hirai of Mitsubishi Petrochemical Co. (see this week's APS Review). Gilbert Jenkins of Energy Business Review gave a presentation on the aviation fuel business, the future role of airline companies, and the market share of Middle East oil companies.

The Soviet Union: Shammas pointed out that, like the Middle East, "the Soviet Union offers the world great opportunities. The demise of Communism presents promoters of global peace with a fateful challenge, however...(because) in setting social standards for the working class, in the capitalist world, the question whether or not Communism was a bad ideology was of little relevance. It was of little relevance to both employers and work-forces. This is just one example of the way capitalism used to benefit from the Communist challenge. Now the collapse of this challenge leaves a vacuum which company managements may find as an opportunity... Communism has been with us for several decades, including two World Wars. Its effect will not vanish with the flick of a TV switch. So those who see opportunity in the collapse of Communism must beware, because time is definitely not on their side. It is my fear that they may not even have the time to enjoy it... To set an order of global consequence one does not simply play it by ear, because we are in crisis. Fighting to make peace should not require another war to keep it, otherwise our crisis would assume dangerous proportions. The world crisis that exists today is a crisis of control... Every stone you overturn will add to the crisis more worms of conscience. Some of these worms date back to the past century...

"Opportunities in Russia, a huge corridor between Europe and the Pacific, have never been greater. They are by far bigger than the opportunities of the Middle East. By the same token the risks in Russia have never been greater, not only for the rich powers but for the world as a whole... Russia today offers the world an historic opportunity. The best, indeed the most serious, opportunity lies in its energy sector. This opportunity by far surpasses the energy resources of the Middle East; and to the extent that we are all concerned about the risks of global conflagration, even Middle East governments should invest in this Russian opportunity.

"The question for Russia lies not in its ability to produce energy but in its potential to save it. It could save most of its energy for the rest of the world. Bringing Soviet energy intensiveness to the OECD level, for example, will mean saving 650 million tons of oil equivalent annually, which is more than its total oil production at present. In effect, its energy saving potential and resultant export possibilities amount to more than half of total OPEC production.

"Far more important for the world is the role Russia can play in making our planet environmentally safe. Dr. Arbatov's proposal merits serious consideration by world leaders, therefore, and we must consider the risks of not responding adequately while we still have the opportunity..."

0174

In fact, Shammas concluded, "the world now has two golden opportunities: one in the Middle East, which is a corridor of opportunities between North and South, and a bigger one in Russia which is a corridor of opportunities between East and West".

-2-

the aps diplomat 

Editor
Pierre W. Shammas

news service

Monday 14/21 October 1991 - 19th Year, Vol. 35, No. 16 SP 185

Middle East Water Crisis Will Make Or Break North-South Peace, Israel Is Warned:

NICOSIA - The following are brief questions and answers about the Middle East perspective until November 1992 gathered from a variety of sources: (1) Will the Arab states unite for a war with Israel over water resources? No. (2) Is any Arab state, or group of states, in a position to confront Israel militarily? No. (3) Will the Arab states unite for a peace and water sharing agreement with Israel? No. (4) Which of the problems is likely to cause the next Arab-Israeli war - water, Palestine, oil or other? Water.

Israeli Radicals Are Probably Honest In Their Warning That President Bush, Or His Peace Initiative, Can Lead To A 2nd Holocaust

The sources consulted by APS include experts in the Middle East, Europe, the Pacific and the US. Middle Eastern sources include Christian, Jewish and Muslim analysts. They all agree that the negotiating position of the Arabs is weaker than that of Israel, with some saying it is at its weakest since the 1940s. They also agree that water shortages will cause a big explosion (see study on the water problem in FAP of this week's package).

The following are brief questions and answers for the perspective in the period between late 1992 and early 1997. (1) Will the Arabs unite for any cause? No. (2) Will the status quo in the Arab World remain unchanged? No. (3) Will there be an Arab-Israeli war? Yes.

But What Is The Alternative To Peace Other Than American Isolation?

The following is a more complex set of questions and answers about the perspective until 1997, all being relevant to the current US peace process and the water problem which is beginning to assume crisis proportions (see overleaf):

1. What purpose will a "super-Israel" serve to the US and other rich powers in the 1990s? The problem is neither side would see it that way, because what would look like a "super Israel" to Arab eyes would still be regarded as a "super-ally" in the US; but it would be a "super-ghetto" to European eyes and to those who are already worried about its nuclear arsenal.

'Super-Israel' Could Be Viable, Provided The Arab World Plunges Into Endless Chaos And Oil Is Priced Out Of OECD Energy

2. Will the next Arab-Israeli war end in a clear Arab defeat or Israeli victory? Neither, because it will symbolise a fight for life among the poor on the one hand, and a fight against a lower standard of living among the rich on the other, i.e., it will spark off a North-South crisis so serious that OECD powers might be compelled to sacrifice Israel. This should explain the worry among Israeli hardliners that the Bush policies could lead to a second holocaust (see this week's Recorder).

0175

Important advisers to President Bush have begun to focus on the water problem in the Middle East. It is on their advice that Washington has persuaded Ankara to postpone a multilateral summit

Published by the Arab Press Service Organisation, Lebanon. APS is an independent centre for Middle East information and research, founded in Beirut in 1972. Ask for APS brochure outlining its publications, consultancy and other services, and for APS "Who's Who".

Annual Subscription to Diplomat Package: US$ 800. Annual Subscription to Full Diplomat & Review Package: US$ 1,200. All APS publications are posted from Cyprus. Apply to: APS, P.O.Box 3896, Nicosia, Cyprus. Fax No. (357-2)-350265.

the aps diplomat news service

Editor
Pierre W. Shammas

Monday 14/21 October 1991 - 19th Year, Vol. 35, No. 16 SP 185

Middle East Water Crisis Will Make Or Break North-South Peace, Israel Is Warned:

NICOSIA - The following are brief questions and answers about the Middle East perspective until November 1992 gathered from a variety of sources: (1) Will the Arab states unite for a war with Israel over water resources? No. (2) Is any Arab state, or group of states, in a position to confront Israel militarily? No. (3) Will the Arab states unite for a peace and water sharing agreement with Israel? No. (4) Which of the problems is likely to cause the next Arab-Israeli war - water, Palestine, oil or other? Water.

Israeli Radicals Are Probably Honest In Their Warning That President Bush, Or His Peace Initiative, Can Lead To A 2nd Holocaust

The sources consulted by APS include experts in the Middle East, Europe, the Pacific and the US. Middle Eastern sources include Christian, Jewish and Muslim analysts. They all agree that the negotiating position of the Arabs is weaker than that of Israel, with some saying it is at its weakest since the 1940s. They also agree that water shortages will cause a big explosion (see study on the water problem in FAP of this week's package).

The following are brief questions and answers for the perspective in the period between late 1992 and early 1997. (1) Will the Arabs unite for any cause? No. (2) Will the status quo in the Arab World remain unchanged? No. (3) Will there be an Arab-Israeli war? Yes.

But What Is The Alternative To Peace Other Than American Isolation?

The following is a more complex set of questions and answers about the perspective until 1997, all being relevant to the current US peace process and the water problem which is beginning to assume crisis proportions (see overleaf):

1. What purpose will a "super-Israel" serve to the US and other rich powers in the 1990s? The problem is neither side would see it that way, because what would look like a "super Israel" to Arab eyes would still be regarded as a "super-ally" in the US; but it would be a "super-ghetto" to European eyes and to those who are already worried about its nuclear arsenal.

'Super-Israel' Could Be Viable, Provided The Arab World Plunges Into Endless Chaos And Oil Is Priced Out Of OECD Energy

2. Will the next Arab-Israeli war end in a clear Arab defeat or Israeli victory? Neither, because it will symbolise a fight for life among the poor on the one hand, and a fight against a lower standard of living among the rich on the other, i.e., it will spark off a North-South crisis so serious that OECD powers might be compelled to sacrifice Israel. This should explain the worry among Israeli hardliners that the Bush policies could lead to a second holocaust (see this week's Recorder).

0176

Important advisers to President Bush have begun to focus on the water problem in the Middle East. It is on their advice that Washington has persuaded Ankara to postpone a multilateral summit

Published by the Arab Press Service Organisation, Lebanon. APS is an independent centre for Middle East information and research, founded in Beirut in 1972. Ask for APS brochure outlining its publications, consultancy and other services and for APS "Who's Who".

Annual Subscription to Diplomat Package: US$ 800. Annual Subscription to Full Diplomat & Review Package: US$ 1,200. All APS publications are posted from Cyprus. Apply to: APS, P.O.Box 3896,

the

Editor
Pierre W. Shammas

fate of the arabian peninsula

14 October 1991 - Vol. 22, No. 4 SP 13

The Water Problem In The Middle East:

Water is the most abundant among the natural resources. But the Middle East and North Africa are among the least blessed areas of the world with respect to the availability of water resources. Vast areas in the Middle East and North Africa are bedevilled by hyper aridity. The following is a study presented at the 5th Annual APS Conference, 'Middle East Strategy To The Year 2004', in Nicosia on Oct. 1-3, by Prof. Elias Salameh of the University of Jordan.

The natural scarcity of water resources in the area is aggravated by human activities such as: (1) Alarming growth rates of population resulting in doubling the population of the different countries every 18 to 30 years. (2) Growing degradation of the available resources thus reducing their utility at their original quality. (3) Increasing demand due to higher standards of living, industrialisation and irrigation.

Domestic Water Use In Different Areas & Countries

Location	Liters/Capita Per Day
1. Bedouins in desert areas	4-5
2. Jordanians	85
3. Arabs in average	125
4. Israelis	275
5. Europeans	250-350
6. North Americans	500-600

This table shows that with the upgrading in the living standards, urbanisation and industrialisation, water demands and uses have increased significantly. The countries and territories of the Middle East and North Africa, i.e., Jordan, Egypt, Saudi Arabia, the Gulf states, Palestine, Libya, Tunisia, Morocco, Algeria, Syria, Iraq and Israel, are at present using or overusing all their annual renewable fresh water resources. Rationing, reducing allocations to agriculture, and damage to sensible groundwater resources are becoming more common.

0177

This fragile situation is greatly aggravated by the fact that over 60% of the area's water resources originate from other areas lying further to the North; Turkey, or further to the South; Ethiopian Plateau. Superimposing water scarcity and water being shared among different countries are the political hostilities and various intentions and interests of the different countries. The link between water and politics can exacerbate political tensions and influence policy decisions. Iraq, for example, receives 66% of its water from other countries. Egypt receives 98% of its water from outside its territories. Syria 34%, Jordan 36%, Sudan 77% and Mauritania 77%. On the other hand, Israel receives 35% of its water supply from aquifers recharged in the West Bank and another 30% from territories occupied in 1967. These facts will add complexity to any future negotiations on Palestinian autonomy or statehood. Also, immigrant populations to the region whether Soviet Jews to Israel or Palestinian and Jordanian refugees from Kuwait and other Gulf states to a Palestinian entity or to Jordan will greatly affect regional demand for this already limited resource, further fuelling the political conflict.

Published by the Arab Press Service Organisation, Lebanon. APS is an independent centre for Middle East information and research, founded in Beirut in 1972. Ask for APS brochure outlining its publications, consultancy and other services, and for APS "Who's Who".

Annual Subscription to Diplomat Package: US$ 800. Annual Subscription to Full Diplomat & Review Package: US$ 1,200. All APS publications are posted from Cyprus. Apply to: APS, P.O.Box 3896, Nicosia, Cyprus. Fax No. (357-2)-350265.

the aps diplomat 

Editor
Pierre W. Shammas

fate of the arabian peninsula

14 October 1991 - Vol. 22, No. 4 SP 13

The Water Problem In The Middle East:

Water is the most abundant among the natural resources. But the Middle East and North Africa are among the least blessed areas of the world with respect to the availability of water resources. Vast areas in the Middle East and North Africa are bedevilled by hyper aridity. The following is a study presented at the 5th Annual APS Conference, 'Middle East Strategy To The Year 2004', in Nicosia on Oct. 1-3, by Prof. Elias Salameh of the University of Jordan.

The natural scarcity of water resources in the area is aggravated by human activities such as: (1) Alarming growth rates of population resulting in doubling the population of the different countries every 18 to 30 years. (2) Growing degradation of the available resources thus reducing their utility at their original quality. (3) Increasing demand due to higher standards of living, industrialisation and irrigation.

Domestic Water Use In Different Areas & Countries

Location	Liters/Capita Per Day
1. Bedouins in desert areas	4-5
2. Jordanians	85
3. Arabs in average	125
4. Israelis	275
5. Europeans	250-350
6. North Americans	500-600

This table shows that with the upgrading in the living standards, urbanisation and industrialisation, water demands and uses have increased significantly. The countries and territories of the Middle East and North Africa, i.e., Jordan, Egypt, Saudi Arabia, the Gulf states, Palestine, Libya, Tunisia, Morocco, Algeria, Syria, Iraq and Israel, are at present using or overusing all their annual renewable fresh water resources. Rationing, reducing allocations to agriculture, and damage to sensible groundwater resources are becoming more common.

0178

This fragile situation is greatly aggravated by the fact that over 60% of the area's water resources originate from other areas lying further to the North; Turkey, or further to the South; Ethiopian Plateau. Superimposing water scarcity and water being shared among different countries are the political hostilities and various intentions and interests of the different countries. The link between water and politics can exacerbate political tensions and influence policy decisions. Iraq, for example, receives 66% of its water from other countries. Egypt receives 98% of its water from outside its territories. Syria 34%, Jordan 36%, Sudan 77% and Mauritania 77%. On the other hand, Israel receives 35% of its water supply from aquifers recharged in the West Bank and another 30% from territories occupied in 1967. These facts will add complexity to any future negotiations on Palestinian autonomy or statehood. Also, immigrant populations to the region whether Soviet Jews to Israel or Palestinian and Jordanian refugees from Kuwait and other Gulf states to a Palestinian entity or to Jordan will greatly affect regional demand for this already limited resource, further fuelling the political conflict.

Published by the Arab Press Service Organisation, Lebanon. APS is an independent centre for Middle East information and research, founded in Beirut in 1972. Ask for APS brochure outlining its publications, consultancy and other services, and for APS "Who's Who".

Annual Subscription to Diplomat Package: US$ 800. Annual Subscription to Full Diplomat & Review Package: US$ 1,200. All APS publications are posted from Cyprus. Apply to: APS, P.O.Box 3896, Nicosia, Cyprus. Fax No. (357-2)-350265.

between the various states. The non-renewable nature of oil puts a time constraint and a sense of urgency on co-operation in this field in order to develop greater levels of interactions to cultivate feelings of mutual trust and interdependence for a lasting stability in the region. Time and oil are, however, running out fast. The Arab oil countries have depleted their oil resources at much faster rates than they were able to build physical and human capital to replace the lost resources.

Development can be best achieved where labour, technology skills, financial and natural resources are in abundance. The oil-poor countries of the Middle East have at their disposal labour, technology and skills which complement the financial resources of the oil-rich countries. The oil states alone represent only a small economic and strategic mass and will always be in need of neighbouring countries as markets and sources of resources and human capital.

The recent three years of drought that have affected Africa and partly the Middle East and the fact of border crossing rivers which these states share and are dependent on, portend an insetting human and environmental crisis which, if unabated, may very well exacerbate an already unstable and crisis-prone region. More urgently than ever, politicians and scientists are arguing that the next Middle East war may be fought over water, having just finished a disastrous war for oil. Scarce resources are increasingly shaping the largely arid, oil-rich Middle East with Turkey emerging as the region's "water super-power" and Saudi Arabia and the Gulf as the region's "oil super-power".

Given the potential for increased dialogue at this time within the Middle East, it is essential that researchers turn towards examining the serious joint economic problems of this area, which can enhance co-operation and put an end to the unfair rivalries over exhaustible, non-renewable resources. The challenge is to plan regionally for co-operative use and better management of energy wealth and other resources, especially water, to overcome the uneven development in the area and to avert looming disasters of resource shortages which could trigger domestic, regional and international conflicts.

Another pressing set of questions focuses on how natural resources management issues interact with conventional macro-economic policy concerns such as structural adjustment, stabilisation measures and trade liberalisation. Much of the problem lies in the contrast between the holistic nature of environmental issues and the fragmented way in which governments, human societies and institutions are structured and function accordingly.

The management options capable of meeting the needs of all the populations in the region are few indeed. The elements that would go into a co-operative management scheme are easy to identify, if difficult for the actors to agree on. First, there must be agreed shares of water from various sources. And there must be equitable conservation schemes that could bring future water needs more into line with potentially available water in order to distribute the burden of shortages in the region. Second, new sources of water must be developed to supplement existing supplies. Third, oil abundance, human and water resources must be brought into line. Finally, some mechanism other than military intervention or retaliation must be devised to resolve the inevitable disputes over whether any management agreement has been violated. This last option, to be effective, must be an institutional framework within which management decisions can be made in the interests of all and as an obligation of each.

0179

In addition to emphasising the application of advanced water-saving technology, any commitment to conservation must de-emphasize agriculture as the social base. If each in the region genuinely accepts the right to co-existence of every other state in the region, the need to occupy land as a measure of military security will diminish. Irrigation uses immense quantities of water while adding very little value to the production of the societies in the region. The ideological dream of making the desert bloom simply cannot be justified in a context where countries with extremely limited economic bases and inadequate water resources can only accomplish their dreams by depriving their neighbours of water. Oil resources should play a major role utilising the human resources in developing the whole area.

Israel... Knowing that Israel is currently utilising all of its renewable water resources and is forecast to have an annual water deficit of 700 to 900 MCM by the year 2005, its occupation of a zone in southern Lebanon up to the western bend of the Litani River is once again raising questions about Israel's hydrological ambitions. On May 11, 1991 Israel declared officially that it would not withdraw from Lebanon without assurances of its "share" of the Litani River. This year, water in Lake Tiberias had dropped to its lowest ever recorded level, and the country's Water Authority was considering emergency measures to restrict water pumping from the lake in order to prevent the water level from dropping below the dangerous point of 212.5 meters below sea level. For the last five years, Israel has been implementing water rationing schemes mostly affecting the politically sensitive farming sector which consumes around 75% of the country's water supply.

The Perestroika of the Soviet Union is likely to aggravate Israel's water problems. In the next decade Israel is expected to receive between 250,000 and 300,000 Soviet Jews (with some estimates putting the total to more than 2 million) for whom Israel is planning to build 100,000 new homes. This is making the Israel Water Works revise their long term plans in order to be able to supply water to the new homes.

Israel's access to the Litani could supplement its annual water supply by 200 to 400 MCM. Another attraction of the Litani River is the high quality of its water compared to that in Lake Tiberias or, the increasingly brackish water from many of Israel's overused aquifers especially those along the coast. Hence the Litani's water would lower the salinity level of Lake Tiberias from which the National Water Carrier takes water to much of the country when reaching the cultivable area in the Negev. The question is, then, can and will Lebanon "share" its water? Will a peace conference in the Middle East persuade the Lebanese to share any additional water they have?

Oil: The Arab Middle East can easily be divided into two groups; oil producing states with abundant financial resources and limited populations, and oil consuming states with large populations and little or no resources. As Arab oil-short countries became increasingly dependent on aid and remittances from the oil producing countries, their resentment, frustrations and disappointments grew in proportion. The expectation was that they would share more equitably in the oil wealth and that they would receive investments to alter their state of poverty and constrained development. (Trade between oil-rich and oil-poor states represents a mere 4% of the oil rich imports. This is because of limited investments by the rich oil states in the poor countries).

Ways Of Co-operation: Much has been written about energy abundance and water shortages in the Middle East, but very little if any has been advanced in terms of ways and instruments about co-operation and interdependence. Advancing water scarcities are a common characteristic of most countries in the Middle East. Therefore, competition between states is increasing over the use of these scarce resources. This competition, due to different goals, values and interests, is gradually leading to conflicts.

Competition over the scarce water resources is aggravated by political hostilities, inconsistencies in the sentiments, purposes, claims, and opinions of social or political entities. This may led to armed conflicts especially between states of extremely different economic capabilities.

The conflict in the Middle East over water resources is still latent. But states initiate conflict usually after evaluating their domestic and international objectives and their abilities relative to nearby states. If benefits outweigh the costs, states may then choose to violently express their opposing interests. However, the resolution of the area conflicts will have greater chances of success if water resources of the areas of conflicts are considered, and co-operative arrangements between the rich and poor states are found.

0180

The situation of co-operation or conflict in the field of oil resources is not substantially different from that of water. But the two types of resources are entirely different in their supply continuity, which changes the entire perspective. The scarce resource, water, is renewable, while the abundant resource, oil, is non-renewable. The abundance of resources is a positive aspect. If properly used and managed it can bring changes in the region and induce co-operation

원 본

외 무 부

암호수신

종 별 :

번 호 : KUW-0694 일 시 : 91 1110 1500

수 신 : 장관(중동일,기정동문)

발 신 : 주 쿠웨이트 대사

제 목 : 쿠웨이트-영국 군사협력협정 가서명 예정

연:KUW-559

1.AL-SALEM 쿠웨이트 국방장관이 11 월말 영국을 방문하여 표제협정에 가서명할 예정인것으로 알려졌는데, 동협정은 쿠웨이트의 영국무기구입시 특혜부여, 영측의 쿠웨이트군 훈련담당과 필요한경우 쿠웨이트 주류 영국에 대한 쿠웨이트측의 병참지원을 골자로 하고있는것으로 알려지고있음.(신문보도)

2. 한편, 영국외무부 대변인은 협종최종문안이 11 월말 가서명을 위해 준비중이며, 동협정은 금번 걸프전쟁을 감안하여 이러한 사태의 재발을 방지코자 여러가지 측면을 고려하고 있다고 언급한것으로 전해짐

3. 또한 영국 하원군사위원회 의장은 동 협정이 영군의 쿠웨이트 주둔을 규정하고 있지않고 있으나, 현재 걸프해역에 있는 해군력에 추가하여 필요시 지원할 수 있는 충분한 병력을 유지하도록 하고있다고 언급하였음.

4. 쿠웨이트는 프랑스와도 유사한 군사협력협정 체결을 추진하고 있는데, 현재 양국 실무진이 이를위해 접촉하고있음.

5. 영국과의 군협문안입수등 상세사항은 추후 다시보고할것임.끝

(대사-국장)

중아국	장관	차관	1차보	2차보	외정실	분석관	청와대	안기부

0181

PAGE 1

91.11.10 21:46

외신 2과 통제관 FM

"소득은 정당하게, 소비는 알뜰하게"

주 카 이 로 총 영 사 관

문서번호 : 주카(정) 20405- 369 1991.11.10

경 유 :

수 신 : 장관

참 조 : 중동아국장, 외정실장, 외교안보연구원장

제 목 : Arab-Soviet 협력

자료응신 :

연 : CAW - 0981

1. 당지 APS의 보도에 의하면 Gorbachev가 이끄는 쏘 연방정부는 Gulf전 (Kuwait 해방전)과 10.30.Madrid 중동평화 개최관련, 그간 온건 아랍측 지지로 GCC제국으로부터 미화 40억$ 차관을 받은 데 이어, 최근 Saudi 정부로부터 12-15개월내로 현금과 신용 총 미화 15억$ 긴급원조 약속을 받았을 뿐 아니라 앞으로 이들 나라들의 대쏘투자도 뒤 따를 것으로 알려지고 있읍니다.

이와같은 Saudi의 대쏘 긴급 구원작전 이면에는 Bush 미 행정부의 보이지 않는 역할과 지난 9월 Primakov특사(현 KGB 국외정보책임자)의 중동순방과 주미 사우디대사 Prince Bandar의 방쏘로 이루어진 것이며,

또한 동긴급 원조금들은 쏘련 연방내의 Russia공화국 Yeltsin대통령의 대외원조 중단 발표(11.1)로 곤경에 빠진 중요 연방 정부기구의 잔존(외무부, 서시베리아 석유 및 가스개발 기구와 긴급 구호 및 식량공급등)에 활용된다는 점과 8.19. Gorbachev축출기도 실패 구테타 시 PLO측, 이락의 Saddam Hussein, 리비아의 Gaddafy를 비롯한 Arab권의 과격 원리주의자들이 동 구테타를 지지한 점을 감안하면 중동평화 추진에 있어 쏘련측보다 온건아랍측에 더 큰 의미가 있는 것으로 풀이되고 있음을 참고로 보고합니다.

2. 관계보도 사본 1부. 끝.

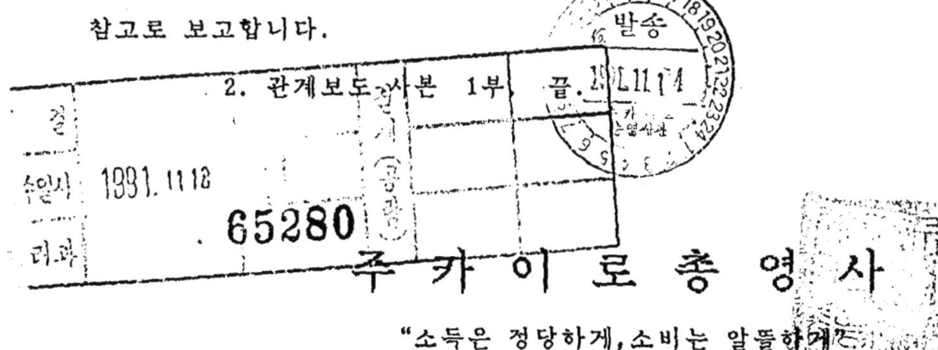

주 카 이 로 총 영 사

"소득은 정당하게, 소비는 알뜰하게"

0182

the aps diplomat news service

Editor
Pierre W. Shammas

Monday 11/18 November 1991 - 19th Year, Vol. 35, No. 20 SP 233

Arab-Soviet Co-operation Will Grow At Bush/Fahd Initiatives - Peace Comes First:

MOSCOW - The government of Saudi Arabia will provide the Kremlin with a total of $1.5 billion in cash and credits during the next 12-15 months. The money will go mostly to the central leadership of Soviet President Gorbachev, rather than to the Russian government of President Boris Yeltsin, according to an authoritative source here.

Gradually, Saudi/GCC Aid Offers Will Be Extended To Include Key Soviet Republics, With Saudi Aramco And SABIC Likely To Set Up JVs In Russia, The Muslim States, The Ukraine, Etc.

The biggest portion of this "emergency aid" amounts to $1 bn. It was pledged to Gorbachev during a recent visit to Moscow by the Saudi Ambassador to Washington, Prince Bandar Ibn Sultan Ibn Abdel Aziz, who was also in Madrid for the peace conference and met with President Bush. But the importance of the news now is that it gives the central leadership in the Kremlin the following assurances:

1. After the meeting in Madrid between Presidents Bush and Gorbachev, the reaffirmation of the Saudi pledge amounts to a "pan-Arab commitment to helping the Kremlin in reasserting its authority" outside the Soviet Union. This is important in view of the Kremlin's role as a co-sponsor of current Arab-Israeli peace negotiations, more important to the moderate camp in the Arab World than to the Soviet side (of course with the exception of Gorbachev's central administration).

2. After President Yeltsin's announcement of a crash programme to free state-controlled prices and push market reforms at a stroke this year, a move which coincided with the meeting in Madrid on Oct. 29 (see Recorder), the renewal of the Saudi aid offer comes as a "guarantee" that important central ministries in Moscow will survive. The emphasis is on the survival of the Soviet Foreign Ministry and its diplomatic network worldwide.

Thus The White House Has A Good Treasurer Able To Operate Anywhere In The World, And In The Final Analysis There Will Be Peace Between Israel, Its Neighbours, President Bush, & So Forth - But Not Before Some Tensions

As Yeltsin announced, from Nov. 1 the Russian government stopped all aid and credits to foreign countries. It began a programme of austerity ceasing to finance most central ministries and institutions. So the Saudi aid can be considered a "rescue operation on behalf of all Arab states and Palestinians involved in the peace process".

0183

The cash will be disbursed to save some central organisations, including "a temporary financing" of those authorities who are involved in West Siberia's producing oil and gas fields. (See OOD in the Diplomat Package and Oil Market Trends of this week's APS Review). A part of this cash will also help finance emergency relief operations and food supplies to be provided by institutions still under Kremlin control.

Published by the Arab Press Service Organisation, Lebanon. APS is an independent centre for Middle East information and research, founded in Beirut in 1972. Ask for APS brochure outlining its publications, consultancy and other services and for APS "Who's Who".

Annual Subscription to Diplomat Package: US$ 800. Annual Subscription to Full Diplomat & Review Package: US$ 1,200. All APS publications are posted from Cyprus. Apply to: APS, P.O.Box 3896, Nicosia, C rus. Fax No. 357-2 -350265.

The credits will be disbursed through the second half of 1992 and will include the supply of chemicals as well as wheat by Saudi Arabia. These supplies will be made directly to Kremlin-controlled institutions. Beyond this pledge, according to the source, Saudi Arabia and fellow GCC states could eventually invest in Russia. They may invest in Kazakhstan, where Saudi Arabia has joined a banking venture, the other Muslim republics and the Ukraine.

The Background & Role Of Primakov: The source points out that the importance of Saudi Arabia's initiative was underlined to all Arab states involved in Madrid. The Arab rulers concerned were visited last September by President Gorbachev's special assistant Yevgeni Primakov. (Now Primakov is the head of the Soviet intelligence, in charge of restructuring what was once known as "the formidable KGB"). Although his Middle East tour was to check on the latest positions of governments concerning the Arab-Israeli peace process, when pressed to tell them what the real priority of his boss was, Primakov smiled, at least to one Arab leader, hinting: "Money, trade and as much money as we can get".

Moscow had previously received a loan of $4 billion from Saudi Arabia, Kuwait and other rich GCC members. That was during the Gulf crisis, as the US was preparing for war to push Iraqi forces out of Kuwait. Since then money has become "king", even among the honest power brokers in Moscow, a message received by the nephew of King Fahd, Prince Bandar. Prince Bandar had flown to the Kremlin earlier in September. President Gorbachev had embraced him like an Arab does to another Arab, and the outcome of that meeting was a request for a fresh GCC loan urgently needed to save his union.

The Soviet role in the Middle East peace process is nothing but positive, therefore, and this is from Washington's standpoint. Gone are the days when the Soviets called the shots in a part of the Middle East that balanced the part which the US used to regard as its sphere of influence. All those generous Soviet ideological and geopolitical actions of good will, together with all the money that went along with them, have been replaced by something different, something which should not upset US President Bush or the Saudi leadership. Most Soviet Ambassadors accredited to Arab capitals have begun to change their attitude accordingly. So in a nutshell the Arabs and Israel are no longer worth the risk of upsetting, or even balancing the actions of, the Bush administration and its allies in the West or in the East - the Cold War having come to an end.

The Soviet Union has established full diplomatic and trading relations with Israel (SP 216), and the PLO has little or no ground to complain about this state of affairs. Indeed there are good reasons for those in the Kremlin and in Yeltsin's own White House not to shed tears for the PLO or for Yasser Arafat. After all the PLO was among those who backed the coup attempt against Gorbachev, although its enthusiasm was way lower than that of Saddam Hussein in Iraq or Col. Qadhafi in Libya.

In Syria President Assad, who still believes he is the most clever among Arab rulers, cares little for what the current leaders in Moscow intend to do. He worries much less about Gorbachev's nods to President Bush and far less about the outcome of Primakov's new mission at KGB headquarters. This was underlined by the fact that, when a visit by Primakov to Damascus was first suggested, Syrian Foreign Ministry officials said President Assad had no time to meet him. They, too, said they had a tight schedule of their own. Of course this was not the way Baker was received in Damascus in recent months, with President Assad always waiting to meet him immediately upon his arrival.

0184

That Moscow is now under the umbrella of 'Pax Americana' might be too much to say, however, because historically the Russians have seldom been comfortable under any foreign umbrella. But now the priority for the Russians is food and many other urgent needs that should be met before winter gets more severe. True, the Soviet central leadership will do its best in keeping its image as a co-sponsor of the Middle East peace conference, but it is more true to say that what makes Kremlin leaders tick nowadays are short-term necessities rather than long-term expediency. It is from this angle that Saudi Arabia is one of the winners and the PLO is one of the casualties of change in the Soviet Union.

관리번호	91/1839

원 본

외 무 부

종 별 :

번 호 : QTW-0253 일 시 : 91 1111 1230

수 신 : 장관(중동일,정보,사본:주사우디대사,주이란대사-중계필)

발 신 : 주 카타르대사

제 목 : 카타르 왕세자 이란방문(자응16)

연:QTW-0249

1.SH.HAMAD BIN KHALIFA AL-THANI 카타르 왕세자겸 국방장관은 11.7-10 간 이란방문종료후,11.10 오후 파키스탄으로 향발함.

2. 양국은 11.10 아래요지의 공동성명을 발표함(당지 GULF TIMES 11.11 자 보도)

-걸프지역의 안보와 안정 강조

-동 지역국가의 주권과 영토 보존존중및내정불간섭 원칙천명

-역내 핵및 대량살상무기 사용금지

-이스라엘에 대한 무기공급의 위험성을 재확인하고 아랍국가에 대한 이스라엘의 침략행위 중지촉구

-팔레스타인 봉기찬양

-OPEC 국가들의 석유생산 쿼타 이행 협력

-동서 냉전종식에 만족하고 동서화해로 인한 지역문제의 평화적 해결과 세계의 안정희망

-GCC 국가와 이란 협력강화

3. 다음 분야의 양자 관계 협정을체결함

-카타르에 대한 이란의 수자원 공급

-교육협력

-사회노동협력

-항공운수협력

-경제, 통상및기술협력

4. 평가 . 걸프전쟁후 이라의 몰락과 관련 페르샤만의 군사강대국인 이란의 영향력 증대를 의식하여, 카타르는 대이란 관계 개선및 유대강화에 주력하여왔음

중아국 차관 1차보 외정실 분석관 청와대 안기부 중계

0185

PAGE 1 91.11.16 13:50

외신 2과 통제관 BW

-90.12 도하에서 개최된 GCC 정상회담에서 GCC 각국 이란간의 협력강화를 도하선언에 반영

. 이란-사우디간 관계정상화를 위한 중재역할 수행

. 양국간 각료급 교류의 빈번화

.GCC 각국과의 유대강화및 영향력 증대를 추구하는 이란으로서는 금번 카타르 와의 수뇌겹 교류로 그 돌파구를 마련하였다고 평가할수 있으며, 카타르로서는 사우디 의존 일변도의 종래 외교노선에서 탈피하여 균형외교를 지향하는 시도로 관측됨. 끝

(대사 유내형-국장)

예고:92.6.30 일반

PAGE 2

0186

원 본

외 무 부

종 별 :

번 호 : KUW-0708 일 시 : 91 1116 1800

수 신 : 장 관(중동일)

발 신 : 주 쿠웨이트 대사

제 목 : 이란 외무차관 쿠웨이트 방문

1.BISHHAITI 이란 외무차관이 라프산자니 대통령의 특사로 친서를 휴대하고 11.10-12간 쿠웨이트를 방문하였음.동 차관은 방문기간 중국왕,수상겸 왕세자등 쿠웨이트지도층 과 면담을 가졌음.

2.동 외무차관은 쿠웨이트 지도층과의 면담시 지역경제,기술협력 공동체구성을제의하였고,기자회견에서

1)이라크의 쿠웨이트 점령은 이란 국민에게도 쓰라린 경험이었으며

2)이라크는 안보리 결의를 준수해야 할것이고

3)이란은 모든 아랍내부 문제에 관여치 않을것이라고 언급하였음.

3.한편,쿠웨이트 정부는 그동안 엄격하게 통제하여 오던 이란인들에 대한 사증발급을 완화,이란인 기술자들에게 사증을 발급할 용의가 있다고 발표하였는데,이란측은 이를 양국관계 개선의 좋은 징조라고 환영하였음.

4.쿠웨이트는 지난 9월 JARRAH 상공장관을 이란에 보내어 이란과의 경제협력 협정 체결을 추진하였고,라프산자니 대통령의 쿠웨이트 방문 초청등 걸프전이후 이란과의 관계개선을 추진한 결과 양국관계가 현저히 개선되었음.끝

(대사-국장)

중아국 장관 차관 1차보 2차보 외정실 분석관 청와대 안기부

0187

PAGE 1

91.11.17 03:27 FN

외신 1과 통제관

원 본

외 무 부

종 별 :

번 호 : KUW-0709　　　일 시 : 91 1116 1800

수 신 : 장 관(중동일,기정)

발 신 : 주 쿠웨이트 대사

제 목 : 쿠웨이트-미국 합동기동훈련

1.쿠웨이트.미국간 군사협력 협정이 체결된 이후 이에따른 양국간 합동기동훈련이 11.12-14간 쿠웨이트시 서북방 100KM 지점에서 실시되었음.

2.이번 훈련에는 미해병대 2,300명과 상륙용주정및 헬기등이 동원되어 이락군이패주할때 버리고간 전차,장갑차등 장비를 목표물로하여 쿠웨이트군의 이락 보유장비에 대한 익숙도를 높이고 배양하기 위한 것이었다고 쿠웨이트군 참모차장이 언급하였음.

3.10.24-25기간중에도 양측간의 소규모 합동기동훈련이 있었는데,쿠웨이트측은 양국간의 협력과 조정을 증진시킬 필요가 있고 또 동훈련이 '양측에 이득이 된다'고 언급한 것으로 보아 앞으로 이러한 훈련은 자주 실시될 것으로 보임.끝

(대사-국장)

중아국　1차보　외정실　청와대　안기부

0188

PAGE 1　　　91.11.17　03:25 FN

외신 1과 통제관

관리번호	91/1842

원 본

외 무 부

종 별 :

번 호 : QTW-0260 일 시 : 91 1118 1300

수 신 : 장관(중동일,정보)

발 신 : 주 카타르 대사

제 목 : 카타르 국왕 오만 방문(자응19)

연:QTW-0256

1. SH. KHALIFA BIN HAMAD AL-THANI 카타르 국왕은 11.16-18 간 오만방문을 마치고 18 일 귀국하였음.

2. KHALIFA 국왕은 오만 방문 마지막날인 11.17 지역안보와 안정, 중동평화 정착등을 비롯한 제반 문제에서 양국간 의견일치를 보았다고 성명을 발표함.

3. 수행원으로는

-SH. AHMED BIN SAIF AL-THANI 법무장관

-SH. HAMAD BIN JASSIM BIN JABOR AL-THANI 도시행정및농업성 장관겸 수전력성 장관대리

-DR.ISSA GHANEM AL-KUWARI 궁내성장관

-MUBARAK ALI AL-KHATER 외무장관

- SH.MOHAMED BIN KHALIFA AL-THANI 재무 석유성 차관임.

4. 평가

-금반 양국 정상의 돌연한 회동에 관하여 공식발표나 상세 보도는 없으나 금년 12월 쿠웨이트에서 개최예정인 GCC 정상회담에 대비한 공동 전략협의로 주목 되는바

-작년 도하 정상회담시 카타르와 오만의 강력한 주장으로 대이란 관계개선을 도하선언에 반영하였으며, 최근에는 카타르 왕세자가 이란을 공식방문하여 양국간 유대를 강화한바, 이로 미루어 보아 카타르와 오만은 GCC 각국과 이란과의 관계긴밀화를 위하여 계속 제휴할것으로 전망됨.

-최근 카타르의 외교동향은 종래 사우디 추종 일변도에서 탈피하여 자주적 적극외교로선을 지향하는 징후를 보이고 있는바 , 이에 대한 사우디및 에집트등 주변 아랍 국가들의 반응이 주목되고 있음. 끝

중아국	장관	차관	1차보	외정실	분석관	청와대	안기부

0189

PAGE 1 91.11.18 20:06

외신 2과 통제관 CD

(대사 유내형-국장)
예고:91.12.31 일반

PAGE 2

0190

정 리 보 존 문 서 목 록					
기록물종류	일반공문서철	등록번호	2020120218	등록일자	2020-12-28
분류번호	772	국가코드	XF	보존기간	영구
명 칭	걸프사태, 1990-91. 전12권				
생 산 과	북미1과/중동1과	생산년도	1990~1991	담당그룹	
권 차 명	V.11 보고 및 자료				
내용목차	* 언론보도 포함				

0001

02

쿠웨이트 사태 관련 각국의 조치

90. 8. 10.

미주국 북미과

1. 미 국

가. 사우디 파병 내역

o 미 지상군 등 12,000명 사우디 도착

- 3개 공정여단(각 2,100명)
- 포병, 헬리콥터 부대
- F-15 전투기 48대
- F-16(지상공격용) 수 미상

o 약 5만명 선까지 증강 계획

* 쿠웨이트내 이라크 병력은 20만명으로 추산

나. 기타 군사조치

o 항모 3척(탑재기 245대) 등 함정 49척 파견

- 항모 Eisenhower : 수에즈 운하 통과, 페르샤만으로 항진중
- 항모 Saratoga : 다음 주말까지 작전지역 도착 예정
- 항모 Independence : 호르무즈 외해에 정박

o 터키 배치 F-111 전폭기 14대, 터키 기지에서 훈련중

- 이라크 국경까지 비행시간 30분 지역

o AWACS 5대 추가 파견

o B-52 폭격기, 인도양의 디에고 가르시아 기지에서 출동 대기중

o 사우디에 F-15 전투기 40대 인도

- 긴급 무기 공여법에 의거한 대통령 행정 명령(8.8)

0002

ㅇ 이라크가 화학무기를 사용할 경우 핵무기 사용등 대량 보복책 고려 (8.9. ABC-TV 보도)

* 주희랍 이라크 대사는 미국이 이라크를 공격할 경우 독가스 사용 경고

다. 외교적 조치

ㅇ Baker 국무장관

- 터키 방문, 이라크의 터키 침공시 NATO의 지원 약속(8.9)
- NATO 국가들이 필요시 미국의 페르샤만 군사 행동을 지원해 줄 것을 요청(8.10. NATO 외상회의에 앞선 사전 접촉)

ㅇ John Kelly 국무부 근동차관보, 8.9. 시리아 방문

ㅇ 8.9. UN 안보리 결의 채택

- 이라크의 쿠웨이트 합병, 또는 쿠웨이트의 지위를 변경하려는 여하한 시도도 무효임을 선언
- 이라크군의 즉각 철군 촉구
- 각국이 이라크의 쿠웨이트 합병 인정, 또는 간접적 승인으로 해석될 수 있는 행동을 자제해 줄 것을 요청

* Bush 대통령은 예정대로 8.10-9.3간 New England에서 휴가

2. 여타 국가

가. 아랍 정상회담 연기

ㅇ 8.9. 개최 예정이었으나, 8.10.로 일단 연기

ㅇ 이라크에서는 제1부총리, 군사 평의회 위원들만 참석

- 효과적 행동에 합의 난망

나. 영국, 전투기 파견(8.9. Tom King 국방장관 발표)

ㅇ 사이프러스 배치 Tornado F-3 전투기 중대, 주말에 사우디로 이동

0003

o 영국 배치 Jaguar 전투기 중대, 걸프지역으로 이동

o 전투기 호위 SAM 미사일, 해양 경비 항공기 파견

o 소해정 3척 동지중해 파견

o 총지원 병력 1,000명

다. 쏘련, 외무부 성명(8.9)

o 이라크의 쿠웨이트 합병 비난

o UN에 의해 군사 행동이 조직될 경우, 동참 고려

- UN 기치하의 집단 대응 촉구

- 미국 등의 파병이 긴장을 고조시키고 있음을 암시

* 쏘 전함 2척 수에즈 운하 통과, 홍해 진입(이집트 소식통)

라. 호주, 해.공군 파견 결정(언론 보도)

마. 요르단, UN안보리 결의에 따른 대이라크 제재 실행 계획(유럽 외교 소식통)

o 홍해의 아카바항으로 통하는 육상 통로 폐쇄

바. 터키, 육.공군 비상대기령

o 병력, 전투기, 미사일 발사대 등 이라크 접경으로 이동

사. 프랑스, Mitterand 대통령 기자 회견(8.9)

o 다국적군에는 불참할 것이며, 아랍권 내부에서의 해결을 희망함.

o 그러나 해결에 실패할 경우, 사우디 등 국가에 물자.기술 지원 제공 예정

아. 중국, 외교부 성명(8.9)

o 아랍국가 스스로에 의한 해결에 찬성

o 외세의 개입은 위기 상황을 심화시킴을 경고

0004

자. 대만, 외무성 발표(8.9)

- 이라크의 쿠웨이트 합병 비난
- 대이라크 제재에 동참하는 방안 신중 검토중

차. 이란, 이라크의 쿠웨이트 합병 비난

0005

쿠웨이트 사태 관련 각국의 군사조치 현황

90. 8. 11.

미주국 북미과

1. 미 국

가. 해군 배치 상황(약50척 배치)

o 페르샤만 : 전함 9척

- Lasalle 전함, 순양함 2척, 구축함, 프리킷 5척

o 지중해 : 전함 5척 및 보조선 2척

o 홍 해 : 항모 Eisenhower호 걸프로 항진중

- 구축함 2척 등 전함 5척이 호위

o 인도양 : 항모 Independence 호 호르무즈 해협 진입설

- 호위 전함 6척

o 대서양 : 항모 Saratoga호 지중해로 항진중

- 다음 주말경 도착 예정

- Wisconsin호 등 전함 9척이 호위

(Tomahawk 크루즈 미사일 32개, 상륙정 5척 등 장비)

o 기 타 : 보급선 수척과 병원선 2척 걸프로 항진중

나. 사우디 파병 내역

o 총 파병 병력수 미상(현재 12,000명 이상 도착)

o 조만간 총파병 병력수가 5만명에 달할 것이며, 20-25만명까지 증파할 수 있는 비상 계획도 있음.(미 국방부 소식통)

0006

o 파병 내역

- 101 공정사단(켄터키) 중 일부
  · 공격용, 대전차 헬리콥터 등 장비
- 24 기계화 보병사단(죠지아) 중 일부
  · 탱크, 전차, 155mm포, 연발 로켓트포 등 장비
- 82 공정사단(노스 캐롤라이나) 중 일부
  · TOW 대전차 미사일 등 장비
- F-15 전투기(버지니아) 48대 이상
- F-16 공격용 전투기 및 A-10 공격용 전투기(사우드 캐롤라이나)
- 기타 C-130 수송기 등

o 병력 수송을 위해 Eastern Airlines 등 민간 항공사 접촉 중

2. NATO 국가

가. 영 국

o Tornado F-3 전투기 12대 사우디 파견

o Jaguar 공격용 전투기 12대 오만(?) 파견

o 전투기 호위 SAM 미사일, 해양 경비 항공기 파견

o 구축함 1척, 프리깃 2척, 지원선박 걸프로 파견
- NIMROD(조기경보기), 유조선 등이 지원

o 소해정 3척 동지중해로 항진중

o 지원 병력 1,000명(지상군 없음)

나. 프랑스

o 항모 Clemenceau 파견 예정
- 순양함 등 6척이 호위

o 지원 병력 3,200명

o 다국적군에는 불참하나, 필요시 걸프국가에 물자.기술 지원 예정

0007

다. 터 키

ㅇ F-16, 병력, Rapier 대공 미사일 등 전진 배치

- 다국적군은 아님

타. 기타 NATO 국가

ㅇ 이태리 : 미 공군의 영공 통과 허용. 수일내 다국적군 참가 여부 결정

ㅇ 카나다 : 함정 3척 파견

ㅇ 서 독 : 소해정 4-5척 동지중해 파견 예정

ㅇ 덴마크 : 여타국의 걸프 파병으로 인한 NATO 지역 방위 부담 인수.
상업선박이 다국적군의 보급선으로 사용되는 것 허가

ㅇ 그리스, 스페인, 포르투갈 : 미군에 기지 제공

ㅇ 화란, 벨지움 : 수일내 다국적군 참가 여부 결정

3. 기타 국가

가. 쏘련

ㅇ 전함 1척, 대잠함 1척 걸프 파견

- 다국적군에는 불참

ㅇ UN에 의한 군사 행동이 결정될 경우 참여 고려(8.9. 외무부 성명)

나. 호주

ㅇ 프리깃 2척, 유조선 1척 파견

다. 이스라엘

ㅇ 이라크군이 요르단 진입하면 이라크 공격(8.7 국방장관 발표)

4. 해상 봉쇄 문제

ㅇ Fitzwater 백악관 대변인 기자 회견(8.10)

- 해상 봉쇄를 거론하기에는 이르지만, 필요시에 대비한 계획은 수립 되고 있음.

0008

o Baker 국무장관 기자회견(8.10. 브럿셀)

- 미국 및 여타국가는 쿠웨이트 왕정의 요청만 있으면, 유엔안보리의 경제 제재 결의 시행을 위해 봉쇄를 실시할 법적 권한이 있음.
- 일부 주요국가가 미국의 이러한 견해에 동의하고 있음.

5. 아랍 연합군 구성 문제

o 8.10. 카이로에서 아랍 정상회담 개최

- Mubarak 이집트 대통령, 아랍 연합군의 사우디 파병 촉구

o 대다수 정상들, 파병에 동의

- 찬성한 국가들은 미확인

6. 화학무기 사용문제

o 이라크는 미국이 이라크를 공격할 경우 독가스 사용 경고(주그리스 이라크 대사)

o 미측은 화학전에 대비하고 있다고 발표하고 있으나, 전문가는 이에 대해 회의적(폭염)

o 이락이 화학무기를 사용할 경우 미국은 핵무기 사용 등 대량 보복책 고려(8.9 ABC-TV 보도)

0009

쿠웨이트 사태 관련 각국의 군사조치

90. 8. 13.

미주국 북미과

〈진전 사항〉

o 미국 등 다국적군 사우디 파병 계속 증가중

o 아랍연합군 사우디 도착

o 미, 해상 봉쇄 의도 명확히 함

1. 미 국

o 사우디 파병 계속(파견 병력수 비상)

o 항모 Kennedy호 내주 투입설(언론보도)

- 신규 증강 또는 Eisenhower호 대체 목적

o 이라크의 사태 해결안 거부(8.12.)

- Hussein 이라크 대통령은 사우디내 미군 등 다국적군이 UN하의 아랍군으로 대체되고, 이스라엘이 점령지로부터 철수하고, 금수조치를 해제할 경우 이라크도 쿠웨이트로 부터 철수 하겠다고 제의(8.12. TV 회견)

- Fitzwater 백악관 대변인은 이라크군의 즉각.완전.무조건 철수 및 쿠웨이트 왕정 복귀를 요구하면서, 이라크의 제안을 묵살

o 해상 봉쇄 문제

- Jaber 쿠웨이트 국왕, 경제제재의 실효성을 확보하기 위한 조치를 미국측에 요청(8.12.)

0010

- Baker 국무장관, 조만간 이라크 출입 선박을 모두 차단할 것임을 발표 (8.12.)
  - 여타 국가 함대와의 협조 시사
  - '봉쇄(blockade)'란 용어는 사용하지 않음.('봉쇄'가 전쟁행위로 해석될 것을 우려)

2. 여타 국가

o 이집트 : 병력 3,000명 사우디 도착
  - 아랍연합군(총10,000명 예상)의 일원

o 벨기에, 스페인 : 함대 파견 예정

o 서 독 : 미국함대의 걸프 파견으로 인한 공백을 메우기 위해 지중해로 함대 파견 고려

o 이스라엘 : 공군에 경계령. 대공미사일 등 요르단 접경지로 이동

o 이 란 : 이라크의 즉각.무조건 철수 요구(8.11. 국가안보회의 성명)

* 북한, 쿠웨이트 사태 관련 입장 발표(8.12.노동신문)
  - 이라크의 쿠웨이트 침공과 미.영 등 외세개입을 동시에 비난
  - 아랍권 내에서의 사태해결 지지

* Bush 대통령 지지도 상승(Newsweek 지 여론조사)
  o Bush 대통령의 금번 사태 대응 지지 : 75%
  o 이라크가 공격할 경우 보복 주장 : 94%

* 쿠웨이트 사태와 미.쏘관계
  o 미국은 금번 사태에 대한 쏘련의 반응에 만족
  o 대쏘 경제원조를 반대하였던 휴스턴 G-7 정상회담에서의 입장을 변경할 가능성 있음.

0011

기협

쿠웨이트 사태 관련 각국의 군사조치 현황

90. 8. 14.

미주국 북미과

1. 미 국

가. 해군 배치 상황(약50척 배치, 탑재기 약245대)

o 페르샤만 : 전함 9척

- Lasalle 전함, 순양함 2척, 구축함, 프리킷 5척

o 지중해 : 전함 5척 및 보조선 2척

o 홍 해 : 항모 Eisenhower호 걸프로 항진중

- 구축함 2척 등 전함 5척이 호위

o 인도양 : 항모 Independence 호 호르무즈 입구에 배치

- 호위 전함 6척

o 대서양 : 항모 Saratoga호 지중해로 항진중

- 주말경 도착 예정

- Wisconsin호 등 전함 9척이 호위

(Tomahawk 크루즈 미사일 32개, 상륙정 5척 등 장비)

o 기 타

- 항모 Kennedy호 분쟁지역으로 출발(8.13.)

- 보급선 수척과 병원선 2척 걸프로 항진중

나. 사우디 파병 내역

o 총 파병 병력수 미상

o 조만간 총파병 병력수가 10만명에 달할 것이며, 20-25만명까지 증파할 수 있는 비상 계획도 있음.(미 국방부 소식통)

0012

° 파병 내역

- 101 공정사단(켄터키) 중 일부
  · 공격용, 대전차 헬리콥터 등 장비
- 24 기계화 보병사단(죠지아) 중 일부
  · 탱크, 전차, 155mm포, 연발 로켓트포 등 장비
- 82 공정사단(노스 캐롤라이나) 중 일부
  · TOW 대전차 미사일 등 장비
- 11 방공사단(텍사스) 중 일부
- 최신예 F-15E 전투기(노스 캐롤라이나) 파견(8.13.)
- F-15 전투기(버지니아) 48대 이상
- F-16 공격용 전투기 및 A-10 공격용 전투기(사우드 캐롤라이나)
- AWACS 5대 추가 파견(기존 5대와 합류)
- 기타 C-130 수송기, 급유기 등

° 병력 수송을 위해 Eastern Airlines 등 민간 항공사 접촉

다. 기 타

° F-11 전폭기 14대 터키 인시르리크에 배치
- 이라크 국경에서 680Km

° B-52 폭격기, 인도양 디에고 가르시아에 배치

° 사우디에 F-15 전투기 40대 인도
- 긴급 무기 공여법에 의거한 대통령 행정 명령(8.8.)

* Bush 대통령은 휴가 중단, 8.14. 백악관으로 돌아올 예정

0013

2. NATO 국가

가. 영 국

- Tornado F-3 전투기 12대 사우디 파견
- Jaguar 충격용 전투기 12대 오만(?) 파견
- 전투기 호위 SAM 미사일 파견
- 구축함 1척, 프리깃 2척, 지원선박 걸프로 파견
  - NIMROD(조기경보기), 급유기 등이 지원 출동
- 소해정 3척 동지중해로 항진중
- 지원 병력 1,000명(지상군 없음)

나. 프랑스

- 항모 Clemenceau 파견 예정(순양함 등 6척이 호위)
- 지원 병력 3,200명
- 다국적군에는 불참하나, 필요시 걸프국가에 물자.기술 지원 예정

다. 터 키

- F-16, 병력, Rapier 대공 미사일 등 전진 배치(다국적군은 아님)

라. 기타 NATO 국가

- 이태리 : 미 공군의 영공 통과 허용. 수일내 다국적군 참가 여부 결정
- 카나다 : 함정 3척 파견
- 서 독 : 소해정 4-5척 동지중해 파견 예정
- 덴마크 : 여타국의 걸프 파병으로 인한 NATO 지역 방위 부담 인수;
  상업선박이 다국적군의 보급선으로 사용되는 것 허가
- 그리스, 스페인, 포르투갈 : 미군에 기지 제공
- 벨지움 : 함대 파견 결정
- 화 란 : 프리깃 2척 파견 예정(8.20.)

0014

3. 기타 국가

가. 아랍 연합군

- ㅇ 총병력 10,000명 예상
  - 이집트군 3,000명 사우디 도착
  - 시리아군 8.13. 출동

나. 쏘련

- ㅇ 전함 1척, 대잠함 1척 걸프 파견
  - 다국적군에는 불참
- ㅇ UN에 의한 군사 행동이 결정될 경우 참여 고려(8.9. 외무부 성명)

다. 이스라엘

- ㅇ 공군에 경계령. 대공미사일 등 요르단 접경지로 이동
- ㅇ 이라크군이 요르단 진입하면 이라크 공격(8.7 국방장관 발표)

라. 기 타

- ㅇ 호 주 : 프리깃 2척, 유조선 1척 파견
- ㅇ 파키스탄 : 사우디 파병 결정
- ㅇ 이 란 : 이라크의 즉각.무조건 철수 요구(8.11. 국가 안보회의 성명)

* 쿠웨이트내 이라크군

- 현재 약14만 추정(6개 대통령 경호사 정예부대 포함)

0015

4. 해상 봉쇄 문제

○ 미　　국 : 8.13. 이라크에 대한 사실상의 전면적 봉쇄에 돌입

- 이라크의 봉쇄를 위해 필요한 모든 조치를 취할 계획(필요시 무력 사용 시사)

○ 영국, 호주 : 미국의 조치에 동참 의사 표명

○ 사 우 디 : 이라크산 원유를 선적하러 온 유조선의 입항을 금지

○ 프 랑 스

- 교전 상태에의 돌입을 뜻하는 해상 봉쇄에 참여하지 않을 것임을 선언
- 해상 봉쇄에는 유엔의 새로운 결의 필요함을 주장

5. 전 망

○ 쿠웨이트내 이라크군의 증강과 미국이 주도한 다국적군과 이집트 등 아랍 연합군의 사우디 파병, 각국 함대의 분쟁지역 파견으로 군사대치는 극에 달해가고 있음.

○ 더우기 8.13.부터 미국이 사실상 해상봉쇄에 들어가고 영국 등 일부 국가가 이에 동참, 무력충돌의 위기는 더욱 심화.

○ 그러나 이라크로서는 다국적군과 아랍연합군에 대해 선제 적대행위를 할 수 없는 입장이며, 미국으로서도 이라크가 사우디의 유전을 공격할 경우 서방 경제에 미칠 영향이 지심하므로 쉽사리 무력 사용을 할 수는 없는 입장.

- 8.13. 이라크 외무장관은 사우디 침공 의사가 없음을 재천명

○ 따라서 이라크군과 다국적군(및 아랍연합군)의 대치 상황은 당분간 계속될 것으로 보이며, 이라크 내부에서의 반 후세인 세력형성 가능성과 이라크에 긴요한 물자를 수송하는 선박의 나포를 둘러싼 우발적 무력충돌이 전쟁으로 확대될 가능성 등이 큰 변수로 남을 것임.

0016

* 화학무기 사용문제

- 이라크는 미국이 이라크를 공격할 경우 독가스 사용 경고(주그리스 이라크 대사)
- 미측은 화학전에 대비하고 있다고 발표하고 있으나, 전문가는 이에 대해 회의적(폭염)
- 이락이 화학무기를 사용할 경우 미국은 핵무기 사용 등 대량 보복책 고려(8.9 ABC-TV 보도)

* 북한, 쿠웨이트 사태 관련 입장 발표(8.12.노동신문)

- 이라크의 쿠웨이트 침공과 미.영 등 외세개입을 동시에 비난
- 아랍권 내에서의 사태해결 지지

* Bush 대통령 지지도 상승(Newsweek 지 여론조사)

o Bush 대통령의 금번 사태 대응 지지 : 75%

o 이라크가 공격할 경우 보복 주장 : 94%

* 쿠웨이트 사태와 미.쏘관계

o 미국은 금번 사태에 대한 쏘련의 반응에 만족

o 대쏘 경제원조를 반대하였던 휴스턴 G-7 정상회담에서의 입장을 변경할 가능성 있음.

o Bush 대통령, 미국 주재 쏘련 기업인 수 제한 철폐(8.13.)

- 쏘련의 상응한 조치 희망
- 1990년도의 미국 주재 쏘련 기업인수는 69명 이하로 제한되어 있었음

0017

(첨 부)

이라크-쿠웨이트 사태 관련 각국의 주요 군사조치 현황

90.8.28 현재

I. 사우디 파병국 및 걸프지역 해군 파견국 현황

1. 사우디 파병국 : 12개국

가. 기파병국(9개국)

미, 영, 이집트, 모로코, 오만, UAE, 카타르, 바레인, 쿠웨이트

나. 파병 예상국(3개국)

방글라데쉬, 파키스탄, 시리아

2. 걸프지역 해군 파견국 : 18개국

가. 기파견국(13개국)

미, 영, 불, 소, 사우디, 오만, UAE, 카타르, 바레인, 쿠웨이트, 호주, 화란, 서독

나. 파견 예상국(5개국)

카나다, 그리스, 벨기에, 이태리, 스페인

3. 참고 사항

o 사우디 파병 아랍 7개국은 이라크의 쿠웨이트 침공이후 파병

o 걸프지역 해군 파견 아랍권 국가의 경우 침공 이전부터 해군력 배치

o 걸프지역 해군 파견국들이 이라크 출입선박 해상 단속 조치에 전부 참여하는 것은 아님

- 호주의 경우, 호주 함정의 presence만 과시하고 실제 작전을 불참

0018

Ⅱ. 각국의 군사조치 현황

1. 미 국

* 페르시아만 파견 미군 총병력 : 11만

가. 해군 배치 상황

o 페르샤만 :

- Lasalle 전함.순양함 2척, 구축함, 프리킷 5척, 병원선 2척

o 지 중 해 :

- 항모 Saratoga호 배치

. Wisconsin호등 전함 5척이 호위, Tomahawk 크루즈 미사일 32개, 상륙정 5척등 장비

- 항모 Kennedy 항진중

. 전함 5척 및 보조선 2척

o 홍 해 :

- 항모 Eisenhower호 및 함대 배치

. 구축함 2척등 전함 5척이 호위

o 아라비아해 :

- 항모 independence호 호르무즈 입구에 배치

. 전함 6척 호위

o 제7함대 소속 수륙양용함 5척(상륙특공대 4,440명 탑승) 사우디 해역에 파견

* 4개 항모 선단의 해군병력 : 3만5천

나. 대사우디 파병 내역

o 총 파병 병력수 : 약7만5천명

- 지상군 3만명

- 해병대 4만5천명

※ 3만5천 병력 추가 배치중

0019

o 파병 내역

- 제1해병 사단(캘리포니아)
- 제7해병 여단
- 제3해병 비행단
- 101 공정사단(켄터키) 중 일부
  . 공격용, 대전차 헬리콥터 등 장비
- 24기계화 보병사단(죠지아) 중 일부
  . 탱크, 전차, 155mm포, 연발 로켓트포 등 장비
- 82 공정사단(노스 캐롤라이나) 중 일부
  . TOW 대전차 미사일 등 장비
- 11 방공여단(텍사스) 중 일부
- 최신예 F-15F전투기(노스 캐롤라이나)
- F-15 전투기(버지니아) 48대 이상
- F-16 공격용 전투기 및 A-10 전차 공격기(사우드 캐롤라이나) 72대
- Stealth 전폭기 22대 파견
- AWACS 5대 추가 파견(기존 5대와 합류)
- 기타 C-130 수송기, 급유기 등
- MI탱크 100대
- 영국 주둔 111F 폭격기 사우디 이동

o 유럽주둔 미군 중동으로 이동 개시

- 서독주둔 제7의료사령부 소속 군인 페만 향진

o 병력 수송을 위해 Eastern Airlines 등 민간 항공사에 동원령

o 40,000 예비군 동원령 발동(8.22)

o 오끼나와 주둔 미해병 선발대 사우디에 도착

- 6천명 사우디 이동 준비중

다. U.A.E 파병 내역

o C130기 5대로 바틴 공군기지에 수송개시(8.20)

0020

라. 기 타

o F-111 전폭기 14대 터키 인시르리크에 배치

- 이라크 국경에서 680Km

o B-52 폭격기 50대, 인도양 디에고 가르시아에 배치

o 사우디에 F-15 전투기 40대 인도

2. NATO 국가

가. 영국

o Tornado F-3 전투기 12대 사우디 파견

o Jaguar 공격용 전투기 12대 파견

o 전투기 호위 SAM 미사일 파견

o 구축함 1척, 프리킷 2척, 지원선박 걸프로 파견

- NIMROD(조기 경보기), 급유기등이 지원 출동

o 소해정 3척 동지중해로 항진중

o 지원병력 1,000명(지상군 없음)

나. 프랑스(다국적군 불참)

o 항모 Clemenceau 파견(순양함등 6척이 호위)

- 지원병력 3,200명, 전투기 40대

o UAE에 약 180여명의 공정대원 파견 예정

o 사우디에 교관요원 파견

* 미테랑 대통령, 자국함대에 발포 허가(8.22)

다. 터키(다국적군 불참)

o F-16, 병력, Rapier 대공 미사일등 전진 배치

0021

라. 기타 NATO 국가

o 이태리 : 함정 3척 파견(다국적 군가담)

o 카나다 : 함정 3척 파견

o 서 독 : 소해정 4-5척 동지중해 파견

o 덴마크 : 여타국의 걸프 파병으로 인한 NATO 지역 방위 부담 인수.
상업선박이 다국적군의 보급선으로 사용되는 것 허가

o 벨지움 : 함대 파견 예정

o 화 란 : 프리킷 2척 파견

o 그리스, 스페인, 포르투갈 : 미군에 기지 제공

o 스페인 : 군함 4척 페르시아만에 파견 결정(8.22)

3. 기타 국가

가. 아랍 연합군

o 파병국 : 이집트, 모로코, 오만, 시리아(파키스탄 파병 결정)

- 총병력 10,000명 예상

. 이집트군 5,000명 파병 천명(3천명 기파병)

나. 쏘련(다국적군 불참)

o 전함 1척, 대잠함 1척 걸프 파견

다. 이스라엘

o 공군에 경계령. 대공미사일등 요르단 접경지로 이동

o 이라크군이 요르단 진입하면 이라크 공격(8.7. 국방장관 발표)

라. 기타

o 일 본 : 비전투요원, 의무병 파견, 재정지원 검토중

o 호 주 : 프리킷 2척, 유조선 1척 파견

0022

o 파키스탄 : 사우디 파병 결정

o 이 란 : 이라크의 즉각.무조건 철수 요구(8.11. 국가안보회의 성명)

o 인도네시아 : UN 요청시 사우디에 파병 용의 표명(8.18)

※ 쿠웨이트내 이라크군

- 현재 약14만 추정(6개 대통령 경호사 정예부대 포함)

0023

90 – 35

主要國際問題分析

이라크의 쿠웨이트 侵攻 : 脫冷戰時代의 地域紛爭

1990. 9. 5

外 務 部
外交安保硏究院

0024

90 - 35 90. 9. 5

主要國際問題分析

이라크의 쿠웨이트 侵攻 : 脫冷戰時代의 地域紛爭

— 內 容 —

1. 이라크의 쿠웨이트 侵攻 : 후세인 大統領의 覇權 追求
2. 美國과 西方의 強硬 對應 : 脫冷戰時代의 國際秩序 確立
3. 아랍圈의 對應 : 地域 勢力均衡 維持
4. 이라크의 孤立 深化와 후세인의 誤判
5. 協商 妥結 可能性 增大
6. 地域情勢 展望
7. 國際 油價와 OPEC 問題
8. 脫冷戰時代의 國際秩序와 危機 管理
9. 我國의 立場과 考慮事項

<附 錄>

本 資料는 韓國外交政策 立案의 參考資料로 作成한 것으로서 外務部의 公式立場과는 無關한 것입니다.

0025

이라크의 쿠웨이트 侵攻 : 脫冷戰時代의 地域紛爭

이라크의 쿠웨이트 侵攻과 合倂 등 후세인 이라크 大統領의 覇權追求로 빚어진 페르샤灣 危機는 脫冷戰時期의 地域紛爭의 중요한 前例가 될 가능성을 내포하고 있음. 國際經濟安定의 중요변수가 되는 에너지 供給의 확보를 위하여 美國과 西方國들은 이라크의 무조건 철수 등 강경한 經濟的·軍事的·外交的 대응을 하고 있고, 이에 대한 UN과 周邊 아랍國들의 支持로 이라크는 軍事的 劣勢와 國際的 孤立에 직면하고 있음. 美·英 등 이라크에 대한 制裁를 주도하고 있는 西方國들의 軍事的 挑戰 가능성과 더불어 이라크는 이라크·쿠웨이트 殘留 外國人들을 인질로 억류함으로써 兩側은 현재 첨예한 對峙狀態에 있음.

최근 美國은 蘇聯의 同意를 얻어 UN 安保理에서 經濟制裁에 이어 軍事力 使用에 있어서 國際的인 正當性을 확보함으로써 軍事行動의 가능성을 높히고 있음.

그러나 한편 이러한 美·이라크의 軍事對立을 協商으로 타개하기 위하여 드케야르 UN 事務總長이 개인자격으로 仲裁에 나서고, 후세인 이라크 大統領이 이를 환영함으로써 協商氣運이 상승되고 있음. 軍事的 對決은 이라크에 있어 자살행위로 인식되고 있으며, 美國 역시 상당한 희생을 감수해야 할 것인 바, 美國이 승리할 경우에도

- 1 -

0026

아랍圈과 國內外 輿論의 비판이 고조될 가능성이 있어 二重的인 負擔이 될 것임. 물론 協商이 후세인의 제거라는 궁극적인 목표에 미치지 못할 가능성이 있으나, 中東地域에서 美國이 長期的 利益을 추구함에 있어서 軍事的 勝利보다는 協商에 의한 이라크軍의 쿠웨이트 撤收가 페르샤만 地域에서의 美軍 駐屯을 가능케 할 것이고, 美國의 影響力 堅持에 도움이 될 것임.

페르샤만 危機로 폭등세를 보이고 있는 國際油價는 戰爭에 의해 페르샤만 産油施設이 대규모로 파괴되는 경우를 제외하고는 危機終熄 後에 배럴당 20-25 달러 선으로 복귀할 것으로 예상되고, 國際經濟 특히 先進工業國에 대한 經濟的 충격은 심각하지 않을 것임. 그러나 韓國과 같은 原油 依存度 및 對外輸出 依存度가 높은 國家에서는 상당한 景氣沈滯 要因으로 작용할 수 있음. 따라서 90年代 中盤부터 예상되는 高油價 時代에 대비한 에너지 정책을 시급히 시행하여야 할 필요성이 대두되고 있음.

페르샤灣 事態 이후에도 中東情勢는 資源(원유, 물), 領土問題와 理念對立 및 政治改革 등의 問題로 계속 不安定할 것으로 전망됨. 이번 事態를 계기로 中東各國은 安保能力을 제고할 것이고, 이에 따른 軍備增大는 地域不安을 더욱 조장할 수 있음. 이라크 견제를 위해 시리아·이란 등이 美國과의 關係를 改善할 가능성이 높아지고, 이와 관련하여 레바논에서의 인질 석방문제가 진전될 可能性이 있음. 한편, 美國과 다수 아랍國家들과의 關係改善은 美國에 큰 부담요인으로 작용하여, 美國은 팔레스타인 문제해결을 위한 協商을 적극 추진할 것으로 보임.

페르샤만 事態를 계기로 脫冷戰時代의 國際秩序는 美·蘇 兩國體制에서 억제되었던 地域紛爭의 增大傾向을 보일 것으로 예상됨. 이에 따라 地域紛爭 管理는 그 중요성에 따라 國際化, 多國化 努力의 양상을 띠게 되고, 美·蘇의 共同參與와 UN의 役割 增大 등이 예상됨. 그러나 蘇聯의 國力衰退와 改革의 信賴度를 構築하기 위한 노력에 비추어, 蘇聯의 적극 介入은 예상되지 않으므로 당분간 美國의 主導下에 危機管理가 행해질 것으로 보임. 따라서 脫冷戰時代에서 美國의 影響力은 감소되기 보다는 오히려 확대될 가능성이 있음.

韓國은 地域紛爭 管理의 國際化 傾向에 대비하여 對UN 外交를 강화하고, UN 單獨加入도 고려해야 할 것임. 美國의 世界的 役割 지속으로 빚어질 防衛分擔 增大 요구에 적절한 對應이 필요할 것이고, 이와 관련하여 韓國의 軍事 現代化를 강력하게 추진하여야 할 經濟的 二重負擔에 직면할 것으로 보임. 한편 地域安保管理를 위한 地域集團安保體制 構築 必要性이 증대됨에 따라 東北亞 6者會談의 當爲性에 대한 關聯國家間 認識도 提高될 것이므로 이의 실현을 위한 外交的 努力이 필요할 것임.

1. 이라크의 쿠웨이트 侵攻 : 후세인 大統領의 覇權 追求

가. 이라크는 기습적인 武力攻擊을 단행하여(1990. 8. 2) 쿠웨이트 王政을 붕괴시키고, 쿠웨이트 合併을 선언하였음(8. 8). 또한, 이라크는 사우디 국경에 군대를 배치하여, 사우디 王政 전복을 위한 聖戰을 선포(8. 10)함으로써 地域紛爭의 확대가 우려되고 있음. 이에 따라 美國과 西方同盟國들이 多國籍軍을 페르샤만에 派兵하였으며, 國際油價가 폭등하여 국제적인 政治·經濟 危機를 야기시키고 있음.

나. 이라크의 對쿠웨이트 侵攻 名分은 쿠웨이트가 OPEC 産油쿼터를 위반하여 過剩生産함으로써 國際油價를 하락시키고, 이란·이라크戰 동안 이라크의 原油를 도굴하여 이라크의 經濟難을 가중(이라크는 이로 인한 손실을 24억 달러라고 주장)시켰다는 것임.

다. 그러나 이라크의 쿠웨이트 侵攻은 國內外 情勢를 감안하여 볼 때, 후세인 이라크 大統領의 政治·經濟·領土的 野慾에 따른 복합적 요인에 기인하고 있으며, 그의 政治的 野望이 主要要因인 것으로 보임.

(1) 후세인 이라크 大統領은 國內的으로 자신의 政治權力을 공고히 하고, 나아가서 아랍圈의 盟主로 부상하려는 의도를 갖고 있음.

· 최근 이라크의 國內事情은 이란과의 長期戰爭으로 빚어진

經濟難과 低油價로 인한 收入 감소, 戰爭으로 비대해진 軍部의 축소문제 및 후세인의 終身制 大統領 채택 등으로 야기된 國內의 政治的 불만을 타개하여야 할 입장임.

· 한편 최근 共産圈의 改革과 政治變化는 中東政治에서 아랍圈의 獨裁 및 王政에 대한 批判으로 나타나고 있으며, 政治改革의 필요성이 아랍人들 사이에서 대두되고 있음. 또한 冷戰終熄과 蘇聯의 改革으로 強硬아랍國들은 蘇聯이라는 강력한 支持 勢力을 잃게 되었고, 蘇聯의 유태人 移民 허용과 東歐의 이스라엘 承認 등은 아랍圈의 무기력함을 노정시켰음.

· 이와 같은 對內外的인 威脅要因의 증대와 國民들의 불만을 쿠웨이트 侵攻으로 전환시킴으로써 후세인은 자신의 權力을 강화하고, 나아가서 아랍人들의 좌절감을 이용하여 汎아랍主義에 소극적이고 親美性向이 짙은 保守 王國들을 위협함으로써 아랍圈의 指導者로 부상하려는 것임.

(2) 經濟的 側面에서 이라크는 이란과의 戰爭으로 누적된 負債問題와 油價下落으로 인한 原油 收入(年 150억 달러) 감소로 經濟建設에 곤란을 겪고 있음. 이에 따라 이라크는 쿠웨이트를 合併하여 世界 原油 保有量의 1/5을 관할하게 되는 産油大國으로 부상하고, 향후 國際油價 動向에 결정적인 影響力을 행사하여, 美國과 西歐에 대항할 수 있는 아랍圈의 經濟·政治大國으로 등장하려는 의도를 가짐.

(3) 이라크의 쿠웨이트에 대한 領土 野慾은 지난 27년간의 領土 紛爭으로 나타나고 있음. 이라크는 쿠웨이트에 대한 領土權을 주장하여 쿠웨이트 獨立(1961)을 2년동안이나 인정하지 않았고, UN 加入과 아랍聯盟 加入을 반대하였음. 이라크는 현재까지 쿠웨이트와의 國境條約을 批准하지 않고 있으며, 페르샤만에 위치한 부비얀島와 와르바島의 반환을 계속 요구해 왔음. 특히 쿠웨이트의 풍부한 石油資源은 이라크의 領土權 主張을 강화하는 요인이 되었음. 또한, 이라크의 쿠웨이트 合倂은 과거 西歐의 植民主義 統治遺産을 청산하고, 아랍圈 統一과 社會主義로의 變革을 도모하는 이라크의 公式統治 理念인 바트 理念에 입각한 革命輸出 努力의 一環으로 볼 수 있음.

라. 이라크의 쿠웨이트 侵攻은 經濟問題에서 빚어진 侵攻이라기 보다는 覇權指向을 위한 事前에 준비된 軍事作戰으로 보이는 바, 그 理由는 다음과 같음.

(1) 이라크는 經濟問題를 外交的 努力으로 해결하려 하지 않았음. 이라크는 7월초부터 OPEC 쿼터위반을 이유로 쿠웨이트와 UAE를 공개적으로 비난하였고, 그후 이집트와 사우디의 仲裁로 개시된 이라크·쿠웨이트간 懸案問題를 해결하려는 협상에서도 非妥協的인 태도를 견지하면서 쿠웨이트 國境에 軍隊를 배치해 왔음.

(2) 이라크는 經濟難이 심각한 상황에서 原油輸出代金의 70%를 軍事部門에 사용하여 왔음.

0031

(3) 이라크 經濟가 극심한 危機에 직면하고 있었다고 볼 수도 없음.

- 이라크의 쿠웨이트·사우디에 대한 債務總額은 정확하게 계산할 수 없으나, 8년간의 戰爭中 매년 150억 달러의 지원을 받았고, 그 가운데 4분의 3은 사우디가 제공한 액수임(쿠웨이트 借款은 대부분 이라크의 原油販賣를 代行한 것임).
- 이와 같은 債務는 이란에 대한 保護資金의 성격을 띠고 있는 것으로, 利子도 없고 期限도 없는 長期 借款 形式으로 中東의 관례로 보아 대부분 갚지 않아도 무방한 것으로 알려지고 있음.
- 또한 사우디의 경우에는 貸與를 贈與로 바꾸었고, 쿠웨이트 支援의 경우에는 個人 資金支援의 경우에만 채무 성격을 띠고 있음.

(4) 이라크는 周邊 아랍國들의 介入을 배제하기 위하여 外交的인 事前 布石을 시도하였음.

- 이라크는 5월부터 라프산자니 이란 大統領에게 親書를 보내 領土問題 등에 이라크의 양보를 提議하는 등 宥和策을 모색하였고, 사우디에 대한 不可侵條約(1989. 3)을 제의하였음.
- 또한 아랍國과 아랍人들의 支持를 획득하기 위하여 이라크는 反美·反이스라엘 態度를 강화하여, 이집트·요르단 등 아랍國들의 지지를 확보하였음.

· 暫定 敵對國인 시리아의 경우에도, 이라크는 蘇聯의 支援 減少와 레바논 派兵으로 시리아의 軍事行動에 한계가 있을 것으로 판단하였을 것임.

(5) 최근 아랍 産油國들 가운데 페르샤만 保守王國들이 非産油國에 대한 經濟支援을 삭감하고, 汎아랍主義 運動에 소극적인 태도를 보이자, 이에 대한 아랍人들의 비난이 증대됨. 훗세인 大統領은 이를 政治的으로 이용함.

· 훗세인 大統領은 아랍 産油量 14mbd에서 1달러씩을 떼어내 아랍地域 發展基金으로 이용할 것을 제의하여 非産油 아랍國들의 支持를 받았음.

· 한편 쿠웨이트는 原油産業을 國際化하여 高油價 政策보다는 市場擴大가 OPEC의 戰略이 되어야 한다는 입장을 취하고 있으며, 사실상 쿠웨이트는 原油收入을 外國投資에 돌려 OPEC國家 가운데 政府豫算의 油價 依存度가 가장 낮음.

· 이러한 배경하에 이라크는 쿠웨이트의 油價政策이 美國과 西歐 帝國主義의 目的에 이용되고 있다고 주장하여, 쿠웨이트에 대한 攻擊을 對美·西方 공격으로 연계시켜 아랍人들의 支持를 얻는데 이용하고 있음.

(6) 이라크는 쿠웨이트의 不可侵條約締結 提案을 2개 島嶼返還을 구실로 거절하였음. 뿐만 아니라 쿠웨이트가 벨리야티 이란 外相을 쿠웨이트에 초청(1989. 7)하여 이란과의 和解를 추구

0033

하는 등의 행동을 취하자, 이를 이라크의 影響力에 도전하는 것으로 인식함.

(7) 또한 美·蘇의 經濟·軍事力 약화로 中東地域에서 勢力空白이 야기되자, 후세인은 이를 이용하여 페르샤만 地域 覇權 政策을 追求함.

2. 美國과 西方의 強硬對應 : 脫冷戰時代의 國際秩序 確立

가. 美國은 이라크의 侵攻 事態에 원상회복이라는 확고한 의지와 일관된 자세로 經濟的, 軍事的, 外交的 압력을 가하고 있음.

나. 美國은 이라크의 즉각적이고 무조건적인 撤收, 原狀回復(알사바 王政의 회복), 사우디 防衛 및 美國人 保護를 목표로 友邦國의 協調와 UN을 통한 國際的 支持를 추구하고 있음.

美國은 UN의 經濟制裁 措置, 外國人 人質 釋放 要求 등 UN 決議案을 실행하기 위한 多國籍軍의 최소한의 武力使用을 허용받는 등 外交的 努力에 성공하고 있으며, 동시에 脫冷戰時代의 美·蘇協力을 실현시키고 있음(UN 決議案 內容은 附錄 참조).

다. 또한 美國은 親美 아랍國들을 설득하여 사우디·UAE, 카타르에 대한 軍事基地 使用權을 얻어냄. 한편 이집트의 주도 아래 아랍聯盟 12個國은 아랍聯合軍의 페르샤만 派兵을 결정·파병하였으며, GCC(걸프만 協力會議) 5個國도 공동 대응하기로 결의하였음.

라. 美國은 原狀回復이라는 원칙에 입각, 이라크의 무조건 撤收를 주장하며 經濟制裁를 통한 「枯死作戰」을 수행하고, 美軍의 增強으로 사우디 防禦에서 軍事攻擊 態勢로 전환하는 등 對이라크 威脅을 증대시키고, 國際的인 協商努力은 이라크軍 撤收에 관한 사항에 국한시킨다는 強硬한 立場을 견지하고 있는 바, 그 理由는 다음과 같음.

(1) 이라크의 쿠웨이트 侵攻은 단순한 地域紛爭과 覇權鬪爭이라는 차원에 그치지 않고, 그 事態 處理 여하가 향후 脫冷戰時代에서 야기될 수 있는 地域紛爭을 해결하고 예방한다는 점에서 紛爭解決의 중요한 前例가 될 수 있다는 것임. 따라서 美國은 美·蘇 데땅트로 紛爭 可能地域에서 勢力眞空狀態가 생기고 있음을 인식하고, 이에 따른 武力紛爭 可能性을 사전에 예방하려는 것임.

(2) 國際經濟體制 維持와 安定과 관련, 미국은 그 중요성이 증대되고 있는 國際原油供給이 후세인 이라크 大統領과 같은 獨裁者의 影響力에 의해서 좌우되는 것을 방지하려 함. 1990년대 중반부터 페르샤만 沿岸 産油國들의 原油 增産能力에 世界原油供給의 依存度가 더욱 높아질 것으로 예상되고 있어, 페르샤만의 地域安定은 國際經濟 安定, 특히 美國과 美國의 同盟國들의 經濟安定에 직접적인 영향을 미칠 수 있음.

(3) 美國은 이번 事態를 계기로 가능하면 후세인과 같은 地域不安定 要因을 제거하고 이라크의 軍事體制를 근본적으로 개조

하여 地域勢力均衡에 대한 威脅要因을 제거하려 함. 美國은 이를 軍事力을 통하여 성취할 수도 있으나, 그것은 엄청난 政治·經濟的 損失은 물론 人的 희생을 수반할 것이므로 經濟制裁 및 國際的 壓力을 통해 후세인을 스스로 屈服시키든지 또는 이라크 國民과 軍部의 불만을 야기시켜 후세인을 재거하는 등의 方法을 택할 가능성이 높음.

마. 과거 아랍圈을 지지해온 蘇聯은 당면한 國內經濟 問題解決에 美國과 西歐의 支援이 필수적이고, 이를 위한 對美·西歐 外交의 성과를 무산시키지 않기 위하여, 美國이 주도하고 있는 對이라크 強硬制裁 措置에 동조하고 있음. 사실 蘇聯은 이라크의 侵攻으로 빚어진 油價上昇으로 經濟的 利得을 보고 있기도 함. 그러나 蘇聯은 美國이 提案한 UN 憲章 42條(武力사용 허용)의 發動에 동의하였으나, UN 合同軍이 형성되지 않는 한, 蘇聯軍의 派遣을 회피하고 武力制裁 보다는 아랍圈의 自力으로 協商에 의한 해결을 강조하는 소극적인 자세로 이라크와의 전통적인 友好關係에 있는 自國의 곤란한 입장을 극복하려 하고 있음. 그러나 蘇聯은 과거에도 페르샤만에서의 原油供給에 대한 美國의 戰略的 利害關係를 인정하여 왔으므로 이번 페르샤만 사태에서 美國의 主導權을 인정하여도 그 정치적 부담은 크지 않을 것임.

3. 아랍圈의 對應 : 地域 勢力均衡 維持

가. 아랍圈은 개전 초기 분열상을 보였으나, 이라크의 사우디 威脅과 사우디의 美國 및 多國籍軍에 대한 軍事基地 사용 허용 등 事態가 급진전하자, 地域內 勢力均衡에 의한 安定을 도모하고, 아랍형제국에 대한 武力侵攻을 응징하기 위하여, 이집트의 주도로 아랍 聯合軍 파견을 결정하였음.

나. 아랍聯盟은 이라크의 無條件 撤收와 原狀回復, 美軍 등 多國籍軍의 사우디 駐屯 支持 등으로 美國의 立場을 支持하고, 이집트, 시리아, 모로코 등이 地上軍을 派兵하였음.

다. 초기 이라크를 지지했던 요르단은 부쉬 美大統領과의 會談 이후 UN 制裁에 동의하고, 이란도 이에 동조함으로써 이라크 支持勢力은 리비아, PLO 등 少數에 그치고 있음.

4. 이라크의 孤立 深化와 후세인의 誤判

가. 이라크는 對쿠웨이트 侵攻直後 가중되는 美國과 西方側의 압력에도 불구하고 쿠웨이트를 合倂하고 國家動員令을 발동하여 사우디와의 國境에 軍事配置를 증강함으로써 일전불사의 決意를 보였음.

0037

나. 이라크는 武力示威外에 사우디와의 對決을 聖戰으로 비유하여 아랍圈의 分裂을 유도하는 心理戰을 폈음. 훗세인은 協商條件으로 이스라엘의 占領地 撤收, 시리아軍의 레바논 撤收, 사우디에서의 美軍 撤收 및 對이라크 經濟制裁 解除 등을 제시하여 아랍圈의 支持를 얻어 外交的 孤立을 탈피하려 하였으나, 아랍聯盟의 아랍軍 派遣 決議로 인해 이라크의 孤立은 더욱 심화되었음.

다. 이라크는 國際的 孤立과 軍事的 劣勢에도 불구하고, 이라크·쿠웨이트에 체류중인 美·英 등 西方人들을 인질로 하여, 이들을 主要戰略施設에 분산시켜 美國의 攻擊에 대한 인간방패로 삼겠다는 威脅을 하고 있으나 이러한 措置는 오히려 國際輿論에 否定的인 影響을 주었음.

라. 훗세인 이라크 大統領의 정치적 야심은 아랍圈 統一과 社會主義로의 變革을 지향하는 바트 理念에 입각하고 있는 바, 이라크의 이러한 바트理念을 바탕으로 한 "革命輸出" 企圖는 다음과 같은 점에 비추어, 國際·地域情勢에 대한 잘못된 판단에 기인하고 있는 것으로 보임.

(1) 前述한 바와 같이 이라크의 쿠웨이트 侵攻은 脫冷戰時代의 國際秩序 構築에 否定的 影響을 미치는 중요한 前例가 되며, 美·蘇 등 西歐勢力의 經濟利益에 중요한 이해가 걸려 있다는 점을 간과함.

0038

(2) 아랍地域 政治에서 전통적인 相互牽制와 勢力均衡이 작용하고 있다는 점을 간과함.

- 이집트는 아랍圈의 政治·文化 中心地이고 軍事的 強國으로서 팔레스타인 문제를 포함한 地域政治에서 主導權을 견지하려는 입장을 취하고 있음.
- 시리아는 蘇聯의 支援減少에도 불구하고 이라크의 軍事威脅에 대항할 능력이 있고, 시리아軍의 레바논 撤收를 요구한 이라크의 主張은 시리아를 자극시켰음.
- 사우디도 軍事·外交·經濟面에서 상당한 저력을 보유하고 있어 무기력한 상대는 아님.
- 요컨대 이들 아랍國들은 周邊國의 國力增強에 민감하게 대응하고 勢力 均衡을 통한 自國 安保를 위해서 이라크의 쿠웨이트 侵攻을 용인할 수 없는 입장임.
- 또한 中東政治에서 아랍 指導者들이 이구동성으로 汎아랍主義를 강조하고 있으나, 이는 다분히 國內政治用으로 이용되어 왔고, 이번의 페르샤만 危機도 이라크의 國內 政治用으로 이용되고 있는 측면이 있음.

(3) 현재 이라크의 쿠웨이트 侵攻으로 빚어진 地域紛爭이 다분히 長期的인 持久戰 양상으로 진행되고 있음을 감안할 때, 후세인은 自國의 國力을 점검하는데 소홀하였음.

- 이라크는 사실상의 內陸國으로 國家收入의 90-95%가 他國領土를 통과하는 送油管에 의한 原油輸出에 의존하고

있으며, 식량의 75%를 輸入에 의존하고 있음. 현재 食糧 備蓄量은 2-3개월분으로 추정되고 있음.

- 또한 戰後 國家建設에 필요한 물자의 대부분을 美國과 EC 등 先進國에 의존하고 있는 바, 이라크는 美國 및 西方國의 經濟 制裁에 극히 취약한 實情임.
- 따라서 이라크의 美國과 西方國을 상대로 한 長期戰 遂行은 사실상 불가능함.

(4) 후세인은 執權初期 2년간을 제외하고는 계속적인 전쟁상태의 지속으로 말미암아 이라크 國民들과 軍人들의 政治的 支持를 더 이상 持續하기 어려운 실정에 직면하고 있음.

마. 이라크는 國際的 孤立을 타파하고 아랍圈의 支持를 얻기 위하여 美國과의 對決 보다는 이스라엘과의 戰爭을 선택할 가능성이 있고, 실제로 對이스라엘 戰爭을 사실상 공언하고 있음. 그러나 다음과 같은 점에서 이라크의 對이스라엘 侵攻은 현실적으로 어려움.

(1) 이스라엘은 이라크의 요르단 國境을 赤色線으로 경고하고 對이라크 전투준비 태세에 있음. 이스라엘과의 戰鬪는 地上軍의 接戰이 거의 불가능하고 空軍力과 미사일 등의 現代戰에서 이스라엘이 絶對的으로 優勢하므로 이라크의 막대한 피해가 예상 될 뿐 승산이 희박함.

(2) 한편 이라크가 主導하는 對이스라엘 戰爭에 아랍強國인 이집트, 시리아가 가담할 가능성도 적음. 이집트는 이스라엘

0040

과의 平和條約 遵守에 더 큰 의미를 부여하고 있고, 또한 시리아가 레바논에서의 旣得權을 희생하면서 競爭國인 이라크를 支援할 가능성은 희박하기 때문임.

5. 協商·妥結 可能性 增大

가. 후세인 이라크 大統領은 戰力의 절대적 劣勢와 世界輿論의 批判으로 協商에 의한 妥結을 모색할 可能性이 크다고 判斷됨.

(1) 현재 이라크의 戰力은 美國과 多國籍軍에 비해 절대적인 劣勢에 있어, 戰爭挑發은 政治的 자살행위가 될 것임. 이라크軍은 제한된 正規戰 經驗을 가졌을 뿐이며, 俸給 支給 지연과 열악한 생활조건으로 기강과 사기가 저하되고 있음.

(2) 또한 이라크가 보유한 스커드 미사일 등 現代 武器도 정확성과 파괴력에서 뒤지고 있음.

(3) 化學武器 使用 威脅은 非武裝 民間人 密集地域에서는 효과가 있으나, 防禦裝備와 機動性을 갖춘 軍事作戰에는 효과가 적음. 또한 이라크의 化學武器 使用은 대량 보복능력이 없는 쿠르드族이나 이란의 人海戰術에 선별적으로 사용되었을 뿐이며, 만일 이라크가 美軍을 상대로 化學武器를 사용할 경우에는 심각한 報復에 직면하게 될 것임.

(4) 對決이 長期化될 경우 美國에게 不利한 점도 없지 않으나, 이라크에게는 치명적일 可能性이 높음.

0041

나. 美國은 軍事力 增強과 對이라크 威脅으로 이라크의 쿠웨이트 撤收를 겨냥하고 있으며, 사우디 侵攻이나 人質에 대한 피해가 자행되지 않는 한, 美國이 戰爭을 挑發할 可能性은 높지 않음. 그러나 美國의 對이라크 戰略目標에 대해서는 強·穩 兩論으로 분열된 意見이 나타나고 있음.

(1) 強硬論은 獨裁者에게 줄 수 있는 敎訓은 패배시키는 것 뿐이라는 주장으로 軍事報復과 후세인 제거를 주장하고 있음.

(2) 穩健論은 사우디 防衛公約을 준수하면서 지속적인 國際的 壓力으로 쿠웨이트 撤收를 유도할 수 있다는 것임.

다. 美國이 軍事的인 劣勢에 있는 이라크에 대한 軍事的 勝利를 추구할 경우, 美國은 政治的으로 이중부담을 안게 될 것임. 戰爭에 따른 상당한 희생은 國內輿論과 11월 中間 選擧에서 부정적으로 반영될 것이고, 나아가서 아랍圈과 世界輿論의 비판을 면하기 어려울 것임. 또한 戰爭에 따른 油價暴騰은 世界經濟에 심각한 충격을 가져다 줄 것임.

라. 현재 드 케야르 UN 事務總長의 仲裁努力을 후세인이 환영하고 있어 쿠웨이트 撤軍과 外國人 人質 석방에 대한 協商妥結 可能性이 높아지고 있음. 美國도 「先撤收 後協商」의 테두리 內에서 協商 妥結을 모색할 경우, 戰略的인 利點을 확보할 수 있을 것임. 美國은 中東地域에서 장기적인 美國의 戰略的 利益을 확보하기 위한 方案을 모색하여야 할 것인 바, 그것은 우선 후세인의 쿠웨이트 撤軍을 誘導하고, 향후의 地域安定을

위하여 사우디·UAE 등 페르샤만 지역에서의 美軍의 駐屯 또는 軍事基地 利用을 확보하는 것임.

마. 9月 9日 개최 예정인 美·蘇 頂上間의 헬싱키會談에서 美國은 「先撤收 後協商」立場을 견지하고 이에 대한 蘇聯의 協調를 요청할 것이나, 中東地域에서의 蘇聯의 影響力 增大를 憂慮하여, 蘇聯의 仲裁役割을 원하지는 않을 것임.

바. 協商은 이라크의 쿠웨이트 撤軍後에 본격화될 것으로 예측되는 바, 구체적인 協商內容은 이라크·쿠웨이트간의 國境條約과 不可侵條約, 이라크의 부비얀과 와르바島의 이용 문제, 이라크에 대한 債務蕩減 및 經濟支援 問題 등으로 될 것으로 보임.

6. 地域 情勢 展望

가. 페르샤만 危機에 따른 美國의 影響力 增大

(1) 協商에 의한 妥結은 地域紛爭 要因의 완전한 해소 보다는 잠정적인 消防措置로 끝날 것으로 보이나, 美國의 對中東 影響力은 제고될 것임. 이에 따라 美國은 과거 소원했던 시리아 및 이란과의 關係改善을 통해 이라크를 견제하고, 나아가서 레바논 인질 석방에 극적인 타결을 이룰 수도 있을 것임. 또한 美國은 親美 아랍國에 대한 武器支援과 經濟協力 강화로 中東에서의 對蘇優位를 견지할 것임.

0043

(2) 아랍圈에 대한 美國의 影響力 強化는 逆說的으로 이스라엘에게는 負擔要因으로 작용할 것임. 美國은 아랍國들의 압력으로 팔레스타인 문제 해결을 위한 이스라엘의 양보를 촉구할 것임. 이와 관련 예상되는 代案의 하나로서 美國은 이스라엘 安保에 대한 美國의 책임과 보장 아래 非武裝 팔레스타인 獨立國 樹立을 추진할 수 있을 것임. 이번 事態를 계기로, 脫冷戰時代의 地域 問題解決에 대한 美國의 影響力은 더욱 제고되고 있음.

나. 中東 各國들의 對應과 立場

(1) 아랍 各國은 自國의 安保를 위한 措置에 특별한 관심을 갖게 되었으며, 이에 따라 아랍國家間 軍備競爭 可能性이 증대되고 있음. 특히 GCC 6개국은 集團安保를 위한 協力을 강화하고, 쿠웨이트도 이에 대해 과거보다는 적극적으로 참여할 것임. 페르샤만 危機 이전에도 世界 武器去來의 40%가 中東地域에서 이루어지고, 美·蘇·中·西歐國家들은 對中東 武器販賣로 상당한 經濟的 利得을 취하여 왔음. 美國은 이번 事態를 계기로 GCC 6個國과 이집트, 터키, 모로코 등에 武器販賣를 강화하여 自國의 影響力 增大와 더불어 아랍國들의 軍備競爭을 더욱 부채질하고 있음. 그러나 向後 中東地域 安定을 위하여 美·蘇와 아랍國들의 軍備 縮小 努力이 倍加되어야 할 것임.

(2) 이라크·시리아의 公式統治理念인 바트理念은 이번 事態를 계기로 아랍圈에서 퇴색될 것으로 보임. 왜냐하면 아랍圈의

統一과 社會主義로의 變革을 추구하는 바트理念은 아랍 형제국을 顚覆하는 好戰的인 革命理念으로 간주되어, 아랍 各國에서 바트理念에 대한 牽制가 강화될 것이기 때문임.

(3) 이번 事態로 요르단은 政治的으로 취약한 입장에 처하게 될 것임. 政治·經濟的으로 이라크에 대한 依存度가 높기 때문에 이라크를 두둔하게 된 요르단은 부시 美大統領과의 會談 이후 UN 制裁에 동참하는 등 二重外交를 추진함. 이로써 요르단은 향후 兩側으로부터 모두 소외될 위협성을 안게 되었음. 앞으로 요르단은 사우디, 이집트 등 反이라크 勢力의 信賴를 잃게 될 뿐만 아니라, 후세인 이라크 大統領의 불확실한 支援과 威脅에 직면하게 될 可能性이 있음. 즉 요르단은 과거 쿠웨이트와 같이 中立的이고 二重的인 對外關係를 추구하고 있으나, 이에 따른 危險負擔은 쿠웨이트 경우와 같이 상대적으로 높아질 可能性이 큼.

(4) 아라파트 PLO 議長의 이라크 支持 態度는 PLO에 대한 穩健 아랍國들의 支持 減少는 물론, 美國과의 對話再開 努力에 부정적으로 작용하여 外交的 孤立을 초래할 可能性이 높음. 이와 같은 孤立을 타개하기 위하여 앞으로 PLO가 對이스라엘 強硬政策을 追求할 可能性도 있음.

다. 地域 紛爭 展望

(1) 資源, 領土, 理念 및 政治改革 要求 등의 복잡 다양한 요인들은 中東地域國家들의 紛爭要因으로 尙存하고 있고, 脫冷戰

時代의 多極化 傾向은 美·蘇의 影響力 減少로 인식되어 地域 紛爭을 可視化시킬 가능성이 높음.

(2) 中東地域의 産油國과 非産油國間의 貧富의 隔差는 汎아랍主義라는 구호 아래 貧·富國家間의 對立으로 발전될 가능성이 높음.

- 現存하는 아랍經濟協力機構들(ACC, GCC, AMU)의 經濟協力은 政治 不安定 등의 투자환경의 미비로 資源配分이나 投資의 移動에 있어 거의 무의미하며, 다만 勞動移動에 의한 經濟利得 配分에 그치고 있음.
- 유럽市場統合은 아랍 經濟 統合을 주장하는 불만 세력에 대한 자극 요인으로 作用할 것임.
- 水資源은 인구폭발과 식량난 해결에 主要資源이 되고 있으나, 나일江, 요르단江, 유프라테스江의 이용을 위요한 隣接國家들 간의 異見도 갈등요인으로 등장할 可能性이 있음.

(3) 西歐 植民統治로부터 獨立하면서 임의로 획정된 新生아랍國들의 國境線과 전통적인 생활방식 및 地理的 特殊性(사막 등)으로 빚어진 領土問題는 앞으로 地域國家間에 심각한 紛爭要因으로 작용할 가능성이 있음.

(4) 이란의 回敎原理主義와 이라크·시리아의 바트理念 등은 保守王政들과의 政治的 對立·葛藤 要因으로 작용할 可能性이 큼.

- 21 -

0046

(5) 中東의 王政과 獨裁統治에 대한 아랍人들의 政治改革 要求는 최근 回教主義者들의 政治得勢를 가져오고, 이들에 대한 아랍人들의 支持 增大는 좌절감에 따른 단순한 「항의투표」 (protest vote) 次元에 그칠 것 같지는 않음.

(6) 이와 같은 아랍國家들 간의 갈등과 軍備統制問題 등을 協議하기 위한 地域協力機構의 創設과 이들의 役割 증대가 요구될 것이나, 현재와 같은 아랍國間의 紛爭과 相互不信 등에 비추어 이러한 努力이 可視化되는데에는 상당한 時日과 共同 努力이 요구될 것임.

7. 國際油價와 OPEC 問題

가. 이라크의 쿠웨이트 侵攻이 國際油價의 폭등을 가져와 國際油價가 쿠웨이트 侵攻 이전의 배럴당 10달러선에서 31달러선까지 폭등하였고, 페르샤灣 事態 進展에 따라 큰 폭으로 변하고 있음. 이러한 의미에서 이라크는 쿠웨이트 侵攻으로 油價上昇을 소극적으로 기다리는 것보다 효과적으로 油價上昇에 성공했으나, 經濟制裁措置로 직접적인 利得을 보지 못하고 있음. 그러나 현재의 國際油價는 需要供給에 의해 合理的으로 형성되고 있다기 보다는 다분히 心理的이고 投機的인 側面에서 형성되고 있음.

나. 현재 페르샤만 危機가 熱戰으로 확산되지 않고(확산될 가능성도 높지 않음), 軍事對峙와 協商이 지속된다면, 油價는 배럴당 20-25달러 線에서 安定될 것으로 보이며, 과거 世界原油의 수급 상황을 고려하면 지속적인 油價暴騰은 예상되지 않음.

(1) 쿠웨이트 事態 이전의 世界原油 供給量은 2.7mdb(日當 270만 배럴)이 공급과잉 상태에 있었고, 지난 몇해동안의 공급과잉으로 原油輸入國들의 비축량은 많음.

(2) 이번 危機와 經濟制裁로 말미암아 世界原油 供給에서 4.3mdb이 감소되고, OPEC의 減産 決定으로 세계원유 수요 64mdb(89년 기준)에 비해 2.1mdb의 부족이 예상되고 있음. 그러나 사우디, UAE 등 OPEC國의 증산과 非OPEC 産油國들의 증산은 供給不足分을 메꿀 수 있고, 西方先進國(OECD)들의 備蓄分(340억 배럴)은 98일간을 지탱할 수 있으므로 向後 2년간 이라크·쿠웨이트의 供給不足分을 대체할 능력이 있음.

(3) 또한 과거 油價暴騰은 中小産油業者들의 市場參與 增大와 原油 輸入國들의 에너지 보존과 代替 에너지 開發 등으로 油價 下落을 가져왔고 OPEC의 권한을 제한하는 要因으로 작용하였음.

다. 따라서 최근의 油價暴騰으로 世界經濟 전반의 인플레·景氣沈滯 등 심각한 經濟難이 야기될 可能性은 그리 크지 않음.

(1) 先進 工業國들은 에너지 절약과 대체 에너지 개발로 에너지 消費 構造를 조정하고 있으며, 油價가 배럴당 50달러 선으로

- 23 -

0048

인상되는 경우에도 先進工業國들은 GNP의 1% 미만 만을 OPEC 收入으로 이전시키게 될 것임(과거 油價暴騰으로 OECD는 GNP의 2%를 이전).

(2) 한편 OPEC 産油國들은 財政赤字 등으로 油價收入을 빨리 지출할 것이므로 과거 石油波動과는 달리 西方經濟에 심각한 충격을 야기시킬 가능성은 적음.

(3) 현재의 經濟狀況을 볼 때, 인플레 요인은 있으나 과거보다 심각하지는 않음.

- 先進工業國들의 인플레는 4% 수준으로(과거 73년, 78년의 1/2) 緊縮財政政策을 취할 필요성이 적고, 국민들이 經濟問題의 심각성을 인식하고 있어 직접적인 충격폭이 크지는 않을 것으로 보임.
- 또한 經濟自由化 政策으로 인한 經濟의 탄력성 증대로 충격 흡수 능력이 높아지고 있음. 물론 油價上昇으로 經濟的 打擊을 받겠으나, 經濟의 規模에서 충격을 완화시킬 수 있을 것임.

라. 그러나 우리나라와 같이 對中東 에너지 依存度가 높고, 에너지 사용도가 높은 産業構造를 지닌 國家에서의 경제적 타격은 先進工業國에 비해서 더욱 심각하게 나타날 것으로 보임.

(1) 에너지 研究院은 油價가 1달러 상승할 경우 GNP 성장율이 0.6%씩 떨어진다고 분석하고 있음.

(2) 또한 오일쇼크에 의한 先進國들의 景氣沈滯는 輸出 依存度가 높은 우리 經濟에 타격을 줄 것으로 예상됨.

0049

(3) 한편 油價上昇에 따른 긍정적인 측면이 있다면, 中東 需要의 增大로 우리 經濟의 對中東 진출 기회가 확대될 수 있다는 것임.

(4) 요컨대 1990년대 중반부터 예상되는 國際油價의 지속적인 상승 추세에 대비하여, 韓國은 合理的인 에너지 需給과 代替 에너지 開發 등 포괄적인 에너지 政策을 강구하여야 할 것임.

마. 向後 OPEC의 機能은 강화될 것이나, 가격문제로 인한 OPEC 國家間의 對立은 지속될 것임.

(1) 세계 에너지 需要의 增大와 供給不足으로 빚어진 高油價 時代는 國際油價問題로 인한 會員國間의 대립상을 완화시킬 가능성도 있음.

(2) 그러나 向後 國際油價決定에서 產油國들과 原油輸入國들간의 經濟的 相互依存性의 增大는 OPEC의 權限을 제약하는 요인으로 작용하고, 이에 따른 갈등이 심각한 國際紛爭으로 발전될 가능성도 배제할 수 없음.

8. 脫冷戰時代의 國際秩序와 危機管理

가. 地域紛爭 增大 傾向

脫冷戰의 전환기적인 國際情勢 하에서 美·蘇의 상대적 影響力 약화와 多極化 趨勢 등으로 美·蘇 兩極體制에서 억제되었던 다양한 紛爭要因이 현재화되고, 이에 따라 地域紛爭 可能性도 增大될 것으로 전망됨.

나. 危機管理의 國際化·多國化

脫冷戰時代의 危機管理는 이번 쿠웨이트 事態와 같이 美·蘇의 協調 등 國際化·多國化 傾向을 띠게 되고, UN의 機能이 강화될 것으로 보임.

다. 美國의 主導的 役割 持續

脫冷戰時代의 地域紛爭 管理는 國際化·多國化 趨勢를 보이고 있으나, 蘇聯의 國力衰退와 改革에 따른 政治不安으로 당분간 美國의 主導 아래 이루어질 것으로 보임.

라. 脫冷戰時代의 集團 安保 傾向

地域紛爭에 대한 효과적인 對應을 위하여 冷戰時代의 유물인 地域安保體制가 다시 강화될 것으로 전망됨.

9. 我國의 立場과 考慮事項

가. 効果的인 外交能力 과시

현재까지 我國의 外交的 對應은 무리없이 진행되고 있음. 國際的으로 이라크에 대한 쿠웨이트 撤軍 要求, UN 制裁措置에의 참여, 多國籍軍에 대한 經濟支援 및 쿠웨이트 大使館

0051

維持 등으로 美國과 西方友邦國 및 다수 아랍國들과 보조를 맞추어, 國際秩序의 基本原則을 준수하고 있음. 한편 現地 我國人들의 安全歸國을 도모하는 등 對이라크 外交에도 성공 하고 있음.

나. 韓國 防衛 위한 二重負擔 增大

地域紛爭 管理에서 美國의 役割 持續으로 美國은 韓國에 대한 防衛分擔 등 危機管理에의 적극 참여를 요구할 것임. 韓國은 美國의 對韓 防衛公約을 강화시키기 위하여 적절한 防衛分擔을 수행하여야 할 것이고, 我國의 國軍 現代化를 지속적으로 추진 하여야 할 것임.

다. 對UN 外交 強化

地域紛爭 管理의 國際化·多國化 傾向으로 UN의 重要性이 부각 되고 있어 我國은 UN 單獨加入 등 對UN 外交를 적극 강화하여야 할 것임.

라. 東北亞 6者會談 實現 可能性 增大

脫冷戰時代에서 地域紛爭 管理를 위한 地域安保體制가 강화될 것으로 보이며, 이와 관련하여 東北亞地域에서도 東北亞地域 安定 등 地域잇슈를 논의할 必要性이 증대될 것으로 예상되는 바, 韓國은 盧大統領의 東北亞6者會談 構想의 具現을 위한 外交的 努力을 경주할 필요가 있을 것임.

1990. 9. 5.

作成 : 研究教授 崔 宜 喆

討論 : 研究部長 玄 熙 剛

研究教授 朴 弘 圭

0053

<附　錄>

決議案 660 號 : 이라크가 쿠웨이트를 侵攻한 2일 安保理는 美國과 쿠웨이트 要請으로 緊急會議를 개최, 이라크軍의 즉각적이고 무조건적인 撤收를 요구하고 4個項 決議案 채택

決議案 661 號 : 6일 美國의 提議로 이라크에 대한 全面的 經濟制裁 措置 결의

決議案 662 號 : 9일 이라크가 쿠웨이트를 合併한 것과 관련, 「이라크가 쿠웨이트를 어떤 구실, 어떤 형태로 合併하든 그것은 전혀 法的 妥當性이 없으며, 따라서 無効로 간주된다」고 만장일치로 결의

決議案 664 號 : 이라크가 이라크와 쿠웨이트內에 잔류해 있던 外國人들에 대한 抑留方針을 밝힌 후 이들의 人質化를 우려해 安保理는 18일 外國人들의 자유로운 出國과 安全 및 健康의 보장을 요구하는 決議案을 18일 만장일치로 채택

決議案 665 號 : 이라크의 쿠웨이트 駐在 外國公館 강제 폐쇄가 임박함에 따라 25일 安保理는 이미 나온 UN 決議案의 즉각 실행과 필요한 경우 多國籍軍에 최소한의 武力使用을 허용하는 5個項의 決議案 채택

0054

이락·쿠웨이트 事態 關聯動向(27)

<90. 9. 6>

1. 9.6 현재 쿠웨이트 事態는

가. 이락이

○ 蘇聯을 방문중인 「아지즈」外相의 고르바초프大統領과의 會談이 성과없이 종료된 가운데

○ 수만명의 豫備軍을 追加 召集(9.6)하고 域內 外國軍隊와의 계속 鬪爭을 선언하는 등 強硬立場 고수

나. 美國은

○ 「베이커」國務長官과 「브래디」財務長官을 각각 中東(9.6 - 사우디, UAE, 이집트) 및 歐洲·亞洲地域(9.4 - 佛蘭西, 英國, 韓國, 일본)에 파견 美國의 軍事活動과 被害아랍國 支援을 위한 외교적 노력을 강화하고 있는 가운데

○ 蘇聯측의 駐이락 軍事顧問團 撤收, 多國籍軍 가담 등을 위한 막후 교섭을 진행하고 있고

○ 「체니」國防長官은 10만명 이상의 兵力과 50여척 함정이 페灣에 배치되었음을 처음으로 확인(9.6) 7예만 10만

29-17

0055

다. 蘇聯은

○ UN安保理 軍事參謀委 構成을 희망하면서 UN軍의 페灣파견 지지 가능성을 시사하고 (9.6 外務省 代辯人)

○ 이락과 蘇聯 軍事顧問團 철수에 합의했다고 언급 (9.7 「세바르드나제」外相)

라. 佛蘭西를 비롯 中國, 이란, 印度, 브라질이 이락에 대한 食糧 및 醫療品 등 인도적 물자의 提供用意를 표명, UN의 對이락 制裁措置가 균열될 조짐.

大國. Regional Hegemony.

2. 主要 關聯動向

가. 이 락

○ 「후세인」大統領, 부시 美 大統領의 이락국민에 대한 TV연설 제의 (9.6 「자심」公報相 발표)

○ 「아지즈」外相, 고르바초프 蘇聯大統領과의 회담직후

- 美大統領앞 메시지 전달 부인

- 美軍과의 계속 鬪爭 재확인 (9.6)

○ 이락 國防部, 37세이하 豫備軍사병 및 轉役후 4년이상 경과한 30대 豫備軍 장교들의 소속부대 복귀 명령 (9.6)

29-18

0056

나. 美　國

○「노울즈」國防省 韓國課長, 韓國이 90년말까지 現金 5,000萬弗과 物資·用役 1억불 지원 및 91.1부터 중동사태 종결시까지 매월 현금 500萬弗과 2,000萬弗의 物資·用役 支援을 해줄 것을 요청할 예정이라고 언급 (9.6)

○ 부시大統領, 이락국민들에게 대한 TV연설 제의 수락 (9.6「피츠워터」白堊館代辯人 발표)

○ 蘇聯측에 駐이락 軍事顧問團 撤收 및 多國籍軍 참여시 대규모 經協支援 제의 (9.6 L. A Times)

○「베이커」國務長官, 軍費分擔 문제 협의를 위한 中東巡訪차 사우디 向發 (9.6)

○ 부시大統領, 中東事態에 대한 美國의 정책 지지 호소차 9.11 上·下兩院 合同演說 예정

○「체니」國防長官, 사우디 및 페灣地域에 10만이상의 병력배치 확인(9.6)

다. 蘇　聯

○「게라시모프」蘇聯 外務部 대변인은

　－ UN軍의 페灣 派遣 지지 가능성 시사 및 UN헌장중 군사참모위원회에 관한 조항 발동 희망

0057

29-19

- 事態의 平和的 解決을 지지하나 UN安保理의 制限的 武力 使用에는 참가할 방침.

○ 세바르드나제 外相, 주이라크 군사고문단 철수 합의 발표(9.7)

라. 西方圈

○ 日本, 페灣 多國籍軍에 보내는 최초의 分擔物品 輸送貨物船 시 비너스號 나고야港 출항(9.6)

○「미테랑」佛蘭西 大統領, 이락의 침공이 없는 한 佛蘭西의 활동을 UN의 禁輸措置 履行에만 국한할 것이라고 언급 (9.6)

○ 대처 英國首相, 中東事態 관련 재정 지원, 페灣 파견병력 증원 및 필요시 무력사용 불사 언급(9.6)

○「콜」西獨首相, 財政的 支援 대신 船舶, 航空機 등의 수송수단 지원방침 언급(9.6)

○ 터키 國會, 터키軍의 해외파견권 · 외국軍의 터키駐屯 허용 권한을 行政府에 부여(9.5)

마. 北 韓

○ 김영남 外交部長, UN安保理決議 661호 이행에 관한 UN事務總長앞 서한(9.1자)을 통해 北韓 · 이락간 관계가 凍結되었음을 지적(9.5 安保理 문서)

0058

29-20

바. 아 랍 圈

○「후세인」요르단 國王은「후세인」이락大統領과 회담, 지난 2주간 유럽 및 아랍國家 巡訪결과 설명(9.6)

○ 이란 언론, UN이 對이락 經濟制裁 決議案에 食糧 및 醫藥品은 포함되지 않는다고 보도(9.6 테헤란 타임즈)

○ 이락 反體制 단체들,「후세인」이락大統領 암살에 합의(9.6 이집트 알 와프드紙)

○「아사드」시리아大統領 , 부시 美 大統領과 전화 통화(9.6)

○ 이집트, UAE派遣軍 제2진 공수(9.6)

사. 其 他

○ 브라질, 對이락 긴급구호식량 제공 계획(9.6「레젝」外相)

○ 유고政府, 14개국 非同盟 外相會議(9.12-13) 대신 유고, 印度, 알제리아 3개국 外相會談을 개최(9.11)키로 결정(9.6)

○ 中國外交部 대변인, 經濟制裁 대상품목에는 食糧 및 醫藥品이 포함되어 있지 않다고 主張(9.6)

3. 評 價

가. 페灣事態는 美·蘇 頂上會談을 앞두고 이락의 對蘇 설득노력

0059

29-21

이 실패로 끝난 가운데 蘇聯측이 美國의 對이락 軍事制裁에 同調할 태도로 轉換하고 있는 局面

나. 蘇聯측이 UN軍 파견 지지 가능성 시사와 함께 駐이락 軍事顧問團 撤收결정은

○ 「아지즈」外相과 고르바초프大統領간의 會談 실패에 따른 強硬立場 선회와 함께

○ 9.9 美·蘇 頂上會談에서 美國으로부터 經協支援을 얻어내려는 意圖도 내포된 것이나

○ 美國의 對이락 軍事膺懲의 주요 장애요인이 제거되었음을 의미

다. 美國의 友邦國에 대한 分擔金 지원요구는

○ 美國의 財政負擔을 덜고 對이락 대응이 友邦國의 지원하에 이루어지고 있음을 국민들에게 주지시킴으로써 페灣事態 대응에 대한 국민 계속적 지지 획득과 아울러

○ 페灣事態의 長期化에도 대비하려는 것이나,

○ 同 問題를 둘러싼 友邦國과의 마찰이 야기되고 있어 注目됨.

0060

29-22

이라크-쿠웨이트 事態의 展望(案)

1990. 9. 17.

外　務　部

0061

I. "페"灣 事態의 展望

事態를 便宜上 短期的으로 90.11.6 美 中間 選擧以前, 中期的으로 앞으로 6個月間 및 長期的으로 91年末까지로 區分 展望해 봄.

1. 短期的 展望(11.6 美中間 選挙以前)

가. 美國은 이라크의 쿠웨이트 無條件 撤收等 目標를 可及的 中間選擧以前에 達成코저 努力中

나. 한편 이라크는 쿠웨이트 併合을 旣定事實化,

금번 事態를 "對美 聖戰"이라는 이락 對 美國 兩者間 對立 方向으로 몰고가려함.

다. 中間選擧前

- 美國은 특히 軍事的 壓力을 高度로 加速化할 것임.
- 만약 이라크側의 挑發이나 制裁에 抵抗하는 行爲가 있을시는 相應하는 軍事的 應懲도 있을 수 있음.
- 또 이라크의 軍事的 衝突 回避 戰略에 대하여는 美軍等에 의한 攻擊的 防禦를 強化하므로서 이락을 軍事的 守勢로 몰고갈 可能性 큼.

0062

ㅇ 時期的으로는, 美軍等 多國籍軍의 配置가 完了되고, 美國 選擧 直前인 10月 中下旬이 軍事的 緊張이 高潮되는 時期로 豫想됨.

라. 만약 軍事的 壓迫戰略이 所期의 實效를 거두지 못하는 경우,

ㅇ 美國은 各國의 世界的 同參과 友邦의 支援을 最大한 廣範圍하게 確保하므로서 이락의 "對美 聖戰" 戰略을 분쇄하고 "對이락 汎世界的 制裁"를 美國 主導下에 成功的으로 遂行한다는 可視的 成果를 美國 選擧民과 世界에 誇示코자 할 것임.

2. 中期的 展望(앞으로 6個月間)

가. 軍事 衝突 可能性

ㅇ 現 段階에서 戰爭 발발시 이라크의 窮極的인 敗北는 確實함으로, 이라크는 쿠웨이트의 合倂 공고화等 現狀維持에 主力하고 軍事的 挑發은 않을 것임.

ㅇ 따라서 戰爭이 있다면 美國側에서 始作한다고 보아야 하는바, 美 中間選擧以前의 軍事的 緊張高潮를 무사히 넘기는 境遇에는, 美側에 의한 戰爭은 美國側에 다음과 같은 不利点이 있어 그 可能性은 적음

- 人質의 犧牲을 包含한 막대한 人命 損失
- 油田 破壞等 世界經濟 困難
- 이라크의 이스라엘 攻擊等 擴戰 可能性
- 蘇聯, EC, 日本, 아랍圈等 世界輿論 不利
- 短期的, 깨끗한 勝利 期待 難望
  . 美國內 輿論 不利, 美國의 威信 損傷
- 事態 解決後 大規模 軍事力의 中東駐屯 名分 弱化

나. 平和的 解決 可能性

ㅇ 早期 解決을 위하여는 美國, 유엔等 反 이라크側이 要求하는 이라크軍의 쿠웨이트 撤收가 必須的 要件임

ㅇ 한편 이라크側은 후세인이 執權하는한 代償이나 名分이 없는 撤軍은 不可能視됨.

ㅇ 따라서 早期 解決을 위하여는 쿠데타等 이라크 內部의 變動이나, 이라크 撤軍의 名分을 살리는 調整이 있어야 하나, 두가지 可能性 모두 극히 적음

3

0064

3. 長期的 展望(1991年末까지)

가. 現狀의 長期化 可能性

ㅇ 反이라크측으로서는 軍事力 및 經濟 봉쇄에 의한 壓力을 加重하면서 다음과 같은 與件을 利用, 長期的, 政治的 解決 努力할 것임.

- 對이락 經濟制裁 効果 最小 3-6個月後 期待
- 費用의 友邦國과의 分擔으로 財政 負擔 輕減
- 사우디를 위시한 GCC國家 및 穩健 아랍國家들과의 關係를 深化시킴으로써 中東에서의 影響力 增大
- 高油價로 인한 經濟的 壓迫은 있지만, 美國의 世界 經濟上 相對的 影響力 強化 機會 增大
- 美國 主導로 世界 主要國家가 支持, 同參하는 새로운 世界秩序 形成, 固着化
- 窮極的으로 이라크의 讓步에 의한 政治的 解決 可能性이 상당히 많음.

나. 長期的 展望

ㅇ 결국에는 이라크의 쿠웨이트 永久合併은 國際 輿論과 反對 勢力에 의해 實現 不能

4

0065

o 平和的 解決:

- 經濟制裁와 軍事的 外交的 壓迫을 持續的으로 加重시켜 이라크의 立場이 弱化된 時点에서 事實上의 原狀回復이라는 反이라크側의 要求 條件 受諾線에서 妥結 可能性 큼.
- 但, 反이라크側의 團合된 勢力이 充分치 못하는 境遇에는 이락側의 要求를 一部 受容하는 妥協도 可能視됨.

o 軍事的 解決 可能性

- 長期的으로는 反이락軍이 이락軍에 壓倒的 優位에 서면서 방대한 軍費는 1991年末까지 일단 確保되고 있으므로, 이라크側이 平和的 解決에 不應할 境遇, 反이락측은 來年後半傾에 軍事的 方法으로 目標達成 試圖 可能性이 있음.

II. 我国의 対応策에 関한 몇가지 意見 提示

1. 原則 固守와 올바른 大局 判断

o 國際法, UN憲章 및 人道主義 違反에 대한 原則 固守와, 美國 中心의 壓倒的 對이락 優位에 비추어 이락側이 勝利하거나 現狀을 固定化 할수 없다는 確固한 大勢觀에 基하여 我國의 立場과 政策을 定立해 나가야 함.

o 이러한 原則과 大勢觀에 立脚, 一時的. 副次的 犧牲에는 毅然히 對處

0066

2. 制裁 参与와 責任 分担 問題

가. 原 則

ㅇ UN과의 特殊 關係 및 傳統的 韓.美 友好 關係 勘案, UN決議와 美側 要請을 積極 受容

- 우리 經濟와 安保 狀況에 비추어 能力 範圍内에서 可能한 最大한 支援
- 이라크側이 이길수 없다는 大勢觀에 立脚, 보다 確固한 姿勢로 우리의 立場을 定立 表明, 施行해감.

나. 時期 및 方法의 問題

ㅇ 美側 要請이 短期的으로는 美中間選擧와 깊은 關聯이 있다는 点을 認識, 配慮

- 選擧前 汎世界的 同參性을 誇示하는데 我國의 先導的 役割 期待에 副應
- 迅速한 軍事 配置와 輸送等 實質的 必要性에 協調
- 時期的 迅速性으로 物量의 制限性을 補完토록 함. 특히 失期로 인한 二重的 失望感을 주지않토록 配慮
- 我國이 보다더 能動的.積極的 姿勢로 對處

다. 責任 分擔의 代償 積極的 追求

ㅇ 中東 및 餘他 建設市場 我國 參與 機會 提供 促求 (사우디 COE 工事와 年間 5,000億弗의 日本 建設市場等)

0067

ㅇ 美國 與論 및 議會内 親韓 무드 造成

ㅇ 韓. 美 安保 體制 공고화

라. 美側 期待와 我國의 與論間隔 縮小 努力

ㅇ 主要紙 社說의 主要論旨 考慮
- 支援 同參 原則은 妥當
- 美 壓力下에 過分한 分擔 不可
- 公明正大한 分擔交涉, 뒷거래 納得 못함.

ㅇ 對美 交涉에 我國 與論을 活用

ㅇ 對國民 與論 對策 樹立 施行 時急

3. 이락 僑民 撤収 및 駐쿠웨이트, 이락 大使館 撤収 問題

가. 僑民 撤收

ㅇ 現況. 9.17 現在
이라크 186, 쿠웨이트 9: 合 195名 殘留
대부분 建設會社 所屬

ㅇ 이라크 建設工事와 유엔 制裁와의 關聯 問題
- 美政府, 9.13字 通報로 外國 業體의 이라크内 勞動써비스 提供이 유엔 安保理 661號 決議 違反으로 解釋, 엄격 規制 要請
- 이로서 이라크 쿠웨이트内 建設工事는 사실상 및 규범상 불가능

7

0068

o 殘留僑民 撤收 積極 促進

- 我國의 制裁 同參 積極化 措置에 따라 이라크의 對我國 僑民 大使館 態度 硬化 豫想

나. 駐이라크. 쿠웨이트 大使館 問題

o 이라크 當局의 駐쿠웨이트 大使 및 官員 出國 不許 措置에 대해 駐韓 이락 大使館에 抗議等

o 駐이라크 大使官員 縮小

o 殘餘 人員은 西方國 外交官과 行動을 같이한다는 原則下에 의연히 對處해 나감.

4. 我国 経済에 미치는 影響과 対応策

가. 現狀이 長期化하는 境遇, 原油價는 $25-30線이란 一般的 豫想에 따른 經濟 및 에너지 政策 樹立이 要請됨.

o 汎國民的 節約風潮 造成 機會로 活用

나. 長期的으로는 이라크보다는 그 以外의 아랍國과의 建設. 通商, 經濟協力 機會가 增大될 것이 豫想되므로, 특히 사우디. 이집트. 예멘. 터어키等과의 建設. 經濟協力 增進해 나감.

o 約 100億弗의 經濟支援이 이집트. 터어키 및 요르단에 集中

o 사우디 軍事 關聯 建設 景氣 豫想

0069

5. 페灣 事態가 가져오는 새로운 国際秩序에의 対応策

가. 美國의 役割 增大와 關係國과의 責任 分擔의 先例化 可能性

- ㅇ 駐韓 美軍 駐屯問題에 影響 檢討 必要

나. 美. 蘇間 協力, 補完 關係와 韓半島에의 影響

- 韓半島에 미치는 直接的 影響 綜合 檢討 必要

다. 아랍勢力 版圖 再編과 "페"灣 石油 價格, 分配 Mechanism의 變化 綿密檢討 對策樹立 必要

9

0070

添 附 資 料

1. "페"灣 事態가 我國 經濟에 미치는 影響

2. 多國籍軍에 軍事的 參加 現況

3. 經費 分擔 現況

4. 各國 最近 動向

5. 各國의 이라크-쿠웨이트 殘留 人員 現況

6. "페'灣 事態에 대한 아랍圈의 反應

0071

수신 : 장관(미북, 미안, 중근동) USW(F) - 2028
발신 : 주미대사
제목 : 걸프만사태(Burden Sharing)

Confrontation in the Gulf: Sharing the Burden

— 7안 —

U.S. Says Gulf Moves' Cost Will Far Exceed $25 Billion

By ANDREW ROSENTHAL
Special to The New York Times

KENNEBUNKPORT, Me., Aug. 31 — The worldwide burden-sharing program for the Persian Gulf operation will require tens of billions of dollars in financial aid to third-world countries, repayment for trade lost to the embargo against Iraq, donations of fuel to American military forces and other contributions, Administration officials said today.

The officials said the price tag cannot yet be estimated exactly. But they said the cost would significantly exceed estimates of $25 billion that were reported today. Much of the program remains to be negotiated by President Bush and Secretary of State James A. Baker 3d and Treasury Secretary Nicholas F. Brady, who plan missions abroad next week.

But officials said the United States expects, among other things, that the oil-producing nations will provide all the fuel for American military forces deployed in Saudi Arabia, that Japan will contribute significantly more than the $1.3 billion it has announced it will give to the program, and that Washington will have to pay a "sizable share" of the cost.

In the Red Sea today, the Pentagon said a United States Naval vessel stopped and boarded an Iraqi oil tanker for the first time since the United Nations authorized the use of the military to enforce the trade embargo on Iraq.

Iraqi Tanker Is Boarded

The guided-missile cruiser Biddle stopped the tanker at 8:36 A.M. Eastern time, found it to be empty and allowed it to proceed, the Navy said. The tanker's captain cooperated and no violence was reported, officials said.

A few countries, including Italy, Finland, Sweden and Greece, reported that a trickle of the foreign citizens held hostage in Iraq and Kuwait were being allowed to leave, or at least to make preparations for doing so.

But the Iraqi Government put new conditions on the departure of others in a group of 237 foreign women and children, including 14 Americans, that Iraq has said would be allowed to leave the country. Baghdad also announced that it had sent more foreign citizens to potential military targets across the country for use as shields against attack. More than two million foreigners were caught in Iraq and Kuwait when Iraq invaded its neighbor on Aug. 2.

The State Department spokeswoman, Margaret D. Tutwiler, said in Washington today that 75 Americans were missing and believed to be among those being used as human shields, including five who were captured ...

'Inhumane and Disgraceful'

Miss Tutwiler said that despite Iraqi promises to let women and children leave Iraq and Kuwait, the Baghdad Government was constantly revising its requirements for their departure.

"This emotional roller coaster is inhumane and disgraceful," she said.

In Kennebunkport, Mr. Bush's vacation home, the White House said today that the President had spoken to the leaders of France, Britain and Saudi Arabia as part of effort to coordinate the "burden sharing" program he announced on Thursday in Washington.

All three countries are expected to play a major role in the effort, which is intended to give financially strapped countries an incentive to adhere to the economic sanctions against Iraq and make it more difficult for President Saddam Hussein to simply hunker down in Kuwait in hopes that the embargo will slowly start to unravel.

The program has two essential elements, they said. One is to help pay for keeping scores of thousands of American soldiers in the Saudi desert, along with dozens of British, Canadian and French warships in the waters around the Arabian Peninsula. Saudi Arabia has been contributing aviation fuel, and the Saudis and other oil producers are eventually expected to provide all the fuel for the American military in the Persian Gulf, officials said.

The other element is to aid countries that are suffering financially from the economic sanctions because they are losing trade with Iraq, income associated with Iraqi oil exports, or the incomes of their citizens who normally work in Iraq. The officials said the first phase of the project will focus on Egypt, Jordan and Turkey, which the United States says have been hardest hit by the gulf crisis.

In the longer term, one official said, assistance will be arranged to another tier of countries, including India, Morocco, Bangladesh, the Philippines and countries in Eastern Europe.

"This crisis hasn't happened in a vacuum," an official said. "If you look at the efforts we've made recently to bring stability to Eastern Europe, we don't want that all to be undone because of what's happening in the Middle East."

A World Bank Objection

In most cases, aid — direct payments, loans, loan guarantees and other programs — will be provided without the requirements of economic revisions usually attached to loans to developing countries, officials said.

"Simply to insist on ideal economic reform policies in a very trying and difficult situation does not make good sense," an official said.

"To be blunt about it, we're trying to stabilize countries and it does not make a lot of sense to ask them to adopt economic policies that will destabilize them," he continued. "We're sensitive to the need for Egyptian economic reform, for example, but not at the price of political stability."

In Washington today, Reuters quoted Barber Conable, President of the World Bank, as expressing concern about the issue. Mr. Conable urged those nations taking part in the financial-aid program not to drop the usual conditions attached to the bank's lending programs.

Administration officials declined to give Washington's targets for contributions from individual countries, although they said a large percentage would come from oil-producing countries. Nations like Britain and France which are already contributing military forces to the region, also are expected to provide financial assistance under the program, officials said.

9.1. NYT

— 1 —

0072

7b3

Allies Split On Military Aid to Gulf

Economic Assistance Is Less Divisive Issue

By William Drozdiak
Washington Post Foreign Service

PARIS, Aug. 31—West Germany and other allies signaled their readiness today to help friendly countries hurt by the economic boycott of Iraq, but some leading European officials expressed skepticism that their governments would approve substantial contributions to pay for U.S. military forces in the Persian Gulf and Saudi Arabia.

Italian Foreign Minister Gianni de Michelis said that West European countries should "dig into our purses" to assist nations such as Turkey, Jordan and Egypt that are suffering from the global ban on trade with Iraq. However, de Michelis said in Rome, "I doubt that it would be easy to bring to the various parliaments a request to saddle themselves with, let's say, 10 or 20 percent of the U.S. military bill."

De Michelis said it was important for wealthy countries to come up with money to alleviate the damage inflicted on Iraq's poor neighbors and trading partners "to sustain the economic-financial choice, along with the military choice that directly involves the United States and many other countries."

President Bush's appeal Thursday for prosperous countries in Western Europe and in Asia to subsidize the enforcement of United Nations sanctions against Iraq seems destined to ignite a potentially explosive debate among America's allies about an equitable distribution of security responsibilities.

Only France and Britain have dispatched sizable contingents of armed forces to the gulf to demonstrate Europe's military commitment to back up the embargo that was set in place after Iraq's Aug. 2 invasion of Kuwait. Other countries, such as Greece, Belgium and the Netherlands, have sent token naval vessels aimed more at providing a symbol of commitment to the embargo than at exercising a meaningful military role.

The divided European response evoked sharp criticism Thursday from British Prime Minister Margaret Thatcher, who told a conference of conservative political parties meeting in Helsinki that the allies cannot "expect the U.S. to go on bearing major military and defense burdens worldwide, acting in effect as the world's policeman."

De Michelis today denounced Thatcher's remarks as "unjustified and ungenerous." Speaking on behalf of the 12 members of the European Community, whose presidency Italy holds until the end of this year, the Italian foreign minister insisted that European countries had responded "effectively and with clarity of intentions and decisions" in the gulf crisis.

But other European political leaders expressed agreement with Thatcher. Denmark's Ulf Elleman Jensen said Thatcher was correct in her assessment. He called on small nations of the world each to dispatch one warship to the gulf as a symbol of their commitment to support sanctions against Iraq.

The primary targets of Bush and Thatcher, in their quest for a bolder and more generous commitment by the allies in the gulf, are the governments in Tokyo and Bonn. Those two nations, citing postwar restrictions on their countries not to engage in military conflicts beyond the need for self-preservation, have been reluctant to become militarily involved in the gulf conflict.

As the two biggest economic powers with no forces in the gulf, Japan and Germany are increasingly regarded by commentators in Britain and France as profiting from their low military profile in order to concentrate on their economic well-being. East and West Germany's recent decision to restrict the size of a united Germany's armed forces to 370,000 was made to reassure its neighbors and allies, which fear a return to the type of German militarism that led the country into two world wars during the first half of the century. Now, however, the decision to limit armed forces is being cited not as proof of a pacifist mentality, but as evidence of a mercantile mentality.

Tokyo announced Thursday that it would provide $1 billion worth of food, water and medical supplies to forces serving in the gulf. Bonn declared today that it would contribute an unspecified amount of financial and material aid in response to Bush's call to share the cost of the embargo.

But those promises, according to some European diplomats, may not be sufficient to satisfy Washington. Those diplomats believe that Washington will seek greater involvement, including military commitments, from both countries.

The ruling parties in Japan and Germany have often cited legal inhibitions barring them from taking any role in the multinational force in the gulf. They also seem anxious about the political risks of leading a parliamentary drive to alter their constitutions to permit deployment of military force abroad.

The Japanese government, having emerged from a bruising election campaign with a narrow victory several months ago, appears reluctant to gamble its slender parliamentary majority by buckling to American and Western pressure and by opening an emotional reassessment of Japan's future military role in the world.

In Bonn, where the process of German unification has overshadowed gulf developments, the task of changing the constitution and setting conditions for German military involvement abroad is looming as the first great political debate once Germany is formally united in early October.

But the heat of political campaigning prior to all-German elections on Dec. 2 is likely to put off any major changes in the country's constitution until a new parliament is seated early next year.

0073

9.1. W.P.

2038 — 0 —

U.S. READY TO SEND ISRAELIS NEW ARMS AS SIGNAL TO IRAQ

UP TO $1 BILLION

Weapons Could Include F-16 Planes, Missiles and M-60 Tanks

By ERIC SCHMITT
Special to The New York Times

WASHINGTON, Aug. 31 — The Bush Administration is preparing to transfer as much as $1 billion worth of advanced weapons to Israel to buttress Israeli defenses against Iraq and offset recent arms sales to Saudi Arabia, Administration officials said today.

Officials said the promise of advanced weaponry to Israel is intended to send a clear signal to President Saddam Hussein of Iraq that the United States intends to stand by its main Middle East ally.

Israel, while keeping a low profile in the Persian Gulf crisis, has placed its military on heightened alert. Israeli and American officials have warned that Iraq, in an effort to shatter Arab opposition to the invasion of Kuwait, might try to draw Israel into the Middle East conflict either by direct missile attack against Israel or by moving military forces into Jordan.

From Stockpiles in Europe

American and Israeli officials are still negotiating final details of the arms package, which could include the delivery of F-15 and F-16 fighter planes, Patriot ground-to-air missiles that can be used to intercept incoming missiles, M-60 battle tanks and Apache tank-killing helicopters, largely from United States stockpiles in Europe.

The idea for additional aid originated with the Israelis, and has been approved in principle by the Defense Department and top national security officials at the White House, Administration officials said. The details and timing of arms deliveries remain to be worked out, with both sides hoping to begin the transfer of some weapons as soon as possible.

The transfer of weapons, through either leases or sales, would come on top of $1.8 billion in American military assistance to Israel planned for this year before the Persian Gulf crisis developed.

Concern About Mideast Balance

Besides Israeli concerns about an Iraqi attack, Israel and its American supporters have expressed longer-term concerns about the need to offset new arms sales to Saudi Arabia, Egypt and other Arab countries that may alter the military balance in the Middle East.

Administration officials in recent days have reaffirmed to leaders of American Jewish groups and members of Congress the longstanding American commitment to maintain Israel's military advantage in the Middle East.

Defense Secretary Dick Cheney met

9.1. NYT (1)

0074

— 2 —

U.S. Is Ready to Send New Arms To the Israelis as a Signal to Iraq

Continued From Page 1

last week with leaders of Jewish groups, and this week a delegation of Israeli military officials, led by David Ivry, the director general of the Israeli Defense Ministry, traveled to Washington to discuss additional American military aid with the State Department and Defense Department.

Washington's relations with Jerusalem have been relatively smooth during the gulf crisis, American and Israeli officials say. Israel has been re-

Israel and its backers seek to preserve the Mideast balance.

sponsive to American requests that it not become directly involved in the conflict, or take any pre-emptive action against Iraq. Washington, in turn, made clear that it was willing to consider added military aid to Israel.

The crisis has deflected attention from the impasse that had been developing between the Administration and Jerusalem over the Israeli Government's reluctance to open a dialogue with the Palestinians on the basis of a compromise formula proposed last spring by Secretary of State James A. Baker 3d.

To bolster Saudi Arabia against a possible attack from Iraq, the Administration announced this week that it would make an emergency sale of $2.2 billion worth of weapons to Riyadh, including 24 F-15 fighter planes, 150 M-60 tanks and 200 Stinger anti-aircraft missiles. In addition, Pentagon officials said the United States would probably sell the Saudis another 24 F-15's early next year.

"The White House and State Department called to say they recognized an imbalance was occurring and that some form of additional weaponry for Israel would be found to remedy that," said Senator Rudy Boschwitz, Republican of Minnesota.

One leader of an American Jewish group, who spoke on the condition of anonymity, said: "Arms to the Saudis pose a real dilemma for the Jewish community. On the one hand Saudi Arabia has legitimate defense needs right now. But this latest package constitutes a clear threat to Israel in the long run. No one knows what will happen to Saudi Arabia in the future. Middle East politics is made up of shifting alliances."

Several hurdles must still be cleared to complete the proposed arms deal. One problem is matching the list of weapons that Israel wants with what the United States can afford to give up.

Soviet Talks May Free Tanks

The Pentagon, for example, expects to have surplus M-60 tanks once arms control talks with the Soviet Union are concluded. The available tanks, however, are an older version of the model the Israelis would like, and would not be available for several months.

In addition, the United States has already earmarked surplus F-15's and F-16's to other nations, including Morocco and the Philippines, as well to reserve units in the United States.

(2) 0075

2078 — 4 —

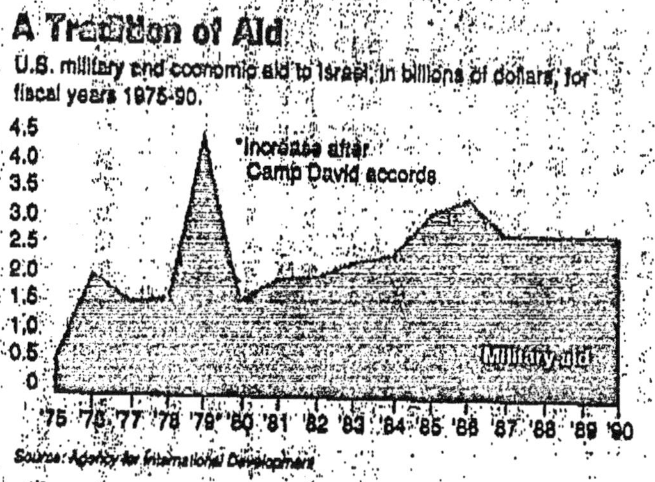

The New York Times

Israel's principal requests include Patriot ground-to-air missiles to counter enemy missiles, and top-of-the-line fighter planes to protect Israel in a multi-front air attack.

Financial terms are also under discussion. Israel cannot afford to pay for the weapons, and the United States is facing its own budget constraints, worsened by the costs of the Persian Gulf military operation, now estimated at $2.5 billion.

Looking at '1,001 Ways'

As a result, "people are looking at 1,001 ways to solve the financing problem," an official said.

The options under study include leasing arms to Israel and positioning American planes and tanks at Israeli bases, transferring ownership in an emergency. An official said the United States might also give or sell at discount general military supplies or ammunition, thus freeing money that the Israelis could spend on weapons.

Creative financing is not new in American military aid to Israel. In the 1970's, the United States lent hundreds of millions of dollars to Israel on favorable terms. The terms were so favorable, said Richard Grimmett, a military analyst with the Congressional Research Service, that many of the loans were completely forgiven.

In the 1980's, the United States has given Israel military assistance with no strings attached. Since 1986, Congress has fixed military aid to Israel, the single largest recipient of American foreign aid, at $1.8 billion.

(3)

0076

-5-

Bush to Forgive $7.1 Billion Egypt Owes for Military Aid

By Patrick E. Tyler
Washington Post Staff Writer

President Bush has decided to forgive Egypt's $7.1 billion military debt to the United States in recognition of Cairo's critical role in supporting the United Nations embargo against Iraq and the massive U.S. military deployment to the Arabian peninsula, administration officials said yesterday.

At the same time, the administration is sending a special envoy, probably deputy national security adviser Robert M. Gates, to tell Jordan's King Hussein that he cannot expect urgent economic assistance from the international community without publicly stating his support for the embargo against Iraq and demonstrating that support by cutting off the remaining traffic to Iraq through Jordan, including food shipments from Jordanian farmers.

These two decisions follow Bush's announcement Thursday that he is launching an international economic plan to pool billions of dollars in donor funds from wealthy nations to help those nations facing severe economic hardship by complying with the embargo.

Jordanian officials expected Hussein to strongly resist a U.S. demand to cut food shipments to Iraq. The king and his advisers in Amman are said to believe that blockading food shipments to Baghdad may be regarded by Iraqi President Saddam Hussein as an act of war.

Another Jordanian concern is the severe domestic impact of a hard break with Saddam. Jordan's farmers have an estimated $200 million in contractual commitments to deliver produce to Iraq in the next few weeks, knowledgeable sources said

See AID, A20, Col. 1

AID, From A1

"They are fearing rot and riot from the farmers if this crop is not delivered," one Jordan expert said.

Some of Jordan's supporters in Washington are suggesting the European Community buy Jordan's crop to forestall a crisis.

The Egyptian debt decision, which requires congressional approval, follows a debate that began during the Reagan administration over whether to forgive some or all of the military debt to key regional allies such as Israel, Egypt, Pakistan and Turkey.

Both the State and Defense departments recommended that Egypt's debt be forgiven, according to U.S. and Arab officials. Bush approved it after a National Security Council meeting Wednesday.

"There were concerns about how this would impact on a number of other countries and that forgiveness would be contagious," one official said. Bush's decision was described as narrowly focused on Egypt.

Egypt's ambassador to Washington, Abdel Raouf Reedy, met yesterday with Robert M. Kimmitt, undersecretary of state for political affairs. Sources said that Kimmitt did not convey Bush's decision but indicated to Reedy that Egypt was about to get good news.

Since Iraq's Aug. 2 invasion of Kuwait, Egypt has extended to the United States overflight rights, staging and transit rights from

9. 1. WP 0077

-028- 6 -

Egyptian air bases and has smoothed the passage of dozens of U.S. warships through the Suez Canal. Egypt refused, however, to base U.S. B-52 bombers, which might be used in strikes against Iraq, officials said.

"They are not going to be puppets, they are going to be partners and there are limits to what we can ask them to do," said one former U.S. official with experience in Cairo.

Politically, Egyptian President Hosni Mubarak led the Arab moderates through a stormy Arab League summit meeting, which overcame Iraqi objections and Jordanian equivocation to reach a resolution condemning Iraq's invasion and calling for a joint Arab military force to defend Saudi Arabia.

"We need to demonstrate to the key Arab party that has stood with us in this crisis that there are benefits to them for staying with us because we are going to be in this for a while," said William B. Quandt, a Middle East scholar who worked on U.S.-Egyptian relations in the Carter administration.

He said Egypt's role also would be crucial in the "post-crisis diplomacy" that seeks to put the Middle East back together after the deep split induced by Iraqi influence over its neighbors and Iraqi intimidation.

Officials from the Treasury Department and Office of Management and Budget expressed concerns about the budget impact of the Egyptian debt decision and the longstanding congressional demand that Egypt undertake tough economic reforms. But Bush, in making the decision, was said to have focused on Egypt's pivotal role in moderate Arab diplomacy throughout the crisis, which justified a "very special" exception to the administration's unwillingness to forgive such debts.

Also yesterday, administration officials said Bush has told his senior advisers that he intends to break the impasse over the deployment of 30,000 additional Egyptian troops to stand with U.S. and other Arab and multinational forces defending Saudi Arabia. White House and Pentagon officials said Egypt has mobilized the two divisions and is ready to send them as soon as "third country" transport can be arranged. The impasse arose when Mubarak and Saudi Arabia's King Fahd could not agree on whether the Saudis had accepted Egypt's offer of two mechanized and armored divisions.

The deployment of a large force of Egyptian troops would help blunt criticism from Congress that the U.S. military is carrying the greatest burden in defending Saudi Arabia. As many as 150,000 U.S. troops will be in the Persian Gulf region by the end of September, while the largest Arab contingent to reach the kingdom so far has been about 5,000 troops.

Morocco, Syria, Pakistan and Bangladesh have committed what some members of Congress have called "token" forces.

Egyptian officials were somewhat embarrassed by criticism from Senate Armed Services Committee Chairman Sam Nunn (D-Ga.) that they needed to send more troops to Saudi Arabia when Mubarak had been offering to do so for weeks, according to Arab diplomats.

"The Egyptians are going in big," one knowledgeable source said. "They are going in with two divisions and everybody has been told, and the Saudis are about to be told," a Pentagon official added.

Bush yesterday spent a relatively quiet day monitoring developments at his summer home in Kennebunkport, Maine, as he began the long Labor Day weekend with a picnic for the visiting press corps.

Bush continued his telephone diplomacy, with calls to British Prime Minister Margaret Thatcher, French President Francois Mitterrand and Saudi Arabia's Fahd to discuss his economic plan.

Secretary of State James A. Baker III and Treasury Secretary Nicholas F. Brady prepared to leave next week for Europe, the Middle East and Asia to round up financial aid to offset U.S. military costs and help nations affected by the crisis.

Staff writer Dan Balz contributed to this report from Kennebunkport.

0078

이라크-쿠웨이트 事態의 展望

1990. 9. 18.

外　　務　　部

0079

I. "페"灣 事態의 展望

1. 短期的 展望(11. 6 美中間 選擧以前)

가. 美國은 이라크의 쿠웨이트 無條件 撤收等 目標를 可及的 中間選擧以前에 達成코저 努力中

나. 한편 이라크는 쿠 併合을 旣定事實化,

금번 事態를 "對美 聖戰"이라는 이락 中心의 回敎圈國家 對 美國間 對決 方向으로 몰고가려함.

다. 中間選擧前

- 美國은 특히 軍事的 壓力을 高度로 加速化할 것임.
- 만약 이라크側의 挑發이나 制裁에 抵抗하는 行爲가 있을시는 相應하는 軍事的 應懲도 있을 수 있음.
- 또 이라크의 軍事的 衝突 回避 戰略에 대하여는 美軍等에 의한 攻擊的 防禦를 強化하므로서 이락을 軍事的 守勢로 몰고갈 可能性 큼.

ㅇ 時期的으로는, 美軍等 多國籍軍의 配置가 完了되고, 美國 選擧 直前인 10月 中下旬이 軍事的 緊張이 高潮되는 時期로 豫想됨.

라. 만약 軍事的 壓迫戰略이 所期의 實效를 거두지 못하는 경우,

ㅇ 美國은 世界 各國의 同參과 友邦의 支援을 最大한 廣範圍하게 確保하므로서 이락의 "對美 聖戰" 戰略을 분쇄하고 "對이락 汎世界的 制裁"를 美國 主導下에 成功的으로 遂行한다는 可視的 成果를 美國 選擧民과 世界에 誇示코자 할 것임.

2. 中期的 展望(앞으로 6個月間)

가. 軍事 衝突 可能性

ㅇ 現 段階에서 戰爭 발발시 이라크의 窮極的인 敗北는 確實함으로, 이라크는 쿠웨이트의 合倂 공고화等 現狀維持에 主力하고 軍事的 挑發은 않을 것임.

ㅇ 따라서 戰爭이 있다면 美國側에서 始作한다고 보아야 하는바, 美 中間選擧以前의 軍事的 緊張高潮를 무사히 넘기는 境遇에는, 美側에 의한 戰爭은 美國側에 다음과 같은 不利点이 있어 그 可能性은 크지 않음.

- 人質의 犧牲을 包含한 막대한 人命 損失
- 油田 破壞等 世界經濟 困難
- 이라크의 이스라엘 攻擊等 擴戰 可能性
- 蘇聯, EC, 日本, 아랍圈等 世界輿論 不利
- 短期的, 깨끗한 勝利 期待 難望
  . 美國內 輿論 不利, 美國의 威信 損傷
- 事態 解決後 大規模 軍事力의 中東駐屯 名分 弱化

나. 平和的 解決 可能性

ㅇ 早期 解決을 위하여는 美國, 유엔等 反 이라크側이 要求하는 이라크軍의 쿠웨이트 撤收가 必須的 要件임

ㅇ 한편 이라크側은 후세인이 執權하는한 代償이나 名分이 없는 撤軍은 不可能視됨.

ㅇ 따라서 早期 解決을 위하여는 쿠데타等 이라크 內部의 變動이나, 이라크 撤軍의 名分을 살리는 調整이 있어야 하나, 두가지 可能性 모두 적음

0082

3. 長期的 展望(1991年末까지)

가. 現狀의 長期化 可能性

ㅇ 反이라크측으로서는 軍事力 및 經濟 봉쇄에 의한 壓力을 加重하면서 다음과 같은 與件을 利用, 長期的, 政治的 解決 努力할 것임.

- 對이락 經濟制裁 効果 最小 3-6個月後 期待
- 費用의 友邦國과의 分擔으로 財政 負擔 輕減
- 사우디를 위시한 GCC國家 및 穩健 아랍國家들과의 關係를 深化시킴으로써 中東에서의 影響力 增大
- 高油價로 인한 經濟的 壓迫은 있지만, 美國의 世界 經濟上 相對的 影響力 強化 機會 增大
- 美國 主導로 世界 主要國家가 支持, 同參하는 새로운 世界秩序 形成, 固着化
- 窮極的으로 이라크의 讓步에 의한 政治的 解決 可能性이 상당히 많음.

나. 長期的 展望

ㅇ 결국에는 이라크의 쿠웨이트 永久合併은 國際 輿論과 反對 勢力에 의해 實現 不能

0083

4

ㅇ 平和的 解決:

- 經濟制裁와 軍事的 外交的 壓迫을 持續的으로 加重시켜 이라크의 立場이 弱化된 時点에서 事實上의 原狀回復이라는 反이라크側의 要求 條件 受諾線에서 妥結 可能性 큼.
- 但, 反이라크側의 團合된 勢力이 充分치 못하는 境遇에는 이락側의 要求를 一部 受容하는 妥協도 可能視됨.

ㅇ 軍事的 解決 可能性

- 長期的으로는 反이락軍이 이락軍에 壓倒的 優位에 서면서 방대한 軍費는 1991年末까지를 目標로 調達하고 있으므로, 이라크側이 平和的 解決에 不應할 境遇, 反이락측은 來年中에 軍事的 方法으로 目標達成 試圖 可能性이 있음.

II. 我国의 対応策에 関한 몇가지 意見 提示

1. 原則 固守와 올바른 大局 判断

ㅇ 國際法, UN憲章 및 人道主義 原則 固守와, 美國 中心의 壓倒的 對이락 優位에 비추어 이락側이 勝利하거나 現狀을 固定化 할수 없다는 確固한 大勢觀에 基하여 我國의 立場과 政策을 定立해 나가야 함.

ㅇ 이러한 原則과 大勢觀에 立脚, 一時的. 副次的 犧牲에는 毅然히 對處

0084

2. 制裁 参与와 責任 分担 問題

가. 原 則

ㅇ UN과의 特殊 關係 및 傳統的 韓.美 友好 關係 勘案, UN決議와 美側 要請을 積極 受容

- 우리 經濟와 安保 狀況에 비추어 能力 範圍內에서 可能한 最大한 支援
- 이라크側이 이길수 없다는 大勢觀에 立脚, 보다 確固한 姿勢로 우리의 立場을 定立 表明, 施行해감.

나. 時期 및 方法의 問題

ㅇ 美側 要請이 短期的으로는 美中間選擧와 깊은 關聯이 있다는 点을 認識, 配慮

- 選擧前 汎世界的 同參性을 誇示하는데 我國의 先導的 役割 期待에 副應
- 迅速한 軍事 配置와 輸送等 實質的 必要性에 協調
- 時期的 迅速性으로 物量의 制限性을 補完토록 함. 특히 失期로 인한 二重的 失望感을 주지않토록 配慮
- 我國이 보다더 能動的. 積極的 姿勢로 對處

다. 責任 分擔의 代償 積極的 追求

ㅇ 中東 및 餘他 建設市場 我國 參與 機會 提供 促求 (사우디 COE 工事와 年間 5,000億弗의 日本 建設市場等)

0085

ㅇ 美國 輿論 및 議會內 親韓 무드 造成

ㅇ 韓.美 安保 體制 공고화

라. 美側 期待와 我國의 輿論間隔 縮小 努力

ㅇ 主要紙 社說의 主要論旨 考慮
- 支援 同參 原則은 妥當
- 美 壓力下에 過分한 分擔 不可
- 公明正大한 分擔交涉, 뒷거래 納得 못함.

ㅇ 對美 交涉에 我國 輿論을 活用

ㅇ 對國民 輿論 對策 樹立 施行 時急

3. 이락 僑民 撤收 및 駐쿠웨이트, 이락 大使館 撤收 問題

가. 僑民 撤收

ㅇ 現況. 9.17 現在
이라크 209, 쿠웨이트 9: 合 218名 殘留
대부분 建設會社 所屬

ㅇ 이라크 建設工事와 유엔 制裁와의 關聯 問題
- 美政府, 9.13字 通報로 外國 業體의 이라크內 勞動써비스 提供이 유엔 安保理 661號 決議 違反으로 解釋, 엄격 規制 要請
- 이로서 이라크 쿠웨이트內 建設工事는 사실상 및 규범상 불가능

0086

o 殘留僑民 撤收 積極 促進

- 我國의 制裁 同參 積極化 措置에 따라 이라크의 對我國 僑民 大使館 態度 硬化 豫想

나. 駐이라크. 쿠웨이트 大使館 問題

o 이라크 當局의 駐쿠웨이트 大使 및 館員 出國 不許 措置에 대해 駐韓 이락 大使館에 抗議等

o 駐이라크 大使館員 縮小

o 殘餘 人員은 西方國 外交官과 行動을 같이한다는 原則下에 의연히 對處해 나감.

4. 我国 経済에 미치는 影響과 対応策

가. 現狀이 長期化하는 境遇, 原油價는 $25-30 前後로 豫想됨.

o 이에 따른 政府의 經濟 및 에너지 政策의 修正. 樹立과 事態의 國民 經濟에 미치는 影響 減少를 위하여 汎國民的 節約風潮 造成이 要請됨.

나. 長期的으로는 이라크보다는 그 以外의 아랍國과의 建設. 通商, 經濟協力 機會가 增大될 것이 豫想되므로, 특히 사우디. 이집트. 예멘. 터어키等과의 建設. 經濟 協力 增進해 나감.

o 約 100億弗의 經濟支援이 이집트. 터어키 및 요르단에 集中

o 사우디 軍事 關聯 建設 景氣 豫想 0087

5. 페灣 事態가 가져올 새로운 国際秩序에의 対応策

가. 美國의 役割 增大와 關係國과의 責任 分擔의 先例化 可能性

ㅇ 駐韓 美軍 駐屯問題에 影響 檢討 必要

나. 美. 蘇間 協力, 補完 關係와 韓半島에의 影響

- 韓半島에 미치는 直接的 影響 綜合 檢討 必要

다. 아랍勢力 版圖 再編과 "페"灣 石油 價格, 分配 Mechanism의 變化 綿密檢討 對策樹立 必要

0088

添 附 資 料

1. "페"灣 事態가 我國 經濟에 미치는 影響

2. 多國籍軍에 軍事的 參加 現況

3. 經費 分擔 現況

4. 各國 最近 動向

5. 各國의 이라크-쿠웨이트 殘留 人員 現況

6. "페'灣 事態에 대한 아랍圈의 反應

0089

添附 1

페灣 사태가 我國 經濟에 미치는 影響

1. 石油市場 動向 및 展望

가. 動向

o 國際原油價, 배럴당 25불이상 수준에서 騰落 거듭

- 現物市場 動向 (Dubai유, $/B)

· 17.20(7.31)→ 25.40(8.7)→31.75(8.22)→ 27.20(8.27)→ 24.75(8.29)→ 28.23(9.6)→27.03(9.10)→ 28.65(9.14)

- 油價上昇原因

· 사우디등의 增産실시 불구, 原油供給 부족 지속 (3/4분기1.2백만D/D, 4/4분기 1.9백만 B/D 不足 예상)

· 사태해결에 대한 전망 不透明 및 冬節期 需要增加 豫想등에 따른 心理的 요인 및 사재기 현상등 작용

o 石油製品의 경우, 페灣 긴장에 따른 軍事用 需要增加와 각국의 輸出減少로 原油에 비해 物量不足 더욱 심각하며 價格上昇幅도 큼

- 燈油의 경우 25.20/B(7.31) 에서 $44.25/B (9.6)로 상승

나. 國際 原油價 展望 ('90)

o 현재의 武力對峙 상태 지속 경우, 國際原油價는 $25-30 사이에서 騰落 持續 展望

o 早期平和的 해결 경우, $21-24/B 전망

o 戰爭勃發경우, 戰爭의 持續期間 및 사우디등 관련국 原油生産施設의 破壞 정도등에 따라 $30-$50/B 油價暴騰 가능

0090

2. 我國經濟에 대한 影響

가. 油價上昇의 波及 効果

o 에너지 海外依存度가 심화 추세에 있고, 石油의 中東依存度가 높음

- 에너지 海外依存度 : 76.2%('85)→85.5%('89)

- 中東石油導入比重 : 57.0%('85)→72.1%('89)

o 産業構造的으로 에너지 節約에 한계

- 鐵鋼, 石油化學, 시멘트등 에너지 多消費 業種이 주요산업으로 成長

o 波及 効果

	국제원유가25$/B 기준	국제원유가30$/B 기준	자료 출처
경제 성장율 하락효과('90)	1.4%	2.0%	에너지 경제연구원
도매물가 상승 효과	3.70%	5.88%	경기원
소비자 물가 상승 효과	0.59%	0.93%	경기원
원유도입 추가 부담(90.9-12)	9 억불	14 억불	동자부

※ 90 上半期 16.5$/B 기준 대비임

※ 90 原油導入計劃 : 3.14억 배럴

나. 이라크·쿠웨이트 工事 管理 問題

o 發注處 허가없이 현장 철수시 契約違反으로 發注處로부터 債權 회수 불능등 문제 발생 우려

※ 쿠웨이트경우, 發注處의 향후 所屬不明으로 債權및 資産 손실회 우려

o 業體 追加 부담 費用 발생

- 금번사태로 工事代金 및 未收金 受領遲延에 따른 金融費用과 人力 撤收에 따른 추가 負擔 발생

- 또한 工事中斷에 따른 裝備資材등 資産의 훼손, 流失이 불가피

0091

o 債權등 資産 및 債務現況

- 債權 : 992백만불 (이라크 920, 쿠웨이트 72백만불)
  - 未收金67, 留保金168, 어음598, 其他159백만불
- 資産 : 68백만불 (이라크49, 쿠웨이트 19백만불)
  - 資材22, 裝備21, 其他 25백만불
- 債務 : 601백만불 (이라크484, 쿠웨이트117백만불)
  - 各種保證281, 現地金融282, 외상매입 38백만불

o 施工殘額 : 837백만불 (이라크755, 쿠웨이트82백만불)

다. 輸出減少('90) : 對 이라크·쿠웨이트 輸出中斷 포함, 페灣 긴장으로
對 中東地域 직접 輸出 2-3억불 減少 예상

0092

添附 2

多國籍軍에 軍事的 參加 現況

(派兵 決定 包含)

90. 9. 17.

國家 軍別	總兵力數	艦艇	航空機
北美 (2)			
미국	155,000	48 척	150 대
카나다	450	3 척	
歐洲 (11)			
영국	6.000	7 척	40 대
불란서	13,000	14 척	100 대
서독		5 척	
이태리		5 척	
화란		2 척	
스페인		3 척	
벨기에		3 척	
희랍		1 척	
폴부갈		1 척	
터키	自國內기지 使用許容	艦艇 派遣 檢討中	
덴마크		民間 輸送線	
中東 (8)			
이집트	19,000		
모로코	1,200		
시리아	15,000		
GCC 5개국	10,000		
亞洲 (5)			
호주		3 척	
일본		民間 輸送線	民間 輸送機
방글라데쉬	5,000(豫定)		
파키스탄	5,000		
인니	地上軍 派兵 用意 表明		
計 (26個國)	229,650	95 척	290 대

※ 蘇聯, 艦艇 2척 派遣

0093

첨부 3

經 費 分 擔 現 況

1. 日本, 40억불

   o 軍費分擔 : 20억불

   o 經濟援助 : 20억불

     . 이집트, 요르단, 터키등 戰線國家에 90년중 6억불 援助(30년 만기, 연리 1%의 차관 형식)

2. 서독, 20억불

   o 軍費分擔 : 10억불 (군사 장비 지원)

   o 經濟援助 : 10억불

     . 2.6 억불 經濟制裁 被害國 援助 基金에 이미 寄與

     . 兩者關係 次元의 戰線國家 經濟 援助

       이집트 : 6.09 억불

       요르단 : 2억불

       터 키 : 68 백만불

   ※ 1.25억불 상당 物品 支援, 7.75억불 開發 援助

3. 이태리, 1.45억불

4. 카나다, 7,500만 카나다불 (250만 카불 기지원)

5. GCC 국가, 120억불

   o 사우디 : 60억불

   o 쿠웨이트 亡命政府 : 40억불

   o UAE등 : 20억불

6. 기타

   o EC, 이집트, 요르단, 터키등 戰線國家에 20억불 經濟 援助 提供 決定

   o 대만, 2-3억불 分擔 約束設

   o 韓國, 0.5-1억불 支援 檢討(9.16. AFP 민자당 소식통 인용 보도)

0094

添附 4

各國最近動向

1990.9.17.

區分	主要動向	備考
1. 이라크	o 經濟 封鎖 打開 努力 - 이란과 外交關係 再開 合議 (9.10) - 라마단 副總理 중국 訪問 (9.6) - 第3世界에 原油 無料 供給 提議 (9.10) o 미국 및 多國籍軍에 對抗 聖戰 促求 o 對西方 宥和 제스처 - 쿠웨이트 殘留 外國 公館員 强制 退去 留保 - 西方 抑留 兒女子 航空機便 出國 許容 o 對 미군 테러 攻擊 可能性 示唆 (9.13) o 쿠웨이트내 게릴라 및 外國人 索出活動 强化 o 팔레스타인人 大學 쿠웨이트 移住 o 쿠웨이트 駐在 불란서, 카나다, 벨기에, 화란등 西方 4個國 公館, 官邸 亂入 (9.13-14, 이라크정부 공식 부인) o 빵, 밀가루 配給制 實施(9.15) - 一日 1人當 빵3個 또는 每月 밀가루 6kg - 內國人, 外國人, 外交官에 대해 同一하게 適用	 9.14. 現在 約 1,150여명

0095

구 분	주 요 동 향	비 고
2. 미 국	o 對 이라크 封鎖 强化 - 미 艦艇, 페르시아만 商船 檢問 檢索 强化	
	o NATO 會員國에 派兵 要請 (9.11)	영, 불外 微溫的 反應
	o 特使 2개반 派遣(국무장관-중동, 재무장관-아주,구주) - 友邦諸國에 軍費 分擔 要請 - 友邦 90년중 200억불 經費 分擔 確約	
	o 長期戰 對應 態勢 - 豫算 뒷받침등 議會 支援 要請 (9.12. 부쉬 대통령 의회 연설)	
	o 議會, 對 이라크 制裁 法案 可決 (9.13)	
	o 180억불 상당 武器 對사우디 販賣 計劃 - F-15 24대, 아파치 헬기 48대, M-1A2 탱크 385대, 裝甲車 4-5백대, 其他 軍用 트럭 및 지프	
3. 소 련	o 中東平和 國際會議 提議 (9.4) - 쿠웨이트 問題, 中東問題 包括 論議 强調 - 쿠웨이트 占領 이라크군을 UN군으로, 사우디 駐屯 美軍을 아랍 多國籍軍으로 代替	
	o 對 이라크 撤軍 壓力 - UN 安保理 決議 移行 促求	
	o 事態 解決後 사우디 駐屯 美軍 撤收 主張 (9.10. 헬싱키 미.소 정상회담)	
	o 美側과 유엔 經濟制裁 效果가 未洽할 경우 追加 措置 合意 (9.10. 미.소 정상 회담)	

0096

구 분	주 요 동 향	비 고
4. 아 랍 권	o 후세인 요르단 國王, 아랍 및 歐洲 巡訪後 이라크 訪問 (9.6)	
	o 가다피 리비아 指導者, PLO 高位 關係者等 平和案 提示 (9.5) - 쿠웨이트 領土 一部 할양후 이라크군 撤收 - 多國籍軍 철수후 아랍 平和軍으로 代替 - 對 이라크 經濟 封鎖 解除	
	o 이집트, 兵力 1만5천명(기갑부대포함) 사우디에 增派 方針	駐 쿠웨이트 大使館 撤收
	o 아랍聯盟 13개국 外務長官 會談 開催 (9.6. 카이로) - 걸프事態의 平和的 解決 方案 摸索	親이라크 8個國 不參
	o 이란 指導者 하메네이, 걸프駐屯 美軍에 對抗 지하드 (성전) 제의 (9.12) - 聖地 美軍 駐屯 反對	
	o 사우디, 쿠웨이트 亡命政府, UAE등 GCC諸國 90년중 120억불 經費 分擔 約束	
	o 시리아, 기갑사단 (병력 1만명, 탱크 300대) 사우디 증파 용의 표명 (9.13. Baker 미국무장관 방문시)	
5. 기 타 E C	o 外相 會議 (9.7) - 터키, 요르단, 이집트에 1991년 20억불 經濟 援助 決議	分擔 提議 內容 . EC가 15% . 사우디, UAE등 65% . 일본, 여타국 20% 3개국 91년 손실 90억불 전망
	o EC-아랍 閣僚級 會談 開催 豫定 (10.6-7 베니스) - 反 이라크 아랍諸國 閣僚	
영 국	o 탱크부대 및 地上軍 派兵 決定 - 海.空軍의 追加 派兵 檢討	기갑여단(8,000여명, 탱크 120여대), 토네이도 전투기 15대

0097

구 분	주 요 동 향	비 고
불란서	o 駐 쿠웨이트 自國 大使官邸 侵入 관련 報復 措置 - 유엔 安保理 召集 要求 - 사우디 派兵(4,000명) 決定 - 駐불 이라크 武官 包含 26명 追放 - 이라크 外交官 파리시내 活動 制限	
이태리	o 自國 駐在 이라크 武官團 追放	
일 본	o 가지야마 日 法務長官 憲法 改正 檢討 言及 (9.13) - 自衛隊 海外 派兵이 可能토록 改正 o 40억불 經費分擔 決定 (군비분담 : 20억불, 경제원조 : 20억불) o 비전투 要員으로 構成된 "국연 협력대" 2,000여명 中東 派遣 檢討 示唆	
서 독	o 20억불 經費 分擔 決定 (9.15)	
인도, 파키스탄	o 自國人 위한 食糧, 醫藥品 供給 決定 - 인도 商船 아크바르호 出港	
U N	o 外交官邸 侵入 관련 이라크 非難 決議 (안보리 결의 667) - 常任理事國, 對 이라크 空中封鎖 및 經濟 制裁 위반국에 대한 制裁 擴大 方案 檢討	

0098

添附 5

各國의 이라크.쿠웨이트 殘留人員 現況

(90.9.14. Reuter 추계)

國別 區分	쿠 웨 이 트	이 라 크
<서 방>		
영 국	1,000 명 이내	400 명 이내
미 국	1,400	200
오스트레일리아	쿠웨이트 및 이라크 160	
오스트리아	미확인	미확인
벨 지 움	7	39
카 나 다	500	200
덴 마 크	35	40
핀 란 드	4	22
프 랑 스	100	300
그 리 스	180	30
아 일 랜 드	50	270
이 태 리	40	310
룩셈부르크	2	4
네 덜 란 드	쿠웨이트 및 이라크 180	
뉴 질 랜 드	쿠웨이트 및 이라크 29	
노 르 웨 이	3	30
포 르 투 갈	4	37
스 페 인	14	19
스 웨 덴	2	70

0099

國別 區分	쿠 웨 이 트	이 라 크
<기 타>		
이 집 트	110,000	120,000
이 란	40,000	미확인
P L O	300,000	170,000
모 로 코	6,000	30,000
튀 니 지	1,000 이내	2,000
터 어 키	2,480	4,000
방글라데쉬	598,000	15,000
인 도	125,000	8,000 (최소한)
파 키 스 탄	40,000	10,000 이내
스 리 랑 카	85,000	미확인
중 국	0	5,000
홍 콩	쿠웨이트 및 이라크 12	
인도네시아	12 (최소한)	미확인
일 본	30	343
필 리 핀	38,000	5,000
중 화 민 국	0	0
태 국	30	3,000
불 가 리 아	미확인	900
체 코	9	257
동 독	쿠웨이트 및 이라크 29	
헝 가 리	0	182
폴 란 드	20	2,000
소 련	0	5,800
유고슬라비아	40	3,500
아르헨티나	쿠웨이트 및 이라크 51	
브 라 질	쿠웨이트 및 이라크 330	
칠 레	쿠웨이트 및 이라크 7	
멕 시 코	쿠웨이트 및 이라크 17	
* 한 국	13	436

※ 9.17 現在, 我國人 殘留 現況 : 쿠웨이트 9명, 이라크 209명

0100

添附 6

"페"灣 事態에 대한 아랍권의 反應

1. 이집트 : 사우디, 시리아등 穩健 아랍國家를 糾合 反이라크 中心國으로 浮上하였으며 이를 통해 美國 및 사우디로부터 莫大한 財政支援 獲得 企圖
   - 사다트 政府의 西歐와 이스라엘과의 分離政策 實施後 西歐와의 關係 緊密
   - 美國으로부터 년20억불 이상 援助 受惠
   - 軍事 및 多分野 制裁 參與 (2,000 코만드등 5,000 派遣, 追加로 15,000명 사우디 增派 方針, 그외에 30,000 多國籍軍 派遣 提議說)
   - 미행정부 71억불 對이집트 軍事借款 탕감 檢討中

2. 사우디 : 이라크의 쿠웨이트 侵攻으로 이라크에 대한 不信 加重 이집트, 시리아등에 莫大한 財政支援을 통해 이라크 侵略 沮止 꾀함
   - 外國 軍隊 駐屯 許容, 이라크 浮上으로 傳統的 均衡 외교 打擊
   - 世界 石油 供給의 40% 이상 支配
   - 對 蘇聯과 外交關係 復交 (9.16. 사우디 외상 소련 방문)
   - 90년 經費負擔 60억불 約束

3. 모로코 : 西歐와 緊密關係 維持
   - 하산2세 王은 수니派로서 이스라엘 關係 仲裁役을 맡아 옴
   - 多國籍軍에 1,200명 派兵

4. UAE : 쿠웨이트와 더불어 OPEC 쿼터량 超過生産 및 油價下落 부추김에 대한 非難 받음
   美國, 英國등 외군 駐屯 許容, 經費分擔 20억불 約束

5. 카다르, 바레인, 오만 : 西方 軍事 駐屯 許容

0101

6. 시리아 : 금번 이라크.쿠웨이트 事態에서 反이라크 路線 加擔으로 國際的
孤立으로부터 脫皮
15,000 派兵 (탱크 300대 및 지상군 1만명) 合意

- 아사드 大統領, 사담 후세인과 中東 覇權을 노리는 競爭者
- 사우디의 財政支援 必要 및 소련 關係 回復 企圖

7. 레바논 : 親이라크계 基督敎側이 대이라크 封鎖措置로 인해 打擊을 받고
있어 親시리아 하라위 政府의 立地가 大幅 强化되어 레바논은
反이라크側으로 기울어짐

8. 요르단 : 가장 複雜하고 어렵게 연루된 國家

- 西方에 대한 仲裁 努力이 이라크측의 代辯人 役割인 듯한 인상을 주어
아랍권 및 西歐로부터의 非難 漸增
- 内部的으로는 짧은 王政 歷史 및 팔레스타인人의 요르단 移住로 인한
不安 加重(전국민의 60% 팔레스타인인)
- 最近 미국의 經濟 支援 등으로 미국側에 기울고 있음

9. PLO :

- 反美등 感情的 次元에서 이라크 支援하나 PLO 財政的 支援國인 사우디,
쿠웨이트 및 餘他 産油國과의 關係로 立場 정립에 어려움 直面
- 팔레스타인 問題 解決 위한 對이스라엘 關係에 있어서 立地 크게 弱化

10. 리비아 :

- 이라크에 의한 西方 人質化 反對
- UN 經濟制裁 또한 反對
- 事態 平和的 解決案 提議
  . 쿠웨이트 領土 一部 할양후 이라크군 撤收
  . 多國籍軍 撤收後 아랍 평화군으로 代替
  . 對 이라크 經濟 封鎖 解除

11. 알제리, 튀니지, 모리타니아 : 美軍의 軍事介入 反對, 아랍연맹 會議 불참
이라크 立場 支持

12. 수단 : 이라크군 700명 駐屯 및 스커드 미사일 配置設

13. 예멘 : 이라크 支持國家로서 쿠웨이트 問題는 아랍 域内 問題로 外勢 介入 反對

0102

美國의 페灣事態 被害國 支援機構 設立 推進動向

1. 부시 美 大統領은 9.25 페灣事態로 인한 被害國 財政支援을 위해 西方先進 7個國(G-7)·EC·GCC(아랍灣 國家 協力會議)·IMF·IBRD등이 참가하는 「페灣事態 被害國 財政支援 調整 그룹」(Gulf Crisis Financial Coordination Group)의 창설을 發表했음.

2. 페灣事態 被害國 支援관련 各國 動向

가. 부시 大統領이

○ 페灣駐屯 美軍 작전비와 被害國 支援費의 友邦國 分擔을 위한 「經濟行動計劃」을 발표(8.30) 하고

○ 「브래디」財務·「베이커」國務長官을 各國에 派遣, 협력을 要請한 데 대해

※ 「브래디」財務, 歐洲(9.4 - 6 英·佛) 및 亞洲(9.6 - 7 韓·日) 訪問

※ 「베이커」國務, 中東(9.6 - 8 사우디·UAE·이집트)·NATO(9.10) 및 歐洲(9.15 伊·西獨) 訪問

0103

28-13

나. 友邦國들은

○ EC가 外相會議에서 被害國에 대한 20億弗 규모의 借款 提供을 결정(9.7)한데 이어 西獨(20億弗) 및 伊太利(1億 4,500만불)도 對美 支援을 表明(9.15)하였으며

○ 日本은 美軍 作戰費(20億弗) 및 被害國 支援費(20億弗)등 總 40億弗 支援방침을 발표(8.29, 9.14)하였고

○ 사우디·UAE 및 쿠웨이트 亡命政府는 美軍 作戰費 및 被害國 支援費로 年間 120億弗을 제공할 것을 約束(9.7)한 바 있음.

3. 이번 美國의 「페灣被害國 財政支援 調整그룹」의 設立은

가. 被害國 支援을 위한 友邦國의 출연금 管理를 위한 것으로서 具體的 內容은 확인되지 않고 있으나

○ 被害國 支援 方式에 대한 日本·EC등의 相異한 立場을 受容, EC와 IMF·IBRD를 構成員으로 包含시키는 가운데

※ 日本은 個別的 支援보다 IMF·IBRD등 國際機構를 통한 共同支援 방안을 주장

0104

28-14

※ 西歐諸國은 共同支援 原則에는 찬성하면서도 EC次元의 獨自的 支援方案이 먼저 마련되어야 한다(9.17 外相會議)는 입장

○ IMF・IBRD등 旣存 國際金融機構의 엄격한 融資條件으로 인해 被害國 支援이 適期에 實施되기 어려운 점을 考慮, 새로운 緊急 融資制度(9.7 「브래디」財務長官 제안)機能을 添加할 것을로 예상됨.

※ 西方先進 7個國 財務相・中央銀行 總裁會議(9.22 워싱턴)와 IMF暫定委(9.24 워싱턴)는 페灣事態 被害國에 대해 IMF의 融資條件을 緩和키로 하는 공동성명을 각각 채택

나. 한편 美측의 同 機構 創設은

○ 事態의 長期化에 따른 友邦 및 國際的 對이락 制裁 共同戰線의 結束 弛緩現象을 防止하고

○ 親이락 國家와 對이락 制裁에 소극적 태도를 보이고 있는 中東地域 國家에 대해서도 壓力手段으로 이용하면서

○ 向後 쿠웨이트事態 終結 후 中東地域 經濟 建設支援 및 域內 安保機構 창설(9.4 「베이커」國務長官) 基盤으로 活用하려는 意圖도 內包되어 있는 것으로 評價됨.

0105

28-15

이락·쿠웨이트事態 關聯動向(46)

1. 10.5 현재 쿠웨이트事態는

가. 이락은

○ 美國등 관련국에 페灣사태를 포함한 中東地域의 포괄적인 平和定着을 위한 대화를 요구(9.30 「후세인」大統領)하고

○ 「후세인」大統領이 이락의 19번째 州로 편입시킨 쿠웨이트를 최초로 방문(10.3)

나. 美國은

○ 부시大統領이 UN總會演說을 통해 이락軍이 쿠웨이트로 부터 無條件 撤收한다면 아랍·이스라엘 문제등 포괄적인 中東平和 문제 해결을 논의할 용의가 있다고 언급(10.1)하고

○ 對이락 經濟封鎖가 실패할 경우 이락에 대한 武力 行使를 승인하는 내용의 UN安保理 決議案 채택작업을 蘇聯과 함께 추진중(9.30 美官吏)인 것으로 알려지고 있는 가운데

○ 페灣에 배치된 18萬 5,000명의 兵力을 10월말까지 23萬명으로 增強시킬 예정(10.2 CNN)

0106

22-14

다. 蘇聯은

○ 고르바초프 大統領이 페灣사태가 戰爭으로 비화될 것이라고는 생각하지 않으며 蘇聯은 끝까지 政治的 解決 노력을 다할 것임을 천명(10.4)한 가운데

○「프리마코프」特使를 이락에 파견(10.4), 이락 정부측과 事態解決 방안을 논의

라. 한편 佛蘭西 미테랑 大統領(10.3 - 4 UAE·사우디)과 日本 가이후 首相(10.2 - 8 이집트·요르단·터키·사우디·오만)도 中東을 방문, 페灣사태의 平和的 解決 위한 외교노력 경주.

2. 主要 關聯動向

가. 이 락

○「후세인」大統領은 9.30「모하메드」誕生 기념메시지를 통해

- 美國등 관련국에게 페灣사태의 공정하고 포괄적인 解決策을 찾기위한 對話를 요구하고

- 對話는 中東地域의 포괄적인 平和定着과 연계된 상태에서 전개되어야 한다고 주장하면서

0107

22-15

- 페灣의 多國籍軍 撤收, UN安保理의 對이라크 經濟封鎖 조치 해제등 이라크의 요구사항에 대해서는 協商하지 않을 것이라고 언급

○ 「후세인」大統領은 이스라엘과의 秘密接觸을 통해 이스라엘에 挑發할 의사가 없다는 내용의 메시지를 전달(10.1 「무바라크」이집트 大統領 언급)

○ 「후세인」大統領은 이라크의 19번째 州로 편입시킨 쿠웨이트를 최초로 방문(10.3)

○ 「라마단」副首相, 가이후 日 首相과의 회담에서 外國軍隊가 아랍땅에 머무는 한 페灣 위기의 외교적 해결은 있을 수 없다고 언급(10.4)

나. 美　　國

○ 美國은 對이라크 경제봉쇄가 실패할 경우 이라크에 대한 무력행사를 승인하는 내용의 UN安保理 決議案 작성 작업을 蘇聯과 함께 추진중(9.30 美 官吏)

○ 부시大統領은 이라크軍이 쿠웨이트로부터 무조건 撤收한다면 67년 中東戰을 통해 이스라엘이 점령하고 있는 시리아 및 요르단의 領土問題에 대한 解決 可能性이 있다고 UN總會演說에서 언급(10.1)

0108

22-16

○ 페灣에 배치된 18萬 5,000명의 兵力을 10월말까지 23萬명으로 增強시킬 예정(10.2 CNN)

다. 蘇　聯

○ 고르바초프 大統領, 페灣사태가 戰爭으로 비화될 것이라고는 생각하지 않으며 同 地域에 이미 충분한 병력이 있는 바 蘇聯은 끝까지 蘇聯의 역할을 이행할 것이라고 언급하면서 페灣에 軍隊를 파견할 계획이 없음을 시사(10.4)

○ 「프리마코프」蘇聯 大統領特使, 바그다드 도착(10.4)

- 페灣사태가 軍事的 衝突로 비화되는 것을 막기위한 政治的인 해결 방안을 찾는 것이 필요하며

- 이락政府가 자신을 초대했는 바 매우 신중한 의견이 교환될 것이라고 언급(10.4)

라. 西 方 圈

○ 미테랑 佛蘭西 大統領, 아랍에미리트(10.3) 및 사우디(10.4)訪問

○ 日本 가이후 首相, 이집트(10.2 - 3)·요르단(10.3 - 4)·터키(10.4 - 6)·사우디(10.6 - 7)·오만(10.7 - 8)등 中東諸國 巡訪코 페灣사태 논의

0109

22-17

마. 아 랍 圈

○ 요르단, 自國領土를 통해서 사우디로 들어가는 모든 트럭의 출입을 봉쇄(10.1)

○ 「후세인」요르단 國王·「아라파트」PLO議長, 「프리마코프」 蘇聯 大統領特使와의 회담에서 이락 大統領과의 대화통로를 열어놓고 페灣위기를 아랍圈내에서 해결하기 위해 노력하고 있으며 페灣사태와 아랍·이스라엘 분쟁이 해결되기를 열망하고 있다고 언급(10.4)

○ 「무바라크」이집트 大統領, 아랍·이스라엘 紛爭 17周年 TV 演說을 통해 「후세인」이락 大統領이 폭탄을 던지고 버스를 공격하기 위해 이집트에 테러團을 파견하고 있다고 주장하고 이들중 일부를 체포했으며 나머지도 체포할 것이라고 언급(10.4).

3. 評 價

가. 페灣사태는

○ 事態勃發(8.2)이래 2개월이 지나도록 이락의 쿠웨이트撤收 不可立場 고수로 해결기미가 보이지 않고 있는 가운데

0110

22-18

○ 美·蘇가 UN安保理의 對이락 武力使用 허용 決議案 채택추진 등으로 軍事壓力을 가중시키는 한편

○ 蘇聯·佛蘭西·日本 등을 중심으로 사태의 平和的 解決을 위한 外交努力이 전개되고 있는 상황

○「후세인」이락 大統領의 페灣사태를 포함한 中東問題의 포괄적 해결주장은

○ 現 페灣사태를 팔레스타인문제, 레바논문제 등과의 連繫를 強調함으로써 아랍內部의 支持擴大를 도모하려는 기존입장을 再確認한 것이나

○「미테랑」불란서 大統領이 제안(9.24)한 페灣平和案을 수락, 西方과의 적극적 對話자세를 表明했다는 점에서 注目

나. 부시 大統領의 페灣사태와 아랍·이스라엘 問題 連繫 가능성 언급은

○「후세인」大統領의 포괄적 中東問題 해결주장에 대한 최초의 肯定的 반응으로서

○ 페灣사태와 中東問題의 별도 해결을 주장해 온 종래 美國의 對中東政策 변화를 示唆하고 있어 注目.

22-19

0111

2. 주요 국제 군사동향

가. 최근 중동사태

이락의 쿠웨이트 침공(8.2) 3개월째에 접어드는 중동 사태는 유엔 소련,일본등에 의한 평화적 해결 노력이 활기를 띠고있어 외교적 성과에 대한 기대심리가 고조되고 있으나 진전없이 사태가 장기화 될 경우 미국의 군사적 응징가능성도 빈번히 거론되고 있어 귀추가 주목되고 있음.(주사우디,일본,미국무관 보고)

< 분석 및 평가 >

o 최근사태 추이

- 이락은 10.8 현재

. 쿠웨이트내에 병력 23만명 및 전차 2,200여대로 군사력을 계속 증강 배치하고

. 이락인 및 친이락 팔레스타인인의 쿠웨이트 이주와 쿠웨이트 화폐 폐지조치로 합병 기정화작업을 주도 면밀하게 추진하는 한편

. 자국이 미국을 비롯한 다국적군의 침공을 받을경우 중동의 유전을 파괴시키고 이스라엘과 친미 아랍국가들을 보복공격 하겠다고 경고(9.30)하는 일방

0112

27 - 11

. 페르샤만 사태의 대화를 통한 해결촉구(9.30)및 프랑스인 억류 인질 부분석방(10.3. 350여명중 9명)등 화전 양면 전략을 계속 구사하고 있음

- 미국은 이락에 대응하여

. 유엔결의를 통한 경제제재(이락은 식량부족 사태로 1인당 월기준 쌀 1.5Kg, 밀가루 6Kg, 설탕 1Kg씩 배급제 실시 및 전 농토에 밀파종 지시, 식량사정 악화로 수개지역에서 반 후세인 시위발생)에 이어 공중 봉쇄 조치(9.25 결의)로 국제적 제재를 더욱 강화하는 동시에

- 자국군 병력을 약 19만명(해상병력 3만5천 포함) 수준으로 증강하고 서방측 다국적군 및 아랍평화 유지군도 약 15만 규모로 증파를 유도하며 우방국들로부터 총 206억$이상의 재정지원도 확보하는등 장기 대응자세로 대이락 군사압력 태세를 계속 강화하는 일방

- 부시대통령의 듀간 공군참모총장 발언 문책 전격 해임(9.16, 대이락 공격시 바그다드 집중폭격, 목표에는 후세인도 포함 발언)및 "군사적 행동은 사용되지 않기를 희망"(10.1 부시 유엔연설)하는등

- 대이락 강경 일변도자세에서 다소 유연한 자세로 신축성을 보이기 시작하고 있음(10.2 베이커 국무장관, 부시대통령이 외교.정치적해결을 강력히 선호하고 있다고 강조)

- 한편 소련은

. 유엔군 후원하에 페르샤만 지역에 대한 파병용의를 표명 (9.29 외상)한데 이어

. 미국과 함께 유엔의 세계적인 대이락 경제제재 조치가 쿠웨이트를 침공한 이락군을 철수시키지 못할경우에 대비 무력행사를 승인하는 내용의 안보리 결의안 작성에 들어간 것으로 알려진 가운데(9.30)

. 고르바초프 대통령의 자문위원회 위원이며 중동문제 전문가인 "에브게니 프리마코프"특사를 바그다드에 파견(10.5)함으로써

. 사태의 정치적해결을 모색하기위한 중재활동에 나섰음

o 미국의 군사적 대응 동향(10.8 현재 군사력증강 현황)

- 지상군:

. 육군 4개사단 : 101공정사단, 82공수사단, 24 기계화사단, 제1기갑(수색)사단,전차900대(M60 및 M1A1)

. 해병 1개원정군 및 3개 원정여단: 제1해병 원정군(캘리포니아), 제7(캘리포니아), 제1(하와이) 및 제4(버지니아) 해병 원정여단, 오끼나와 해병 원정부대(2,500)

- 해 군: 인디펜던스(페르샤만), 사라토가(동지중해), 케네디 (홍해)등 항모 3척을 비롯한 총 43척

0114

27 - 13

- 공 군: 전술기 약 800대(디에고 가르시아 기지 B-52전략 폭격기 10대 포함)

- 병력증강: 미군병력은 일일평균 1,000명씩 도착중이며, 현재병력 및 장비는 요구분의 80%정도로 10월말까지 23만수준에 도달할 예정

- 배치현황

사우디의 지형은 중요한 지형지물이 없는관계로 각국간 작전 책임지역의 전투지경선은

. 이락국경과 50Km남방에 평행하게 연결 설치된 송유관을 중심으로

. 북쪽은 사우디군, 남쪽은 아랍평화군, 동부해안 지역 및 도로는 미군과 서방 다국적군이 각각 담당

. 사우디주둔 미군은 현재 6개지역에 병영시설 건축계획을 추진

.. 시설규모: 1개여단병력 수용시설(5,000명 규모)

.. 계획지역: 담맘, 파디리, 브카이크, 하니드, 알.쿠브라안.누아이리야

- 지휘체계

. 사우디 주둔 미군은 중앙사령관이 장악하고

. 서방 다국적군은 기본적으로 각기 독립적인 지휘체계를 유지하고 있으나 긴밀 협조관계를 유지하며(영국군 경우에는 미군 지휘하에 편입 허용 용의표명)

. GCC 및 아랍평화군은 사우디군 사령관의 지휘를 받게됨

0115

27 - 14

o 다국적군 및 아랍평화군과 비용 분담

- 미국을 제외한 30개국에서 약 10만병력 파병 GCC 및 EC와 일본,서독,대만,한국등에서 206억$ 상당의 재정분담 (한국: 2.2억$)

- 병력파견국 및 재정분담국 현황

구 분	군 사 력 파 견 국	경 제 지 원 국
나 토 국 가 (13개국)	미국,영국,프랑스,이태리, 폴튜갈,서독,카나다,벨지움, 네델랜드,놀웨이,그리스, 터키,스페인 * 미참가국: 덴막,아일랜드, 룩셈브르크	서독: 20.8억$ 이태리: 1.45억$ EC: 20억$(분담액 미합의)
아 랍 국 가 (9개국)	GCC 6개국, 이집트, 시리아, 모로코 * 이락지원국: 수단,리비아, PLO, 요르단	사우디: 60억$ 쿠웨이트: 40억$ U A E: 20억$
아시아 국 가 (3개국)	방글라데시,파키스탄,인도네시아 * 일본: 비무장 자위대원 1000-2000명 규모의 유엔 평화협력대 파견 추진	일본: 40억$ 한국: 2.2억$ 대만: 2-3억$
기 타 국 가 (5개국)	소련,알젠틴,체코,폴랜드, 호주	호주: 800만$

0116

27 - 15

o 사태전망

- 유엔을 통한 대이락 제재조치 강화에 병행, 외교적 노력에 의한 사태해결 모색을 적극화 할것으로 예상되나

- 이락:	. 사우디 국왕 및 유엔 사무총장과 협상용의
	. 쿠웨이트 합법정부수반에 "사바"국왕 배제조건
- 미국:	. 이락군의 쿠웨이트 무조건 철수 요구 견지
	. 사태의 평화적.외교적 해결 추구 강조
- 소련:	. 이락이 쿠웨이트 철수 동의 경우
	. 침공이전 제기했던문제 협의방침
	(부채 100억$ 탕감, 전략요충 "부비얀"도 조차등)
- 일본:	가이후 수상 요르단 방문 이락부수상과 회담

- 경제적제재 및 외교적노력(정변에 의한 후세인 퇴진포함)이 실패하고 사태가 장기화 될경우 군사적 응징을 단행할 가능성도 있는바

. 실시될경우 병력 요구수준(20만명 이상)이 충족되는 10월 중순 이후부터는 이락에 대한 모든형태의 공격작전이 가능하게 되어 그 시기는 정치적 결단에 따라 결정할수 있을 것이며

. 중간선거에 부담이 없고 중동 현지기온도 다소 서늘해지는 11월 6일이후 성탄절 이전 가능성도 유력한 시기의 하나로 고려할수 있을것임

0117

이라크 사태 관련 각국의 군사조치 현황

90.10.18.

I. 군대 파견국 현황

1. 지상군 파병국

   o 미, 영, 불, 이집트, 모로코, 방글라데시, 파키스탄, 시리아, 체코, 폴란드, 불가리아, 루마니아

   * 일본 : 비무장 자위대원 1,000-2,000명을 유엔 평화협력대 이름으로 파견 추진중

2. 해군 파견국

   o 미, 영, 불, 소, 사우디, 호주, 화란, 서독, 스페인, 이태리, 카나다, 벨기에, 덴마크, 그리스

II. 각국의 군사조치 현황

1. 미 국

   가. 해군(총 전함 43척)

   o 페르시아만

   - 항모 Independence(전함 6척)
   - Lassale 전함, 순항함 2척, 구축함, 프리킷 5척

0118

o 지중해

- 항모 Saratoga(Wisconsin 호등 전함 5척)

o 홍 해

- 항모 Kennedy(전함 5척, 보조선 2척)

o 제7함대 기함 블루릿지호 페만 향진(일본 모항)

o 제7함대 소속 수륙양용함 5척(상륙특공대 4,440명 탑승)

나. 지상군(총병력 : 약23만명)

o 기갑부대, 공정대, 해병이 주력

o 탱 크 900대

다. 공 군

o 전술기 800대

라. 기 타

o F-111 폭격기 14대 터키 인시르리크에 배치

- 이라크 국경에서 680km

o B-52 폭격기 50대 인도양 디에고가르시아에 배치

* 참고 : 미국의 대 사우디 무기판매

. F15 전투기 40대(91년 24대 추가 파병 예정)

. M60 탱크 150대

. 스팅어 미사일 200기(발사대 50기)

2. NATO 국가

가. 영 국(총병력 11,000명)

o 기갑여단(8,000여명, 탱크 120대)

o 함정 7척

0119

2. 이라크 군사력 현황

o 정규군 총병력 : 100만명

o 육 군 : 955,000명

- 탱크 5,500대
- 경탱크 100대
- 포 및 미사일 3,700문
- 무장 헬리콥터 160대

o 공 군 : 40,000명

- 전투.폭격기 510대

o 해 군 : 5,000명

- 프리깃함 5척
- 미사일 적재함 8척

※ 참 고

o 쿠웨이트내 이라크군

- 현재 약 23만 추정(탱크 : 2,200대)

o 60개사단(80만) 병력 및 다량의 화학무기 사우디.이라크 국경지역에 배치

0120

o 노르웨이 : 수송선 수척

o 파키스탄 : 지상군 11,000명, 고문관 1,000명

o 방글라데시 : 지상군 5,000명

o 체　　코 : 지상군 170명

o 폴 란 드 : 지상군 소수

Ⅲ. 참고사항

1. 각국 경제지원 현황

o 아시아국가

- 한국 : 2.2억불
- 일본 : 40억불
- 대만 : 약2억불
- 호주 : 800만불

o 나토국가

- EC : 20억불
- 서독 : 20.8억불
- 이태리 : 1.45억불

o 아랍국가

- 사우디 : 60억불
- 쿠웨이트 : 40억불
- UAE : 20억불

0121

o 재규어 전투기 12대, Tornado 전투기 27대, Nimrod 해상초계기 수대

나. 불란서(총병력 13,000명)

o 지상군 8,000명 파견

o 함정 16척(항모 1기, 프리깃 4등)

다. 기타 NATO 국가

o 서 독 : 함정 5척

o 이 태 리 : 함정 6척, Tornado 전투기 수대

o 화 란 : 프리깃 2척, F16 전투기 18대

o 벨 기 에 : 함정 3척

o 스 페 인 : 함정 4척

o 덴 마 크 : 함정 1척

o 그 리 스 : 프리깃 1척

o 포르투갈 : 수송선 3척

o 카 나 다 : 함정 3척, CF-18 전투기 1편대, 교관요원 450명

3. 기타 국가

가. 아랍 국가

o 이집트 : 지상군 20,000명(탱크, 방공무기)

o 모로코 : 지상군 6,200명

o 시리아 : 지상군, 4,000명, 탱크 300대

나. 기 타

o 소 련 : 전함 2척

o 호 주 : 프리깃 2척

0122

대이라크 제재 조치 실효화를 위한 방안

1. 배 경

o 이라크의 국제적 고립 탈피 및 쿠웨이트 침공에 대한 국제적 비난 여론을 분열시키기 위한 일관된 노력 경주

- 외국 사절들의 이라크 방문 초청과 이에 대한 대가로 억류 외국인 인질 석방
- 이라크의 유화 태도 선전을 위한 사절들의 해외 파견 노력도 병행
- 평화안 협상 진행중 추가 UN 결의 논의의 불필요성을 강조키 위해 UN 안보리 이사국 외교사절의 이라크 방문 초청

o 이라크측은 프랑스 및 소련측 평화안이 국제적 공감대와는 구별됨을 부각시키는데 관심 집중

- Tariq Aziz 이라크 외상 10.23. 소측 중재 노력 평가
- 이와 대조적으로 대미, 대영 비난 공세는 계속

o 이라크측의 유화적 태도에 대한 보도는 이라크측 공식 성명과는 상치됨.

- 8.12. 후세인 발표 강경 입장 고수

2. 논 점

o 이라크의 정치.경제 및 군사적 고립 상테 인식 조집

- 사절단의 해외 파견 및 외국 인사들의 방문 초청 증가
- 이에 대한 대가로 억류 외국인 인질 일부 석방

o 상기와 같은 이라크측의 유치한 술책은 소련, 프랑스 등으로 부터도 냉소적 반응을 받고 있음.

- 프랑스, 인질 관련 어떠한 협상도 거부하며 이라크에 의한 UN 결의 이행을 촉구

0123

o 이라크측이 국제적 압력을 느끼고 있다는 조짐이 나타나고 있음.

- 대이라크 정치.경제 및 군사적 고립화 계속 필요

o 이라크측의 억류 인질 일부 석방에 대한 대가 부담은 절대 불가함.

- 모든 당사국은 억류 외국인 인질 전원의 즉시 출국 허용을 촉구해야 마땅

o 이라크측으로 하여금 쿠웨이트로 부터의 부분적이고 조건부 철수로도 충분하다는 인식을 갖지 않도록 해야 할 것임.

- 모든 당사국은 이라크측의 UN 결의 완전 이행을 촉구 필요

o 유화적 태도를 주장하는 이라크 관리들에게는 억류 외국인 인질에 대한 즉각적 출국 허가, 쿠웨이트 합법 정부의 회복 및 쿠웨이트로 부터의 완전하고 무조건적 철수만이 해결 가능 조건임을 인식케 해야 함.

o 금번 사태의 평화적 해결을 위한 최선의 방법은 상기와 같은 국제사회의 확고한 의지를 이라크 지도자들에 전달하는 것임.

0124

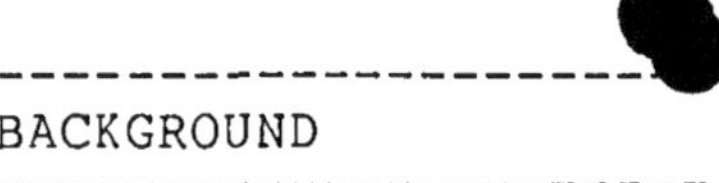

BACKGROUND

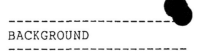

THE IRAQI GOVERNMENT IS MAKING A CONCERTED EFFORT TO REDUCE ITS ISOLATION AND CREATE CRACKS IN THE INTERNATIONAL CONSENSUS OPPOSING ITS OCCUPATION OF KUWAIT. ONE UNUSUALLY CYNICAL TACTIC IS TO PROMOTE VISITS BY FOREIGN ENVOYS TO BAGHDAD. BRITISH, SWEDES, ARAB-AMERICANS, FINNS, SPANISH, BULGARIANS AND OTHERS HAVE

BEEN INVITED TO IRAQ AND "REWARDED" BY THE RELEASE OF SOME OF THEIR FOREIGN NATIONALS.

THE IRAQIS HAVE ALSO BEEN SENDING ENVOYS TO FOREIGN CAPITALS WHO HINT AT "FLEXIBILITY" IN THE IRAQI POSITION. IN SOME INSTANCES, IT IS A QUESTION OF TONE. IN OTHERS, A WILLINGNESS OF IRAQI ENVOYS TO DISCUSS CONDITIONAL OR PARTIAL WITHDRAWAL. IN ANOTHER VERSION OF THIS TACTIC, THE GOI HAS CALLED IN DIPLOMATS FROM UNSC MEMBER STATES IN BAGHDAD TO ARGUE AGAINST FURTHER UN RESOLUTIONS WHILE PEACE PROPOSALS ALLEGEDLY ARE "ON THE TABLE."

THE IRAQIS HAVE BEEN PARTICULARLY INTERESTED IN PORTRAYING FRENCH AND SOVIET INITIATIVES AS DISTINCT FROM THE INTERNATIONAL CONSENSUS. IRAQI FOREIGN MINISTER TARIQ AZIZ OCT. 23 WELCOMED CONTINUING SOVIET EFFORTS (THE CURRENT MISSION OF SOVIET ENVOY PRIMAKOV TO THE MIDDLE EAST) AND LINKED THEM TO FRANCE. AZIZ REFERRED TO THE LATE OCTOBER MEETING OF GORBACHEV AND MITTERRAND IN PARIS AS AN OPPORTUNITY TO PURSUE PEACE. IN CONTRAST, BOTH AZIZ AND SADDAM HUSSEIN HAVE CRITICIZED THE U.S. AND UK FOR OBSTRUCTING PEACE.

AT THE SAME TIME, THE REPORTS OF IRAQI FLEXIBILITY ARE NOT REFLECTED IN OFFICIAL STATEMENTS. OFFICIALLY, THE IRAQIS CONTINUE TO BASE THEIR POSITION ON SADDAM HUSSEIN'S HARDLINE PROPOSAL OF AUG. 12 WHICH SUBORDINATES THE KUWAIT ISSUE TO THE LEBANESE CONFLICT AND THE ARAB-ISRAELI CONFLICT. NOR IS ALLEGED IRAQI FLEXIBILITY REFLECTED BY ANY CHANGE ON THE GROUND. ON THE CONTRARY, IRAQ CONTINUES TO DIG IN MILITARILY AND PROCEED WITH THE IRAQ-IZATION OF KUWAIT WHICH EFFECTIVELY MEANS DISPOSSESSING HUNDREDS OF THOUSANDS OF KUWAITIS.

POINTS

-- THERE ARE INDICATIONS THAT THE POLITICAL, ECONOMIC AND MILITARY ISOLATION OF IRAQ IS BEGINNING TO TELL. THE IRAQI GOVERNMENT HAS RECENTLY DISPATCHED ENVOYS AND

0125

INVITED MANY FOREIG[N P]ERSONALITIES AND GROUPS T[O B]AGHDAD TO REDUCE ITS ISOLAT[IO]N, PROBE FOR CRACKS IN THE INTERNATIONAL CONSENSUS AND PLAY FOR TIME. IN MANY CASES, IRAQ HAS SHAMELESSLY USED PARTIAL RELEASES OF ITS FOREIGN HOSTAGES AS "REWARDS."

--THESE CYNICAL IRAQI GAMBITS HAVE GENERALLY BEEN

RECOGNIZED FOR WHAT THEY ARE. THE INTERNATIONAL CONSENSUS, INCLUDING THE SOVIETS AND FRENCH WHO HAVE BEEN SINGLED OUT FOR ATTENTION BY THE IRAQIS, REMAINS FIRM. DURING HIS RECENT VISIT TO WASHINGTON, SOVIET ENVOY PRIMAKOV REITERATED "WE SHOULD LOOK FOR POSSIBILITIES TO AVOID MILITARY CLASHES BUT NOT REWARD IRAQ FOR ITS ACTIONS." IN RESPONSE TO AN IRAQI PROPOSAL TO RELEASE ALL FRENCH HOSTAGES, THE GOF REJECTED ANY NEGOTIATIONS FOR HOSTAGES AND CALLED FOR FULFILLMENT OF UNSC RESOLUTIONS WHICH REQUIRE COMPLETE AND UNCONDITIONAL WITHDRAWAL FROM KUWAIT.

--THE SIGNS FROM BAGHDAD INDICATE THAT THE IRAQI GOVERNMENT IS FEELING THE PRESSURE. THE MOST EFFECTIVE ACTION THAT THE INTERNATIONAL COMMUNITY CAN TAKE NOW IS TO HEIGHTEN IRAQ'S POLITICAL, ECONOMIC AND MILITARY ISOLATION.

--IRAQ SHOULD RECEIVE NO REWARD FOR PARTIAL RELEASES OF HOSTAGES. RATHER ALL INTERLOCUTORS SHOULD INSIST MORE STRONGLY THAT ALL FOREIGN NATIONALS BE ALLOWED TO DEPART.

--SIMILARLY, IRAQ SHOULD NOT BE ENCOURAGED TO BELIEVE THAT PARTIAL OR CONDITIONAL WITHDRAWAL WILL BE SUFFICIENT. RATHER, ALL INTERLOCUTORS SHOULD INSIST THAT NOTHING SHORT OF COMPLETE IMPLEMENTATION OF UNSC RESOLUTIONS IS ACCEPTABLE. LINKAGE OF WITHDRAWAL TO OTHER ISSUES IS AN IRAQI DEVICE TO DEFER PROGRESS INDEFINITELY.

--IRAQI ENVOYS WHO PROFESS FLEXIBILITY" SHOULD BE ASKED POINT BLANK WHETHER IRAQ IS PREPARED TO RELEASE ALL FOREIGN NATIONALS AND WHETHER IRAQ IS PREPARED TO WITHDRAW IMMEDIATELY, UNCONDITIONALLY AND COMPLETELY FROM KUWAIT AND PERMIT THE RESTORATION OF THE LEGITIMATE KUWAITI GOVERNMENT.

--FIRM AND ENDURING INTERNATIONAL RESOLVE EFFECTIVELY CONVEYED TO IRAQ'S LEADERSHIP IS THE BEST MEANS OF PROMOTING A PEACEFUL SOLUTION TO THE CURRENT CRISIS.

0126

이라크 宥和손짓…戰雲걷힐까

撤軍·油田할양, 교환등 잇단 제스처

이 "빈손撤收아니면 체면유지"
"反戰"시달리는 美 수락가능성
美매파 「조건붙는協商 반대」가 變數로

유엔이 내년 1월15일을 철수시한으로한 對이라크 무력제재결의안을 승인한후 이라크의 협상용의제스처가 잇따르고 있어 주목된다. 특히 미국은 베이커美국무장관과 아지즈이라크외무장관의 교환방문이란 협상방안을 밝힌후엔도 이라크의 先철수를 전제조건으로 강력히 요구하고 있다. 그러나 이라크의 잦은 협상신호나 미국의 「무반응」은 오히려 공개협상을 앞둔 마지막 신경전이며 더나아가선는 양측간에 막후에서 이미 얘기가 오가고 있는게 아니냐는 관측을 낳기에 충분하다.

때마침 4일 영국의 한 방송이 사담·후세인 이라크대통령의 타안으로 알려진 평화안을 보도한 것도 이같은 분석을 뒷받침한다.

위성중계 뉴스전문인 영국의 스카이뉴스 TV는 이날 후세인대통령이 서방국의 아라크不侵보장을 전제로 루마일라유전을 제외한 쿠웨이트로부터의 철군, 알·사바王政복고등 조건을 제시했다고 밝혔다.

이방송은 또 베이커美국무장관의 바그다드방문시 이조건을 놓고 양측이 심도깊은 대화를 나눌것이라고 전망했다.

같은 날 장·피에르·슈베느망 佛국방장관도 「전쟁을 피할 기회가 있다면 모색해야한다」며 「후세인이 쿠웨이트철군을 선언할경우 쿠웨이트의 종전국경선을 재조정할수도 있을것」 이라고말해 이같은 조건제시의 신빙성을더하고있다.

더욱이 유엔안보리 상임이사국들이 이라크가 쿠웨이트철수·王政복고·인질석방을이행하면 이라크에대한 공격배제를 제안하고 후세인정권을 보장할 태세가 돼있다는 4일자 英가디언紙보도역시 무력이라는 「최후수단」 에앞서 이러한 막후협상이 활발히전개되고있을 가능성을 짐작케시사해주는것이다.

이라크의 루마일라 유전등을 제외한 철수용의는 페灣사태발생초기부터 있어 왔지만 협상분위기와 맞물려 그 의미를 더해가고 있다고 볼수 있다.

루마일라유전지대는 1차대전이전 쿠웨이트자체가 자국의 영토였다는 이라크측의 주장이나 역사적 뒷받침은 차치하고라도 대부분이 이라크에 있고 南과 국경을부터 3.2㎞에 걸쳐 쿠웨이트쪽에 위치해 있다.

이 유전지대에 쿠웨이트가 시추공을 박아 연간3억달러 이상의 원유를 도둑질했다는게 이라크의 주장이다.

이라크로서는 페灣으로의 절로목에 있는 와르바, 부비안등 무섬도 전략 가치상 쉽사리 포기하기는 힘들다. 그러나 최소한 루마일라유전이라도 확보하면 사태이후 정권유지에 급급해야할 후세인의 「체면」은 세워진다고 볼수있다.

또 주변국도 그정도는 양해할수 있을것이라는 전망이다. 후세인은 두섬에 대해서는 복고된 쿠웨이트왕정으로부터 임대하겠다는 생각이다.

현재 이라크가 쿠웨이트에 구축한 방어현태를 살펴보더라도 루마일라에 대한 이라크의 애착이 그대로 설명된다. 부비안등에는 예비사단을 배치한 대신 루마일라에는 15개사단규모의 최정예공화국수비대를 밀집투입, 결사항전의 의지를 다지고있다.

한편 쿠웨이트망명정부의 태도도 주목된다. 쿠웨이트정부는 그간 이라크축출을위한 무력사용을 거듭 촉구하면서도 이라크와의 협상을 수용하겠다는 이중적 자세를 취해왔다. 특히 최근 한각료는 「이라크침공이전에도 이미 영토문제에대해 이라크와 협상하려했다」고 전제, 루마일라등 분쟁지역을 이라크측에 할양할 가능성마저 시사했었다.

따라서 문제는 무조건철수를 요구해온 미국이 후세인의案을 수용할수있느냐는 점이다. 그간 미국이 보여온 결의로서는 「패배가 분명한 협상案」이기 때문이다.

미국내 매파여론을 리드하고있는 헨리·키신저 前국무장관은 「조건이 붙는 협상을 할바에 뭣하러 40만명씩이나 파병할 필요가 있느냐」고 행정부를 공박했다.

이는 후세인정권을 존속시키면 중동지역의 불안요인이 여전히 남기때문이다.

또 이라크의 위협을 두려워하는 사우디, 이집트 등의 군비증강도 계속돼 세계평화기류가 형성되는 시점에도 이 지역은 계속해「세계의 화약고」로 남게된다.

알·사바왕정이 복고되더라도 이미 점령5개월째 접어든 이라크측이 그간 팔레스타인등 親이라크계 아랍인의 이주정책을 지속해와 왕정이 쉽게 붕괴되고 그 여파가 사우디등 주변 절대군주제국가에 전해질우려도높다.

하지만 당장 눈앞의 현실이 꼭 미국에 유리하다고 할수 없다.

특히 국내에서는 反戰기운이 고조되면서 심각한 의회의 견제를 받고있다.

인질문제만 하더라도 공동대응이라는 사전약속은 깨진지 오래다. 각국들이 앞다투어 정부차원이 아닌 민간특사형식의 유력인사를 파견, 개별적으로 자국인을 귀국시키고 있는 실정이다.

이렇게 될때 「우선 이라크가 무조건 철수한후 주권독립국인 쿠웨이트가 어떻게 할지는 미국권한밖」이라는 한 美국무부 고위관리의 말이 시사하는 바가 크다.

실제로 양측의 막후협상이 이처럼 서로의 체면을 살려주고 사후보장을 약속하는식으로 전개될 가능성이 높다고도 볼 수 있다.

【尹碩敏기자】

이라크
루마일라
유전
바스라
이란
와르바
부비안
최정예 공화국 수비대 15개사단
쿠웨이트
쿠웨이트市
이라크軍43만
페르시아灣
이라크방어선
전차방호진지
대전차해자
철망 및 지뢰지대
사우디아라비아
다국적군

0127

90. 12/6
한국일보

한국일보 1990年12月6日 (木曜日) (4)

후세인 "조건부撤軍 용의"

"루마일라油田 확보땐 西方측 불가침 보장도"

英TV보도

【런던 AP AFP=聯合】 이라크는 쿠웨이트와의 분쟁대상이던 루마일라 유전을 계속 보유할 수 있도록 허용된다면 쿠웨이트 대부분 지역으로부터 철수할 용의가 있을지도 모른다고 영국의 스카이 TV방송이 보도했다.

이 방송은 사담·후세인 이라크대통령이 예브게니·프리마코프 소련특사를 비롯, 중동사태 중재차 이라크를 방문한 여러 고위인사들과 만난 자리에서 이같은 협상 입장을 설명했다고 말했다.

이방송은 협상내용을 잘아는 한 소식통의 말을 인용, 이같이 보도했다.

후세인 대통령은 서방측이 이라크를 공격하지 않는다는 보장과의 교환조건으로 쿠웨이트와의 접경지에 있는 루마일라 유전만 제외하고 쿠웨이트 전지역에서 철군할것임을 밝혔다고 이방송은 전했다. ★관련기사5면

후세인 대통령은 또 쿠웨이트가 전략요충지인·부비얀섬과 웨르바 섬을 이라크에 대여해주는 협상을 할 의향이 있다면 이들 섬도 반환할 것이라고 밝히는 한편 쿠웨이트 철군이후 이라크가 축출한 쿠웨이트왕가의 복귀도 허용할 것이라고 말했다.

0128

90-1443

제4 유

분류기호 문서번호	중근동 720-2113	협조문용지 ( )	결재	담당	과장	국장
시행일자	1990. 12. 12.					
수 신	수신처 참조	발 신	중동아프리카국장 (서명)			
제 목	걸프 정세 및 전망 분석자료 송부					

당국에서 작성한 '걸프 정세 및 전망' 자료를 별첨 송부 하오니 업무에 참고 하시기 바랍니다.

첨 부 : 걸프정세 및 전망 1부. 끝.

수신처 : 장.차관실, 외교안보연구원장, 제 1, 2 차관보, 각 실.국장.

1991.6.30. 에 예고문에 의거 일반문서로 재분류됨

0129

1505 - 8 일 (1) 190mm × 268mm (인쇄용지 2 급 60g / m²)

19/120

걸프 情勢 및 展望

1990. 12. 11.

外 務 部
中東아프리카局

0130

目 次

0131

1. 狀 況

가. 유엔의 武力使用 決議 및 美國의 協商 提議

걸프事態는 11.29. 유엔 安保理가 이락에 대한 武力使用을 承認하고 사담후세인 이락 大統領이 이에 絶對 不服할 것임을 밝힘으로써 武力 對決의 危險이 성큼 다가오는듯 하였으나 ①이틀후 부쉬 大統領이 이락과의 直接 協商을 電擊的으로 제의하고 ②사담후세인 大統領이 이를 受諾한데 이어 ③12.6. 西方人質 全員을 釋放 決定 하므로써 平和的 解決의 曙光이 비치기 시작 하였음.

나. 外交的 努力의 展開

이와 함께 ①유엔安保理는 中東平和 國際會議 開催를 討議하고, ②一部穩健 아랍국가들은 쿠웨이트 領土의 割讓과 多國籍軍을 아랍군으로 代置하는 方案을 가지고 仲裁에 積極 나서고 있어 일단 武力衝突의 危險은 상당히 적어지고 相對的으로 平和的 解決의 可能性이 크게 높아진 것으로 보겠음.

다. 軍事的 動向

이에 앞서 11.8. 美國의 兵力 15萬名 增派 決定에 이어 이락은 25萬 兵力의 쿠웨이트 增派를 發表하므로써 이에 對應한바 있음. 또한 英國도 11.21. 1만4천명의 兵力 增派를 發表 하였음.

2. 分 析

가. 美國의 外交的 壓力

1) 걸프事態 發生 直後 美國은 美軍의 사우디 派兵에 즈음하여 ①美國人 人命 保護 ②이락軍의 쿠웨이트 撤軍 ③쿠웨이트 合法政府의 復歸와 ④걸프地域의 安保를 4大 政策目標로 設定하고 특히 人質釋放, 撤收 및 合法政府 復歸는 결코 協商의 對象이 될수 없다는 斷乎한 立場을 表明해 왔음.

2) 이러한 立場을 貫徹하기 위해서는 이락에 대한 軍事的, 外交的 壓力을 極大化 할 必要가 있다는 判斷下에 安保理가 武力使用 承認 決議案을 採擇하도록 베이커 國務長官은 물론 부쉬 大統領까지 前面에 나서서, 특히 經濟 制裁 效果를 위해서는 좀더 시간이 必要하다는 立場에서 武力使用에 留保的 態度를 취했던 蘇聯, 佛蘭西, 中國等 安保理 常任 理事國 說得에 全力을 투구한 結果, 美國이 安保理 常任 理事國 議長職을 예멘에게 引繼하기 이틀前인 11.29. 同 決議案 採擇에 成功 하였음.

3) 美國이 武力使用 決議 採擇을 위해 큰 努力을 하게된 背景은 ①當初 1-2개월이면 效果가 나타날 것으로 보았던 經濟 制裁 措置가 豫想과는 달리 이락에 대해 決定的인 打擊을 주지 못하고 있다는 結論에 이르고 ②美軍을 包含한 多國籍軍의 配置만으로는 사담후세인으로 하여금 多國籍軍이 實際로 이락을 공격 하리라고 믿게 하기가 어렵다는 것이 西方側의 共通된 分析이었고 ③美國이 실제 軍事行動을 취해야 할경우, 國內外的 支持 基盤을 튼튼히 할 必要가 있다는 점이었음.

4) 美國이 武力使用 承認 決議案을 成立시킨 直後 다시 電擊的으로 이락과의 直接 對話를 提議한 것은 ①美行政府의 事態의 平和的 解決 意志를 부각시켜 美國內 反戰 輿論을 撫摩 하므로써 對話가 決裂되는 경우 武力使用이 不可避하다는 것을 美國民에게 說得할 必要가 있다는 考慮와 ②사담후세인 大統領에 대해 撤收할수 있는 名分을 주어 國內外的으로 體面을 維持하도록 할 必要가 있다는 考慮가 作用한 것으로 보임.

나. 이락의 心理戰

1) 이락이 美國의 協商 提議를 受諾한 背景으로는 ①安保理가 時限까지 정하여 武力使用을 承認 함으로써 美國의 戰爭 遂行 決意를 새로히 認識하게 되었다는 점 ②經濟 封鎖가 産業部門에는 아직 큰 打擊을 주지 못했지만 國民 生活에는 相當한 정도까지 打擊을 주고 있다는점 ③對美 協商을 지금까지 主張해 오던대로 팔레스타인 問題를 포함한 包括的인 中東平和 協商으로 이끌어 가도록 하여 時間을 벌어보자는 점을 들수 있을것임.

2) 한편 종래 多國籍軍이 攻擊을 敢行하지 않는다는 保障을 하면, 크리스마스로 부터 3.15 까지 3개월에 걸쳐 人質을 釋放하겠다는 條件附 人質 釋放 立場을 바꾸어 이락이 西方人質을 크리스마스 以前 全員, 無條件 釋放할 것을 電擊 發表한 背景은,

① 유엔의 武力使用 承認 成立으로 나타난 美國의 一戰不辭의 결의로 보아 人間 防牌로서의 人質의 戰略的 價値가 크게 떨어져 人質의 繼續 抑留는 오히려 世界的 敵對感만 招來하고 있다는점

② 對美, 對西方 平和제스처로 美國內 反戰 輿論을 부추기고 多國籍軍의 結束을 弛緩시켜 戰爭 反對 움직임을 擴散시킬수 있다는점

③ 人質釋放이 12.4. 이락, 요르단, 예멘, PLO 頂上會談의 結果임을 부각시킴으로써 걸프事態를 아랍 內部에서 解決할 수 있다는 것을 對外에 誇示하고자 했던점

④ 또한 形式上 이락 議會가 사담후세인 大統領의 決定을 承認하도록 함으로써 이락 國民의 總意에 의한 決定이라는 점을 强調하여 對內的인 結束을 圖謀할 수 있다는점 등이 考慮되었을 것임.

다. 對이락 軍事的 壓力

1) 美國은 이락과의 協商 提議를 하는 한편, 12.4. 사우디 駐屯 美軍과 사우디 陸軍의 合同作戰으로 이락 國境 南部에서 大規模 訓鍊을 실시 하고 旣存의 防禦 姿勢에서 攻擊 態勢로 轉換 하였음을 發表 함으로써 ①이락에 대한 心理的 壓迫을 加重시키고 ②有事時 指揮體制 確立과 美軍의 沙漠戰 適應을 圖謀한 것으로 봄.

2) 한편 이락은 11.20. 쿠웨이트에 兵力 25만을 追加 派遣키로 決定하고 우선 7개 사단을 이동 配置하는 한편 豫備軍 15만명을 동원 하였음. 이로써 45만명의 이락군이 쿠웨이트에 배치된 것으로 추정됨.

3) 美軍을 包含한 多國籍軍의 兵力은 11.8. 美軍 약 15만명의 增派 發表와 11.22. 英國軍 1만4천명의 增派 發表等을 감안할때 兵力 配置가 완료 되는 1월 초순경까지는 약 55만 兵力이 될 것으로 일단 推定되나 안보리 決議가 採擇된 以後에는 總兵力 規模에 대한 報道, 특히 西方言論의 報道가 없어 과연 美側이 發表한대로 兵力 增派가 繼續되고 있는지 一抹의 疑問이 있음.

3. 展 望

가. 이락의 選擇

1) 쿠웨이트의 이락化 繼續 推進

가) 이락은 쿠웨이트 侵攻以後 4개월이상 推進해온 쿠웨이트의 이락化 政策을 加速化하여 쿠웨이트 王政이 復歸 되더라도 有效한 統治가 事實上 어렵게 되도록 繼續 努力할 것임.

나) 이락의 쿠웨이트 侵攻의 目的은 ①8년간의 이.이戰으로 인한 經濟的 逼迫에서 脫皮 ②原油 輸出을 위한 걸프만 港口 確保 ③7.25. 사담후세인 大統領의 終身制 改憲에 대한 國民의 비판을 外部로 돌리고 ④예멘, 요르단등과 提携하여 中東의 覇權을 確立 하는것 이었음으로 이 目的의 達成을 위해서는 쿠웨이트의 合倂 내지는 隸屬化가 可能만 하다면 最善의 方策일 것임.

2) 領土 一部 割讓 妥協

가) 쿠웨이트 侵攻 名分중의 하나가 이락의 쿠웨이트 全國土에 대한 영유권 主張이었으나 侵攻의 重要한 目的이 經濟的, 戰略的인 것이었고 실제로 사담후세인 大統領이 8.12. 平和회담 條件으로 내세운것도 ①이락國境 루마일라 油田地帶의 領土 할양과 ②걸프만으로 나가는 戰略的 要衝地인 부비얀섬과 와르바 섬의 租借 要求였던점에 비추어 이러한 두가지 要求가 全部 充足될수 있다면 좋겠지만 部分的 으로라도 充足되어 體面만 維持될수 있다면 사담후세인 大統領은 유엔이 정한 明年 1.15. 에 臨迫해서 쿠웨이트로+부터 自進 撤收할 可能性이 있음.

나) 실제로 亡命 쿠웨이트 政府側과 사우디 國防長官等은 이락군이 撤收하는 境遇, 쿠웨이트 領土 一部 할양 問題도 協商 可能할 것임을 示唆한바 있었으며 그후 사우디의 公式 否認이 있기는 하였으나 割讓 可能性이 繼續 擧論되고 있는것이 事實임. 다만, 와르바섬 租借의 경우 軍事的, 經濟的 理由에서 이란은 이에 상당한 抵抗을 할 것으로 보임.

3) 中東平和 國際 會議

가) 이락이 쿠웨이트로 부터 撤軍하는것에 대한 諒解 事項으로 쿠웨이트 問題를 包含한 中東問題의 包括的 解決을 위하여 國際會議 開催를 主張할 可能性이 있음. 이는 아랍권의 呼應을 받을수 있을 것이며 유엔 安保理에서도 美國을 除外한 蘇, 佛, 中等 常任 理事國들이 이미 中東平和案 摸索을 위하여 適切한 時期에 國際會議를 開催한다는 決議案 採擇에 원칙적으로 합의한 것으로 알려지고 있어 쿠웨이트 問題를 包含한 中東平和 國際會議가 91년에 열릴 可能性도 큼.

나) 사우디를 비롯한 걸프 沿岸 産油國들도 武力 解決 不辭 立場을 表明하고는 있으나 內心으로는 걸프 地域에서 武力 衝突을 바라지 않고 있어, 쿠웨이트로 부터 이락군이 撤收 한다면, 쿠웨이트 문제를 이스라엘의 팔레스타인 占領 問題와 連繫시켜 解決하자는 이락의 主張을 反對하지는 않을 것이므로 美國, 이락 協商에서 이 問題가 擧論될 것이 確實視 됨.

다) 美國은 지금까지 팔레스타인 問題와 쿠웨이트 撤軍이 別個의 事案 이라는 立場을 固守하여 왔으나 사담후세인 大統領이 쿠웨이트 撤軍의 前提로 이 問題를 들고 나올때 유엔 安保理 決議를 理由로 이락의 條件없는 撤軍과 사바 王政 復歸를 主張하고 있는 美國으로서도 이스라엘의 유엔 決議 不履行을 論議하게 될 國際會議 開催를 拒絶할 수 없는 難處한 立場에 처하게 될 것임.

나. 美國의 選擇

1) 美軍 또는 아랍 平和 維持軍의 繼續 駐屯

가) 美國은 이락이 쿠웨이트에서 撤收하고 쿠웨이트 王政만 復歸 된다면 일단 一次的 目標는 達成할 수 있다고 보나, 걸프地域의 安保를 保障한다는 窮極的인 目標는 이락의 軍事力을 弱化 시키기 전에는 성취할수가 없으므로 이락의 쿠웨이트 領土 할양의 代價로 美軍 또는 多國籍軍을 代置할 美國 影響下의 아랍 平和軍을 域內에 常駐 시키고자 試圖할 可能性이 있음.

5

0136

나) 그러나 이경우 軍事 大國으로서의 이락의 位置는 弱化되지 않는다는 어려움이 있을것임.

2) 經濟 封鎖의 繼續

가) 美國은 어떠한 理由를 들어서라도 이락에 대한 經濟制裁 특히 武器, 戰略 物資에 대한 國際的인 禁輸措置를 斷行함으로써 이락의 軍事力 특히 核武器, 化學武器, 미사일 攻擊能力을 弱化 내지 除去 시키고자 할 可能性도 있음.

나) 이 경우 이락이 쿠웨이트에서 撤收하면 유엔 決議에 의한 經濟 封鎖는 더이상 妥當性을 喪失하게 되므로 다른 理由를 들어 리비아에 대한 禁輸措置와 유사한 措置를 施行해야 될 것임.

3) 武力 使用 可能性

가) 美國은 유엔이 정한 時限을 遵守하지 않았다는 理由로 이락 軍事力의 弱化라는 窮極的 目標를 達成하는 方法으로 武力 使用을 選擇할 可能性도 排除할수 없는바, ①目標를 가장 確實하게 達成할수 있고 ②人質釋放 및 駐쿠웨이트 美大使館員 撤收로 民間人 犧牲에 대한 負擔이 없어졌으며 ③大規模의 多國籍軍을 派兵하고 많은 나라에 軍費까지 分擔시킨 狀態에서 쉽게 撤收하기가 어렵다는점 등이 考慮될 것임.

나) 그러나 武力使用 경우 ①막대한 人命被害 ②이스라엘의 戰爭 介入으로 인한 擴戰 憂慮 ③美國과 世界 經濟에 미칠 影響 ④名分없는 戰爭 主張이라는 批判的 輿論등을 역시 考慮하지 않을수 없을것임.

다) 다만 戰爭을 할 경우에는 奇襲的, 電擊的, 短期的인 大量 攻擊이 豫想됨.

外務部 걸프事態 非常對策 本部

題 目: 日日 報告 (17)

1991. 1 . 22 .
14:00

I. 전 황

1. 다국적군

o 대규모 공습 계속

- 8,100 여회 전투기 출격
- 핵원자로 4기, 화생방 무기시설, SCUD 이동식 발사대 16기 파괴
- 현재까지 계획대로 잘 진행되고 있다고 평가

o 이스라엘 방위 강화

- Patriot 미사일 6개 포대 배치 완료 (1포대 32개 미사일 발사 가능)
- 항모 포레스톨(플로리다 소재) 동지중해 배치 예정
  (걸프 미 항모 총7척)

o 보병 부대 전진 배치 계속

- 아파치 헬기 부대, M1 A1 탱크 부대등

o 미해병대, 쿠웨이트내 이라크 포대에 포격 개시

o 미헬기 이라크 사막 미해군 실종 조종사 구조 성공

- A-10 전투기 2대 참여
- 8시간 작전중 실종 조정사에 접근중이던 이라크군 트럭 1대 파괴

2. 이라크군

o 사우디 동부에 대한 SCUD 미사일 2기 발사 공격

- 1.22. 07:00 발사 1기는 걸프 해역에 피해없이 떨어짐
- 1.22. 09:05 발시 1기는 미측 미사일에 의해 요격됨.
  (파편 부상자 12명 발생)

0138

政府綜合廳舍 810號 電話 : 730-8283/5, 730-2941.6.7.9, (구내)2331/4, 2337/8 Fax : 730-8286

3. 양측 피해

가. 다국적군 발표

o 다국적군 전투기 격추 : 총 16대
  미국 9, 영국 4, 쿠웨이트 1,
  이태리 1, 사우디 1대

o 다국적군 조종사 피해 : 총 21명 실종, 1명 사망
  실종 : 미국 12(3명 포로 추정),
  영국 5, 이태리 2,
  쿠웨이트 1, 사우디 1

o 이라크군 전투기 격추 : 17대

o 이라크군 포로 : 23명

나. 이라크군 발표

o 다국적군 전투기 : 160대

o 다국적군 포로 : 25명

o 이라크인 피해 : 민간인 40명 사망, 군인 31명 사망
  부상자 150명

II. 각국 동향

1. 이 라 크

o 다국적군 포로들의 인간 방패화 선언(경제, 사회, 교육 시설)
  - 다국적군의 경제, 사회, 교육시설 공격으로 이라크 민간인 피해 주장

o 사우디와의 불가침 협정 폐기를 포함한 모든 관계 단절 선언

o 고르바초프 대통령의 철군 종용 및 평화 해결 제의 거부 발표

0139

2. 미　　국

ㅇ 부쉬 대통령, 이라크의 포로 방패화 선언 강력 비난

- 포로의 전쟁 목적 이용은 전쟁 범죄를 구성함을 경고

- 체니 국방장관, 이라크 전술로 다국적군 공격 계획 영향받지 않을것임을 확언

- 국무성, 주미 이라크 대사대리를 3일째 초치, 제네바 협정 준수 촉구 (이라크도 동 협정 서명국)

ㅇ 이글버거 국무부 부장관 이스라엘 폭격 지역 시찰

- 이스라엘의 자위권 인정 및 이스라엘 보복 자제 찬양

ㅇ 1.23. 부터 공습 일층 강화 시사

- 기상 조건 호전 예상

ㅇ 여론조사 결과 흑인 47%, 백인 80% 전쟁 지지

- 그러나 18%만 단기전 낙관

ㅇ 미 예비군 20,000명 추가 동원 (총 131,890명)

ㅇ Iowa주 2,000여명 반전 시위

ㅇ 해외 여행자 격감

- TWA 해외 노선 운항 50% 축소

- 주요 회사 해외 여행 금지 조치

3. 영　　국

ㅇ 메이저 수상, 이라크의 다국적군 포로 인간 방패화 선언 비난

ㅇ 이라크군의 방공 체제가 아직 완전히 파괴되지 않았다고 평가

- 전쟁 참혹성 및 장기화 경고

ㅇ 일부 병사, 사우디군의 임전태세 미비 불만 토로 (미군병사들도 같은 반응)

0140

4. 불 란 서

o 이라크와 이스라엘이 심리전 전개 중이라고 평가

- 이라크의 심리전

. 화학전 포함 대규모 파괴 능력이 있음에도 불구, 소규모 미사일 공격만 감행

. 민간 목표 공격으로 이스라엘 자극, 참전 유도중

- 이스라엘의 역심리전

. 첨예 레이다망으로 공격 사실 감지할수 있었음에도 방치

. 국제적 동정을 얻기 위한 고도의 역심리전 전개중

5. 오스트리아

o 테러 용의 이라크인 10-11명 체포

6. 터 키

o 나토 사무소 폭탄 2개 폭발

7. 리 비 아

o 터키의 다국적군 공군 기지 사용허가 관련 경고

Ⅲ. 평화적 해결 위한 각국 외교 노력

1. 이 집 트

o 리비아 및 시리아에 특사 파견, 유엔 최후 통첩 형식의 이라크군 철수 및 잠정 휴전안 제의 실현 노력중

2. 파키스탄

o 평화 해결 모색위해 수상이 중동제국 방문 예정

0141

3. 이 란

o 인도, 유고, 알제리등과 더불어 비동맹의 중재 노력 전개 시사

IV. 다국적군 군비 추가 지원 동향 (G-7 뉴욕 재무부장관 회의)

1. 일 본

o 난민 수송위한 군수송기 파견 결정

o 추가 분담금 100억불 가량 지원 예정 시사

2. 독 일

o 액수 미상이나 추가 분담금 지원 조만간 발표 예정

3. 미 국

o 회의 참가국 지원 약속에 만족 표명

V. 유가 및 주가 동향

1. 유가

가. 뉴욕 (Light) : $ 2.05 상승 ($ 21.30)

나. 동경 (Brent) : 변경 없음 ($ 19,25)

2. 주가

가. 뉴욕 : 17.57 포인트 하락 (2,629.21)

나. 동경 : 98.54 포인트 하락 (23,253.65)

0142

2. 17
한국일보 字

모호한 이라크의 終戰案

다국적군의 공개된 전략과 언느 점도 공개적인 스케줄에 따라 진행되고 있는 걸프전쟁은 여러가지 면에서 선례가 드문 전쟁이다. 애초에 전세계를 상대로 군사적 도발을 시작한 이라크측의 무모한 전쟁이라는 뜻에서도 수수께끼같은 전쟁이었다. 게다가 이라크 혁명평의회가 15일 쿠웨이트로부터 철수하겠다는 제안을 내놔 또 한바탕 세계가 분주하게 움직이고 있다. 대체로 말해서 세계는 이라크 혁명평의회가 「조건부 철군」을 내놓은 진의가 어디에 있는지 의혹과 기대를 가지고 「추리」를 하고있는 상황이다. 형식상 5개항으로 이루어진 이라크의 조건부 철군제의는 사실상 10개항으로 돼있다. 한마디로 말해서 팔레스타인문제 연계조건등 종전의 입장보다도 더 요구조건이 늘어난 제안이다.

이라크에 동정적인 입장에서 보자면 이제의는 이라크가 처음으로 유엔 안전보장이사회의 무조건 철수요구 결의를 받아들였다는 뜻에서 전쟁의 평화적 해결가능성을 암시하는 것이다. 「제3자」의 입장에서 본다 하더라도 역사상 수많은 終戰협상이 흔히 서로 받아들여질 수 없는 조건의 제시로부터 출발했다는 사실을 생각해 볼수 있다. 더구나 다국적군측의 평가에 의하면 이라크군의 전쟁능력은 3분의1쯤이 이미 파괴된 상태다. 앞으로 2주내에 이라크군은 쿠웨이트에서 지상전을 수행할수 없을 정도로 약화될 것이라고 했다. 지난 1월 17일 開戰초 미군사당국의 폭격전과평가의 실수로 미국측의 발표는 상당히 조심스럽게 받아들여지는 것이 통례로 돼있다. 그러나 압도적인 기술적 우위와 제공권을 쥐고있는 다국적군이 지상전에서도 승리할것을 의심하는 사람은 없다. 또 지상전은 늦어도 회교도의 단식기간이 시작되는 3월17일 이전에 결판이 나야할 것이다.

이런 상황속에서 이라크의 후세인대통령은 그의 정치적생명을 보전할수 있는 한도안에서 그나름대로 「명예로운終戰」을 생각해야할 것이다. 그것은 아마도 스스로 저지른 6·25전쟁을 「휴전」으로 끝낸 지난날 김일성의 입장과 엇비슷하다고도 볼 수 있다. 이라크가 이번에 내놓은 제안의 핵심은 쿠웨이트로부터의 철수요, 그것을 아홉가지의 꽃다발로 장식한 것일 수도 있다. 적어도 전쟁보다 타협을 주장하는 세계의 「비둘기파」들에겐 그렇게 보여질수도 있을 것이다. 사실 유엔의 안정보장이사회 결의를 지지한 나라가운데서도 소련·이란뿐만 아니라, 프랑스도 엉거주춤한 양다리걸치기자세를 보여주고 있다. 이들 제3의 집단들이 행동하기에 따라서는 이라크가 요구한 팔레스타인문제연계조건에 「중재자의 보증」을 담보로 후세인이 사실상의 白旗를 들수도 있을 것이다. 그러나 이것은 지나치게 낙관적인 시나리오일 가능성이 크다. 그 키를 쥐고있는것은 후세인이다. 비극적인 유혈을 뜻하는 지상전까지 남은 시간은 결코 길지않다. 후세인이 만약 다국적군의 戰列교란을 위한 「여론플레이」를 노리고 있다면 참극은 불가피할 것이다.

0143

2. 17 조선일보

0144

유엔결의 660號

유엔안보리결의안 제660호는 이라크가 쿠웨이트를 전격침공했던 지난해 8월2일 긴급소집된 유엔안보리에서 채택됐다.

당시 회의에 불참했던 예멘을 제외한 14개회원국이 찬성으로 채택된 유엔안보리결의안660호의 내용은 다음과 같다.

<유엔안보리는 1990년8월2일 이라크가 무력으로 쿠웨이트를 침공한데 대해 경고를 발한다.

유엔안보리는 이라크의 쿠웨이트침공이 국제평화와 안전에 대한 침해라고 규정한다.

이에 유엔안보리는 유엔헌장 제39조와 제40조에 의거, 다음과 같은 행동을 취한다.

1. 이라크의 쿠웨이트침공을 비난한다.

2. 이라크에 대해 8월1일이전의 상태로 모든 병력을 무조건 즉각 철수하기를 촉구한다.

3. 이라크와 쿠웨이트는 즉각 양국사이의 이견을 해소하기위한 집중적인 협상에 착수할 것을 촉구하며 이문제에 관한 모든 노력, 특히 아랍연맹회원국들의 노력을 지지한다.

4. 이 결의안의 이행을 위한 추후조치가 필요할 경우 다시 회의를 개최키로 결정한다>

부시의 聲明 요지

이라크의 성명은 유감스럽게도 이라크인들이나 전세계인들이 가진 희망을 꺾었으며 「잔인한 속임수」에 지나지않는 것으로 보인다.

이라크측의 성명이 발표되자 바그다드에서는 축하분위기가 있었던것같다. 이는 전쟁이 끝나기를 바라는 이라크국민들의 희망을 반영했던 것으로 생각된다. 이라크의 성명은 받아들일수 없는 이미 오래된 조건들뿐만 아니라 일련의 새로운 조건까지 달고있다. 우리는 또이라크 연합전선에 가담하고있는 동맹국들과 접촉을 가졌으며 그들도 이라크가 쿠웨이트에서 철수해야 한다는 점을 추호도 양보할 것은 없다는 기본입장에 전혀 변함이 없다는 점을 인식하고 있다.

이라크는 쿠웨이트에서 아무런 조건없이 철수해야하고 유엔안보리의 결의사항들이 완전히 이행되어야 하며 정치적 다른 문제와 이번 전쟁이 연계되어서는 안된다. 그리고 쿠웨이트의 합법적인 통치자들이 다시 쿠웨이트로 돌아가야한다는 점을 다시 한번 강조하고자한다.

이라크가 쿠웨이트에서 대량으로 철수하기전까지 다국적군은 유엔 결의 678호에 의거, 이같은 결의를 관철시키기위한 노력을 계속할 것이다.

그러나 약탈사태를 피할수 있는 다른 방안도 있다. 이는 이라크군과 국민들이 직접나서 독재자 사담·후세인을 권좌에서 퇴진시키고 유엔 안보리의 결의를 수용, 평화를 사랑하는 국가사회에 다시 복귀하는 것이다. 전쟁은 예정대로 진행되고 있다는 점을 분명히 하고싶다.

우리 모두가 전쟁이 조속한 시일내에 끝나기를 바란다. 이는 후세인이 유엔의 결의를 무조건적으로 수용, 그가 유엔군에 했어야만 했던 일들을 시행하면 이루어 질수 있다.

이라크의 撤軍조건

▲지난해 8월2일 이라크의 쿠웨이트침공전·후 걸프 및 중동지역에 파견된 모든 군대와 함정, 무기들이 철수할 것.

▲군대와 무기들의 철수는 휴전후 1개월이내에 실시되어야 하며 이후 걸프지역에는 지역국가들이 스스로의 안보를 담당하는 「외국군사 기지없는 지대」로 선포될 것.

▲이스라엘은 팔레스타인 점령지구와 골란고원, 레바논에서 철수할 것.

▲걸프사태를 이유로 이스라엘에 제공된 모든 무기와 장비들이 철수될 것.

▲쿠웨이트에 대한 이라크의 역사적인 영토·영해권이 보장될 것.

▲쿠웨이트에서 정권은 왕·사바 왕가가 아닌 국민들의 자유로운 민주적 관행에 따라 민주주의와 선택이 보장될 것.

▲유엔의 對이라크 경제제재및 결의들이 철폐되고 각국가 또는 집단적으로 이라크에 대해 취했던 각종 조치들도 철폐될것.

▲다국적군에 가담한 국가들은 이라크가 입은 전쟁피해의 복구에 필요한 비용을 지불할 것.

▲다국적군에 가담한 국가들에 대한 이라크의 모든 부채는 탕감할 것.

▲외국군의 외세의 침략으로 파괴된 일부 국가들에 이제도 지원에 착수할 것.

外務部 걸프事態 非常對策 本部

題 目 : 日日 報告 (72)

1991. 2. 20 06:00
작성자 : 정진호 과장

I. 이라크, 소련 평화안 수락 가능성 시사

1. 소련 평화안 요지

   o 소련 평화안의 자세한 내용은 밝혀지지 않았으나 지금까지 밝혀진 내용을 종합하면 아래와 같음.

     i) 유엔 안보리 결의 660호에 의거, 쿠웨이트로부터 무조건 철수

     ii) 이라크 국경선 보장

     iii) 전후 이라크 및 사담 후세인 대통령에 대한 보복 금지

     iv) 팔레스타인 문제를 포함한 모든 중동지역 문제 협상

2. 소련의 입장

   o 이라크는 쿠웨이트에서 무조건 철수할 태세가 되어 있는 것으로 보며, 소련 평화안의 성사 여부에 대해 '낙관적'이라고 평가 (프리마코프)

   o 이라크측의 조속한 회답 (2일 이내) 촉구

   o 전후 국제사회에서 이라크가 중요한 역할을 수행하기를 희망

3. 이라크의 반응

   o 아지즈 외상은 2.19 이라크로 귀환, 혁명평의회에서 소련 평화안을 검토후 회답을 가지고 모스크바 재방문 예정

   o 이라크는 안보리 결의 660호에 따른 소련 평화안 수락함으로써 협상을 심각하게 모색하고 있다고 발표

4. 미국의 반응

   o 부시대통령은 소련안이 요구조건에 '몹시 미흡하다' 고 일축하고 협상이나 양보 가능성을 배제한다고 발표

   o 영국 수상도 소련안이 유엔 결의 충족에 미흡한 것으로 평가

5. 기타 각국 반응

   o 이 란

     - 외교적 해결 지지 확산위해 외무장관 독일 파견

     - 이라크가 유엔 결의 660호에 의거, 무조건 철수할 것을 확신한다고 발표

0145

政府綜合廳舍 810號 電話 : 730-8283/5, 730-2941. 6. 7. 9, (구내)2331/4, 2337/8 Fax : 730-8286

- 군사적 해결보다 정치적 해결에 노력 집중하여야 함.
- 이라크가 내건 조건들은 철수와 연계된 조건이 아니라 거론되어야 한다는 것을 밝힌 것에 불과함.

o 독 일
- 전후 중동지역에서 소련의 강력한 역할에 지지 표시
- 소련은 중동지역 신질서 형성에 동등하게 참여할 권리 보유하고 있음. (겐셔 외무장관 언급)

o 요 르 단
- 소련 평화안 환영

Ⅱ. 지상전 개시 임박

1. 이라크가 소련 평화안을 수락할 가능성을 시사하고 있음에도 불구하고 다국적군의 지상전 개시가 임박한 징후가 나타나고 있음.

o 부시대통령 언급
- 소련 평화안에 냉담한 반응, 지상전 개시 암시
- 목표는 정해졌으며 전쟁은 계속되고 있음.

o 영국 수상도 미국과 협의후 군사작전 계속키로 결정했다고 의회에서 발표

o 미군 사령부는 소련의 평화안이 군사작전에서 아무런 변화도 줄 수 없으며 지상전 준비는 예정대로 진행되고 있음을 강조

o 다국적군 함대 쿠웨이트 해안 접근중

o 다국적군, 지상전 준비단계로 공화국 수비대를 포함한 전선의 이라크 군사 목표물에 대한 공중.지상 폭격 계속

2. 지상전 개시 여건 성숙

o 향후 며칠간은 상륙작전에 적합한 만조시기이며, 아울러 고성능 야간 작전에 유리한 달이 없는 기간임.

3. 소련의 지상전 반대 경고

o 소련 외무장관은 지상전 개시시 상호 막대한 희생만 날뿐, 아무런 결과도 얻지 못할 것이라고 경고

0146

Ⅲ. 기타 주요 동향

1. 이라크 인명 피해 상황 발표

   o 이라크는 전쟁 개시 26일간 총 피해 상황을 처음으로 언급

   - 사망자 : 2만여명, 부상자 : 6만여명
   - 군인, 민간인 피해 구분하지 않았음.
   - 총 피해액수 : 2000억불

   o 상기 숫자는 종전 이라크 공식 발표보다 20배나 많은 숫자임.

2. 한국 군수송단 파견

   o 한국 군수송기와 비전투병력이 다국적군에 참여하기 위해 2.19 출발 (국방부 대변인 발표)

3. 이라크, 이스라엘 대한 SCUD 미사일 공격

   o 1.19 저녁 이스라엘 중부지역에 SCUD 미사일 1대 발사

   o 재래식 무기 장착, 피해여부 밝혀지지 않음.

4. 인도, 미군용기 재급유 금지 발표

   o 인도정부는 걸프전 참가위해 인도를 통과하는 미군용기에 대해 재급유를 금지한다고 발표

   o 이에 대한 구체적인 이유는 밝히지 않음.

5. 불란서.리비아의 역할

   o 걸프전 종전 및 중동지역 안보문제 협의차 리비아를 방문중인 불란서 하원 외무위원장은 불란서와 리비아가 '중요한 역할'을 수행하고 있다고 발표

0147

外務部 걸프事態 非常對策 本部

題 目: 日日 報告 (75)
- DAY 36 -

1991. 2. . 22 .
06:00
작성자 : 김동억서기관

I. 사담후세인 연설 (2.22 00:00 한국시간)

1. 연설 요지

o 이라크는 승리의 자신감을 가지고 계속 투쟁할 것이며, 그들은 (미국등 지칭) 이라크의 항복을 기대하고 있으나 실망할 것임.

o 걸프사태는 40여년간의 팔레스타인 숙제를 결부시키지 않고는 해결될수 없음.

o 이라크는 협상을 통한 해결을 모색했으나 사우디, 쿠웨이트 등의 비타협적 태도로 실패하게 되었음.

o 미국 등이 당초의 쿠웨이트 철수 요구에 추가하여 계속 새로운 요구 조건을 내걸고 있는데 이는 결국 이라크의 모든 힘과 능력을 제거하려는 그들의 의도를 나타낸 것임.

o 아직 본격적인 지상군 교전이 없어 누구도 이라크 지상군의 진정한 전력을 정확히 모르고 있음.

2. 각국의 반응

가. 미 국

o Fitzwater 백악관 대변인

- 사담 후세인 연설에 실망함. 동 연설은 이미 전세계가 수차 들은바 있는 같은 독설(same invective)을 되풀이 한것이고, 유엔 결의를 무시하는 것임.

o Foley 하원의장

- 실망함. 전혀 다른 내용의 이야기가 있을 것이라고 생각하였음.

나. 영 국

o 사담 후세인의 연설로 한가닥의 희망이나 타협가능성이 사라졌음. 지상전은 불가피함.(Major 수상)

0148

政府綜合廳舍 810號 電話 : 730-8283/5, 730-2941. 6. 7. 9, (구내)2331/4, 2337/8 Fax : 730-8286

다. 이스라엘

o 도발적, 비타협적 내용의 연설임. 사담 후세인은 이라크 군.민을 절망적인 전쟁에 몰아 넣으려하고 있음(Avi Pazner 수상 보좌관)

라. 쿠웨이트

o 사담 후세인의 연설은 국제사회의 총의를 무시한 것이며, 지상전을 초래했음.(주유엔 대사)

마. 이 란

o 외교에는 자제와 신중함이 필요 사담후세인이 강경 연설을 행한 것은 미. 영이 소련 평화안에 부정적인 반응을 보인데도 연유가 있다고 생각함. 다만, 소련 제안에 대한 이라크의 최종적 입장은 Aziz 외무장관에 의해 밝혀질 것으로 봄.(주유엔 대사)

바. 예 멘

o 혁명 평의회의 이름을 빌리지 않고 사담 후세인이 직접 쿠웨이트 철수를 언급했다는 점에서 긍정적인 면도 있음(주유엔 대사)

II. 소련 평화안 관련동향

1. Aziz 이라크 외무장관 2.22 새벽(한국시간) 모스크바 도착

o 이라크 혁명 평의회, 2.21 사담 후세인 주재 야간 회의 개최

- 소련 평화안에 대한 이라크 입장 결정(내용 미상)
- Aziz 외무장관 소련 파견 결정

2. 미국의 입장

가. Baker 국무장관, 이라크의 즉각, 무조건, 전면 쿠웨이트 철수 및 걸프사태 관련 유엔 제결의 이행 재촉구

나. Bush 대통령, Gorbachev 소대통령에게 소련 평화안에 하기 3개 조건 추가 요구설(2.21 워싱톤포스트 보도)

o 미국의 추가요구 3개 조건 내용

- 합의 도달후 4일내 이라크군의 쿠웨이트 철수 완료
- 전쟁포로 전원 석방
- 모든 지뢰밭의 위치 공개

0149

o 외교 소식통, 4일내 철군완료 요구는 이라크로 하여금 탱크 상당수를 철수시킬수 없도록 하려는 미측의 의도로 분석

o 상기3개조건이 충족 안될 경우 Bush 대통령은 지상전 즉각 개시 결정 예상

3. Velayati 이란 외무장관, 이라크의 회답지연 관련 사태의 평화적 해결 전망에 다소 비관적 견해 표명

4. "전기침" 중국 외무장관, 미국에 소련 평화안 수락 촉구

o 중국 외교부 성명, 이라크에 즉각 철군개시 촉구 및 걸프전 문제와 팔레스타인 문제간의 연계에 원칙적 거부 입장 표명

5. 유럽의 반응

가. 유럽 의회, 소련 평화안 지지 결의안 채택 전망

o 2.21 밤(현지시간) 표결 예정인바, 대다수 의원 지지 표명

나. 교황청, 소련 평화안에 대한 지지 표명(교황청 대변인 성명)

다. Eyskens 벨기에 외무장관, 이라크가 즉각 철수개시 보장할경우 안보리에서 걸프전 정전안에 지지 용의 표명

o 벨기에, 안보리 비상임이사국

6. 비동맹 4개국, 2.23 테헤란 회합 예정

o 사담후세인에게 소련 제안 수락을 요청키 위한 대표단 이라크 파견 가능성

o Sadoun Hammadi 이라크 부수상, 비동맹 대표단과의 대화 용의 표명

7. 소련 평화안의 문제점(유엔 외교 소식통)

o 이라크의 쿠웨이트 철군에 관한 명확한 시간표가 없음.

o 전쟁포로 문제, 쿠웨이트 정부 복귀, 이라크의 전쟁 배상에 대한 언급이 전혀 없음.

o 이라크의 쿠웨이트 침공이래 유엔안보리가 채택한 12개 결의 모두를 이라크가 이행해야 한다는 명확한 요구가 없음.

0150

III. 전쟁관련 동향

1. 다국적군 지상전 준비 강화

o 지상 공격 현황(미중앙사 2.21. 정례브리핑)

- 공화국 수비대, 통신망, 전략목표물, 지휘 시설에 대한 개전이래 최대 규모의 포격
- 2.21 사우디군 포함 다국적군이 개전이래 최초로 국경을 넘어 공격 감행
- 이라크 벙커 공격에서 이라크군 435명 생포(장교20명, 대대장1명 포함)

o 체니 미 국방장관, 상원 군사위원회 증언에서 사상 최대규모의 지상공격 준비 완료 발표

* 참 고 : 미측 전과분석에 혼선
  - CIA, 쿠웨이트 주둔 이라크 군의 탱크, 대포등 10-15% 파괴 평가 (국방부의 30% 파괴 주장과 상치)

2. 이라크 반격 동향

o 이라크, 후세인 연설 1시간전 Scud 미사일, 사우디 중북부에 발사
- Patriot 에 요격됨. 사상자 없음.

o Frog 미사일 2발 발사 : 세네갈 군인 8명 부상

3. 쌍방 피해현황

o 다국적군 발표
- 전과
  . 포로 1,780여명, 항공기 격추 141대
- 피해
  . 전사 36명(미 17, 사우디 19)
  . 실종 51명(미30, 영10, 이태리1, 사우디10)
  . 포로 13명(미9, 영2, 이태리1, 쿠웨이트1)
  . 항공기 상실 41대

o 이라크측 발표
- 전과
  . 항공기 격추 180대, 포로 20여명
- 피해
  . 사망 20,000명, 부상 60,000명

0151

IV. 기타 동향

1. Shamir 이스라엘 수상, 이스라엘은 걸프전 참전에 적극적이 아니나 부득이 참전이 필요해 질지도 모른다고 언급

   o 이라크가 화학무기 공격을 가하거나 대량인명 손실이 발생할 경우에는 이스라엘의 보복이 불가피함.

   o 걸프전을 통해 이스라엘에 대한 이라크의 안보 위협이 제거되고 걸프지역 평화가 회복되기를 기대

2. 쿠웨이트 망명 정부의 전후 대책(Al-Awadi 관방장관 언급 요지)

   o 3-6 개월의 비상통치 기간을 설정, 동 기간중 이라크 동조자 색출 등 치안 회복에 중점. 이후 정상적 왕정 회복

   o 최초 90일간 의료시설, 식량.식수 공급, 통신시설 복구 등에 약 8억불 투자 계획

     - 완전 복구에는 5년간 최대 1,000억불 소요 예상

   o 기타 사항

     - 현재 쿠웨이트 잔류 쿠웨이트인 약30만, 해외 거주 약50만 (절반이 사우디 체재중) 추산

     - 이라크 침공이래 약 25,000명의 쿠웨이트인 실종(이라크 당국에 의해 억류 또는 처형 추정)

V. 군수송단 2진 출발

o C-130 3대(84명 탑승)

o 91. 2. 22 05:30 서울 공항 출발

  - 제1진 2대는 UAE 알아인 기지에 2.21 무사히 도착함.

0152

日日 報告 (76)

- DAY 37 -

2 23
06:00
작성자 : 김의기 과장

1. 주요 동향

가. 부쉬 대통령 대이라크 최후 통첩 주요 내용 (00:40분 KST)

o 이라크는 쿠웨이트로 부터 2.23.(토) 정오까지 즉각적이고 무조건적인 철수를 개시하여야 함.

o 미국과 다국적군 국가들은 후세인 대통령에게 즉각적이고 무조건적인 철수를 요구하는 유엔 결의안을 강행키로 했음.

o 소련 평화안은 너무 많은 조건이 있어 수용할수 없으며 무조건 철수를 요구한 유엔 안보리 결의안 660호와도 부합되지 않음.

o 이라크는 모스크바에서 회담이 진행중인 동안에도 이스라엘에 미사일을 공격하고 쿠웨이트에서 초토화 작전을 수행하였음.

〈참 고〉 백악관 대변인이 발표한 미국의 종전 관련 주요 제의 내용

o 2.22. 정오(워싱턴 시간)까지 철군 개시

o 1주일 이내에 철군 완료 (쿠웨이트시로 부터는 48시간 이내에 철군하고 쿠웨이트 합법정부의 복귀를 허용함)

o 48시간 이내에 모든 전쟁포로 및 민간인 인질 석방

o 쿠웨이트내에 매설된 모든 폭발물 및 지뢰 제거

나. 고르바쵸프 소련 대통령 6개항의 새로운 평화안 제의

o 이라크의 쿠웨이트로 부터의 조속한 무조건 철수

o 휴전후 24시간 이내에 철군 개시

o 이라크는 쿠웨이트시로 부터 4일 이내에, 쿠웨이트 전역으로부터 21일 이내에 철군 완료

o 휴전후 72시간 이내에 모든 전쟁포로 석방

o 철군이 완료되면 모든 대이라크 유엔 안보리 제재 해제

o 평화안 이행을 감시하기 위한 유엔안보리 옵서버 파견

0153

다. 평 가

o 미국 부쉬 대통령이 성명 내용에 소련 평화안이 철군 관련 너무 많은 조건이 있어 수락할수 없다고 하였으나 소련의 노력에 대해서는 평가 한다고 언급 하였으며 소련이 부쉬 성명 발표후 곧 새로운 평화안을 제의한점을 보아 아직도 지상전을 피할수 있는 협상 여지는 있는 것으로 보임.

o 미측은 소련의 철수 기간 21일이 너무 길어 이라크측이 철수시 무기등 군사장비를 반출할수 있어 종전후에도 이라크의 군사력이 상당수준 유지될수 있을 가능성을 우려하고 있는 것으로 관측됨.

2. 전 황 (2.22. 현재 쌍방 피해 현황, 로이타 집계)

o 다국적군 발표

<다국적군 피해>

- 인 명 : 전사 84명, 포로 또는 실종 64명
- 항공기 : 47대 (미국 35, 영국 7, 사우디 3, 쿠웨이트 1, 이태리 1)

<이라크 피해>

- 인 명 : 전사 80명 포로 또는 실종 1,907명
- 항공기 : 135대
- 선 박 : 73척

o 이라크군 발표

<다국적군 피해>

- 인 명 : 전사 53명
- 항공기 : 329 대

<이라크 피해>

- 인 명 : 전사 90명
- 항공기 ; N/A
- 민간인 피해(공식) : 사망 967명, 부상 480 명
- 민간인 피해(비공식) : 사망 20,000명, 부상 60,000명

0154

3. 기타 동향

o 프랑스, 쿠웨이트 전후 복구사업 참여 교섭단 파견 예정
(2.22. 파리발 로이터)
- 프랑스 정부는 3월중 Jean-Marie Rausch 통상장관을 단장으로한 대표단을 사우디에 파견, 쿠웨이트 망명정부와 전후 복구사업 참여 교섭 예정.
- 동 대표단에는 프랑스 건설업계, 대표들도 참여
- 불정부 및 건설업계, 미국의 전후복구 참여 독립적 계약 우려
- 쿠웨이트 복구사업에는 500억달라 소요

o 쿠웨이트 유정 140여개 파괴 (사우디 미군 중앙사 Neal 준장 발표)
- 이라크는 2.22. 하루동안 140여개의 유정을 파괴함.
  . 쿠웨이트에는 약 950개의 유정이 있음.
- 쿠웨이트 유전의 약 25%가 검은 연기에 싸여있음.
- 쿠웨이트 원유생산 시설이 체계적으로 파괴되고 있어 이라크는 초토화 작전을 개시한 것으로 보임.

o 부쉬 대통령 대 이라크 최후 통첩후 유럽 금융시장 동향 (2.22.)
- 4월 선적 예정 북해산 원유가 : 배럴당 16.57 불 (28센트 하락)
- 금 (1온스) : 358,75불 (2.21. 종가 대비 4.50불 하락)
- 런던 파이낸셜 타임스 주가지수 : 2,314.3 (1.9 포인트 상승)
- 파리 CAC-40 주가지수 : 1,716.88 (개장시에 대비 7.16 포인트 상승)
- 독일 DAX 주가지수 : 1,582.52 (16.20 포인트 상승)

0155

1. 고르바쵸프 소련 대평령(이라크 외무장관과 회담후)의 휴전안 (91. 2.22. 08:30)

1) 이락은 무조건 전면 철수에 합의

2) 휴전후 제 2일부터 철수 개시

3) 철수는 시한을 정해 시행

4) 2/3 철수후 경제 제재 해제

5) 철수 완료후 모든 유엔 결의 무효 선언

6) 휴전후 전쟁 포로의 석방

7) 참전국 이외 국가와 유엔이 철군 감시

8) 세부 문제는 계속 유엔에서 논의

2. 미국의 제의 내용 (91. 2.23. 00:40)

1) 2.23. 정오(워싱턴 시간)까지 철군 개시

2) 1주일 이내에 철군 완료 (쿠웨이트시로 부터는 48시간 이내에 철군하고 쿠웨이트 합법정부의 복귀를 허용함)

3) 48시간 이내에 모든 전쟁포로 및 민간인 인질 석방

4) 쿠웨이트내에 매설된 모든 폭발물 및 지뢰 제거

3. 고르바쵸프 소련 대통령 6개항의 새로운 평화안 제의 (91. 2. 23.)

1) 이라크의 쿠웨이트로 부터의 조속한 무조건 철수

2) 휴전후 24시간 이내에 철군 개시

3) 이라크는 쿠웨이트시로 부터 4일 이내에, 쿠웨이트 전역으로부터 21일 이내에 철군 완료

4) 휴전후 72시간 이내에 모든 전쟁포로 석방

5) 철군이 완료되면 모든 대이라크 유엔 안보리 제재 해제

6) 평화안 이행을 감시하기 위한 유엔안보리 옵서버 파견

0156

소련.이라크간 합의 8개항 평화안에 대한 분석

2 22

1. 휴전의 시점에 대한 언급이 없는바 이것은 미국등 다국적군의 동의가 있어야 하므로 일방적으로 결정할수 없는 사항이었기 때문일것임.

2. 철군 시한을 정한다고만 되어있을뿐 철군의 시간표는 제시되지 않음.

3. 처음에는 유엔 결의의 효력 정지로 발표되었으나 후에 무효로 수정되었는바 확실한 표현은 미상임.

4. 휴전후 포로의 석방을 수용한것은 미국의 요청을 포함시킨 것으로 보임.

5. 소련.이라크 평화안은 대체적으로 문제의 해결 장치를 유엔의 테두리 안에 두려는 의도가 보임.

6. 대체적으로 당초 소련의 평화안 4개항을 기초로 하였으며 포로의 석방, 유엔 결의의 무효 선언, 유엔에서의 계속 논의등 새로운 항이 추가된 반면 당초 소련 평화안에 포함되었던 것으로 알려진 팔레스타인 문제를 포함한 중동문제 전반에 관한 협상 개최에 관한 언급이 없음.

7. 유엔 결의중 쿠웨이트 왕정 복귀, 전쟁 피해에 대한 이라크의 책임등에 관한 언급이 없음.

8. 선휴전 후철군의 형식을 채택하고 있고, 유엔결의의 무효선언을 통해 쿠웨이트 합법정부의 복귀, 전쟁배상등을 사실상 거부하고 있으므로 미국으로서는 수락하기가 어려울 것이나, 대부분 EC등과 소련의 동정적 입장때문에 현시점에서 지상전 개시도 역시 어려울 것으로 보임.

0157

外務部 걸프事態 非常對策 本部

題 目: 미, 이라크의 소련 수정평화안 수용을 거부(속보) 1991. 2.23 23:30

(워싱턴 AFP 보도)

- 미국, Aziz 이라크 외무장관이 이라크는 휴전후 21일내 쿠웨이트로 부터의 무조건 완전 철수라는 소련의 수정제안을 전적으로 수용한다는 발표 직후, 이를 거부(2.23)

- 거부이유는 동 수정제안이 ① 유엔결의안인 즉각적이고 무조건적인 철수에 대한 분명한 언질이 없고 ② 다른 유엔 안보리 결의의 완전한 이행이 불가능하기 때문에 무효임.

- 이라크측의 수용선언은 아무런 효력도 없으며 미국은 현재 다국적군의 최후 통첩에 대한 이라크의 반응을 계속해서 기다리고 있음.

- 워싱턴의 이러한 단호한 입장은 부쉬 대통령이 금요일 내놓은 GMT 17:00시 제한시간 7시간 전에 나옴

- 한편, 이라크의 Aziz 외무장관은 이라크의 철수가 1주내 완결되어야 하며 이라크군은 철수개시후 48시간내 쿠웨이트시로 부터 철수하여야 한다는 다국적군의 최후 통첩에 대해 상금 불언급

0158

政府綜合廳舍 810號 電話 : 730-8283/5, 730-2941. 6. 7. 9, (구내)2331/4, 2337/8 Fax : 730-8286

外務部 걸프事態 非常對策 本部

題 目: 이라크, 미국 종전안 수락 시사 (속 보) 1991. 2.24 03:00

ㅇ 유엔 주재 유리보론초프 소련대사, 아지즈 이라크 외무장관이 미 부쉬대통령의 중전안에 대한 일부조건에 긍정적 반응을 보였다고 유엔안보리 회의시에 언급 (이란 및 카나다 외교관 말 인용)

ㅇ U.N 안보리, 이라크의 쿠웨이트 철수시한 직전 걸프사태 관련 공식 비공개 회의 개시

ㅇ 이라크 철수관련 미국측 주장과 일치하는 철수조건 목록을 동 소련대사가 동 회의에서 발표

ㅇ 이라크 외무장관이 긍정적 반응을 나타냈으나, 이것이 모든 조건을 포함하는 것인지는 불분명한 것으로 알려짐.

ㅇ 피크링 유엔 주재 미국대사, 동 이라크측의 철군조건에 대해 분명하게 구체화 할 것을 요청

ㅇ 미측은 미국 종전안과 관련, 사우디, 이라크 및 쿠웨이트 국경과 쿠웨이트로 부터 48시간 이내 이라크군 철수, 1주일내 철수 종료할 것을 언급

0159

政府綜合廳舍 810號 電話: 730-8283/5, 730-2941. 6. 7. 9, (구내)2331/4, 2337/8 Fax: 730-8286

247
249

外務部 걸프事態 非常對策 本部

題 目: 부쉬 미대통령, 지상전 개시 시사(속 보) 1991. 2.24 04:30

ㅇ 다국적국가가 제시한 이라크 철수시한이 만료됨에 따라, 쿠웨이트 해방을 위해 다국적군의 군사행동을 계획에 따라 예정대로 계속할 것임.

ㅇ 이라크의 쿠웨이트 무조건 철수에 대한 U.N 결의 이행을 위해 사담 후세인이 아무런 행동을 취하지 않은 점에 유감표명

ㅇ 슈바르츠코프 미군사령관이 다음 단계의 전쟁을 위해 걸프 지상전 전개 전권을 수임(미국합성 고위관리 언급)

0160

政府綜合廳舍 810號 電話 : 730-8283/5, 730-2941.6.7.9, (구내)2331/4, 2337/8 Fax : 730-8286

外務部 걸프事態 非常對策 本部

多國籍軍 現況

題 目: 1991. 2 25

多國的軍 構成에 관한 駐美, 駐英, 駐佛, 駐사우디, 駐카이로 公館의 報告와 外信報道를 基礎로한 分析結果는 아래와 같음.

1. 多國籍軍 參加國數

- o 多國籍軍 參加國數에 대한 一致된 意見은 없으며 一般的으로 가장 많이 言及되고 있는 28個國도 그 構成에 있어서는 共通된 意見이 없음.
- o 開戰 初期에는 美國 支持 聯合國들의 規模를 誇示하기 위해서 多國籍軍 參加國에 대한 數字를 重視하였지만 일단 汎世界的으로 反이라크 連帶가 形成된 이상 多國籍軍 參加國 數字는 그 意味가 退色한 것으로 보임.
  - 26個國 : 駐 사우디 大使館
  - 28個國 : 부쉬 大統領 年頭 敎書, 盧泰愚 大統領 年頭記者會見, 美國務部 近東局, 美國防部, 駐英大使館
  - 29個國 : 美國務部 代辯人室.政治軍事局, 駐佛 大使館
  - 31個國 : AP 通信
  - 32個國 : 駐 카이로 總領事館
  - 36個國 : 駐 英 大使館

2. 分 析

가. 共通 包含 國家 : 25個國

- 西方 3個國(美國, 캐나다, 濠洲)
- 西歐 8個國 (英, 佛, 伊, 벨기에, 和, 스페인,希, 덴마크)
- 아랍8個國 (사우디, 쿠웨이트, 오만, 카타르, 바레인, UAE, 이집트, 시리아)
- 아시아 2個國 (파키스탄, 방글라데시)
- 아프리카 3個國 (모로코, 세네갈, 니제르)
- 南美 1個國 (아르헨티나)

나. 論難 對象國家

1) 獨 逸

. 駐美 大使館 및 駐 카이로 總領事館 報告에 의하면 地中海

0161

政府綜合廳舍 810號 電話 : 730-8283/5, 730-2941.6.7.9, (구내)2331/4, 2337/8 Fax : 730-8286

東部에 掃海艇 派遣한 것으로 되어 있으나 戰鬪目的은 아니고 觀察 目的으로 보임.

. 美國務部 代辯人室.政治軍事局 및 NSC 는 包含, 美國務部 近東局, 美國防部는 不包含.

2) 뉴질랜드

. AP 通信 報道에 의하면 C-130 軍輸送機를 派遣한 것으로 되어있음.

. 美國務部 近東局.政治軍事局은 包含, 美國務部 代辯人室, 美國防部는 不包含.

3) 포르투갈, 노르웨이, 체코

. 美國政府는 3個國 모두 不包含.

. AP 通信은 3個國 모두 艦艇내지 兵力을 派遣한 것으로 報道하고 있으며 大使館 報告는 대체로 3個國을 多國的軍에 包含하고 있음.

4) 蘇聯, 터키

. 美國 政府는 不包含.

. 기타 대부분 報告는 兩國을 艦艇 派遣國으로 把握하고 있으나 美國은 同 艦艇을 戰鬪 目的이 아닌 觀察 目的으로 把握하고 있음.

5) 폴랜드

. 美國務部 代辯人室은 包含, 近東局.政治軍事局 및 美國防部는 不包含.

. 기타 報告는 不包含, 駐佛 大使館만 艦艇 2隻 派遣으로 報告

. 폴란드가 醫療陳 派遣國으로 分類되어 있고 同 醫療陳에 病院船 2隻이 包含되어 있음에 비추어 볼때 駐佛 大使館 報告는 이 病院船을 艦艇으로 把握했을 可能性이 있음.

6) 온두라스

. 駐 카이로, 駐 佛 報告에는 150名 規模의 兵力 派遣國으로 把握되어 있는바, 주 과테말라 大使館에 確認한 結果, 當初 計劃이 있었으나 野黨 反對와 經濟 事情으로 議會同意 要請 節次도 保留한 狀態라 함.

7) 루마니아

. 2.7. 議會에서 360名 規模의 醫療支援團과 180名 規模의 對化學戰 部隊를 사우디아라비아에 派遣하는 同意案 議決, 通過시킴.

. 루마니아의 上記 決定은 最近의 것으로서 어느 公館 報告에도 集計되지 않고 있음.

0162

다. 기타

- 美國防部는, 2.16. 反 이라크 聯合國이 33個國이라고 發表함으로써 支援國 5個國(韓國,中國,獨逸,헝가리,뉴질랜드)을 包含시킴. 中國이 包含된 理由에 대해서는 具體的 答辯을 回避하고 있는바 다분히 事務錯誤일 것으로 推測된다는 駐美大使館 報告가 있음.
- 駐美.英 大使館 報告에 의하면 韓國은 "戰鬪兵力 派遣國"은 아니지만 "戰鬪 支援 兵力 派遣國"과 "財政支援 供與國"에 包含됨.
- 日本은 어느 分類에도 包含되지 않은것이 눈에 뜨이는바 美, 英은 財政 支援國에 包含시키고 있음.
- 參考로 醫療團 派遣國은 韓國, 헝가리, 싱가폴, 필리핀, 시에라리온, 불가리아, 루마니아(派遣豫定)等 7個國

添 附 1 : 多國籍軍 現況表

添 附 2 : 해밀턴 英國 國防長官 下院提出 書面資料 (駐英 大使館 報告)

0163

<添附 1>

多 國 籍 軍 現 況

(*표는 醫療團도 派遣한 國家)

連番	國 別	本 部 把 握	駐사우디大使館報告	駐카이로總領事館報告	駐佛蘭西大使館報告	A P (2.7字)	NSC 資料 / 備考
1	*미 국	. 병력 : 492,000 . 탱크 : 2,000 . 항공기 : 1,300 . 함정 : 60 (항공모함 6척)	. 병력 : 약500,000 (육.해.공군 파견)	. 병력 : 425,000 . 탱크 : 2,500 . 항공기 및 헬기 1,800 . 함정 : 100 (항공모함 6척)	. 병력 : 430,000 . 탱크 : 2,000 . 전투기 : 1,300 . 전투헬기 : 1,500 . 함정 : 55 (항공모함 6척)	. 병력 : 500,000 . 탱크 : 2,000 . 항공기 : 1,780 (항모탑재기 480대 포함) . 헬기 : 1,700 . 함정 : 120 (항공모함 6척)	. 육.해.공군 파견
2	*캐 나 다	. 병력 : 2,000 . 항공기 : 24 . 함정 : 3	. 해.공군 파견	. 항공기 : 24 . 함정 : 3	. 병력 : 1,700 . 항공기 : 18 . 함정 : 3	. 병력 : 1,850 . 항공기 : 18 . 함정 : 3	. 육.해군 파견
3	*호 주	. 함정 : 3	. 해.공군 파견	. 함정 : 3	. 함정 : 3	. 함정 : 2	. 해군 파견
4	*영 국	. 병력 : 35,000 . 탱크 : 170 . 항공기 : 72 . 함정 : 16	. 병력 : 30,000 . 탱크 : 130 . 항공기 : 50 . 함정 : 16	. 병력 : 25,000 . 탱크 : 170 . 항공기 : 63 . 함정 : 15	. 병력 : 35,000 . 탱크 : 170 . 전투기 : 72 . 함정 : 16	. 병력 : 35,000 . 항공기 : 70 . 함정 : 16	. 육.해.공군 파견
5	프 랑 스	. 병력 : 10,000 . 탱크 : 40 . 항공기 : 40 . 함정 : 14	. 병력 : 15,000 . 항공기 : 38 . 함정 : 14 (항공모함 1척)	. 병력 : 10,000 . 탱크 : 72 . 항공기 : 38 . 함정 : 9	. 병력 : 15,200 . 탱크 : 40 . 장갑차 : 300 . 야포 : 18 . 전투기 : 60 . 전투헬기 : 120 . 함정 : 14	. 병력 : 12,000 . 항공기 : 3개 비행대대 . 함정 : 12-14	.육.해.공군 파견
6	이 태 리	. 항공기 : 8 . 함정 : 6	. 해.공군 파견	. 항공기 : 7 . 함정 : 6	. 전투기 : 8 . 함정 : 6	. 함정 : 6 . 공군 파견 : 8 (터키 배치)	. 해.공군 파견
7	*벨 기 에	. 함정 : 3	. 해군 파견	. 함정 : 3	. 함정 : 3	. 항공기 : 18 (터키 배치) . 함정 : 2	. 해군,터키배치 공군
8	*네덜란드	. 함정 : 3	. 해군 파견	. 함정 : 3	. 함정 : 3	. 함정 : 2	. 해군,터키배치 공군
9	스 페 인	. 함정 : 3	. 해군 파견	. 함정 : 4	. 함정 : 3	. 함정 : 3	. 해군 파견
10	그리이스	. 함정 : 1	. 해군 파견	. 함정 : 1	. 함정 : 1	. 함정 : 1	. 해군 파견
11	*덴 마 크	. 함정 : 1	. 해군 파견	. 함정 : 1	. 함정 : 1	. 함정 : 1	. 해군 파견

0164

連番	國 別	本 部 把 握	駐사우디大使館報告	駐카이로總領使館報告	駐佛蘭西大使館報告	A P	NSC 資料 / 備考
12-17	GCC국(사우디,오만, 쿠웨이트, 바레인, UAE, 카타르)	. 병력 : 150,500 . 탱크 : 800 . 항공기 : 330 . 함정 : 36	. 육.해.공군 파견	. 병력 : 50,000 . 탱크 : 520 . 항공기 : 334	. 병력 : 165,300 . 탱크 : 750 . 항공기 : 260 . 전투헬기 : 203	. 병력 : 150,500 . 탱크 : 800 . 항공기 : 330	. 육.해.공군 파견
18	이 집 트	. 병력 : 35,000 . 탱크 : 400	. 병력 : 35,000	. 병력 : 35,000 . 탱크 : 450	. 병력 : 35,600 . 탱크 및 장갑차 400 . 함정 : 16	. 병력 : 38,500	. 육군 파견
19	시 리 아	. 병력 : 19,000 . 탱크 : 300	. 병력 : 30,000	. 병력 : 20,000 . 탱크 : 270	. 병력 : 19,800 . 탱크 : 300	. 병력 : 21,000	. 육군 파견
20	*파키스탄	. 병력 : 7,000 (6천명 추가파견 예정)	. 육군 파견	. 병력 : 8,000	. 병력 : 5,000	. 병력 : 13,000 (군사고문단6,000)	. 육.해군 파견
21	*방글라데시	. 병력 : 2,000 (3천명 추가파견 예정)	. 육군 파견	. 병력 : 6,000	. 병력 : 2,500	. 병력 : 2,000	. 육군 파견
22	모 로 코	. 병력 : 1,700	. 병력 : 1,700	. 병력 : 1,500	. 병력 : 6,700	. 병력 : 1,700	. 육군 파견
23	세 네 갈	. 병력 : 500	. 육군 파견	. 병력 : 500	. 병력 : 500	. 병력 : 500	. 육군 파견
24	니 제 르	. 병력 : 480	. 육군 파견	. 병력 : 500	. 병력 : 500	. 병력 : 480 . 1개 비행대대	. 육군 파견
25	아르헨티나	. 병력 : 100 . 함정 : 2	. 해군 파견	. 함정 : 2	. 병력 : 100 . 함정 : 2	. 병력 : 100 . 함정 : 2	.육군 파견
26	포르투갈	. 함정 : 1		. 함정 : 1	. 함정 : 1	. 함정 : 1	미국정부는 불포함
27	노르웨이	. 함정 : 1	. 해군 파견	. 함정 : 1		. 함정 : 1	미국정부는 불포함
28	*체 코	. 병력 : 200		. 병력 : 300	. 병력 : 200	. 병력 : 200	對화학전 부대 미국정부는 불포함
29	소 련	. 함정 : 2 (관찰목적)	. 함정 : 철수시킴	. 함정 : 4	. 함정 : 2	. 함정 : 2	미국정부는 불포함
30	터 키			. 함정 : 2			자국방위군
31	*폴 란 드				. 함정 : 2		미국무부 근동국, 정치군사국은 불포함
32	*뉴질랜드					. 항공기 : 2 (C-130 수송기)	미국무부 근동국, 정치군사국은 포함

0165

連番	國別	本部把握	駐사우디大使館報告	駐카이로總領事館報告	駐佛蘭西大使館報告	A P	NSC 資料 / 備考
33	독 일			. 함정 : 5		. 항공기 : 18 (터키 배치)	미국무부 근동국, 미국방부는 불포함 미국무부대변인실, 정치군사국은포함
34	온두라스			. 병력 : 150	. 병력 : 150		미국정부는 불포함
계		총 28개국 . 병력 : 755,480 . 탱크 : 3,710 . 항공기 : 1,774 . 함정 : 153 (항공모함6, 1척 추가파견 예정)	총 26개국	총 32개국 . 병력 : 581,950 . 탱크 : 3,982 . 항공기 : 2,266 (헬기포함) . 함정 : 159 (항공모함 6)	총 29개국 . 병력 : 718,250 . 탱크 : 3,660 . 항공기 : 3,541 (헬기포함) . 함정 : 163 (항공모함 6)	총 31개국 . 병력 : 781,030 . 탱크 : 2,800 . 항공기 : 3,944 이상 (헬기포함) . 함정 : 172 (항공모함 6)	

0166

(添 附 2)

해밀턴 英國 國防長官 下院 提出 書面 資料

陸.海.空軍, 醫療支援團 派遣 및 實質的 支援 供與國 (36個國)

1. 西方 4個國 (美, 캐나다, 濠州, 뉴질랜드)
2. 西歐 11個國 (英, 佛, 伊, 벨기에, 和, 스페인, 希, 덴마크, 노르웨이, 스웨덴, 포르투갈)
3. 아랍 8個國 (사우디, 쿠웨이트, 오만, 카타르, 바레인, UAE, 시리아, 이집트, 시리아)
4. 아시아 4個國 (파키스탄, 방글라데시, 韓國, 싱가폴)
5. 아프리카 4個國 (모로코, 세네갈, 니제르, 시에라리온)
6. 南美 1個國 (아르헨티나)
7. 東歐 4個國 (체코, 루마니아, 폴란드, 헝가리)

0167

1/2L
(외신기관
참고)

外務部 걸프戰 事後對策班

題 目 : 유엔 安保理의 걸프戰 正式休戰 決議案 採擇

91. 4. 4.
中 東 1 課

1. 槪 觀

ㅇ 유엔 안보리는 4.3 저녁(뉴욕시간) 걸프전 정식 휴전 결의(687호)를 찬성 12, 반대 1(쿠바), 기권 2(예멘, 에쿠아돌)로 채택함.

ㅇ 미.소등 안보리 상임이사국 5개국은 지난주 걸프전의 정식휴전 (formal ceasefire)을 이룩하기 위한 결의안 내용에 합의를 보고, 그동안 비동맹 이사국들과 문안내용에 대한 협의를 가진바있음.

2. 決議 主要 內容

ㅇ 이라크.쿠웨이트 국경문제는 63년 양국간의 합의의사록에 따른 국경선을 존중한다는 원칙하에 유엔 안보리가 이를 보장

ㅇ 유엔 감시단(UN observer unit)의 이.쿠 국경 배치 및 다국적군 철수

ㅇ 이라크의 생.화학무기,사정거리 150km 이상의 탄도미사일, 핵무기능력을 완전 제거하고 재래식 무기 금수도 계속 시행

ㅇ 이라크의 원유 수출 대금중 일정액을 공제, 배상금으로 충당

ㅇ 이라크의 테러리즘 포기

ㅇ 이라크가 상기 제조건을 수락함을 공식 통보하는대로 정식 휴전 발효

3. 分析 및 評價

ㅇ 이번 안보리 결의는 걸프전의 잠정휴전을 이룩한 지난번 결의 686호에 이어 정식 휴전을 발효시킴으로써 유엔차원에서 걸프전을 공식적으로 종결시키기 위한 결의로서, 결의 내용중 주요 쟁점은 이라크의 군사력 제한 문제와 이라크-쿠웨이트간 국경문제였음.

ㅇ 이번 결의 내용은 무력도발 행위를 자행한 이라크에 대해 응징을 가하려는 미국측의 초안을 거의 대부분 반영하였는바, 이러한 결의를 채택함에 있어 미국이 연합군에 참여한 영, 불은 물론 소련과 중국의 동의를 받아냈다는 점은 걸프전 이후 높아진 미국의 국제적 위상을 다시한번 확인한 것으로 평가됨.

0168

o 이라크-쿠웨이트 국경문제에 관한 유엔 결의 내용은 63년도 「우호관계 회복 및 관련문제에 관한 합의의사록」에 따른 양국간의 국경선 합의를 국제적으로 보장하는 것인바, 비동맹 국가들은 국경문제는 이라크, 쿠웨이트 양국이 협상해야 할 사안이고 더우기 유엔 안보리가 이러한 국경선 인정과 보장을 하는 것이 전례없는 일임을 들어 반대입장을 표명한바 있음.

o 금번 결의는 이라크의 군사력 제한 문제에 관하여 상세하게 규정하고 있는바, 골자는 이라크의 화학.생물무기 및 사정거리 150km 이상의 탄도미사일과 핵무기 능력등 주변국에 중대한 위협이 되는 군사력을 철저히 제거하고, 그외에 재래식 무기 금수조치도 당분간 지속시키자는 것임. 이번 결의에 따라 유엔 조사팀이 이라크 영내에서 동 무기의 현장조사 및 파괴, 제거작업을 하게될 것으로 예상되는바, 이 경우 전쟁 패배 사실을 이라크 국민에게 직접적으로 강조하는 결과가 되어 사담 후세인 정권의 입지가 더욱 어려워질 가능성이 큼.

o 상기 결의로 이라크에 대한 식품, 민수용 필수품 공급은 가능하게 되었으나, 쿠웨이트 유전방화등을 포함 걸프전 관련 피해에 대한 이라크의 배상책임을 공식 확인하고 석유 수출 대금중 일정 비율을 배상금 재원으로 사용하도록 규정하였으며 대이라크 경제제재 조치도 당분간 대부분 유지키로 함으로써, 사담후세인 현정부가 존속하는한 이라크에 대한 압력을 늦추지 않겠다는 미국과 연합국의 의사가 충분히 반영됨.

o 이번 결의는 가장 길고 복잡한 내용을 담은 유엔 결의로서 특히 이라크에 대해서는 'demand','require'등 강경한 용어를 사용하는등 매우 엄격한 내용이며 전쟁피해 배상의무를 규정하는등 1차대전 이후 패전국에 대한 강화 조약과 유사한 점도 있는바, 이는 불법무력 도발행위를 철저히 응징하려는 미국을 비롯한 전승국가들의 결의가 투영된 결과로 보임. 끝.

0169

<table>
<tr><th colspan="6">정리보존문서목록</th></tr>
<tr><td>기록물종류</td><td>일반공문서철</td><td>등록번호</td><td>2020120223</td><td>등록일자</td><td>2020-12-29</td></tr>
<tr><td>분류번호</td><td>772</td><td>국가코드</td><td>XF</td><td>보존기간</td><td>영구</td></tr>
<tr><td>명 칭</td><td colspan="5">걸프사태, 1990-91. 전12권</td></tr>
<tr><td>생 산 과</td><td>북미1과/중동1과</td><td>생산년도</td><td>1990~1991</td><td>담당그룹</td><td></td></tr>
<tr><td>권 차 명</td><td colspan="5">V.12 Press Release</td></tr>
<tr><td>내용목차</td><td colspan="5">1. 주한이라크 대사관
2. 주한사우디아라비아 대사관
3. 기타</td></tr>
</table>

0001

1. 주한이라크 대사관

0002

Embassy of
The Republic of Iraq
Seoul

سفارة الجمهورية العراقية
سيئول

The position of the Government of the Republic of Iraq on the recent development in Kuwait is as follows ;

1. The events currently occuring in Kuwait are an internal affair with which Iraq has no relation.

2. The Interim Free Government has asked Iraqi Government to extend assistance for the maintenance of law and order with a view to sparing the people of Kuwait any harm. The Iraqi Government has decided to extend the assistance requested on the basis of this consideration and non other.

3. The Iraqi Government vigorously reaffirms that Iraq harbours no special objectives in Kuwait and is desirous of establishing relations of fraternity and good neighbourliness with it.

4. It is up to the people of Kuwait themselves to determine in the end their own affairs. The Iraqi forces will be withdrawn as soon as the situation is settled down and as soon as the Free Government of Kuwait has so wished. We hope that this will be a matter of a few days or a few weeks at the latest.

5. We reject any foreign interference in the current events. Such interference will only aggravate the situation.

Iraq looks forward to seeing the situation restored back to normal in Kuwait quickly and by the people of Kuwait themselves without any foreign interference.

0003

Embassy of
The Republic of Iraq
Seoul

سفارة الجمهورية العراقية
سيئول

PRESS OFFICE

NO. 13/90

PRESS RELEASE

SEOUL, August 2nd, 1990

0004

이락 혁명 평의회 성명서
1990. 8. 2

이락 혁명 평의회는 다음과 같은 개요의 성명서를 발표하였다;

모든 사람들이 알고 있듯이, 전 아랍 세계는 붊신에 대항하여, 그리고 외부로부터 자신을 보호하기 위하여 결속되어왔다. 하지만 쿠웨이트의 통치자와 그의 추종자들은 위의 원칙에, 특히, 아랍 국가들간의 관계를 감독하는 원칙에서 이탈하여왔다.

혁명은 바로 쿠웨이트인들 자신들에 의해서 익루어졌는데, 이 혁명으로 그들은 쿠웨이트의 통치자와 그를 둘러싼 도당들을 타도하였다. 혁명을 일으킨 이들은 평화적인 임시 정부를 수립하였고, 이락 정부에 쿠웨이트 국민의 평화와 안보를 증강시키기 위한 지지를 요청하였다.

이락 혁명 평의회는 상황이 정상으로 돌아오는대로, 쿠웨이트 정부의 요청이 있으면 즉시 철수할 것입을 알리면서, 쿠웨이트 정부의 요청을 수락하였다. 이느 수일 내지 수주일 이상 걸리지는 않을 것이다.

혁명 평의회는, 정규군 및 의용군과 함께 전 이락 국민은 쿠웨이트와 함께 설 것이며, 어떠한 침략과 공격에서라도 쿠웨이트를 보호할것이라고 했다.

0005

Embassy of
The Republic of Iraq
Seoul

سفارة الجمهورية العراقية
سيئول

PRESS OFFICE
No. 14-90

PRESS RELEASE

SEOUL, AUGUST 4, 1990

0006

A STATEMENT
BY
THE REVOLUTION COMMAND COUNCIL
OF THE REPUBLIC OF IRAQ
ISSUED ON AUGUST 3, 1990

The Iraqi Government, Friday, August 3, 1990, announced that it will begin withdrawing Iraqi forces from Kuwait as of Sunday, August 5, 1990. A revolution Command Council Spokesman said in Baghdad yesterday, Friday, August 3, 1990, referred to the Council's statement of August 2, which outlined the reason and circumstances which prompted Iraq to extend help to the Free Provisional Government of Kuwait saying that the Iraqi forces had fulfilled their honest national and pan-Arab duties in maintaining security and stability with high degree of sincerity and discipline. The spokesman added that in the light of the Revolution Command Council's statement of August 2, and in accordance with the understanding between Iraq and the Free Provisional Government of Kuwait, Iraqi Government laid down a plan to stand withdrawing Iraqi forces in accordance with a timetable as of Sunday, August 5, unless something happens that proves a threat to the security of Kuwait and Iraq.

The spokesman, however, said that in so doing, Iraq does not mean to respond to the fun made here or there by certain hostile circles.

The Iraqi spokesman sternly warned any party that may try to attack Iraq or Kuwait, whatever its size or colour that it would be forced with a firm stand by Iraq and that "its hand would be chopped from the shoulder."

The Revolution Command Council's Spokesman stressed that they will be no going back to the outmoded era (of Al-Sabah regime) and that the relationship between Kuwait and Iraq in the present as well as in the future will be decided by the the peoples of both countries.

0007

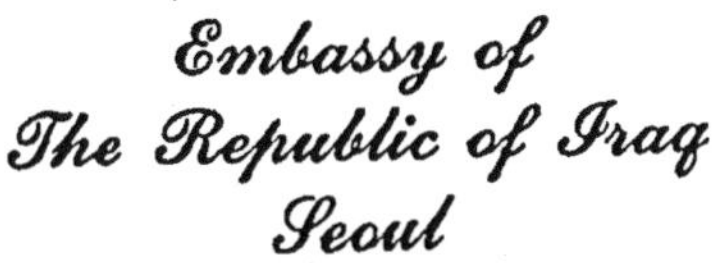

سفارة الجمهورية العراقية
سيئول

PRESS OFFICE

NO. 15/90

PRESS RELEASE

SEOUL, August 9, 1990

0008

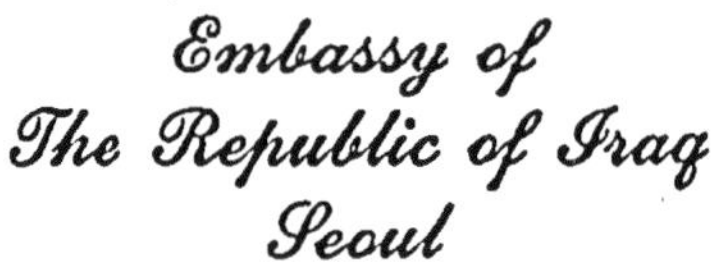

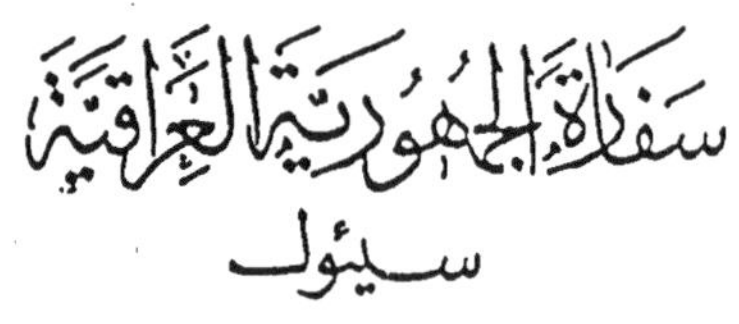

성 명 서

1990. 8. 8, 미대통령의 성명서에 관한 논평에서, 이라크 혁명 평의회의 한 대변인은 다음과 같이 말했다. ;

미국 대통령은, 자신은 사우디 아라비아의 요청에 의하여 미국 병력을 파견하며, 이 병력은 이라크의 날조된 침략으로부터 사우디 아라비아를 방어할 것임을 선언하였다. 이라크는 이러한 거짓말을 전적으로 부인한다.

사담 후세인 대통령이 바그다드에 있는 미국 대리대사를 통해서, 이라크는 이라크를 공격하거나 그 지역에서 미국이 그릇된 의도를 수행할 구실로서 미국에 의해 사용될 지도 모를 어떠한 오해나 관심사를 명백히 밝히기 위하여 현 사태에 관하여 누구에게나 무엇이든지 설명할 준비가 되어 있다는 점을 확인하는 메시지를 미국 대통령에게 전달했음에도 불구하고, 미국 정부측은 이러한 조작 사실을 선전 하고 반복하기를 고집했다.

결론적으로, 이라크 대변인은, 이라크의 모든 군사적 행동은 제국주의자들과 시온주의자들의 침략으로부터 자신을 방어하기위한 방어적 성격이라고 했다. 이라크는 자신과 국민, 그리고 아랍 세계를 위한 자기 방어이외에는 누구에 대항해서라도 군사적 침략을 감행할 계획은 없다. 이라크는 사우디 아라비아나 다른 어떤 나라에 대해서도 야욕은 없으며, 쿠웨이트에서 발생한 사건은 전적으로 다른 경우들과는 다른 것이다. 왜냐하면 쿠웨이트는 이라크의 일부이며, 그들사이에는 특별한 역사적 배경이 있다. 이러한 관계는 다른 어떤 나라와도 함께하지 않는 것이다. 또한, 이라크는 사우디 아라비아와 불가침 조약을 체결하였고, 이를 존중한다. 사담 후세인 대통령은 이라크가 사우디 아라비아와 우호적 관계를 유지할 것임을 강조했다. 대변인은 이락을 공격할 구실로 사용하기 위하여, 미국이 이러한 조작을 선전하고 주장한다는 우리의 결론은 애초부터 정확했다고 덧붙였다.

대변인은 유감을 표명했는데, 왜냐하면 사우디 아라비아의 관리들은 미국의 이러한 그릇된 주장에 영향을 받고 있기 때문이다.

0009

08/14/90 18:33 ☎ 02 792 66.. IRAQIYA-SE... P.02

Embassy of
The Republic of Iraq
Seoul

سفارة الجمهورية العراقية
سيئول

PRESS RELEASE

NO. 19-90 August 14, 1990

AZIZ EXPOSES US DOUBLE STANDARDS

Iraq's Deputy Premier and Foreign Minister Mr. Tareq Aziz on Monday said that the rejection by the U.S. and Israel of President Saddam Hussein's initiative to establish peace in the whole Middle East revealed that double-standard policy of the rejectionist.

Mr. Aziz said that only hours after the declaration of President Hussein's initiative on Sunday, the White House, Britain and Israel announced their rejection of the initiative.

President Hussein's initiative included immediate withdrawal of all occupation forces in the Middle East region and the implementation of all Security Council resolutions in connection with these cases.

President Hussein also proposed that any party failing to withdraw should face UN sanctions similar to those being imposed on Iraq now.

Mr. Aziz said President Hussein's initiative called for the adoption of the same principles in dealing with world problems on the basis of equity and justice. He added that the rejection by America, Britain and Israel of the Iraqi peace initiative sheds light on all aspects of the conspiracy against Iraq.

The rejection "uncovers the real stands of the United States and its allies in adopting double standards and a selective approach in dealing with the problems of the region and the world," Mr. Aziz said.

"While they keep silent over Israel's occupation of Arab and Palestinian territories despite all resolutions issued by the UN Security Council, the General Assembly and world organizations, they hastily, and in a few hours, issue a series of unjust resolutions against Iraq."

All Iraq did was supporting an uprising for liberation and responding to a historical call for unity with a part (Kuwait) that had been unjustly partitioned from Iraq, said Mr. Aziz.

"The stand of the White House, London and Israel reveals the real attitude of Arab regimes which alligned themselves with the former in plotting against Iraq," Mr. Aziz added.

"This affirms the direct responsibility of these Arab regimes for continued Zionist occupation of Palestine and Arab territories."

"These regimes follow the steps of their masters in the White House and London by resorting to the most perfidious means to harm Iraq while they ignore Zionist occupation of Arab territories. One of these regimes, Egypt, in fact recognizes the Zionist entity."

0010

Embassy of
The Republic of Iraq
Seoul

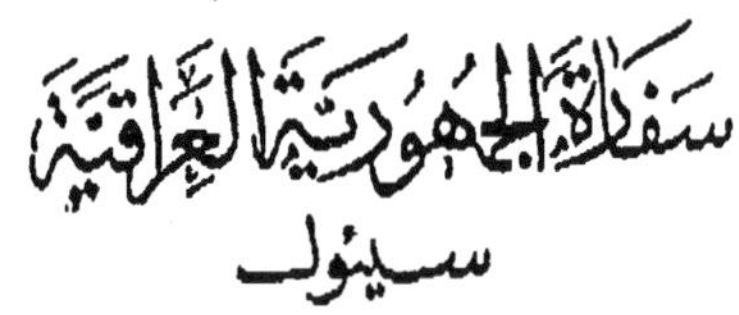

Mr. Aziz called on world states and peoples to reconsider anti-Iraq stands which were influenced by the United States campaign of distortion against Iraq.

The Foreign Minister called on world states to adopt fair stands based on the principles of justice and responsibility towards peace and security in the world.

Mr. Aziz said world states, peoples and forces of freedom have in the past rejected double-standard and policies through which the United States has sought to impose on the United Nations and the world community.

He said they should realize the true motives behind the resolutions taken against Iraq at the UN Security Council through US pressure.

A copy of the text of President Hussein's initiative was handed to the UN Secretary General Mr. Javier Perez de Cuellar by Iraq's Permanent Representative to the United Nations.

Meanwhile, Iraq has reiterated its denial of allegations that it is poised for an attack on Saudi Arabia as totally unfounded.

In a letter to the United Nations Secretary General Mr. Javier Perez de Cuellar on Monday, Iraq's Deputy Prime Minister and Foreign Minister Mr. Tareq Aziz said the United States and its allies, as well as some Arab states, particularly Saudi Arabia, were still repeating false claims that Iraq was taking military action against the Kingdom of Saudi Arabia.

"These claims are totally baseless and unfounded," said Mr. Aziz. "The claims are lies which everybody has become aware of."

Mr. Aziz challenged those making such claims to produce any proof or evidence to support their claims. He attributed the aims behind such claims to the search for a cover for the military presence of the US and its allies on Arab territory.

He said the aim was to create a pretext for an armed military aggression against Iraq by the US, its allies and some Arab states collaborating with them.

"Iraq has not acted in any form nor taken any measure that may pose a threat to the Kingdom of Saudi Arabia, whether directly or indirectly."

Mr. Aziz explained that Iraq and Saudi Arabia had signed an accord stipulating non-interference in the internal affairs of either country by each and refrainment from use of force between the two states.

"Iraq is still committed to this accord if Saudi Arabia honours its commitment," said Mr. Aziz.

He added that Iraq had informed Saudi Arabia directly and through top Arab officials that it had no intention to launch any military act against Saudi Arabia if the latter did not initiate any military act against Iraq.

Iraq has assured Saudi Arabia of its attitude on various occasions, most recently during the Cairo summit last week, said Mr. Aziz.

"Iraq expressed its readiness before all Arab leaders to extend the required guarantees through bilateral means or through the Arab league to reassure the Kingdom of Saudi Arabia."

0011

08/16/90 12:14

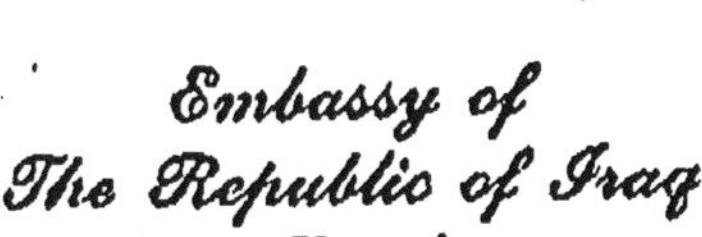

NO. 21-90 **PRESS RELEASE** August 16th, 1990

Iraq has decided to withdraw its forces from the areas facing Iran as from Friday, August 17, 1990, and to start releasing the Iranian prisoners of war (POWs) as from the same date.

This was contained in a message sent by President Saddam Hussein to Iranian President Ali Akbar Hashemi Rafsanjani, and which included a comprehensive settlement to the relations between Iraq and Iran.

The message said that within the frame of confirming desire of Iraq and his people for peace and as a result to the direct contacts made between Iraq and Iran following the president message to messrs: Ali Khameini and Ali Akbar Rafsanjani on April 21, 1990, and in conformity with the spirit of the president initiative and as a final and clear solution we decided the following;

One. Approving your proposal which was contained in your reply message dated August 8th, 1990 and which was received by our representative in Geneva, Mr. Barazan Ibrahim Al-Tikriti from your representative Mr. Syros Naseri on endorsing the agreement of 1975 linked with the bases included by our letter on 30th July, 1990, especially as concerns the exchange of POWs and articles 6 and 7 of the Security Council Resolution No. 598.

Two. On the bases of what was included in para one of this letter and your letter of July 30, we are ready to despatch a delegation to Tehran or that an Iranian delegation visits us in Baghdad to arrange agreements and getting prepared for signing them on the level to be agreed on.

Three. As an initiative of good intent, our withdrawal will start as from Friday, August 17, and we will withdraw our forces facing Iran along the borders with the exception of what would be token forces together with the police and borders guards for implementing daily duties in normal circumstances.

Four. An immediate and comprehensive exchange of all POWs in both Iraq and Iran will take place and across the land borders along Khanaqin-Qasr Shireen Road and other outlets to be agreed upon. We will take the initiative and start that as from next Friday.

President Hussein's message added that in our decision, everything has become clear and everything you wanted was realized and nothing has remained but to exchange documents from a position overlooking new life prevailed by cooperation in the shade of principles of Islam and to respect each other rights and also to distance those of bad intentions from our coasts, and maybe we will cooperate for keeping the gulf a lake of peace and safety free from foreign threats and forces which are after us.

The President message expounded that after removing all what could obstruct the path for brotherly relations with all moslims and for opening the way for a serious interaction with all believers for confronting evil forces which are after harming Muslims and the Arab nation and for keeping Iraq and Iran away from the blackmail and games of the evil international forces and their lackeys in the region and in conformity with the spirit of our initiative announced on August 12, 1990, in which we wanted the realization of lasting and comprehensive peace in the region and so that to remove any pretext that coule prevent interaction and maintain precaution and also for boosting Iraq's potentials in the field of the great duel and mobilizing them towards the objectives which all Muslims and honourable Arabs were unanimous that they were right so that good people could find their way for normal relations between Iraq and Iran, this decision was made.

0012

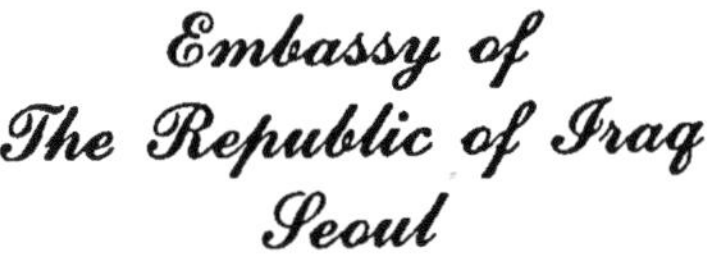

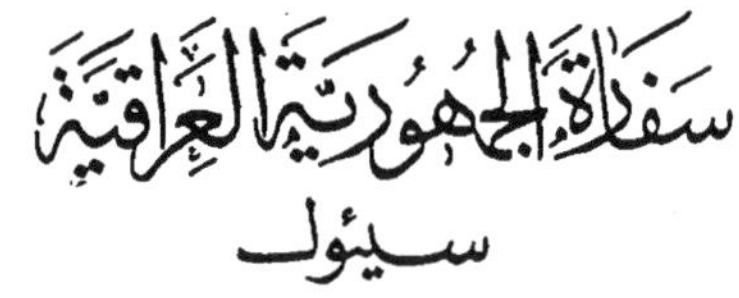

No. 109-90

The Embassy of the Republic of Iraq presents its compliments to the Ministry of Foreign Affairs of the Republic of Korea and has the honour to enclose herewith a letter of H.E. President Saddam Hussein's, addressed to the president of the Islamic Republic of Iran, H.E. Ali Akbar Hashemi Rafsanjani.

The Embassy of the Republic of Iraq avails itself of this opportunity to renew to the Ministry of Foreign Affairs of the Republic of Korea the assurances of its highest consideration.

SEOUL, August 17, 1990

TO THE MINISTRY OF FOREIGN AFFAIRS
OF THE REPUBLIC OF KOREA

0013

Embassy of
The Republic of Iraq
Seoul

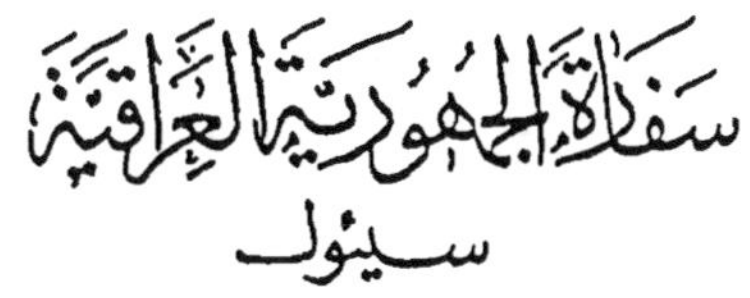

PRESS RELEASE

NO. 25-90

Date 20/8/1990

United Nations
Is
Against American
Military Intervention

On August 16, 1990, the Secretary General of the United Nations said that military force by any country to enforce U.N. sanctions on IRAQ would be a breach of the U.N. Charter as long as the Security Council did not approve the use of force.

We quote him ;
"Any intervention, whatever the country, would not be in accordance with either the letter or the spirit of the U.N. Charter."

We may add to what the Secretary General said, that we believe very strongly that the whole American presence in the area is useless, because it will complecate the situation rather than putting an end to it.

0014

Embassy of
The Republic of Iraq
Seoul

سفارة الجمهورية العراقية
سيئول

PRESS RELEASE

NO. 25-90 1990/8/20

UN, 미국의 군사개입 반대

1990년 8월 16일, UN 사무총장은, 안전 보장 이사회가 무력 사용을 승인하지않는한은 이라크에대한 UN의 제재를 강화하기 위한 어떠한 나라의 무력 사용도 UN 헌장에 위배되는 것이라고 밝혔다.

그는 다음과 같이 말했다 ;
" 어떠한 나라의 어떠한 간섭도 UN 헌장의 정신과 법문에 입치하지 않을 것이다."

사무총장의 발언에 우리는 다음과 같이 덧붙이고자 한다. 즉 이 지역내 모든 미국인의 존재는 무익하다고 우리는 확신한다. 왜냐하면, 이는 사태를 종결짓기보다는 더욱 복잡하게 만듭 것이기 때문이다.

0015

08/16/90 12:14 ☎ 02 792 ...

Embassy of
The Republic of Iraq
Seoul

سفارة الجمهورية العراقية
سيئول

NO. 21-90

PRESS RELEASE

August 16th, 1990

Iraq has decided to withdraw its forces from the areas facing Iran as from Friday, August 17, 1990, and to start releasing the Iranian prisoners of war (POWs) as from the same date.

This was contained in a message sent by President Saddam Hussein to Iranian President Ali Akbar Hashemi Rafsanjani, and which included a comprehensive settlement to the relations between Iraq and Iran.

The message said that within the frame of confirming desire of Iraq and his people for peace and as a result to the direct contacts made between Iraq and Iran following the president message to messrs:
Ali Khameini and Ali Akbar Rafsanjani on April 21, 1990, and in conformity with the spirit of the president initiative and as a final and clear solution we decided the following;

One. Approving your proposal which was contained in your reply message dated August 8th, 1990 and which was received by our representative in Geneva, Mr. Barazan Ibrahim Al-Tikriti from your representative Mr. Syros Naseri on endorsing the agreement of 1975 linked with the bases included by our letter on 30th July, 1990, especially as concerns the exchange of POWs and articles 6 and 7 of the Security Council Resolution No. 598.

Two. On the bases of what was included in para one of this letter and your letter of July 30, we are ready to despatch a delegation to Tehran or that an Iranian delegation visits us in Baghdad to arrange agreements and getting prepared for signing them on the level to be agreed on.

Three. As an initiative of good intent, our withdrawal will start as from Friday, August 17, and we will withdraw our forces facing Iran along the borders with the exception of what would be token forces together with the police and borders guards for implementing daily duties in normal circumstances.

Four. An immediate and comprehensive exchange of all POWs in both Iraq and Iran will take place and across the land borders along Khanaqin-Qasr Shireen Road and other outlets to be agreed upon. We will take the initiative and start that as from next Friday.

President Hussein's message added that in our decision, everything has become clear and everything you wanted was realized and nothing has remained but to exchange documents from a position overlooking new life prevailed by cooperation in the shade of principles of Islam and to respect each other rights and also to distance those of bad intentions from our coasts, and maybe we will cooperate for keeping the gulf a lake of peace and safety free from foreign threats and forces which are after us.

The President message expounded that after removing all what could obstruct the path for brotherly relations with all moslims and for opening the way for a serious interaction with all believers for confronting evil forces which are after harming Muslims and the Arab nation and for keeping Iraq and Iran away from the blackmail and games of the evil international forces and their lackeys in the region and in conformity with the spirit of our initiative announced on August 12, 1990, in which we wanted the realization of lasting and comprehensive peace in the region and so that to remove any pretext that coule prevent interaction and maintain precaution and also for boosting Iraq's potentials in the field of the great duel and mobilizing them towards the objectives which all Muslims and honourable Arabs were unanimous that they were right so that good people could find their way for normal relations between Iraq and Iran, this decision was made.

0016

Embassy of
The Republic of Iraq
Seoul

سفارة الجمهورية العراقية
سيئول

NO: 45 / 90

Press Release

Date:13/9/1990

IN REPLY TO THE U.S. PRESIDENT GEORGE BUSH'S SPEECH BEFORE THE AMERICAN CONGRESS, THE IRAQI DEPUTY PREMIER AND FOREIGN MINISTER TAREQ AZIZ STATED TO IRAQI NEWS AGENCY -INA- THAT THE AMERICAN PRESIDENT'S ADDRESS CONTAINED MANY SOPHISTRIES AND ASPECTS THAT NEED TO BE EXPOSED. THE AMERICAN PRESIDENT ASSERTS IN HIS SPEECH THE AMERICAN IMPERIALIST TENDENCY FOR LEADING THE WORLD AND IMPOSING AMERICA'S DICTATORSHIP ON IT.

THE FOREIGN MINISTER HAS FURTHER SAID THAT THE AMERICAN PRESIDENT SHOULD REALIZE THAT THE WORLD DOES NOT RECOGNIZE THIS LEADERSHIP AND IF A NUMBER OF AGENT OR WEAK GOVERNMENTS ACCEPTS TO RECEIVE ORDERS FROM THE AMERICAN ADMINISTRATION, THE MAJORITY OF THE WORLD NATIONS, PARTICULARLY THE ARAB NATION AND ISLAMIC PEOPLES, CATEGORICALLY REJECT THAT AND INSIST ON PRESERVING THEIR INDEPENDENCE AND THEIR FREE WILL.

ON THE OTHER HAND, AND REGARDING THE ATTITUDE VERSUS IRAQ, THE AMERICAN PRESIDENT HAS PURPOSFULLY RESORTED TO LIES AND DISTORTION OF REALITIES AND FACTS WHEN HE REPEATED THE AMERICAN ALLEGATIONS WITH REGARD TO IRAQ'S INTENTIONS AGAINST SAUDIA AS A JUSTIFICATION OF HIS MILITARY CAMPAIGN IN THE REGION, MR AZIZ FURTHER CLARIFIED.

BUSH HAS NOT PUT FORWARD AN EVIDENCE FOR THESE ALLEGATIONS AND THE AMERICAN SATELLITES ARE AWARE OF THIS FACT. ALSO, THE AMERICAN MILITARY CIRCLES HAVE CONFIRMED IN MANY STATEMENTS THAT THE IRAQI MILITARY ARRANGEMENTS HAVE BEEN DEFENSIVE ARRANGEMENTS,THE MATTER WHICH INDICATES UNDERESTIMATION BY THE AMERICAN PRESIDENT OF THE AMERICAN PEOPLE'S MINDS AND ALSO THE MINDS OF THE CONGRESS MEMBERS.

THE IRAQI FOREIGN MINISTER HAS FURTHER ADDED ''WE CHALLENGE THE AMERICAN PRESIDENT TO PRESENT THE MATERIAL EVIDENCE OF THIS CLAIM AND WE ALSO REQUEST FROM THE OTHER STATES THAT POSSESS MEANS OF PHOTOGRAPHY BY SATELLITES, SPECIALLY THE SOVIET UNION, TO TAKE PART IN THE PROCESS OF PRESENTING THE EVIDENCE OR DENYING IT.''

PRESIDENT BUSH HAS TRIED IN HIS SPEECH TO FRIGHTEN THE AMERICAN PEOPLE AND CONGRESS FROM IRAQ'S POSESSION OF 20 PERCENT OF THE WORLD RESERVE OF PETROLEUM, MR AZIZ FURTHER SAID.

BEFORE AUGUST 2, 1990 IRAQ WAS IN POSSESSION OF 10 PERCENT OF THE WORLD'S RESERVES OF PETROLEUM BUT HAS NOT THREATENED ANYBODY NEITHER AMERICA NOR OTHERS AND ONE THIRD OF THE IRAQI EXPORTED OIL WAS BEING EXPORTED TO AMERICA ITSELF, SO WHAT WILL CHANGE IF IRAQ'S RESERVES WERE AMOUNTED TO 20 PERCENT?

0017

THE AMERICAN PRESIDENT CANNOT, HERE TOO, OFFER THE EVIDENCE ON HIS ALLEGATIONS IN SCARING HIS PEOPLE FROM THIS FACT PARTICULARLY THAT IRAQ'S POLICY IN THE FIELD OF OIL HAVE BEEN WELL KNOWN DURING TWO DECADES, AS JUST AND RESPONSIBLE POLICY.

THE IRAQI DEPUTY PREMIER HAS ALSO SAID THAT BUSH'S TALK WITHIN THIS CONTEXT AROUSES A NUMBER OF SERIOUS QUESTIONS WITH REGARD TO WHAT THE WORLD COUNTRIES POSSESS OF POTENTIALS AND RESERVES.

PRESIDENT BUSH'S LOGIC ASSUMES THE EXISTENCE OF PROPORTIONS, ACCEPTABLE OR NOT PERMITTED, REGARDING POSSESSION OF RESERVES OF MATERIALS SIGNIFICANT TO THE WORLD, FOR INSTANCE IRON, COAL OR GAS OR CAPABILITY OF GRAINS PRODUCTION. AND IF PRESIDENT BUSH'S LOGIC IS APPLIED IT WILL INCLUDE MANY COUNTRIES LIKE CANADA, AUSTRALIA AND OTHER COUNTRIES IN AFRICA AND ASIA AND EVEN IN EUROPE, THEREFORE, IT IS NECESSARY THAT THE AMERICAN PRESIDENT TO EXPLAIN HIS AIMS BEHIND THE PROMOTION OF THIS LOGIC AND WHETHER THE WORLD HAS FOR INSTANCE TO ENDEAVOUR TO DIVIDE AMERICA SO THAT IT WILL NOT POSSESS THE CAPACITY OF EXPORTING HALF OF THE WHEAT IN THE WORLD. AND IN ALL EVENTS WHEAT IS MORE SIGNIFICANT FOR HUMANITY THAN PETROL.

DEPUTY PREMIER TAREQ AZIZ HAS FURTHER SAID ONCE AGAIN THE AMERICAN PRESIDENT REPEATS LIES OF HIS EMPLOYEES IN THE REGION LIKE HUSNI MUBARAK, AND WE CHALLENGE BUSH AND THE WHOLE WORLD TO PROVE THAT WE HAVE TOLD LIES TO ANYBODY DURING 22 YEARS OF OUR LEADERSHIP OF IRAQ. WE HAVE EXPLAINED CONCOMITANTS OF THE LIE THAT HUSNI MUBARAK HAS PROPAGATED AFTER HIS VISIT TO BAGHDAD, BY PRESENTING DOCUMENTED STATEMENTS, AND WE HAVE PROVED THAT HUSNI MUBARAK HAS PUT BUSH AND HIS ALLIES IN AN UNPLEASANT SITUATION, SO DOES BUSH STILL INSIST ON CONTINUING IN THIS INVOLVEMENT INSPITE THAT BUSH KNOWS VERY WELL THE OPINION OF KING HUSSEIN WHO HAS VISITED IRAQ AT THE SAME PERIOD AND DEALT WITH THE SAME SUBJECT?

IN HIS STATEMENT TO INA, THE FOREIGN MINISTER HAS ALSO SAID THAT THE AMERICAN PRESIDENT'S EMPHASIS ON RAISING MONEY FROM OTHER COUNTRIES FOR FUNDING HIS AGGRESSIVE MILITARY CAMPAIGN IN THE REGION CONFIRMS AND DISCLOSES AMERICA'S POLICY OF PLUNDERING RICHES OF THE GULF AND USING THEM ON THE WIDEST SCALE IN SERVICE OF THE AMERICAN IMPERIALIST ENDS. IN HIS STRESS ON ISSUES OF THE BUDGET AND OTHERS, PRESIDENT BUSH IS DECEIVING THE AMERICAN PEOPLE AND PEOPLES OF THE WORLD FROM WHOM HE IS COLLECTING MONEY.

THE FOREIGN MINISTER HAS WONDERED WHY DOES NOT BUSH STOP HIS AGGRESSIVE MILITARY CAMPAIGN, WITHDRAW HIS TROOPS AND LESSEN THE AMERICAN EXPENSES, AND WHY DOES NOT HE URGE HIS ALLIES TO SPEND THE MONEY HE IS COLLECTING FOR AGGRESSION ON DEVELOPMENT OF THE COUNTRIES THAT ARE IN NEED OF THEM, INCLUDING COUNTRIES OF THE REGION TO WHICH HE HAS DISPATCHED HIS MILITARY FORCES TO THREATEN AND DOMINATE THEM, THE MATTER WHICH WILL ACTUALLY CONSOLIDATE SECURITY AND STABILITY.

THE IRAQI FOREIGN MINISTER HAS CONCLUDED HIS STATEMENT BY SAYING THAT THE AMERICAN PRESIDENT'S ADDRESS IS AN EXEMPLARY SPEECH OF AN IMPERIALIST SELF-OPINIONATED RULER WHO WANTS TO IMPOSE HIS CONTROL ON THE WORLD BY THE WAY OF LIES AND COUNTERFEITING FACTS AND OBJECTIVES.

THE REALITIES WILL PROVE THE ERROR AND FAILURE OF THIS APPROACH, FOR PEOPLES WILL NOT BE DEFEATED BY SUCH ATTEMPTS AND THEIR WILL FOR FREEDOM, INDEPENDENCE AND JUSTICE WILL BE VICTORIOUS. 0018

Embassy of
The Republic of Iraq
Seoul

سفارة الجمهورية العراقية
سيئول

NO. 46-90

Press Release

15/9/1990

김서기관
조사무관
박서기관

STATEMENT

IRAQI Spokesman denied, categorically, what was circulated by French and Dutch authorities, that IRAQI troops had penetrated the headquarters of the previous diplomatic missions in the province of Kuwait. The Spokesman said that there are strict instruction for not entering these places, though they are no more diplomatic missions as of August 24, 1990. The Spokesman clarifies that the IRAQ authorities is binding itself delicately towards this matter, to preserve certain consideration, and not in accordance with Vienna Agreement, because Vienna Agreement does not cover the previous missions in the province of Kuwait. IRAQ, strictly implements this Agreement towards the accredited missions in it.

0019

Embassy of
The Republic of Iraq
Seoul

سفارة الجمهورية العراقية
سيئول

NO: 47 / 90

Press Release

Date:17/ 9/1990

The people of Iraq is being subjected to the fiercest campaign ever to be launched against it by the U.S.A and its allies, with a view to starving, blackmailing and threatening it. Only recently , the U.S Administration has exerted pressure on the UN to impose on the International Community a resolution of its own making, calling for blockading Iraq, starving its people and depriving it of food and drugs. The U.S.A also deployed its military forces to occupy and desecrate sacred Arab Lands, in violation of international norms and conventions, including heavenly laws.

This unjust campaign is the making of a super-power claiming keenness on the maintenance of world peace and security, and the defence of human rights and freedoms. yet the reality of the situation shows that the U.S.A is exactly the opposite . The U.S Administration is starving Iraqi Children by depriving them of their basic food-milk, and is threatening a whole nation with annihilation , without a fault being committed by the Iraqi people against the U.S.A .

You are fully aware of America's involvement in all the catastrophies affecting peoples and progressive regimes of the World. The U.S.A prohibits the permissible and permits the prohibitable in such a manner as to serve its narrow - minded interests, without due regards to the feelings and aspirations of people, and without any sense

0020

of moral and humane responsibility. The U.S.A came to our region as an occupying force under the pretext of protecting its agents and interests, and reinstalling the family of vice and brutality -i-e Al-Sabah ruling puppets in Kuwait . In so doing, the U.S.A.is acting against the will of the people, who has chosen to be united in a merger between Iraq and Kuwait, the latter being historically and legitimately an integral part of Iraq, separated from motherland, Iraq, by British intelligence and colonialist forces.

The real aim behind the presence of foreign troops in our region is no longer secret. It is to do with U.S plans to impose hegemony on the region with a view to dominating , controlling and stealing the region's wealth, particularly Oil , and also to launch an aggression on Iraq, under the protext that our country is a threat to peace and security in the region and the world !!

Dear Friends,

Our Organization appeals to you on behalf of the children, Women and the elderly of Iraq, and in the name of humanity, just and conscience , to exercise your moral and humane responsibilities, in confronting this smear campaign of starvation and annihilation. Our children look forward to a humanitarian stance to be taken by Iraq's friends, in order that this evil campaign is foiled . We also appeal to you , in the name of all values, laws and conventions, to act quickly and effectively with a view to preventing the U.S.A.from waging a war of destruction in the region. Such a war will have drastic repercussions in the region and the world at large.

Kindly raise your voices with just against falshood, and record your humanitarian stances, proving to the enemies of peoples and humanity that peoples' steadfasness cannot possibly be broken, and that the enemies' adventurism will be met with total failure. Our Children are awaiting positive stances from you- stances enabling them to have their food and milk, and making them feel secured and happy.

Best regards,

Organization of Friendship, Peace
and Solidarity in Iraq

Baghdad / September 1990

0022

on 4b

Embassy of
The Republic of Iraq
Seoul

سفارة الجمهورية العراقية
سيئول

No. 130-90

Dear Sir,

Enclosed, herewith, please find the text of the letter dated September 4th, 1990, sent from H.E. Tariq Aziz, Deputy Prime Minister, Minister of Foreign Affairs to Ministers of Foreign Affairs of the Nations.

The letter including many historical facts concerning current events taking place in Arab Gulf.

Please accept my best regards.

Press Attache
Embassy of the Republic of Iraq

<u>S E O U L</u>, September 18th, 1990

0023

Greetings

Amidst the developments witnessed in the Arab Gulf region, I find it necessary and useful to present some of the facts which I believe will help you to understand the background to the events that have occured in this region.

Iraq, is known to have always been a political entity and the seat of many states throughout millenia. It has always been a coastal state and a major trading centre. The small village established some two centuries ago on the banks of the Arab Gulf under the name of "Kuwait", an Iraqi term for "a small settlement of people", had remained throughout the nineteenth century and up to the First World War, an Iraqi Qadhas' (district) belonging to the province of Basrah. Under Ottoman administrative law, Kuwait was an integral part of Iraq, subject to the Province of Basrah.

In 1897, the governor of Basrah, Muhsin Pasha, informed the Sheikh of Kuwait, Mubarak al-Sabah, of the Sultan's decree appointing him as Qa'im-Maqam (district administrator) of the Qadhaa' of Kuwait, a district of the Province of Basrah. By then, Mubarak had been instigated by the British to kill his two elder brothers, Mohammed and Jarrah, who had opposed the British plan to turn Kuwait into an entity under British dominance.

In 1899, Britain goaded Mubarak al-Sabah into signing a secret agreement under which the British were to provide him with protection even though he was a vassal of the Ottoman Empire and, accordingly, had no authority to sign any international accord. The agreement was therefore strongly rejected by the Ottoman Sultan, which forced Mubarak to retreat and declare his allegiance and subordination to the Ottoman Sublime Porte in 1901.

Britain never ceased these attempts, but continued to establish bases in various parts of the Arab Gulf in order to consolidate its colonial grip over this region, the strategic importance of which had increased both militarily and politically, within the framework of the competition with the Ottoman Empire, and economically as it constituted an important trade route and was known by the British to contain vast oil reserves. In order to secure the interests of the British Empire by weakening all major states in the region, Britain focused its influence on Kuwait and drew artificial boundaries as they did later, together with their French ally, in the Sykes-Picot Agreement of 1917. By so doing Britain pernitiously severed a part of Iraq in a manner that deprived a country ancient in its civilization, and great in its land and population, of its natural access to the waters of the Arab Gulf, the access which it had possessed throughout history.

It was through such artificial colonial machinations that an artificial entity, called Kuwait, was founded for the first time in history under British domination and given artificial boundaries which have no historical or geographical foundations.

Since its establishment in 1921, the State of Iraq has refused to accept this artificial entity. All successive Iraqi governments continued to demand the return of this severed part of Iraq and historical and geographical justice be done to Iraq to guarantee its commercial and economic interests and provide it with the requirements necessary for the defence of its national security. This was the position adopted by successive Iraqi governments, despite the fact that the Iraqi regime at the time was closely linked to Britain.

Britain had also vigorously opposed any project which would bring the one people of Iraq and Kuwait close together and in coastout contact with each other. The project to provide Kuwait with water from Shatt al-Arab, the Kuwait railway project, the project to establish an Iraqi port in Kuwait City were all rejected. These projects continued to meet with British procrastination and/or outright rejection throughout the period from the early 1920s to the early 1960s.

Then Britain consistently pressurized Iraq into accepting the fait accompli. When the British government forced the Prime Minister of Iraq in 1932 to exchange letters with the British Commissioner in Baghdad, regarding the demarcation of the boundaries on the basis of the draft agreement proposed between the Ottoman and British governments, the agreement which had remained unsigned because of the outbreak of the world war I, the Iraqi House of Representatives refused, in its capacity as the country's legislative authority, to ratify the said letters.

During the 1930s, popular demand increased for the return of Kuwait to Iraq. The national press adopted those demands and began supporting them articles and historical document affirming the inevitable return of Kuwait to Iraq. In 1933, the British Political Representative in Kuwait, Colonel Dickson, warnen, in his letters to the British Political Resident in the Gulf, against any approachment between the people in Kuwait and Iraq, and called for their sepation.

0025

In 1940, the ruler of Kuwait replaced the Iraqi administration of the post office in Kuwait with British staff. In 1949, the Iraqi school curricula applied in Kuwaiti schools were replaced by Egyptian curricula.

King Ghazi, the second monarch of Iraq, supported enthusiastically the necessity of the unification of Kuwait with Iraq. He expressed his desire to visit Kuwait in return to an earlier visit made to Iraq by Sheikh Ahmed al-Sabah in 1932. Britain, however, did not encourage the visit, and endeavored to prevent Iraq and Kuwait from reaching any agreement.

In April 1938, Mr. Tawfiq al-Suwaidi, Iraq's then Foreign Minister, informed the British ambassador in Baghdad, Mr. Peterson, that; "the Anglo-Ottoman Agreement of 1913 had recognized Kuwait as a district belonging to the province of Basrah, and since sovereignty over Basrah had been reliquished by the Ottomans to the state of Iraq, then that sovereignty should be extend to include Kuwait as provided for in the agreement of 1913. Iraq, therefore, does not recognize any change in the status of Kuwait."

The Iraqi popular demand for the return of Kuwait to Iraq was met with wide favourable response from the population in Kuwait. The Kuwaiti youth took an active part in the call for Kuwaiti unification with Iraq. In May 1938, a group of "free Kuwaitis" submitted a petition to the Iraqi Government inviting Iraq to help them achieve their aspirations regarding the return of Kuwait to Iraq. To this end, a "national coalition" was established to call upon Ahmed al-Sabah, the Sheikh of Kuwait to set up a legislative council representing the free people of Kuwait. He was forced to accept this demand, but when members of the new Council expressed their demand for the return of Kuwait to Iraq. The Council's demand displeased the ruler of Kuwait and he disolved the Council on 21 December 1938, and waged a campaign of arrest and oppression against its members.

Nevertheless, the free people of Kuwait continued to demand the return of Kuwait to Iraq. They sent many telegrams to pitition King Ghazi. One of those telegrams, which was broadcast on Baghdad radio on 7 March 1939, called upon King Ghazi to intervene, saying "Our history confirms the integration of Kuwait with Iraq. We shall live and die under the Iraqi flag. Ghazi! help your brothers in Kuwait!"

The situation escalated into a sweeping uprising led by the youth of Kuwait against the authorities on 10 March 1939. The ruler of Kuwait had to resort to armed force to disperse the youth, a great number of whom he then arrested and imprisoned.

King Ghazi tried to intervene in order to secure the release of the prison ers. He warned the Sheikh of Kuwait against the continued harassment and imprisonment of the "free Kuwaitis". In consequence, King Ghazi and the then Iraqi Government were subjected to intensified British pressure to desist from Iraqi demands for the integration of Kuwait. To this end, ambassador Peterson had several secret meetings with King Ghazi shortly before latter's sudden death, in an attempt to press him to give up the claims to Kuwait. King Ghazi was killed in a mysterious accident on 5 April 1939, giving every reason to believe that Britain was behind his death because of his strong advocacy of the return of Kuwait to Iraq.

Following the assasination of King Ghazi, Britain's collaborators seized power in the country. Then, with the outbreak of the Second World War and the following years, Iraq and the region witnessed a series of successive changes and developments including the creation of Israel, the Arab-Israeli war and the revolution in Egypt. All these developments gave the British colonialists the pretext to concentrate their influence in Kuwait while severing its political and human links with Iraq.

On 9 March 1956, while, Sellwyn Llyod, the British Foreign Secretary was on a visit to Baghdad attending a consultative meeting of the Permenant Council of the Baghdad Pact, Prime Minister Nouri al-Said of Iraq raised the subject of accession of Kuwait to the Arab Union which was being formed at the time. Llyod promised to put the matter before the British cabinet. Britain's reply, which was delivered via the British ambassador in Baghdad, Michael Wright, was that Britain was prepared to grant Kuwait independence, and Kuwait would have the freedom to decide the question of joining the Union. In order to present Britain with a fait accompli, Iraq dispatched Deputy Prime Minister, Tawfaq al-Suwaidi, in April 1957, to Shtura in Lebanon, where Sheikh Abdullah al-Salim al-Sabah was staying, in order to negotiate with him about the necessity of Kuwait's accession to the Union which was to be established. That effort, however, did not produce any positive result.

Early in 1958, Prime Minister Nouri al-Said of Iraq submitted to the Baghdad Pact the necessity of the integration of Kuwait with Iraq, at a meeting attended by the representatives of Turkey, Iran, and Pakistan along with the US

Secretary of State, John Foster Dulles, who attended the meeting as an observer.

No success was achieved at that meeting because of Britain's persistent objection. Following the establishment of the Arab Union between Iraq and Jordan on 14 February 1958, King Faisal II, joined by Prime Minister Nouri al-Said and the Foreign Minister of the new Union, Tawfiq al-Suwaidi, raised the issue of unity with Kuwait once again with the British Foreign Secretary Mr. Sellwyn Llyod. The British, however, still rejected the Iraqi position.

When Abdullah al-Salim al-Sabah, the Sheikh of Kuwait, visited Baghdad on 10 May 1958, King Faisal II and Prime Minister Nouri al-Said, raised with him the issue of Kuwait's entry to the Arab Union. The Sheikh of Kuwait responded by saying that he had to consult the British and seek cheir advice on the matter.

On 5 June 1958, the Government of the Union presented a confidential note to the British Embassy in Baghdad proposing the accession of Kuwait to the Arab Union. The note stated that

> The land of Kuwait had, from the point of view of international law, been under the sovereignty of the Ottoman Empire, as a qadhaa' (district) belonging to the province of Basrah. This sovereignty had never been subject to doubt or dispute from the point of view of either the local authorities in Kuwait or the British Government. Indeed, the latter had recognized this fact in the Anglo-Turkish Agreement signed in London on 29 July 1913, which stated, in article 6, the right of the Sheikh of Kuwait to exercise his authority invested in him as an Ottoman district administrator subordinate to the Province of Basrah.

As a result of this, the Iraqi Government and the Government of the Arab Union became convinced that Britain was behind the obstacles preventing the achievement of this objective. This generated tension in Iraqi-British relations and led Iraq to intensify its efforts and increase its pressure upon Britain. An official note was prepared by the Iraqi Government to be published on 12 July 1958, with documented evidence supporting the necessity of Kuwait's entry into the Arab Union. But the British ambassador requested that the publication of that note be postponed and conveyed to Foreign Minister Tawfiq al-Suwaidi Britain's approval, in principle, of the idea of the entry of Kuwait into the Arab Union, provided that the details of the matter be discussed at a meeting which was set to be held in London, on 24 July 1958, between the Prime Minister and the Foreign Minister of the Arab Union, on the one hand and their British counterparts. On the other the meeting, however, did not take place because of the Iraqi Revolution on 14 July 1958.

In 1961, Britain decided to grant the artificial entity of Kuwait what it called "independence", a decision which prompted the then Prime Minister of Iraq to declare, in a press conference on 25 June 1961, that Iraq considered Kuwait an integral part of its territory and that Iraq does not recognize the special relationship agreement between Britain and Kuwait which the Sheikh of Kuwait, Abdulla al-Salim al-Sabah, had signed with Colonel M.J. Mead, the British Political Resident in the Gulf, on 19 June 1961. Following that declaration, Britain deployed its armed forces in the area to confront Iraq and protect its new creattion, the so-called "State of Kuwait."

Had it not been for the mistake made by Iraq's Foreign Minister at the time, Hashim Jawad, when he withdrew in angry protest from the meeting of the Arab League Council, which was considering the entry of the so-called "State of Kuwait" into the League of Arab States, thereby allowing a decision to be adopted, on 20 July 1961, to accept Kuwait as a member of the Arab League, this artificial entity would have remained outside the League; and hence out of the international organizations, as the admission of a new member to the League of Arab States is subject to a unanim ous vote of approval.

The Iraqi Foreign Ministry issued statement on 21 July 1961, declaring that Iraq considered decision No. 35-1777, accepting Kuwait as a member of the League of Arab States, to be a flagrant violation of the League's Charter which stipulated that such a decision could only be adopted by unanimity. Iraq also declared the said decision to be null and void and made clear its position that Kuwait would remain an integral part of its territory and that Iraq would not abandon its endeavours to restore this part by all legitimate means.

The Government of the former regime in Kuwait also failed in its efforts between 1961 and late 1963 to be granted membership in the United Nations.

Following the downfall of the political regime which ruled Iraq between July 1958 and February 1963, the Prime Minister of the former Government of Kuwait visited Baghdad in circumstances of political confusion and instability in Iraq. A joint comminique was issued on the basis of the correspondence of 1932. However, the National Council of Revolutionary Command (NCRC), the highest Iraqi legislative authority according to the interim constitution of 1963, did not ratify that comminique.

This historical review shows that none of the successive governments of Iraq has accepted the severence of the Kuwaiti part from the land of Iraq or signed a border treaty with the artificial entity created therein. No constitutional law has ever been promulgated to describe the border.

Such was the situation prevailing in Iraq by the time the Revolution of 17 -30 July 1968. The revolutionary government leading Iraq since that date has been keen, under instruction from President Saddam Hussein, to settle this issue in a manner that would secure for Iraq a reasonable measure of its historical rights and remove at least a limited part of the injustice done to it since the beginning of the century.

During the 1970s, Iraq was the party that took the initiative in approaching the former rulers of Kuwait to find such a settlement. But those rulers, encouraged by their foreign allies, insited that Iraq accept the measures imposed by British colonialism. The Foreign Minister of Iraq visited Kuwait City a number of times in 1972 and 1973 to discuss this issue. The Interior Minister, too, visited Kuwait for the same purpose on 16 May 1978, several committees were formed without achieving any results.

This chapter on the discussions of this issue was put aside following the outbreak of the Iran-Iraq war. Immediately after the liberation of Faw, however, and while attending the Algiers Arab Summit, I took the initiative in informing the Foreign Minister of the fromer regime in Kuwait of our genuine desire to settle the border issue. We were astonished, when there was no prompt response from the regime and we had to wait until early July 1988, when the Foreign Minister of the former regime visited Iraq to agree that the subject be discussed by the two Foreign Ministers.

The talks between the two sides were delayed becauses of my preoccupation with the Iraq-Iran negotiations following the ceasefire. The President of Iraq decided to send the vice-Chairman of the Revolution Command Council, Mr. Izzat Ibrahim to Kuwait city, on 6 December 1988, to urge the former regime there to resume the talks. It was agreed that our RCC Vice-Chairman would represent our side while the Crown Prince of the former regime would represent theirs.

The visit of Vice-Chairman Ibrahim was returned by Sa'ad al_Abdullah on 6 February 1689, but it was clear that he was not prepared to consider conceding even the minimum of Iraq's legitimate demands.

On 27 March 1989, Sa'ad al-Usaimi, the Minister of State for External Affairs of the former regime, visited Baghdad and officially proposed that the talks on this issue be postponed. During the visit made by the Sheikh of Kuwait to Baghdad in September 1989, President Saddam Hussein proposed to him that the border talks be resumed. It was agreed that the matter be pursued between Deputy Prime Minister Sa'doun Hammadi and the Foreign Minister of the former regime. Dr. Hammadi visited Kuwait city on 19 November 1989 to discuss the subject. The Foreign Minister of the former regime did not reciprocate the visit until February 1990.

It ought to be mentioned here that the former rulers of Kuwait had in fact exploited the situation throughout the period during which the settlement of this issue remained pending. They exploited Iraq's internal and regional preoccupations, the last and most pressing of which being the Iran-Iraq war which lasted eight years. They expanded northwards, setting up police-posts, military installations, farms and oil rigs. In 1963, for instance, the check-point for crossing from Kuwait to Basrah was a place called al-Miltaa' where passports were stamped. But during the time in which Iraq was preoccupied with internal and regional problems, this check-point was gradually moved up to a place more than seventy kilometers to the north of al-Mitlaa' to present Iraq with a fait accompli.

Dear Colleague,

As to the political and economic aspects of the issue, I wish to point out the following;

In February 1990, President Saddam Hussein delivered a speech at the Amman Summit in which he warned against the continued presence of the US navy in the Arab Gulf, now that the war between Iraq and Iran had come to an end. President

Hussein stated that :

The continued US presence in the Gulf is due to the fact that the Gulf, in view of the developments witnessed in international politics and in the prospect of the oil market and of the increasing need for oil by the United States, Europe, Japan, and perhaps even the Soviet Union, has become the most important spot in the region. Indeed it may have become the most important spot in the whole world. The country therefore, that succeeds in wielding the biggest share of influence over the region, through the Arab Gulf and its oil, will secure to itself an unchallenged supremacy as a superpower. This means that unless the people of the Gulf and all the Arabs are aware, the Gulf region will become subject to the will of the United States. The situation may get to the point where, if the debilitation and unawarenes continue the United States will try to dictate the level of oil and gas production for each country, the amount sold to this or that country, and the price at which it is to be sold, all accordance with the special interests of the United States and regardless of the interests of others.

Following the President's speech, a feverish campaign was launched against Iraq by US and other Zionist-influenced circles in the West. It soon became clear that those circles intended to corner Iraq politically and in the information media in preperation for a military strike to be implemented by Israel to destroy Iraq's military power which those circles considered to upset the strategic balance in the region, and which previously in Israel's favour.

The price of oil, at the time of the President's speech in Amman was somewhere between $18 and $21 per barrel. Immediately afterwards we saw the rulers of Kuwait, supported by those of the Emirates, suddenly announced their demand for an increase in their OPEC quotas. Before waiting for the matter to be discussed in OPEC, they proceeded to flood the oil market through overproduction, bringing about a sharp fall in prices and rapid decline in Iraq's already debilitated revenues. The price of oil went down to $11 per barrel, which meant a reduction of several billion dollars in Iraq's income, at a time when the country was encountering the very heavy economic burden left by the coasts of the war.

Iraq sought to draw attention, by diplomatic means and through bilateral contacts, to the destructive consequences its economy because of this policy. Iraq dispatched envoys to Kuwait, the Emirates, Saudi Arabia and other countries; but all was to no avail.

At the Baghdad Arab Summit Conference, which was held over the period 28-30 May 1990, President Saddam Hussein, in the presence of all the leaders, warned against this policy during a closed session on 30 May 1990. The President said ;

War occurs sometimes through soldiers and damage is infected by explosives killings or coup attempts: at other times it occurs through economic means... to those who do not intend to wage war against Iraq, I say that this is a kind of war against Iraq.

The befhaviour of the former rulers of Kuwait and of the Emirates, however didnot change. They continued to flood the market with oil and to destablize the oil prices. Iraq again took the initiative, late in June 1990, in sending Deputy Prime Minister Sa'doun Hammadi to deliver letters from President Saddam Hussein to King Fahd, Jabir al-Ahmed and Sheikh Zayid. Iraq proposed that a summit meeting be held amongst the four parties (Iraq, Saudi Arabia, the Emirates and Kuwait), with a view to arriving at an acceptable settlement of the problem. King Fahd, however, and both the former ruler of Kuwait and the ruler of the Emirates, evaded such a meeting and accepted instead that the meeting should be on the level of oil ministers. The four oil ministers met on 10 July 1990, and the Saudi, Kuwaiti and Emirate ministers pretended to accept a return to the level of production as agreed in OPEC quotas.

No sooner had the meeting ended than the oil minister of the former regime in Kuwait announced that his regime would again demand an increase in its share in October next. This was meant to sabotage the positive results of the meeting in order to continue the conspiracy to destroy the Iraqi economy.

In his national address of 16 July 1990, President Saddam Hussein reiterated his warning against the new type of conspiracy being perpetrated against Iraq through certain Arab quarters. The President said;

Because the people of Iraq, who have suffered this deliberate injustice, have enough faith in their right to self-defence and the defence of their rights, they shall never forget the saying: "Rather heads be cut off, than sustenance." If words fail to provide protection, then decisive action must be taken to restore the usurped rights to their owners.

President Hussein pointed out in that same address that the loss incurred by Iraq, since the beginning of the slump in oil prices from $28 to $11 per barrel, had amounted to $14 billion. All this was due to the policy of flooding the world market with cheap oil which in turn replenished the strategic reserves of the United States whose need for imported oil had already witnessed a marked increase in recent times. This policy caused huge damage to the national economy and was a treacherous stab in the back for Iraq.

For, although Iraq emerged victorious from a very long and costly war, it was burdened with huge debts which had to be repaid. Iraq had also to continue its development plans and provide food for its people' who had endured much and sacrificed the flower of its youth in defending its national and pan-Arab security and in protecting the Gulf region from advancing the Iranian danger.

Prior to that, His Excellency the president had voiced a clear warning on 9 July 1990, when he received Mr. Hisham Nazir, the Saudi oil minister to whom the President said :

> I shall not allow myself to accept for the people of Iraq to go hungery and for the women of Iraq to go naked of need.

On 15 July 1990, I delivered a detailed note to the Secretary-General of the League of Arab States in Tunis, a note substantiated by facts and figures confirming the involvement of the former rulers of Kuwait in the conspiracy to destroy the economy of Iraq, and exposing their delibrate and incessant violations, over the years, of the rights and vital interests of Iraq.

Amongst the things pointed out in that note, copies of which were sent to you through our diplomatic channels, was the following;

> The aggression of government of Kuwait, against Iraq has been twofold; by encroaching upon our territories and oilfields, and by steal

ing our national wealth, such action is tantamount to military aggression. The Kuwaiti government's deliberate attempts bring down the Iraqi economy is an aggression no smaller, in its consequences, than a military aggression.

Following President Hussein's address of 16 July 1990 and my note of 15 July 1990 to the Secretary-General of the Arab League, a number of Arab leaders intervened to help resolve this issue. It was agreed that a meeting be held on 30 July 1990 in Jeddah between His Excellency the Vice-Chairman of the Revolution Command Council and the Crown Prince of the former regime of Kuwait.

Many true Arabs who were eager to see an acceptable settlement being achieved, expected the rulers of Kuwait would in that meeting abandon their arrogance, intransigence and their attempts to harm Iraq. The behaviour of the delegation of the Kuwaiti regime during the meeting was marked, however, by their prevarication, procrastination and a flagrant denial of Iraq's obvious and legitimate rights.

Thus the conclusion was confirmed that the former regime in Kuwait was bent on perpetrating its design to destroy the Iraqi economy and destabilize its political system. It is inconceivable, that such a small regime could entertain the perpetration of a conspiracy of this dimension against a big and strong country like Iraq without being supported by a great power. That power was the United States of America.

This dangerous conspiracy against Iraq led us to extend military assistance to the young revolutionaries of Kuwait in their uprising on 2 August 1990. On the following day, His Majesty King Hussein of the Hashimite Kingdom of Jordan, visited Iraq and informed President Saddam Hussein that he had made intensified contacts with a number of Arab leaders, and that there was a proposal for a small summit to be held in Jeddah on the 4th or 5th of August and attended by Iraq, Jordan, Egypt, Yemen and Saudi Arabia. President Saddam Hussein accepted the idea of this summit which was also confirmed during the visit made to Iraq on 4 August 1990, by His Excellency Mr. Ali Abdullah Saleh, President of the Republic of Yemen.

This summit, which was to be held during the evening of Saturday, the 4th of August, or on Sunday the 5th, did not take place because of the intervention of the United States of America. On the very day for which the Arab Summit had been scheduled, President Bush asked his Defence Secretary to visit Saudi Arabia seeking the King's approval for US forces to be invited to Saudi Arabia. The US Defence Secretary arrived in Jeddah in the morning of 6 August and the US forces began entering Saudi Arabia on 7 August, the very next day. The speed with which the operation was started confirms two basic facts. The first, is that there was already a US military plan to ensure US domination of the Gulf region, (This has been confirmed by former US officials including Zbigniew Brzezinski), and this was the right time for its implementation. The second fact is that the United States deliberately aborted an Arab solution to the problem as was planned for the Summit to be held in Jeddah on 5 August 1990.

One day after the arrival of the US forces in Saudi Arabia, the government of Egypt proposed, on 8 August, that an Emergency Arab Summit Conference be held in Cairo. The call for this summit was made without prior consultation with Iraq at least ascertain whether President Saddam Hussein would be able to go to Cairo. Neither did we receive an official invitation from the host country nor from the Secretariat of the League of Arab States as required by the regular proceedures.

Despite this aberrant behavior on the part of the Egyptian Government, an Iraqi delegation went to Cairo, headed by RCC member and First-Deputy Prime Minister Mr. Taha Yassin Ramadhan and including two other RCC members, DPM and Foreign Minister Tariq Aziz and DPM Dr. Sa'doun Hammadi. On arrival in Cairo, the Iraqi delegation requested a meeting with President Mubarak. During the meeting, the Egyptian President assured the head of the Iraqi delegation that the objective of the summit was to conduct a "dialogue". Before the openning session on the next day, and prior to any consultation being conducted amongst the leaders present, the member-states of the Gulf Cooperation Council, along with Egypt and other states, presented a paper supporting the Saudi invitation to the US forces to Saudi Arabia and calling on other Arab states to send forces there too. This created resentment amongst the other leaders attending the summit, and they demanded that the paper be withdrawn in order to enable the conference to enter into a serious dialogue. The Egyptian President, however, prevented the holding of any dialogue in search of an acceptable solution. He forced the draft paper to a vote in a manner unprecedented in Arab conferences. This was how the second attempt at an Arab solution to the problem was aborted. The states either voted against, abstained or expressed their reservations; Jordan, the Yemen, Palestine, the Sudan, Libya, Algeria, Mauritania and Tunisia which had boycotted the meeting altogether.

Dear colleague,

This historical and factual presentation makes clear the fact that the issue in question is not merely a dispute over ordinary economic or border matters. We had tolerated such differences or disputes for twenty years, a period during which we were seeking to maintain the best of relations with the former rulers of Kuwait, in spite of their wicked conduct against Iraq. What we are dealing with now is a premeditated conspiracy, in which the former rulers of Kuwait participated wilfully and in accordance with a plan supported by the United States of America, to destabilize the Iraqi economy and undermine its defence capabilities and the potential with which to face the Israeli-Imperialist scheme of aggression and expan sionism against the Arab homeland, the scheme aimed at imposing US hegemony over the region and its oil wealth in partniicular. This was in fact, as described in President Hussein's statement at the Baghdad ARab Summit and in my letter to the Secretary-General of the League of Arab States, a war waged against Iraq.

As regards Iraq's relations with the other states of the region, including Saudi Arabia, none of them offer a case similar in any way to that of Kuwait both from the point of view of history and in terms of the nature of the bilateral relations. We have been keen to establish normal relations with all these states, and have been committed to all our obligations towards them within the framework of our fraternal links. We are keen to maintain these commitments for as long as the states concerned maintain their commitments.

In view of the spurious allegations concerning the so-called Iraqi threats to Saudi Arabia, we have affirmed in every way available to us that there is no Iraqi threat to Saudi Arabia or to any other country in the Gulf. We have made clear our willingness to provide all necessary guarantees that effect, whether on the bilateral level or within the framework of the League of Arab States. We have also stated that we would not object to Saudi Arabia calling in Arab forces for assistance or protection, if the Saudis were afraid, although we still see no basis whatsoever for this fabricated fear.

Another chapter of the problem is to do with the Security Council and the position it has adopted. On the first day of the events, the United States pushed the Security Council into adopting a resolution against Iraq on the basis of Chapter VII of the UN Charter. I am referring here to resolution 660 of 2 August 1990, which has no precedent of its kind in the whole history of the Security Council. The Council adopted this resolution without even giving Iraq the chance to be heard. It has always been normal practice in the Security Council, while dealing with international crises, to invite the Foreign Ministers of the parties concerned to attend the Council meetings before a resolution is adopted. It was obvious that everything was being conducted under feverish US pressure. On the 6th of August another unprecedented resolution was adopted to impose unjust sanctions against Iraq. Then three other resolutions were adopted for the same purpose. These were resolution 662 (9 August), resolution 664 (18 August) and resolution 665 (25 August, 1990). It was obvious that the United STates had launched a full-scale campaign in which it exercised overtly and covertly, all forms of pressure, intimidation and threats, economic and otherwise, in trying to get member-states to vote for those resolutions proposed by the United States.

On 12th August 1990, President Saddam Hussein announced an initiative in which he called for all outstanding issues in the region to be settled on the basis of the same criteria and principles. He expressed his genuine hope that this intiative would open the door for just and peaceful solutions of all the problems in the region. Western countries, however, rejected this initiative even before inquiring about it or asking for a copy of the text, thus confirming the double-standard they apply to regional and international disputes in comparison to their position towards Israel. These countries have never urged the Security Council to implement against Israel the many resolutions already adopted on the question of Palestine, its people and their rights. This has been their position despite the fact that Israel has been occupying the land of Palestine for several decades and continues to massacre the Palestinian people in all brutality while still occupying the Golan Heights of Syria and Southern Lebanon.

Iraq hereby warns against the dangers of the US scheme to impose hegemony on the Arab nation, plunder its resources and prevent its development and progress. To allow the United States a free hand indealing with regional problems in such a manner arrogant and contemptuous, while implicating other countries along with it, is a matter that constitutes a grave threat to international peace and security, the damages of which will not be confined not only to the interests of the developing third world countries, but will also affect Europe, Japan and all countries seeking to achieve independence in their positions and decisions.

As I address this message to Your Excellency, I trust that the situation shall be studied carefully, taking all facts and factors into consideration. I also hope that the efforts of the international community shall cooperate in their efforts to confront the policy of aggression and adventurism being imposed by the United States of America upon Iraq and the region as a whole; the region that has, for decades bitterly suffered from the US policy of hegemony and blackmail, and the infamous alliance forged between the United States and Israel.

I hope that shall consider dealing seriously with the historic intiative announced by President Saddam Hussein on 12 August 1990, and with the sincere Arab efforts aimed at finding comprehensive Arab solutions to the problems of the region.

I assure you that Iraq, with its faith in peace and justice, shall remain faithfull to its belief in dialogue and in the constructive exchange of views with regard to all bilateral, regional and international issues.

Please accept, Excellency, the assurances of my highest consideration.

(signed)
Tariq Aziz
Deputy Prime Minister and
Minister of Foreign Affairs of
the Republic of Iraq
Baghdad
14 Safar, 1411 H.
4 September, 1990 A.D.

0039

Embassy of
The Republic of Iraq
Seoul

سفارة الجمهورية العراقية
سيئول

No. 202-91

Press Release

20/9/1991

AN OFFICIAL SOURCE IN THE IRAQI ATOMIC ENERGY COMMISSION COMMENTS ON THE STATEMENT MADE IN THE SECURITY COUNCIL BY MR. ROLF EKEUS, CHAIRMAN OF THE SPECIAL COMMISSION

We have become used by now to hearing statements issued by heads of the international inspection teams, and by officials in the International Atomic Energy Agency (IAEA) and in the Special Commission, in which they repeat using expressions like: "the Iraqis are very cooperative" and "there is a good level of trust". Yet, they keep retorting the old question: "what is hidden?" and add the sentence that "they still need more time to gather information and assess the programme."

The statement recently issued by Mr. Ekeus, Chairman of the Special Commission, is no exception to this approach. Indeed, the statement is full of contradictions. While he says that "good progress had been made in the Commission's work", he returns to claim once again that "he could not say that Iraq had fully cooperated in any of the major areas of that work", and that "the Commission lacked a forthcomming attitude from the Iraqi side". Yet he says in another place that "Iraq's cooperation on the technical level with regard to declared material was good", and that "there was a good spirit between the inspectors" who were given good access. Then Mr. Ekeus returns to contradict himself by claiming that "in the area of what remained to be diclosed

It seems that certain limits have been drawn to Mr. Ekeus and others whenever they have to refer to the good cooperation extended by Iraq, and that neither he nor the others are allowed to go beyond those limits. Indeed, it seems that something negative has to be inserted in order to minimise the significance of Iraq's cooperation and present Iraq as being unwilling to comply with the resolutions of the Security Council, with a view to creating pretexts for the prolongation of the economic blockade imposed upon the Iraqi people.

The official IAEC source added:

We notice that there are amongst the heads and members of the inspection teams those we seek stardom in the political arena of the respective countries, believing that such stardom could be acchieved through the mistreatment of Iraq. So when they find themselves forced to say something about the full cooperation extended by Iraq, they begin to employ vague or non-commital language in order to minimize the importance of such cooperation.

We hope that Mr. Ekeus will not be drawn into the open auction for stardom; for he is in no need of it. Othewise, how can we interpret Mr. Ekeus's claim that "the Commission was missing what could be referred to as the 'master plan'", at a time when Iraq has give all the the technical and planning information it has in the nuclear field.

Amongst the first observations that we made about the work of the inspection teams was that they lacked a master plan for each team. This was not a surprise to us, for these teams are here to implement a strange and unprecedented resolution for which they have neither the experience nor the practice.

During the visit made to Iarq last June by Mr. Ekeus with the Director-General of the International Atomic Energy Egency heading a high level committee, the President of the Iraqi Atomic Energy Commission pointed out that the IAEA had not specified exactly what it wanted from Iraq until that we had to use our discretion in supplying the information. The IAEC President added that even the data forms were drawn up by the Iraqi side. The IAEA Director-General conceded to that fact and promised to review the matter.

0040

To speak of the lack of the master plan after all these months is indeed a matter that raises questions. What is the purpose of the master plan, and what details should it contain? Hasn't Mr. Ekeus at least seen the minutes of the meeting between the President of the Iraqi Atomic Energy Commission and the head of the fourth inspection team during which the IAEC President went through the plan of the Iraqi nuclear programme? Moreover, didn't the Deputy President of the IAEC present sufficient detailed explainations to the third and fourth inspection teams? What is meant by the master plan?

It is most obvious now that the Special Commission and its inspection teams want to turn Iraq into a training labortary in which to practice inspection activities and learn about such technologies as may be of use to the big powers, especially after they discoverd how original Iraqi inventivness has been. Whenever they knew of an advanced Iraqi invention or development in this field, they began dispatching their experts to acquire Iraqi knowhow under various international techrical titles. The last case in point has been that of chemical enrichment.

After Iraqi experts had presented a detailed account of this subject to the third nuclear inspection team, whose visit to Iraq was concluded on 19 July 1991 and whose members left the country so satsfied with what they had heard and observered that they raised no further questions, the fouth inspection team arrived in the country to ask that a similar technical presentation be given, once again, to its members. The Iraqi side responded positively to the request, and the presentation was repeated in August with additional detailed documents, even including even progress reports. Yet no mention whatsoever was made of this whole subject in the report submitted by this inspection team.

Finally, we have received this week the fifth inspection team and discovered that amongst its members is a French expert in chemical enrichment. The team has asked that this particular expert conduct discussions with his Iraq counterparts on this subject.

The fact that must be pointed out here is that the Chairman of the French atomic energy authority, who visited Iraq in 1979 in the company of the then Prime Minister of France, invited the Iraqi side to particpate in French chemical enrichment research programme and purchase the technology related to it from France. By then, Iraq had not yet acquired sufficient experience and knowhow; but as the Iraqi programme moved ahead during the eighties, Iraqi researchers worked on their own and achieved good results in this method. This explains the reason why the big powers want to obtain Iraqi knowhow in this method. And this is the real reason behind the arrival of the French expert amongst the fifth nuclear inspection team. Many other instances can be given to demonstrate this kind of practice.

Vague and general statements such as that about the absence of a master plan, etc., are naked and flimsy pretexts meant to obscure other objectives. Some of those objectives are technical to do with stealing knowhow, while the others political and meant to provide some cover of technical international legitimacy for the continuation of the war of destruction and starvation waged against thr Iraqi people and its economic infrastructure. It is most regrettable to see Mr. Ekeus indulge in technological illiteracy when he speaks of the Iraqi uranium enrichment programme as being "intended for non-peacful purposes", simply "due to the nature and the economics" of the enrichment activities. Does this mean that all states should call off their enrichment activities due to the nature of such activities? It seems that wisdom, common sense and scientific objectivity are giving way to the logic of the absurd. It is really amazing to see Mr. Ekeus issue arbitrary figures in the billions about the Iraqi nuclear programme, and then ask what "was the idea behind all those investments."

Mr. Ekeus would have been wiser, had he inquired about these supposed investments directly from the sources concerned, instead of letting loose his imagination or relying on press reports for his information.

The official sources of the Iraqi Atomic Energy Commission have supplied the true and total figures of all their projects, whether those completed by French and Italian companies during the seventies or those completed during the eighties. The figures are not as extravagant as Mr. Ekeus wants to make them. In fact the real figures are no where near any of the figures he gives.

What was given to the French and Italians during the seventies was much higher than the figures of the eighties. The French and Italian governments, which had given their respective companies theier seal of approval to work in Iraq, never questioned the wisdom of those investments. Indeed they found the investments most feasible at the time. But since the projects of the eighties were completly indiginous, they did not look as wise or as feasible as those of the seventies from the point of view of those used to exploiting other peoples and plundering their resources.

If Iraq had spent its oil wealth not on projects of scientific or technological value, with a view to ensuring a future of independence and prosperity for its people, free from foreign hegemony, and if the oil revenues were squandered on gambling tables and in bribery and corruption deals, as has been done by some so-called Arabs, then this would have brought comfort to those who want to presrve the picture of the Arab as a backward creature ignorant of how to employ his own wealth except by squandering it in the West and losing it to western banks.

Iraq has placed all its resources in the hands of its peolpe in order to build the scientific, technological and industrial base with which to face the future and the challanges it usually unflods. Had it not been for this base, the people of Iraq would not have been able to achieve this rapid reconstruction of their country's infrastructure which was destroyed as a result of the thirty-state aggression against Iraq.

The goal of the thirty-state aggression was, and still is, to push Iraq back into the middle-ages. But the aggression has failed due to th resolve of the Iraqi people and their determination to remain strong and continue the reconstruction process.

What we find difficult to understand, and indeed continue to resent, is how the Iraqi human factor can become a source of concern for Mr. Ekeus, when this factor can only be Iraq's real guarantee for a future of technological progress and economic prosperity. Yet, Mr. Ekeus shows no concern when US tanks bury alive this human factor with full knowledge, and indeed under the instructions, of the US military and political leaderships!!

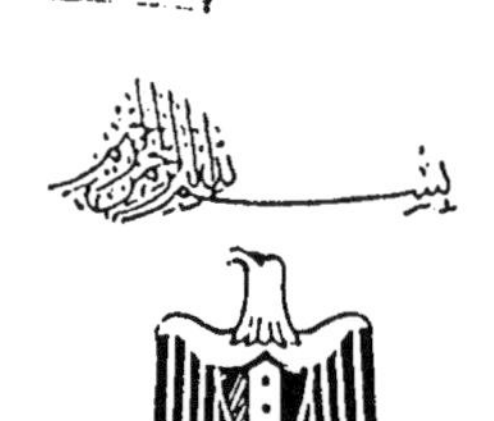

Embassy of
The Republic of Iraq
Seoul

سفارة الجمهورية العراقية
سيئول

NO. 84/90

Press Release

1/12/1990

귀하께서는 안전 보장 이사회가 이라크에 실행한 경제 봉쇄 결의안의 성급하고 부당한 태도를 알고 계신줄로 확신합니다. 이 결의안의 내용과 정신은, 정의와 평등을 보장하는 평화적인 방법으로 그 곳에서의 갈등을 해결하기 위하여 극히 민감한 상황을 말하려고 하는것 같지 않다는 것을 보여 줍니다.이 결의안들은 차라리 미국의 음모와 압력의 산물인데, 그들의 주된 목적은 인본적인 국제 법률의 고려에 상관없이 가혹한 처벌의 강압적인 조치를 취하는 것이었읍니다.

안보리의 결의안들은 우리의 식량과 유아용 우유 수입 전반에 걸쳐 광범위한 제재를 가하였읍니다. 이 봉쇄 조치의 결과 이라크 국민들의 기아가 초래되었는데, 이는 단지 자신의 생존과 권리를 지키기위해 외부의 압력과, 또한 그 자원과 더 나아가서는 전반적인 운명을 제어하려는 패권 정책을 직면함으로써 일어난 것이었읍니다.

귀하께서는 1949년 제 4회 제네바 회의에서 채택된 인본적인 국제 법률을 알고 계시리라고 믿습니다. 그리고 그것의 1977년 최초의 첨가 원안은 무력 투쟁의 한 수단으로써 민간인의 기아를 금하고 있읍니다. 그러나 안보리는 순전히 정치적인 목적으로, 이러한 국제적으로 승인된 합법적인 조항을 무시하고 기아의 정책을 채택하였읍니다 UN이 남아프리카나 로디지아에대해 비록 봉쇄 조치를 단행하기는 했으나 그러한 방책을 채택하지 않은 점은 매우 흥미롭습니다.

이러한 조치는 인권 위반이며, 그 결의안을 의문시하고, 그에 반대하며, 그 비합법적인 결과의 조명을 위해 일하도록 하는 신성한 종교적 가르침에도 위배됩니다.

미국의 대이라크 유아용 분유 수출의 금지압력을 통해 부과된 압박으로 이라크 정부는 신생아에게 분유 공급을 중단해야만 했는데, 이는 영양실조로 인한 유아 사망율의 현저한 증가를 초래하였읍니다. 의료 공급에대한 봉쇄 조치도 역시 사망율의 증가를 가져왔읍니다.

인간 결속의 원칙에서부터, 이러한 비인간적인 결의안들은 다시 생각되어지고, 현재 이라크 국민의 기아를 가져온 이러한 범죄가 종결되어지도록 노력하기를 바라며, 이 문제를 귀하앞에 놓는 바입니다.

주한 이라크 대사관

0043

Embassy of
The Republic of Iraq
Seoul

سفارة الجمهورية العراقية
سيئول

NO. 84/90

Press Release

1/12/1990

Dear Sir,

You are no doubt aware of the hasty and unjust manner in which the Security Council has imposed the resolutions of economic boycott and blockade against IRAQ. The texts and spirit of these resolutions show that they have not been adopted to address a highly sensitive situation with a view to resolving the complexities involved therein in a peaceful manner which ensures justice and equality. These resolutions were rather the product of the US policy of blackmail and pressure whose prime objective was to impose coercive measures of sheer punishment regardless of the considerations by humantarian international law.

The resolutions of the Security Council have imposed a comprehensive embargo over all our imports of foodstuffs and infant milk. The outcome of this embargo is the starvation of our people simply because it has risen to defend its very existence and rights to face external aggression and all the policies of hegemony aimed at controling its resourses and consequently its whole destiny.

You are no doubt aware that humanitarian international law, cited in the fourth Geneva Convention of 1949, and its first additional protocol of 1977 prohibits the starving of civilians as a measure in armed conflicts. Yet, the Security Council has adopted for purely political ends, a policy of starvation in disregard of these internationally accepted legal provisions. It is most interesting that the United Nations adopted no such policy against South Africa or Rhodesia although the UN imposed sanctions against the regimes of those entities.

These measures represent a violation of human rights and are contrary to the teachings of divine religions, which makes it incumbent upon the faithful everywhere to condemn the resolutions in question, oppose them and work for the illumination of their illegitimate consequences.

The constraints imposed through US pressure to prevent exports of infant-milk to IRAQ has forced the Iraqi authorities to halt milk supplies to new-born babies, which has led to a marked increase in infant mortality caused by malnutrition. The embargo on medical supplies has likewise led to an increase in the fatality rate.

Proceeding from the principles of human solidarity, I wish to place this matter before you, hoping that efforts will be made to see to it that these inhuman resolutions are reconsidered and that the crime currently perpetrated to starve the people of IRAQ is brought to an end.

Accept, please the assurances of highest consideration.

Embassy of the Republic of IRAQ

0044

Embassy of
The Republic of Iraq
Seoul

سفارة الجمهورية العراقية
سيول

Press Release

NO. 85/90

3/12/1990

IRAQ REJECTS US RESOLUTION VOWS TO CRUSH AGGRESSION

Iraq on Friday rejected a US-imposed Security Council resolution which set an ultimatum for Iraq to withdraw from Kuwait by mid-January, vowing to crush any aggression and teach the United States and its allies a hard lesson unprecedented in history.

A joint meeting of the Revolution Command Council and the Regional Command of the Arab Ba'th Socialist Party chaired by President Saddam Hussein issued a statement stressing Iraq's rejection of ultimatum and threat.

The statement said Iraq would not bow to the policy of arrogance and terrorism. It accused the United States of pressuring members of the UN Security Council to pass the resolution.

"The resolution issued by the Security Council on Thursday, November 29, is illegal and null and void", the statement said.

"It is first and foremost an American decision in which a group of countries participated only under US pressure at this stage when the United States practises the highest degree of hegomony and arrogance vis-a-vis the world community in the wake of the latest developments in international scene", the statement said.

"Money was paid by America's allies to a number of Security Council member governments, and immense pressure was put on them directly from the President of the United States of America and his Secretary of State", the statement said.

"These clear and tangible facts prove that this resolution is illegal and that it does not express the principles of the United Nations Charter," it added.

"It is a disgraceful resolution and tarnished with shame the nations which helped issue it, placed the Security Council under US hegemony, turned it into an oppressive instrument to car-

0045

ry out the evil American aims and made the Council theatre for dirty deals".

The statement said that the countries which made the Security Council adopt a resolution granting legitimacy for US aggression against Iraq and the Arab nation had not moved towards confronting the Israeli aggression against Palestine.

These countries pursued a policy of manipulation and delay in dealing with the usurpation of Jerusalem and Arab territories and with the brutal crimes committed in a systematic manner by the Israeli occupation forces against the Arab Palestinian people, the statement said.

"They had kept silent about US occupation of Panama and Grenada", it said.

The statement said that the double-standard policy practised by those countries in dealing with Arab issues are now exposed openly, in the same way as the hypocricy of some major powers in dealing with international issues.

"The United States has garnered all its potential in an unprecedented manner, practised pressure and terrorism and paid, with its agents, bribes to make a number of Security Council members to issue a resolution granting false legitimacy for its military presence (in the Gulf region) and its evil intentions of aggression against Iraq, the Arab nation and Moslems".

The statement added that for these reasons Iraq the Arab nation, Moslems and all peace-loving people in the world had every right to denounce the disgraceful course followed by those countries. They also had every right to refuse to recognise the legitimacy of the American resolution which was issued in the name of the Security Council, it said.

The statement expressed appreciation of the stand taken by a number of the Security Council members which rejected US means of pressure and intimidation.

The statement said that because of US hegemony and

0046

the stands of some member states with illegitimate interests, the Security Council had ignored the Palestinian question for tens of years. The Security Council did not pursue the implementation of piles of resolutions it had issued on the Palestinian question and other issues related to peoples of the Third World, but kept watching occupation, usurpation and crimes being committed by Israel, it said.

It is this Council itself, which under US pressure over some of its members, that is working day and night in pursuit of Iraq and issuing one unjust resolution after the other, the statement said. It added that Iraq, the Arab nation, the Moslems and all fair-minded people of the world rejected these double standard which stem from arrogance and from illegitimate interests.

"If the Security Council really wants to carry out its tasks as specified in the UN Charter, it should adopt the same standards and be fair and just in dealing with Arab issues, the Palestinian question in the forefront, and all other international issues which are the cause of injustice and suffering for many peoples of the world, the statement said.

The statement stressed that the Iraqi people are highly prepared to defend their territory and historical rights. It warned that the Iraqi people and war-hardened army would teach the aggressors a lesson unprecedented in history if they waged aggression against Iraq.

"In the heat of battle, Iraq will wipe out the dwarfs who are supporting America, especially the treacherous (Saudi King Fahd), who turned the land of sanctities which he is ruling into a springboard of aggression against Iraq", the statement stressed.

"If those criminals sitting in the corridors of the White House and Pentagon base confrontation on technical and theoretical calculations, then the Iraqis, and with them all Arabs and Moslems will turn these miscalculations upside down.

"On the battle arena, they will prove that victory will be for right over wrong, faith over blasphemy and honour over disgrace and corruption, and that God is on the side of the faithful", the statement said.

It said that Iraq believes in its inalienable rights and in the rights of the people of Palestine and the Arabs to freedom, justice, integrity and peace for all peoples of the world on equal basis.

It stressed Iraq's firm stand that equal dialogue is the means to discuss the situation in the Middle East region.

In order to be well-intentioned and just, the call to respect Security Council resolutions should be addressed to all those concerned with these resolutions, in the same language, and should be implemented in the same spirit, the statement said, adding that Security Council resolutions shouldnot be selective.

The statement stressed that Iraq considered President Saddam Hussein's August 12 peace plan as expressing its stand that there would be no peace in the region without solving all its problems in accordance with uniform principles and standards that secure peace, justice and security for all peoples of the region so as to reflect positively on international peace as a whole. In the forefront of these solutions, the legitimate rights of the Arab Palestinian people should be restored, the statement said.

The statement said the United States had violated Arab and Moslem sanctities and occupied Arab territories in a manner unprecedented in history. The US had supported Israeli expansion and occupation of Jerusalem, the rest of Palestine, the Golan Heights and southern Lebanon, said the statement, adding that the US had brought its military forces to the region to impose its hegemony and control the resources of the Arab nation.

Embassy of
The Republic of Iraq
Seoul

سفارة الجمهورية العراقية
سيئول

No. 110/90

Press Release

28/12/1990

'Iraq subject to US-led unjust campaign, blockade'

President Saddam Hussein has said that the people of Iraq are being subjected to an unjust campaign spearheaded by US President George Bush with the help of World Zionism and also to an economic blockade that has deprived Iraqis of medicine and baby powder milk.

In a message to the International Gathering of Peacemakers on Tuesday, President Hussein said Bush has brought his army over thousands of miles and mobilised the most up-to-date technology of destruction and death to defeat the will of a people that has decided to defend its legitimate rights.

He told peacemakers that the evil powers have mobilised all this formidable force just to defend petro-sheikhs who belong to the era of backwardness, the sheikhs who have been turned into guards at the oil wells of world monopolies to help them continue their pillage and hegemony of the world.

The President wondered whether the world is living a time when oil has become more precious than human life and values. He warned against the consequences of these regimes and rulers greed. These wealth-thirsty rulers can think of nothing but their self-interests, he said.

The President added that as the twentieth century draws to a close, Palestinians remain scattered out of their homeland for more than 40 years. No world form or international meeting is unaware of the Palestinians' plight and the injustice done to them.

Scores of UN General Assembly and Security Council resolution have been passed on the Palestinian issue but none of them has been implemented because of the bias of successive US administrations and their Israeli allies and because of their disregard to the will of the international community. They have resorted to the use of pressure, terrorism, bribery and double standards, the President stressed.

He concluded his message by reminding all fair-minded people in the world that injustice breeds war and that peace can be achieved through equitable dialogue that seeks to achieve justice.

0049

Embassy of
The Republic of Iraq
Seoul

سفارة الجمهورية العراقية
سيئول

No. 111-90

Press Release

28/12/1990

US policy - now too vulnerable

Following a marathon process, the UN Security Council last week issued a resolution on the protection of Palestinians under Israeli occupation. The resolution was a diluted form of a draft initiatied by Non-aligned members of the Council calling for a conference on the Middle East and the dispatch of a UN ombudsman to monitor the Israeli treatment of Palestinians.

Although the resolution has fallen short of Palestinian and other fair-minded parties' hopes, it can still be viewed as and initial gain for the Palestinians.

After eight postponements, the US fought tooth and nail to block any provision for a Mideast conference on the Palestinian issue. The US representative dug in his heels insisting that either the conference issue is eliminated or a veto would be used.

The Americans finally accepted a lesser of two evils by having the Non-aligned sought conference in a separate nonbinding statement.

The Bush administration's dilemma was undoubtedly caused by Iraq's call for linkage between the Gulf crisis and the Palestinian issue. On August 12, President Saddam Hussein called for a blanket solution of all Middle East problems, chief among which is the Palestinian question.

It could be the first time the US representative found himself hand-tied as to the options he had. He could either accept the final resolution, which in itself, was still a bitter pill to swallow the veto in which case be would have embarrassed Arab allies, namely Egypt and Saudi Arabia, the two main partners in Bush's anti-Iraq coalition.

Iraq's unwavering stand towards the agony of Palestinians living under Israeli occupation for the last 43 years has put to test the US credibility about the "international legitimacy"

In a record period, the UN issued a record number of Security Council resolutions against Iraq under cover of the "international legitimacy." But the UN Council, now under the power monopoly of the US, has failed to see scores of UN resolutions respected by Israel. It took the Council a fortnight to issue this US-blessed watered-down resolution on an issue which signifies the most blatant challenge to the Geneva convention and the UN Charter.

All the credit should go to Iraq which has for the first time forced the US to bow, sightly this time, to an international storm. Such a resolution would not have been allowed to see the light had it been debated before August 12.

0050

Embassy of
The Republic of Iraq
Seoul

سفارة الجمهورية العراقية
سيئول

No. 112/90

Press Release

31/12/1990

Nass Al-Bayaan:

All Friends, Progressive Organisations, and
Peace-loving People of the World

STATEMENT

On December 26, the "Peace Boat" was subjected to American piracy in the Arab sea. The boat was heading for Umm Qasr port in Iraq. On its board were defenceless children and women calling for peace, and waving the Olive branch. The boat of peace was also carrying a quantity of baby powder milk, medicines and foodstuffs. American and other allied troops fired at the boat, and landed on it, thus terrorizing the passengers in a barbaric manner unprecedented in the history of contemporary world. It was indeed a sheer aggression on advocates and messengers of peace.

The boat was searched thoroughly, and its loads of food and medicine were confiscated. The crew of the boat was arrested and the boat towed to another port. A number of invading forces insulted the passengers, and inflicted physical harm on them. It was an act of sheer piracy that reminds the world of stone-age.

The Organizations of Friendship, Peace and Solidarity in Iraq, while strongly condemns this barbaric act of piracy and oppression against the defenceless children and women, calls upon the United Nations Secretary General to exercise the authorities vested in him, to demand the immediate release of the boat and its passengers and the load. This act violates the simplest principles of human rights. It is indeed an act of criminal nature against humanity at large. the United States is acting as the terroristic policeman of the world and as such, it is jeopardizing the principles of peace.

We also appeal to all friend, progressive organizations, the human rights organizations, and peace-loving peoples of the world, to condemn this oppressive and inhumane act and to raise their voices loudly and clearly for freeing the boat and its passsengers. This act is a crime against human rights. It unveils the ugly face of the United States of America and its terroristic policies. It is a violation of the international law, and norms and conventions, in heaven and on earth.

Expose U.S. hypocracy and double-standards. Expose the ill-intentions of the U.S.A. and its allies before the peoples of the world.

Condemn the U.S. and its allies for violating the charter of the United Nations.

Show the world that the rule of hegemony, domination, and arrogance is over.

Stand by the right against falsehood.

Stand by justice against injustice.

0051

Adnan Dawood Salman
Chairman of the Organization of Friendship, Peace and Solidarity in Iraq

Embassy of
The Republic of Iraq
Seoul

سفارة الجمهورية العراقية
سيئول

No. 1/91

Press Release

3/1/1991

Don't be too confident, Mr Bush

President Bush told Time magazine that he "is not will- ; to sacrifice American lives" in a confrontation in the ılf. He also said he was confident he had chosen the ;ht course in the Gulf crisis. He added that he had a ut feeling" Iraq would withdraw from Kuwait.

But does Mr Bush not think that he is over-confident? ›w would he guarantee that his servicemen would come : unscathed? Or is he expecting a brief war in the Gulf?

The Bush administration has pushed to the Gulf the gest American force since the Vietnam war, and only a l would think that such a US military presence in the a would not lead to a huge loss of life.

Mr Bush should be aware that if a war breaks out in the a, it would be hell on earth for the Americans. Such a r would drag on for longer than Mr Bush would want. t seems that Mr Bush is repeating the same misjudge- at his predecessors had made in Indochina. The erican administrations of the time thought they would ıble to crush the peasants and poorly-equipped guer- as of Vietnam.

erhaps Mr Bush needs to be reminded of the night- res and stress disorders Vietnam veterans have been ıg with for years now. Let him go and ask those who still receiving treatment at veterans' rehabilitation ıres about their fighting experience in an alien land, ng two enemies: people and nature.

hese veterans must have an abundance of horror stor- o tell Mr Bush. And perhaps they will give him a very · piece of advice: to go and watch "Coming Home," ocalypse Now" or "Born on the Fourth of July" to see himself the devastating effect of having to fight in a war.

Like Bush's, former US administrations eluded themselves into believing that they would break up peoples' resistance to American dreams of hegemony over other peoples' sovereignty and wealth. However, the United States was defeated in its reckless adventures, particularly those in Vietnam where thousands of servicemen were killed or left with psychological scars. And let the Americans not forget the 1983 explosion in Beirut that left dozens of US soldiers dead, some beyond recognition.

Citing incidents like these might be useful especially that Bush's soldiers, mostly inexperienced, are facing battle-hardened Iraqis who are determined to hold on, no matter the sacrifice, in the face of the armies of the "civilized world." And they are not alone as Mr Bush tried to picture them. They have behind them the Arabs and Moslems of the world who have vowed to join the Iraqis against aggression.

So, Mr Bush, why all this over-confidence?

0052

Embassy of
The Republic of Iraq
Seoul

سفارة الجمهورية العراقية
سيئول

Press Release

No. 11/91 22/1/1991

SUMMARY OF COMMUNIQUE NO. 11 OF
THE GENERAL COMMAND OF THE ARMED FORCES
ON JANUARY 20, 1991

In the Name of Allah, the Merciful, the Compassionate

With the help of Allah, the Almighty and out of the conviction of noble and humanitarian principles, the Iraqi heroic people, under the leadership of our beloved President Saddam Hussein, continued the endeavor of defending the homeland against American-Zionist-Western barbaric aggression.

1. The barbaric forces of evil, led by the criminal Americans, continued their cowardly air raids against the Iraqi civilian and innocent people from 8:30 a.m. until 2:45 p.m. of January 20, 1991 on the following locations:

* The Province of Thee Qar (twice).
* The Province of Anbar (twice).
* The Province of Arbil (from Turkey).
* The City of Nasiria.
* The City of Kuwait.
* The holy City of Najaf (twice).
* The Province of Tameem.

2. At 12:25 p.m., an enemy convoy of 25 vehicles committed aggression against our border's posts with Saudi Arabia.

3. An AWACS plane crossed our border with Saudi Arabia at 1:10 p.m.

4. Eight Cruise missile attacks were launched against the Iraqi cities and towns of Tikrit, Mendili, Beiji and Al-Abyadh. These attacks were launched from three direction: from Turkey in the north, from the Zionist entity in the west, and from Saudi Arabia in the south.

5. Ten air targets (planes and missiles) were knocked down by the heroic Iraqi air defends.

6. The total number of enemy planes shot down until issuing this communique amounted to 160 planes.

0053

Embassy of
The Republic of Iraq
Seoul

سفارة الجمهورية العراقية
سيئول

No. 12/91 **Press Release** 22/1/1991

SUMMARY OF COMMUNIQUE NO. 12 OF
THE GENERAL COMMAND OF THE ARMED FORCES
ON JANUARY 21, 1991

In the Name of Allah, the Merciful, the Compassionate

Our valiant armed forces, blessed by God the Almighty, have been able to stand against the American-Zionist-Western aggression and thwart their designs.

1. American-Zionist-Western barbaric air raids continued against Iraqi civilian population during the period 8:05 till 15:55 on January 20 on the following locations:

* The ancient city of Hatra in Ninews Province (two times).
* Province of Baghdad (three times).
* Province of Kuwait.
* Province of Anbar (three times).
* Province of Kirkuk (from Turkey).
* City of Imara.
* City of Naseria.

2. Our victorious army was able to shoot down 18 air targets (planes and missiles).

3. In response to the barbaric aggression of the enemy in hitting our civilian cities, our units launched a deadly missiles attack against the enemy position inside Saudi Arabia namely in Al-Khfji area.

0054

Embassy of
The Republic of Iraq
Seoul

سفارة الجمهورية العراقية
سيئول

No. 13/91

Press Release

23/1/1991

SUMMARY OF COMMUNIQUE NO. 13 OF
THE GENERAL COMMAND OF THE ARMED FORCES
ON JANUARY 21, 1991

In the Name of Allah, the Merciful, the Compassionate

While the barbaric aggression, spearheaded by the Bush administration and its stooges Al-Saud continued unabated, the brave people of Iraq under the leadership of our valiant leader, President Saddam Hussein, proved beyond any doubt the fallacy of the enemy so-called technological superiority, through humilating the Americans and their stooges.

1. Our mobile rocket launchers attacked, on the eve of 20/21 January, slected targets in Dhahran base, the Capital Riyadh and Dammam in Saudi Arabia.

2. The American-Zionist-Western aggressors carried out barbaric air raids on the civilian between 7:50 a.m. until 11:00 p.m. on the following locations:

* The Province of Anbar (three times).
* The Province of Nassiriya (two times).
* The Province of Simawa.
* The Province of Baghdad (four times).
* The Province of Basrah (two times).
* The Province of Tameem.
* The Province of Kuwait where one Beduin was martyred and 11 other womwn and children were wounded.
* The Province of Tikrit.
* The Province of Thee Qar.

3. 13 enemy air targets were shot down by the valiant air defenders of Iraq.

4. Our brave forces launched deadly rocket attack on enemy position during the night in Al-Khafji area and in front of Al-Wurfa oil field of Saudi Arabia.

5. A number of the enemy pilots were captured and bodies of others were spotted.

0055

Embassy of
The Republic of Iraq
Seoul

سفارة الجمهورية العراقية
سيئول

No. 14 /91

Press Release

23/1/1991

SUMMARY OF COMMUNIQUE NO. 14 OF THE GENERAL COMMAND OF THE ARMED FORCES ON JANUARY 22, 1991

In the Name of Allah, the Merciful, the Compassionate

God Is Great

The Iraqi people have set another heroic example of undermining the allegations and claims of the American-Zionist-Western barbarians by directing unrelenting retaliatory strikes and humilating them.

Military activities between 1:00 a.m. and 8:30 a.m. were as follows:

1. The barbaric enemy continued raiding civilian targets and killing innocent Iraqi people with their deadly bombs on the following locations:

   * The Province of Baghdad (six times).
   * The Province of Tameem (twice from Turkey).
   * The Province of Kuwait (three times).
   * The Province of Missan (four times).
   * The Province of Anbar (four times).

2. Our surface to air missile forces were able to shoot down ten enemy air targets (planes and missiles).

0056

Embassy of
The Republic of Iraq
Seoul

سفارة الجمهورية العراقية
سيئول

No. 29/91

Press Release

24/1/1991

SUMMARY OF COMMUNIQUE NO. 15 OF
THE GENERAL COMMAND OF THE ARMED FORCES
ON JANUARY 22, 1991

In the Name of Allah, the Merciful, the Compassionate

The valiant people of Iraq went on unhindered to extract the evil teeth of American Imperialists and further expose the arrogance of the Bush Administration, through successive lethal Iraqi retaliations.

1. The savage American enemy went on with its cowardly bombardment and missiles against Iraqi civilian population during the period 11:30 hours till 16:21 hours on the following locations:-

   * Province of Baghdad
   * City of Mendely
   * Province of Anbar (Three times)
   * Province of Salahiddin

2. Five air targets (planes and missiles) were downed by our valiant armed forces.

3. A number of American pilots were captured and dead bodies of others were spotted.

4. Three Iraqi soldiers managed to stand against a group of cowardly American tanks, further shattering the morale of the vicious enemy.

0057

Embassy of
The Republic of Iraq
Seoul

سفارة الجمهورية العراقية
سيئول

No. 30/91

Press Release

24/1/1991

SUMMARY OF COMMUNIQUE NO. 16 OF

THE GENERAL COMMAND OF THE ARMED FORCES

ON JANUARY 23, 1991

In the Name of Allah, the Merciful, the Compassionate

The volcano of the Iraqi anger continued to hammer on the rotten heads of the American Imperialists. The Iraqi vàliant people under the leadership of President Saddam Hussein is determined to allow those cowards to experience the taste of defeat.

1. During the period between 22:10 hours January 21, till 21:15 hours January 22, our missiles brought death and destruction on the following targets:-

   * Jabal AL Saudi (Saudi Arabia).
   * Riyadh (Saudi Arabia)
   * Dhuhran (Saudi Arabia)
   * Baqeeq Oil Complex (Saudi Arabia)
   * In revenge for the Palestinian Children of the Stone, and to show the Zionists the bitterness of holy Jihad, Tel Aviv was the target of our missiles.

2. The degenerate Americans and their subservients perpetrated the crimes of bombarding Iraqi civil populations as of 6:45 hours till 22 hours against:

   * Province of Salahidin (Twice)
   * Province of Baghdad (Three times)
   * Province of Anbar (Twice)
   * Province of Thee Qar (Twice)

3. Four enemy air targets (planes and missiles) were downed.

0058

Embassy of
The Republic of Iraq
Seoul

سفارة الجمهورية العراقية
سيئول

NO. 44-91

Press Release

28/1/1991

Annex

Letter dated 24 January 1991 from Mr. Tariq Aziz, Deputy Prime Minister and Minister for Foreign Affairs of Iraq, addressed to the Secretary-General

Since the imperialist United States, NATO and Zionist aggression against our country began at 0230 hours on 17 January 1991, the attacking forces have been committing heinous premeditated crimes against Iraqi citizens and against the economic, cultural, scientific and religious assets of our great people, which is one that has made a centuries-old contribution to human civilization.

On all occasions - in the course of our meeting at Amman on 31 August 1990 and during your visit to Baghdad on 11 and 12 January 1991 - we have constantly indicated and have explained to you in a clear and detailed manner that the basic fact with regard to the events which preceded and followed 2 August 1990 is that the imperialist United States, NATO and Zionist alliance and its treacherous adherents among the régimes of the region have had the objective, as they continue to do, of destroying resurgent Iraq, which is pursuing a free and independent policy and which proudly rejects imperialist and Zionist hegemony over the region and over its resources. Everything that has happened has taken place within the framework of a conspiracy hostile to the hopes of peoples for freedom, sovereignty, independence and relations of equality, which are the very principles and objectives for the achievement and defence of which the United Nations is supposed to have been established.

The deliberate and brutal attacks launched on behalf of the United Nations by the forces of the criminal Zionist-imperialist alliance on civilian economic, humanitarian, medical, cultural and religious targets and on citizens and their families in all parts of Iraq - documented examples of which are provided to you in the present letter - give cogent proof of the fact that the Governments participating in this alliance have the sole objective of taking vengeance on the proud people of Iraq and its militant leadership because of their opposition to the imperialist goals of those Governments.

It is indeed shameful for the United Nations that these premeditated crimes should be committed under the cover provided by resolutions adopted by the Security Council. The most recent of these is Security Council resolution 678 (1990), which the United States of America succeeded in having adopted by means of pressure, blackmail and bribery. The facts with respect to the receipt of bribes by States members of the Council and by leaders in those States are common knowledge.

Hundreds of millions of people in the world, in Asia, Africa and Latin America, who have suffered from the oppression and the crimes of the former colonialists and the new imperialists, are today finding the so-called new international order of which the arrogant former colonialists and new imperialists are speaking to be a dark age of intimidation and threats against those peoples aspiring to freedom and independence and fighting for relations of equality. The removal of the balancing role formerly played by the Soviet Union opens wide the

0059

way for the arrogant former colonialists and new imperialists once again to impose hegemony and intimidation, not only by the use of new and innovative methods, as is well known, but also by the old methods, namely aggression and open military occupation. What is new is that the colonialist technique as witnessed in past centuries has this time been used under the cover provided by iniquitous resolutions fabricated in the name of the United Nations which the Governments of the imperialist colonialist alliance succeeded in having adopted by means of pressure, intimidation, blackmail and bribery.

The States that endorsed those resolutions did so for the motives indicated. You, personally, bear responsibility to history and to mankind for the heinous crimes being committed against the free and militant people of Iraq. Examples are given hereunder of the savage and premeditated acts of aggression committed by the aggressor forces between 17 and 21 January 1991.

Baghdad Governorate

I. 17 January 1991

1. A pasteboard factory and a plastic foam factory in Za'faraniyah bombed.

2. Homes in the Urdunn, Bunuk and Wahdah quarters set on fire.

3. The Postal Department at Bab al-Mu'azzam set on fire and two citizens wounded.

4. A civilian vehicle set on fire near Al-Sha'b bridge.

5. The civil defence centre for the [illegible] area bombed

6. Abu Nawwas Street bombed.

II. 18 January 1991

1. A clinic bombed; one killed and 10 wounded and four ambulances damaged.

2. The 7 Nisan residential area bombed; seven killed.

3. The residential Kasrah area bombed.

4. The vegetable-oil factory bombed.

5. Al-Sha'b sports stadium bombed.

III. 19 January 1991

1. The Iwadiyah area bombed, resulting in the wounding of one citizen, the collapse of a restaurant and damage to neighbouring shops.

2. The Ma'rifah residential district bombed; three wounded.

0060

3. A building in the Kasrah area bombed; four civilians killed.

4. The Madinat Saddam residential area bombed; two homes damaged.

5. The Jazirat Baghdad tourist centre bombed; two killed and seven wounded; one home destroyed.

6. A building under construction for the Council of Ministers bombed.

7. The Al-Rashid Hotel area bombed; four homes damaged.

8. The Iraqi Museum bombed; six killed and 10 wounded; large-scale damage to the museum building.

IV. 21 January 1991

1. Five killed and homes damaged in a residential neighbourhood in Baghdad.

2. The Civil Defence Directorate building in the Al-Sha'b area bombed; two of the staff killed and five wounded; five vehicles damaged.

V. 22 January 1991

1. Homes in the 52 Street area bombed; two killed and three wounded.

2. Residential neighbourhoods bombed in Nuayrah, Kiyyarah, the Qadisiyah quarter and the Dur al-Shuhada' quarter.

3. Madinat Saddam bombed and homes set on fire.

4. The Karradat Maryam area bombed; two killed and four wounded; four homes destroyed; a number of neighbouring homes damaged.

VI. 23 January 1991

Residential neighbourhoods in the Waziriyah area and the Amin II area bombed.

<u>Salah al-Din Governorate</u>

I. 17 January 1991

One killed and nine wounded in the Khudayrah area of the Balad district as a result of the explosion of time-delay bombs dropped from aircraft.

II. 21 January 1991

1. Air attack on the Biji - Qaryat al-Bujwari district, wounding six.

0061

2. Attack on the Dur district, in the heavily populated southern region, killing 22 and wounding 33 and causing large-scale damage to 112 homes and 30 vehicles and damage to the Al-Abbasi Mosque.

3. Missile falling in a field in the Faris district, killing one woman and wounding two other citizens, one of them a woman.

4. The Tikrit district bombed with cluster-bombs dropped by two BRM-3A/As.

III. 22 January 1991

Residential centres bombed in the town of Tikrit and the Samarra' and Biji districts.

Ninawa Governorate

19 January 1991

The historic St. Thomas's Church bombed and damaged.

Wasit Governorate

I. 17 January 1991

Air attack on the provincial capital, killing nine and wounding nine others and damaging eight homes.

II. 18 January 1991

Attack on residential neighbourhoods in the city of Kut, killing a woman and wounding 29 other citizens and damaging six homes and six civilian government offices.

Babil Governorate

I. 18 January 1991

1. Residential areas bombed in the Latifiyah subdistrict; one woman wounded; a home damaged.

2. Attacks on the Musayyib district, damaging homes there.

II. 19 January 1991

The provincial capital and the Musayyib, Mahmudiyah and Iskandariyah areas were subjected to air attacks in which the textile plant at Hillah was damaged and two of the workers were killed and 14 wounded and homes in Mahmudiyah were damaged.

0062

III. 21 January 1991

1. The health centre in the provincial capital bombed from the air; 24 wounded; extensive damage to the centre building, the Civil Defence Directorate building and neighbouring homes.

2. The Tall al-Dhahab area bombed; one wounded; homes damaged.

IV. 22 January 1991

Residential areas bombed in the Mahmudiyah and Musayyib districts and the Iskandariyah subdistrict; four civilians wounded.

Anbar Governorate

19 January 1991

1. A food storage warehouse containing vegetable-oil and rice for the civilian inhabitants bombed in the Abu Ghurayb area.

2. Residential centres bombed in the Bubali area of the provincial capital; four children and two women killed; 16 other citizens wounded, including six women and five children; two homes destroyed; and a fire started.

3. The Nukhaym subdistrict bombed; 25 killed; nine wounded.

20 January 1991

1. Attack on the phosphate plant at Qa'im, killing three and wounding others.

2. A warehouse containing foodstuffs, meat and vegetable-oil bombed at Ramadi; two killed and seven wounded.

21 January 1991

1. The Hit district bombed; one killed and three wounded; homes damaged and destroyed; two civilian vehicles destroyed.

2. The Azrakiyah area in the Saqlawiyah subdistrict bombed; a woman killed and four other citizens wounded.

3. A home hit by a missile fired by an aircraft, killing three and wounding nine, all of them women and children.

4. A home hit by a missile fired by an aircraft, destroying the house and a civilian vehicle.

5. An infant formula factory bombed in the Abu Ghurayb area.

6. A poultry farm bombed in the provincial capital.

Qadisiyah Governorate

17 January 1991

1. Residential centres in the provincial capital bombed; four killed and 23 wounded.

2. A residential building bombed, the governorate office building, the civil defence building, a number of shops and houses and four civilian vehicles damaged and an ambulance set on fire.

Muthanna Governorate

18 January 1991

Air attack on a train travelling from Baghdad to Basra; three killed and 21 wounded.

Maysan Governorate

18 January 1991

1. Air attack on civilian areas in the Qal'at Salih and Kahla' districts, killing four in the Ka'bi area and wounding five others.

2. The sugar factory bombed.

Najaf Governorate

I. 18 January 1991

Agglomerations of nomadic Bedouin bombed in the Huwaymal area near Umm Tayyarah; 20 killed, including 12 children and 5 women.

II. 21 January 1991

1. The Kufa cement factory bombed.

2. The water purification plant for the civilian inhabitants bombed; five killed, including a woman, and 22 wounded.

3. Residential neighbourhoods in the cities of Najaf and Kufa bombed; 14 killed, including four children and three women; 24 wounded, including three children and 16 women; a number of homes destroyed and damaged in the Amir quarter of Najaf, where 130 citizens were killed, and in the Al-Mutanabbi quarter of Kufa.

0064

Dhi Qar Governorate

I. 17 January 1991

Air attacks, killing two and wounding five in the Batha' - Qaryat Al Budayr area and wounding two and damaging two homes and a vehicle in the provincial capital.

II. 18 January 1991

Spherical bombs dropped on the Suq al-Shuyukh and Batha' areas, killing two and wounding two.

III. 19 January 1991

One child killed in the Budur area in the course of an air attack.

Qadisiyah Governorate

19 January 1991

1. The State Vehicle Company complex bombed.

2. The food storage warehouse and flour factory bombed; damage caused; 10 killed and 22 wounded; two homes in the Mu'allimin quarter destroyed.

Karbala' Governorate

19 January 1991

1. Residential neighbourhoods bombed in the provincial capital.

2. The Karbala' cement factory bombed, causing large-scale damage.

22 January 1991

A residential neighbourhood bombed in the provincial capital.

Basra Governorate

17-19 January 1991

1. The provincial capital bombed, including areas of the city of Basra, Barjasiyah and Al-Asma'i and neighbouring residential apartments, and Atabat Bin Ghazwan; 28 wounded; 40 shops and some homes and civilian vehicles damaged.

2. The Harithah and Assafiyah areas bombed; six killed and 11 wounded, including a child aged three; six homes, an apartment and four shops destroyed; six shops and 15 vehicles damaged.

0065

3. The Faw district bombed; one wounded; 40 homes damaged.

4. The Qurnah district bombed; two killed and six wounded; a number of homes damaged.

5. The Zubayr district bombed; 17 killed and another 17 wounded; 12 homes destroyed; six civilian vehicles damaged.

(Signed) Tariq AZIZ
Deputy Prime Minister and
Minister for Foreign Affairs
of the Republic of Iraq

0066

Embassy of
The Republic of Iraq
Seoul

سفارة الجمهورية العراقية
سيئول

No. 29/91

Press Release

31/1/1991

SUMMARY OF COMMUNIQUE NO. 29 OF

THE GENERAL COMMAND OF THE ARMED FORCES

ON JANUARY 29, 1991

In the Name of Allah, the Merciful, the Compassionate

1. Our valiant armed forces carried out a blitz in the middle sector of the southern theatre, against enemy fortifications and its advanced forces through our borders with Saudi Arabia in the district of Arar. The two-pronged attack by our forces managed to kill a great number of enemy thugs and capture huge amounts of enemy intact war equipments and destroyed its fortifications, before withdrawing safely to bases.

2. One of our patrols destroyed a number of enemy observation posts on the borders of our 19th Province with Saudi Arabia.

3. The vicious enemy carried out 24 air sorties against the populated areas of our beloved Iraq.

0067

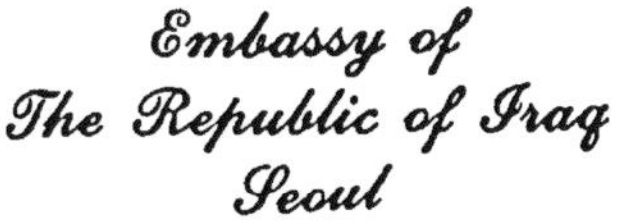

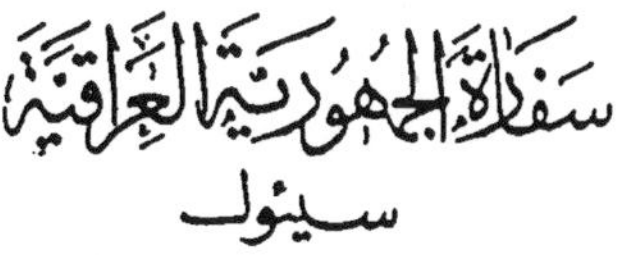

No. 30/91

Press Release

31/1/1991

SUMMARY OF COMMUNIQUE NO. 30 OF

THE GENERAL COMMAND OF THE ARMED FORCES

ON JANUARY 30, 1991

In the Name of Allah, the Merciful, the Compassionate

Now, that the imperialists and Zionists have exhausted all their vicious means of aggression against the peace-loving people of Iraq, our valiant patriots are still standing firm in the face of aggression and fully determined to follow the Iraqi leadership in the holy Jihad to safeguard the sovereignty and integrity of our homeland.

1. The cowardly enemy continued bombarding innocent citizens in Iraq, through 127 sorties.

2. It is now established beyond any doubt that 34 Zionist combat aircraft have crossed insided Turkey in order to participate from there in the aggression against Iraq.

3. Three enemy planes were downed.

0068

Embassy of
The Republic of Iraq
Seoul

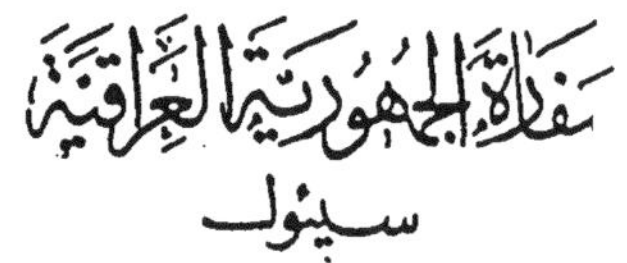

No. 31/91

Press Release

31/1/1991

SUMMARY OF COMMUNIQUE NO. 31 OF THE GENERAL COMMAND OF THE ARMED FORCES ON JANUARY 30, 1991

In the Name of Allah, the Merciful, the Compassionate

The Victory of Allah is at hand!

O' Great People of Iraq!

O' Magnaminous People of Najd and AL-Hijaz!

O' Peoples wherever You are!

Allah is our Witness, we didn't want it. But Fahd, the traitor, the American agent wanted it. He transformed the holy land into an operation theatre of the blasphemous and committed his treacherous crime in collaboration with Bush, the enemy of Allah. They are bombarding the innocent people of Iraq on a daily basis, killing women and children and other good people of Iraq.

Your valiant forces have now unleashed a blitz inside Najd and AL-Hijaz and succeeded by the help of Allah to enter the city of Khafja. Thus Allah opened the way for the Believers for destroying the front of blasphemy.

O' People of Najd and AL-Hijaz!

We have no ambitions in your land. We are your brothers. We are all in the same side against the side blasphemy, crime and corruption, the side of Bush and Fahd.

We are not invading your territories. Entering your land is a strategic necessity, directed against the armies of infidels and aggression, which transformed your homeland into a base of aggression.

Allah is Great.

0069

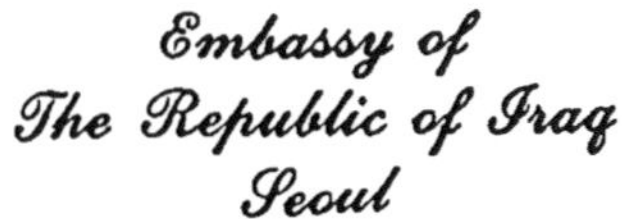

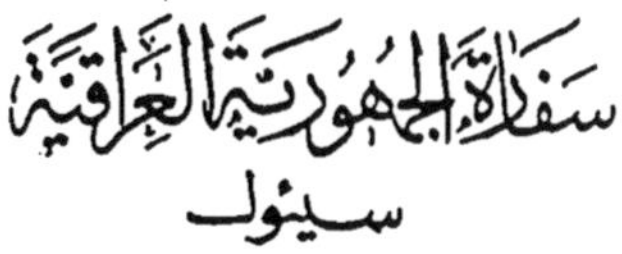

No. 52/91

Press Release

31/1/1991

STATEMENT OF A MILITARY SPOKESMAN

ON JANUARY 29, 1991

In the Name of God, the Merciful, the Compassionate.

In line with the series of crimes which the American administration and its Atlantic allies are now perpetrating against the valiant people of Iraq, three missiles were launched on the evening of January 29, 1991 along with a number of air raids targetting an Industry Ministry's establishment in Baghdad and resulted in the death of one of the captured pilots residing in that quarter.

We hereby declare to the Wolrd public opinion that the United States alone bears the responsibility of this heinous crime against our citizens and against the captured pilots whom Iraq host. We have repeatedly warned against the danger of hitting cities and civilian targets, in consideration of the safety not only of our citizens but also of those whom the savagery of Bush forced them to participate in the aggression gainst Iraq.

We appeal to all peace-loving people, including the families of POWs to raise their voices in condemnation of the crimes committed by Bush, and that crime in particular which indicate the irresponsibility and inhuman nature of the American politicians.

0070

Embassy of
The Republic of Iraq
Seoul

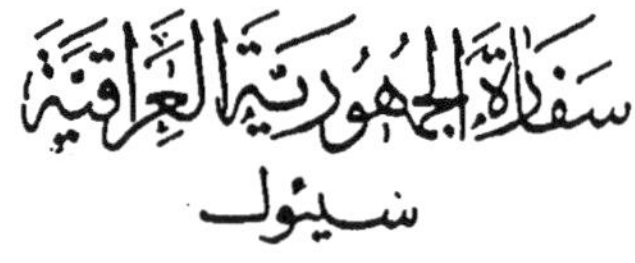

No. 54/91

Press Release

1/2/1991

STATEMENT OF A MILITARY SPOKESMAN ON JANUARY 30, 1991

In the Name of God, the Merciful, the Compassionate.

In pursuance to the Communique No.30 of the General Command of the Armed Forces on January 30, 1991, the American-Zionist vicious enemy continued the air raids against our homeland, from Saudi and Turkish territories. So far the cowardly enemy carried out 76 raids and 2 missiles.

Our valiant air defenses were able to down three air targets (planes and missiles).

Allah bless our courageous defenders.

Allah be praised for His victories.

0071

NEWS OF THE MOTHER OF ALL BATTLES

JANUARY 30, 1991

H.E. President Saddam Hussein presided over a meeting, on January 26, 1991, attended by Mr. Izzat Ibrahim, vice-chairman of the Revolutionary Command Council (RCC), and a number of the RCC members including Mr. Taha Yaessin Ramadhan, First Deputy Prime Minister, Mr. Tareq Aziz, Deputy Prime Minister and Minister of Foreign Affairs, Dr. Sa'dun Hamadi, Deputy Prime Minister, and Mr. Latif Nissayif Jassim, Minister of Information.

The meeting was also attended by Mr. Hussein Kamil, Minister of Industry and Military Industry, Staff Lieutenant General Sa'di Tu'ama Abbas, Minister of Defence, and a number of Senior army Commanders.

During the meeting, a plan for a ground offensive against the American-Atlantic-Zionist Forces of aggression was drawn up.

* On January 27, 1991, H.E. President Saddam Hussein visited the Governorate of Basra where he met army commenders of the Battle field. The President gave his instructions to implement the ground's offensive plan.

NEWS OF THE MOTHER OF ALL BATTLES

JANUARY 31, 1991

* Iraqi News Agency learned from a reliable military source that our valiant forces which entered the city of Khafji after defeating enemy forces are the brave forces of Mohammed Al-Qassim commanded by Staff-Brigadaire Yaseen Falih Al-Ma'eeni.

INA also learned that the American, Saudi and other prisoners of war of other blasphemous "alliance" are still in the city of Khafji with our forces and they will stay there untill further notice.

INA learned as well, that among the POWs captured by our intrepid forces which occupied the Saudi city of Khafji on the night of 29/30 of January 1991, there are American female soldiers who receive good treatment in accordance with the tradition and in compliance to the magnificent Islamic laws.

0072

SUMMARY OF COMMUNIQUE NO. 32 OF

THE GENERAL COMMAND OF THE ARMED FORCES

ON JANUARY 31, 1991

In the Name of Allah, the Merciful, the Compassionate

O' Great People!
O' Heroic Believers of the Armed Forces!
O' Peoples who are working for welfare, love and peace!

Bush, the modern-day Satan was preaching treachery and murder and providing his Congress and Senate with the results of his crimes by utilising remote-control tecnnology.

Though fighting is not our only choice, we found ourselves forced to fight to safeguard our values against the aggression waged by the enemies of Allah.

Bush has been too coward to confront our brave ground forces in a manly manner. Thus he resorted to remote-control technology, imagining that he could realise his sick dreams of victories against the people of Iraq.

The valiant Believers decided to make Bush and his sebservient, Fahd know the extent of their own degradation, through a blitz by our valiant armed forces who entered the city of Khafji.

Some of the forces of blesphemy were killed, others fled and a number of American males and females were captured.

On the night of 30/31 of January, a counter attack by the desperate forces of evil was repulsed and humiliated by the heroic forces of Mohammed AL-Qasim.

Allah be praised for His victory!
O' valiant men of our armed forces!

The Glorious battle of Khafji is the gate to the grand victory of the Believers which will hamper the will of Satan. Victory is yours and for our valiant brothren in Najd and AL-Hijaz, plagued by the traitor of the Two Holy

0073

Shrines who caused the confrontation with their brothren, the Iraqis.

This battle, O' valiant Believers. will be the prelude to liberate the holy Tomb of the Prophet, Palestine, Lebanon and all other territories.

God is Great.

STATEMENT OF A MILITARY SPOKESMAN

ON JANUARY 31, 1991

In the Name of God. the Merciful. the Compassionate

At 14:00 hours on January 31, a number of enemy aircraft attempted a raid on the populated areas in our beloved Iraq. Our valiant eagles confronted this aggression and, in a spectacular dogfight, downed, with the help of Allalh, one plane and hit another, while other enemy planes fled in panic of our eagles.

Allah preserve the hands of our eagles!

The coming days shall, by the will of Allah, witness more and more heroic deeds by our eagles.

Victory of Allah is at hand.

0074

Embassy of
The Republic of Iraq
Seoul

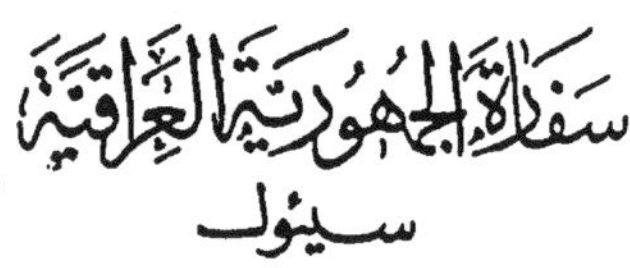

No. 61/91 **Press Release** 5/2/1991

SUMMARY OF COMMUNIQUE NO. 37 OF

THE GENERAL COMMAND OF THE ARMED FORCES

ON FEBRUARY 4, 1991

In the Name of Allah, the Merciful, the Compassionate

The Americans, Zionists and their so-called "allies" have exhausted all technologically advanced means of destruction against our people. But they miscalculated the will of the Almighty and the power of Man, supporting Iraq in one trench. Criminal Bush and his stooges have not been able yet to comprehend the determination of the Iraqis who are standing under the banner of Allah, carried by our valiant Leader Saddam Hussein.

The forces of darkness will kneel before the forces of right, the forces of Iraq which are bound, without any doubt, to liberate our sanctities in Palestine and Najd and Hijas.

The vicious enemy continued the bombardment of the populated areas in our homeland and the attempts to hit our armed forces from afar, with an aggression of 150 air sorties through Turkey, Saudi Arabia and, in violation of the Iranian airspace, through Iran.

Our valiant air defenses downed thirteen enemy combat aircraft in the Syrian territories and in the waters of the Arabian Gulf.

Victory is ours.

0075

Embassy of
The Republic of Iraq
Seoul

سفارة الجمهورية العراقية
سيئول

No. 63/91

Press Release

7/2/1991

SUMMARY OF COMMUNIQUE NO. 38 OF
THE GENERAL COMMAND OF THE ARMED FORCES
ON FEBRUARY 6, 1991

In the Name of Allah, the Merciful, the Compassionate

The conspircy against the people of Iraq in all the details of aggression and mass destruction against the innocent civilians of Iraq and its religious, cultural and other sites, has been meticulously anticipated by the mind of the great Leader of Iraq and the Arab Nation, President Saddam Hussein. No wonder the Iraqi valiant people has succeeded in repulsing the aggression and rendered the American-Zionist-Western vicious "dreams" into a collosal "nightmare". No wonder also that, out of their cowardice and fear to confront our forces, the degenerate enemy concentrates his air raids against the Iraqi women and children.

We are proud to say that we are now much stronger and more capable to crush the aggressors with the help of the Almighty.

O' Sons of Iraq!
O' Brethren in Arabism!

The criminal enemy continued their savage air raids against populated areas last night in 371 air sorties. With the help of Allah, our courageous air defenses succeeded in downing nine enmy aircraft.

Allah be praised!

0076

Embassy of
The Republic of Iraq
Seoul

سفارة الجمهورية العراقية
سيئول

No. 64/91

Press Release

8/2/1991

Statement of the Assembly of the Islamic Cleric in the Most Honoured Najaf On January 25, 1991

In the Name of Allah, the Merciful, the Compassionate

"Those, who are told that people had mobilised against you and you should fear them, have their faith strengthened and said we are satisfied that Allah is on our side, and He is the best guarantor" Allah's is the word of Truth.

The Moslem people of Iraq is subject these days to a savage and unfair attack by the armies of aggression and blasphemy, their hypocritical agents, and their allies with intention of invading our holy land and blemish our sanctities and heritages and destroy our traditions.

The Islamic Cleric Assembly in the Most Honoured Najaf, while regarding aggression against any Moslem people as an aggression against ALL Moslems and insulting them as insulting the great religion of Islam, appeal to the Moslems all over the World to shoulder their responsibilities and confront the Blasphemous, in defending the sanctities and holy places which are now violated in Iraq in general and the Most Honoured Najaf and Holy Karbala in particular.

The Islamic Cleric Assembly condemns resorting to the assistance of blasphemous forces for the cheap benefit and the temporary interest. To do this is a grand sin in Islam. Allah, the Almighty said "Warn the hypocrites that painful torture is in store for them, for they have the Blasphemous for their leaders instead of the Believers for the purpose of finding glory, but glory is exclusively Allah's." Allah's is the word of Truth.

Singed by:

Seyid Mohammad AL-Sadir, Seyid Mohammed Mahdi AL-Kharsan,
Seyid Ala'a AL-Din Bahr el-ILoom,
Seyid Izz AL-Din Bahr el-ILoom, ALi AL Musawi AL-Razwari,
Muheyi AL-Din AL-Ghareeqy, Ahmed AL-Bahadly,
Ridha Al- Musawi AL-Khilkhali, Ali AL-Azzawi, Hadi Fiadh,
Hassan Taha Tabai' AL-Hakeem.

0077

Embassy of
The Republic of Iraq
Seoul

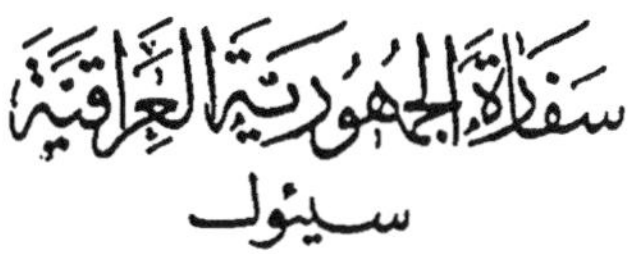

No. 65/91

Press Release

9/2/1991

SUMMARY OF COMMUNIQUE NO. 39 OF

THE GENERAL COMMAND OF THE ARMED FORCES

ON FEBRUARY 7, 1991

In the Name of Allah, the Merciful, the Compassionate

While the valiant forces of Islam are waiting like lions for the decisive hour when battle of liberating the sanctities of Islam gets closer, the forces of darkness and their Arabic speaking subservients carry out with unprecedented savagery their air raids against populated areas in our homeland.

1. Our courageous forces launched a devastating strike with AL-Hussein missile against Dhehran, the symbol of submission and treason of AL-Saud.

2. The cowardly enemy carried out through the borders of Saudi Arabia 284 air sorties against innocent population and, from afar, against our armed forces.

3. Our valiant air defense forces downed six enemy air targets (planes and missiles).

Praise to Allah! Glory for Iraq!

0078

Embassy of
The Republic of Iraq
Seoul

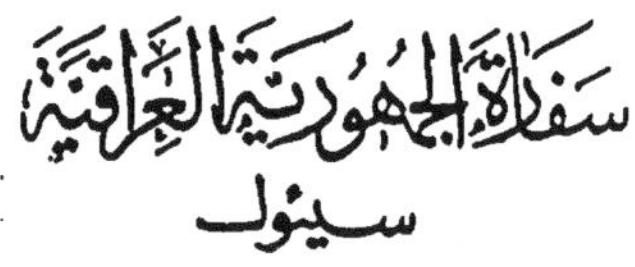

No. 68/91

Press Release

9/2/1991

SUMMARY OF COMMUNIQUE NO. 41 OF THE GENERAL COMMAND OF THE ARMED FORCES ON FEBRUARY 8, 1991

In the Name of Allah, the Merciful, the Compassionate

On the occasion of 8 February Revolution, the Armed Forces extend heartiest congratulations to the Supreme Commander of the Armed Forces, President Saddam Hussain and to the valiant Iraqi people, begging the Almighty to preserve Iraq against the forces of Blasphemy.

Our Armed Forces renew, on this occasion, to the victorious Leader and the Iraqi people their determination to crush the rotten heads of the aggressors and to revenge the martyrs in Iraq and in all the Arab nation.

1. In retaliation to the treachery of Al-Sauds, a missile strike was launched last night against Al-Riyadh, the Capital of the infidel Al_Saud. All missile launchers returned to base safely.

2. The mean enemy carried out 192 air sorties against populated areas in our homeland.

3. With the help of Allah, our valiant air defenses downed three enemy combat aircraft.

Allah is Great.

0079

Embassy of
The Republic of Iraq
Seoul

سفارة الجمهورية العراقية
سيئول

No. 70/91

Press Release

11/2/1991

SUMMARY OF COMMUNIQUE NO. 42 OF

THE GENERAL COMMAND OF THE ARMED FORCES

ON FEBRUARY 9, 1991

In the Name of Allah, the Merciful, the Compassionate

The voice of truth from Iraq shall not be overcome by the lies and fabrications of the American-Zionist-Western aggressors. Now the whole World knows that the aim of aggression is to destroy the power of the Arab nation, through trying to destroy Iraq. But, every passing day, the valiant Iraqis, under the leadership of Saddam Hussain who is supported by Allah, Moslems, and all peace-loving peoples of the World, are proving that victory, Allah willing, is at hand.

1. Since the Zionist entity is the prime instigator of the aggression, and systemstically trying to wipe out our people in Palestine, a devastating Al-Hussain missile attack was launched against Tel Aviv. All missile launchers returned to their bases safely.

2. Our valiant armed forces launched a series of missile attacks against concentrations of enemy forces, destroying a sizeable number of his equipements and personnel.

3. The barbaric Americans carried out 345 air raids against our civilized country through Saudi Arabia, and violated our eastern borders.

Glory is for Allah and for our Great Leader Saddam Hussain under the banner of Allah is the Greatest.

0080

Embassy of
The Republic of Iraq
Seoul

سفارة الجمهورية العراقية
سيئول

No. 71/90

Press Release

11/2/1991

Annex

Letter dated 1 February 1991 from the Deputy Prime Minister and Minister for Foreign Affairs of Iraq addressed to the Secretary-General

On 24 January 1991, I wrote you a letter to inform you that, since the commencement of their aggression at 2.30 p.m. on 17 January 1991, the forces of the United States, NATO and Zionist alliance have been committing heinous and premeditated crimes against Iraqi citizens and against the economic, cultural, scientific and religious institutions of the Iraqi people.

In that letter I presented a long list of tangible facts concerning such crimes committed in the period from 17 to 21 January. Those facts were subsequently confirmed and reported by neutral press agencies, and were widely discussed in political and media circles throughout the world.

We find it strange that the Secretary-General of the United Nations has not expressed his view in this regard, as expected not only by the Iraqi people but by all just and free persons throughout the world, who regard the United Nations as an institution whose purpose is to defend human values. Instead, you have remained silent concerning these crimes which, for the first time in history, are being committed in the name of the United Nations and under the cloak of groundless and unjust Security Council resolutions, the most recent of which is resolution 678 (1990). The whole world is aware that those resolutions were adopted as a result of pressure, blackmail and bribery by the United States and its allies, thereby bringing shame on the Security Council, the United Nations and the countries which received bribes and yielded to United States pressure and blackmail. Your silence in the face of these crimes will merely increase the shame of the United Nations, which is now being used by the imperialist Powers to subjugate peoples, muffle their free and independent voice, impose full control over oil and perpetuate Israeli hegemony over the region. Indeed, the very goals that the United Nations is supposed to embody are being violated before the eyes and with the knowledge of the Secretary-General of the United Nations, who utters not a word. Numerous free voices have denounced the crimes that are being committed against the people of Iraq, and officials of some countries participating in the aggression have protested against it and have declared that what is happening far exceeds the intended purpose of the resolutions adopted in the name of the United Nations, notwithstanding the fact that those resolutions are groundless and unjust. However, you still remain silent.

In this letter I am presenting further facts concerning the crimes that are being committed against the Iraqi people and which took place after the date of my first letter. It is a record for history, and the judgement of history is harsh and merciless.

0081

Baghdad governorate

I. 26 January 1991.

Air bombardment in which five citizens were wounded, one of whom subsequently died.

II. 28 January 1991.

1. An air raid on residential areas in which 10 citizens were wounded.

2. Bombardment of the Radio and Television Building, in which two citizens were wounded.

III. 29 January 1991.

Bombardment of Al-Jumhouriya Bridge in Baghdad.

IV. 30 January 1991.

1. An air raid on the Central Bank, which suffered damage and in which two citizens were wounded.

2. Missile attack on the Ministry of Justice.

Salah al-Din governorate

I. 23 January 1991.

1. Time-fuse bombs were dropped on agricultural areas in the district of Balad, as a result of which one citizen was killed and two others were wounded.

2. 25 January 1991.

Air raid on residential areas on the Baghdad-Nineveh road and on Qadisiya quarter and the village of Arbida in the subdistrict of al-Alam, as a result of which five citizens were killed and nine others wounded.

Anbar governorate

I. 21 January 1991.

Bombardment of a desert area in Kebisa district, as a result of which three citizens were killed and one wounded.

II. 23 January 1991.

1. A missile fell on a house in the district of Abu Ghurayb.

0082

2. A missile fell on al-Furat village in the district of Hit and another fell in the al-Boukamal area in the subdistrict of al-Karmah. Seven cluster bomb canisters were dropped in the district of al-Rutbah.

III. 26 January 1991.

An air raid on al-Ramadi city and the districts of al-Qaim, al-Rutbah, Haditha and Hit killed eight citizens and wounded seven others.

IV. 22 January 1991.

An air raid on al-Nakhib subdistrict killed four citizens and wounded one woman.

V. 26 January 1991.

Bombardment of the Qadisiya Irrigation Dam, which was damaged.

VI. 27 January 1991.

Air raids on al-Ramadi city including al-Ramadi city centre and the districts of al-Rutbah, al-Qaim, Haditha, Hit and the subdistrict of al-Ameriya, in which two citizens were killed and another wounded.

VII. 28-29 January 1991.

1. Air raids on al-Ramadi city centre and the districts of al-Rutbah, al-Qaim, Haditha, Hit and the subdistricts of al-Ameriya and Kebisa.

2. Air raids on 28 January 1991 on the highway between al-Qaim and Akashat, in which four Jordanians were killed and seven persons wounded, including two Jordanians and one person from Thailand.

VIII. 30 January 1991.

1. Bombardment of the al-Kindi Company for Medical Vaccines, the subdistricts of al-Nasr and al-Salam in Abu Ghurayb district and a Customs office, in which one citizen was wounded.

Dhi Qar governorate

22 January 1991.

Two citizens were wounded by a missile fired from an enemy aircraft.

Najaf governorate

23 January 1991.

Bombardment of residential areas at Najaf, Kufa and al-Manadhira.

0083

Basra governorate

20 January 1991.

Bombardment of al-Najibiya residential area, in which 15 citizens were killed, 19 others wounded and 19 residential buildings destroyed. Four occupants of those buildings were wounded and two shops and a civilian vehicle were damaged.

Ta'mim governorate

20-25 January 1991.

An air raid on densely populated residential areas at Imam Qasim, al-Andalus, Azadi, Arafa and Bey Hasan quarters and al-Dibs district resulted in the death of 15 citizens, including 12 children and 2 women. Six citizens, including four children and a woman, were wounded.

Babil governorate

I. 23 January 1991.

1. Four missiles fired at the residential areas of the modern village in the subdistrict of Iskandariya killed 20 citizens and wounded 25 others.

2. Bombardment of residential areas in the district of al-Mahmoudiya killed three citizens and wounded four others.

II. 24 January 1991.

Two air raids on the Musayyib district, targeting residential areas at Jurf al-Sakhr, resulted in the death of two civilians.

III. 26-27 January 1991.

An air raid on the principal city in the governorate and on the districts of Musayyib and Hashimiya and the subsdistrict of Iskandariya killed eight citizens and wounded 36 others in the principal city of the governorate.

Karbala governorate

25 January 1991.

Bombardment of Karbala Cement Plant.

Arbil governorate

I. 24 January 1991.

Bombardment of houses in the principal city of Arbil governorate killed two citizens and wounded 20 others, including seven women and four children.

0084

II. 26 January 1991.

Bombardment of residential areas in the Basterma area of Harir subdistrict resulting in the death of 13 citizens, including eight women, four children, and wounded 85 other citizens.

Wasit governorate

24-25 January 1991.

An air raid on the al-Badriya area in Wasit governorate killed two citizens and wounded another.

(Signed) Tariq AZIZ
Deputy Prime Minister
and Minister for Foreign Affairs
of the Republic of Iraq
Baghdad

0085

Embassy of
The Republic of Iraq
Seoul

سفارة الجمهورية العراقية
سيئول

No. 72-91

Press Release

12/2/1991

SUMMARY OF COMMUNIQUE NO. 43 OF

THE GENERAL COMMAND OF THE ARMED FORCES

ON FEBRUARY 10, 1991

In the Name of Allah, the Merciful, the Compassionate

The enemy will be defeated.. Their sick thoughts will be defeated in front of the genuine, humanatrian and national beliefs.. Their history, which is full of shame and atrocities will be defeated in front of the rich Arab-Islamic history.. Their barbarism and brutalism will be defeated in front of Iraq's civilization.. Their vile will, their leaders, their agents and their coward forces will be defeated in front of the will of God, the inginuity and courage of the historic hero Saddam HUSSEIN and the valiant men of Iraq.

With full readeness and holding their deadly weapons with strong arms, our forces are preparing to put an end to the American colonialism and imperialism and to avenge the pure Arab blood.

The barbarians continued their cowardly aggression against our peaceful residential areas but are still freightened of confronting our heroic army.

1. The enemy launched 165 air raids against our civilian targets in Iraq.

2. Our valiant air defenders shot down three enemy planes.

0086

Embassy of
The Republic of Iraq
Seoul

سفارة الجمهورية العراقية
سيئول

No. 74/91

Press Release

12/2/1991

STATEMENT OF DEPUTY PRIME MINISTER, MINISTER OF FOREIGN AFFAIRS ON FEBRUARY 9, 1991, REGARDING THE VISIT OF THE PAKISTANI PRIME MINISTER TO A NUMBER OF ARAB & ISLAMIC COUNTRIES

After the huge demonstrations all over Pakistan, through which the Pakistani people denounced and condemned the American-Atlantic-Zionist aggression against the people of Iraq, the Pakistani Prime-Minister paid visits to a number of Arab and Islamic countries and is now visiting another number of Arab Maghreb countries. During these visits the Prime-Minister of Pakistan pretends to be endeavouring for what he calls the settlement of the crises.

Obviously these visits and the statements isssued in the meanwhile are but an attempt to absorb the wrath of the Pakistani People and other Pakistani patriotic forces due to the policy of the government of Mr. Nawaz Sherif, which sides with aggression.

Any government which has sent troops in support of the American-Atlantic-Zionist aggression cannot be categorized as sincere in an honourable settlement.

We condemn the policy of the current Pakistani Government, because it serves the conspiracy of aggression by the American-Atlantic-Zionist alliance against Iraq, which has always reserved the best brotherly relations with the Moslem People of Pakistan. We salute the principled attitude of the people of Pakistan, in strong solidarity with Iraq which is now valiantly confronting the flagrant aggression by the United States, its allies and the Zionist entity.

0087

Embassy of
The Republic of Iraq
Seoul

سفارة الجمهورية العراقية
سيئول

No. 77/91

Press Release

13/2/1991

THE MERCENARIES OF THE "NEW" INTERNATIONAL ORDER!

From the outset of the American-Zionist-Western intervention in the Holy land of Najd and Hejaz, their conspiracy with their servants in the area like King Fahd & his Gulf Sheikhs & Emirs, President Mubarak and President Assad of Syria, has been very clear.

It was popularly stated by the people of the Arab Peninsula that while the King is acting as an obedient servant of Bush, the ruling Saudi family will leave the fighting to their "white slaves'! Thus the American-Zionist-Atlantic axis deployed their mercenaries on the Arab-Muslem Holy land and started passing the hat to cover their expenses.

Now the "white slave" theory has become a reality. For it is established beyond a shadow of doubt that the Saudi rulers are obliged to pay the sum of US$ One Million for each American family who loses a member perishing as dead in the process of the barbaric aggression against the people of Iraq. Those notorious rulers compensate also the American families for the wounded and the prisoners of war whom they lose in their miserable attempts to defend the doomed autocratic rulers of the Gulf.

It is also an established fact that the forces of the unholy American-Atlantic-Zionist "alliance" finance their evil aggression against our homeland, through humbly begging for contributions from the Gulf regimes and the defunct ruler of "Kuwait".

What more obvious evidence there is that those forces are no more than mercenaries, who trade and make their living out of spilling the blood of the innocent!

Out of the conviction that Allah is on our side, the side of the right, the mercenary "alliance" of evil will be doomed and end up with the shame of devastating defeat.

0088

Embassy of
The Republic of Iraq
Seoul

سفارة الجمهورية العراقية
سيئول

No. 78/91 **Press Release** 13/2/1991

SUMMARY OF COMMUNIQUE NO. 44 OF
THE ARMED FORCES GENERAL COMMAND
ON FEBRUARY 11, 1991

In the Name of Allah, the Merciful, the Compassionate

Our enemies have made public in word and deed that they are the enemies of the Arabs and Muslems and that they will not accept our right in progress and unity. Our enemies are doing their utmost to keep the region in backwardness and strengthen their hegemony on man, land and resources. Those enemies endeavour, in collaboration with the corrupt rulers to paralize the movement of our nation and help the treacherous rulers drain the public coffer on extravagance and sensuous pleasures.

Under the banner of our great Leader Saddam Hussein, the Iraqi will continue, aided by the strength and honour of the Arabs and Muslems, to confront and humiliate the vicious enemy.

O' Brethern,

The barbaric enemy carried out 28 air sorties against civilian targets such as bridges, roads and water supplies. The vicious enemy also carried out 35 sorties against our valiant armed forces in the South.

Allah willing, Iraq will continue to fight till the victorious end.

0089

Embassy of
The Republic of Iraq
Seoul

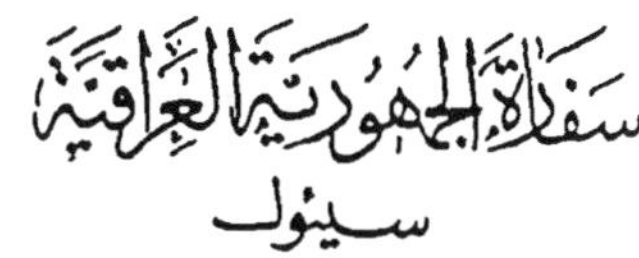

No. 79/91

Press Release

13/2/1991

U.S. COMMITS WAR CRIMES IN IRAQ BOMBING

NEW YORK (Reuter) - Former U.S. attorney general Ramsey Clark accused the United STates on Monday of committing war crimes in Iraq by causing extensive civilian casualties and damage.

"The damage that we saw was staggering in its expanse," he told a news conference on his return from a week-long visit to Iraq.

Clark said the head of the Iraqi Red Crescent, Dr. Ibrahim al-Noori, estimated that between 2,000 and 7,000 civilians had died so far in the allied bombing, aimed at forcing president Saddam Hussein to withdraw from Kuwait.

"This is an attack on the people of Iraq, the economy of Iraq." Clark said. He was giving an account of what he said he saw while driving more than 2,000 miles (3,200 Km) through the country, including visits to Baghdad and Basra, the two biggest cities.

"These are violations of the Hague Conventions, they are violations of the Geneva Conventions, they are violations of Nuremberg, they are war crimes," he said, alluding to the legal code applied to Nazi leaders at trials in Nuremberg after World War II.

Clark, who served as attorney general under the late president Lyndon Johnson but later strongly opposed the Vietnam war, is a frequent critic of U.S. foreign policy.

He said he went to Iraq because he feared the large number of air sorties being carried out must have resulted in extensive civilian casualties. He obtained "significant cooperation" from the Iraqi government and was accompanied by an Iraqi-American, whom he did not identify but who he said had family in Baghdad and Basra.

He also took along a television crew, but the Iraqis did not inspect the film footage, either through oversight or because "they trusted me."

It was not shown at the news conference.

"When President Bush talks about pinpoint bombing, let me tell you I didn't see any collateral military damage," Clark said. He was making an ironic allusion to U.S. claims that attacks on military targets might sometimes produce "collateral" or unintended civilian damage.

"The bombing is a violation of international law which all of us should always remember protects civilians. You don't kill civilians..."

"And they are not hitting military targets. If they are, why can't you find some shreds of soldiers' clothing? What you find is the people's clothing scattered around, and their possessions scattered around, in their residential areas."

0090

Embassy of
The Republic of Iraq
Seoul

سفارة الجمهورية العراقية
سيئول

Press Release

NO. 79/91 — 13/2/1991

미국은 이라크를 폭격하면서 전쟁 범죄를 자행하다

뉴욕 (로이터)- 전 미국 법무 장관 램시 클라크는 일요일, 미국이 막대한 민간인 사상자와 재해를 일으킴으로 이라크에서 전쟁 범죄를 자행하고 있다고 비난했다.

"우리가 목격한 손상은 어마어마한 것이었다" 라고, 일주일간의 이라크 방문후 가진 기자회견에서 그는 말했다.

그의 말에 의하면, 이라크 붉은 초생달의 지도자인 이브라힘 압 누리 박사는 사담 후세인 대통령이 쿠웨이트에서 철수하도록 하는데 목적을 둔 지금까지의 다국적군의 폭격으로 2천명에서 7천 명사이의 이라크 민간인이 사망했다고 추정했다.

"이것은 이라크 국민과 이라크 경제에 대한 공격이다"라고 클라크는 말한다. 그는 이라크 최대의 도시인 바그다드와 바스라를 포함하여 나라 전역에 걸쳐 2천 마일 (3,200 KM) 이상을 차를 타고 가며 자신이 본 것을 보고하고 있다.

"이것은 헤이그 협정의 위반이며, 제네바 협정의 위반이고, 또한 뉴렘베르크의 위반이다. 이들은 전쟁 범죄이다."라고 그는, 제 2차 대전후 뉴렘베르크 재판에서 나치 지도자들에게 적용된 법률을 언급하면서 말했다.

고 린든 죤슨 대통령 시절 법무 장관을 지냈고, 후에 베트남전을 강력하게 반대했던 클라크는 미국의 대외 정책에 대한 단골 비평가이다.

그는, 현재 진행중인 다수의 비행 출격은 막대한 민간이 사상자를 초래하였음이 틀림없다고 생각하였기 때문에 이라크에 갔다고 한다. 그는 이라크 정부로 부터 "의미심장한 협조"를 받았고, 신원은 알 수 없지만, 가족이 바그다드와 이라크에 살고 있다고 한 이라크계 미국인의 수행을 받았다.

그는 또한 일단의 방송인들을 데리고 갔는데, 이라크는 실수로인지 혹은 그를 믿기때문이었는지, 필름을 조사하지는 않았다.

그것은 기자회견에서는 보여지지 않았다.

"부시 대통령이 정밀조준 폭격에 대해서 말할때, 나는 어떠한 부수적인 군사파괴 도 보지 못했다는 사실은 이야기하고자한다."고 클라크는 말했다. 그는 군사 목표물에 대한 공격에, 때때로 부수적인, 또는 고의가 아닌 민간 희생이 일어날 지도 모른다고 한 미국의 주장에 반어적인 암시를 하고 있다.

"이 폭격은, 항상 민간인은 보호해야한다는, 우리 모두가 기억해야 할 국제법의 위반이다. 민간인은 희생되어서는 안된다..."

"그리고 그들은 군사 목표물을 공격하고 있지 않다. 만일 그렇다면, 왜 군복 한 조각도 발견되지 않고 있는가? 발견되는 것은, 주거지에 여기 저기 흩어져 있는 민간인 옷들 뿐이며, 그들의 소유물이다."

Embassy of
The Republic of Iraq
Seoul

سفارة الجمهورية العراقية
سيئول

NO : 80

Press Release

Date : 14/2/1991

SUMMARY OF COMMUNIQUE NO. 45 OF THE ARMED FORCES GENERAL COMMAND ON FEBRUARY 12, 1991

In the Name of Allah, the Merciful, the Compassionate

Our people are heroicaly confronting colonialism with all its aggressive means.

What the Iraqis are doing today should be a pride, not to the Iraqis only, but to all of who seek freedom, progress, justice and for the Arab, Moslem and Third World nations.

While our forces stand as a solid fence along our borders challanging, with pride, the enemies of Arabs and Moslims, the enemies have been cowardly reverting to low means of attacking our civilian town and villages. Meanwhile, Iraq, angered by the barbarian American-Zionist-Atlantic aggression, continues to pound, with the strength of justice, the strongholds of the aggressors.

Followniq are our activities and the enemy's acts of aggression against out people last night and this morning:

1- To punish the Zionists, who in their vile means, started and ttaking part in this war, a devastating Al-Hussein missile attack was launched against Tel Aviv yesterday evening.

2- A second Al-Hussein missile offensive was launched yesterday after mid night against Tel Aviv.

3- In order to punish the treacherous infedels of Al-Saud, another Al-Hussein missile offenssive was launched against the capital of evil, Al-Riyadh. Our brave missile forces returnd to theri base safe.

4- The barbaric enemy continued its aggression against our cities, towns, and villages targetting our residential quarters, civil establishments, and a number of military targets.

The enemy carried out 42 air raids aimed at cars bridges, one public hospital, a maternity hospital, a kindengarden, a drinking water tank, tents inhabited by shephreds, and a number of residential houses and commercial shops in some of our towns and villages.

0092

The enemy carried out 135 air raids against the military targets in the southern sector of the

Embassy of
The Republic of Iraq
Seoul

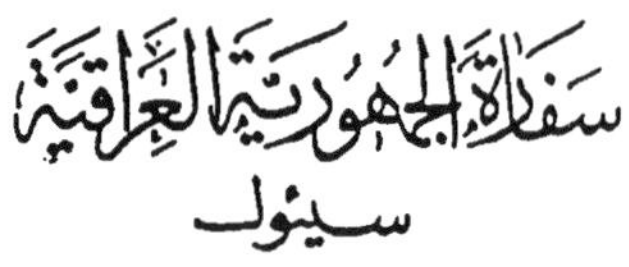

NO : 81

Press Release

Date : 14/2/1991

SUMMARY OF COMMUNIQUE NO. 46 OF THE ARMED FORCES GENERAL COMMAND ON FEBRUARY 13, 1991

In the Name of Allah, the Merciful, the Compassionate

While our great people continues showing its brave steadfastness, our valiant armed forces are fully prepared to crush any attempt by the barbaric aggressors to desecrate the pure land of Iraq.

Contrary to what the criminal American, British and French agressors claim, their combat planes continue to attack populated areas in Iraq with the clear intention of destroying our homeland and its civilisation.

The enemy carried out today and last night 86 air sorties against various residential areas in Iraq, targeting bridges, store and numerous civilian places which have nothing to do with the military. The criminal enemy also carried out 92 air sorties against military targets in the South. Our air defenses downed one enemy combat plane.

Let Bush, his unholy allies and the criminals of Al-Saud know that their crimes will not go unpunished and their atrcities will not affect the determination of the Iraqi people to destroy the enemies of Allah.

0093

بسم الله الرحمن الرحيم

Embassy of
The Republic of Iraq
Seoul

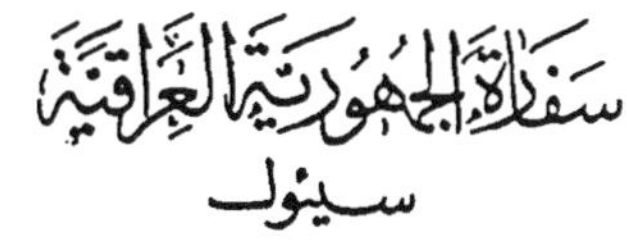

NO ; 82

Press Release

Date ; 14/2/1991

UNOFFICIAL TRANSLATION

LETTER OF THE DEPUTY PRIME MINISTER, FOREIGN MINISTER OF IRAQ ADDRESSED TO THE SECRETARY-GENERAL OF THE UNITED NATIONS

Excellency,

I have the honour to inform you and other members of the United Nations that the American-Atlantic-Zionist forces of aggression which have been waging a dirty war against Iraq for continuous four weeks, have, at dawn today, February 13, 1991, committed a heinous and dirty crime through deliberately targeting a civilian shelter in AL-Amiria district in Baghdad. In that shelter there were about 400 civilian citizens comprising mainly of women, children and elderly.

The International Networks and foreign correspondents in Baghdad have witnessed this crime. This heinous crime will be added to the criminal black record of the American-Atlantic-Zionist aggression against our steadfast and chivalrous people who are well known now to all fair and honest peoples of the world, inspite of all the hectic efforts, made by the governments of the states participating in the aggression, to veil the truth and allow lies and misleadings.

We demand that the United Nations and you personally condemn this heinous crime and endeavour to expose the facts of aggression which are waged by the traditional leaders of colonization and Imperialism against Iraq. To try to justify these crimes is a shame on the United Nations.

We hereby remind that the states which supported Security Council Resolution 678 bear especial legal, political and moral responsibilities for these crimes. For, by submission to the American will and supporting this evil resolution, these states have paved the way in front of the principal criminal, the United States, to commit these crimes. Those states will continue bearing these responsibilities unless they stand honourably and firmly for the purpose of stopping aggression and the crimes committed by the United States against humanity.

The Iraqi People hold all those participating in these crimes, whether in allowing the crimes or executing them, fully responsible in front of history and humanity.

Accept my highest consideration.

Tareq Aziz
Deputy Prime Minister,
Minister of Foreign Affairs
Baghdad, February 13, 1991

0094

Embassy of
The Republic of Iraq
Seoul

Press Release

NO: 83/91

DT: 15/2/1991

SUMMARY OF COMMUNIQUE NO. 47 OF THE ARMED FORCES GENERAL COMMAND ON FEBRUARY 14, 1991

In the Name of Allah, the Merciful, the Compassionate

Those who claim to be the defenders of civilization and civil rights; those who pretend to be the guardians of the free and democratic world; those who mustered their armies and armadas under the pretence of protecting Saudi Arabia and liberation, desecrating the sanctities of Islam and exercised corruption and moral degeneration in the land which houses the Holy House and the Grave of the Messenger of Allah.

They are now exposed as they really have been, as criminal and rogues, the enemies of liberity and democracy, the enemies of Man.

We hereby present a unique example unprecedented in the history of wars, or the history of crime.

Last night February 12/13, the cowardly air force of degenerate Bush carried out a raid against our beloved capital, Baghdad. They targeted with clear intention and premeditation, as their spokesman declared, a shelter in AL-Ameria district for the protection of civilians from air raids.

It is very well known, legally, morally, ethically and from humanitarian view point, that such places are not military targets. But those criminals committed their crimes in order to unveil their reality as the enemies of the valiant citizens of Iraq, including the elderly, women and children.

In the shelter, when it was targeted, there were hundreds of civilians mostly women and children. So far 64 martyrs were dug out mostly women and children, and a great number of wounded. Salvation is still going on and we will inform you with final results of the crime in a following statement.

We swear by the Almighty that the enemy will pay dearly for this crime.

0095

O' Our Great People,

O' Sons of Our Great Arab Nation,

O' Moslem Brethren,

O' Honourable Peoples of the World,

While this heinous crime were shocking the world, those criminals continue raiding the civilian populations in our homeland targeting with 29 air sorties the holy cities in Iraq, like Karbala and AL-Najaf, where the Graves of Imam Ali and Imam Hussain Allah Bestow His Satisfaction on Them. In Basra, they targeted the Mosque of Our Lord Othman Bin Affan (A.B.H.S.H.).

The vicious enemy's air sorties against populated areas in various parts of country totalled 135 sorties.

Our valiant air defenses downed one enemy combat plane.

Allah Bestow Mercy on the Souls of our Martyrs, and fast recovery for our Wounded.

0096

Embassy of
The Republic of Iraq
Seoul

سفارة الجمهورية العراقية
سيول

Press R~lease

NO: 84/91 15/2/1991

February . 1991

Secretary-General Javier Perez de Cuellar
The Secretariat
United Nations Plaza
New York, NY 10017

Dear Mr. Secretary General:

During the period February 2 to February 8, 1991 I traveled in Iraq to assess the damage to civilian life there resulting from the bombing [illegible] the embargo, including civilian deaths, injuries, illness [illegible]nd destruction and damage to civilian property. I was [illegible]ccompa[illegible]d by an experienced camera team that has filmed war and its destructive[illegible]ess in many countries including Afghanistan, Angola, Cambodia, El Salvador, Nicaragua, the Philippines and Vietnam. Their film documents most of the damage I mention in this letter and some I do not. In our party was an Iraqi-American guide and translator who has family in Baghdad and Basra and is personally familiar with those cities and many other areas of Iraq. He had last visited Baghdad, Basra and Kuwait City in December 1990.

We traveled over 2000 miles in seven days to view damage, learn of casualties, discuss the effects of the bombing with government officials, public health and safety agency staffs and private families and individuals. We had cooperation from the government of Iraq including Ministers, Governor[illegible], health and medical officials and civil defense personnel. The bombing in all parts of Iraq made travel difficult, requiring caution for bomb craters and damage to highways and roads and making night driving especially hazardous.

The damage to residential areas and civilian structures, facilities and utilities was extensive everywhere we went. Every city and town we visited or that was reported to us had no municipal water, electricity or telephone service. Parts of Baghdad had limited delivery of impure water for an hour a day.

The effect of damage to municipal water systems on health and safety is tremendous. The Minister of Health considered potable water for human consumpt[illegible] the single greatest health need in the country. Tens of thou[illegible]ands are known to suffer diarrhea and stomach disorders. There are believed to be hundreds of thousands of unreported cases Several thousands are believed to have died.

0097

Secretary-General de Cuellar   Feb. 12, 1991

He adds to the toll thousands of deaths from failure to obtain adequate supplies of infant formula and medicine, contaminated water and from increased death rates from stress, heart attacks and similar causes.

While I applaud your recent initiative in designating a U.N. mission to Baghdad to carry medical supplies and ascertain the health needs of the Iraqui people, I urge you to seek major funding now or release of Iraqui funds for supplying 2500 tons of infant and baby milk formula, greatly needed medicines and sanitation supplies, municipal water system restoration and water purification.

The bombing constitutes the most grievous violation of international law. It is intended to destroy the civilian life and economy of Iraq. It is not necessary, meaningful or permissible as a means of driving Iraq from Kuwait.

No UN resolution authorizes any military assault on Iraq, except as is necessary to drive Iraqi forces from Kuwait. The bombing that has occurred throughout Iraq is the clearest violation of international law and norms for armed conflict, including the Hague and Geneva Conventions and the Nuremberg Charter. It is uncivilized, brutal and racist by any moral standard. With few if any exceptions we witnessed, the destruction is not conceivably within the language or contemplation of Security Council Resolution 678/44.

I urge you to immediately notify the Member States of the General Assembly and the Security Council of the information herein provided. I urge you to ask for the creation of an investigative body to examine the effect of U.S. bombing of Iraq on the civilian life of the country. Most urgent, I ask you to do everything within your power to stop the bombing of cities, civilian population, public utilities, public highways, bridges and all other civilian areas and facilities in Iraq, and elsewhere. If there is no cease fire, bombing must be limited to military targets in Kuwait, concentrations of military forces in Iraq near the border of Kuwait, operational military air fields or identified Scud launching sites or mobile missile launchers in Iraq. If a cease fire is not achieved, the immediate cessation of this lawless bombing of civilian and non combatants is essential.

0098

The effect of the bombing, if continued, will be the destruction of much of the physical and economic basis for life in Iraq. The purpose of the bombing can only be explained rationally as the destruction of Iraq as a viable state for a generation or more. Will the United Nations be a party to this lawless violence?

I will briefly describe destruction to residential areas in some of the cities and towns we visited. In Basra Governor Abdullah Adjram described the bombing as of February 6 as worse than during the Iran-Iraq war. We carefully probed five residential areas that had been bombed.

1. A middle class residential area was heavily damaged at 9:30 p.m. on January 31. 28 persons were reported killed, 56 were injured, 20 homes and 6 shops were destroyed.

2. On January 22, an upper middle class residential neighborhood was shattered by three bombs destroying or extensively damaging more than 15 homes reportedly injuring 40 persons, but without any deaths.

3. On January 24, an upper middle class neighborhood was bombed, killing 8, injuring 26 and destroying 3 homes and damaging many others.

4. On February 4, described by officials as the heaviest bombing of Basra to February 6, at 2:35 a.m. 14 persons were killed, 46 injured and 128 apartments and homes destroyed or damaged together with an adjacent Pepsi Cola bottling plant and offices across a wide avenue. The area devastated was 3 blocks deep on both sides of streets. At least fifteen cars were visible, crushed in garages. Small anti personnel bombs were alleged to have fallen here and we saw what appeared to be one that did not explode imbedded in rubble. We were shown the shell of a "mother" bomb which carries the small fragmentation bombs.

5. On January 28, about eighteen units in a very large low cost public housing project were destroyed or severely damaged, killing 46 and injuring 70. The nearby high school was damaged by a direct hit on a corner. The elementary school across the street was damaged.

0099

On the evening of February 5 at 8:30 p.m. while our small group was dining alone by candlelight in the Sheraton Basrah, three large bomb blasts broke glass in the room. We went upstairs to the roof. From there I saw one bomb fall into the Shaat-Al-Arab beyond the Teaching Hospital to the South throwing a column of water high into the air; another bomb hit near the Shaat. As agreed upon earlier, civil defense officials came to take us to the blast sites. They were 1.2 km down the street near the Shatt Al Arab. I had walked by the area about 6:30 p.m.

We found two buildings destroyed. It is an apartment and residential home area. One was a family club, the other a night club. If either had been open scores of people would have been killed. Palm trees were sheared off and shrapnel, rocks, dirt and glass covered the street for several hundred feet. We were unable to enter the buildings that night.

We returned the next morning and were told both buildings were empty at the time by the owners who were looking at the damage. The teaching hospital, about 150 yards distant, which had been closed for a week following earlier bombing was without windows. It apparently received no new damage. As with all the other civilian damage we saw we could find no evidence of any military presence in the area. Here, there was no utility, or facility that are frequent, if illegal, targets either. There were only homes, apartments and a few shops, grocery stores and other businesses found in residential areas, plus too small bridges connecting the hospital to the mainland.

We were informed by a variety of sources including visual observation during extensive driving in Basra, that many other residential properties had been hit and that the five areas we filmed were a minor fraction of the civilian damage that had occurred.

At the central market where more than 1000 shops and vendors sell fruits, vegetables, fish, meat, foodstuffs and other items, a bomb leaving a huge crater, had demolished a building with a grocery store and other shops and damaged an entry area to the market at about 4:00 p.m. It reportedly killed 8 persons and injured 40.

We examined the rubble of a Sunni Moslem Mosque, Al Makal, where a family of 12 had taken sanctuary. The minaret remained standing. Ten bodies were found under the rubble and identified by a family member who had returned from his military post when informed of the tragedy. The dead included his wife and four young children.

0100

In Diwaniya, a smaller town, we examined the same types of civilian damage we witnessed elsewhere and that was reported everywhere. In the town center, apparently seeking to destroy the radio telephone relay equipment in the post office, bombing had damaged the tower and the office. We saw many similar, or identical relay towers in the region that had not been attacked. Adjacent to the Post Office on the central circle of the city, 3 small hotels of 30 to 50 rooms were destroyed together with a host of shops, cafes, and offices including those of doctors and lawyers. We were told 12 people were killed and 35 injured. More damage could be seen across the circle among business and apartment buildings from one or more bombs that fell there.

Near the outskirts of town 4 more or less, contiguous residential areas had been bombed. 23 persons were reported killed and 75 injured. Two schools were badly damaged. There was no water, electricity or telephone service. A water irrigation station was destroyed. Other damage was witnessed while driving around the town. On the outskirts an oil tank was on fire, one of more than a dozen we saw burning during our travels.

Baghdad has been more accessible to foreign observation than Basra and other places in Iraq. It will only be highlighted. We examined extensive damage on a main street in the blocks next to and across the street from the Ministry of Justice which had all its windows on one side blasted out. I know that area as a busy poor commercial residential area from walking through it on the way to the National Museum and visiting the Justice Ministry. A large supermarket, eight other stores and six or eight houses were destroyed or badly damaged. Across the street, one bomb hit on the sidewalk and another was a direct hit on housing behind the street front properties. Six shops, a restaurant and several other stores plus 9 or 10 homes were destroyed, or badly damaged. We could not get an agreed account of casualties from the forty or fifty people standing around the damage. Some said as many as thirty died and many more were injured.

We visited a residential area where several homes were destroyed on February 7th. Six persons in one family were killed in an expensive home and several [illegible] One 500 lb. bomb had failed to explode and the tail was seen above the thick concrete roof when a member of our team first drove by. When we returned, the bomb had been removed. Our camera team visited the hospital where the injured were taken later that afternoon. The critically injured father from the home where the bomb failed to explode was there. This was one of four hospitals treating persons injured in bombings that we visited.

0101

[illegible]

A bus station was hit by a bomb and the stained glass in a [illegible] we drove by on our arrival.

We saw five different damaged telephone exchanges while driving around Baghdad and many destroyed and damaged government and private buildings. Bridges in Baghdad were a frequent target though damage to them was minimal when we left. The bridges are not a legitimate military target. Even Defense Ministry buildings are occupied by non-combatants. The telephone exchanges run by civilians are overwhelmingly processing non military calls. The military has the most extensive independent communications capacity in the country. These are not legitimate targets and the effort to bomb them necessarily takes civilian lives.

Damage in Basra appeared to be considerably more extensive than in Baghdad and the actual bombing there was much more intensive than at any time we were in Baghdad. There were civilian deaths every night we were in Baghdad.

Visits to the towns of Hilla, Najaf and Nasseriya by press corps representatives and our crew found civilian casualties in residential areas of each, damages to a medical clinic, 12 deaths in one family, and 46 deaths in one night of bombing in one town. A small town was bombed a few minutes before we passed through on our drive back from Basra. We saw no military presence there. Smoke could be seen from three fires.

Over the 2000 miles of highways, roads and streets we traveled, we saw dozens, probably several hundred, destroyed vehicles. There were oil tank trucks, tractor trailers, lorries, pickup trucks, a public bus, a mini-bus, a taxicab and many private cars destroyed by aerial bombardment and strafing. Some were damaged when they ran into bomb craters in the highways, or road damage caused by bombs and strafing. We found no evidence of military equipment or supplies in the vehicles. Along the roads we saw several oil refinery fires and numerous gasoline stations destroyed. One road repair camp had been bombed on the road to Amman.

0102

Embassy of
The Republic of Iraq
Seoul

سفارة الجمهورية العراقية

Press Release

No. 93/91 18/2/1991

In the name of God, the Merciful, the Compassionate,

Declaration issued by the Revolution Command Council

O glorious Iraqi people,

Noble Arabs,

Muslims, true believers in Islam,

Free and noble people of the world,

Ever since the United States, the Zionists and America's Western colonialist allies have realized that a Power was coming into being in an Arab Muslim country, Iraq, a Power capable of counterbalancing the Zionist hegemony supported by imperialism in the region, a free and noble Power, determined with sincerity and self-denial to confront the aggression and the Zionist ambitions and to reject imperialist domination of the region, the United States, the Zionists and all the colonialist forces full of hatred for the Arabs and the Muslims have begun to take measures and decisions and to launch campaigns of intrigue and incitement against Iraq in order to prevent the formation and growth of this Power, to isolate, contain and punish Iraq because it had, with faith, determination and competence, overstepped the bounds drawn for it by the United States, the Zionists and the colonialist forces of the countries of the region.

In 1988 and 1989 there were constant attacks in the press and media, and on the part of officials in the United States and other colonialist countries, paving the way for the achievement of these wicked aims.

In 1990 these attacks escalated at a feverish and accelerating pace and on an ever-widening scale. The aim was patently obvious to us and to all conscious Arabs and true Muslims, to all free and noble people who believe in freedom and justice in the world. The aim was to prepare for the destruction of this rising Power and to restore predominance in the region to the United States, Zionists and the colonial Powers, this predominance which had for decades continued to prevent the Arabs from recovering their rights and their usurped and occupied territories in Palestine, the Golan and Lebanon, just as it had prevented the Arab nation from achieving its hopes of advancement, progress and justice in order that it might occupy the natural position it deserves in the world by reason of its glorious history and great contribution to human civilization.

During the first months of 1990 these attacks intensified and broadened and acquired a hysterical character. They began to urge daily that Iraq should be attacked and its leadership liquidated, and that it should be deprived of the means of advancement and progress. The United States, together with other colonialist countries, adopted a series of unfair decisions and measures prohibiting the export of everything which might contribute to the development of Iraq, and to its scientific and industrial advancement. These decisions comprised an effective economic boycott, one of the effects of which was the cancellation of foodstuff

0103

contracts in March 1990. It was also clear that the United States was making preparations, in coordination with the Zionist entity, to strike at scientific and industrial facilities and sites and to liquidate the faithful national leadership of Iraq. When the United States discovered that this scheme, which depended to a large extent on the Zionist military capability, was insufficient to achieve its evil objectives, it recruited to the conspiracy its agents and protégés among the corrupt and imperious rulers in the region, the enemies of God.

The role of the latter was to weaken and exhaust the economy of Iraq, and bring it to the brink of economic collapse. At the same time the United States began to reinforce the network of the colonialist alliance in order to set up an American-NATO political and military coalition with the aim of attacking Iraq and gaining control of the region, since it had been afforded the opportunity to do so following the withdrawal of the Soviet Union from world affairs in order to pursue internal matters.

Iraqis,

Arabs,

Muslims,

Free and noble people of the world,

The essence and purpose of the events of 2 August 1990 were not as portrayed by American and colonialist propaganda nor as recounted by the treacherous rulers and followers of America. They constituted a patriotic, national, Islamic uprising against the conspiracy and against the imperious, an uprising against oppression and decadence, against corruption and the imperialist, Zionist and colonialist hegemony over the region, against the imperious rulers, whose role had been revealed in the American Zionist conspiracy. This is why the imperialist Zionist NATO alliance revealed its true aims and intentions from the very first hours of those events. It massed its armies and forces and organized the most evil campaign of delusion, lying and deception the world has witnessed in recent times. This evil, tyrannical imperialist, Zionist, NATO alliance coerced the United Nations into issuing against Iraq, with unparalleled rapidity, a series of iniquitous and unprecedented resolutions. At the same time, this Organization has for decades been incapable of satisfying the simplest claims of the Arab nation and of preserving the simplest rights of the Arabs in Palestine, despite the clarity of the Arab right and the violence of the tragedy endured by the heroic people of Palestine and from which other Arabs suffer, including the oppressed people of Lebanon.

This iniquitous alliance imposed its will on the world, pursued methods of intimidation, blackmail and bribery and employed all the means of viciousness, falsehood and deception in the arsenal of the imperialists, Zionists and forces of colonialism in order to prepare the way for aggression against Iraq.

/...

0104

O glorious Iraqis,

O noble Arabs,

O believing Muslims,

O those in the world who are noble and honourable,

The aggression that has befallen the courageous, proud, combatant, believing and steadfast country of Iraq, has no counterpart in history. In the entire history of mankind, there is no record of the likes of such a coalition, in which there participated the United States, two major Powers and many other States, some 30 in number, against combatant, courageous, steadfast Iraq, whose population does not exceed 18 million. It is indeed an evil, iniquitous, malicious and disbelieving alliance against the stronghold of faith and principle, an alliance against the seat of freedom and the call for justice and fairness. For an entire month, the United States and its allies together with the Zionist entity, which has participated in the aggression from the outset, have been launching savage and devastating attacks against the people of Iraq, against its economic, scientific, cultural and services-related assets and its religious centres and against the country's sites of ancient civilization. History has not seen its like for intensity of fire nor means of slaughter and destruction, launched in the name of the United Nations, a fallacious international legitimacy and the new world order that they intend will be one of United States and NATO hegemony over the world.

The United States and the parties to the evil coalition have delivered, with aircraft that fire their missiles from afar and with long-range missiles, enormous quantities of bombs and explosives against women, children and elderly persons in all the towns and villages of Iraq and even the nomadic Bedouin of the desert. They have struck, in a premeditated manner, mosques, churches, schools, hospitals, civilian factories, bridges and major highways, telephone exchanges, electricity and water installations, irrigation dams, cultural centres and archaeological landmarks in the country. They have struck targets that have no connection of any kind whatever with the military effort or with the arena of the military clash of which they have spoken. The most recent such crime was that vile and heinous crime committed in the deliberate bombing of a civilian shelter, which killed and incinerated hundreds of women, children and elderly persons. The objective of this brutal act of aggression was abundantly clear, and it was to advance the process of destruction that was their intention, and to punish the proud, noble and combatant people of Iraq because it had chosen the way of freedom, independence and honour and rejected humiliation, degradation and subjection to the will of colonialism and zionism.

The United States and its allies have launched a vile and cowardly war against a courageous and believing people. The history and destiny of peoples and nations are not determined by the material possessions of States and ruling regimes. Throughout history, many a strong and wealthy empire has fallen because it adopted the way of shame, cowardice, oppression and dissoluteness. This is the destiny of iniquitous America and its vile regimes, and it is the destiny of zionism and all the forces of colonialism, God willing. Iraq has triumphed in this confrontation. It has triumphed because it has remained steadfast, courageous, believing, noble,

/.

0105

and strong-willed. It has triumphed because it has maintained principles and spiritual values derived from its true religion and its centuries-old heritage. Its losses in terms of material assets in this battle, despite their enormity, are of slight importance when set against its preservation of its resolute spirit, its faith deeply rooted in principle and its strong determination to pursue the road of resurgence and progress.

O noble Iraqis,

O honourable Arabs,

O Muslims ... who truly believe in Islam,

O those in the world who are noble and perceptive,

On the basis of this strongly entrenched feeling and of this assessment of the character of the conflict, in order to deprive the vicious United States, Zionist and NATO alliance of the opportunity to achieve its planned destructive goals, in appreciation of the initiative of the Soviet Union conveyed by the envoy of the Soviet leadership, and in keeping with the principles set forth in the initiative of President Saddam Hussein, announced on 12 August 1990, the Revolution Command Council has decided to announce the following:

I. Iraq's readiness to deal on the basis of Security Council resolution 660 (1990) with a view to reaching an honourable and acceptable political solution, including withdrawal. The first step that must be taken, as an undertaking on Iraq's part with regard to the matter of withdrawal, is linked with the following:

(a) A complete and comprehensive cease-fire on land, at sea and in the air;

(b) That the Security Council should, from the outset, decide to annul its resolutions 661, 662, 664, 665, 666, 667, 669, 670, 674, 677 and 678 and all the consequences to which they give rise. Similarly, the annulment of all decisions and measures of boycott and embargo and the other adverse decisions and measures adopted by certain States against Iraq, jointly and severally, prior to 2 August 1990, and which were the true cause of the Gulf crisis, so that matters may be restored to their normal status as if nothing had happened and without any adverse consequences for Iraq for any reason whatever;

(c) The United States, the other States participating in the aggression and all States that have dispatched forces to the region shall withdraw from the Middle East region and the Arabian Gulf region all the forces, armaments and matériel that they introduced before and after 2 August 1990, whether they are on land, at sea, in the oceans or in the gulfs, including the weapons and matériel provided by certain States to Israel on the pretext of the crisis in the Gulf, it being understood that the withdrawal of such forces, armaments and matériel shall take place within a period not to exceed one month from the date of the cease-fire;

(d) That Israel should withdraw from Palestine and from the Arab territories it is occupying in the Golan and in Lebanon, in implementation of the resolutions of the Security Council and the General Assembly of the United Nations. In the

/...

0106

event that it should refuse to do so, the Security Council shall apply against Israel the same resolutions that it adopted against Iraq;

(e) The guarantee of Iraq's full and undiminished historical rights on land and at sea in any political solution;

(f) The political arrangement to be agreed upon shall be based on the will of the people in accordance with genuine democratic practice and not on the acquired privileges of the House of Al Sabah. On this basis, national and Islamic forces must participate in a fundamental manner in the political arrangement to be agreed upon.

II. Those States that have participated in the aggression and in financing it shall undertake to rebuild that which the aggression has destroyed in Iraq, in accordance with the highest specifications for each of the activities, projects and installations targeted by the aggression, at their own expense and without Iraq's incurring any financial outlays.

III. Cancellation of all the debts incurred by Iraq, as well as by the States of the region damaged by the aggression which have not participated in it either directly or indirectly, to the Gulf States and those foreign States which participated in the aggression; the establishment of relations between the poor and wealthy States of the region and of the world based on justice and fairness so as to confront the wealthy countries with unequivocal obligations for the achievement of development in the poor countries and for the elimination of their economic sufferings, on the basis of the principle that the poor have a right to the resources of the wealthy; and a halt to the use of double standards in dealing with issues affecting peoples and nations, whether on the part of the Security Council or on the part of one State or another.

IV. To the States of the Gulf, including Iran, shall be left the freedom and the duty to establish security arrangements in the region and to organize relations among themselves without any external interference.

V. The declaration of the Arabian Gulf region as a zone free of foreign military bases and of any form of foreign military presence; and universal commitment to that effect. This is our case, and we have announced it to the world. We have set it forth clearly and plainly to the treacherous and perfidious and their imperialist masters. Our fundamental assurance, having placed our trust in the One and Only God, is in our mighty Iraqi people, in its combatant and valiant armed forces, and in those who have believed in the road that we are taking in resisting oppression and the oppressors. In the coming days, victory over the oppressors shall be assured, just as it was assured in former days. God is most great. May the infamous be driven out.

Revolution Command Council

29 Rajab A.H. 1411
15 February 1991

0107

Embassy of
The Republic of Iraq
Seoul

سفارة الجمهورية العراقية
سيئول

No. 94/91

Press Release

18/2/1991

TRANSCRIPT OF MEETING HELD ON SUNDAY EVENING, 13 JANUARY 1991,BETWEEN H.E. PRESIDENT SADDAM HUSSEIN AND H.E. PEREZ DE CUELLAR, SECRETARY GENERAL OF THE UNITED NATIONS.

After an exchange of courtesies, Mr. de Cuellar said: I am happy to see you again. I have seen H.E. President Saddam Hussein three times, all of them in difficult circumstances. One day I shall come to Iraq to enjoy your hospitality in a different way, as a tourist, and to acquaint myself with the cultural heritage of your country.

H.E. the President-Leader said: There were circumstances in which there were no problems, but you didn't come.

The Secretary-General: It is my hope to come as a tourist, and I shall avail myself of my friendship with Mr. Tariq Aziz to see all the important archaeological sites in this country. All civilized peoples acknowledge that this country is the cradle of civilization.

The President-Leader: Except Bush.

The Secretary-General: In any case, Mr. President, I should like to say that I have come to Iraq without being charged with any mandate; I am entrusted with no specific task either by the Security Council or the United Nations. I have, however, been encouraged to make this trip not only by heads of States and governments, but also by the Pope and by humble citizens who have asked me to take advantage of our position, particularly its moral aspect, to work for the establishment of peace in this region. It may surprise you, Mr. President, that among those who have wished success for my mission is the President of the United States with whom I have met and talked four times since last Saturday. But I wish to assure you that I do not carry any message and I am no one's messenger. I represent only myself. I have had the honour to meet with you twice, and I think President Saddam Hussein will remember the neutral, impartial way we tried to use in mediating between you and

0108

Iran. Today, I meet with Your Excellency in the same spirit. I should like you to know that I wish to leave tonight, since I must be in Europe tomorrow: Although I am charged with no mandate by the Security Council, my duty requires that I should be there. Your Excellency, as a military man, will know what it means to abide by one's duty.

The President-Leader: For the information of the Secretary-General, I haven't had even a single day of military studies. I am a lawyer, in terms of the conventional accounting of specializations.

The Secretary-General: We are colleagues. I, too, have studied law. You, however, are the Commander-in-Chief of the Armed Forces, and so we say you are a military man. It is my duty to submit a report to the Security Council on the discussions I am to have with Your Excellency today. Since Your Excellency is a lawyer, there is competition with my friend, Mr. Tariq Aziz.

The President-Leader: You would cooperate.

The Secretary- General: Your Excellency will be aware that you are a Member of the United Nations, and this Organization acts by resolutions. Now resolutions adopted by the General Assembly are recommendations, but those adopted by the Security Council are mandatory on Member States.

Unfortunately, the history of the United Nations makes it clear that some resolutions of the Security Council have not been implemented. I am fully aware of your feelings on the matter; however, as a friend of your country, I should like to say that bad examples should not be followed.

It is not within my duty to reiterate or read out all the resolutions which the Security Council has adopted, for I know that you are a very well-informed statesman. The only matter on which I should like to offer assistance is how to avoid any confrontation or war as a result of this crisis.

I know that there have been many visits by important prominent personalities who might have reflected their own concerns or the concerns of their countries and peoples. I have, however, grown old as a Secretary General: in a few days I shall be 71 years old; and I should like to make use of the independence I enjoy for peace.

My colleague Tariq Aziz has given me a clear explanation of the position of your government. I respect that, and I agree with him in many areas. I believe

I am not going to enter into arguments with Your Excellency, but I should like to know in what reasonable way can one achieve peace.

Before coming to Iraq, I had met a week ago with President Bush and informed him of my decision to meet with you ... I wanted, before doing so, to listen to him and to ascertain his wish with regard to finding a peaceful solution to the crisis.

I cannot guarantee intentions, but all he said to me, knowing I was going to meet with you, was that he wanted a peaceful solution to the crisis, desperately. That was before the Geneva meeting between your Minister of Foreign Affairs and Mr. Baker. After the Geneva meeting, President Bush contacted me through the private telephone link between us to say that he had approved of all that was positive between the two Ministers. Later on, and after my discussions with him, that is to say, on the day I left for Baghdad, I had a discussion with him by telephone, and I said to him: "I am going to meet President Saddam Hussein, so can I say that you want a peaceful solution?" He said, in spite of the impression given by the information media in considering me responsible for finding a peaceful international solution: "I prefer the peaceful solution of the crisis".

While it is not part of my task to convey this message, I consider it a necessary background. There are some ideas which can be used to find a peaceful solution to this crisis.

I know that you are a lawyer and that you respect legality. I can say that in this world of ours we need not only peace but peace and justice, since peace is not enough to realize the aspirations of our peoples.

Of course there are many resolutions which have been adopted by the Security Council. And you know that I am not responsible for these resolutions. I am only a witness, since I do not vote on them. But I am convinced that it is possible to read the Security Council resolutions in a positive manner.

You have taken certain initiatives, an important and constructive one of which was your decision to release the foreigners, by which you removed an obstacle in the way of the relaxation of tension in the area.

The 12 August initiative has not been well understood, but it figures in one form or another in the first of the Security Council resolutions, which specifically referred to the Arab League and its participation in any solution. I believe that to be a positive thing. On that basis something can be done.

And you have done something, as I have told your Minister of Foreign Affairs I consider that you have done a great deal for the question of Palestine: you have put the fate of the Palestinian people on the agenda. Being of Spanish descent, I feel close to the Arab world and the Palestinian people. Afterwards, I did not hesitate to call the attention of the United Nations to the Palestinian problem, working for convening an international conference in keeping with six or seven resolutions of the General Assembly of the United Nations. Only yesterday, I announced that I was going to appoint a Special Representative to be responsible for this question and to deal with it in accordance with resolution 242. I am happy that my friend Yassir Arafat has found that to be a positive decision, considering it to give a new push to the solution of the problem.

Your Excellency, before coming here I had a meeting with the twelve Ministers of Foreign Affairs of the European Community. What gave me great satisfaction was that all the Ministers, although in varying degrees, were inclined to have this problem settled. Even your colleague Mr. Bush, when I saw him on Saturday, acknowledged the pressing need to settle the Palestine crisis. He said he hadn't forgotten the statement he made before the General Assembly on the first of October in which he said there might be an opportunity for all States to find a solution to the problem which had divided the Arabs and Israelis. I don't want to argue, Mr. President, but you deserve all the credit for this achievement for the question of Palestine.

Now, Mr. President, I am eager to build on what has been achieved so far, modest though it might be. What is important is not to lose the opportunity of helping our Palestinian brothers. I said to your Minister of Foreign Affairs yesterday that the fate of the question of Palestine depended on peace in the region. Apart from that, on 20 December a statement by the President of the Security Council was finalized and approved by the United States, the only country besides Israel which has a problem with holding an international conference. That statement says an international conference on peace will be arranged at an appropriate time and should facilitate the efforts aiming at achieving a peaceful settlement and a comprehensive and lasting solution in the area of the Arab-Israeli conflict

Again, this was brought about as a result of efforts made by you, and it is only natural, to achieve such a result, that we should have your help in finding a solution to the problem.

I know your courage and your generosity, and you know how I have followed up the Iraqi-Iranian war and the unilateral initiatives you offered to put an end to that war. I hope that you will, in the same spirit, offer something to put an end to this conflict.

Of course, in order to do so, we must see our way through to compliance with the United Nations resolutions, especially resolutions 660 and 678. At the same time, there should be an indication as to how the future role of the United Nations is to be perceived with regard to what will happen after this crisis in the area of security in the region and security for your country. This was emphasized by

President Bush. They realize that you want guarantees and that your country needs such guarantees not only from the Permanent Members of the Security Council but also from others. This matter can be discussed.

Should it be your wish, I can develop some ideas relating to the post-crisis period. I have in this paper certain ideas which I would sum up as follows:

You will remember what was said by President Mitterand of France ... he said: "If we are able to implement the Security Council resolutions, everything will be possible".

The important matter or the important concern is that if a decision is taken to that effect then it is the duty of the United Nations to ensure that there will be no threat to your country. There is something else said by Mr. Bush which I put down on a small piece of paper. It is this: "The United States will not attack Iraq or its armed forces if withdrawal from Kuwait has been achieved and the situation has returned to what it was prior to 2 August. The United States does not want to keep ground forces in the region; it will support negotiations between the parties concerned, and I shall accept any decision taken by those parties".

[The same passage re-translated:]

"The United States will not attack Iraq or its armed forces if withdrawal from Kuwait has taken place and the situation has been restored to what it was prior to 2 August. The United States has no intention to keep its ground forces in the region; it will support negotiations between Iraq and the parties concerned, and will work for the relaxation of the sanctions imposed on Iraq if it complies with the Security Council resolutions".

This was what was said to me by President Bush before I left for Baghdad. I am in a position to urge [the adoption of measures ensuring] that there will be no threat to the security of your country, such as the creation of United Nations forces which will be recruited from acceptable countries and will come to the region to help in restoring the situation existing before 2 August and to ensure the safety of Iraq's boundaries. I can also work for further guarantees to be offered by the Security Council.

We believe that the important thing is to work for setting up special arrangements for the region with a view to consolidating regional security and cooperation. Your Excellency will recall that resolution 598 which you were kind enough to accept referred in its paragraphs 7 and 8, currently under implementation, to the need for ensuring security and stability in the region.

The President-Leader: And we got nothing from it.

The Secretary-General: We shall work for its implementation, while the possibilities of action available to the United Natioins have expanded agreat deal. Also, by profiting from Your Excellency's initiative, we should work for the elimination of all weapons of mass destruction in the region. Finally, as I have said, we should work for] setting up such arrangements between the countries of the region as are necessary for promoting their development and improving the general atmosphere and conditions there. In referring to that, I am referring to the elimination of weapons of mass destruction in Israel.

Mr. President, these are our modest aspirations by which we hope to contribute to finding a solution to the crisis. Now I am not so naive as to imagine that we shall resolve this problem tonight. But I wish to be in a position to go back with something we can build up on to reduce tension and deprive the warmongers of their opportunity. These are the ideas which I wish to share with you. Thank you very much.

[Here, H.E. the President-Leader asked Mr. de Cuellar: "Do you take unsweetened coffee? This kind of coffee doesn't help you sleep through the night." Mr. de Cuellar answered: "I travel a great deal, and I am used to what is called jet lag. I am old, but I am quite strong for my age. The head is in control of everything." The President-Leader said: "The head is the organizer".

The President-Leader (continuing): I wouldn't conceal from you, I wanted you to come and not to come to Baghdad. You are the Secretary-General of the United Nations. We are all one family in the United Nations. We are part of this world family, and it is only natural that we should be concerned that the United Nations should assume its role in the life of States.

Now I wanted you to come because you know us. You have dealt with us in the past, and would remember our characteristic ways of thinking. On the other hand, I was apprehensive about your coming because you would be coming in the circumstances of a situation in which recourse to arms at the earliest possible moment is being advocated by the powerful who, when you are unable to offer them what they want, may thus find in your visit an excuse for reinforcing the argument for going to war. In listening to you, however, I found many positive elements in your discourse. I agree with you that with regard to such a complex issue, it s not to be expected to find solutions in a single meeting, but it is necessary to discuss matters in depth and comprehensively.

I should like to say that we are not about to give up our membership in this international family of the United Nations, by which I mean our responsible role in it. Such a statement could be made by President Bush or the Soviet Union or France just as it was made by me; but a statement has as much merit as its corroborating evidence. When we state that we want to be a part of the family of the United Nations, and to be a responsible part in circumstances such as these, we must provide evidence that this is the case, and here is the evidence:

You have followed up the war between Iran and Iraq at a certain stage. We met you twice. Then the Minister of Foreign Affairs conducted talks with you, and not with Iran, on the agreement of 8 August 1988. Later, there came our letter to the Iranians in April 1990, in which we invited them to a dialogue at the Summit level and assured them of our desire for peace. You will remember the military state of Iran in 1988 and you know our military state then and now in 1990. Why so?

It is that we always take peace initiatives with regard to Iran because we want peace, and because we know that we can build our country in the right way only under the banner of peace. All this building activity which you see around you, including the thriving city of Baghdad, is the product of our own and no one else's efforts; and he who knows how to build and has a passion for building does not want war. But when our security, the opportunities for building and the free choice of our beliefs were threatened by Iran, we fought. When the Iranians were threatening Basrah, when all countries thought that they were on the verge of occupying Basrah in 1987 (they had already occupied Fao), and we were presented with a draft sponsored by the French or the Soviets for a ceasefire, they were told by the Minister of Foreign Affairs: "We do not want a ceasefire". They said to him: "But Basrah will fall". He said: "No, it will not fall; and even if it should fall, we shall fight on. What we want is comprehensive peace, not a ceasefire". Thus we fought in East Basrah to repel some of the most ferocious attacks that have ever been known, but we never asked for a ceasefire.

When, on 8 August 1988, the opportunity arose for a ceasefire as a gateway to a comprehensive peace, you and the Minister of Foreign Affairs reached agreement thereon by telephone ... and that agreement, as I think, has thus been the most easily arranged agreement to have ever been concluded in connection with a case like this within the framework of the United Nations. Why did that agreement take place? the answer is because Iraq wanted it and because Iraq cooperated with you. This, then, is evidence from recent history that we are a constructive not a destructive or troublesome member of the United Nations family.

Can any other, particularly the United States, offer similar evidence taken from the history of their relations with the United Nations? So, the latest evidence in the United Nations shows that it is the Iraqis who have pioneered the way in a major issue involving eight years of hostilities. We are proud and pleased that this has been the case.

As to the issue of Kuwait: it would have been possible to live with the situation existing prior to 2 August as we had always done before. We did not just all of a sudden remember that Kuwait had been part of Iraq severed by Britain to be made a protectorate, then to be converted into a state in 1961. We know this, and we also know that none of the Kings or Presidents who have ruled the Iraqi State since 1921 has ever said that Kuwait is not part of Iraq. You, Secretary-General, will know that, up to 2 August 1990, you have no document signed by the two parties that designates boundaries between Iraq and Kuwait.

What has brought matters to the point reached after 2 August? It is the threat we feel as a result of the fact that Kuwait has been converted into an American base for hatching plots against us. It is only natural in such circumstances that we should call to mind the historical background with all its underlying premises. Even so, we continued to proceed with caution in deference to the legal aspects of the matter. Kuwait was not immediately annexed to or unified with Iraq although, as you know its former rulers fled and control over it was achieved on the very first day, and a government was formed by a number of Kuwaiti army officers of whom the most senior had the rank of major. We sought thereby to defer to to the legal aspects in consideration of the fact that we are members of the United Nations family. We agreed to a summit conference to be held in Saudi Arabia by five countries, namely, Iraq, Yemen, Jordan, Saudi Arabia and Egypt, out of a wish to have all the complexities discussed and resolved within the Arab environment.

Then what happened? The five-State conference was not held; instead, it was cancelled by Saudi Arabia and Egypt, and it was agreed with the United Sates to have its forces land in Saudi Arabia. The opportunity for finding an Arab solution was thus lost. The Americans so acted without a resolution by the Security Council. When the Americans came to Saudi Arabia they did so on the basis of an American decision. The forces then began to increase.

It was unreasonable to expect lower-ranking army officers with little experience to be able to administer Kuwait and confront the American forces in order to defend Kuwait. The unification measures were therefore accelerated and did not take the due form that would satisfy the legal concerns of the West. Although the decision to rush the American forces to Saudi Arabia had already been announced, we dealt positively with Security Council resolution 660. While it is true that we did not recognize that resolution, we did deal with its contents. We clearly announced that . would withdraw our forces on 4 August; and we did not stop at a mere announcement but actually withdrew some of our forces: I think we withdrew a whole brigade although our force at the time was not as big as it is today.

But when the American escalation continued and the strength of the arriving American forces kept increasing, we stopped the withdrawal. As I have previously stated, we then announced the unificationto to say to the Iraqis and to the Iraqi Army: "Kuwait is now part of your country. Fight to the death to defend it." Iraqis would not fight to defend Kuwait with a provisional government at its head as hard as they would when they are told that Kuwait is now part of their country. Had there been no such development in the actions taken by the United States, the unification would perhaps have taken a longer time, thus allowing all to acquaint themselves with the legal steps involved in the unification process.

Who is responsible for all this? It is the United States, which has introduced many complexities into the matter: of course when Kuwait has been unified with Iraq, we have had to discuss all the background as to how Kuwait was part of Iraq; how it was separated; how King Ghazi was killed , and all the other matters which the Minister of Foreign Affairs must have talked with you about.

Meanwhile, more and more forces were arriving to the Moslem's sacred lands, and, as they arrived, there was more and more provocation to the sensibilities of Moslem Arabs. Along with this, the Security Council was passing resolutions at an increasingly quicker pace, to the point that no one in the region had an opportunity to give thought to resolving the impasse into which matters have been allowed to fall. This is unprecedented in the history of the Security Council, as you are well aware as a veteran diplomat.

We find nothing unusual when we are disagreed with on legal aspects relating to the subject of Kuwait's unification with Iraq or on the use of the army in Kuwait. But we want to be heard by all so that they may acquaint themselves with the background of these developments and ask us for the documentation in support of every word we say to be able to ascertain our position. We know that we will not receive the applause of the international community for the disappearance of a Member State of the United Nations, but that community ought to acquaint itself with the facts.

Let us go back to the matter of law. How can a Member of this family be converted into an accused party without it being given a chance to be heard in self-defence? You are the Secretary-General of the United Nations, yet you have not been able to ensure the arrival of the plane carrying the Iraqi Minister of Foreign Affairs to arrive at the United States for him to be able to attend and defend the point of view of Iraq.

<u>The Secretary-General</u>: I tried; I said tht was not in keeping with the Headquarters Agreement with the United States.

The President-Leader: Yes, I know that; but the Americans did not listen to the voice reminding them of legality in a most elementary matter, namely, the Minister's attendance to exercise his right to defence. You know there is no case in the whole world said to have been conducted in accordance with the law in which the accused has not been granted the right to self-defence. In cases involving accusations the whole membership of a court would visit the scene of the alleged offence to have the help of eyesight as well as sound reasoning to reach a fair decision! How could one then prevent an accused who himself would want to attend to defend himself from doing so? We have ample evidence indicating that international law has become American law rather than the law of the United Nations or that America has taken to putting the law to in the service of political aims rather than to exercise it objectively which is the most important condition for its impartial application.

We respect peace with justice and not peace without justice, because this is to our interest both as Iraq and as an Arab nation which has been wronged under international law. Palestine is occupied. Al-Jawlan is occupied. Both Al-Quds [Jerusalem] and Al-Jawlan have been annexed to Israel by an official decision of the Israeli government, but no armies have been marshalled against Israel, nor has it been placed under an economic embargo or boycott.

It may be said that all this belongs to the past. Very well. Let us cite other evidence that this conduct continues and is not part of the past. The idea of protecting the Palestinians from suppression by the occupiers has recently been put forward. You are aware that it took 84 days for this idea to become a resolution, and you know how that idea was squeezed and squeezed until it lost all its flavour and all strength. Who has done this? It is the United States. What has it had to say on the subject? It declared openly that it "opposes the idea of holding an international conference to prevent Saddam Hussein from scoring a political victory". The United States, then has made justice contingent upon political tactics, and it does not seek peace with justice; otherwise, and had it had any respect for justice with peace, it would have seen to it that the Palestinian people are granted its rights regardless of the Gulf crisis or the the way the crisis develops.

What are they saying now? -- Let Iraq withdraw from Kuwait, then we shall convene an international conference to discuss the issues involved. This is not a categorical promise; it is only a possibility.

We want peace with justice, but not all Members of the United Nations want peace with justice. On 12 August, we offered an initiative. We did not imagine that it would be accepted in its entirety; but we did not imagine, either, that it would be left without being examined. The President of the United States rejected that initiative while aboard his plane only two hours after it was announced and before learning anything about its contents. Is this right? As to the Soviet Union, after issuing comments to the effect that the initiative contained positive elements, backed out from any further involvement in the matter when faced with the strong reaction on the part of the United States.

We then submitted the initiative of 16 August, based on the initiative of 12 August. We stated, in terms of the new initiative, that if the international community was unprepared to deal with the subject as whole, then it should leave the Arabs to solve their own problems and provide the proper environment for that. This initiative was also rejected.

The meaning of all this is that there is an insistence on a particular course through which it is intended to achieve certain political and military goals. Accordingly, there is no point in discussing or thinking of initiatives. We know that the United Nations cannot, prima facie, approve anything illegal. The United Nations, however, is a political Organization and not the International Court of Justice in the sense that the United Nations takes for a basis for its actions to achieve security with justice. Should it find that this objective can be achieved by this means rather than by that it should change its means and ways. Even law gives the judge ample latitude to adapt his decisions in the light of the circumstances of the accused and the implications of the law. The United Nations has always dealt with complex issues on the basis of this ABC of politics and international law. While its resolutions might provide for withdrawal, this principle would always be set within a framework of negotiations and dialogue, rather than of pre-conditions, to facilitate cooperation among the parties to an issue.

We have stated and continue to emphasize that we desire peace and are prepared to bear our responsibility as a part of the international family of the United Nations. But are the others equally prepared to bear their responsibility on the same basis? Are they prepared to apply interntional legality and international law to the issues of the Middle East and with regard to each and every issue, taking into account the background of these issues and the questions of justice and equity they involve.

Just look at the American President: see how he talks about matters of form and fails to touch on substantive issues of concern to us as a wronged nation; how he talks about the possible withdrawal of land forces and fails to mention a thing about the withdrawal of the air and naval forces; and how he talks about the possible relaxation of some economic measures and fails to talk with any sincere conviction about cumulative measures.

The Secretary-General: These are not my resolutions but the Security Council's resolutions.

The President-Leader: These are American resolutions. This is an American era. What America wants today goes, not what the Security Council wants.

0118

The Secretary-General: I am on your side, as far as I am concerned.

The President-Leader: Let us see now. You, Secretary-General, have no aircraft and no tanks. You act in accordance with the requirements of law and morality and the responsibility devolving on the Secretary-General in relation to the international community. We want a true United Nations. We want to have international law and international legality truly applied.

The Secretary-General: Allow me, Mr. President. There is an International Court of Justice. Perhaps it can work for a settlement of such a problem.

The President-Leader: In any case, let us give dialogue its due; let us give it all the room needed to identify all the complexities involved in the various issues so as not to say that the human mind is incapable of finding solution to these and other issues. The important thing is willingness. All that we have been told so far is implement this and that and that. This is not the same as talks or dialogue: this is an imposition of will.

What was there in Bush's letter to Saddam Hussein? We are being surprised daily that the Americans do not know us. How could have Bush imagined that there is a possibility of even one percent that Saddam Hussein fears threats? Was he tempted by the notion that his capture of the President of Panama to put him on trial in the United States would make all Heads of State fear his threats?

Such tactics on his part do not have the effect of making us willing to enter into dialogue with him, because our Iraqi people will not allow us to stay in

0119

power one more day if they should discover that we fear threats. It is the human duty of our people to know that those in charge of administering their affairs are acting responsibly in their behalf with regard to international law and peace and security in the world. Our people know their legal responsibilities: they are inculcated in them by their history upon reading the laws of Hammurabi which, enacted over four thousand years ago, represent the first code to prescribe human rights and duties.

I am glad you have come to Baghdad because of what I have heard about you. If the others have opened opprtunities for you to assume your role in this issue, you know we are the kind of people who would facilitate your task. You have had your experience with us. You made peace by telephone, a matter which has never happened in the world before.

In the present instance, matters are not in our hands. In August 1988, we used to tell you "yes, we agree with Iran", and that "yes" meant we agreed on peace, not on war. Now look at the latest resolution which Bush insisted on forcing out of the Senate and the House of Representatives. He had tried similar pressures to force out resolution 678: we know that he had told a number of Security Council Members that what was intended by that resolution was to put pressure on Iraq, not to have it used. He has now played the same game with the American Senate and House of Representatives, and has got his resolution by hinting that the resolution is not necessarily for use but to face the Iraqis with a threat which will make them withdraw.

The Iraqis, however, will never withdraw in the face of threats. Bush will therfore be pushed day by day into a corner, and he will be obliged to resort to arms because he who is busy preparing the requirements for the use of arms could not occupy his mind fully with thinking about how to find alternatives to avoid the use of arms.

We are not responsible for this. America has brought matters to this level. Had American leaders been patient, had they sought other means than those into which they have pushed matters, the state of affairs would not have come to such a point either before or after 2 August 1990.

At present, we have good relations with Iran, and we praise God for this. It is our hope, and our determination, to improve these relations in all fields. All our people know that we have given half of Shatt-al-Arab to Iran and have released all prisoners of war without waiting for the release of ours. When Iraqis asked me: "Why all this?", I answered: "For the sake of peace. Now that Kuwait is part of Iraq, you have all that long cost of your own, and there is no longer a need for us to shove one another for Shatt-al-Arab". Then we withdrew our army from this front to Kuwait.

Do you see these complexities created by the United States? It has entangled one thing with another. Even those who call for the withdrawal of Iraq do not explain where to, leaving aside Iraq's views on the subject.

[At this point, the President-Leader turns to explaining on a map certain matters relating to the absence of boundaries between Kuwait and Iraq, and how has Kuwait expanded at the expense of Iraq.

[Pointing to the map, he says: here were Kuwait's lines when it was a protectorate. It then expanded to this point, then to this point, where the lines were at a place called Al-Mitlaa (which I suggest you take down). This was the state of affairs until 1963. Mr. Yassir Arafat's passport is stamped at Al-Mitlaa. For our part, we have corroborating documents and thousands of passports.

[In the years 1963 - 1968, Iraq was ruled by two weak brothers during whose rule the Shaikhs of Kuwait marched again in the land from Al-Mitlaa to this point. During the period of the war with Iran they further advanced in the land to exploit oil fields known from the beginning to be within pre- 2 August 1990 Iraq.

[When Kuwait city was within the wall here (pointing at the map), a British subject was killed within the wall, and the British government asked the Shaikh of Kuwait to investigate the incident. The shaikhs of Kuwait had the victim's corpse thrown outside the wall, and the Shaikh of Kuwait wrote to the British government that since the offence had taken place outside the wall, it fell within the responsibility of the government of Baghdad, and the Baghdad government did actually undertake an investigation.

[Furthermore, the Mab'outhan (the Ottoman Turkish Parliament) approved the status of Kuwait as a protectorate only within the wall. The relevan documents are all there.]

In the light of this complexity, when it is suggested that Iraq should withdraw, where is it supposed to withdraw to?

The Secretary-General: If you have such a good case, you may have recourse to the International Court of Justice.

The President-Leader: I wanted to explain these matters to help you. I am sure that had the Americans heard from us after resolution 660, they wouldn't have hurried to have all that heap of resolutions which have placed them in an impasse. The British know all these facts which they have in their files. Mr. Heath knows them, too.

The Secretary-General: My colleague here confirms what you have said. (Mr. de Cuellar is referring to a side exchange he had with one of his aides during the President's latter discourse). You stated at the outset that you had doubts about my visit ...

The President-Leader: They weren't doubts.

The Secretary-General: This mission may have a character which runs counter to the course of peace. As you have stated, those who want war and not peace will take advantage of the fact that I shall return with nothing. What I am asking for is not in the name of the United Nations but in the name of the international community which wants you to give me something which could relax tensions and be a way out not only for the region but also for the world.

The President-Leader: every point we have discussed involves giving you something.

The Secretary-General: I shall give thought to all that you have discussed, in all sincerity, and shall include it in my report. I am afraid, however, that what I shall take with me will not be considered concrete enough to relax the threat dangling, like a sword, not over my head but over the "head of the world", so to speak.

You will be aware of the many expectations and hopes attached on my visit. You have been visited by a large and significant number of personalities, but none of them had the global mission I have. I remember at the press conference he held following the Geneva meeting, Mr. Tariq Aziz was asked: Is this the last chance for peace? So I should like to ask if this is the last chance for peace. I should also like to say I am afraid if I should return with nothing along with the important matters you stated, that would not be enough to stop the slide towards confrontation not only in the region but in the world atlarge. This is my fate; wherever I go they think I carry the solution.

The President-Leader: You said you came without being charged with a mandate by anyone. You came having nothing in your hands except a wish to have peace prevail and the spectre of war banished. This is the first meeting we have with you after the events and the first time you yourself hear from us. Consequently, you ought to discuss the publicly stated point to the effect that Iraq announce withdrawl after which "everything will be possible", to quote Mitterand and not Bush who has come to make war. It is obvious that even this cruel matter involves no guarantee, whether from Bush, Mitterand, or the United Nations, that would have for its basis some part of the Arab of Iraqi issues.

I should like to say something of vital importance to Mr. de Cuellar. Iraqis know Kuwait to be the the nineteenth province. If you ask anyone in the street from elementary schoolchildren to university professors, they will all say to you that they want peace and a dialogue leading to a just peace; that they are willing to assume their responsibilities with regard to peace and to offer their share of sacrifices for peace if the others are willing to do the same, but that they are at the same time willing to fight if attacked, confidently relying on the depth of a fighting experience extending over a period of 8 years. They also know that if matters were to the point of the breakout of hostilities, they will suffer huge losses not because the opponent has more courage or has a just and legitimate but because he has more sophisticated weapons than ours. They are, however, as sure as though they have the outcome in the grip of their hands that, in the end, the aggressor will be defeated.

Hence, even if we were to be granted all the priveleges, any priveleges, in the world, I should say when the two armies, the Iraqi and the American (the likelihood of war is now a matter of hours), no one will ever utter the word withdrawal, because to utter the word withdrawal when war is likely is to prepare the psychological ground for the victory of the enemy. Now isn't this what the Americans want? They know what it means; but this will never happen, never.

What will happen is to be the outcome of our willingness to discuss a whole package. You are aware of our insistence on the principle of the whole package in the Iraqi-Iranian war, and you know that this insistence led in the end to the achievement of peace. Since we want peace and not partial or provisional solutions, we insist on the principle of the whole package in which no one can deceive anyone and all know their duties as well as their rights and know what sacrifices and gains they are making. The fragmented treatment of issues without comprehensive linkage between them will in the end have for an outcome deceivers and deceived and winners and losers. We do not believe this will serve peace.

The Secretary General: If I understood you well, your position on Kuwait is irreversible, in which case the principle of the package cannot be applied.

The President-Leader: I didn't say this, you said it. If you find the Americans in a position wherein they are looking for a way out of their impasse without losing or necessarily realizing all that they have in mind, it is possible to set down certain principles then charge the Arabs to look for a solution in keeping with those principles. Or you as a capable, experienced diplomat might sound other parties for their points of view.

The Secretary-General: You are a party, too.

The President-Leader: Then you might submit proposals which you will discuss with the principal parties, including us. in the hope of reaching an agreed solution.

The Secretary-General: Do you authorize me to tell the Security Council that you want continuous discussions to be conducted through the Secretary-General?

The President-Leader: I regard this as given on the basis of your offer. That is why I have said there is a positive aspect to all the points you discussed. there may emerge a package as result of continuity.

The Secretary-General: Thank you for the trust you have given me as a Secretary-General. I must reflect on the points and include them in my report to the Security Council. I shall try to do that in the best possible way. I shall maintain contact with the Iraqi Minister of Foreign Affairs and keep him informed of the reactions to what you have offered. I shall communicate that to all those concerned in this crisis, especially in view of the fact that yours is a defensive and not an offensive position.

The President-Leader: Peace can be achieved only when both parties want it.

The Secretary-General: Thank you for your hospitality and for the time you have allocated for me. I also thank you for your attitude of undertanding concerning my coming here on an independent visit in order to achieve peace together.

The President-Leader: I wish you success.

The Secretary-General: We must think of our Palestinian brothers.

The President-Leader They are slaughtering the children and women of Palstien every day.

The Secretary-General: I know that very well.

The President-Leader: 't is necessary that you should discharge your responsibility with regard to food and medicine for Iraq.

The Secretary-General: I told your Minister oif Foreign Affairs that the World Health Organization intdnds to come here to evaluate the situation with regard to providing Iraq with medicine and food. My colleague will come here to ascertain the situation. Another concerned person in WHO will come over. The Sanctions Committee has now a new president, the Austrian Ambassador, and I will tell him of the problem.

The President-Leader: Welcome to all.

0125

بسم الله الرحمن الرحيم

Embassy of
The Republic of Iraq
Seoul

سفارة الجمهورية العراقية
سيئول

No. 102/91 **Press Release** 24/2/1991

STATEMENT OF SPOKESMAN OF THE

REVOULTION'S COMMAND COUNCIL ON FEBRUARY 22, 1991

In the Name of Allah, the Merciful, the Compassionate.

Bush, the enemy of Allah, tried through his statement today, and in harmony with his degenerate character, to illustrate or insinuate that what Mr. Tariq Aziz the Foreign Minister has agreed upon in Moscow is one thing, and the statement of President Saddam Hussein is another.

Bush here wanted to deceive himself, because Mr. Aziz was fully authorized by the President to be committed to whatever it is agreed upon with the Soviet Union.

Bush also attempts to send Quixotic ultimatums for Iraq to withdraw by noon tomorrow, as he says. We don't know whether Bush wanted in his shameful ultimatum to create the impression that the peace initiative is the outcome of his ultimatum, or claim to the world that he and his miserable allies have prevailed over Iraq! He pretends that the world does not know that all he and his allies have done since the night of 16/17 January 1991 was executing a cowardly devastating plan to destroy personal properties of civilian Iraqis and demolish Mosques and Churches, in addition to shelters such as that of Al-Ameria and those in Faluja, Mosul, Nassiriya, Basrah and other cities, towns and villages, including Beduins and Camel-herders.

Bush and his collaborators who committed cowardly crimes avoided initiating their aggression with our valiant ground forces, because they have realized that they lack legality which gives them the capability to confront the army of Faith and Jihad.

It is possible that Bush wanted to speed things up so that he might enjoy his weekend, thus giving the satisfaction of continuing his evil aggression.

We would like to stress that Iraq seeks peace and has seriously endeavoured to support the Soviet initiative and facilitate its success, not out of fear from Bush's threats or out of respect for him, for we neither respect him nor are we afraid of him. He has tried with us his miserable 0126 luck, supported by the spilled blood caused by his criminal equipments and weapons.

In adopting such an attitude, we express our respect for what we believe in and what we consider as necessary for our people and the whole humanity. We adopt this attitude out of respect to people whom we respect and who do not include Bush, the enemy of Allah and friend of Satan.

Bush's talk about the destruction of property in Kuwait is also miserable. It seems that Bush doesn't know what was destroyed in Kuwait or in any other place in Iraq, be that Oil installations ot others. No other vandalists or invaders in history surpassed Bush in his lust for destruction. He thus, is not among those who are entitled to evaluate or accuse. If Bush denies his devastating crimes against oil and economical installations which are related to transportation, exploitation or production of Petrol in Iraq or Kuwait, then we call upon the Security Council to form a neutral committee including China, the Soviet Union and other countries to be named by the Council provided they are not party or supporters in the war. The task of the committee should be to asses the level of civilian or economical destrction whether in Kuwait or Iraq as a whole and to conduct the verification of which destruction was done as a military necessity.

The talk about Iraqi missile strikes which Bush calls "Scud missiles" is indeed rediculous. As if Bush, who portrays himself as "supervisor general" over the operations of aggression for the so-called Desert Storm, pretends that he does not know about the continuing aggression, day and night, of his air and ground forces which escalated their criminal actions after the disclosure of the Soviet initiative.

Where is, after all, cease-fire agreements which made Bush criticise Iraq for hitting specific targets with missiles? Can it be that Bush imagines that Iraq has to exert self-restraint, while he aggresses and makes some childish despicable statements?

0127

Embassy of
The Republic of Iraq
Seoul

سفارة الجمهورية العراقية
سيئول

No. 103/91

Press Release

24/2/1991

SUMMARY OF COMMUNIQUE NO. 57 OF THE ARMED FORCES GENERAL COMMAND ON FEBRUARY 22, 1991

In the Name of Allah, the Merciful, the Compassionate

Those, who were frustrated by the overall progress achieved by the Iraqi Revolution, have missed no opportunity to conspire against these achievements and never missed achance to destroy them. But the people of Iraq, under the banner of valiant Leader Saddam Hussain, have been more determined every day to liberate the occupied Arab land and safeguard the Arab and Iraqi interests.

1. A degenerate British force attempted to approach our valiant forces in the Al-Mensour Sector of operations, and was swiftly repulsed by our heroic forces who inflicted heavy losses on the enemy in personnel and equipments.

2. In revenge against the treachery of Al-Saud, our forces carried out two devastating missile strikes against the Khalid town and military airport. All missile launchers returned to base safely.
3. The criminal enemy carried out 23 air sorties against residential areas, bridges and dams in our homeland.

4. Our air defences downed five enemy aircraft, including two helicopters.

SUMMARY OF STATEMENT OF A MILITARY SPOKESMAN ON FEBRUARY 22, 1991

In the Name of Allah, the Merciful, the Compassionate.

1. By the help of Almighty, our heroic missile forces launched at dawn today, three devastating missile strikes against concentrations of enemy combat planes in Issa military airport, from which enemy planes take off and hit our civilians. All missile launchers returned to base safely.

2. Our forces carried out, just before midnight yesterday, a lethal missile strike against the military city of Khalid.

3. In pursuance to our Communique No. 57 of today's afternoon, it was learned that another enemy combat plane, which had targetted residential areas in Baghdad, was downed.

0128

Embassy of
The Republic of Iraq
Seoul

سفارة الجمهورية العراقية
سيئول

No. 104/91

Press Release

24/2/1991

SUMMARY OF COMMUNIQUE NO. 58 OF THE ARMED FORCES GENERAL COMMAND ON FEBRUARY 22, 1991

In the Name of Allah, the Merciful, the Compassionate

Allah is Great, and will bestow His assistance and victory.

O' Brethren,

O' Valiant Armed Forces,

O' Children of the Glorious Arab Nation.

After our forces had repulsed the British attempts against our forces, the enemy continued its skirmishes with our forces. At 9:15 hours this morning, the enemy started its preparatory bombardments in the same Operation Sector, with more skirmishes. This signifies without any doubt that the ground battle has begun.

We declare to the whole world that the American administration and its allies in the region are responsible of this grave developments which might destroy all peace opportunities, welcomed by Iraq. They are responsible infront of Allh and history of any blood that will be spilled in their war of aggression.

Iraq will remain committed to peace and determined to defend and safeguard its territories and sovereignty, inflicting, Allah willing, defeat and humiliation on the enemy.

Our armed forces renew, infront of Allah, to the heroic Leader Saddam Hussain, the pledge to drown the enemy in the swamp of defeat and humiliation.

Victory is at hand, Allah willing.

0129

SUMMARY OF
STATEMENT OF A MILITARY SPOKESMAN
ON FEBRUARY 22, 1991

In the Name of Allah, the Merciful, the Compassionate.

In pursuance to our Communique No: 58 of today's afternoon, we declare to our people, our valiant Armed Forces and the International public opinion the following:

1. The enemy has, as of this morning, been attacking our forces in many directions in the Soutern Operation Sector, which included Al-Hamza forces, in addition to the Al-Mansour forces.

2. Our intrepid armed forces confronted the enemy with various weapons, inflicting heavy losses and forcing a part of the enemy to retreat.

Victory over the forces of Blasphemy, Allah willing, is at hand.

0130

Embassy of
The Republic of Iraq
Seoul

سفارة الجمهورية العراقية
سيئول

No. 105/91

Press Release

24/2/1991

SUMMARY OF COMMUNIQUE NO. 59 OF THE ARMED FORCES GENERAL COMMAND ON FEBRUARY 23, 1991

In the Name of Allah, the Merciful, the Compassionate

Our armed forces, in these decisive moments in the history of our nation, are poised to fulfil the sacred duty, believing in the divine victory by the help of Allah, our capabilities and the strategic depth which includes the whole Arab nation.

If the Blasphemous enemy has refused peace initiatives to realize their intentions against our homeland, then we will not hesitate to render the ground war which they are seeking, a hell consuming their troops.

We have full confidence in our efficient and wise leadership, and in the zeal of our people who are very well aware of the noble cause we are fighting for.

1. In pursuance to our Communiques Nos. 57 & 58 of yesterday, in which we announced the start of the ground war and the victories of our armed forces against the forces of aggression, the enemy made three more attempts to approach our armed forces at 20:15 Hrs. and 23:00 Hrs. on February 21 and at 14:30 Hrs. of February 22 in the hope of compensating for his previous losses. The forces of Al-Hamza and Al-Mansour succeeded, by the help of Allah, to repulse all these enemy attempts inflicting heavy losses in his personnel and equipments. Despite his repeated failure, the enemy is continuing his futile attempts at the same front and our Al-Mansoor and Al-Hamza forces continue to inflict significant losses in his pesonnel and equipment and is completely in control of the situation.

2. In addition to the successful Holy Jihad of our ground forces, our missile forces continued launching devastating strikes as follows:

A) Al-Hussain missile strike against the Capital of Al-Saud.

B) Fahd Airport was devastated by Al-Hussain missiles. 0131

All missile launchers returned to base safely.

3. Our valiant armed forces in the Southern Sector of operations launched a series of devastating tactical missile strikes against the oil and military town of Al-Khafji.

4. The degenerate enemy carried out 39 air sorties and missile attacks, targetting residential areas, bridges and other civilian targets. The enemy also carried out 210 air sorties against military targets in the South.

With the help of Allah, one enemy air target was downed.

0132

Embassy of
The Republic of Iraq
Seoul

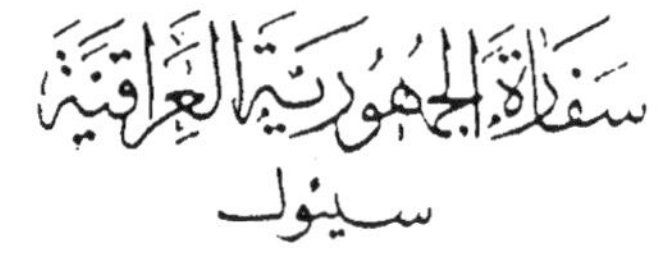

No. 109/91

Press Release

26/2/1991

SUMMARY OF COMMUNIQUE NO. 62 OF THE ARMED FORCES GENERAL COMMAND ON FEBRUARY 25, 1991

In the Name of Allah, the Merciful, the Compassionate

Fierce battles raged last night all along the front. After completely destroying enemy assault, the forces of the Third Corps, commanded by Lt. General Salah Abood initiated an all out counterattack, which resulted in coomplete repulsion of enemy forces, and restored all positions along the Third Corps front. Enemy forces were completely beaten and retreated in front of the valiant attack of the forces of Mohammed AL-Qasim, commanded by Brigadier Yasin Flaih AL-Maini and the forces of Salah Al-Din, commanded by Brigadier Hasan Zaidan.

Among the defeated were the American Second Armoured Division, and the Fourth Armoured Division belonging to the agent regime of Husni Mubarak, who has participated in the American-Atlantic aggression against Iraq.

SUMMARY OF COMMUNIQUE NO. 63 OF THE ARMED FORCES GENERAL COMMAND ON FEBRUARY 25, 1991

In the Name of Allah, the Merciful, the Compassionate

After announcing to you in our Communique No. 62 of today's afternoon, regarding the victories scored by the heroic soldiers of the Third Corps against the aggression of the Americans and their allies, who suffered tremendous losses, our forces repulsed more attacks, increasing the losses of the enemy.

Our valiant armed forces are now heroically confronting the enemy's attempts in Failakah Island.

Let it be clear that the enemy, by refusing all peace initiatives, is responsible for all the losses inflicted on their own forces.

Let it also be known that our armed forces will continue performing their sacred duty to defend the homeland against aggression.

0133

Embassy of
The Republic of Iraq
Seoul

سفارة الجمهورية العراقية
سيئول

No. 112/91 **Press Release** 27/2/1991

SUMMARY OF
STATEMENT OF A MILITARY SPOKESMAN
ON FEBRUARY 27, 1991

In the Name of Allah, the Merciful, the Compassionate.

inspite of the fact that the enemy interferred in the withdrawal process of our forces, the withdrawal was completed by all the Iraqi corps in accordance to the President's speech and the statement of yesterday morning.

The first light of today February 27, 1991, marked the withdrawal of the last unit of our valiant forces.

0134

Embassy of
The Republic of Iraq
Seoul

سفارة الجمهورية العراقية
سيئول

No. 118/91

Press Release

14/3/1991

STATEMENT OF THE SPOKESMAN OF THE MINISTRY OF FOREIGN AFFAIRS ON MARCH 13, 1991

A spokesman of the Ministry of Foreign Affairs said on March 13, 1991, that American security authorities violated, last Friday, the Iraqi Chancery and Residence of the Ambassador in Washington.

The spokesman told Iraqi News Agency that the American authorities closed the Iraqi Chancery and Residence in Washington after ordering the head of the Iraqi Interest Section to leave it on Friday March 8, 1991.

In the same evening, the American security authorities forced open the building without any permission of the head of the Iraqi Interest Section, and stayed inside for a while. They again entered it on Monday March 11, 1991.

The spokesman stressed that this American measure is a violation of the Geneva Convention on Diplomatic Relations of 1961 which stipulates that the Chancery and the Residence are inviolable and that the officers of accrediting state shall not enter them without the consent of the head of mission.

The spokesman also stressed that the American authorities committed this flagrant violation of the Vienna Convention without any legal justification, while the American Chancery and Residence in Baghdad have never been subject to any interference whatsoever by the Iraqi authorities, since the American envoys left them on January 12, 1991. These premises are still enjoying full diplomatic immunity and inviolability, ensured by the Iraqi security authorities.

0135

Embassy of
The Republic of Iraq
Seoul

سفارة الجمهورية العراقية
سيئول

No. 142/91 **Press Release** 26/4/1991

Letter From Iraqi President of Environment Protection Council to the Executive Director of U.N. Environment Programme on April 24, 1991

Dr. Mustafa TALBA,
Executive Director,
United Nations Environment Programme

Mr. Executive Director,

Greetings

I have the pleasure to send you this letter, with the request that your Organization exercise its role in averting an environmental catastrophe that might beset Iraq and the Arab Gulf.

Following are the details:

The State Department of the United States contacted the Head of the Iraqi Interest Section in Washington on April 1, 1991, and informed him of the leak of an oil slick from Iraqi Al-Bakr Terminal oil storage in the Arab Gulf. This 40-mile long slick. the State Department added, was heading southward. The State Department requested that the Iraqi Government take all measures possible to stop the source of the oil leakage.

Since this leakage was a result of the Allied bombardment against Iraqi oil installations, and because Al-Bakr Terminal is within the area controlled by American ground and air forces, the Head of the Iraqi Interest Section in Washington requested the State Department on April 15, 1991, to allow an Iraqi technical team to visit AL-Bakr Terminal by helicopters or boats in order to asses the causes of the leakage and try to repair it. Unfortunately, the American authorities have been procrastinating about the permission to visit this area, with the leakage going on in the meanwhile in the Arab Gulf.

Mr. Executive Director,

0136

We are submitting these facts about an issue which threatens not only the environment in Iraq and the Arab Gulf, but might also adversely affect the world at large if not immediately tackled. This is added to the other environmental catastrophes caused by the Americans when they bombarded the Kuwaiti oil installations and terminals, resulting in the largest oil slick in the history of sea pollutions.

The leakage from the oil storages from the Iraqi Al-Bakr Terminal imposes on the world and its hygenic and environmental organizations, in the forefront of which, is your organization, the responsibility of interferring for the purpose of averting this catastrophe. My country is fully prepared to cooperate with whoever your organization delegate to tackle this situation, now that the American authorities have been hindering the efforts of the Iraqi technical authorities to stop the leakage.

Accept, Sir, my highest consideration.

Signed:
President of Environment
Protection Council
of the Republic of Iraq

0137

Embassy of
The Republic of Iraq
Seoul

سفارة الجمهورية العراقية
سيئول

Dear H. E. Moon Dong-suk,

이락 내의 최근 사태에 관해 귀하에게 알려드리게 됨에 무한한 영광을 느낍니다.

미, 영 행정부는 UN 안보리의 당면 결의문에 대한 그들의 이제까지의 맹종에도 불구하고, 이락에 대한 지속적인 제제를 주장함으로써 이락의 국민들에게 막대한 고통을 가하는 데 목적을 둔 그들의 정책을 계속하고 있습니다.

현 이락의 상황에 대한 놀라운 사실들을 알기 위해 UN 사무총장의 PERSONAL REPRESENTATIVE 인 MARTY IHTISARY 의 1991. 3. 30 일자 보고에 의하면, 하버드 대학의 한 의료진이 최근 이락을 방문하여서 수십만의 어린이들이 대이락 공습의 복합적 영향과 지속적이 제제의 결과로 죽음에 직면 해 있다는 사실을 발견했습니다. 하버드 의료진을 대표하여 ROB NOODLE 박사는 이락의 11개 도시에 대한 현장작업에 근거를 두고 관찰한 결과, 5세 미만 어린이들의 치사율이 170,000 명 더 추가 될 것이라고 말했으며, 이러한 이락의 상황을 "국민 건강의 큰 재앙"으로 기술했습니다.

이락은 현재 전쟁 이전 전력의 20% 밖에 생산하지 못하고 있습니다. 발전소, 방송망과 관제기관을 용의주도하게 겨냥한 미 주도의 폭격때문입니다. 그 결과, 하수도 처리, 식수 공급, 약품의 냉장 및 의료 수술등이 극히 어렵거나 거의 불가능하게되었습니다. 더운 계절이 다가오면서 콜레라와 장티푸스가 현재 유행성 질병의 비율에 이르고 있습니다. 심각한 영양실조가 만연하고 있으며, 하버드 의료팀은 기근이 있을 수도 있다고 생각합니다.

0138

하버드 의료진의 이 무시무시한 예견은 UNISEF 의 EZIN MURZIL 박사에 의해 확증 되었는 데 그는 1세 미만 어린이의 80%가 이미 영양실조에 걸려 있다고 했습니다. 국제 적십자사의 DOMINICK DUTOUR 박사는 덧붙이기를, 만일 의약품이 없다면 남부 이락의 약 94,000 명의 어린이들이 단지 설사와 식수 매개의 전염병 때문에 죽을 수도 있다고 했습니다.

1991년 5월 20일 그리고 6월 18일에 다시 부시 대통령은 사담 후세인 대통령이 권좌에 있는 한, 이락에 대한 제제를 계속해서 할 것이라고 선언 했습니다. 똑 같은 입장이 이미 메이저 영국 수상에 의해 공표 되었었습니다. 전 세계에 민주주의를 설교하는 사람들은 이락 국 들의 선택을 먼저 존중 해야만 합니다.

이락 국민들은 전 세계로부터의 인도주의적 원조에 깊이 감사를 드립니다. 그러나, 이 모든 원조가 전쟁 이전의 이락의 수요 - 5억 불의 의약품 수입과 식량의 70% 이상의 수입 의존 - 을 전부 감당 할 수는 없습니다. 따라서, 경제 봉쇄가 즉시 해제 되어 이락이 석유를 판매하여 긴급한 식량, 의약품 및 다른 기본적인 민간 필수품들을 구입 할 수 없다면, 수백 만의 무고한 시민이 죽게 될 것입니다. 가장 위협을 받고 있는 것은 어린이들입니다.

이락에 부당하게 지속되고 있는 비인간적인 경제 봉쇄를 즉각 해제 할 것을 요구함으로써, 이락 국민들의 고통을 종식시키는 긴급한 조치를 취해 주시기를 인도주의의 이름으로 간곡하게 요청하는 바 입니다.

이락 국민들의 기본적인 궁핍을 덜어주기 위해 필요하리라고 생각되는 것과 더불어, 귀하께서는 인도주의적 관심을 이락 국민들의 어려운 상황에 돌려 주시리라고 확신합니다.

1991년 7월 3일

주 한 이 락 대 사 관

0139

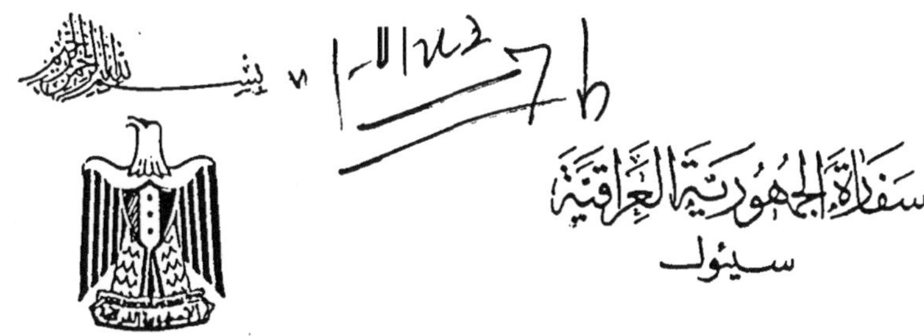

Embassy of
The Republic of Iraq
Seoul

NO. 169-91 **Press Release** 29/7/1991

1990년 8월 2일 사태이후, 이라크는 UN의 모든 결의문을 받아들였고, 전후의 모든 공약을 이행하였다. 이제 경제 제재 조치를 해제하는 것이 UN의 의무이다. 왜냐하면 위의 제재는 이라크 국민들에게 막대한 고통을 가져다 주기 때문이다. 미국, 영국 양국이 다른 국가들과 함께, 고의적으로 이라크 국민들을 죽음으로 몰아넣고, 이라크의 경제, 사회, 문화 구조를 파괴하는데 목적을 두었 두었다는 것은 나날이 명백해지고 있다. 이것은 가장 기본적인 인도주의적 가치와 국제법에 위배된다. 또한 국가들간의 명백한 근본 방침들도 위반하고 있다.

우리는 모든 국민들과 국가들에게 대이라크 금수 조치의 해제를 요구함으로써, 그들의 책임을 짊어질것을 호소하는 바이다. 왜냐하면, 이미 이전에 언급한 바와 같이, 이라크가 UN의 결의문을 모두 이행한 지금, 경제 제재에 대한 정당성은 더이상 없기 때문이다. 그뿐만이 아니라, 다수의 민간적, 국제적 인도주의 기관에 따르면, 지속적인 경제 제재 조치는 수천명의 이라크 어린이들과 노인들의 생명을 앗아갈 것이 확실하다.

0140

Embassy of
The Republic of Iraq
Seoul

سفارة الجمهورية العراقية
سيئول

NO. 201-91 **Press Release** 19/9/1991

- "신 연방주의자" 초고에서 -
- 이라크인들을 생매장 ; 드러난 더 많은 미국의 전쟁 범죄 -

조셉 부르타

워싱턴 9월 14일 (EIRNS) - 미 육군 1개 사단이 걸프전에서 지상전 개시 2일동안 수 천명의 이라크 군인들을 생매장시켰다고 뉴욕 롱 아일랜드의 한 일간지가 폭로했다.
롱 아일랜드 뉴스 데이에 따르면, 제 1 기계화 사단의 3개 여단은 탱크 위에 설치한 쟁기를 사용하여 사우디아라비아와 이라크 사이의 국경선에 걸쳐 있는 중립지대 끝을 따라 70 마일의 참호속에 있는 약 6,000 여명에 다다르는 이라크 병사들을 매장시켰다. 국제 여론은 미군의 연극에 의해 방해를 받아왔었다. 1948년 제네바 협정과 전후 뉴렘베르크 재판에서 선언된 국제법에 악명높게 위배되는 이 행위는 미국 정부의 전쟁 범죄 행위를 상징 한다.

이라크에 대한 범죄 행위가 여전히 진행중 이라는 사실은 이라크 보건 장관의 최근 보고서에서 보여지고 있는데, 이보고서는 말할 나위도 없이 현 시점에서, 미국이 부과한 대 이라크 경제 제재 및 봉쇄 조치로부터 기인하여 일어나는 대규모의 사망을 보여 주고 있다.

- 용의주도하게 의도된 대량 학살 -

9월 12일자뉴스 데이의 계산에 의하면, "거대한 붉은 자"로 알려 진 탱크위에 쟁기를 설치한제1 기갑사단이 전투 지상요원들과 함께 참호속에 있는 수 천명의 이라크 병사들을 2월 24-25일 생매장 시켰다고 한다. 70마일이나 되는 참호들은 8천 여명의 군인들에 의해 방어되고 있었는데, 단 2천명만이 살아 남았다.

"우리가 일단 그 곳을 통과하여 가면, 항복한 자 이외에는 아무것도 남아있지 않았다"고 배니 윌리암스 대위가 뉴스 데이에서 말했다. 그는 이 전투로 은성 훈장을 수여 받았다. 이공격에서 단 한명의 미군도 희생되지 않았다.

"내가 알기로는, 우리는 수 천명을 죽일 수 있었다...." 고 가장 격렬한 저지를 받았던 제 2여단 사령관인 안토니 모레노 장군은 말했다.

모레노의 진술에 의하면, 대부분의 경우 참호선의 각 소대는 거대한 이빨처럼 생긴 쟁기를 단 아브람 주 전투 탱크 2대씩에 할당되었다. 탱크들은 참호들의 앞 부분을 점령하였는데 그 범위는 폭 3피트, 깊이 6피트였다. 그리고나서 전투용 차량과 캐리어로 무장한 화포가 참호를 공격하여 이라크 병사들에게 화력을 퍼부었다.

0141

" 나는 그 선봉대 바로 다음으로 지나왔다. 보이는 것은 사람들의 팔과 그들을 계뚫고 있는 것들이 있는   파묻힌 참호들이었다." 고 모레노가 말했다.

민간 요원 조 퀸은 지상요원들과 함께 죽은 병사들을 파묻는 그의 입무로 청동 훈장을 받았다. " 많은 사람들이 겁을 먹었지요. ' 그러나, 나는 그것을 즐겼지요." 하고 퀸은 뉴스 데이에서 말했다.

그 사단은 실제 공격이전에 전술상 능란하게 수행할 수 있도록 이라크 군 참호의 복제를 건설했었다.

- 미 국무성은 살인을 정당화하다 -

이 내용이 발행된 다음 날, 미 국무성 대변인은 그 수치가 사실임은 인정했으나, 뻔뻔스럽게도 그들의 행위가 전쟁의 긴박함으로 정당화된다고 주장했다. " 살아있는 사람들을 파묻는다는 것은 좋게 들리지는 않습니다." 제 1 사단의 론 마가트 장군은 기자들에게 말했다. ' " 하지만 대부분의 사람들은 지상전이 얼마나 격렬한 지 알지 못 합니다." - 30개국의 무장 군인들을 대면하여 몹시 질려있는 이라크 군인들에 대한 학살이 마치 군사적으로 필수적이었던 것처럼.

국무성 대변인은, 지상전 후반기에 쿠웨이트로부터 이라크로, 고속도로를 따라 후퇴하고 있던 이라크 병사들에 대한 학살을 정당화 할 때도 똑같은 이론적 해석을 사용하였다. 똑같은 형태의 이론이 또한, 미국의 민간인 공습 대피소, 유아용 의약품 공장, 교량들을 폭격한 직후에 사용되었다. 왜냐하면 작은 이라크는 " 세계에서 4번째 규모의 군사력"을 가지고 있으니까.

당시 미 공군 참모총장 마이클 듀간이 1990. 9. 16 뉴욕 타임즈에 미국은 이웃 민간인들을 공습하게 될지도 모를 것이라고 말 했을때,미국이 전쟁에 대한 모든 규범을 위반하리라는 것은 전쟁이전부터 이미 명백하였었다. 미군 사령관 노만 슈와츠코프 장군과 조지 부시에 의해 이라크 군인들은 " 인간이 아니라는" 취지의 반복된 말들은 미군들이 그들의 지도자가 명령한 범죄를 이행할 수 있는 요건을 이루어 주었다.

- 이라크의 큰 재앙 -

반면, 13개월간의 UN의 경제 제재와 봉쇄 조치를 겪고있는 이라크 내 사정은 어떠한가? 이라크 보건부 장관이 지난 주 발표한 자료에 의하면, 그 곳에서의 재앙은 계속되고 있으며 더욱 극심해지고있다.

보건부의 보고서는, UN의 의약품 부족 부과 조치의 결과로(경제 봉쇄 조치 결과로), 16,000명의 이라크 암 환자들은 적절하게 치료를 받을 수 없으며, 또한 많은 경우에 있어서 지난 해 동안 전혀 치료를 받을 수 없었다. 5세 미만의 어린이가 단지 의약품 부족으로 14,000명이 넘게 죽었다. 1990년 같은 기간을 비교해 볼 때, 봉쇄 조치로 인한 의약품과 마취제의 부족으로 지난 6개월 동안 새로운 실맹이 1,000 % 증가하였다.

0142

불길하게도, 오래 전에 이라크에서 사라졌던 콜레라가 미 공군의 이라크 하수시설과 전력시설의 폭격으로 거대한 하수 웅덩이가 모이면서 다시 나타났다. 이라크 보건부는 전쟁 이후 1,640 건의 콜레라를 보고했다. 이라크의 건강 모니터 체계는 (역시 공습때문에) 불능 상태이다. 표준 유행병 검진도 현재 불가능하다 - 콜레라 희생자의 수는 아마도 보고되어진 것 보다 훨씬 클 것이다. 히바드 의대의 계산에 따르면, 수 십만의 이라크 이들이 질병과 기아로 죽게 될 것이다.

2. 주한사우디아라비아 대사관

0143

ROYAL EMBASSY OF SAUDI ARABIA

NEWS BULLETIN

No. 2/91 January 18, 1991

PRESS OFFICE
1-112, Shinmoon-ro, 2-Ka
Chongro-gu, Seoul 110-062,
Republic of Korea

0144

KING FAHD ADDRESSED THE MEMBERS OF THE EXECUTIVE BUREAU OF THE ISLAMIC POPULAR CONFERENCE EXPOUNDING ON MATTERS CONCERNING THE GULF SITUATION

Custodian of the two Holy Mosques King Fahd Ibn Abdulaziz received here on Saturday Ulema, Sheikhs and members of the Executive Bureau of the Islamic Popular Conference which concluded its deliberations in Makkah on Friday and expressed delight over the Conference.

In an address before them, King Fahd expressed regret that Baghdad and some of its allies are speaking too much about the deployment of foreign troops in the Kingdom of Saudi Arabia and other Gulf states.

"They have been speaking about these armies as if these armies are invading forces, but at the same time, they ignore a key factor behind the presence of these armies which are invited by the Kingdom and other Arab Gulf states in view of the vicious Iraqi invasion of Kuwait and Baghdad's threats to other states in the region," the Saudi monarch said.

King Fahd told the audience that what happened on August 2, 1990, has taken all Islamic states, particularly the Kingdom of Saudi Arabia and Egypt, with surprise because no one could imagine at the time that Iraq would make such an aggression on an Arab, Islamic and neighbouring state regardless of any backgrounds.

King Fahd cited the early efforts made by him and Egyptian president Hosni Mubarak when they had sensed that matters were heading for the worst. "But neither me nor President Mubarak had ever thought for a moment that Iraq would invade Kuwait, which had provided big assistance to the neighbouring Iraq," the Saudi monarch said.

"Moreover, before August 2, 1990, Saddam Hussein had never missed an occasion to highlight the generous, fraternal, moral and material support extended by the Kingdom of Saudi Arabia and Kuwait to the Iraqi brothers when in need," King Fahd said.

0145

The Iraqi ruler had been a usual admirer of Saudi and Kuwaiti cordial stands toward Iraq in a manner that dismissed any doubt, that one day, he would try to insult any one of them," the Saudi monarch added.

King Fahd said he had dispatched Prince Saud Al-Faisal again on a similar mission when he noticed the continuation of the Iraqi mobilizations and again the Iraqi president had repeated the same words.

Then, King Fahd had notified President Hosni Mubarak on the matter and that the Egyptian president had proposed to visit Baghdad and talk to the Iraqi president.

"When President Mubarak met with Saddam in Baghdad, the Iraqi president repeated to him what he had conveyed to the Kingdom in this context. Then President Mubarak proceeded to Kuwait where he had assured Sheikh Jabir and his government on the intentions of Iraq," the Saudi monarch said.

He said President Mubarak told him later that he had noticed a gap in relations between Iraq and Kuwait which might generate into some impacts or complicate matters if not settled by amicable means and that the Iraqi ruler had agreed on a meeting between the delegations of the two countries in the Kingdom on August 1, 1990 meeting and had proposed that the two delegations, led by Sheikh Saad Al-Abdullah, the Kuwait heir apparent and prime minister and Izzat Ibrahim, the Iraqi vice president, would meet fact-to-face without any mediation.

After several hours meeting, the two delegations were invited for a dinner banquet, the King said, "I was glad that the leaders of the delegations came in one car with signs of satisfaction," the Saudi Monarch added.

"During the banquet, I had welcomed a proposal made by the head of the Iraqi delegation before his Kuwaiti counterpart, Sheikh Saad, that the next meeting would be held in Baghdad on next Saturday to settle the matters and if needed, another one could be held in Kuwait during the week or the next one," the Saudi monarch said.

King Fahd expressed regret that despite Iraq's repeated promises, the Iraqi forces invaded Kuwait in the early morning of the next day (Thursday August 2, 1990) and the Saudi Arabian Embassy in Kuwait had confirmed the sad, unbelievable and surprising event.

"In the following hours, I had tried in vain to contact the Iraqi president by telephone but I had been informed that Saddam was on leave and resting at an area with no telephone service. But no one would believe that a head of state has no telephone service in such circumstances. As such, I had been convinced that he did not like to speak to me," the King added.

"When the Iraqi leader contacted me by telephone later on Thursday, he told me that the telephone discussion may not be adequate and that he will send his deputy to explain the matter.

"When the Iraqi Vice President Izzat Ibrahim arrived, he told me that President Saddam's message is that what had happened is a natural event and that Kuwait is part of Iraq and has returned to its natural position," the King said.

He said the Iraqi delegate had shown no further discussions and had no authority to do anything but to convey the message of Saddam Hussein.

The King said he had briefed the Iraqi delegate on his stance over such critical circumstances.

King Fahd expressed deep regret over what had happened and recalled the generous assistances provided by the Kingdom and Kuwait to the Iraqi people and army. "After all this, Iraq had shown its complete determination that there is nothing called Kuwait," the monarch said.

King Fahd also spoke about different justifications made by the Iraqi leadership on invasion and annexation of Kuwait. "However, the Kingdom had been convinced that the matter is merely an invasion and nothing else," the Saudi monarch said.

Giving a summary of the background about the dispute between Iraq and Kuwait that started more than 50 years ago and efforts made by the Arab League to settle the matter with peaceful means, King Fahd pointed out the historical fact that Iraq did never govern Kuwait during the last 250 years as far as he knows, until Iraq, under the rule of late president Ahmad Hassan Al-Bakar recognized Kuwait as an indepedent and sovereign state. The documents of the recognition are now deposited with the Arab League and the United Nations leaving no justifications whatsoever for Iraq to claim that Kuwait is a part of it, the King said.

The real reason behind the invasion of Kuwait is the ambitious Iraqi expansionist plots over the Arab Gulf states, he said.

King Fahd told the Islamic gathering that the huge mobilizations of the iraqi forces in Kuwait, proved that the Kingdom of Saudi Arabia might be the next step despite a bilateral no aggression convention signed by the two countries during King Fahd's last visit to Baghdad.

During the signature ceremony in Baghdad, King Fahd said President Saddam Hussein had assured him that the agreement was only meant to reinforce and dedicate the close and fraternal ties between the two countries.

"Saddam had also reassured me that the Iraqi army is built to defend Arab rights and to repulse any aggression that might be sustained by any Arab state. Even if the Iraqi army shows any bad behaviour, other Arab armies should fight it," the Saudi monarch added.

"After all Iraq should pull out its forces from Kuwait and if there are any legal border claims, they would be settled through arbitration of Arab or Islamic leaders who might be accepted by the two conflicting sides," King Fahd said.

He cited the dispute between the two countries over Al-Rumellah Oil Field and said the dispute could be settled by amicable means by Arab, Islamic bodies or the International Court of Justice which has been set-up for such cases.

"What Iraq wants? It has much oil, two rivers, much cultivable lands and a population with much experience that could exploit such natural wealth," the King said. "It was not the responsibility of the Kingdom of Saudi Arabia or Kuwait if Iraq had not utilized such huge human and natural resources," he added.

"After the Iran-Iraq war came to an end, the Iraqi president could have exploited the huge resources of Iraq for the welfare of his people, but it has been proved he wants to breach all promises and Islamic charters and give the worst example in the Islamic history," he said.

Referring the Islamic style of rule, King Fahd said the Islamic faith has given the best principles for a democratic rule and the most sophisticated system ever known by the mankind that calls for brotherhood, mercy and cooperation.

King Fahd expressed pride that the Islamic faith is now speaking all-over-the-globe without the need for the use of force.

The Saudi monarch expressed hope that the Iraqi president would realize that he made a mistake and come back to the right path and respond to the international unanimous will.

"Even those who earlier supported Iraq, have announced that they do not approve the occupation of Kuwait regardless of any justifications," he said.

King Fahd made it clear that the Kingdom of Saudi Arabia does not need fighting with Iraq but it wants that the Iraqi ruler would undertake a responsible and wise decision and orders his forces to get out of Kuwait and remove the mobilized forces along the Saudi borders.

He said some Arab, Islamic and friendly states sent their troops to the Kingdom voluntarily after the Kingdom and other Arab Gulf states realized the Iraqi threats and that the invitation of foreign troops is legalized by the Islamic teachings.

King Fahd refuted the iraqi allegations that the mobilization of the multinational forces are threatening Iraq and said the Iraqi leader forgot the fact that the mobilizations of the international forces were ordered for the implementation of resolutions adopted by the U.N.'s Security Council in response to a request from Kuwait, a member of the U.N. which sufferred the aggression, and it order to normalize the situation over there and to prevent similar aggression in future.

He said it is the aggression of the Iraqi regime against Kuwait and its mobilization along the Kingdom's borders that made it necessary for the Kingdom to seek the help of the multinational forces.

"I could frankly say that it is not easy for me to see the Iraqi people and army defeated, but what elase could we do, the solution is in the hands of one man, that is Saddam Hussein, who is the only one to tell the Iraqi forces to pullout from Kuwait," the King said.

The King said Saddam could have undertaken a decision within minutes like the one he had undertaken in terms of its relations with Iran.

As an eye witness, the King gave a background on the Iraq-Iran dispute since 1975, when he was delegated by the late King Faisal to attend negotiations which led to an agreement between the two sides.

Citing the earlier close friendship and brotherly ties with Saddam Hussein, King Fahd said when the Iraqi leader spoke to him one day about Iranian provocations along the common borders, " I had advised him not to make similar provocations because Iran was undergoing problems of a changing power. I had also advised him not to interfere in the domestic affairs of Iran," the Saudi monarch said.

"Saddam did adhere to the advice. But, then the costly and useless eight-years war broke out. Now why the Iraqi president decided to return to the agreement this time," the Saudi monarch said.

King Fahd said the Iran-Iraq conflict has been settled by the United Nations's Security Council and that they were about to reach an agreement whereby no party would extend concessions to the other one but the Iraqi ruler had undertaken a personal decision in less than 15 minutes to recognize the Algiers Agreeement and to give Iran all lands it demanded according to the Agreement.

"I have no objection whatsoever over the decision made by the Iraqi ruler and does not want to interfere in his affairs. But I want to ask him one question whether it is not possible to give similar concession over Kuwait and pullout his occupation forces from Kuwait. And if there are any claims afterwards, they could be resolved through arbitration," he added.

King Fahd denied categorically the false reports that the two holy Harams and other holy sites are under the control of foreign troops and assured the gathering that Makkah and Madinah are located 1,500 kms away from the sites where the multinational forces are deployed. "The Kingdom is capable to providing adequate protection to the holy cities," the Saudi monarch said.

Referring to the problems being faced by some Islamic states who are suffering from impacts of colonization, King Fahd vowed that the Kingdom of Saudi Arabia would extend every possible support to them.

- 0 -

0152

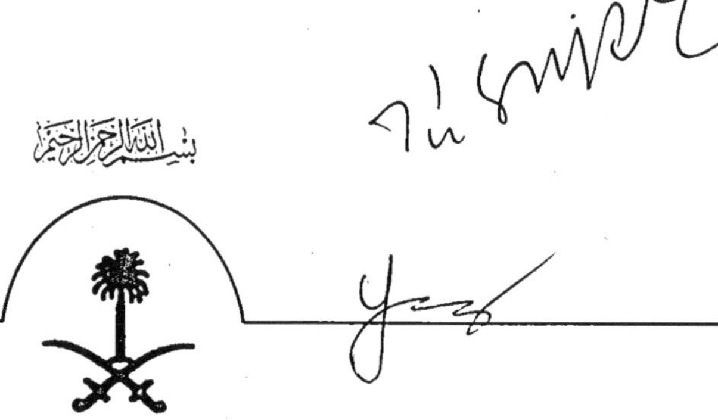

ROYAL EMBASSY OF SAUDI ARABIA

NEWS BULLETIN

No. 3/91 January 18, 1991

PRESS OFFICE
1-112, Shinmoon-ro, 2-Ka
Chongro-gu, Seoul 110-062,
Republic of Korea

0153

KING FAHD ANSWERED HUSSEIN'S OPEN MESSAGE

In reply to an open message carried by Radio Baghdad for Custodian of the Two Holy Mosques King Fahd Ibn Abdulaziz, from Iraqi President Saddam Hussein, the Saudi monarch said:

"In the name of God, the most gracious, the most merciful:
The Almighty God said in the Holy Q'uran: There is a type of man whose speech about this world's life may dazzle thee, and he calls God to witness about what is in his heart, yet he is the most contentious of enemies".

President Saddam:

It is not our habit to address anyone even if he uses impolite style as you have done in your message, except with good words and morals and in line of the teachings of Islam because the Holy Q'uran says:
When the ignorant address them, they say "Peace".

In order to clarify facts, I reply some of your message's contents, which contained lies and distortion of facts.

Why do you try to ignore the direct cause of what has happened in the Arab arena, the division of ranks, turmoils and tragedies since your vicious aggression on an Arab, Muslim and secure country which supported your country when it faced difficulties?

Why did you not fulfill your promise to me and Egyptian President Hosni Mubarak that you would not launch an aggression on Kuwait?

After only few days from your pledge, you committed the most vicious crime in the history of mankind when you crept in with your army in the darkness and shed blood and expelled an entire nation to the desert in violation of all norms and values?

0154

Why did you mass troops and military equipment along the borders of the Kingdom of Saudi Arabia which supported you during your eight years of war whose fruits were lost in eight minutes along with bloods of one million persons killed in the war? Now you ask about the causes of the presence of the forces of the fraternal and friendly countries in the Kingdom ignoring your crimes?

I have tried to tackle the problem wisely and by good words taking into consideration the bonds of friendship which existed between me and you. And I did a lot to realize your desire when dispute erupted between you and the officials in Kuwait and the United Arab Emirates about the petroleum production and prices and I had called for an urgent meeting after consultations with the brothers in the GCC member states. Moreover, in coordination with my brother Hosni Mubarak, I did my best to contain the dispute about the issue of borders with Kuwait and made arrangements for the meeting of your envoy Izzat Ibrahim with Shaikh Saad Al -Abdullah Al-Sabah, the Kuwaiti heir apparent in Jeddah to enable the two sides review aspects of dispute, hoping to reach a solution acceptable by the two parties.

The meeting between the two parties was held in Jeddah without our interference. The two delegations (of Iraq and Kuwait), and we were hopeful that the second round of talks would be held in Baghdad but after hours, we were caught by surprise when the Iraqi forces invaded Kuwait on Thursday, August 2, 1990. When I heard the sad news, I immediately exchanged telephone calls with you to contain the problem and you dispatched to me Izzat Ibrahim who said to me that Kuwait is part of Iraq.

Hosni Mubarak called for the convening of an extraordinary Arab Summit in Cairo to give you a chance for an honourable retreat. I did my best in collaboration with the good-hearted Arab leaders to heal the rift, uplift injustice and return of the normal situation. Realizing the importance of the Arab solidarity and unity, and devoting efforts for the service of the main Arab causes, particularly the Palestinian problem. But you were planning something unknown to us. We were caught by surprise at the Arab League when some tried to support the injustice and aggression. This has a bad impression in the hearts of the sincere Arab leaders and people. This injury which you have caused will continue to bleed for years to come.

In unanimity, the entire world through the Arab, Islamic and international resolutions called for your immediate and unconditional withdrawal from Kuwait and the restoration of legitimacy to Kuwait as well as the withdrawal of your troops massed along the Kingdom's borders. Mediators from different countries have exerted intensive efforts to convince you to remove injustice and restore the situation that had prevailed before August 2, 1990, but you have rejected and insisted on continuing aggression claiming that Kuwait was part of Iraq. God knows that Kuwait was never under the Iraqi rule and the members of the family of Al-Sabah were rulers of Kuwait since about 250 years.

You say in your message - in a style which we will not match it - who authorized me to call the Arab, Islamic and friendly troops to the Kingdom. I have called these forces to the Kingdom realizing my responsibility towards the defence of my country. I have taken the right decision at the suitable time.

But who has authorized you to involve the Iraqi army and people in a bloody and fruitless war with Iran? Who authorized you to kill a million Iranian and Iraqi Muslims? Who authorized you to give up all the gains for what you had fought for in few moments? Who authorized you to occupy Kuwait and kill its sons, rape its women, loot its property and destroy its landmarks? No doubt, Satan and your covetousness have urged you to do so at the expense of the Arab Gulf countries which were proud of the Iraqi army.

The Almighty God says in the Holy Q'uran: "For those who ascribe false things to God, will never prosper".

You said in your message that we had only extended to you 11.53 million Dinar to contribute to the reconstruction of Al-Basra in addition to one million Dinar worth of equipment to reconstruct Fao.

But we would like to make facts clear:

Oh! ruler of Iraq, the Kingdom extended to your country $ 25,734,469,885.80 as follows:

Non-repayable aid	$ 5,843,287,671,23
Soft Cash Loans	$ 9,246,575,342.46
Development Loans	$ [illegible],[illegible]95,890,410.95
Military Equipment and Logistics	$ 3,739,184,077.85
Petroleum Aid	$ 6,751,159,583
Value of Industrial Products for Reconstruction of Al-Basra	$ 16,772,800
Due Payments for SABIC from Iraq	$ 20,266,667
Trucks, tractors, caterpillars, asphalt rollers (270 vehicles)	$ 21,333,333,50
TOTAL: Twenty Five Thousand and Seven Hundred and Thirty Four Million and Four Hundred and Sixty Nine Thousand and Eight Hundred and Eighty Five Dollars	$25,734,469,885.80

You said agreements and conventions are concluded between us including non-aggression agreements and non-interference in domestic affairs. Have you honoured these agreements when you massed your forces along the Kingdom's borders? How can we have confidence on a man who has violated his pledges and occupied a secured country for marginal dispute? Where are the conventions and where is the credibility of men?

You said in your message you are ready to make what has happened as an unhappy dream that will not prevent the return of the Saudi-Iraqi relations to their right and proper framework: No aggression and no foreigner, relations ruled by the Book of Allah and on the bases of the values of brotherhood and friendship and departure of the foreigner immediately, I would like to say as the Holy Q'uran said: "Produce your proof if you are truthful". The proof we are looking for, alongwith other countries of the world is your announcement for an immediate withdrawal from Kuwait to pave the way for the return of the normal situation under the leadership of Shaikh Jaber Al-Ahmed Al-Sabah, the Emir of Kuwait, and his government. And consequently, withdraw your forces from the Kingdom's borders. When you do so, all things will be solved.

I conclude my message by reiterating our just demand by asking you to take a brave decision and prove to the world that you are worthy of responsibility you are shouldering in ruling Iraq. If you do so, ,you will record an eternal stand which will be mentioned by history because by doing so, you would have avoided bloodshedding and preserved the souls of the innocents as well as the wealthy of the Arab and Muslim nations.

The Almighty God says in the Holy Q'uran: "Verily, never will God change the condition of a people until they change it themselves (with their own souls)".

-0-

0158

Royal Embassy of
Saudi Arabia
Seoul

93/1/436

January 21, 1991

Excellency,

I have the great honour and privilege to transmit herewith the Statement of the Government of the Custodian of the Two Holy Mosques concerning the initiation of military operations to liberate the brotherly State of Kuwait, and to restore its legitimate government, as issued on January 18, 1991. I am enclosing for this purpose a copy of the Statement in its original Arabic text and unofficial English translation.

I would like to convey likewise my sincerest appreciation and gratitude for Your Excellency's kind attention on this matter.

Please accept, Excellency, the assurances of my highest esteem and most cordial regards.

Sincerely yours,

Mohammed A. Al-Shewaihy
Ambassador

encls.: as stated

His Excellency
Lee Sang ock
Minister of Foreign Affairs
Republic of Korea

0159

Royal Embassy of
Saudi Arabia
Seoul

سفارة المملكة العربية السعودية
سيئول

Unofficial Translation

STATEMENT BY THE GOVERNMENT OF THE CUSTODIAN OF THE TWO HOLY MOSQUES CONCERNING THE INITIATION OF MILITARY OPERATIONS TO LIBERATE THE BROTHERLY STATE OF KUWAIT AND TO RESTORE ITS LEGITIMATE GOVERNMENT (January 18,1991)

* According to the execution of the Arab, Islamic and international resolutions especially the UNSC resolution no. 678 (1990), authorizing the use of all necessary measures to support and implement its resolution no. 660 (1990), and all the following resolutions in this regard, as long as Iraq does not implement these resolutions completely by January 15, 1991 or earlier, and the restoration of international peace and safety in the region; thus the armed forces of the Kingdom of Saudi Arabia, brotherly and friendly countries started their military operations to liberate the State of Kuwait from Iraqi occupation and restore its legitimacy, stressing in this regard its full commitment to the international treaties concerning military conflicts, and its awareness to lessen the civilian casualties as much as possible.

* The Kingdom of Saudi Arabia took this decision with consultations with the Governments of the brotherly and friendly countries which shouldered its historical responsibility in accordance with the UNSC resolution no. 678 (1990), and proved its commitment to the liberation of Kuwait from Iraqi occupation, if possible - peacefully, and by war, when there is no alternative left except war.

0160

* The Kingdom of Saudi arabia and many other peace and justice-loving countries of the world continued and concentrated their efforts to convince the Iraqi leadership to lift the oppression inflicted on the State of Kuwait, and to return the situations prevailing before the 2nd of Augst 1990. Initiatives followed initiatives and requests followed requests from the world leaders to achieve the legitimate and justified calls for the withdrawal of Iraqi occupation forces from the Kuwaiti territory and the return of the Kuwaiti legitimate government; but all these efforts and initiatives were met unfortunately by the insistence of the Iraqi leadership on the continuation of aggression and refusal to abide by the Arab, Islamic and international will. This was clearly evidenced lately when the Iraqi regime refused the personal efforts exerted by the Secretary General of the United Nations in his mission to Baghdad on January 12 and 13, 1991, as the Iraqi leaderhisp had refused before and after all the efforts which were supported by the Arab, Islamic and the European community, the non-aligned movement and many other popular and Islamic leaderships.

* Whatever any delay in the liberation of Kuwait will lead to, not only in the increase of sufferings of the brotherly people of Kuwait, the Arab and Islamic nations, and in the forefront - the brotherly Iraqi people themselves; and due to the insistence of the Iraqi regime on the choice of military confrontations, the Kingdom of Saudi Arabia found no way except to prove its

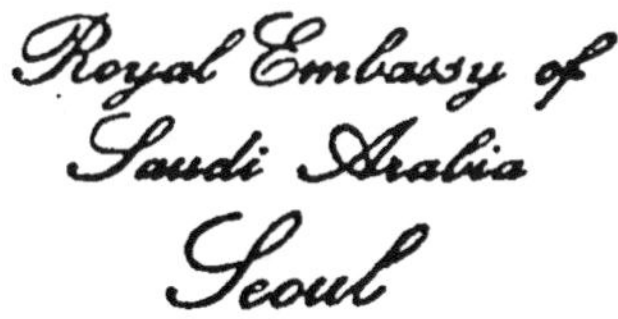

capabilities and confrontation, confirming at the same time its readiness to take the decision for peace and harmony when the Iraqi regime take the decision of peace, so that the brotherly people of Iraq may avoid more sufferings and destruction.

* The Kingdom of Saudi Arabia expresses its appreciation to the support and assistance given by the international community for the cause of righteousness, justice and legitimacy. The Kingdom confirms its willingness for the continuation of cooperation and consultation with the governments of brotherly and friendly countries for the restoration of righteousness, and expresses its hope for the end of military operations as quickly as possible so that peace and tranquility will prevail in this vital region of the world. We pray to God for support, success and victory. He is all Hearing and Answering.

-0-

0162

Room 801 –
기마늘
803
과업1만스원
이 담 두약인

بسم الله الرحمن الرحيم

Royal Embassy of
Saudi Arabia
Seoul

سفارة المملكة العربية السعودية
سيئول

بيـــــــــان

١٨ / ١ / ١٩٩١م

صادر عن حكومة خادم الحرمين الشريفين حول بدء العمليات

العسكريه لتحرير دولة الكويت الشقيقه واعادة الحكومه الشرعيه اليها

× انفاذا للقرارات العربيه والاسلاميه والدوليه وعلى الاخص قرار مجلس الامن الدولي رقم ٦٧٨ لعام ١٩٩٠م القاضي باستخدام جميع الوسائل اللازمه لدعم وتنفيذ قراره رقم ٦٦٠ لعام ١٩٩٠ وجميع القرارات اللاحقه ذات الصله ، مالم ينفذ العراق هذه القرارات تنفيذا كاملا في ١٥ كانون الثاني / يناير ١٩٩١ او قبله واعادة السلم والامن الدوليين الى نصابهما في المنطقه ، فقد بدات القوات المسلحه للمملكه العربيه السعوديه والدول الشقيقه والصديقه عملياتها العسكريه لتحرير دولة الكويت من الاحتلال العراقي الغاشم واعادة الشرعيه اليها ، موءكدة في هذا الصدد التزامها الكامل بالمعاهدات الدوليه النافذه بشان النزاعات المسلحه ، وحرصها على تقليل الخسائر المدنيه بقدر الامكان .

× لقد اتخذت المملكه العربيه السعوديه قرارها هذا بالتشاور مع حكومات الدول الشقيقه والصديقه التي تحملت مسوءوليتها التاريخيه وفق قرار مجلس الامن رقم ٦٧٨ لعام ١٩٩٠ ، واثبتت بذلك تصميمها على تحرير الكويت من الاحتلال العراقي سلما ما امكن السلم وحربا حين لا يبقى سوى الحرب .

× ولقد بذلت المملكه العربيه السعوديه والعديد من دول العالم المحبة للسلام والعدل جهودا متواصله ومكثفه لاقناع القياده العراقيه برفع الظلم عن دولة الكويت وعودة الامور الى ما

0163

Royal Embassy of
Saudi Arabia
Seoul

(٢)

كانت عليه قبل الثاني من اب / اغسطس ١٩٩٠ وتتالت المبادرات تلو المبادرات والمنشدات تلو المنشدات من القاده والزعماء لتحقيق المطالب العادله والمشروعه بانسحاب قوات الاحتلال العراقي من الاراضي الكويتيه وعودة الحكومه الشرعيه الكويتيه ، الا ان كل هذه الجهود والمبادرات والمناشدات قوبلت بكل اسف واسى باصرار القياده العراقيه على مواصلة العدوان واستمرار رفضها الامتثال للاراده العربيه والاسلاميه والدوليه ، وتجلى ذلك بوضوح موءخرا عندما رفض النظام العراقي الجهود الشخصيه المخلصه التي بذلها امين عام الامم المتحده في مهمته الى بغداد يومي ١٢ - ١٣ كانون الثاني / يناير ١٩٩١ ، كما رفض من قبل ومن بعد الجهود الاخرى التي ساندتها الدول العربيه والاسلاميه والجماعه الاوروبيه وحركة عدم الانحياز وكثير من القيادات والزعامات الشعبيه والاسلاميه .

× وحيث ان اى تاخير في تحرير دولة الكويت سيوءدى ليس فقط الى زيادة معاناة الشعب الكويتي الشقيق بل الى زيادة معاناة الامه العربيه والاسلاميه وفي مقدمتها الشعب العراقي الشقيق نفسه ، وامام اصرار النظام العراقي على اختيار قرار المجابهه العسكريه لم تجد المملكه العربيه السعوديه بدا من اثبات قدرتها على المجابهه ، موءكدة في الوقت نفسه استعدادها لاتخاذ قرار السلام والوئام عندما يتخذ النظام العراقي قرار السلام ليجنب بذلك شعب العراق الشقيق المزيد من الدمار والالام .

× والمملكه العربيه السعوديه اذ تعرب عن تقديرها للدعم والتاييد والمسانده التي قدمتها الاسره الدوليه مناصرة للحق والعدل والشرعيه ، فانها توءكد رغبتها في الاستمرار بالتعاون والتشاور

0164

(٣)

مع حكومات الدول الشقيقه والصديقه ليعود الحق الى نصابه ، وتعرب عن املها في انتهاء العمليات العسكريه باسرع وقت ممكن ليعود السلم والامن الى ربوع هذه المنطقه الحيويه من العالم ،   والله نرجو ان يمدنا بعونه وتوفيقه ونصره انه سميع مجيب .

....

0165

ROYAL EMBASSY OF SAUDI ARABIA

NEWS BULLETIN

No.7/91 February 22,1991

PRESS OFFICE
1-112, Shinmoon-ro, 2-Ka
Chongro-gu, Seoul 110-062,
Republic of Korea

0166

KING FAHD EXPRESSED DISAPPOINTMENT OVER ASTRAYED ARAB LEADERSHIPS AND RECALLED SAUDI ARABIA'S EFFORTS TO HAVE PREVENTED THE WAR

King Fahd ibn Abdulaziz, Custodian of the Two Holy Mosques, in his speech on February 18, 1991, before the "Jihad" Convention, organized by Imam Mohammed ibn Saud Islamic University in Riyadh, said that over six months the Arab and Islamic nation has experienced great sorrow and tribulation that has deeply affected faithful Muslims everywhere.

In his speech, read on his behalf by H.R.H. Prince Sultan ibn Abdulaziz, Second Deputy Premier, Defense and Aviation Minister and Inspector General, the monarch added, "Indeed six months ago, Iraq unleashed its troops along the Saudi borders, acts which shook the conscience of ordinary human beings worldwide."

"As a matter of fact, the Iraqi regime had cast aside all noble principles and values before embarking on its inhuman invasion and its despicable act of war. And yet, inspite of all this, we fondly imagined that it could well be a horrendous act of misjudgement which would soon be followed by an act of withdrawal."

The monarch added, "With these thoughts uppermost, we gave full rein to diplomatic efforts and all good offices to try our bounden best to prevent the evils of war which have embroiled the Arab Gulf Region today."

"Later on, when the crisis grew, I expressed my willingness to act as an honest mediator between Iraq and Kuwait in a bid to defuse the matter. President Saddam seemed to welcome this suggestion of mine. I therefore got in touch immediately with Shaikh Jaber of Kuwait, who in turn, welcomed the suggestion. Further support was also readily forthcoming from my brother President Hosni Mubarak. But it was all in vain and sad to say, we all found ourselves in the midst of an Arab tragedy - the like of which was completely unknown throughout Arab history. It was, in fact, a terrible tragedy of gigantic proportions - a heinous crime that has shamed the entire Arab world."

0167

King Fahd pointed out, "Contacts with all parties and well-wishers everywhere were multiplied over and over again. A vast miscellany of regional and international calls (redolent of brotherly goodwill and deep compassion) were continuously made by world leaders and prominent personalities all over the globe to avert the internecine strife and to avert impending bloodshed - but the Iraqi leadership went on in its intransigent way. Iraq seemed to think that the pursuit of peace was an act of sheer weakness and utter powerlessness on the part of the peacemakers."

"At this point, we had no option but to face down the aggressor by calling on Arab and Islamic states together with many friendly countries to support our Saudi Armed Forces in defending the Kingdom and taking part in freeing the State of Kuwait."

King Fahd added, "Now, what hurts me is to witness Arab leaderships that have gone astray, and that have cast their lot in with the aggressor by supporting him to the hilt."

"I really don't know why these Arab leaderships have taken their strange stands behind Saddam Hussein who has been judged by the entire world as the root cause of all the catastrophes that have engulfed the Arab world, and who has been held solely responsible for bypassing all opportunities for effecting withdrawal, and who has blatantly and wilfully insisted on continuing the occupation of Kuwait."

"It is indeed strange to see these leaderships today shedding tears over Saddam Hussein's failures to stem the tides of destruction that are overwhelming his country and his army. These misguided sympathizers of his are stopping their ears against the scores of missiles fired against the cities of the peace-loving inhabitants of Saudi Arabia who have been honoured by Almighty God to serve, alongside the Kingdom's government, the needs of the two Holy Cities (Makkah and Madinah), and the Two Holy Mosques - when all the while Saddam Hussein falsely asserts that he is defending Islam and all it stands for."

The monarch went on to say, "It is within the capacity of the Iraqi regime to avoid further horrors that clearly await its nation, and indeed, the entire Gulf Region by the simple expedient of a total unconditional and immediate withdrawal from Kuwait and from the Saudi borders."

"This auspicious occasion which Imam Mohammed ibn Saud Islamic University has brought about today is living evidence of our insistence on continuing our struggle (Jihad) without any hesitation or lukewarmness whatsoever. Indeed, this joyous occasion is also clear evidence of the oneness that pervaded our nation - that has purposed in its heart to continue till the defense of our homeland is assured and full withdrawal attained."

"I am also most happy to witness the many visitors from the Kingdom and abroad who are gathered here in our midst to share in our joy."

King Fahd added," It is also germane to the issue here to state that men of knowledge and culture, journalists and information media specialists as well as poets - all these and their ilk are warriors who are faithfully serving in the realms of thought and considered opinion, as well as warriors in the cause of faith."

"Finally, I beseech Almighty God to preserve this our homeland from all ills and grant it full security on all sides forevermore.

HIGHLIGHTS OF INTERVIEW WITH H.R.H. PRINCE BANDAR IBN SULTAN IBN ABDULAZIZ, SAUDI AMBASSADOR TO WASHINGTON AS FEATURED IN " LARRY KING LIVE " (CNN)

His Royal Highness Prince Bandar ibn Sultan ibn Abdulaziz, Saudi Ambassador to Washington was interviewed for a full hour in "Larry King Live", aired by CNN on the eve of February 14, 1991.

Prince Bandar, known for his eloquent manner of speaking and sharp, honest and straightforward comments, touched on several issues pertaining to the Gulf War.

The prince was very optimistic that the coalition will win the war, saying that the activities to liberate Kuwait were going very well for the allied forces. " I think right will prevail over wrong. I think Saddam Hussein will lose. That I know for sure. The question is we hope he lose with minimum bloodshed. And we are trying our best to communicate with the Iraqi troops in Kuwait, - by pamphlets, by loud speaker, by other means...But, we hope that we can get them to give up the fight to their Arab brothers."

Along this line, Prince Bandar expressed , " It is sad that it had come to war. We hoped that Saddam Hussein will come to his senses and spare us all the tragedy of war. He didn't...

Prince Bandar, who is also a fighter pilot, remarked that he was surprised to see the lack of Iraqi response since the war began, " I have great respect for the Iraqi people and the Iraqi armed forces, both the soldiers and the pilots, and I did not expect to see the performance of lack of it, that we have seen. This tells me one thing. Their hearts and guts are not in it. They know they are not fighting for a justified cause. It's not a strategy." The prince further commented on the Iraqi soldiers' suffering from low morale and lack of motivation "since Saddam Hussein went through an eight year war with Iran, lost half a million dead, killed half a million brother Muslims dead, and at the end of all of that he gave away everything that he won over night. So, the Iraqi soldier right now is saying -"Should I loose my life in Kuwait, and then he will give it away? Is it worth fighting for? And these are legitimate reasons."

As for the bombing of Iraq on February 13, 1991, the prince expressed his indignation, " It was tragic. Anytime innocent civilians are killed, that is tragic and sad. But I am not only sad. I am angry. I am angry at Saddam Hussein for putting his own people and his own country - his whole country - in harm's way only to satisfy his own ego." Prince Bandar went on further to say that this act of the Iraqi regime was a military set up, and there's no doubt about it.

When reminded that Saddam Hussein might be watching the show that night, and that it might be a mistake for Prince Bandar to attack the Iraqi leader, lest it angers him, the Prince very bravely explained, "...People say don't demonize Saddam Hussein. Don't call him Hitler. ...The fact is that Hitler became a Hitler because we allowed him to continue to be. Saddam Hussein is in his early stages of being a Hitler. He is a Hitler. If we appease him now, we will end up with a Hitler."

Prince Bandar went on to say that Saddam Hussein had really lost his credibility. He recounted an incident which happened in April, proving that the dictator is really a liar. Prince Bandar further explained that in the wake that Saddam Hussein was bombing civilian areas in Israel and Saudi Arabia," I have always believed that Saddam Hussein was never going to attack Israel in a serious way...Because he told me so. I was with Saddam Hussein and this is important for my Arab brothers who are watching and particularly the Palestinians who think this guy is the champion of their cause. He isn't. " The prince recalled that two days later after Saddam Hussein stated that he would burn half of Israel, the prince saw him at the Iraqi President's request. Saddam Hussein wanted Prince Bandar to "go assure President Bush and Prime Minister Thatcher that he didn't mean it, and that he said it just to mobilize his people." Prince Bandar finally threw a question, "Now, is this the man that now tells us that he is championing the Palestinian cause.?"

In line with this Israeli issue, Prince Bandar criticized Saddam Hussein as wanting to make the Gulf conflict appear to the Arab masses as an Arab-Israeli conflict, which has nothing to do with it. "The truth of the matter, the most damage that has been done to the Arab cause vis-a-vis the Palestinian-Israeli conflict was done not by Israel but by Saddam Hussein. We had won the world support and fifty percent of the Israeli public support for the fact of the inadmissibility of acquiring land by force and annexing it. And here comes Saddam Hussein, a brother Arab, occupied an Arab country. That is the most - I think that is the most devastating thing aybody could have done to the Palestinians and guess who did it, - Saddam Hussein."

Prince Bandar also sharply criticized the people who have taken sides with Saddam Hussein. For King Hussein of Jordan for instance, the prince commented, " He is irrelevant now. He has betrayed us as his friends for 40 years and took the side of Saddam Hussein and therefore he earned our disrespect." The prince did not discount the possibility that King Hussein might have been worried that Saddam Hussein might go to Jordan. Ironically, Prince Bandar commented that if that was the case, King Hussein should have joined the winning side, not the losing side. Prince Bandar even recalled that although Iraq has the world's largest fourth army in the world, King Fahd stood up and said no to Saddam Hussein, unlike King Hussein who didn't have the guts to say no.

As for the position of the other countries towards the war, Prince Bandar affirmed that "the meeting of President Gorbachev with the Kuwaiti foreign minister is a positive sign and it just shows that all respectable countries of the world still recognize Kuwait as a state-nation regardless of what Saddam and his friends feel. I must say that President Gorbachev and the Soviet Union have been very positive on the Gulf policy..." As for Iran, the prince remarked, " I believe that Iran could play a very positive role if they continue in their public stated position, which is neutrality and which is non-acceptance of the occupation of Kuwait." Concerning rumors that Syria might be rethinking of leaning differently towards Israel, Prince Bandar explained that "Syria is a very important country not just now, but for the peace process in the future."

Prince Bandar stressed that Saudi Arabia is a strong advocate of peace. "We would like to have peace in the Middle East. Peace in our part of the world means better for everybody, not just for my country or for Israel, but for the Palestinians and everybody. King Fahd has been a champion of peace in the region. In 1981, he had what was called as the Fahd plan which then became the Fez declaration which is the first ever the Arab world collectively at the summit level says we want to solve the Middle East problem by peaceful means. So, Saudi Arabia and King Fahd personally have been champions of peace. I believe that the elimination of Saddam Hussein and his kind and what he represents will mean a better chance for peace and I promise you, Saudi Arabia will be in the forefront of working hard to achieve peace in the Middle East."

Prince Bandar emphatically said however, that in case Kuwait will be liberated, either if Saddam Hussein leaves or he be forced out, Saddam Hussein's fate rests on the Iraqi people themselves. "I believe the best vindicator for all of us are the Iraqi people. They know what this man is and know what he has done to them." He added that it will not be the Iraqi people's problem to take care of Saddam Hussein, but it will be their privilege, on the other hand.

The prince stressed that Saudi Arabia and its friends will do whatever it takes to liberate Kuwait. He rejected the term burden-sharing in referring to the cost of the war. "We don't consider defending our country a burden. We think the appropriate term is that we must have responsibility sharing. If King Fahd and the Saudi people are willing to put the lives of our soldiers on the line, expose the citizens of our country to harm's way, then obviously money and dollars are not going to be more expensive than human lives. Within that context, we are grateful and appreciative to the American Congress for supporting us in our moments of need and we don't think therefore that any amount of dollars will be too expensive to help our friends and pick up part of the burden."

Finally, Prince Bandar expressed hope that the war will end sooner than later. "I think the American people, the coalition countries and the world at large should rest assured that we are on the right side against wrong, we represent international legality, and we have the moral high ground, and we will prevail against this evil. This man is not just a tyrant. He is a criminal, and we must not be, not let our spirit be dampened when people like some of the voices that support him attack us."

-0-

0173

3. 기 타

0174

"No Democracy Without Popular Congresses"

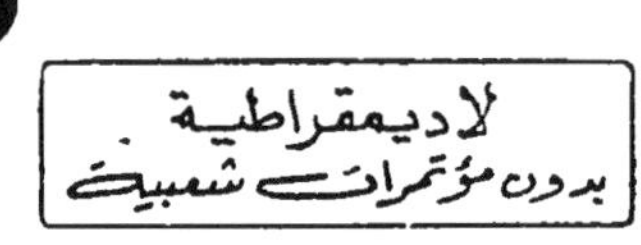

PEOPLE'S BUREAU OF
THE SOCIALIST PEOPLE'S LIBYAN
ARAB JAMAHIRIYA
SEOUL.
C.P.O. BOX NO. 8418
TEL. 797-6001~7 6

المكتب الشعبى
للجماهيرية العربية الليبية
الشعبية الاشتراكية
سيــول

Our Ref. 22
Ref.

Date

The People's Bureau of the Great Socialist People's Libyan Arab Jamahiriya in Seoul presents its compliments to the esteemed Ministry of Foreign Affairs of the Republic of Korea and has the honour to inform the Ministry that the Secretary for Public Unilities and Public Works was appointied Head of Libyan Arab Joint Committee in succession to the Secretary for Health.

The People's Bureau of the Great Socialist People's Libyan Arab Jamahiriya avails itself of this opportunity to renew to the Ministry of Foreign Affairs of the Republic of Korea the assurances of its highest consideration. علم

Seoul January 11. 1991

To : Ministry of Foreign Affairs
of the Republic of Korea

0175

With the Compliments

of the Hungarian Embassy

0176

Embassy of the Republic of Hungary

Seoul

HUNGARY NEWS January 23, 1991

The Ministry of Foreign Affairs of the Republic of Hungary has released the following government statement:

The Government of the Republic of Hungary on the basis of her historical experience and as a matter of principle is unable to accept actions in flagrant violation of the sovereignty of individual states, rejects all forms of aggression and firmly stands for the maintenance or, if necessary, the restoration of international legal order.

On the basis of these principles Hungary has deeply condemned the annexation of and the aggression against the state of Kuwait in August, 1990. Hungary has been committed to and has fully implemented all UN Security Council resolutions regarding the Iraqi aggression against Kuwait in the sincere hope that the united stand of the international community will compel the Iraqi leadership to dismantle the consequences of aggression.

The Iraqi leadership in defiance of the will of the international community refused to adhere to the norms and stipulations of international law. Up until the final deadline set by the UN Security Council Iraq had shown no readiness to withdraw its troops from Kuwait and had given no indication at all that it intended to seek a peaceful settlement of the conflict. All diplomatic endeavours proven to be unsuccessful, all opportunities to find a negotiated settlement had been exhausted. Thus, the international forces encorporating Arab units deployed in the region have become compelled to make use of the authorization of the UN Security Council to uphold international law and employ all means at their disposal to enforce the mandatory resolutions of the United Nations.

The Hungarian people are aware that war is an undesirable solution to conflicts, a necessary evil even in the most righteous cause. The Hungarian people are, however, also conscious of the lessons of human history: aggression must be arrested, aggressors must be stopped irrespective of sacrifices.

0177

The Government of the Republic of Hungary sincerely hopes that the military operations aimed at the liberation of Kuwait will remain limited both in time and scope, and will lead to the restoration of the sovereignty, territorial integrity of Kuwait and the security of all countries in the region with the least loss of life and damage. In keeping with her possibilities Hungary will contribute to these efforts, and all her steps taken will continue to be aimed only at the elimination of aggression and its consequences and will in no way be directed against the people of Iraq.

The Republic of Hungary is confident that in the wake of the just solution of the conflict new opportunities will open up to restore and enhance cooperation with Iraq and the other states in the region, to the creation of a regional security system, to solve decades old conflicts.

0178

بسم الله الرحمن الرحيم

Sultanate of Oman
Ministry of Communication
Telex : 3390 MWASALAT ON
Cable : Communications
P.O. Box : 684
MUSCAT

سلطنة عمان
وزارة المواصلات
تلكس : ٣٣٩٠ مواصلات اوان
برقيا : المواصلات
ص.ب : ٦٨٤
مسقط

Our Ref. :   اشارتنا :

Date :   التاريخ :

PRESS RELEASE

Ministry of Communication announces, there was no truth in reports repeated by some air and marine transport authorities about Omani air space and territorial waters last week. These reports claimed that there were restsictions on the use of Omani air space and territorial waters for international traffic.

The Ministry confirms: Omani airports and Sea Ports are open to international traffic on continuous basis and were never closed.

Omani airport and Sea ports are operated in high efficiency and according to International Standards. The Ministry said and added " Omani Ports are not included and sited out areas restricted by military activities presently going on in the Gulf Northern Areas". MOC express its hopes that Air and maritime Companies will find a definite reply on all arisen questions and promised to grant them all help and assistance whether their Cargo are exported to Oman or other areas in the Gulf in cluded that one listed nowdays as restricted area.

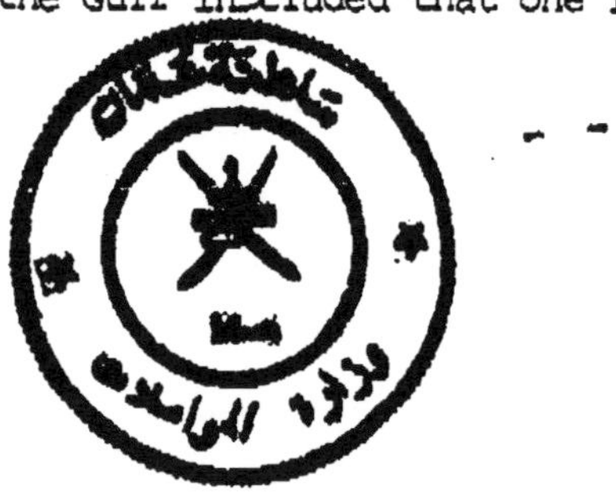

0179

2. 7 11:35 교통부 항공국 FAX 송부
2. 7 11:40 해운항만청 해운국에 FAX 송부

Embassy of
the Sultanate of Oman
R. of Korea - Seoul

سفارة سلطنة عمان
في جمهورية كوريا
سيئول

Ref.: 2171/22170/131701/67/91 الرقم:

Date: Feb. 6, 1991 التاريخ:

The Embassy of the Sultanate of Oman in Seoul presents its compliments to the Ministry of Foreign Affairs of the Republic of Korea and has the honour to enclose herewith a press release from the Ministry of Communication of the Sultanate of Oman which stresses the fact that the Omani Airports and Sea ports are open to International traffic on continuous basis and were never closed.

This Embassy will be greatful if this press release is circulated to the concern authorities of the Korean government.

The Embassy of the Sultanate of Oman in Seoul avails itself of this opportunity to renew to the Ministry of Foreign Affairs of the Republic of Korea the assurances of its highest consideration.

Ministry of Foreign Affairs
Republic of Korea
Seoul

Encl: stated above

0180

외교문서 비밀해제: 걸프 사태 31

걸프 사태 전망 및 분석, 안보협력 문제, 언론 자료 2

초판인쇄 2024년 03월 15일
초판발행 2024년 03월 15일

지은이 한국학술정보(주)
펴낸이 채종준
펴낸곳 한국학술정보(주)
주 소 경기도 파주시 회동길 230(문발동)
전 화 031-908-3181(대표)
팩 스 031-908-3189
홈페이지 http://ebook.kstudy.com
E-mail 출판사업부 publish@kstudy.com
등 록 제일산-115호(2000. 6. 19)

ISBN 979-11-6983-991-4 94340
979-11-6983-960-0 94340 (set)

책에 대한 더 나은 생각, 끊임없는 고민, 독자를 생각하는 마음으로 보다 좋은 책을 만들어갑니다.

우루과이라운드

지적재산권 협상

우루과이라운드

지적재산권 협상

한국학술정보

| 머리말

우루과이라운드는 국제적 교역 질서를 수립하려는 다각적 무역 교섭으로서, 각국의 보호무역 추세를 보다 완화하고 다자무역체제를 강화하기 위해 출범되었다. 1986년 9월 개시가 선언되었으며, 15개 분야의 교섭을 1990년 말까지 진행하기로 했다. 그러나 각 분야의 중간 교섭이 이루어진 1989년 이후에도 농산물, 지적소유권, 서비스무역, 섬유, 긴급수입제한 등 많은 분야에서 대립하며 1992년이 돼서야 타결에 이를 수 있었다. 한국은 특히 농산물 분야에서 기존 수입 제한 품목 대부분을 개방해야 했기에 큰 경쟁력 하락을 겪었고, 관세와 기술 장벽 완화, 보조금 및 수입 규제 정책의 변화로 제조업 수출입에도 많은 변화가 있었다.

본 총서는 우루과이라운드 협상이 막바지에 다다랐던 1991~1992년 사이 외교부에서 작성한 관련 자료를 담고 있다. 관련 협상의 치열했던 후반기 동향과 관계부처회의, 무역협상위원회 회의, 실무대책회의, 규범 및 제도, 투자회의, 특히나 가장 많은 논란이 있었던 농산물과 서비스 분야 협상 등의 자료를 포함해 총 28권으로 구성되었다. 전체 분량은 약 1만 3천여 쪽에 이른다.

2024년 3월

한국학술정보(주)

| 일러두기

· 본 총서에 실린 자료는 2022년 4월과 2023년 4월에 각각 공개한 외교문서 4,827권, 76만여 쪽 가운데 일부를 발췌한 것이다.

· 각 권의 제목과 순서는 공개된 원본을 최대한 반영하였으나, 주제에 따라 일부는 적절히 변경하였다.

· 원본 자료는 A4 판형에 맞게 축소하거나 원본 비율을 유지한 채 A4 페이지 안에 삽입하였다. 또한 현재 시점에선 공개되지 않아 '공란'이란 표기만 있는 페이지 역시 그대로 실었다.

· 외교부가 공개한 문서 각 권의 첫 페이지에는 '정리 보존 문서 목록'이란 이름으로 기록물 종류, 일자, 명칭, 간단한 내용 등의 정보가 수록되어 있으며, 이를 기준으로 0001번부터 번호가 매겨져 있다. 이는 삭제하지 않고 총서에 그대로 수록하였다.

· 보고서 내용에 관한 더 자세한 정보가 필요하다면, 외교부가 온라인상에 제공하는 『대한민국 외교사료요약집』 1991년과 1992년 자료를 참조할 수 있다.

| 차례

정 리 보 존 문 서 목 록					
기록물종류	일반공문서철	등록번호	2019090032	등록일자	2019-09-05
분류번호	764.51	국가코드		보존기간	영구
명 칭	UR(우루과이라운드) / TRIPs(지적재산권) 협상 그룹 회의, 1991. 전2권				
생 산 과	통상기구과	생산년도	1991~1991	담당그룹	다자통상
권 차 명	V.1 2-6월				
내용목차					

0001

분류번호 | 보존기간

발 신 전 보

번 호 : WGV-0188 910207 1559 FK 종별 :

수 신 : 주 제네바 대사. 총영사 대리

발 신 : 장 관 (통기)

제 목 : UR / TRIPS 주관부처 변경 통보

UR/TRIPS 협상의 주관부서가 아래와 같이 변경 되었으니 참고바람.

1. 이관대상 업무 : GATT/UR 지적재산권 협상 전반

2. 이관내역

   o 현 행 : 경제기획원 대외조정실

   o 변 경 : 특허청 기획관리관실

3. 이관일시 : 1991. 1.14일부터

4. 이관사유 : 지적소유권 분야의 협상이 마무리 단계에 있음을 감안, 향후 국내 관련제도 개선 및 보완의 효율적 추진을 도모할 수 있는 특허청에서 동 협상을 전담. 끝.

(통상국장 김삼훈)

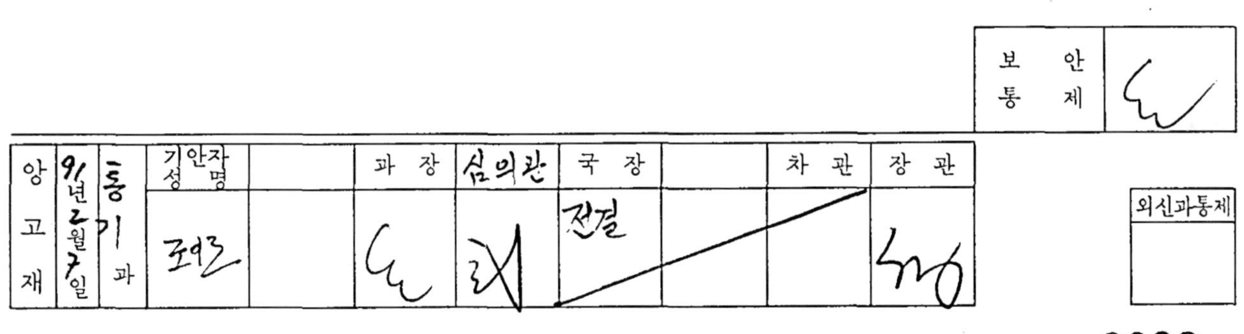

0002

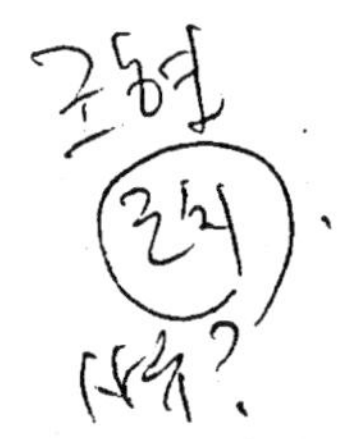

특　　　　허　　　　청

국협 28140- 528　　　　568-6077　　　　1991. 2. 5.

수신 외무부장관

참조 통상국장

제목 UR/TRIPs 주관부처 변경통보 의뢰

UR/지적재산권 협상의 주관부처가 별첨문서 사본과 같이 경제기획원으로부터 특허청으로 이관되었음을 알려드리오니 업무에 참고하시기 바라며, 동 내용을 주제네바대표부에 아래와 같이 통보하여 주시기 바랍니다.

아　　　　래

1. 이관대상 업무 : GATT/UR 지적재산권 협상 전반
2. 이관내역
   - o 현 행 : 경제기획원 대외조정실
   - o 변 경 : 특허청 기획관리관실
3. 이관일시 : 1991. 1. 14일부터
4. 기타 사항
   - o UR/지적재산권 협상에 특허청 파견 주재관 활용

첨부 경제기획원 관련문서 사본 1부.

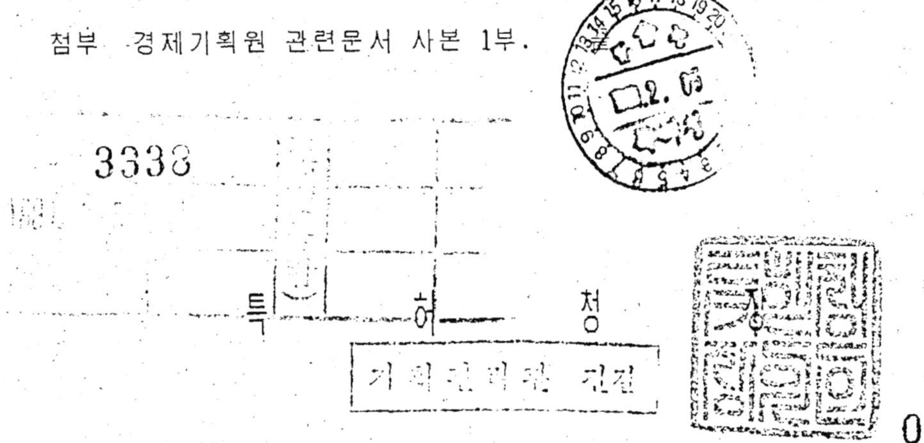

3338

특　　　허　　　청

0003

경 제 기 획 원

통조삼 10502- 32　　　503-9149　　　1991. 1. 14.

수신 특허청장

참조 국제협력과장

제목 UR/TRIPs협상 주관의뢰

1. UR/지적소유권협상과 관련하여 그동안 당원에서는 협상대응방안 및 아국입장 정립을 위하여 관련부처 및 귀청과의 협의하에 지적소유권분야 의제를 주관하여 왔는바,

2. 지적소유권분야의 협상이 마무리 단계에 있어 향후 국내관련제도 개선 및 보완의 보다 효율적인 추진측면에서 귀청에 UR/TRIPs협상의 주관을 의뢰하니 귀청은 향후 협상대책과 국내보완책을 마련하여 계속 추진하여 주시기 바랍니다.　끝.

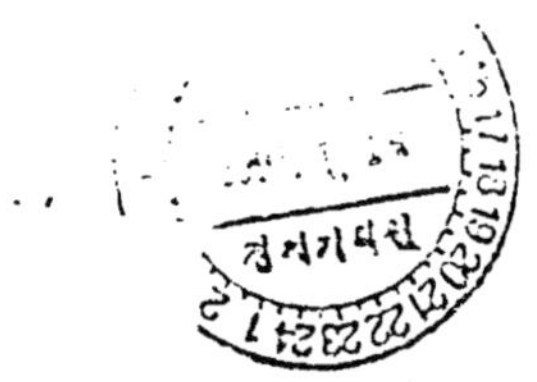

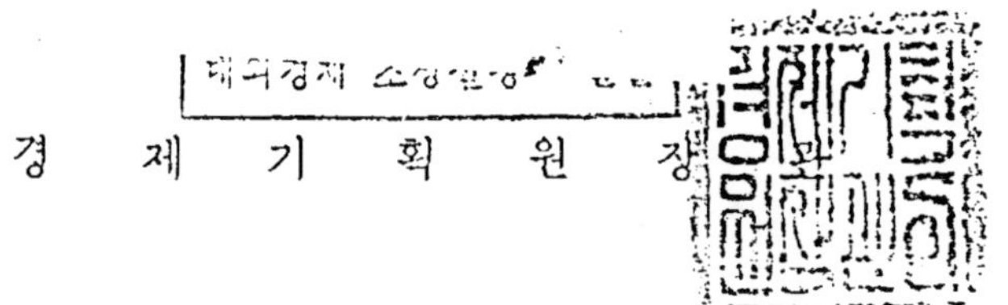

경 제 기 획 원 장

0004

오인

→ 회

주인도대사관

인도(상)2065-134　　　　　　　　　　　　　　　　91.2.22

수신 : 외무부장관

참조 : 통상국장, 주제네바 대표부대사(본부경유), 상공부 국제협력관

제목 : U.R. 관련자료 송부

인도의 National Working Group on Patent Laws 로부터 별첨과 같이 U.R. 관련자료를 송부하여 왔아오니 참고 하시기 바랍니다.

첨부 : U.R. 관련자료 1부.　끝.

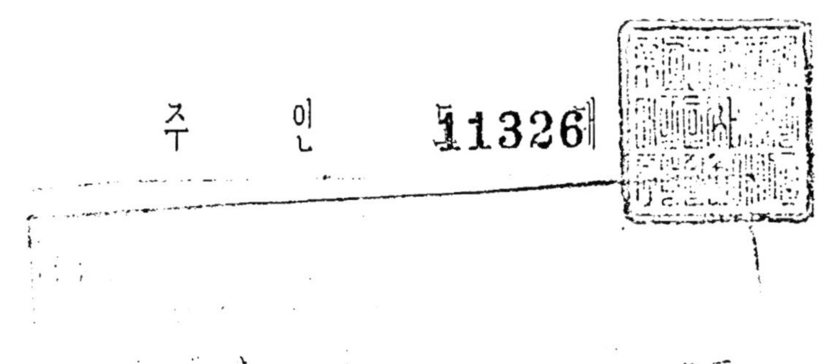

0005

National Working Group on Patent Laws

79, Nehru Place (First Floor), New Delhi-110 019 (India)

M. H. Kim

FEBRUARY 14, 1991

CHAIRMAN
DR NITYA NAND
Ex-Director
Central Drug Research Institute

CO-CHAIRMAN
DR SURENDRA J PATEL
Ex-Director
United Nations Conference on Trade & Development

CONVENOR
MR B K KEAYLA
Forum For Preservation of Indian Patent Laws

CONVENOR CORE GROUP
DR RAJEEV DHAVAN
Public Interest, Legal Support & Research Centre

JOINT CONVENOR
MR DINESH ABROL
CSIR Scientific Workers' Assn

JT. CONVENOR CORE GROUP
DR BISWAJIT DHAR
Res & Infn. System for Non-Aligned & Dev. Countries

MEMBERS
PROF S K MUKERJEE
Ex-Head & Prof of Em IARI

DR AMIT SEN GUPTA
Delhi Science Forum

DR MIRA SHIVA
Voluntary Health Assn of India

DR V PANIKULANGARA
Pub Int Law Service Society

DR N N MEHROTRA
Academy of Young Scientists

MR N I GANDHI
Indian Drug Mfrs Assn

WING COMDR SATNAM SHAH
Consumers Forum

MR K ASHOK RAO
National Confn. of Officers' Assn. of P S. Undertakings

MR BALRAJ MEHTA
Senior Journalist

MR L P.S. SRIVASTAVA
Forum For Financial Writers

MR DINESH PATEL
Forum For Preservation of Indian Patent Laws

MR J S MAJUMDAR
National Compaign Committee on Drug Policy

MR HARDEV SINGH
All India Lawyers Union

MR V KRISHNAN
International Marketing Forum

Dear H.E. Mr. Kim,

In our letter dated January 8, 1991 (copy attached) we had informed you about the Brain-Storming Workshop on 'Proposals Before the Uruguay Round of GATT Negotiations' organised by our Group on 30th December, 1990. Copies of the Resolution and the Statement adopted at the Workshop were sent to you for transmitting them to the concerned Officials who represented your country at the Multilateral Trade Negotiations of the Uruguay Round held at Brussels in December, 1990.

The papers presented by various experts during the Workshop have since been published in a book entitled ' GATT Negotiations : Economic Sovereignty in Jeopardy'. ~~Four~~ Three copies of this publication are sent herewith. Kindly have them passed on to the following officials of your country :

1. H.E. Mr. ~~Pil Soo Park~~ Bong Suh Lee,
   ~~Ambassador, Minister~~
   Minister of Tarde and Industry
2. H.E. ~~Sang Ock Lee~~ Soo Gil Park,
   Ambassador,
   Permanent Observer to the United Nations Office and
   Permanent Representative to the International Organizations,
   Geneva

We hope these officials would find this publication useful in assessing the serious implication of GATT proposals on the economic sovereignty of the developing countries.

Thanking you and with kind regards,

Yours sincerely,

(B. K. KEAYLA)
CONVENOR

Encls : As above

H.E. Mr. Taezhee Kim,
Ambassador,
Embassy of the Republic of Korea,
NEW DELHI

Phone : 641-5089 Telex : 031-62110, Fax : (91-11) 6430633

0006

National Working Group on Patent Laws

79, Nehru Place (First Floor), New Delhi-110 019 (India)

JANUARY 8, 1991

Dear

The National Working Group on Patent Laws (India) organised a Brain-Storming Workshop on 'Proposals before the Uruguay Round of GATT Negotiations' on December 30, 1990 in the Conference Room of India International Centre, New Delhi. The Workshop was divided into the following four Sessions :

SESSION-I 09.30 AM- 10.30 AM	:	OVERVIEW OF LATEST GATT PROPOSALS
SESSION-II 10.45 AM- 01.00 PM	:	SECTORAL ISSUES : TRIPS
SESSION-III 02.00 PM- 03.45 PM	:	SECTORAL ISSUES : TRIMS, SERVICES AND OTHER ISSUES
SESSION - IV 04.00 PM- 05.00PM	:	CONCLUDING SESSION

A large number of eminent Scientists, Legal Experts, Economists and representatives of Voluntary Organizations, Industry and Trade Unions, etc. participated in the Workshop.

The Workshop extensively deliberated on the agenda during the four Sessions and unanimously adopted a Resolution and a Statement on Proposals in the Uruguay Round of Negotiations in GATT.

Three copies of the Resolution and Statement are sent herewith. On behalf of the National Working Group, I would request you to kindly transmit these copies to the following officials of your country for their use. We find that they represented your country at the Multi-lateral Trade negotiations of the Uruguay Round held at Brussels early last month :

We hope that you would kindly give due importance to our request and forward these papers to the above-mentioned officials urgently.

Thanking you and with kind regards,

Yours sincerely,

(B. K. KEAYLA)
CONVENOR

0007

Phone : 641-5089 Telex : 031-62110, Fax : (91-11) 6430633

2 copy-인

원 본

외 무 부

종 별 :

번 호 : GVW-0347 일 시 : 91 0222 1830

수 신 : 장 관(통기,경기원,재무부,농림수산부,상공부,특허청)

발 신 : 주 제네바 대사대리

제 목 : UR/TRMIS 및 TRIPS 협상

2.22(금) DUNKEL 의장 (TNC 의장 자격)은 브랏셀 회의 결과 의장이 부여한 MANDATE에 따라 표제 회의를 개최한다고 선언하고 아래 요지와 같이 향후 회의일정 및 회의 진행절차에 관해 설명하였음. (참석 박영우 공사,엄낙용재무관,김준규서기관)

1. TRIMS 및 TRIPS 협상에 관한 회의를 91.3.18(월) 오후에 개최함.

2. TRIMS: 브랏셀 회의에 제출할 합의된 협상기초가 없었고 COMMENTARY (갓트 문서 MTN.TNC/2/35/REV.1 페이지 238)만 있었다고 말하고 각국대표들이 TRIMS 협상에 대한 의견 개진과동 COMMENTARY 에 의거 기술적 차원에서의 협상을 진행토록 제의함.

TRIPS: 브랏셀 회의에 제출한 협상문서 (갓트문서 MTN.TNC/W/35.REV. 1 페이지194-195)가 향후 협상의 기초가 될것이며 협상진행은 현재까지의 TRIPS 협상 현황을 검토하고 현단계에서 진행할 기술적 차원의 작업분야 확인등을 의제로 토의를 진행토록 제의 함.

첨부: 의장 발표문 1부

(GVW(F)-0077). 끝

(대사대리 박영우-국장)

통상국 2차보 경기원 재무부 농수부 상공부 특허청

PAGE 1 91.02.23 09:25 WG

외신 1과 통제관 0008

.91
10.30

GVW(F)-0077
10222 1800
GVW-JC7 724

TRIMS AND TRIPS

Friday, 22 February 1991, a.m.

Note for Chairman

1. In his closing remarks at the Brussels Ministerial Meeting, Minister Gros Espiell requested me to pursue intensive consultations with the specific objective of achieving agreements in all the areas of the negotiating programme in which differences remain outstanding. These consultations will, he said, be based on document MTN.TNC/W/35/Rev.1, dated 3 December 1990, including the cover page which refers to the Surveillance Body and the communications which various participants sent to Brussels. He added that I would also take into account the considerable amount of work carried out at the Brussels meeting, although it did not commit any delegation.

2. I suggest that the meeting first address TRIMs and then take up TRIPs.

Trade-Related Investment Measures

3. Unlike in most other areas of the negotiations, it did not prove possible to transmit a draft text of an agreement on TRIMs to Ministers in Brussels. The commentary on TRIMs on page 238 of MTN.TNC/W/35/Rev.1 simply enumerates the points on which basic divergences of view exist. These are: coverage; level of discipline; developing countries and restrictive business practices.

4. When work restarts on TRIMS on Monday, 18 March in the afternoon I suggest that the delegations be given an opportunity to comment on the present status of negotiations on TRIMs. We should also try to identify technical work that can usefully be done in this area at the present stage of our negotiations.

0003

On this latter point, I suggest that agreement could be assisted by discussions of a technical nature, building as appropriate on work already undertaken as reflected in the draft texts referred to in the commentary on page 238 of W/35/Rev.1. Technical discussions to elaborate a workable "effects test" would, for example, be a useful contribution in the level of discipline area.

Trade-Related Aspects of Intellectual Property Rights

6. The text sent forward to Brussels in TNC/W/35/Rev.1 listed on pages 194-195 the outstanding issues on which decisions were required in the TRIPs negotiations. These issues remain unsettled, and the basis for future work is the draft text as contained in that document.

7. When work restarts on TRIPs - again in the afternoon of 18 March - I suggest that delegations be given an opportunity to consider the present state of the negotiations in this area, taking into account the work done in Brussels, and to identify any areas in which technical work could usefully be undertaken at this stage.

77-2-2

TOTAL P.01

060 P01 LENINPROTOCOL '91-02-23 02:31 0010

특 허 청

국협 28140-867 568-6077 1991. 3. 2.

수신 수신처참조

제목 UR/TRIPs 대책회의 개최

UR/TRIPs (우루과이 라운드 지적재산권협상) 의 대책마련을 '91년부터 우리청이 주관하게 됨에 따라, 주요의제에 대한 의견조정 및 앞으로의 협상 대책방향 수립을 위해 동 협상의 주요내용을 직접 담당하고 있는 관련부처의 실무자급 대책회의를 다음과 같이 개최하고자 하오니 참석하여 주시기 바랍니다.

다 음

1. 일 시 : '91. 3. 8 (금) 15:00 - 17:00
2. 장 소 : 특허청 소회의실 (강남구 역삼동 풍림빌딩 14층)
3. 참석범위 : 특 허 청 기획관리관 (회의주재)
   - 특 허 청 국제협력담당관
   - 경제기획원 통상조정 3과장
   - 외 무 부 통상기구과장
   - 상 공 부 전자부품과장
   - 농림수산부 통상협력담당관
   - 보건사회부 약무과장
   - 문 화 부 저작권과장
   - 과학기술처 정보산업기술담당관

0011

국협 28140-867　　　　　　　　　　　　　　　　　　91. 3. 2.

4. 논의내용

o 주관 변경에 따른 부처간 의견조정 방안

o TRIPs 협상 기본대책 방안

o 주요 의제별 논의내용 및 담당부처 의견

5. 부처별 관련사항에 대하여는 별첨 쟁점사항을 참조, 의견내용을 작성하여 회의시 제출하여 주시기 바랍니다.

첨부　부처별 쟁점 사항서 1부.　　끝.

특　　　허　　　청　　　장

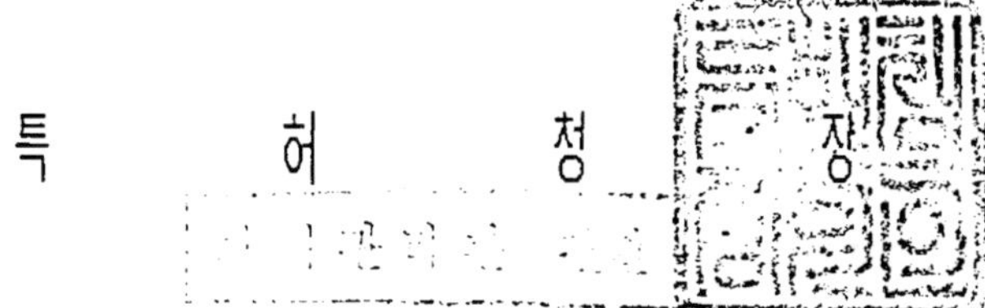

수신처 : 경제기획원장관, 외무부장관, 상공부장관, 농림수산부장관,
　　　　보건사회부장관, 문화부장관, 과학기술처장관.　　　　0012

부처별 주요쟁점

1. E P B

o UR 협상의 전체구도를 고려한 TRIPs 협상대처 기본방향 (전향적 대응정도 여부)

2. 외 무 부

o EC, 일본과의 쌍무협상 (미시판 물질특허보호 및 보정인정 문제)을 고려한 경과 규정(73조)의 수용

3. 문 화 부

o 대여권 (제11조) 인정

o 음반의 소급 보호 (15조, 16조)

4. 과학기술처

o 컴퓨터 프로그램의 어문저작물 간주 (제10조)

o 컴퓨터 프로그램에 대한 대여권 인정 (제11조)

5. 농림수산부, 보사부

o 영업비밀중 의약, 농약 판매허가를 위한 정부 제출자료 비밀유지 의무 (제42조 4A)

6. 상 공 부

o IC 선의 구매자의 보호 (39조, 40조)

o 반도체 칩 보호법 입법관련 TRIPs 규정 배치 여부

0013

TABLE OF CONTENTS

2. For the purposes of this Agreement, the term "intellectual property" refers to all categories of intellectual property that are the subject of Sections ... to ... of Part II.

3. PARTIES shall accord the treatment provided for in this Agreement to the nationals of other PARTIES.[1] In respect of the relevant intellectual property right, the nationals of other PARTIES shall be understood as those natural or legal persons meeting the criteria for eligibility for protection under the Paris Convention (1967), the Berne Convention (1971), the Rome Convention and the Treaty on Intellectual Property in Respect of Integrated Circuits. Any PARTY availing itself of the possibilities provided in Articles 5.3 or 6.2 of the Rome Convention shall make a notification as foreseen in those provisions to the Committee established under Part VII below.

Article 2: Intellectual Property Conventions

1. In respect of Parts II, III and IV of this Agreement, PARTIES shall not depart from the relevant provisions of the Paris Convention (1967).

2. Nothing in this Agreement shall derogate from existing obligations that PARTIES may have to each other under the Paris Convention, the Berne Convention, the Rome Convention and the Treaty on Intellectual Property in Respect of Integrated Circuits.

Article 3: National Treatment

1. Each PARTY shall accord to the nationals of other PARTIES treatment no less favourable than that it accords to its own nationals with regard to the protection of intellectual property, subject to the exceptions already

---

[1] When the term "national" is used in this Agreement, it shall be deemed, in the case of Hong Kong, to mean persons, natural or legal, who are domiciled or who have a real and effective industrial or commercial establishment in Hong Kong.

provided in, respectively, the Paris Convention (1967), the Berne Convention (1971), the Rome Convention and the Treaty on Intellectual Property in Respect of Integrated Circuits. Any PARTY availing itself of the possibilities provided in Article 6 of the Berne Convention and Article 16.1(a)(iii) or (iv) or Article 16.1(b) of the Rome Convention shall make a notification as foreseen in those provisions to the Committee established under Part VII below.

2. PARTIES may avail themselves of the exceptions permitted under paragraph 1 above in relation to judicial and administrative procedures, including the designation of an address for service or the appointment of an agent within the jurisdiction of a PARTY, only where such exceptions are necessary to secure compliance with laws and regulations which are not inconsistent with the provisions of this agreement and where such practices are not applied in a manner which would constitute a disguised restriction on trade.

Article 4: Most-Favoured-Nation Treatment

With regard to the protection of intellectual property, any advantage, favour, privilege or immunity granted by a PARTY to the nationals of any other country shall be accorded immediately and unconditionally to the nationals of all other PARTIES. Exempted from this obligation are any advantage, favour, privilege or immunity accorded by a PARTY:

(a) deriving from international agreements on judicial assistance and law enforcement of a general nature and not particularly confined to the protection of intellectual property rights;

(b) granted in accordance with the provisions of the Berne Convention (1971) or the Rome Convention authorising that the treatment accorded be a function not of national treatment but of the treatment accorded in another country;

(c) deriving from international agreements related to the protection of intellectual property which entered into force prior to the entry into force of this agreement, provided that such agreements are notified to the Committee established under Part VII below and do not constitute an arbitrary or unjustifiable discrimination against nationals of other PARTIES;

[(d) exceeding the requirements of this Agreement and provided in an international agreement to which the PARTY belongs, provided that such agreement is open for accession by all PARTIES to this Agreement, or provided that such PARTY shall be ready to extend such advantage, favour, privilege or immunity, on terms equivalent to those under the agreement, to the nationals of any other PARTY so requesting and to enter into good faith negotiations to this end.]

Article 5: Multilateral Agreements on Acquisition or Maintenance of Protection

The obligations under Articles 3 and 4 above do not apply to procedures provided in multilateral agreements concluded under the auspices of the World Intellectual Property Organization relating to the acquisition or maintenance of intellectual property rights.

Article 6: Exhaustion[1]

Subject to the provisions of Articles 3 and 4 above, nothing in this Agreement imposes any obligation on, or limits the freedom of, PARTIES with

---

[1] For the purposes of exhaustion, the European Communities shall be considered a single PARTY.

respect to the determination of their respective regimes regarding the exhaustion of any intellectual property rights conferred in respect of the use, sale, importation or other distribution of goods once those goods have been put on the market by or with the consent of the right holder.

Article 7: Objectives

The protection and enforcement of intellectual property rights should contribute to the promotion of technological innovation and to the transfer and dissemination of technology, to the mutual advantage of producers and users of technological knowledge and in a manner conducive to social and economic welfare, and to a balance of rights and obligations.

Article 8: Principles

1. Provided that PARTIES do not derogate from the obligations arising under this Agreement, they may, in formulating or amending their national laws and regulations, adopt measures necessary to protect public health and nutrition, and to promote the public interest in sectors of vital importance to their socio-economic and technological development.

2. Appropriate measures, provided that they do not derogate from the obligations arising under this Agreement, may be needed to prevent the abuse of intellectual property rights by right holders or the resort to practices which unreasonably restrain trade or adversely affect the international transfer of technology.

0018

[**Article 14: Definition of Public**

The term "public" shall not be defined in the domestic law of PARTIES in a manner that conflicts with a normal commercial exploitation of a work and unreasonably prejudices the legitimate interests of right holders.]

Article 15: Protection of Works Existing at Time of Entry into Force

The provisions of the Berne Convention (1971) concerning the protection of works existing at the time of entry into force shall apply in respect of the rights secured under that Convention.

Article 16: Protection of Performers, Producers of Phonograms (Sound Recordings) and Broadcasts

[1. In respect of a fixation of their performance on a phonogram, performers shall have the possibility of preventing: the fixation of their unfixed performance; and the reproduction of such fixation. Performers shall also have the possibility of preventing the broadcasting by wireless means and the communication to the public of their live performance.]

2. Producers of phonograms shall enjoy the right to authorise or prohibit the direct or indirect reproduction of their phonograms.

[3. Broadcasting organisations shall have the right to authorise or prohibit the fixation, the reproduction of fixations, and the rebroadcasting by wireless means of broadcasts, as well as the communication to the public of television broadcasts of the same. Where PARTIES do not grant such rights to broadcasting organisations, they shall provide right holders in the subject matter of broadcasts with the possibility of preventing the above acts.]

4. The provisions of Article 11 shall apply <u>mutatis mutandis</u> to right holders in phonograms.

appropriate. In consultation with the World Intellectual Property Organization, the Committee shall seek to establish, within one year of its first meeting, appropriate arrangements for co-operation with bodies of that Organization.[1]

Article 72: International Cooperation

PARTIES agree to co-operate with each other with a view to eliminating international trade in goods infringing intellectual property rights. For this purpose, they shall establish and notify contact points in their national administrations and be ready to exchange information on trade in infringing goods. They shall, in particular, promote the exchange of information and co-operation between customs authorities with regard to trade in counterfeit goods.

Article 73: Protection of Existing Intellectual Property

1. PARTIES shall apply the provisions of Articles 3, 4 and 5 of Part I, of Sections 2, 3, 7 and 8 of Part II, of Part III and of Part IV to subject matter under protection in a PARTY on the date of application of the provisions of this Agreement for that PARTY as defined in Part VI above.

2. PARTIES are not obliged to apply the provisions of Sections 1, 4, 5 and 6 of Part II to subject matter under protection in a PARTY on the date of application of the provisions of this Agreement for that PARTY, subject to the provisions of Article[s] 15 [and 16.6]. Subject matter in respect of which the procedures for the acquisition of rights have been initiated as of that date for which, however, the intellectual property title has not yet been granted shall [not] benefit from the provisions of this Agreement. Nothing in this Agreement shall affect other subject matter covered by these Sections which is already in existence and not under protection in a PARTY on the date of application of the provisions of this Agreement for that PARTY, subject to the provisions of Article[s] 15 and [16.6].

[1] This provision depends on the decision to be taken regarding the institutional arrangement for the international implementation of this Agreement.

0020

3. The application of Articles 2 and 6 of this Agreement to existing intellectual property shall be governed by paragraphs 1 and 2 of this Article, as appropriate to the intellectual property right in question.

Article 74: Review and Amendment

1. PARTIES shall review the implementation of this Agreement after the expiration of the transitional period referred to in paragraph 2 of Article 68 above. They shall, having regard to the experience gained in its implementation, review it [-] years after that date, and at identical intervals thereafter. The PARTIES may undertake reviews in the light of any relevant new developments which might warrant modification or amendment of this Agreement.

2. Amendments merely serving the purpose of adjusting to higher levels of protection of intellectual property rights achieved, and in force, in other multilateral agreements and accepted by all PARTIES may be adopted by the Committee.

[Article 75: Reservations

A PARTY may only enter reservations in respect of any of the provisions of this Agreement at the time of entry into force of this Agreement for that PARTY and with the consent of the other PARTIES.]

報 告 畢

長 官 報 告 事 項

1991. 3. 2.
通 商 局
通 商 2 課(14)

題 目 : 韓. EC 知的所有權 問題

> 韓.EC 知的所有權 問題의 解決方案 協議를 위한 關係部處 對策 會議가 91.3.2(土) 開催된 바, 同 結果 아래 報告드립니다.

1. 會議 槪要

o 日時 및 場所 : 1991.3.2(土) 11:00-13:00

o 參 席 : 經濟企劃院 對調室長(主宰), 및 經企院, 外務部(通商局長)
保健社會部, 商工部, 文化部, 科學技術處, 特許廳 擔當局課長

2. 討議 內容

(背 景 說 明)

o 對調室長 : - 90.10 關係部處 會議時 UR 結果에 따라 韓.EC 知的所有權 問題를 解決키로 方針을 정하고 EC側에도 通報한바 있으나, UR 妥結 展望이 不確實해지고, 最近 EC側으로 부터의 解決 壓力이 加重되고 있어 我側立場의 再檢討 必要

o 通商局長 : - 最近 各種 채널을 통한 EC側의 解決 要求 說明 및 全般的인 韓.EC 關係增進을 위해 同件의 可能한 早期 解決 必要性 言及

0022

(各部處 立場)

o 經 企 院 : - 韓.EC 關係를 위해 同件의 圓滿解決이 필요하나, 現在까지의 UR 協商에서는 知的所有權 遡及保護가 排除될 可能性(著作權은 遡及保護가 대세) 이 많으므로 UR 結果대로 解決하는 것이 바람직

- EC와 雙務交涉에 의해 妥結時, 日本.EFTA에도 同等保護가 不可避한바, 國內外的 問題點 많음

o 商工部,特許廳: - UR 協商에서의 遡及保護排除 展望이 不透明하므로(마지막 段階에서 EC側이 遡及保護를 貫徹시킬 可能性)雙務交涉에 의한 懸案의 早期 解決이 바람직

o 保 社 部 : - 國內業界, 國會等의 强力한 반발 및 막대한 로얄티 支給等 現實的으로 우리에게 미칠 影響을 勘案, 遡及保護附與反對

- 아직까지 EC에 한해서는 一部 遡及保護를 許容할 수 있다는 立場을 취해왔으나, 最近에 國內業界 環境變化로 EC에게도 附與하기 어려운 狀況

(日本.EFTA에 대해서는 여하한 境遇에도 不可)

- UR 結果대로 解決하면 國內的으로 큰 문제없음

o 文 化 部 : - 著作物에 대한 行政指導 方法 能力이 現實的으로 전혀 없는 狀況에서 對 EC 遡及保護附與 約束 不可

o 科 技 處 : - EC 및 日本, EFTA에 대한 software 遡及保護는 별 문제 없음

o 通商局長 : - UR 展望이 불투명한 점에 비추어, EC와 雙務交涉 再開 必要

- 我側의 誠意 있는 解決 努力이 없을 경우, 同 件은 韓.美間 通商摩擦처럼 韓.EC間 政治問題로 비화될 可能性

0023

- 아직까지 我側이 主張해온 GSP 停止 措置의 報償은 EC의 制度上 不可能하므로, 同 件 解決의 代價로 醫藥分野 技術 移轉 및 向後 一定期間 GSP 供與 保障等을 EC측에 要求 (保社部 檢討 要請)
- 著作權은 EC측에 旣約束한 事項이며, 國內外的 명분상으로도 許容함이 妥當

(結 論)

o 各部處 立場差異가 너무 현격하여 今日 會議時 어떠한 決定은 내리지 못하고, 保社部, 文化部等에서 對 EC 遡及保護時 우리에게 미칠 利害 得失을 좀 더 具體的으로 檢討한 후, 가까운 時日內 재회합, 論議키로 함
o 保社部는 對 EC 雙務交涉時 EC側에 要求할 技術移轉 希望 品目 檢討
o 著作權에 대해서는 文化部를 제외한 모든 部處 參席者들이 遡及保護 필요성에 認識을 같이함

3. 向後 計劃

o 가까운 時日內에 關係部處會議를 재소집, 我側 立場 確定토록 經企院側과 緊密 協議
  - 實務先에서 合意가 어려울 경우, 長.次官會議에 上程
o 同 方針이 정해지는대로 EC側과 交涉 再開. (끝)

0024

외 무 부

1991. 3. 8.

통 상 기 구 과

0025

한.EC 지적재산권 보호 협상을 고려한 TRIPs 의장 초안 73조(기존 지적재산권 보호 규정)의 수용 여부 문제

o 한.미 지적재산권 협정 내용이 차별적이고, 정당화 할 수 없는 협정으로 해석되어 상기 MFN 대상이 됨으로써 1986.8 한.미간 합의사항의 EC에의 자동확산이 우려되나 특별조항 우선 원칙에 의거 불소급 원칙(73조 3rd sentence) 적용됨에 따라 EC등 제3국에 대해 대부분 소급효 부여 의무 면제 가능하고, 한편 계류중인 제법특허의 물질특허로의 전환, 보정청구 문제는 73조 2항 2nd sentence의 shall(not)의 bracket 제거로 shall not을 주장함으로써 해결 가능. 끝.

0026

UR/TRIPs 대책회의 자료

1991. 3. 8

특 허 청

0027

I. UR/TRIPs 협상 전망

1. UR 전반 최근 동향

o 최대 관건인 농산물 협상이 2. 20일 재개되고, EC 측이 종래의 global approach 로 부터 국내 보조, 수출보조, 수입장벽 철폐의 3개구분 협상 방식에 동의함으로써 협상의 재개 움직임.

o 2.26일 실무자급 TNC 에서 기존 협상그룹(15개)를 7개 협상그룹으로 재구분 협상재개를 합의

o 협상 참여국의 이러한 노력은 미행정부의 Fast-track 연장 요청의 명분을 제공하기 위한 것으로 평가되며, 논란이 있으나 실제적인 협상은 3월중 technical matters 를 그룹별로 논의한 후 미 의회의 Fast-track 연장이 결정될 5-6월 이후 에야 개시될 것으로 전망

o 브럿셀 각료회의 실패 및 걸프전쟁 등으로 UR에 대한 기대는 다소 떨어졌으며, 미국, EC도 협상 진전이 어렵거나, 애초 목표를 달성할 수 없는 분야는 신속한 협상 종결을 모색할 것으로 예상 되며, 특히 미국의 경우 UR 에 기대할 수 없는 분야에 대해서는 UR Plus 방식으로 쌍무협상을 강화할 우려

0028

2. TRIPs 협상 전망

o 조정 7개 협상그룹중 GNG 중의 New Issue 를 통합한 TRIPs/TRIMs 그룹으로 위치

o Brussel 에서 최종 의장보고서가 TNC 에 제출 되기는 했으나 많은 쟁점사항이 정리되지 않은채 남아있는 상황으로 실제적인 논의가 이루어지지 못하였고 3.18(월) 로 예정된 Technical matter 논의에서도 큰 변화는 없을 것으로 예상

o TRIPs/TRIMs 그룹은 모두 UR 에서 최초로 논의 되기 시작한 New Issue 로서 TRIPs 는 협상의 출발이 되는 GATT Ability 문제, TRIMs 는 투자 제한조치의 다양성에 따라 전체적 규정 마련이 어려워 완전한 타결은 어려울 것으로 예상되며, UR 협상의 주력이 농산물과 Service 쪽으로 집중됨에 따라 비중이 감소될 것으로 관측

IPR trade-off의 대상이 될 가능성

o 미국, EC등은 TRIPs의 타결과 관계 없이 쌍무적 압력을 강화함으로써 소기의 목적을 달성하고자 할 것이며, 그간 UR 타결 결과를 따르기로 연기 해놓은 쌍무간 현안과제를 더이상 방치하지 않을 것으로 예상됨.

0029

II. TRIPs 대책수립의 기본 구조

1. Brussel 까지의 대책

o TRIPs는 광범위한 Coverage 로서, 부처간 조정이 필요한 동시에 중요 통상문제로서 EPB에서 주관

o 전체 협상 구조상 농산물분야에 협상력을 집중키로 함에 따라 전향적으로 대처할 Group 으로 분류, 유화적 대처 대상으로 결정

o 가장 중요한 교역대상인 미국과의 관계에서 대부분 TRIPs 규정 이상의 보호를 약속한 바 있고, 또 현행 산업재산권 4법과 저작권법의 규정과 크게 상치되는 부분이 없으며, 현행 제도에 없는 분야도 조만간 입법을 추진하고 있어 타 협상보다는 대부분의 쟁점에 대해 국내제도가 최종 예상 타결 결과에 접근하고 있는 것으로 평가

2. 앞으로의 대처 방안

o 기본 전제

- UR 타결과 관계 없이 향후 주요 교역대상국의 아국에 대한 지적재산권의 보호 요청수준은

0030

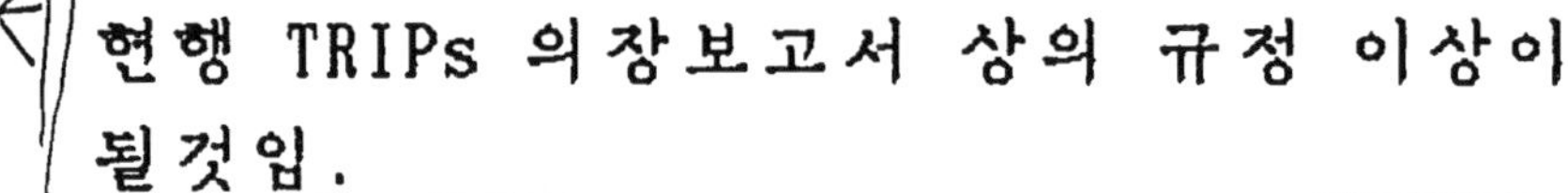
현행 TRIPs 의장보고서 상의 규정 이상이 될것입.

- 따라서, 전체적으로 가급적 전향적 자세를 유지, 타결을 도모하도록 하되, 유관 산업계의 급격한 피해가 예상되는 부분을 선정, 반드시 관철해야할 사항과 필요하면 Trade-off 할 수 있는 사항, 양보함으로써 차후 협상 기여도에 대해 긍정적 평가를 도모, 양자간 통상문제에 유리하게 작용할 수 있는 사항, 일본등 타국이 강력히 주장함으로써 편승할 수 있는 사항등으로 주장의 정도를 grading 하도록 함.

o 특허청의 입장

- '91년 1월 이후 TRIPs 주관부처로 업무 이관

- 우리청 소관분야는 Brussel입장과 변동 없음.

- 타부처 소관업무는 해당부처의 최종 입장을 수용하되 타결가능성과 통상에 미치는 영향 및 양자관계를 고려, 우선순위에 따라 관철의 정도 단계화

- 부처간 최종 합의 사항은 EPB UR 대책반에 통보토록 하고, 전체협상 구도상 문제는 EPB와 협의 조정토록 할 예정

0031

3. 행정사항

o 회의 및 부처 의견 문의시 협조 요망

- 소관이 뚜렷한 분야에 대해서는 해당부처의 명확한 입장 표명 요망

- 소관이 중첩된 분야에 대해서는 회의를 통해 입장 정리

- 신규입법 또는 소관업무에 대해 TRIPs 논의 내용을 참고해야할 부분이 있는 경우 UR과 국내 제도가 괴리되지 않도록 주의를 요함.

o 추후 협상 회의 참가

- 3. 18일 TRIPs 회의는 현지 대표부 대처

- 협상 진행에 따라 주요논점이 부각되면 해당 부처 관계자 참석 요망

- 소관분야에 대해 정확한 입장을 미리 확정해 둠으로써 회의 참석자가 명확히 대처할 수 있도록 함.

0032

o EPB UR 협상 중간보고서 작성

- 지금까지의 논의내용에 따른 중간보고서를 작성할 계획으로, EPB의 자료 요청시 신속히 대처할 수 있도록 준비 요망

o 유관업계 홍보 및 의견 수렴

- 각 부처는 업계에 UR 논의내용을 홍보, 의견을 수렴함으로써 정부의 대책부재라는 인식을 불식토록 적극 대처 필요

III. 부처별 주요입장 정리 필요사항

1. EPB

o UR 협상의 전체 구도를 고려한 TRIPs 협상 대처 기본 방향

- TRIPs의 UR 협상상의 비중 및 대처 기본차세
- 양보의 수준 및 전향적 대응정도 여부
- 특허청과 EPB의 향후 협조 방안

0033

2. 외무부

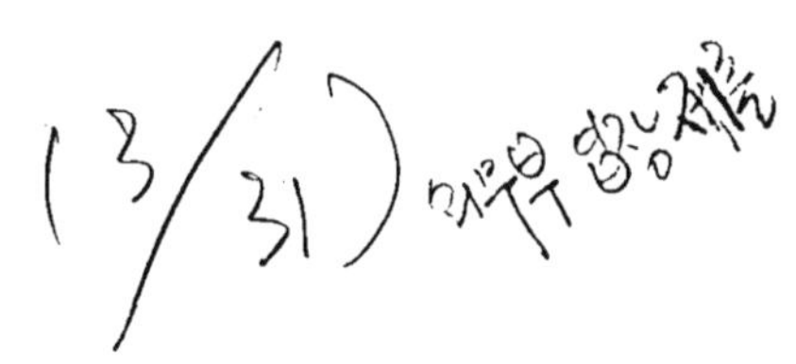

o EC, 일본과의 쌍무 현안문제와 경과규정(73조) 의 수용 여부

- 대미 양허사항(제법특허의 물질특허 보정, 미시판 특허물질의 소급보호)에 대한 EC와의 협상시 UR 결과에 따라 협상토록 한 바 있고, 일본에 대하여는 구체적 협상이 이루어지지 못하고 있음.

- TRIPs에서는 73조 제2항 후반에 "조약 발효일전 존재하나 보호받지 못하는 Subject matter는 본조약을 적용하지 않는다." 로 규정, PP는 보호하지 않아도 되는 근거조항으로 인식

- 보정문제는 73조 제2항 전반에 "절차는 개시했으나 아직 권리화 되지 못한 경우는 본 조약에 의해 이익을 받을 수 있다(없다)"로 규정, "있다"로 될 경우 MFN 조항과 함께 EC 출원 제법특허('87년 7월 이전)중 절차 종료되지 않은 것의 보정인정 문제 발생

- 양자관계와 UR을 동시에 고려한 최종입장의 신속한 정리가 필요하며 EC에 대한 양보 필요성에 따라 UR 에서의 경과 규정 수용 여부를 검토(경제기획원 공동사항)

0034

3. 문화부

o 대여권 인정 여부(과기처 공통사항)

- CP와 영상저작물에 대한 대여금지권과 보상 청구권 인정

- 미국은 이외에 CD, 음반에 대해서도 대여권 인정 주장

- 문화부 기존 입장 : 유통질서 혼란 및 규정의 집행가능성 문제로 반대

- 미국은 일본의 CD 대여업 성행에 대하여 큰 불만이 있으며 우리나라의 경우 현재 Video tape에 문제가 있으나, CD 업계의 성장에 따라 미국 IIPA등은 Special 301조 업계의견 제출시 한국에 대해 CD 에 대한 대여금지 조처를 취할 것을 미 정부에 청원

o 음반의 소급보호

- 저작권의 보호는 Bern 협약의 규정을 채택, 소급효를 인정

- 저작인접권에 관하여는 로마조약에 따라 소급효과 없는 것으로 규정

0035

- 미국은 음반에 대해 소급보호를 강력히 주장

- 타결시 피해 예상 및 현 업계의견 조정 필요

4. 과기처

o 컴퓨터 프로그램의 어문저작물 간주

- 기존 컴퓨터 프로그램보호법 규정상의 문제점 도출

- 어문저작물의 10년 소급보호('86. ROU) 감안

5. 농수산부, 보사부

o 정부 제출자료 비밀유지의무

- 의약, 농약의 판매허가시 제출되는 기술 data의 5년간 타 품목허가 이용금지 및 영구공개 금지

- 타결시 제약허가등에 선진국 실험자료를 이용할 수 없어 어려운 실험 자료를 직접 작성 해야 하는 우려

0036

- 정부가 인허가시 기제출 자료를 이용할 수 없고, 위반시 손해배상이 정부에 대해 청구됨.

- 농수산부, 보사부는 현행 의약, 농약판매 허가 과정에 있어 실제 관행을 조사, 피해 파악 필요

6. 상공부

o IC 보호

- 워싱톤 반도체칩 보호 조약 이상의 보호수준 (Washington plus) 문제

- IC 선의구매자의 보호 방안

- 반도체칩 보호법 입법 추진현황과 TRIPs 규정과의 상호 관계

- 협상 대처 방안

0037

IV. 추후 활동내역

o 본 회의에서 결정된 사항을 토대로 각부처는 최종 입장을 정리, 3월말경 회의 재개

o EPB 중간보고서 원고 작성을 위한 자료 제출

o 협상 진전상황에 따른 현지 협상 참석범위 확정

o 관련 정보의 수집시 특허청 송부 요망

o 특허청장 주재의 국장급 회의 개최 검토

0038

UR/TRIPs 협상의 주요내용

91. 3. 8.

특 허 청

0039

Ⅰ. TRIPs 의장 보고서의 주요내용

1990. 12. 벨기에 브랏셀 각료회의에 제출된 TRIPs 협상 그룹 의장보고서의 주요내용

Part Ⅰ : 기본원칙 (내국민 대우, 최혜국 대우)

Part Ⅱ : 보호기준 (저작권,특허,의장,상표,지리적표시,반도체 칩 설계배치, 영업비밀의 7개분야별 권리내용 및 남용규제)

Part Ⅲ : 시행절차 (권리 행사를 위한 국내, 국경조치, 가처분 조치)

Part Ⅳ : 지적재산권의 획득 및 유지 (합리적 기간내에 권리획득 이루어져야함).

Part Ⅴ : 분쟁해결

Part Ⅵ : 경과조치 (개도국 우대조항)

Part Ⅶ : 관리기구 ; 부칙

Ⅱ. 주요쟁점

항 목	의 장 보 고 서 내 용	비 고
1. 저작권		
o 컴퓨터프로그램 데이타 편집물	베른조약상의 어문(literary) 저작물인정(10조)	
o 대여권 인정범위	컴퓨터프로그램 영상저작물, 음반(11조 16조4항)	
o 기존저작물의 보호	베른조약(소급보호원칙)적용 (15조)	
o 음반의 소급보호	베른조약적용(16조 6항)	
o 실연자 음반재작저 및 방송사업자보호	실연자, 음반제작자 : 50년 방송사업자 : 25년 (16조 5항)	

0040

항 목	의 장 보 고 서 내 용	비 고
2. 집적회로설계배치		
o 최종제품 포함여부	포함 또는 제외(39조)	국내입법 추진중
o 선의 구매자의책임	보상책임 인정 또는 불인정(40조)	
o 보호기간	10년 (41조)	
3. 영업비밀		
o 상업적 가치있는 비밀보호	국내법으로 보호의무(42조 2항)	국내입법 추진중
o 약품,농약,판매 허가시 제출되는 자료를 정부가 경쟁제품 허가시 이용할 수 없음.	최소 5년간 보호 (42조 4항)	
4. 분쟁해결		
o 패널보고서 불이행시 제재여부	3가지 대안제시 (부칙) I 안 (사무국안) ┐ GATT 에 따른 보복허용 II 안 (선진국안) ┘ III 안 (개도국안) : 권고에 그침	
5. 조약의무발생일		
o 선진국	조약체결후 [X]년후	
o 개도국 및 동구 사회주의국	" [X+Y]년후. 단,내국민 대우, MFN 은 [X]년후	
o 최빈국	" [X+Y+α] 년후 (68조, 69조)	
6. 기존 발명의 보호		
o 계류중인 특허출원	적용 또는 부적용	별첨 對 EC 관련사항 참조

0041

UR/TRIPs 협상 내용중 對 EC 관련사항

==

I. P/P 보호

o 제1차 보고서에서부터 제3차 의장보고서(제36조)까지에는 미국의 주장을 반영하여 미시판 물질을 특허처럼 보호하는 규정이 있었으나 제4차 보고서 이후로는 삭제하였음.

o 보호방법

- TRIPs 협정발효일 이후 특허가능하게된 발명(예: 화학물질, 의약품)에 대해
- 가맹국중 어느 한 당사국(예: 스위스)에서 특허받았으면
- 보호를 하는 당사국(예: 브라질)에서 시판되지 않았던 품목에 대해 특허권자이외 제조,사용,판매할 수 없음.

o P/P 보호안이 미국이외의 국가에게서는 지지를 받지 못해 재론되기는 어려운 것으로 보임.

II. MFN 및 그 예외

o 제1차 보고서 이후 계속해서 강력한 MFN 규정이 주장되어져 왔으며, 극히 제한된 예외만이 인정되고 있음.

o 예외

- 사법공조 협정
- 베른조약, 로마조약에서 인정되는 경우
- TRIPs 발효이전 체결된 지적재산권 협정으로 자의적(arbitrary)이거나 부당(unjustifiable)하지 않은 협정

0042

* 당초 아측은 『TRIPs 발효이전 체결된 (모든)지적재산권 협정』으로 grandfathering 을 주장하였으나, GATT 원칙의 하나로 인정되는 강력한 MFN 원칙 주장에 밀려 성공하지 못하였음.

- TRIPs 의 요건을 상회하는 협정으로, 모든 TRIPs 체약국에 개방되어 있거나 동등대우를 위한 선의의 협상이 재시되는 협정
  * 본 예외는 EC 의 제안에 따라 5차 의장보고서 이후에 대안의 형태로 제시된것으로 아직 주요국의 지지를 받지는 못하고 있음.

Ⅲ. 계류중인 출원에 TRIPs 적용여부(경과조치)

o TRIPs 발효시점에 가맹국에서 계류중인 특허출원에 대해 동 조약을 적용하게 되면 계류중인 EC. 일본의 제법 특허에 대해 MFN 원칙이 적용되어 미국의 경우와 같이 대우해야 하므로 아측의 관심 사항임.

o 아측은 MFN grandfathering 이 어려워지자 경과 조치 규정을 통한 문제 해결을 위해 사무국과의 활발한 접촉 등 노력집중

- 2차보고서에는 『존재하나 보호받지 않고 있는 대상』은 TRIPs 적용 않는다는 규정(part Ⅶ. 1.6.)삽입
- 제3차 보고서(제72조), 제4차 보고서(제71조)에서는 같은 표현 존치
- 제4차 보고서 토의시부터 동 규정에 각국 관심 고조로 점차 상세한 내용 토의됨.
- 제5차 보고서(제71조)에서는 계류중인 출원에 대해 보호기준을 규정한 Part Ⅱ 의 규정들을 적용 않는다고 만 제안되어 있어서 Part Ⅰ. 의 내용인 MFN 은 적용하여야 하는 것으로 해석되었음.
- 아측의 사무국과 접촉후 제6차 및 제7차 보고서에서는 계류중인 출원에 대해 TRIPs 협정전체(MFN 포함)를 적용 않는 것으로 제안하였음.(제73조) 다만, 6차,7차 보고서에서는 협정전체를 적용 또는 부적용하는 두가지 대안 모두가 제시됨.

0043

- 브랏셀 각료회의 개시직전 90. 12. 2. 미국이 73조에 대해 자국 관심 사항인 지리적 표시 등에 관해 경과 규정을 명확히 하는 제안을 하였는바, 계류중인 특허출원에 대해서는 협정 전체를 적용하는 규정이 포함되었음.

  o 각료회의 기간중 73조는 Gradin 의장이 Small drafting group 에서 논의할 Technical issue 로 분류되어 논의하였는바, 미국은 계류중 특허출원에서 TRIPs 적용을 강력히 주장하지는 않고 있으나 EC. 스위스 등이 강력 주장 아국 포함한 개도국 반대 주장 대립 있었음.

0044

특 허 청

국협 28140- 886 568-6077 1991. 3. 11

수신 수신처참조

제목 UR/TRIPs 대책회의 결과 통보

1. 국협 28140 - 862 (91. 3.2) 관련입니다.

2. 표제관련 3.8(금) 회의의 결과를 별첨과 같이 통보하오니, 별첨 "4.나항"의 중요쟁점중 귀부처 소관사항에 대한 의견을 별첨 양식에 따라 3. 30(토) 까지 통보하여 주시기 바랍니다.

첨부 1. UR/TRIPs 대책회의 결과 1부.

2. 양식 1부. 끝.

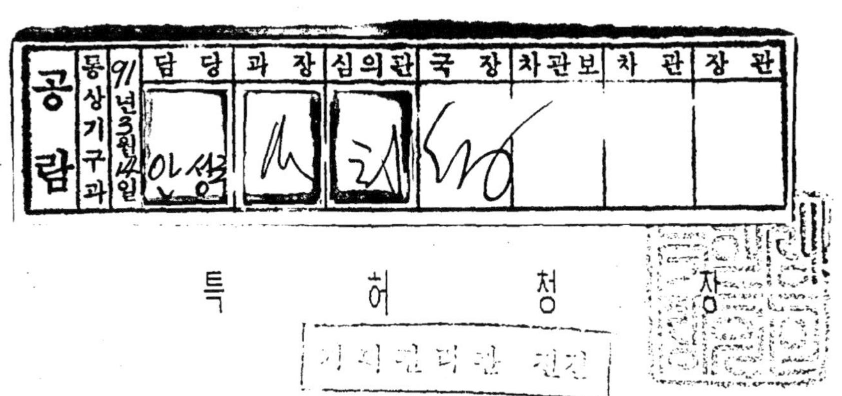

공람	통상기구과	91년 3월 14일	담당	과장	심의관	국장	차관보	차관	장관
			안성국						

특 허 청 장

수신처 경제기획원(통상3과), 외무부(통상기구과), 상공부(전자부품과), 농수산부(생활방역과, 가축위생과), 문화부(저작권과), 보사부(약무과), 과기처(정보산업기술담당관).

6487

0045

UR/TRIPs 대책회의 결과

1. 회의일시 : 1991. 3. 8(금) 15:00 - 17:00

2. 장 소 : 특허청 기획관리관실

3. 참 석 자 : 특 허 청 기획관리관 (주재)

   " 국제협력담당관, 유기화학심사담당관실

   경제기획원 통상 3과

   외 무 부 통상기구과

   상 공 부 전자부품과

   농림수산부 생활방역과, 가축위생과

   문 화 부 저작권과

   보 사 부 약무과

   과학기술처 정보산업기술담당관실

4. 회의 내용

가. 특허청 향후 협상대책 수립 기본방침

o TRIPs 대책수립 방향

- 전향적 자세로 대처함을 전제로 관련부처의 의견을 종합하여 타결 가능성 및 중요도 별로 주장강도를 단계화할 예정

- 각부처는 의견제출시 관련제도를 상세히 설명하고 가급적 계량화된 자료를 첨부토록하여 특허청의 최종안 확정시 구체적인 비교가 가능토록 협조 요망

- 현재 입법 또는 개정이 추진중인 것은 TRIPs 의 논의사항을 충분히 감안 국내제도와 UR 의 거리를 좁히도록 함.

0046

o UR 전체 협상과의 관련

- 특허청의 최종 TRIPs 협상대책은 UR 전체 협상구도상 양보쪽으로 선회될 가능성이 있으며, UR 이 일괄타결 방식으로 진행되므로 타 협상과의 중요성 비교에 따라 Trade-off 될수 있음.

나. 주요 쟁점별 논의 내역

o 대여권 인정

- 대여금지 또는 자유대여후 보상중 택 1로서 VTR Tape 의 경우 관련업계의 피해가 막대

- CD 의 경우 아직 시장규모가 크지 않으나, 확대에 대비 추가적 검토가 요청됨.

- 최근 Laser Disk 가 등장 이것이 음반인지 영상저작물인지 논란의 우려가 있음.

o Berne 협약가입 및 소급보호

- Berne 협약 가입은 문화부에 검토된바 없음.
- 아국의 경우 Berne 협약에 가입하였으나 UCC 가입전의 저작물에 대해서는 소급을 인정하지 않았으며, 말레이시아의 경우 소급효가 있는 것으로 가입

o 반도체 칩 보호

- 반도체 칩 보호는 Washington 조약의 내용을 기본으로 입법을 추진중이며, TRIPs 에서의 우리측 주장내용인 선의의 구매자 보호, 최종제품의 제외등도 입법내용에 포함할 예정임.

0047

o 정부 제출자료의 비밀유지 의무

- 의약의 경우, 선제출 자료가 후원 약품의 허가에 5년간 이용될수 없다함은, 우리업계가 직접 실험을 하여 제약허가를 받아야 하는것을 의미하므로 실험기관과 설비가 취약한 우리 업계의 경우 5년을 기다려 허가를 받아야 할 것이므로 피해는 막중하며, 이는 오히려 PP 문제보다 더심각한 것으로 생각됨.

- 더구나 특허기간, generic drug 에 의한 특허기간 연장 이외에 또한번의 보호기간을 설정해주는 결과가 되어, 우리 업계의 신물질개발은 사실상 불가능해질 것임.

- 농약의 경우은 더욱 심각하여, Life-cycle 이 짧고, 업계가 영세하여 장기간 허가를 받지 못할 경우 타격은 막대할 것으로 예상

o 컴퓨터 프로그램의 어문저작물 간주

- 특징상 어문저작물 간주는 모순이며, 우리 법제와는 크게 다름.

o 경과규정과 EC.일본과의 협상

- EC 협상문제는 EPB 로 업무가 이관되었으며, 3.2 회의시 논의된바 있음을 참고 바람.

- 통상마찰 해소 차원에서의 선협상을 주장하는 EPB, 외무부, 상공부, 특허청의 입장과 UR 타결로써 이의 자연스러운 해결을 바라는 보사부, 문화부의 입장이 대립중

- 본 규정은 우리에게 UR 에서 가장 중요한 의미를 가진 것으로 현재 소기의 목적은 달성한 것으로 판단되나 협상진행에 따라 불리하게 진행될 우려도 큼.

0048

다. 향후 대책

o 논의된 사항에 대한 입장을 재정리하여 특허청에 제출토록 함. (3월말까지)

o 가급적 피해여부를 가시적으로 판단할 수 있도록 계량화 하여 줄것을 요망

o 향후 특허청의 최종입장 정리시, 관철가능성 및 주장의 합리적 근거를 고려하여 주요 추진사안을 마련할 것이므로 신중을 기하여 주기 바람.

o 특허청장 주재로 국장급 회의를 개최, 최종입장을 수립토록 할 예정임.

라. 기 타

o TRIPs 논의내용은 전문적인 사항이고 업계의 관심이 적은 분야로서, 정확한 판단이 어려우나 그럴수록 정부의 신중한 판단이 요구되며, 각 부처는 소관 업계 이익과 종합적 협상구도를 다같이 고려해야 할것임.

o 회의 논의내용중 추가적 검토의 필요성이 있는 사안에 대해서도 의견이 있으면 제안해 주기 바라며, 특허청도 기타사항에 대해 제안토록 할것임.

0049

협 상 대 책

주요쟁점	내 용	
	주장국 의 도	
국내 제도 (현행 또는 입법 추진)		
타결시 파급효과	업 계	
	제 도 조 정	
협상대책	검 토 의 견	
	주 장 가능성	
	근 거	
기 타		

0050

UR / TRIPs 관계부처 대책회의 결과 보고

1. 일 시 : 1991. 3. 8.(금) 15:00-17:00

2. 장 소 : 특허청 소회의실

3. 참 석 자 :

- 특 허 청 기획관리관 (회의 주재)
- 특 허 청 국제협력담당관
- 경제기획원 통상조정3과 담당사무관
- 외 무 부 통상기구과 담당사무관
- 상 공 부 전자부품 과장
- 농림수산부 통상협력담당관
- 보건사회부 약무과장
- 문 화 부 저작권 과장
- 과학기술처 정보산업기술담당관

4. 논의 내용

가. 주관부처 변경 (경제기획원 →특허청)에 따른 부처간 의견 조정 원활화를 위한 협조 요청

나. 1990.12. 브랏셀 각료회담시 TRIPs 협상 아국 입장 브리핑 (특허청 김성기 심사관)

o 전체 협상 구조상 농산물 분야에 협상력을 집중키로 함에 따라 전향적으로 대처할 Group으로 분류, 유화적 대처 대상으로 결정

공람	통상기구과	91년 3월 11일	담 당	과 장	심의관	국 장	차관보	차 관	장 관
			안성국	(서명)					

0051

o 가장 중요한 교역대상인 미국과의 관계에서 대부분 TRIPs 규정 이상의 보호를 약속한 바 있고, 또 현행 산업재산권 4법과 저작권법의 제도에 없는 분야도 조만간 입법을 추진하고 있어 타 협상보다는 대부분의 쟁점에 대해 국내제도가 최종 예상 타결 결과에 접근하고 있는 것으로 평가

다. 향후 TRIPs 협상 전망 및 대책 설명 (특허청 국제협력담당관)

o Brussel에서 최종 의장보고서가 TNC에 제출되기는 했으나 쟁점사항이 정립되지 않은채 남아있는 상황으로 실제적인 논의가 이루어지지 못하였고 3.18.(월)로 예정된 Technical matter 논의에서도 큰 변화는 없을 것으로 예상

o TRIPs/TRIMs 그룹은 모두 UR에서 최초로 논의되기 시작한 New Issue로서 TRIPs는 협상의 출발이 되는 GATT Ability 문제, TRIMs는 투자 제한 조치의 다양성에 따라 전체적 규정 마련이 어려워 완전한 타결은 어려울 것으로 예상되며, UR 협상의 주력이 농산물과 Service 쪽으로 집중됨에 따라 비중이 감소될 것으로 관측

o UR 타결과 관계없이 향후 주요 교역상대국의 아국에 대한 지적재산권의 보호 요청 수준은 현행 TRIPs 의장보고서상의 규정 이상이 될 것임.

o 따라서, 전체적으로 가급적 전향적 자세를 유지, 타결을 도모하도록 하되, 유관 산업계의 급격한 피해가 예상되는 부분을 선정, 반드시 관철해야할 사항과 필요하면 Trade-off 할 수 있는 사항, 양보함으로써 차후 협상 기여도에 대해 긍정적 평가를 도모, 양자간 통상문제에 유리하게 작용할 수 있는 사항, 일본등 타국이 강력히 주장함으로써 편승할 수 있는 사항 등으로 주장의 정도를 grading 하도록 함

라. 외무부 관련사항

✓ o 협정의무 발생일을 지연시킬 수 있도록 아국이 개도국으로 분류 가능토록하는 논리 창출을 외무부가 담당할 것을 요청

- TRIPs 협정 의무 발생일

0052

. 선진국 조약체결후 〔X) 년후

. 개도국 및 동구사회주의국 조약체결후 (X + Y) 년후

단, NT, MFN 부여 의무는 (X) 년후

. 최빈국 조약체결후 (X + Y + α) 년후

o 의장 초안 73조는 한.EC 지적재산권 협상과 관련하여 계류중인 특허 출원의 의장 초안 부적용(73조 2항 2번째 문장의 Shall [not] 에서 bracket 배제)을 분명히 한다면 아국은 수용 가능. 끝.

0053

원 본

외 무 부

종 별 :

번 호 : GVW-0503 일 시 : 91 0319 1000

수 신 : 장관(통기, 경기원, 재무부, 농림수산부, 상공부, 특허청)

발 신 : 주 제네바 대사

제 목 : UR/TRIMS.TRIPS 주요국 비공식 협의

3. 18. DUNKEL 사무총장 주재로 개최된 표제 협의토의 결과 아래 보고함. (본직, 엄재무관, 김준규 서기관 참석)

1. 무역관련 부자 조치

0 의장(DUNKEL 총장)은 MTN/TNC/W/69 의 37개내지 39항의 내용을 상기 시키면서이를 기초로 하여 향후 기술적 분야에 대한 논의를 진행할 예정인바 구체적 논의대상에 대한 발언을 요청함.

0 이에 대해 스웨덴은 구체적인 정의 규정 및 COVERAGE 등에 대한 합의가 없는상태에서논의 대상인 기술적인 부문을 정하기는 어려운 문제이나 W/69 에 언급된부자조치의 EFFECT TEST가 가능한 논의 대상임을 제안한바 미국, EC, 일본등이 이를 지지함.

0 호주, 인도는 기술적인 문제와 정치적 결정을 요하는 문제간에 그 구분 한계가 불분명하여 기술적 분야에의 논의는 정치적 결정을 요하는 부문에 곧 접하게 되므로 스웨덴이 제안하는 접근 방법에 부정적 입장을 표명하였으며, 브라질, 멕시코, 이집트, 필리핀 등도 EFFECT TEST 가 기술적 부문에 대한 논의의 출발점이 될수있다는데는 반대하지 않았으나 COVERAGE 에 대한 합의가 없는 상태에서의 이들 부문에 대한 논의 진행의 실익에 의문을 표시 하였음.

0 의장은 차기 협의 의제를 1990. 11.9 의장 초안중 CHAPTER II 에 규정된 4가지 유형의 무역 왜곡효과 분석. 검토로 정하기로 하고 그 이외 무역 왜곡효과 LIST에 관심이 있는 국가는 이를 제출할수 있다 하였음.

2. 무역관련 지적 재산권

0 던켈 의장은 MTN/TNC/W/69 의 40 및 41항에 관한 내용을 언급하고 앞으로 TRIPS 협상을 더욱 진전시키기 위해 구체적으로 논의할 사항에 관하여 각 대표들에게발언을

통상국 경기원 재무부 농수부 상공부 특허청

PAGE 1 91.03.19 22:52 DA

외신 1과 통제관

0054

요청함.

0 이집트는 아직 TRIPS 협상에서 기술적인 문제에 관해 개도국을 위해 타협된 것이 없으며, 향후 토의에서 선.개도국 간에 이문제에 관한 구체적 토의가 진행되어야 할것이라 제안하자 이에 대해 스위스는 지금까지 실질적인 문제에 관해 합의된것이 없으며, 어느것이 기술적인 문제에 해당하는지 그 범위를 한정하기 어렵다고함.

0 놀웨이는 제 73조 (기존 지적 재산권 보호)에 관하여 기술적인 토의보다 정치적인 토의가 진행되어야 한다고 언급하고 현단계에서 다른협상 그룹의 진전상황과병행하여 TRIPS 협상을 진행해야 한다고 하였으며, 콜럼비아는 협상 균형면에서 볼때 보호수준이 증대 되었음을 지적하고 개도국에 대한 경과조치(제 6장), 분쟁해결 절차등에 관해 토의가 진행되어야 한다고 언급함.

0 던켈 의장은 TRIPS 에 관해서는 실질적이고 진전된 TEXT 를 만들어야 하며, 현단계에서 기술적인 문제에 관해 토의할 생각을 강하게 느끼지 않고 있으나 TRIPS 협상에 도달하기 위한 DEADLINE 이 없으며, 토의가 진전되지 않을 것이므로 토의진전을 위해 DEADLINE 설정의 필요성을 검토할 것이라고 함.

3. 차기 회의 일정

0 추후 통보 예정이라 하고 금번 회의 종료함.

끝

(대사 박수길-국장)

원 본

외 무 부

종 별 :

번 호 : GVW-0509 일 시 : 91 0319 1750

수 신 : 장 관(통기,경기원,재무부,농림수산부,상공부,특허청)

발 신 : 주 제네바 대사

제 목 : UR/ 협상 비공식 협의 일정

연: GVW-0375

연호 일정이후 계속되는 DUNKEL 사무총장 (TNC 고위급 의장) 주재 비공식협의 일정은 아래와 같음.

- 3.20(수): 분쟁해결.최종의정서
- 3.21(목): 시장접근
- 3.25(월)-26(화): 규범제정
- 3.26(화): 향후 협상 계획
- 4.8(월)-12(금): 써비스
- 4.15(월)- 19(금): 농산물. 끝

(대사 박수길-국장)

통상국 2차보 경기원 재무부 농수부 상공부 특허청

PAGE 1

91.03.20 10:01 WG

외신 1과 통제관

0056

기 안 용 지

분류기호 문서번호	통기 20644- 13479	(전화: 720 - 2188)	시 행 상 특별취급	
보존기간	영구. 준영구 10. 5. 3. 1.	장 관		
수 신 처 보존기간		대결		
시행일자	1991. 3.27.			

보조기관	국 장	전 결	협조기관		문서통제
	심의관				검열 1991. 3. 28 통제관
	과 장	(서명)			
기안책임자		안 성 국			발 송 인

경 유 수 신 참 조	특허청장 국제협력과	발신명의	
제 목	UR/TRIPs 협정초안에 대한 입장 통보		

대 : 국협 28140-986

TRIPs 협정 의장 초안 73조(경과 규정)에 대한 당부 입장을 별첨과 같이 통보하오니, 업무에 참조하시기 바랍니다.

첨 부 : 협상 대책 1부. 끝.

0057

협 상 대 책

주요쟁점	내 용	TRIPs 협정 73조(경과 규정) 수용 여부
	주장국 의 도	MFN 조항(TRIPs 의장초안 4조)을 기존 지적재산권 보호에 적용함으로써 지적재산권 관련 1986.8. 대미 양허사항(계류중 제법특허의 물질특허로의 보정청구, 미시판 특허물질의 소급보호)의 EC, EFTA, 일본등에로 자동확산을 노림.
국내 제도 (현행 또는 입법 추진		
타 결 시 파급효과	업 계	
	제 도 조 정	
협상대책	검 토 의 견	73조 2항 둘째 Sentence의 Shall[not]에서 bracket 배제를 분명히 함으로써 계류중인 제법특허의 물질특허로의 보정청구문제와 관련한 MFN 원칙적용을
	주 장 가능성	방지할 수 있고, 73조 2항 세째 Sentence는 미시판 특허물질의 소급보호 불가를 의미하므로 상기 Shall [not]에서의 bracket 배제가 확보되는 경우 73조
	근 거	규정은 그대로 받아들여도 EC와의 지적재산권을 둘러싼 양자교섭에서의 우리나라 기존입장은 그대로 유지되는 것으로 볼 수 있음.
기 타		

0058

13 November 1990

PROPOSAL FOR THE ESTABLISHMENT OF DISPUTE PREVENTION SYSTEM IN RESPECT OF TRANSFER OF TECHNOLOGIES(2)

Encouraged by positive responses from various delegation and in light of the comments offered by the representatives of Brazil, Canada and Australia, the Delegation of the Republic of Korea hereby submits a second Proposal for the Establishment of Dispute Prevention System in Respect of Transfer of Technologies ("Proposal"), which is an expanded and refined version to its earlier text dated 8 November 1990, as follows.

I. PROPOSAL

It is proposed to add, under PART V: DISPUTE PREVENTION AND SETTLEMENT, the following provision.

Article 66 bis: Prevention of Disputes Between Undertakings

1. Private undertakings of different PARTIES engaged in the negotiation of a voluntary license agreement involving patent and/or know-how* may, through their respective government, request the Committee on Trade Related Aspects of Intellectual Property Rights for an advisory opinion with regard to whether such license agreement, either in part or as a whole, constitutes an abuse of the patents and/or know-how or has an adverse effect on competition in international trades, subject to the following provisions.

2. Within two years from its first meeting, the Committee shall, through consultations with PARTIES and in cooperation with bodies of the World Intellectual Property Organization as provided in Article 71, promulgate a Guideline for the Prevention of Abusive Practices in License Agreement Involving Patents and/or Know-how.

---

* Know-how, for the purpose of this Article, shall mean a body of Undisclosed Information which has an industrial application.

3. Immediately after the establishment of such Guideline and upon receipt of such request, the Committee shall establish and commission a License Review Board(s) comprising a panel of experts selected from the roster referred to in Article 66, Para.2 for the purpose of reviewing such request and rendering its advisory opinion based on the Guideline.

4. The Committee shall also be authorized to issue an Implementation Regulation relating to:

   (1) organization and other institutional arrangements for the License Review Board; and

   (2) procedures for filing and examination of the request.

5. The License Review Board shall issue within 6 months from the referral of the request a written opinion accompanied by the reasons therefor. The Committee shall publish the opinion unless either PARTY, at the time of filing the request, submits a written objection to the publication.

6. The opinion shall not be binding upon any PARTY; and shall not affect any PARTY in adopting its national legislation and carrying out such appropriate measures as referred to in Article 42, Para. 2.

7. Notwithstanding Para. 6 above, PARTIES shall not prevent their undertakings from voluntarily agreeing to be bound by the result of the opinion.

II. EXPLANATION OF THE PROPOSAL

A. In General

It is truistic that disputes between the PARTIES involving a right-holder's abusive practices originate from a private contract between the right holder and another individual party. Accordingly, in order to minimize the occurrence of disputes between the PARTIES, it is only logical to control the occurrence at the origin: i.e., the private contracts. This obvious conclusion forms the very foundation of this Proposal, which is designed to prevent the disputes between private parties negotiation a license agreement involving patent rights and/or know-how.

B. Related Provisions in the TRIPs Agreement

(1) As pointed out in our earlier text, Article 8. Para.2. recognizes the need to employ "appropriate measures" in order "to prevent the abuse of intellectual property rights or the resort to practices which unreasonably restrain trade or adversely affect the international transfer of technology."

As one of such appropriate measures, this Proposal envisages a dispute prevention system by way of allowing PARTIES on behalf of their respective undertakings to seek an advisory opinion from the License Review Board established and supervised under the aegis of the TRIPs Committee.

(2) Article 43.3B provides that:

> Each PARTY shall enter, upon request, into consultations with any other PARTY which has cause to believe that an intellectual property right owner that is a national or domiciliary of the PARTY to which the request for consultations has been addressed in undertaking practices in violation of the requesting PARTY's laws and regulations on the subject matter of this Section, and which wishes to secure compliance with such legislations, without prejudice to any action under the law and to the full freedom of an ultimate decision of either PARTY. The PARTY addressed shall accord full and sympathetic consideration to, and shall afford adequate opportunity for, consultations with the requesting PARTY, and shall to cooperate through the supply of available information of relevance to the matter in question, subject to and depend upon the assurances of confidentiality given by the requesting PARTY unless the party providing the information agrees to its disclosure or disclosure is compelled by law.

The above provision contemplates a situation wherein a right holder who is a national or domiciliary of PARTY A is engaged in abusive practices in the territory of PARTY B in violation of the national law of PARTY B.

The above geographical confinement is a built-in limitation for an effective operation of the consultative mechanism. For instance, an agreement for international transfer of technology may not even involve any patents registered in PARTY B or know-how that exists in PARTY B. In this instance, Article 43.3B may not apply.

Furthermore, it is not clear as to what the obligations of PARTY A are; and, in the absence of satisfactory response from PARTY A for whatever reasons, disputes between the PARTIES will likely occur. In short, the efficacy of this provision is highly uncertain, if any.

(3) On the other hand, Article 66 authorizes the TRIPs Committee to render recommendations and rulings for the settlement of disputes between the PARTIES by way of establishing a panel of experts drawn from an existing roster of experts.

Since the nature of disputes arising out of a particular clause in a patent/know-how license agreement on the question of an abusive practice is bound to be highly technical, they can be an ideal task for the panel of experts. In other words, the panel of experts envisaged in Article 66 can also be called upon rendering an advisory opinion prior to the occurrence of disputes between the PARTIES.

(4) The language contained in Article 71 is broad enough to include, within the scope of the Committee's responsibilities and activities, the assignment of establishing an License Review Board and having it issue an advisory opinion on the propriety of a patent/know-how license agreement, in addition to the promulgation of a Guideline to be used by the Board. Specifically, Article 71, in relevant parts, reads:

> The Committee shall...afford PARTIES the opportunity of consulting on matters relating to trade related intellectual property rights. It shall carry out such other responsibilities as assigned to it by the PARTIES, and it shall, in particular, provide any assistance requested by them in the context of dispute settlement procedures. In carrying out its functions, the Committee may consult with and seek information from any source they deem appropriate.

In short, the proposed dispute prevention mechanism does not require any other additional personnel or resources than those already envisaged for the purpose of carrying out the dispute settlement.

III. EXPLANATION OF ARTICLE 66 bis

A. Para.1: Scope of Request

(1) Para.1 makes it clear that the subject matter for which an advisory opinion is sought is limited to contractual clauses contained in a license agreement involving patents and/or know-how. In other words, the subject matter does not include a license agreement of such other IPRs as trademark or copyrights, although they can be an ancillary part of a patent/know-how license agreement. The provision also excludes non-voluntary license agreements.

(2) The request for an advisory opinion is submitted not by the private undertakings but by the PARTIES where the licensor and the licensee reside. This is consistent with the existing procedures for consultations and settlement of disputes under GATT.

This procedural requirement will accord the PARTIES an opportunity to consider the desirability and appropriateness of not only making the request under this Article but also carrying out consultations and cooperation as provided in Article 43.3B.

B. Para.2: Establishment of Standards for Determination of Abusive Practices

The last sentence of Article 71 mandates the TRIPs Committee to establish, within one year from its first (organization) meeting, appropriate arrangements for cooperation with WIPO. Para. 2, therefore, contemplates a period of 2 years as sufficient to formulate and promulgate the Guideline. There are a number of reasons for this relative optimism.

First, in order for the Committee to effectively carry out the settlement of disputes under the mandate of Article 66, they need to employ, in consultation with the panel of experts, certain standards or norms. It is expected that large parts of such standards will be equally applicable to the dispute prevention procedure under Article 66 bis.

Secondly, the existing laws and regulations in various countries that govern the abusive or anti-competitive practices of IPRs are relatively uniform. Especially, the principles established in those countries which have historically administered strict controls over anti-competitive practices, notably the U.S. and the European Community, are of high standards, developed over long periods of time through numerous court decisions applied and tested in a plethora of differing circumstances. It is believed that most, if not all, of these principles can serve as an excellent reference for the establishment of the Guideline.

C. Para.5: Evolution and Refinement of Standards through Case Law Approach

(1) Even though the formulation and "legislation" of legal norms, i.e., the Guideline, may be rather easily accomplished, the task of applying them to an international contract in the context of the TRIPs Agreement will be a totally different matter.

In this connection, the approach taken by the European Community is highly instructive: that is, they have accomplished the harmonization of not only the IPR statutes but also their interpretation through the case law approach. This case law approach adopted by EC did not go unchallenged, however.

In fact,the fiscal senate of the German Supreme Court held that certain decisions of the European Court of Justice were not binding upon it because the European Court had reached its conclusions by relying on its earlier decisions. However, the German Constitutional Court held that:

> development of the law on a case law basis is fully in conformity with European legal traditions because not only had the common law development been in England in this way, but also had Roman Law, German Gemeines Recht and French Administrative Law.*

As can be seen above, there is nothing novel in employing a case law approach even in civil law countries: as a matter of fact, the dynamic nature of IPRs together with diverse differences in the culture, philosophy, level of technology and economy of PARTIES makes it a compelling case where the case law approach can be best utilized for harmonizing the "law" that will govern the control of abusive practices in international transfer of technologies and its interpretation.

To adopt the stare decisis method, however, publication of written decisions fully supported by reasons therefor is essential. PARTIES should be, therefore, encouraged not to object to the publication of the opinions for an effective development of international law governing anti-competitive practices in exercising industrial property rights.

(2) Needless to say, these should be a time limitation for the issuance of the opinion by the License Review Board as the private undertakings cannot be kept inactive too long. The current clearance system practiced by EC has a 6-month period.

D. Para.6: National Regimes not Preempted

One possible concern that PARTIES may express might be the preemptive effect of this procedure on their national regime and procedures established for reviewing and approving a license agreement. In response to such concern, the following comments may be offered.

First, inasmuch as the request to the TRIPs Committee is to be made through the government where the concerned individual undertaking resides, the PARTY has the control or opportunity to consider the desirability and possible consequences which may result from making the request.

Secondly, there are situations where an intervention by the government of the licensee will only produce negative effects on the transfer of technology.

---

* In re Frau Kloppenburg (1988) CMLR 1.
See also John Richards, "10 Years of Substantive Law Development in the European Patent Office," JPTOS, PP320-342 (1989).

Thirdly, as stated previously, if the patents to be licensed and foreign patents, there is not much that the licensee's government can do, especially when the licensor's government is reluctant to interfere with the licensor's affairs.

Fourthly, the advisory nature of the opinion does not affect in any way for each PARTY to apply its national law, where appropriate, in regulating the licensor's unlawful conduct.

E. Para.7: Restriction on PARTY's Undue Influence

In order for the TRIPs Agreement to be viable and successful, it must be assumed that the advisory opinion rendered under the auspices of the TRIPs Committee is reasonable and proper. Therefore, it only behooves the PARTIES to encourage their respective undertakings to respect and accept the Committee opinion to the maximum extent possible. Should, however, PARTIES be allowed to step their willing nationals from adhering to the opinion, the very integrity of the whole TRIPs Agreement may be in jeopardy.

Thank you Mr. Chairman,

I would like to take this opportunity to express our basic position briefly on the GATT Uruguay Round TRIPs negotiation.

At the outset, I would like to make it clear that Korea has been and will continue to be, supportive of the inclusion of the intellectual property framework within the GATT not only because we believe that such a framework is necessary to bring about an enhanced protection of intellectual property worldwide, but also because it may provide a workable mechanism for deriving multilateral solution to IPR problems and disputes, which is far more desirable than a bilateral approach.

We do, however, recognize that there exist certain obstacles to be overcome in order to reach a satisfactory accord in this final stage of TRIPs negotiations. One of such obstacles appears to stem from the fact that overly ambitious goals of certain Parties may have been reflected in the TRIPs negotiation. For a successful conclusion of the TRIPs Agreement, therefore, we believe that the participating Members should make conscientious efforts to make it successful by way of making maximum concessions in a most cooperative and constructive manner.

A second deficiency, in our opinion, that exists in the current TRIPs proposal is that it fails to fully take into account the need of technology transfer for developing countries. In this context, Korea has proposed a pre-clearance system or dispute prevention system in respect of transfer of technologies by way of minimizing anti-competitive practices, on one

0067

hand, and providing objective standards in determining such practices, on the other hand. This and other device may be utilized in striking a balance, within the TRIPs Agreement, between the need to provide an effective protection of IPR's and the need to guard against abusive practices of right holders, leading to an early successful conclusion of the Agreement.

Turning now to the specipic provisions contained in the Chairman's 7th draft prepared for the Brussels Conference, in most of the areas, Korea should be able to accommodate the draft provisions as they are either compatible with the existing Korean laws and regulations or, at least, consistent with the direction toward which we are moving. However, there still remain a number of items which we do feel strongly about. Our reservations include the following provisions:

(a) rental rights, which we oppose on the basis of, among other things, the theory of exhaustion of rights.
A potentially devastating aspect of Article 11 (rental rights) lies in the fact that it authorizes the original right owner to prohibit the rental business altogether,

(b) retroactive protection of phonograms, which is contradictory to the principle of non-retroactivity as embedded in the Rome Convention,

(c) protection of well-known trademark, which is exceptional case to the registration system of trademark,

(d) inclusion of animal and plant varieties within the scope of patentable subject matters,

0068

(e) limitation on the export of product produced under a non-voluntary license, which restricts the right of a later inventor,

(f) extending protection to assembled products in the case of semi-conductor chips and requiring payment of royalties by innocent purchasers, which go beyond the scope of the Washington Treaty,

(g) protection of undisclosed information involving test data submitted in connection with acquiring a product license of new pharmaceutical or agrochemical products, a de facto exclusive right given in addition to patent, and

(h) extending a border closing measure to patent dispute cases as well, which is entirely contrary to the basic tenet or fundamental principle underlying the TRIPs Agreement. That is, instead of promoting fair trades, it may contribute toward economic regionalization and engendering economic warfares.

As for future TRIPs negotiations schedule, in our view, since there are so many substantive issues to be discussed and negotiated, I believe that we should concentrate on such textual matters, leaving such political matters as GATTability to the ministerial level discussions and decision.

In closing, it is believed that the new intellectual property regime under the GATT should ultimately aim at achieving a balance between the policies that promote global diffusion of new science and technology and those that emphasize the proprietary interests of researchers, companies and nations. Toward this goal, I would like to express our Delegation's assurances that Korea is firmly committed and is fully prepared to work with other participants in a most cooperative spirit.

0069

UR/TRIPs 협상대책(안)

1991. 6.

특 허 청

0070

I. UR/TRIPs 협상전망

1. 최근 동향

o 1991. 5.24 미 행정부의 신속승인권 (fast-track authority) 연장을 의회에서 승인함으로써 6월부터 본격적인 협상 개시

- 6.7 TNC 회의 소집하여 분야별 그룹 회의 일정 토의
  * TRIPs 회의일정 : 6.27 - 28 Geneva 에서 개최 예정

- 분야별 협상이후 7.29 주간에 TNC 회의를 개최하여 협상결과에 대하여 논의할 예정

o '91.6.4 OCED 회의에서 GATT/UR 에 우선순위(priority)를 두고 올해안 타결 촉구토록 합의

- EC, Andriessen 부집행위원장 : Service, IPR 에 중점

2. TRIPs 협상 전망

o 각 쟁점에 대해 각국의 입장은 이미 명백화되어 있는 상태이나 Brussels 회의이후 입장의 변화는 보이지 않음.

o 미국은 걸프전쟁등을 통해 확보한 국제경제, 사회에서의 지도력을 통해 협상을 강력하게 추진할 것으로 보이나, 협상이 부진할것에 대비 Fast-track authority 연장에 따른 명분을 확보하기 위하여 양자협상도 병행, 가속화할 움직임.

- EC 도 TRIPs 가 타결되지 않자 쌍무적 현안과제를 해결하기 위한 압력 가중 (91.5.27, 한.EC 고위협의회)

o 농산물, 서비스등 미국.EC등 선진국내에서 쟁점에 해결에 따라 TRIPs도 타결될 전망 (Hills USTR, 올해안 UR 타결 촉구)

Ⅱ. 협상대응의 방향

1. 기본 전제

o 양자협상에 의한 결과보다 UR 등 다자협상을 통한 결과가 아국에 유리

o 아국의 법률제도가 TRIPs 에서 논의되는 대부분의 내용을 수용 가능

- '90.12, 산업재산권 관련 법률 개정
- 반도체 집적회로, 영업비밀등 새로운 보호논의에도 대응하여 입법활동 추진중
- 저작권 보호를 위한 Berne 조약에도 가입을 검토중

o 선.개도국간의 조정자적 입장에서 협상의 조속타결을 위해 노력

2. 협상대응의 방향

o 최종 순간까지 입장고수 분야, 양보가능 분야, 양보분야르 각 쟁점을 grading 화 하여 협상에 대처

o 협상의 조속 타결을 위해 전향적 입장을 취할 분야 개발

o 입장 고수분야에 대해서는 대응논리 개발 및 심화

o 양보 가능분야에 대해서는 타국에 대해 dealing 할 분야 모색

o 협상타결을 예상하여 국내제도, 법률 정비 및 기업에 대한 대비책 촉구

Ⅱ. 협상대책(안)

1. 주요 협상대상 분야 (요약)

분 야	대 응 논 리
<제 1 안> : 1 - 17	
1. Public 의 정의	
- "Public" 용어의 국내법 위임한계 설정 (정상 관행)	- 권리의 균형과 공공목적의 실현을 위한 각국의 노력에 부당한 압력을 가하므로 반대
2. 특허권의 보호기간	
- 출원일로부터 최소 20년	- 동일한 보호기간 설정위해 단일기간 20년
3. 입증책임의 전환	
- 입증책임 전환 요건을 다음과 같이 규정 . 신물질인 경우, 실질적 유사성이 있는 경우	- 입증책임의 전환규정은 특별한 예외 규정이므로 제한적으로 운용되어야 함.
4. 권리남용 및 반경쟁적 행위	
- 반경쟁적 행위에 대해 국내법상 조치 (계약실효등)	- 권리남용, 반경쟁적 행위는 규제 필요
5. 컴퓨터 프로그램 및 자료 편집물	
- 컴퓨터 프로그램을 어문저작물로 보호	- 컴퓨터 프로그램은 어문저작물과 다른 특성을 갖고 있음(기술성, 산업연관성)
<제 2 안> : 6 - 17	
6. 대여권 (보상청구권)	
- 최소한 음반컴퓨터 프로그램 및 영상 저작물에 한해 보상청구권 인정	- 권리자의 동의에 의해 시판된 저작물에는 권리자의 권리가 소진되어 자유사용 가능

관 철 분 야	대 응 논 리
7. 외국유명상표 보호	
- 유명상표 판단기준은 관련업계에 알려진 정도, 국제교역증대에 따른 결과 반영	- 등록되지 않은 유명상표 보호는 예외적인 것으로 당해국내에서 유명한 것이어야 함.
8. 불특허대상	
- 동.식물 변종 - 핵전환 제법에 의한 발명	- 경제, 기술수준, 대상자체의 문제점에 따라 불특허대상을 규정할수 있어야 함
9. 특허의 강제실시권 실시범위	
- 국내수요 충족만을 위해 실시	- 권리자가 국내에서 특허를 사용하지 않으면 적정한 조건하에 국가가 강제실시권을 부여할수 있어야 함. (이용발명에 대한 강제실시권의 경우 수출도 가능)
10. 분쟁예방 절차	
- 기술이전 검토위원회 설치 - 기술이전에 관한 지침 설정	- 권리자의 권리남용을 방지하기 위해 기술이전에 관한 지침설정과 검토를 통해 분쟁의 신속한 처리 및 해결
------------------------------------	------------------------------------
<제 3 안> : 11 - 17	
11. 경과규정	
- TRIPs 발효시점에 존재하나 보호되지 않는 subject matter 는 TRIPs 규정 적용 제외	- 저작권등 지적재산권에 광범위하게 인정되고 있는 public domain (공중의 영역, Berne 조약 제7조)의 법리를 이용해서 지지 확보
12. 국경조치 적용범위	
- 위조상표 부착상품, 저작권 침해물품은 권리자의 청구에 의해 세관에서 통관 유예조치 발동 가능	- 특허, IC등 복잡한 기술분야에 피고(수출입업자)에게 항변할 기회도 부여않고 비전문인인 세관에서 침해여부를 판단하여 통관유예 조치를 발동하는 것은 새로운 무역장애를 조래하므로 위조상표, 저작권에 한정

관 철 분 야	대 응 논 리
13. IC 보호의 범위	
- IC 를 내장한 완제품도 보호 (권리를 침해한 IC가 계속 내장되어 있을 경우만)	- IC 가격과 IC를 내장한 제품과는 현격한 가격차이가 발생하므로 침해 IC 를 이유로 완제품을 유통정지하면 교역에 증대 장애 초래 - IC 만 제거하면 유통정지 하지 않아야 할것.
14. 정부제출 자료의 공개금지	
- 제약, 농약의 판매허가시 제출되는 기술자료 (ex. 임상실험자료)를 최소 5년간 타품목허가시 원용(rely on) 금지	- 저약가 정책을 위해 복사품목에 대해 품목허가를 신청하는 경우 기존자료를 원용하도록 하는 것이 국제관례이므로 반대 (미.일)
15. 음반소급 보호	
- TRIPs 발효당시 존재하고 있는 음반 보호	- 음반에 관해 규정하고 있는 Rome 협약(제20조), 음반협약(제7조 3항)에도 불소급효 규정
16. IC 선의의 구매자에 의한 행위	
- 선의로(침해한 IC 라는 것은 모르고) 구매한 IC 재고품을 사용한 제조행위에 대해 royalty 지급	- royalty 지급은 당연하나 IC 제조업자에게 직접 청구하는 것이 바람직하며, 최종제품 제조업자가 부담하는 것은 과부담이 됨.
17. 대여권 (대여금지권)	
- 최소한 음반, 컴퓨터 프로그램 및 영상저작물에 한해 대여금지권 인정	- 권리자의 동의에 의해 시판된 저작물에는 권리자의 권리가 소진되어 자유사용 가능 - 보상청구권은 인정 가능하나, 대여금지권은 불가

2. 주요쟁점 내역별 협상대책

가. 양보가능분야 (I)

1) 컴퓨터 프로그램 및 자료편집물 (제10조)

가) 규정내용 : 컴퓨터 프로그램 및 자료편집물을 일반 어문저작물 (literary works)로 보호

나) 현행 국내제도 : 컴퓨터 프로그램은 특별법(컴퓨터 프로그램 보호법)에 의해 보호

다) 협상대책

o 제1단계 : 컴퓨터 프로그램은 일반 어문저작물과 다른 특성(기술성, 보호기간, 등록주의등)이 있으므로 일반 어문저작물에 의해 보호하는 것은 반대

- 어문저작물로 보호할 경우 저작인격권(공표권, 동일성 유지권등)을 인정해야 하는 문제점 발생

o 제2단계 : 선진국안 수용

- 컴퓨터 프로그램의 특성상 보호기간의 장기화는 의미가 없으며 (life-cycle이 짧음)

- 컴퓨터 프로그램이 어문저작물과 달리 등록주의를 채택하고 있으나, 등록이 권리발생 요건이 아니라 제3자 대항요건에 불과하므로 일반 저작물과 구분의 실익은 적음.

2) Public 의 정의 (제14조)

가) 규정내용 : Public 용어의 국내법 위임 한계 설정 (정상적 상업 목적 사용에 어긋나게 권리제한 해서는 안됨)

6 0076

나) 현행 국내제도 : Public 개념을 도입해서 저작권자의 권리를 제한하고 있음. (ex. 학교교육 목적 복제, 비영리목적 공연, 방송, 시사보도를 위한 이용등)

* Public 개념 도입해 저작권을 제한하는 것은 세계각국의 현실

다) 협상대책

o 1 단계 : 반대

- 복제권에 적용되는 최소제한의 범위가 저작권 전분야에 적용 된다면 권리의 균형과 공공목적 실현을 위한 각국 노력에 부당한 압력이라는 면에서 반대가 가능하나,

o 2 단계 : 수용

- normal commercial exploitation (정상적 상업목적 사용)에 위배 되지 않으면 되므로 공공목적을 위한 사용은 문제없다고 해석 가능

3) 특허권의 보호기간 (제36조)

가) 규정내용 : 출원일로부터 최소 20년

나) 현행 국내제도 : 출원공고 혹은 등록일로 부터 15년 (단, 출원일로부터 20년 초과 불가)

다) 협상대책 : 수용

o 1 단계

- 동일발명에 대한 보호기간의 통일화를 위한 단일기간인 20년을 주장하나,

o 2 단계

- 최소 20년 이라는 조건을 단일기간 20년이 충족 가능하므로 수용 가능

4) 입증책임의 전환 (제37조)

가) 규정내용 : 제법특허 침해소송시 입증책임의 전환요건을 다음과 같이 규정 [해야 한다], [할수 있다].

- 신물질인 경우, 실질적 유사성 (substantial likelihood) 이 있는 경우

나) 현행 국내제도 : 신물질(new product)인 경우만 인정

* 특허법 129조 (생산방법의 추정) : 제법특허의 경우에 그 물건이 특허 출원전에 국내에서 공지된 물건이 아닌때(new product) 에는 그 물건과 동일한 물건은 그 특허된 방법에 의해 생산된 것으로 추정

다) 협상대책

o 1 단계 : 반대 (신물질인 경우만으로 한정)

- 입증책임의 전환은 특별한 예외 규정이므로 제한적으로 적용되어야 함.

. 실제 known product 에는 수많은 process 가 존재할수 있으므로 실질적 유사성만 있는 경우에도 인정하는 것은 과한 것임.

o 2 단계 : 수용

- [할수 있다(may)] 로 하면 선택권이 있으므로 수용 가능

5) 권리남용 및 반경쟁 행위 (제43조)

가) 규정내용 : 반경쟁적 행위에 대해 국내법상 조치 (강제실시, 계약 실효등) 가능

나) 현행 국내제도 : 없 음

8

0078

다) 협상대책 : 수용

o 1 단계 : 개도국안 지지

- 권리자의 권리남용, 반경쟁적 행위에 대해 규제가 필요하다는 개도국 의견에 원칙적으로 지지 가능하나,

o 2 단계 : 입장 유보

- 동 내용은 강제실시권 규정에 포함되므로 삭제되어야 한다는 선진국안 수용 가능

나. 양보가능 분야 (II)

1) 대여권 (rental rights) (제11조)

가) 규정내용 : 최소한 컴퓨터 프로그램 및 영상저작물에 한해 대여금지권 또는 [보상청구권] 인정

나) 현행 국내제도 : 없 음

다) 협상대책

o 제1단계 : 규정반대

- 권리자의 의사에 의해 시판된 저작물에 대한 행위에 대해 권리자가 권리를 주장할수 없음 (exhaustion of right 이론)

o 제2단계 : 선진국안 수용 (보상청구권만)

- 대여권이 인정된다 해도 일부 대여요금 상승의 효과만 가져올 것이며, 실제 가격상승은 저작권자와 대여업자의 계약에 의해 결정될 것이므로 선진국안 수용

- 대여금지권은 불가 (입장고수분야 참고)

2) 외국 유명상표 보호 (제18조 2)

가) 규정내용 : 관련업계에 알려진 정보, [국제교역 증대에 따른 결과]를 반영한 기준에 의해 유명한 상표를 등록이 안되었어도 보호

나) 현행 국내제도 : 국내에서 유명한 상표 보호

* '86 한.미 양해각서: 국내에 알려진 정도와 관계없이 외국상표 보호
→ '90.6.1 심사기준 개정: 국외에서만 유명한 상표도 보호

다) 협상대책

o 제1단계 : 당해국내에서 유명한 상표 보호를 주장

- 등록되지 않은 유명상표 보호는 그 상표가 국내외에 널리 알려져 있어 타인이 그 유명상표를 사용할 경우 소비자의 혼동을 초래할 염려가 있어서 보호하는 예외적인 조치이므로,

- 당해국내에서 소비자가 혼동을 일으킬 만큼 유명해야 함.

o 제2단계 : 선진국안 수용

- 유명성 판단과 그 심사에 어려운 점은 있으나, '90.6.1 심사기준 개정으로 실제 국외에서의 유명성 정도 입증을 통해 심사에 반영하고 있으므로 수용 가능

3) 불특허대상 (제30조 3)

가) 규정내용 : [동.식물 변종], [핵전환 제법에 의한 발명]을 특허대상에서 제외

나) 현행 국내제도 : 동물, 식물(유성번식 식물) 변종, 핵전환 제법에 의한 발명을 특허대상에서 제외

다) 협상대책

o 제1단계 : 불특허대상 규정

- 발명자의 연구활동에 보상을 주기 위해 특허대상은 가급적 넓게 규정해야 하나, 대상 자체의 문제점, 개도국의 경제.기술 수준에 따라 불특허대상을 규정해야 함.

. 동물변종 : 윤리성, 안정성(stability)에 문제가 있으며,

. 식물변종 : 농업정책적 문제가 있으며

o 제2단계 : 선진국안 수용

- 불특허대상을 별도로 규정 않더라도 발명인가의 여부 (발명의 정의), 특허요건중 "산업상 이용 가능성" 을 이유로 불특허할 수 있으며 (미국.EC 의예)

- 동.식물 변종은 특별법으로 보호할 가능성이 부여되므로 수용 가능 (may)

4) 특허의 강제실시권 실시범위 (제34조)

가) 규정내용 : 일정조건하 강제실시권 규정 둘수 있으며

- 국내수요 충족만을 위해 실시권 부여 (제34조 f)

나) 현행 국내제도 : 강제실시권 제도 있음 (국내수요 충족만을 위해 실시해야 한다는 제한 없음)

다) 협상대책

o 제1단계 : 강제실시를 통해 생산된 제품 수출 가능

- 불실시, 불충분한 실시를 이유로한 강제실시권의 경우는 선진국의 안을 수용할 수 있으나,

- 기술이 복잡화 함에 따라 선발명을 기본으로 하는 후발명이 많아지고 있으므로 이용발명을 이유로 한 강제실시권의 경우는 선진국안이 후발명자의 권리를 과도하게 제한하는 것이므로 반대

  * 이용발명을 이유로 한 강제실시권 : 후발명자가, 관련있는 선발명자의 허가가 없어 생산, 판매행위를 할수 없을 경우 후발명자에게 후발명 실시를 위한 선발명의 실시권을 강제로 부여

o 제2단계 : 선진국안 수용

- 강제실시권은 국내적 목적을 위해 허가되는 것이 일반적이므로 선진국안 수용 가능

5) 분쟁예방절차 (아국제안) - 의장보고서에 규정화 되지는 않았음.

가) 제안내용 : 기술이전에 관한 지침설정, 기술이전 검토위원회를 설치
기술이전 계약을 심사함으로써 분쟁을 사전예방하고 신속하게 해결

나) 협상대책

o 제1단계 : 제안 반영 주장

- 분쟁해결 절차로 가기전에 사전에 분쟁예방 절차를 둠으로써 효율적인 기술이전 도모

o 제2단계 : 제안 후퇴 (유보)

- 기술을 가진 권리자의 반경쟁적 행위를 제한하고 분쟁을 신속히 처리한다는 의미만 반영

다. 입장고수 분야

1) 최혜국대우(MFN) 및 경과 규정

가) 규정내용

A) Art.4. MFN - 지적재산권 보호에 관한 이득, 특혜, 면책등을 타국에 즉시 무조건적으로 적용 B) Art.73. 기존 지적재산권의 보호 (경과규정) a) 특허, 의장, IC등 계류중인 것은 TRIPs 규정을 적용할 수 있다[없다] b) TRIPs 발효시점에 존재하나 보호되지 않는 subject matter는 TRIPs 규정 적용 제외

나) 규정의 파급효과

① MFN

'86 한.미 양해각서상의 조치와 조약 923호 (제법특허출원의 물질특허에로의 보정허용)에 따른 대미 수혜조치를 타국(EC.일본등)에 자동확산 적용할 의무를 지게됨.

② 경과규정

- b(아국제안)를 관철하게 되면, 최소한 '86 한.미 양해각서상의 pipeline products 보호(미시판물질 보호)는 동 규정에 해당하게 되어 TRIPs 규정(MFN)에 의해 타국에 확산 적용하지 않아도 됨.

다) 협상 대책

o 강력한 최혜국대우(MFN) 원칙 주장

- 미국 이외 타국에 차별적이고 폐쇄적인 특성을 가진 대미 수혜조치 (pipeline products 보호, 보정조치)를 MFN 의 예외로 할것을 주장하여 관철될 가능성이 희박하므로,

- 예외조항을 두지 않도록 주장하는 것이 바람직

o 대신, 경과조치에서 아국주장을 관철하여 대미 수혜조치의 자동 확산 적용을 막음.

- TRIPs 발효시 계류중(심사중)인 특허, IC, 의장등에는 TRIPs 규정을 적용 않도록 하고,

- TRIPs 발효시 존재하나 보호받지 않고 있는 물질등 (보호대상, subject matter)은 public domain(공중의 영역)의 논리를 원용하여 타당성을 주장함.

* public domain 논리의 적용

. pipeline products 의 경우 물질은 개발되어 있으나, 보호제도가 없어 보호받지 않는 상태에 있는 것 (public domain에 있는것을 한.미 양해각서에 대해 행정적으로 보호해주고 있는 것)이므로 EC.일본등 타국의 물질은 공중의 영역(public domain)에 있는 것임.

2) 통관유예조치의 적용 범위

가) 규정내용

Art. 54 통관유예조치 위조상표 부착상품, 저작권 침해물품은 권리자의 청구에 의해 세관에서 통관유예 가능

나) 규정의 파급효과

o 현재의 규정대로면 큰 문제가 없으나 선진국은 통관유예조치의 대상을 전 지적재산권 (특허, IC, 영업비밀등) 침해물품으로 확산할 것 주장

o 선진국의 주장대로 채택되면 아국의 수출품을 선진국 세관에서 특허권등 침해를 이유로 손쉽게 통관유예 시킬수 있음.

- 현재 미국의 관세법 第337조에 의한 조치보다 강력 (권리자의 청구에 의해 ITC 결정에 따라 통관유예조치 발동)

다) 협상대책

o 통관유예조치의 적용범위를 상표, 저작권 침해상품으로 한정

- 기술이 전문화, 복잡화 되어가고 있는 시대에 수출입업자에게 항변할 기회도 부여하지 않고 비전문인인 세관에서 권리자의 청구만으로 권리침해여부를 판단하여 통관유예조치를 발동하는 것은 자유무역의 흐름에 오히려 장애를 초래할 것임.

- 특허, IC 등의 경우 권리의 범위, 침해여부의 판단은 매우 전문적인 지식을 필요로 하며, 통관유예조치가 잘못 발동될 경우 손해보상의 조치가 마련되어 있기는 하나 이미 치명적인 손해 (파산, 실업) 를 가져온 수출입자에게는 소용 없는 것임.

- 수출입 단계에 있는 물품에 국내 단계에 있는 물품에 대한 조치보다 손쉬운 조치를 발동함은 피해가 내국인보다 주로 외국인에게 부여 된다는 것을 전제로 할때 불공정한 것임.

3) 반도체 집적회로 보호의 범위

가) 규정 내용

> Art. 39 보호범위
>
> 집적회로 배치설계 및 배치설계를 결합한 IC 또는 [제품]의 사용에 대한 배타권을 가짐 [IC를 내장한 제품의 경우는 제품속에 침해한 IC를 계속 포함할 경우만 그 제품에 권리가 미침]

나) 파급효과

o 단순히 IC 를 내장한 완제품 (ex. 컴퓨터, TV 등 전자제품) 에도 권리가 미치면 완제품 속의 어느 하나 IC 라도 권리를 침해한 것이라면 유통정지, 통관정지 조치 발동 가능

o 2~20 달러에 불과한 IC 를 이유로 300~30,000달러 이상의 제품의 유통이 중지되거나 통관정지가 되는 효과가 발생하므로 전자제품 수출에 장애를 초래

다) 협상대책

o 제품(전자제품)의 경우 제품속에 권리를 침해한 IC가 계속 포함되어 있을 경우만 제품에 권리가 미친다고 주장

- IC 와 IC 를 내장한 제품과는 현격한 가격 차이 발생

- 따라서 침해한 IC를 이유로 제품 자체를 유통정지, 통관 유예하는 것은 무역장애를 초래함.

- 제품속에 있는 침해한 IC만 제거(교체)하면 제품이 유통, 통관될수 있어야 함.

4) 정부제출 자료의 공개 금지

가) 규정내용

Art. 42. 4A 정부제출 자료 공개 금지
제약, 농약의 판매허가시 제출되는 기술자료를 [....최소 5년간 타 품목 허가에 원용(rely on) 할수 없으며].... 공개되어서는 안됨.

나) 파급효과

o 신약개발 능력이 전무한 상태인 국내 제약업계에서 royalty 를 지불하고 license 를 받은 일부 품목을 제외하고는 특허기간이 만료된 generic drug 의 copy 품목 생산에 의존하고 있는 실정

- 따라서 상기 규정이 채택될 경우 외국 다국적 기업의 시장독점 효과 발생

∵) 국내제도: copy 품목 제조 판매허가시 외국기업이 제출한 임상실험 자료를 원용하고 생물학적 동등성에 관한 시험자료만 제출하고 있음.

bio-equivalence test.

다) 협상대책

o 선진국 주장의 부당성을 제기해서 반대

o 대응의 논리

① 특허기간이 만료된 generic drug 의 경우

- 미국에서도 generic drug(미국에서도 특허기간이 만료된 약품)

. 미국에서도 Waxman-Hetch 법에 의해 복사품목에 대해 타 업자가 품목허가를 신청하는 경우 보편적으로 생물학적 동등성 시험자료 제출을 요구하는 것이 국제 관례임. (미.일.EC.한국)

- 미국에서는 generic drug 이 안된 경우 (미국에서는 특허기간이 만료 되지 않았으나 타국의 보호기간이 짧거나 보호제도가 없어 타국에서 generic drug 이 된 경우)

  . 행정보호 형태의 추가적인 보호를 외국에 강요하는 결과가 되어 소급보호의 결과를 초래하게 됨.

② 특허기간이 만료되지 않은 일반 의약, 농약품의 경우

- 임상실험의 raw data 원용

  . 특허권이 유효한 품목과 동일한 품목을 생산하기 위해서는 권리자의 허가(license) 를 받아야 하므로 이 경우는 license 계약시 임상 실험 raw data 를 권리자가 제공할 것이므로 문제가 없으며 전적 으로 license 계약상의 문제임.

- 임상실험의 결과만 원용 (결과만을 타품목 제조허가시 원용하는 경우는 많음) ex) 제품 설명서상의 부작용, 작용 효과등

  . 제품설명서에 나온 결과는 공표를 통해 public domain 에 빠진것임.

  . 신약개발 능력이 없는 대다수 국가에 royalty 부담을 가중시켜 약품가격 상승의 효과를 초래 → 개도국의 국민 보건에 지대한 영향

5) 음반의 소급보호

가) 규정내용

Art. 16. 6 [음반에 있어서 음반제작자 및 실연자의 권리에 제15조 (Berne 협약 상의 소급보호 준용 규정) 를 준용한다.]

나) 파급효과

o TRIPs 발효 이전의 외국 음반에 관한 권리를 보호해야 하는 의무를 짐.

o 따라서, 외국의 classic 명곡, 유행가(popular song)등 음반제작에 관해 royalty 부담의 증가

다) 협상 대책

o Berne 협약상 보호받는 저작물이 아닌 음반의 보호에 대해 Berne 협약상의 소급보호에 관한 규정을 적용하는 것은 타당치 못함.

- 저작인접권 관련 Rome 협약 제20조, 음반협약 제7조 3항에서도 음반의 불소급보호 원칙 선언

6) 선의의 IC 구매자에 의한 행위

가) 규정내용

Art. 40. 선의의 IC 구매자에 의한 행위 선의로 (권리를 침해한 IC라는 것을 모르고) 구매한 IC를 최종제품 (전자제품)에 결합하는 업자가 침해사실을 통고받은후 IC 재고품을 최종제품에 결합하는 경우 [권리자에게 royalty를 지급해야 함]

나) 파급효과

o 대량으로 IC를 구매한 후 제조행위를 하는 것이 관례임.

- 실제 권리자는 권리를 침해한 IC 제조자 보다 최종제품 제조자에게 royalty 를 청구하는 문제가 많이 발생하고 있음 (royalty 부담액이 큼)

. IC 제조업자간의 분쟁에 제조업자가 피해를 보는 경우가 발생함.

- 따라서 선의로 구매한 IC 재고품 사용에 대해 royalty 를 지급해야 되면 최종제품 제조자에게 과도한 부담을 주는 것임.

다) 협상 대책

o IC 가 권리를 침해한 것임을 통보받은 이후의 제조행위에 대해 실제 권리를 침해한 IC 제조업자에게 royalty 를 청구하는 것이 바람직하나 선의의 최종제품 제조자에게 청구하는 것은 바람직 하지 못함.

7) 대여권 (대여금지권)

가) 규정내용

Art. 11. 대여권 (rental rights) 최소한 컴퓨터 프로그램, 영상저작물, 음반에 대해 대여금지권 [또는 보상청구권] 인정

나) 파급효과

o 대여금지권을 인정할 경우 국내관련업계 (비디오, Compact Disc 업계) 가 극심한 공황에 빠짐.

- 국내의 대여업을 금지하고 외국업계가 직접 운영 가능성

* 비디오 업계 현황 ('90 한국전자연감)

. VTR 보급대수 : 400만대 → 1,000만대 ('95)

. 비디오 shop : 25,000 여개소

. 외국 비디오 수입 : 약 4,000종

- 1종당 2,000～20,000 복제, 편당 10～20회 대여

다) 협상 대책

o 보상청구권은 협상에 따라 수용 가능하나 대여금지권은 불가

- 권리소진이론을 근거로 주장

특　　허　　청

국협 28140- 770　　568-6077　　1991. 6. 11.

수신 수신처참조

제목 UR/지적재산권 협상분야 실무 소위원회 개최

1. UR/지적재산권 협상에 대비, 표제회의를 다음과 같이 개최함을 통보하오니 참석하여 주시기 바랍니다.

2. 아울러, 동 회의 결과를 토대로 협상대책을 마련, UR 대책 실무위원회에 보고후 확정할 계획임을 통보합니다.

다　　음

가. 일 시 : 1991. 6. 14, 15:00 - 17:00

나. 장 소 : 특허청 14층 회의실

다. 참석범위 : 특 허 청　기획관리관 (회의 주재)

　　　　　　　　"　　　국제협력과장

　　　　　　경제기획원　통상조정 3과장

　　　　　　외 무 부　통상기구과장

　　　　　　문 화 부　저작권과장

　　　　　　상 공 부　전자부품과장

　　　　　　보 사 부　약무과장

　　　　　　과 기 처　정보산업기술과장(무순).

0092

국협 28140-2790 1991. 6. 11.

특 허 청 장

수신처 경제기획원장관(대외경제조정실장), 외무부장관(통상국장), 문화부장관(어문출판국장), 상공부장관(전자전기국장), 보사부장관(약정국장), 과학기술처장관(기술정책관).

0092-1

원 본

외 무 부

종 별 :

번 호 : GVW-1126 일 시 : 91 0618 1630

수 신 : 장 관(통기,경기원,문화부,특허청)

발 신 : 주 제네바 대사

제 목 : UR / TRIPS 공식 회의 개최

6.27-28 간 제네바 갓트에서 표제회의를 별첨 의제에 따라 개최되므로 아래 사항을 참고하여 본부대표의 참가등을 필요 조치 바람.

1. 동 회의 진행은 6.27(목) 10:00 공식회의를 개최(오전)하고 브랏셀 각료회의이후 TRIPS 협상의 상태에 관한 토의 및 각국 대표에게 주요 관심 사항 및 입장을 발표할 기회가 부여될것임.

2. 공식회의에 이어서 별도로 주요국별 비공식협의회(오후)를 갖고 각국의 주요관심사항, 향후협상 방법등에 관해 토의할 것임.

3. 6.28(금) 공식회의를 다시 소집, 각국별 비공식협의 결과를 참고하여 향후 협상 진행방법 및 협상 일정을 토의 결정할 것임.

4. 차기 공식 회의는 잠정적으로 9월에 개최할것이라고 함. 끝

첨부: 회의 의제 1부 (GVW(F)-210)

(대사 박수길-국장)

통상국 2차보 문화부 경기원 특허청

PAGE 1 91.06.19 08:04 FO

외신 1과 통제관

0093

GVW(F)-0210 10618 1630

"GVW-1126 첨부"

GATT/AIR/ 17 JUNE 1991

SUBJECT: URUGUAY ROUND NEGOTIATING GROUP ON THE TRADE-RELATED ASPECTS OF INTELLECTUAL PROPERTY RIGHTS, INCLUDING TRADE IN COUNTERFEIT GOODS

1. A MEETING OF THE NEGOTIATING GROUP ON TRADE-RELATED ASPECTS OF INTELLECTUAL PROPERTY RIGHTS, INCLUDING TRADE IN COUNTERFEIT GOODS, WILL BE HELD ON 27 AND 28 JUNE 1991 IN THE CENTRE WILLIAM RAPPARD. THE MEETING WILL BEGIN ON MONDAY 27 JUNE AT 10 A.M. THE FOLLOWING AGENDA IS PROPOSED FOR THE MEETING:

A. REVIEW OF THE STATE OF THE NEGOTIATIONS;

B. ORGANIZATION OF FURTHER WORK;

C. OTHER BUSINESS.

2. GOVERNMENTS PARTICIPATING IN THE MULTILATERAL TRADE NEGOTIATIONS, AND INTERNATIONAL ORGANIZATIONS WHICH HAVE PREVIOUSLY ATTENDED PROCEEDINGS OF THIS NEGOTIATING GROUP, WISHING TO BE REPRESENTED AT THIS MEETING ARE REQUESTED TO INFORM ME AS SOON AS POSSIBLE OF THE NAMES OF THEIR REPRESENTATIVES.

A. DUNKEL

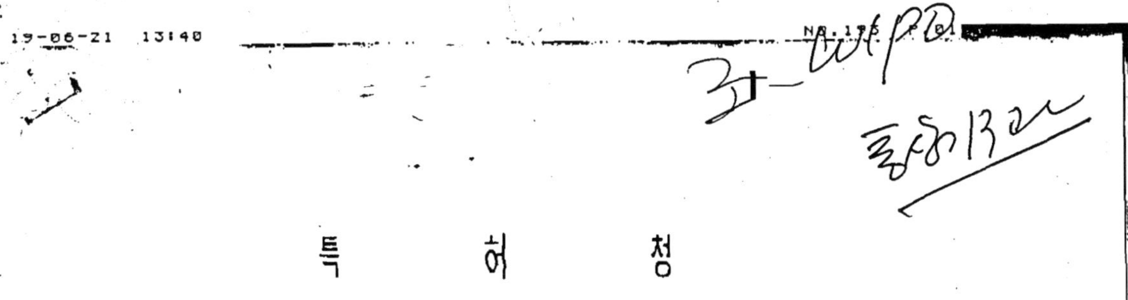

특 허 청

조사 02101 - 568 - 0121 1991. 6. 21.

수신 수신처참조

제목 영업비밀 보호입법을 위한 관계부처 (단제) 실무자 회의

1. 최근 기술혁신과 경제사회의 정보화, 서어비스화 추세에 따라 기술상 또는 경영상의 노우하우등 영업비밀이 대량생산되고, 거래또한 활발해 지면서 그관리와 유출이 새로운 사회적 문제로 제기되는등 그중요성이 날로 증대되고 있어, 이에 대한 적절한 보호제도의 마련이 불가피한 실정입니다.

2. 특허청에서는 '88. 8월부터 영업비밀 보호제도 연구반과 입법추진 위원회를 구성, 2차에 걸친 공청회 및 세미나, 6차에 걸친 법안 심의과정을 거처 영업비밀 보호를 위한 부정경쟁방지법 개정초안을 마련하고 이에 대한 관계부처 및 경제단체 실무자 의견을 수렴코자 아래와 같이 회의를 개최하오니 적극 참석하여 주시기 바랍니다.

가. 일 시 : '91. 6. 26 (수) 14:00

나. 장 소 : 특허청 14층 회의실

(서울 강남구 역삼동 823번지)

다. 대 상

1) 관계부처 : 과장급

2) 경제단체 : 임원급

라. 회의자료 : 당일배부.

0095

조사 02101 - 2557 1991. 6. 21.

특 허 청

수신처 총무처, 외무부, 내무부, 교육부, 경제기획원, 과학기술처, 재무부, 법무부, 농림수산부, 상공부, 동력자원부, 건설부, 체육청소년부, 보건사회부, 노동부, 환경처, 공보처, 문화부, 교통부, 체신부, 조달청, 농촌진흥청, 산림청, 수산청, 공업진흥청(25), 대한무역협회, 전국경제인연합회, 중소기업중앙회, 대한상공회의소, 한국정밀화학공업진흥회, 한국기계공업진흥회, 한국전자공업진흥회, 한국섬유산업연합회, 대한방적협회, 한국신발산업협회, 한국전기공업진흥회, 한국자동차공업협회, 한국공업표준협회, 한국생산성본부, 한국발명특허협회(15)

0096

UR/TRIPs 협상(안)

1991. 6.

특 허 청

0097

I. 기본입장 (훈령안)

o 재개되는 GATT/UR 지적재산권 협상에 참가, 아국의 기본입장을 설명하고 각국의 입장과 동향을 파악하여 향후 협상대책 수립에 효율적으로 반영하고자 함.

o 특히, 선진국의 과도한 주장에 대해 부당성을 제기하고 이에 대한 지지를 확보하여 아국에 유리하게 타결되도록 노력할 것임.

o 이번 협상의 재개가 GATT 내에 지적재산권등 새로운 분야를 포괄한 새로운 자유무역 체제를 탄생시킬 수 있느냐의 여부를 시험하는 무대가 될것임을 강조하여 선.개도국의 양보를 촉구함.

o "기술이전에 관한 분쟁예방 절차" 마련을 위한 제안을 공식 제안함으로써 아국의 협상력을 강화하고 선.개도국간 중재자 역할을 강화해 나감.

0098

Ⅱ. 세부입장

1. GATT ability

o 실질적으로 지적재산권 분야에 해결해야 될 무역관련 쟁점이 많이 발생하고 있으므로 이를 무역관련 기구인 GATT 내에 TRIPs 협정을 마련하여 해결하는 것이 바람직함.

2. 향후 협상일정

o 협상 순서

- 재개된 TRIPs 협상에도 아직 논의되어야 할 쟁점이 많이 존재하고 있기 때문에 기술적인 문제 (technical matters)를 먼저 논의하여 성과를 거둔 다음에 political matters 를 나중에 논의해야 한다고 봄.

o 협상시한 설정

- 올해안에 TRIPs 협상이 종료되는 것이 바람직함.

3. 주요쟁점 분야 입장

1) 컴퓨터 프로그램 및 자료편집물 (제10조)

o 제1단계 : 컴퓨터 프로그램은 일반 어문저작물과 다른 특성(기술성, 보호기간, 등록주의등)이 있으므로 일반 어문저작물에 의해 보호하는 것은 반대

- 어문저작물로 보호할 경우 저작인격권(공표권, 동일성 유지권등)을 인정해야 하는 문제점 발생

0099.

o 제2단계 : 선진국안 수용

- 컴퓨터 프로그램의 특성상 보호기간의 장기화는 의미가 없으며 (life-cycle이 짧음)

- 컴퓨터 프로그램이 어문저작물과 달리 등록주의를 채택하고 있으나, 등록이 권리발생 요건이 아니라 제3자 대항요건에 불과하므로 일반 저작물과 구분의 실익은 적음.

2) Public 의 정의 (제14조)

o 1 단계 : 반대

- 복제권에 적용되는 최소제한의 범위가 저작권 전분야에 적용된다면 권리의 균형과 공공목적 실현을 위한 각국 노력에 부당한 압력이라는 면에서 반대가 가능하나,

o 2 단계 : 수용

- normal commercial exploitation (정상적 상업목적 사용)에 위배되지 않으면 되므로 공공목적을 위한 사용은 문제없다고 해석 가능

3) 특허권의 보호기간 (제36조)

o 1 단계

- 동일발명에 대한 보호기간의 통일화를 위한 단일기간인 20년을 주장하나,

o 2 단계

- 최소 20년 이라는 조건을 단일기간 20년이 충족 가능하므로 수용 가능

0100

4) 입증책임의 전환 (제37조)

o 1 단계 : 반대 (신물질인 경우만으로 한정)

- 입증책임의 전환은 특별한 예외 규정이므로 제한적으로 적용되어야 함.

. 실제 known product 에는 수많은 process 가 존재할수 있으므로 실질적 유사성만 있는 경우에도 인정하는 것은 과한 것임.

o 2 단계 : 수용

- [할수 있다(may)] 로 하면 선택권이 있으므로 수용 가능

5) 권리남용 및 반경쟁 행위 (제43조)

o 1 단계 : 개도국안 지지

- 권리자의 권리남용, 반경쟁적 행위에 대해 규제가 필요하다는 개도국 의견에 원칙적으로 지지 가능하나,

o 2 단계 : 입장 유보

- 동 내용은 강제실시권 규정에 포함되므로 삭제되어야 한다는 선진국안 수용 가능

6) 대여권 (rental rights) (제11조)

o 제1단계 : 규정반대

- 권리자의 의사에 의해 시판된 저작물에 대한 행위에 대해 권리자가 권리를 주장할수 없음 (exhaustion of right 이론)

o 제2단계 : 선진국안 수용 (보상청구권만)

- 대여권이 인정된다 해도 일부 대여요금 상승의 효과만 가져올 것이며, 실제 가격상승은 저작권자와 대여업자의 계약에 의해 결정될 것이므로 선진국안 수용

- 대여금지권은 불가 (입장고수분야 참고)

0101

7) 외국 유명상표 보호 (제18조 2)

o 제1단계 : 당해국내에서 유명한 상표 보호를 주장

- 등록되지 않은 유명상표 보호는 그 상표가 국내외에 널리 알려져 있어 타인이 그 유명상표를 사용할 경우 소비자의 혼동을 초래할 염려가 있어서 보호하는 예외적인 조치이므로,

- 당해국내에서 소비자가 혼동을 일으킬 만큼 유명해야 함.

o 제2단계 : 선진국안 수용

- 유명성 판단과 그 심사에 어려운 점은 있으나, '90.6.1 심사기준 개정으로 실제 국외에서의 유명성 정도 입증을 통해 심사에 반영하고 있으므로 수용 가능

8) 불특허대상 (제30조 3)

o 제1단계 : 불특허대상 규정

- 발명자의 연구활동에 보상을 주기 위해 특허대상은 가급적 넓게 규정해야 하나, 대상 자체의 문제점, 개도국의 경제.기술 수준에 따라 불특허대상을 규정해야 함.

. 동물변종 : 윤리성, 안정성(stability)에 문제가 있으며,

. 식물변종 : 농업정책적 문제가 있으며

o 제2단계 : 선진국안 수용

- 불특허대상을 별도로 규정 않더라도 발명인가의 여부 (발명의 정의), 특허요건중 "산업상 이용 가능성" 을 이유로 불특허할 수 있으며 (미국.EC 의예)

- 동.식물변종은 특별법으로 보호할 가능성이 부여되므로 수용가능 (may)

0102

9) 특허의 강제실시권 실시범위 (제34조)

o 제1단계 : 강제실시를 통해 생산된 제품 수출 가능

- 불실시, 불충분한 실시를 이유로한 강제실시권의 경우는 선진국의 안을 수용할 수 있으나,

- 기술이 복잡화 함에 따라 선발명을 기본으로 하는 후발명이 많아지고 있으므로 이용발명을 이유로 한 강제실시권의 경우는 선진국안이 후발명자의 권리를 과도하게 제한하는 것이므로 반대

* 이용발명을 이유로 한 강제실시권 : 후발명자가, 관련있는 선발명자의 허가가 없어 생산, 판매행위를 할수 없을 경우 후발명자에게 후발명 실시를 위한 선발명의 실시권을 강제로 부여

o 제2단계 : 선진국안 수용

- 강제실시권은 국내적 목적을 위해 허가되는 것이 일반적이므로 선진국안 수용 가능

10) 분쟁예방절차 (아국제안) - 의장보고서에 규정화 되지는 않았음.

o 공식제안을 함으로써 제안이 반영되도록 주장

- 분쟁해결 절차로 가기전에 사전에 분쟁예방 절차를 둠으로써 효율적인 기술이전 도모

* 제안에 대해서는 Ⅲ 참조

0103

11) 최혜국대우(MFN) 및 경과 규정

o 강력한 최혜국대우(MFN) 원칙 주장

- 미국 이외 타국에 차별적이고 폐쇄적인 특성을 가진 대미 수혜조치 (pipeline products 보호, 보정조치)를 MFN 의 예외로 할것을 주장하여 관철될 가능성이 희박하므로,

- 예외조항을 두지 않도록 주장하는 것이 바람직

o 대신, 경과조치에서 아국주장을 관철하여 대미 수혜조치의 자동 확산 적용을 막음.

- TRIPs 발효시 계류중(심사중)인 특허, IC, 의장등에는 TRIPs 규정을 적용 않도록 하고,

- TRIPs 발효시 존재하나 보호받지 않고 있는 물질등 (보호대상, subject matter)은 public domain(공중의 영역)의 논리를 원용하여 타당성을 주장함.

* public domain 논리의 적용

. pipeline products 의 경우 물질은 개발되어 있으나, 보호제도가 없어 보호받지 않는 상태에 있는 것 (public domain에 있는것을 한.미 양해각서에 대해 행정적으로 보호해주고 있는 것)이므로 EC.일본등 타국의 물질은 공중의 영역(public domain)에 있는 것임.

12) 통관유예조치의 적용 범위

o 통관유예조치의 적용범위를 상표, 저작권 침해상품으로 한정

- 기술이 전문화, 복잡화 되어가고 있는 시대에 수출입업자에게 항변할 기회도 부여하지 않고 비전문인인 세관에서 권리자의 청구만으로 권리 침해여부를 판단하여 통관유예조치를 발동하는 것은 자유무역의 흐름에 오히려 장애를 초래할 것임.

0104

- 특허, IC 등의 경우 권리의 범위, 침해여부의 판단은 매우 전문적인 지식을 필요로 하며, 통관유예조치가 잘못 발동될 경우 손해보상의 조치가 마련되어 있기는 하나 이미 치명적인 손해 (파산, 실업) 를 가져온 수출입자에게는 소용 없는 것임.

- 수출입 단계에 있는 물품에 국내 단계에 있는 물품에 대한 조치보다 손쉬운 조치를 발동함은 피해가 내국인보다 주로 외국인에게 부여 된다는 것을 전제로 할때 불공정한 것임.

13) 반도체 집적회로 보호의 범위

o 제품(전자제품)의 경우 제품속에 권리를 침해한 IC가 계속 포함되어 있을 경우만 제품에 권리가 미친다고 주장

- IC 와 IC 를 내장한 제품과는 현격한 가격 차이 발생

- 따라서 침해한 IC를 이유로 제품 자체를 유통정지, 통관 유예하는 것은 무역장애를 초래함.

- 제품속에 있는 침해한 IC만 제거(교체)하면 제품이 유통, 통관될 수 있어야 함.

14) 정부제출 자료의 공개금지

o 선진국 주장의 부당성을 제기해서 반대

o 대응의 논리

① 특허기간이 만료된 generic drug 의 경우

- 미국에서도 generic drug(미국에서도 특허기간이 만료된 약품)

0105

. 미국에서도 Waxman-Hetch 법에 의해 복사품목에 대해 타 업자가 품목 허가를 신청하는 경우 보편적으로 생물학적 동등성 시험자료 제출을 요구하는 것이 국제 관례임. (미.일.EC.한국)

- 미국에서는 generic drug 이 안된 경우 (미국에서는 특허기간이 만료되지 않았으나 타국의 보호기간이 짧거나 보호제도가 없어 타국에서 generic drug 이 된 경우)

  . 행정보호 형태의 추가적인 보호를 외국에 강요하는 결과가 되어 소급보호의 결과를 초래하게 됨.

② 특허기간이 만료되지 않은 일반 의약, 농약품의 경우

- 임상실험의 raw data 원용

  . 특허권이 유효한 품목과 동일한 품목을 생산하기 위해서는 권리자의 허가(license) 를 받아야 하므로 이 경우는 license 계약시 임상실험 raw data 를 권리자가 제공할 것이므로 문제가 없으며 전적으로 license 계약상의 문제임.

- 임상실험의 결과만 원용 (결과만을 타품목 제조허가시 원용하는 경우는 많음) ex) 제품 설명서상의 부작용, 작용 효과등

  . 제품설명서에 나온 결과는 공표를 통해 public domain 에 빠진것임.

  . 신약개발 능력이 없는 대다수 국가에 royalty 부담을 가중시켜 약품 가격 상승의 효과를 초래 → 개도국의 국민 보건에 지대한 영향

15) 음반의 소급보호

o Berne 협약상 보호받는 저작물이 아닌 음반의 보호에 대해 Berne 협약상의 소급보호에 관한 규정을 적용하는 것은 타당치 못함.

- 저작인접권 관련 Rome 협약 제20조, 음반협약 제7조 3항에서도 음반의 불소급보호 원칙 선언

0106

16) 선의의 IC 구매자에 의한 행위

o IC 가 권리를 침해한 것임을 통보받은 이후의 제조행위에 대해 실제 권리를 침해한 IC 제조업자에게 royalty 를 청구하는 것이 바람직하나 선의의 최종 제품 제조자에게 청구하는 것은 바람직 하지 못함.

17) 대여권 (대여금지권)

o 보상청구권은 협상에 따라 수용 가능하나 대여금지권은 불가

- 권리소진이론을 근거로 주장

Ⅲ. 기술이전에 관한 분쟁예방 절차 마련을 위한 제안

(별첨 참조)

0107

기 안 용 지

분류기호 문서번호	통기 20644-	(전화 : 720 - 2188)	시 행 상 특별취급	
보존기간	영구. 준영구 10. 5. 3. 1.	차 관	장 관	
수 신 처 보존기간		전결		
시행일자	1991. 6.22.			

보조기관		협조기관		
국 장		제2차관보		문 서 통 제
심의관				
과 장				
기안책임자	조 현			발 송 인

경 유 수 신 참 조	건 의	발신명의		
제 목	UR/TRIPs 협상 정부대표 임명			

91.6.27(목)-28(금)간 제네바에서 개최되는 UR/TRIPs 협상에 참가할 정부대표단을 "정부대표 및 특별사절의 임명과 권한에 관한 법률"에 의거, 아래와 같이 임명할 것을 건의하오니 재가하여 주시기 바랍니다.

- 아 래 -

0108

1. 회 의 명 : UR/TRIPs 협상

2. 회의기간 및 장소 : 91.6.27(목)-28(금), 제네바

3. 정부대표

o 본부대표

- 특허청 기획관리관 노영욱

- 특허청 국제협력과 사무관 이찬우

- 경제기획원 통상조정2과 이승길

o 현지대표 : 주 제네바 대표부 관계관

4. 출장기간 : 91.6.25-7.1 (6박7일)

5. 소요경비 : 특허청 및 경제기획원 소관예산

6. 훈 령

o 아국의 기존 입장에 따라 UR/TRIPs 공식 회의 및 주요국별 비공식 회의에 적극 참가하고, 각국의 입장 및 협상 동향을 파악, 향후 협상 대책 수립에 반영토록 함.

- 2 - 0109

o 협상의 원만한 타결을 위하여 일부 입장 대립 분야에서 선.개도국간의 양보를 촉구하고, 특히 공공개념의 확대 해석등 선진국의 과도한 주장은 적절하게 이의 부당성을 지적토록 함.

o 현지 실정에 따라 "기술이전에 관한 분쟁예방 절차"에 관한 아국 입장을 공식 제안하여 아국의 협상력을 강화토록 함.

첨 부 : "기술이전에 관한 분쟁예방 절차" 제안 검토서. 끝.

기술이전에 관한 분쟁예방절차 마련을 위한 제안

1. 제안 이유

o 기술이전 계약에 있어서 권리자의 권리남용에 의해 불공정한 계약이 많이 발생

o 그러나, 세계적인 지적재산권 보호체제 마련을 위한 TRIPs 협상에서는 보호수준의 향상으로 기술 공급자인 권리자의 이익을 보호하는데 중점을 두는 반면, 기술 수요자의 측면을 고려되지 않고 있음.

o 따라서 기술이전 계약에 있어 권리자의 반경제적 행위를 규제하고, 발생 가능한 분쟁을 사전에 예방하고자 함.

2. 제안 내용

가. 제안내용 요약

제66조의 2 : 기업간의 분쟁예방 (Prevention of Disputes Between Undertakings)

1. 특허, know-how 에 관한 자발적 license 계약협상을 하는 다른 체약국간의 사기업은 그들의 정부를 통해 license 계약의 전체 혹은 부분이 권리남용 혹은 국제무역에서의 경쟁에 위배되는지 여부의 판단을 아래 규정에 의거 TRIPs 위원회(위원회)에 요청할 수 있음.

2. 위원회는 첫 회의이후 2년내에 체약국들의 협의, 69조에 따른 WIPO 의 협조를 얻어 특허, know-how license 계약에서의 권리남용행위 방지에 관한 guideline 을 제정해야 함.

3. 위원회는 guideline 설정과 요청이 있은 직후 요청을 심사하고 guideline 에 기초한 자문을 하기 위해 제66조 2(C)에 따른 명부에서 전문가를 선출해 기술이전 계약검토위원회(License Review Boards)를 구성함.

0111

4. 위원회는 다음과 관련한 시행규칙 (Implementation Regulation)을 제정할수 있음.

(1) 기술이전계약 검토위원회 (License Review Board)의 조직

(2) 요청의 제출과 심사

5. 검토위원회는 요청이후 6개월이내 이유를 포함한 서면 의견을 제시해야 함. 위원회는 당사국(PARTIES)이 요청시 의견의 공포를 반대한다는 서면의사를 제출 않는한 의견을 공포함.

6. 상기 의견은 체약국을 구속하지도 않고 각 국내법에 영향도 주지 않음.

7. 6항에 불구하고 체약국은 그들의 사기업이 그 의견에 자발적으로 따르는 것을 막지 않음.

나. 제안내용 설명

o 제1항 : 요청의 범위 (Scope)

- 요청대상 : 특허와, know-how 에 대한 license 계약 (강제실시권을 배제)

- 요청주체 : 체약국이 대행

. 체약국이 사기업의 요청을 걸러주는 역할 담당

o 제2항 : 권리남용 여부 결정의 기준 설정

- 제71조 (TRIPs 위원회)의 mandate 에 의해 1년이내 WIPO와 협력방안 설정

. 따라서 2년내에 전문가의 의견을 들어 기준설정 가능

- 미국.EC등 IPR 분야 독점금지에 관한 규정, 제도를 참고로 하면 설정 가능

0112

o 제5항 : 판례에 의해 기준의 개발

- IPR 분야는 동적으로 변화하고 있기 때문에 판례법에 의해 기준을 세련화 하고 개발할 수 있음.

. 대륙법계 국가도 영.미버계와 마찬가지로 가능
ex) 독일연방 헌법재판소의 판결

o 제6항 : 국내에 대한 구속력

- 국내에 대한 구속력이 없음.

o 제7항 : 사기업에 대한 영향력

- TRIPs 협정이 성공적이라면 TRIPs 위원회의 자문의견은 적절한 의견일 것임.
- 따라서 사기업이 자발적으로 동 의견에 따르는 것을 막을수는 없음.

3. 제안의 효과

o 기술 수입국인 아국이 선진국과 기술도입 계약을 체결할때 특허, know-how 기술의 독점적인 성격으로 부당한 계약을 체결하는 경우가 많음.

o 이에 반해 선진국은 자국내에 기술 license 계약시 독점금지법을 통해 각종 규제를 가하고 있지만 대 외국 계약시에는 별다른 규제수단이 없음.

o 따라서, 동 제안을 함으로써 선진국과의 기술이전 계약시 TRIPs 위원회가 제정한 guideline 에 근거하여 기술이전 계약을 함으로써 정당한 조건으로 기술도입이 가능하게 됨.

0113

o 물론, guideline 과 위원회의 자문의견이 구속력이 있는 것은 아니나 선언적인 효과를 갖게되는 것이며,

- 개도국의 제안인 PART Ⅱ, Section 8 (권리남용 및 반경쟁적 행위)이 채택되지 않는다 해도 동 제안에 의해 아국의 실익을 확보할 수 있음.

o 아국의 제안은 중도국 (캐나다.호주등)의 지지를 받고 있는 내용으로 제안을 함으로써 아국이 TRIPs 협상에서 선.개도국간의 조정자 역할로서의 협상력을 강화할 수 있는 것임.

0114

특 허 청

국협 28140-2552 568-6077 1991. 6. 21.

수신 외무부장관

참조 통상국장

제목 '91 제1차 GATT/UR TRIPs 협상그룹 회의참가

'91. 6.27 - 28간 스위스 제네바에서 개최되는 표제회의의 당청 참가자를 아래와 같이 선정하여 추천하오니 필요한 조치를 취해 주시기 바랍니다.

아 래

1. 회 의 명 : '91 제1차 GATT/UR TRIPs 협상그룹 회의
2. 기간 및 장소 : '91. 6.27(목) - 28(금), 스위스 제네바 GATT 본부
3. 참 가 자

소 속	직 위	직 급	성 명	비 고
특 허 청	기획관리관	부이사관	노 영 욱	수석대표
"	WIPO 주재관	서 기 관	김 준 규	대표 (현지참석)
"		행정사무관	이 찬 우	대 표

첨부 1. 회의의제 1부.
2. 세부일정 및 활동계획서 1부.
3. 소요경비 내역 1부.
4. 국.영문 이력서 각 1부.
5. 아국입장 1부. 끝.

특 허 청 장

0115

1. 회의 의제

o 협상의 상황 검토

o 향후 협상계획

o 기 타

0116

2. 세부일정 및 활동계획서

일 자	시 간	일 정	비 고
6. 25 (화)	12 : 40	서울 발 (KE 907)	
	17 : 55	런던 삭	
	20 : 00	런던 발 (SR 837)	
	22 : 30	제네바 착	
26 (수)		협상대책 회의	
27 (목) / 28 (금)		TRIPs 회의 참석	
29 (토)		협상결과 및 향후 협상대책 논의	
30 (일)	18 : 45	제네바 발 (SR 728)	
	19 : 50	파리 착	
	21 : 30	파리 발 (KE 902)	
7. 1 (월)	17 : 30	서울 착	

0117

3. 소요경비 내역

(단위 : $)

구 분	항공료	일 비	숙박비	식 비	판공비	계
국장 노영욱	2,125	175	474	322		3,096
5 급 이찬우	2,125	140	396	294		2,955
계	4,250	315	870	616		6,051

o 노영욱 기획관리관 (6박 7일)

- 항공료 : $ 2,125
- 일 비 : $ 25 x 7일 = $ 175
- 숙박비 : $ 79 x 6박 = $ 474
- 식 비 : $ 46 x 7일 = $ 322

계 : $ 3,096

o 이찬우 (6박 7일)

- 항공료 : $ 2,125
- 일 비 : $ 20 x 7일 = $ 140
- 숙박비 : $ 66 x 6박 = $ 396
- 식 비 : $ 42 x 7일 = $ 294

계 : $ 2,955

0118

경 제 기 획 원

통조삼 10502- 428 503-9149 1991. 6. 22.

수신 외무부장관 〈통상기구과〉

제목 UR/지적재산권 협상그룹회의 참석

스위스 제네바에서 6.27-28 양일간 개최되는 UR/지적재산권협상회의에 아국대표단 일원으로 참석할 당원 대표를 다음과 같이 추천합니다.

다 음

가. 인적사항

소 속	직 급	성 명
경제기획원 대외경제조정실	사 무 관	이 승 길

나. 출장기간: '91.6.25~6.30 (5박 6일)

다. 경비부담: 당원

첨부: 출장일정 1부. 끝.

〈기 FAX 송부〉

경 제 기 획 원 장

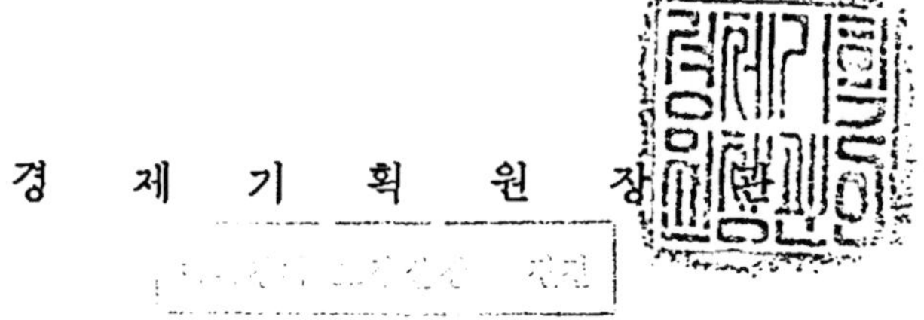

0119

출 장 일 정

'91. 6. 25(화)	13:50	서울 발 (KE 903)
	20:00	프랑크프르트 착
	21:05	프랑크프르트 발 (SR 545)
	22:10	제네바착
6. 26(수)		제네바 대표부 방문 대책회의
6. 27(목) ~ 6. 28(금)		UR/지적재산권 협상참가
6. 29(토)	18:35	제네바 발 (SR 836)
	19:15	런던 착
	20:30	런던 발 (KE 908)
6. 30(일)	17:30	서울 착

0120

2S919

기 안 용 지

분류기호 문서번호	통기 20644-	(전화: 720 - 2188)	시 행 상 특별취급	
보존기간	영구. 준영구 10. 5. 3. 1.	장 관		
수 신 처 보존기간				
시행일자	1991. 6.22.			
보조기관 국 장	전 결	협조기관		문서통제
심의관				접수 1991. 6. 25 통제관
과 장	대결			
기안책임자	조 현			발 송 인
경 유 수 신 참 조	경제기획원장관, 특허청장	발신명의		발송 1991. 6. 25 외무부
제 목	UR/TRIPs 협상 정부대표 임명 통보			

1. 91.6.27(목)-28(금)간 제네바에서 개최되는 UR/TRIPs 협상에 참가할 정부대표단이 "정부대표 및 특별사절의 임명과 권한에 관한 법률"에 의거 아래와 같이 임명 되었음을 통보합니다.

- 아 래 -

가. 회 의 명 : UR/TRIPs 협상

- 1 -

0121

나. 회의기간 및 장소 : 91.6.27(목)-28(금), 제네바

다. 정부대표

o 본부대표

- 특허청 기획관리관 노영욱

- 특허청 국제협력과 사무관 이찬우

- 경제기획원 통상조정2과 이승철

o 현지대표 : 주 제네바 대표부 관계관

라. 출장기간 : 91.6.25-7.1 (6박7일)

마. 소요경비 : 특허청 및 경제기획원 소관예산

2. 상세 출장 결과 보고서는 본부대표단 귀국후 2주일이내 당부로 송부하여 주시기 바랍니다. 끝

0122

Thank you Mr. Chairman.

The Korean delegation wishes to state briefly its basic position on the GATT Uruguay Round TRIPs negotiation.

At the outset, I would like to make it clear that Korea has been and will continue to be supportive of the inclusion of the intellectual property framework within the GATT not only because we believe that such a framework is necessary to bring about an enhanced protection of intellectual property worldwide, but also because it may provide a workable mechanism for deriving multilateral solution to IPR problems and disputes, which is far more desirable than a bilateral approach.

We do, however, recognize that there remains to be certain obstacles to be overcome in order to reach a satisfactory accord in this final stage of TRIPs negotiations. One of such obstacles appears to stem from the fact that overly ambitious goals of certain participating countries may have been reflected in the TRIPs negotiation. For a successful conclusion of the TRIPs Agreement, therefore, we believe that these participants should make conscientious effort to make it successful by way of making maximum concessions in a most cooperative and constructive manner.

A second deficiency, in our opinion, that exists in the current TRIPs proposal is that it fails to fully take into account the need of technology transfer for developing countries. In this context, Korea has proposed a pre-clearance system or dispute prevention system in respect of transfer of technologies by way of minimizing anti-competitive practices, on one hand, and providing objective standards in determining such practices, on the other hand. This and other device may be utilized in striking a balance, within the TRIPs Agreement, between the need to provide an effective protection of IPR's and the need to guard against abusive practices of right holders, leading to an early successful conclusion of the Agreement.

Turning now to the specific provisions contained in the Chairman's 7th draft prepared for the Brussels Meeting, in most of the areas, Korea should be able to accommodate the draft provisions as they are either compatible with the existing Korean laws and regulations or, at least, consistent with the direction toward which our IPR system is moving. However, there still remain a number of items which we do feel strongly about. Expecially, our reservations include the following provisions:

(a) rental rights, which we oppose on the basis of, among other things, the theory of exhaustion of rights.
A potentially devastating aspect of Article 11(rental rights) lies in the fact that it authorizes the original right to prohibit the rental business altogether,

(b) retroactive protection of phonograms, which is contradictory to the principle of non-retroactivity as embedded in the Rome Convention,

(c) inclusion of animal and plant varieties within the scope of patentable subject matters,

(d) limitation on the export of product produced under a non-voluntary license, which restricts the right of a later inventor,

(e) extending protection to assembled products in the case of semi-conductor chips and requiring payment of royalties by innocent purchasers, which go beyond the scope of the Washington Treaty,

(f) protection of undisclosed information involving test data submitted in connection with acquiring a product license of new pharmaceutical or agrochemical products, a <u>de facto</u> exclusive right given in addition to patent, and, finally,

(g) extending a border closing measure to patent dispute cases, as well, which is entirely contrary to the basic principle underlying the TRIPs Agreement. That is, instead of promoting fair international trade, it may contribute toward economic regionalization and engendering economic warfares.

As for future TRIPs negotiations schedule, in our view, since there are so many substantive issues to be discussed and negotiated, I believe that our future work should be concentrated on such matters where brackets still remain, leaving such political matters as GATTability to the ministerial level discussions and decision.

In closing, it is believed that the new intellectual property regime under the GATT should ultimately aim at achieving a balance between the policies that promote global diffusion of new science and technology and those that emphasize the proprietary interests of researchers, companies and nations. Toward this goal, I would like to express our Delegation's assurances that Korea is firmly committed and is fully prepared to work with other participants in a most cooperative spirit.

UR/TRIPs協商會議 關聯 對策檢討

1. 會議槪要

- 會議日程 및 主要議題

  o 6.27 午前: 公式會議 開催 (협상진행상황 토의 및 각국 입장 발표)
  o 6.27 午後: 主要國別 非公式 協議會
  o 6.28: 公式會議 (향후 협상일정 및 진행방법 토의결정)

  * 次期會議: '91.9월 예정

- 我國代表 參與計劃

  o 特許廳 企劃管理官(또는 주제네바 대사)이 TRIPs協商에 대한 我國立場 開陳 (현지 사정에 따라 伸縮性있게 對應)

  o 이에 대응하여 特許廳에서는 UR/TRIPs 實務小委를 2회 開催하여 關係部處 의견수렴

2. 我國代表 演說 主要內容

- UR/TRIPs協商이 先進國 및 開途國 모두가 참여하여 成功的으로 妥結될 수 있도록 努力

- 我國의 關心分野 (입장고수 분야를 우회적으로 表現)

  ① Pre-clearance system 도입
  ② 貸與權: 권리소진 이론에 의거 반대

0127

② 關聯部處 協議問題

- 2차에 걸친 實務級(관계부처 사무관) 會議를 거쳤다하나 他部處의 최종적인 의견수렴 의문

- 我國政府 最終立場은 최소한 UR對策實務委員會 또는 對外協力委員會에서 審議決定 必要

<對應方案>

① 我國 立場固守分野 적절히 反映

(1안) 立場固守分野를 豫示的으로만 提示하여 향후 協商餘地 確保 (特許廳 修正案)

(2안) 旣存 我國主張 17個部門 모두 포괄 (協商寄與不足)

② 公式發言 與否

(1안) 修正案대로 發言

(2안) 현지 判斷에 따르되 他參加國이 具體的인 對應方案을 提示하지 않을경우 具體的事項에 대해서는 發言自制

0128

③ 음반의 遡及保護: Rome협약에 규정된 不遡及原則에 위배
사항으로 반대

④ 動物 및 植物變種의 特許對象 범위포함문제

⑤ 強制實施權 附與에 의해 생산된 상품의 수출제한문제

⑥ IC 保護範圍 및 善意의 IC 購買者에 대한 로얄티 지급문제

⑦ 政府에 提出된 資料(의약품, 농약)의 원용 및 공개금지

⑧ 通關 유예품목대상 범위문제

<特技事項>

- 我國立場中 立場固守分野만 言及
  - o 당초 立場固守分野中 소급보호에 대한 經過規定除外
  - o 당초 讓步可能分野中 不特許對象, 특허의 강제실시권 실시범위를 立場固守分野로 反映
  - o 有名商標保護(양보가능분야) 除外

3. 檢討意見 및 對應方案

<檢討意見>

① 全體 UR協商動向과 관련하여 我國의 전향적 立場表明의 시의성 문제

- 현재 各分野別 協商은 각국의 基本立場을 반복하는 수준에서 進行

- 현싯점에서 我側이 전향적 입장을 提示할 必要가 있는지 檢討必要 (9월이후 협상본격 진행전망)

0129

	분류번호	보존기간

발 신 전 보

번 호 : WGV-0818 910624 1646 DU 종별 : 암호송신

수 신 : 주 제네바 대사. 총영사

발 신 : 장 관 (통 기)

제 목 : UR/TRIPs 협상

대 : GVW-1126

1. 6.27-28간 개최되는 표제회의에 참가할 정부대표를 아래 임명 하였으니, 귀관 관계관과 함께 참석토록 조치바람.

가. 본부대표

o 특허청 기획관리관 노영욱

o 특허청 국제협력과 사무관 이찬우

o 경제기획원 통상조정2과 이승길

나. 훈 령

o 아국의 기존 입장에 따라 UR/TRIPs 공식회의 및 주요국별 비공식 회의에 적극 참가하고, 각국의 입장 및 협상 동향을 파악, 향후 협상 대책 수립에 반영토록 함

보안 통제	

앙 고 재	91 년 6월 22일	통기 과	기안자 성명		과 장	심의관	국 장		차 관	장 관
			조현				전결			

외신과통제

0130

o 협상의 원만한 타결을 위하여 일부 입장대립 분야에서 선.개도국간의 양보를 촉구하고,(특히 공공개념의 확대해석등 선진국의 과도한 주장은 적절하게 이의 부당성을 지적토록 함.)

o 현지 실정에 따라 "기술 이전에 관한 분쟁 예방 절차"에 관한 아국입장을 공식 제안하여 아국의 협상력을 강화토록 함.

2. 상기 "기술 이전에 관한 분쟁 예방 절차"에 관한 아국의 공식제안 준비 서류는 본부대표가 지참 예정인 바, 귀지에서 동 내용을 검토하고 현지 협상 진행 상황 및 분위기를 파악, 필요시 공식 제안 바람. 끝.

(통상국장 김 삼 훈)

0131

발 신 전 보

분류번호	보존기간

번 호 : WGV-0823 910625 1612 ED 종별 : 암호송신

수 신 : 주 제네바 대사. 총영사

발 신 : 장 관 (통 기)

제 목 : UR/TRIPs 협상

연 : WGV-0818

연호 나항 TRIPs 협상의 훈령을 아래와 같이 수정 통보함.

1. 첫째항(아국의 기존 입장에 .... 반영토록 함)을 아래로 대체

o 정부대표는 UR 대책 실무위원회에서 결정한 대책안을 중심으로 현지 협상 동향을 감안하여 아국 입장을 신축성있게 개진토록 하는 한편 공식회의 및 주요 비공식 회의에 적극 참여하여 각국의 입장 및 협상 동향을 파악 향후 협상 대책에 반영토록 함.

2. 두번째항 후반부 "특히 공공개념 ..... 지적토록 함"을 삭제. 끝.

(통상국장 김 삼 훈)

보안통제	

앙고재	91년 6월 25일	통기과	기안자 성명		과 장	심의관	국 장		차 관	장 관
			조현				전결			

외신과통제

0132

* 經濟企劃院 [illegible] 合意內容
('91. 6. 25)

① 금번 UR/知的財産權 會議에 參加하는 정부대표는 UR對策 實務委員會에서 결정한 對策案을 중심으로 현지 協商 動向을 감안하여 我國立場을 伸縮性있게 開陳토록 하는 한편 公式會議 및 主要 非公式會議에 적극 참가하여 各國의 立場 및 協商動向을 파악 향후 協商對策에 反映 토록 함.

② 協商의 원만한 妥結을 위하여 一部 立場對立分野에서 先.開途國間의 讓步를 촉구토록 함.

③ 현지 協商雰圍氣를 把握하여 필요시 紛爭解決節次에 관한 我國立場을 公式提案하여 我國의 協商力을 強化 토록 함.

0133

지적재산권 (TRIPs)

1. 협상 목표 (푼타 델 에스테 각료선언)

   o 지적재산권의 효과적이며 적절한 보호의 필요성을 감안하여 지적재산권의 국제교역에 있어서 왜곡과 장애를 완화함.

   o 그러나 지적재산권 보호를 위한 시행조치 및 절차 그자체가 정당한 무역에 장애가 되지 않도록 함.

   o 이를 위해 동 협상은 갓트 규정을 명료화 하거나 필요한 경우 새로운 규칙과 규율을 마련함.

   o 위조상품의 국제교역 문제를 취급할 다자간 규범을 개발함.

   o WIPO 및 기타 관련 국제기구의 보완적 노력을 저해하지 않도록 함.

2. 협상 현황

   가. 1989.4. TNC에서 TRIPs 협상의 기본 방향에 관한 합의 도출

      o 협상 대상, 협상시 고려사항 및 협상 결과의 관할에 관한 기본적인 협상 추진 방향에 관해 합의

   나. 1990.7. TNC에서 TRIPs 협상 진전상황 점검

      o 실질적 합의사항 없이 향후 협상의 기초로 대안만을 나열한 의장보고서 제출

      o 의장보고서상의 주요의제

         - 기본원칙

         - 보호기준 (보호대상 및 보호수준)

            . 저작 및 인접권

            . 상 표

            . 지리적 표시

0134

다. 협상 결과의 관할

o TRIPs 협상 결과를 관할할 국제기구(GATT 또는 WIPO)에 대해 예단하지 않고 협상을 진행

4. 미합의사항 및 주요쟁점

가. 주요 미합의사항

o 기본원칙 부문중 MFN (최혜국 대우) 문제

o 보호기준 부문중 저작권 및 저작인접권 문제, 지리적 표시, 특허, 반도체, 영업비밀등의 주요 쟁점사항

o 시행절차 (특히 국경조치)

o 분쟁해결 절차 (분쟁담당기구 및 대상)

o 경과 조치 (개도국 유예기간)

나. 주요쟁점

(선) : 선진국, (개) : 개도국

구 분	쟁 점	각국 입장	아국 입장
1.협정형태	o GATT에 포함 여부	(선) - 전체협정을 GATT의 일부로 포함 (개) - 위조상품 교역 규제 부분만 GATT에 포함 - 보호기준, 시행절차등 기타사항은 별도 협정 제정	- 전체협정을 갓트에 포함
2.기본원칙	o 내국민 대우, 최혜국 대우, 명료성등 갓트 일반원칙 수용 여부	(선) - 갓트 일반원칙 수용 주장 - 단, EC는 관세동맹, FTA는 최혜국 대우 원칙의 예외 주장 (개) - 내국민 대우원칙만 수용 주장	- 갓트 일반원칙 수용 - 관세동맹의 최혜국 대우 원칙 예외에 반대
	o 내국민 대우 원칙	(선) - 불리하지 않는 대우 (no less favourable) (개) - 동등한 대우 (the same treatment)	- 동등한 대우 주장

0135

구　분	쟁　점	각국　입장	아국 입장
3.보호기준			
가. 저작권	o 저작인격권(moral rights) 포함(9조)	(미) - 반 대 - 자국 저작법에서 불인정, 경제적 권리 (eonomic rights)에 한정 (기타) 찬성	- 포함시 주장 베른협약
	o 컴퓨터 프로그램 어문 저작물(literary Works) 인정 및 50년간 보호 (10조, 12조)	(선) 찬성 (저) 반대-보호기간 장기화 우려(25년 주장)	- 수용 가능
	o 대여권(Rental rights) 범위 (11조, 16조4항)	(미) 컴퓨터 프로그램, 음반 (EC) 영상저작물 추가 (개) 불인정-유통질서 혼란	~~영상저작물 및 음반 포함 반대~~ - 대여행위는 (보상청구가능시) 가능
	o 베른조약의 개도국 우대조항(13조)	(선) 제한 (개) 현행 유지	입장없음.
	o 공중전달의 정의 (14조)	(미) 정의규정 신설 (기타) 반대	반대.
	o 음반의 소급보호 (16조6항)	(선) 소급주장(특히 미국) (개) 반대(로마조약 원칙 고수)	- 반대
	o 실연자 방송사업자 보호범위 및 기간 (16조)	(EC) 50년 (미) 50년, 실연자 불인정 (개) 20년, 실연자 불인정	- 국내법 위임
나.상　표	o 색책 상표의 보호 (17조 1항)	(선) 찬성 (개) 반대-판별에 어려움	보호 찬성.

0136

구 분	쟁 점	각국 입장	아국 입장
	o 저명상표 판단 기준 (18조 2항)	(선) 국제무역을 통한 소비자 인식으로 유명하면 저명상표 인정 (개) 국내소비자에 저명해야 인정	- 수용 가능
	o 상표사용 요건(22조)	(선) 타상표와 사용 요구 불가 (개) 각국 위임	선진국 입장
다. 지리적 표시	o 주류에 관한 지리적 표시의 보호 - 소비자의 오인, 혼동없이도 타역 제품에 사용 금지되는 상품의 범위(25조)	(EC, 스위스) 전상품, 적어도 포도주, 주정 (미) 포도주 (남미) 반대 (아시아) 이해관계 없음	이해관계 없음
	- 지리적 명칭으로 된 상표의 계속 사용(26조)	(EC, 스위스) 등록상표 취소 (미, 남미) 등록취소 불가	
	o 지리적 표시 국제 등록 절차(27조)	(EC) TRIPs 발효후 협상 개시 (기타국) TRIPs 발효후 필요성 검토	〃
라. 의 장	o 의장의 요건 (28조 1항)	(EC) New or original (미) New and original	이해관계 없음
	o 섬유의장(28조 2항)	(미, EC, 스위스) 출원, 등록, 비용, 절차에서 실질적 보호 (개) 산업별 차별 반대	〃
마. 특허	o 선 발명주의 적용 방법(30조 1항)	(EC, 일) 발명지에 무관하게 적용 (미) 미국내의 발명에 한하여 적용 - 특허법 통일화 협상에서 취급 주장	아국: 선출원주의 주장.

0137

구 분	쟁 점	각국 입장	아국 입장
	o 불특허사항 (30조 3항)	(미) 불요(모든 발명특허 주장) (EC) 진단 및 치료방법, 동물변종 * 식물변종은 특허 또는 UPOV (개) 동.식물, 미생물, 화학물질, 의약품, 식품, 원자핵물질	
	o 제법특허의 효력범위(31조 1항(a))	(선) 제법의 사용, 제법으로 생산된 제품 (개) 제법의 사용에 한정	
	o 특허권자 실시 의무 (32조 2항(a))	(선) 수입도 국내실시 (개) 국내실시는 생산에 한정	
	o 강제실시권 및 정부사용(34조)		
	- (f) 국내공급 한정	(개) 반대	
	- (g) 허여사유 종료시 실시권 실효	(개) 반대	
	- (h) 보상의 기준	(개) adequate (선) fair and equitable	
	- (m) 제법특허의 강제 실시권 요건	(선) 기술진보 및 경제적 중요성 (개) 기술진보	
	- (n) 수입의 국내 실시 인정	(선) 찬성 (개) 반대	
	- (o) 정부사용의 요건	(개) 강제실시권 보다 완화 (선) 강제실시권과 동일한 제한	
	o 특허기간(36조)	(선) 최소 20년 (개) 각국 위임	

0138

구 분	쟁 점	각국 입장	아국 입장
	o 입증 책임전환(37조)	(미) 신규 동일물질 또는 특허권자의 상당한 노력 (개) 신규 동일물질	
바.집적회로 설계배치	o 권리자의 범위 : 최종제품 포함 여부 (39조)	(선) 포함 (개) 최종제품 포함 반대 배치 설계 및 집적회로에 한정	- 포함 반대 (워싱턴 조약 기준)
	o 선의의 구매자 책임 (40조)	(선) 권리자로부터 통지후에는 과거 구매제품에 대해서 배상의무 (개) 반대	- 보상의무 반대 (워싱턴조약)
	o 보호기간(41조)	(선) 10년 (개) 8년	- 선진국안 수용 가능
사.영업비밀	o 지적재산권으로 인정 여부	(선) 찬성 (개) 반대	찬성.
	o 의약, 농약 판매 허가시 제출하는 기술자료가 부정 경쟁행위에 이용되지 않도록 하고, 최소 5년간 정부도 이를 타품목 허가에 이용할 수 없음	(선) 찬성 (개) 반대	반대.
아.권리남용 또는 반경쟁적 행위	o 기술이전 계약 규제 TRIPs에 포함	(선) 반대 (개) 찬성	찬성
	o 권리 남용으로 추정하는 행위 규정 (수출제한, 가격 지정등)	(선) 반대 (개) 찬성	"
4.개도국 유예기간	o 개도국 및 동유럽 국가들에 대한 의무 이행 유예기간 산정 (내국민 대우, MFN은 유예기간 불인정)	(선) 단기 (개) 장기, 동구권과 별도 취급	

0139

구 분	쟁 점	각국 입장	아국 입장
	o 유예기간 동안의 보호 약화 불가 (Standstill) 및 국별 입법 계획 제출		
5.경과조치 (충분한 논의 없었음)	o 조약 발효 당시 존재하는 보호대상의 취급 - 이미 보호중인 대상은 조약무관 - 특히 IC 의장 출원중인 것의 본조약 적용 - 이미 존재하면서 보호받지 못하고 있는 대상은 조약 무관 단, 저작물 음반은 베른조약 적용 소급보호원칙	(스) 찬성 (일, 남미) 반대 (미) 입장 불명 (EC) 상표, 지리적 표시 이외는 양안 모두 수용 가능 (개) 반대	- 반대('87 대미 특별 조치 관련) - 반대
6.분쟁해결	o 사무국안, 개도국안 선진국안 각각 부록에 첨부 o 아국 제안의 분쟁 예방 절차는 의장 cover letter에 언급		cross retaliation

5. 아국 입장

가. 기본 입장

o TRIPs 협상의 결과가 가능하면 많은 개도국들이 참여하는 형태의 협정을 도출할 수 있도록 지적재산권의 보호와 함께 사용자의 권익을 보호하는 균형적인 접근을 견지

o 한.미간 협정('86.8)과 관련 소급 보호사항의 MFN 적용을 통한 타선진국 (EC, 일본, 스위스등)으로의 확산 방지를 위하여 우선적인 협상력 집중

0140

o 수출의존도가 높은 홍콩, 싱가폴과 함께 국경조치에 있어 세관의 권한을 제한하는 규정의 강화 주장

o IC 설계 부문은 IC가 내장된 제품을 대량생산 및 수출하는 아국 전자산업의 주요 관심사항으로 아국 제안 관철을 위한 노력 경주

o TRIPs 협정 형태 및 담당기구, 분쟁해결절차, 경과조치등은 선.개도국간의 입장이 첨예하게 대립되고 있는 분야들로서 아국은 신축적으로 대응

나. 아국의 주요 관심사항

o MFN 적용문제

- 협상의 전반적 추세가 강력한 MFN으로 기울고 있으므로 기본원칙 부문에서의 MFN 예외 인정은 매우 어려울 것으로 전망
- 아국은 대 미국 지적재산권 특혜조치(86.8)와 관련, 의장보고서의 제71조(존재하나 보호받도 있지 않은 subject matter에 대해 TRIPs 협정 적용 면제)를 적용, MFN 의무.면제를 관철토록 추진

o 국경조치

- 통관정지 대상은 위조상표 및 해적판에 한정(개도국 입장 지지)
- 통관 압류 조치를 당한 상품 소유권자가 세관조치의 무효화를 위한 소송 제기시 자동적 압류 연장 불가

o IC 설계

- 보호대상으로 회로설계 및 IC까지만 인정(개도국 입장 지지)
- IC가 내장된 제품까지의 보호대상 확대(선진국안)에는 반대

o 경과조치

- 가급적 많은 개도국의 TRIPs 협상 참여가 바람직하므로 장기간의 경과기간 부여

0141

o 분쟁해결 절차

- GATT 일반협정의 분쟁해결절차 적용을 주장하는 선진국안의 수용이 불가피할 것으로 예상되나, 가급적 많은 개도국의 협정 참여를 유도하기 위하여 분쟁 예방조치의 추가를 주장

o 특허의 강제실시권 및 취소 여부

- 강제실시권의 실시 요건 완화 및 특허취소 가능(개도국 입장 지지)

o 저작권의 대여권

- 아국의 현행 컴퓨터 프로그램 보호법은 대여권을 인정
- 컴퓨터 프로그램 이외의 대여권 인정 : 음반 대여권(미국 주장)은 수용 가능하나 Video 저작권(EC 주장)은 현행 유통 관행에 미치는 국내영향이 큰 점을 감안, 반대

o 음반의 소급보호

- 미국만이 음반의 소급보호 인정을 주장하나, 대다수국의 반대 추세에 맞추어 소급보호 불인정 입장 견지

o 영업비밀

- 영업비밀을 보호대상에서 제외할 것을 주장하되 부득이한 경우 부정경쟁 방지 법규에서 보호인정(일본과 동일 인정)

6. 협상 전망

o 선진국들은 TRIPs 협상을 UR 협상 그룹중 최우선 관심분야의 하나로 선정, 협상 타결에 강력한 의지를 보이고 있는바, TRIPs 협상은 어떤 형태(일반협정문 개정방식 혹은 Code 방식)로든 지적재산권 보호에 대한 합의를 도출해낼 것으로 전망

o 현재 예상 가능한 협상 결과

- TRIPs 협정의 GATT 체재내에서의 시행

0142

- 기본원칙 부문은 내국민대우 및 강력한 MFN 적용
- 보호기준으로는
  . 저작권에 있어 대여권(최소한 컴퓨터 프로그램) 인정
  . 원산지 보호의 강화
  . 강제실시권의 허여 요건 강화
  . 제약 및 식물변종의 특허 인정
  . IC 설계의 보호대상으로 내장된 제품까지 포함
  . 영업비밀 보호 강화
- 시행절차(국경조치)에 있어 최소한 위조상표 및 해적판제품은 통관 정지 대상으로 규제
- GATT 일반협정의 분쟁해결 절차 적용으로 상품과의 교차 보복 허용

o 개도국은 TRIPs 협상 내용, 특히 경과조치 부문의 유예기간 인정등 개도국 우대조항 및 여타 UR 협상 의제와 연계하여 협정 참여 여부를 결정할 것으로 전망

0143

. 의 장

. 특 허

. 집적회로 배치 설계

. 영업비밀

- 시행절차

- 분쟁방지 및 해결절차

- 경과 규정

- 타국제기구(또는 협약)와의 관계

- 위조상품 교역

다. 1990.11. 브랏셀 각료회의에서 전체 UR 협상의 결렬로 TRIPs 협상도 교착상태 봉착

o 브랏셀 각료회의 이후 기술적 사항에 관한 논의는 계속하고 있으나, 협상의 큰 진전은 이룩하지 못하고 있는 상태 지속

o 브랏셀 각료회의에 의장보고서 [제3차 수정안] 제출

3. 합의사항

가. 협상 대상 (coverage)

o 갓트의 일반원칙과 관련 국제협약들의 기본원칙 적용 가능성 검토

o 무역관련 지적재산권의 적정한 보호기준 정립

o 각국의 상이한 지적재산권 보호 관계법을 고려, 적절한 시행절차 마련

o 갓트의 분쟁해결 절차 적용 가능성을 포함한 국제분쟁 방지 및 해결 절차 마련

o 다수국의 참여 유도를 위한 경과 조치 채택 여부 및 그 내용 설정

나. 협상시 고려사항

o 개도국의 개발목표 및 기술목표를 포함한 공공정책 목표를 충분히 고려

o WIPO등 관련 국제기구와 갓트간의 상호 보완적 관계 유지

0144

원 본

외 무 부

종 별 :

번 호 : GVW-1208 일 시 : 91 0628 1530

수 신 : 장 관(통기,경기원,상공부,보사부,문화부,과기처,특허청)

발 신 : 주제네바대사

제 목 : UR/TRIPS(지적재산권 협상) 회의(1)

대: WGV-8023

6.27(목) 10:00 갓트에서 개최된 표제회의 내용을 하기 보고함.

(아국대표단 참석: 특허청 기획관리관 노영욱, 김준규주재관, 사무관 이찬우, 경기원 사무관이승길)

1. 공식회의(6.27 오전)

0 ANELL 의장은 금번회의의 목적이 협상의 현상황 점검과 향후 협상 계획을 논의하기 위한 것이라고 설명하고 구체적이고 세부적인 사항은 9월회의에서 논의하자고하고 브랏셀 각료회의 이후 6개월이 지난 현 싯점에서 각국의 입장 및 의견을 개진토록 하였는바 각국의 발언 내용은 아래와 같음.

0 이집트는 의장 보고서에 아직 현저한 문제점이 많아 잔존하고 있으며 개도국의 이해를 충분히 고려한 균형적이고 유연한 협정이 되어야 한다고 주장함.

- 인도, 방글라데시, 브라질등 개도국이 이에 동조함.

0 특히, 태국, 파키스탄, 방글라데시는 미국의 301조에 의한 일방적 제재 조치가그들의 입장을 악화시키고 있으며, 이는 PUNTA DEL ESTE 선언에도 위배되는 것이라고 주장함.

0 아국대표는 먼저 GATT 내 다자간 협정에 의한 지적재산권 문제의 해결이 바람직함을 주장하고, 의장 보고서에 아직 문제가 있는 내용이 많이 존재하고 있으므로성공적인 협상 타결을 위해서는 입장이 대립되고 있는 분야에 대하여는 선.개도국간의 양보가 있어야 할것이라고 촉구하고, TRIPS 협상이 기술확산과 권리자 보호의 양측면에 균형을 유지하여야 할것임을 지적함.

- 그리고, 정치적 문제(POLITICAL ISSUES)는 고위급 회의에서 논의하는 것이 바람직하다고 주장하고 세부적인 아국의 관심사항에 대한 입장표명은 일단 유보함.

통상국 2차보 보사부 문화부 경기원 상공부 과기처 특허청

PAGE 1 91.06.29 08:17 WH

외신 1과 통제관

0145

0 EC 는 시장보고서에 대해 불만족을 표시하고 진전이 적은 분야, 진전이 전혀 없었던 분야에 대해 언급함.

- 진전이 적었던 분야로

. 반도체 칩 보호

. 상품(권리내용, 특히 유명상표 보호)

. 컴퓨터 프로그램, 대여권

. 제한적인 지리적 표시 보호

. 충분한 논의가 적었던 특허의 강제실시권분야

. 시행절차 분야를 들고

,- 전혀 진전이 없었던 분야로

. 저작인접권, 특허대상, 영업비밀 보호 및 MFN규정을 열거함.

- 특히 매우 기술적인 분야인 73조(경과규정)는REDRAFTING 이 필요하다고 주장함.

- 향후 협상은 이러한 분야를 중심으로 논의 하는것이 바람직하다고 함

0 EC 의 주장에 대해 이집트는 시행절차가 각국의 사법제도를 제약하는 것이라고 언급함.

2. 아울러 홍콩의 요청으로 아국 및 호주, 뉴질랜드, 태국, 브라질, 말레이지아,멕시코등 8개국이 참가한 비공식 오찬에서 각국은 불특허대상, 강제실시권, 컴퓨터프로그램, 대여권, 분쟁해결 절차등에 대해 논의하고 73조(경과규정)에 대해 아국과입장을 같이하는 등 상당한 관심을 표함.

0 한국은 분쟁예방 절차(PRE-CLEARANE SYSTEM)제한이 권리자의 권리남용을 규제할 수 있을것 이라고 설명하고 이에 대한 지지를 요청함.

0 오전 공식회의에서의 아국대표의 발언에 대해 뉴질랜드, 홍콩, 호주등이 지지한다는 입장을 표명함.

0 홍콩은 향후 협상계획에 대해서는 7차 의장보고서를 중심으로 토의되어야 할것이라고 입장을 표명하고 ANELL 의장이 이에대한 각국의 의견을 청취할 필요가 있다고 말함.

3. 비공식 회의(6.27 오후)

0 ANNEL 의장은 지난 BRUSSELS 회의에서 농산물, 서비스, 시장접근등 타협상 그룹의 논의때문에 GRIPS 에 대한 논의에 진전이 없었다고 설명하고 협상의 출발점을 어디로 할것인가에 대해 논의하자고 함.

- 새로운 ELEMENT 를 제시하는 것을 반대하지는 않으나 제 7차 의장보고서를 논의의 출발점으로 하는것이 효율적일 것이라고 설명함.

0 홍콩은 작년 12월 브랏셀회의 이후 협상의 진전이 없음에 비추어 7차 의장보고서가 9월 실질토의의 기초로 되어야 할것임을 주장하였으며

,0 말레이지아, 인도 및 태국등 개도국은 7차의장보고서에 BRUSSELS 회의에서 논의된 사항을추가해 새로운 의장 보고서를 만들어 토의하자고 함.

- 인도는 구체적으로 자국의 관심사항이

. 특허대상(PATENTABILITY), 기본원칙, 시행절차, 지리적 표시, IC, 상표, 저작인접권, 영업비밀, 경과규정, 강제실시권에 있다고 설명하고

0 한국은 7차 의장보고서에 BRACKET 으로 남아있는 사항을 중심으로 논의하고 GATT ABILITY등 정치적인 문제는 고위급 회의로 미루는 것이 바람직하며, 협상 타결을위해서는 의장이 각국의 양보를 촉구하는 노력이 있어야 할 것이라고 주장함.

0 ANELL 의장은 7차 의장 보고서에 대해 미국, EC 등이 불만족을 표시하고 있는상황에서 새로운 ELEMENT 는 도입 않는것이 바람직하다는 의견을 제시함.

4. 아국대표단은 공식회의에 앞서 6.26.15:00HARTRIDGE GATT 무역정책 국장을 면담하였는 바 그 요지는 아래와 같음.

0 HARTRIDGE 국장은 이번 회의에서 각국의 입장을 확인하고 양자, 혹은 SMALL GROUP회의등을 조직할 계획이라고 설명함.

0 협상의 전망은 사견을 전제로 농산물등 타협상그룹에 비해 상당한 진전이 있었으며 장애가 상대적으로 적으므로 금년내 타결될 수 있을 것이라고 전망함.

0 작년이후 미국은 업계의 압력으로 입장이 많이 강화되었으며,

- 브라질, 멕시코, 아르헨티나는 미국과의 양자협상결과에 의해 입장이 상당히 약화되었다고 판단하고 있다고 말하고

,- 인도, 이집트, 탄자니아등이 강경 개도국의 입장이나 점점 고립화 되어가고 있으며 계속 강경입장을 고수할 경우 고립화 시킬수 밖에 없을 것임을 강조함.

0 협상의 참여도에 대해서는 아르헨티나등 개도국은 기술적인 사항인 TRIPS 에 대한 관심과 참여도가 약화되고 있으나, 스위스등 기술역점 국가는 관심도가 높아지고 있다고 설명함.

0 아국의 제안(분쟁예방 절차)에 대해서 9월의 분쟁해결 절차에 대한 실질토의에 대비 아주 적절하다고 말함.

0 HARTRIDGE 국장은 아국관심사항에 대해 질의하고 다음회의는 9.16 주간이 될것이라고설명함. 5. 6.28 오전 비공식 회의는 10 더하기 10 방식(종전1 더하기 1 방식과 동일)으로 진행되며 오후에는 공식회의가 계속될 예정인바

,0 아국대표단은 분쟁 예방 절차에 관한 대호 서면제안을 6.28 속개되는 공식 회의에서 정식 제안할 예정임.끝

(대사 박수길-국장)

암 → 2

원 본

외 무 부

종 별 :

번 호 : GVW-1223 일 시 : 91 0701 1500

수 신 : 장 관(통기,경기원,상공부,보사부,문화부,과기처,특허청)

발 신 : 주 제네바 대사

제 목 : UR/TRIPS(지적재산권 협상)회의(2)

1. 비공식회의(6.29 오전)

0 ANELL 의장은 9월 회의에서는 의견이 대립되고 있는 기술적 분야 (TECHNICAL MATTERS)를 먼저 논의하고, 73조 (경과 규정)와 분쟁해결 절차는 정치적인 문제 (POLITICAL MATTERS) 이면서 기술적인 문제이므로 이에 대해서도 논의할 것과 9월 회의는 9.16 주간에 개최할 것을 제의함.

0 EGYPT 는 이에 대해 TEXT 의 모든 조항들을 검토해야 할 것이라고 주장하고 브랏셀 회의의 결과와 이의 평가도 제시해 줄것을 요구함.

0 인도는 브랏셀 회의에서 논의된 사항을 모든협상 참가국에게 알려 줄것을 요구함.

0 ANELL 의장은 9월 회의에서 모든 조항을 검토하기는 힘드므로 7월의 TNC 회의등의 결과를 고려하여 9월회의 방향이 결정될 것임을지적함.

2. 공식회의(6.28 오후)

0 ANELL 의장은 비공식회의 및 각국과의 접촉결과를 보고하면서 9월 회의의 잠정적 일정을 아래와 같이 제의하였음.

- 정치적인 문제는 뒤로 미루고 의견이 대립되고있는 기술적인 문제를 중심으로 논의함과 아울러 정치적인 성격을 갖고 있으나 기술적인 내용을 갖고 있는 73조 (경과규정)과 분쟁해결절차에 대해서도 논의함.

- 시간이 허용할 경우 개도국의 요청대로 전체조항을 모두 논의하도록 노력함.

- 회의의 기초는 브랏셀회의에 제출한 7차 의장보고서로 함.

- 회의는 9.16 주간 (1주일) 에 개최할 것을 제안하고 TRIPS 회의가 타협상 그룹보다는 협상속도가 늦어서는 안될것이라고 말하고 그러나 농산물, 서비스 및 시장접근 분야의 협상진전상황이 TRIPS 에도 크게 영향을 미칠것이라고 전망함.

통상국 2차보 보사부 문화부 경기원 상공부 과기처 특허청

PAGE 1 91.07.02 08:54 WG

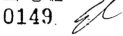

외신 1과 통제관

0149

- 아울러 개도국이 요청한 브랏셀회의 결과는 9월회의에서 자세하게 구두로 전달할 것임을 약속함.

0 인도는 ANELL 의장의 제안에 대해 동의를 표시하고 의제중 분쟁해결 절차가 세가지 대안이있는데 어떻게 논의할 것인가에 대해 질의한바, ANELL 의장은 세가지 대안에 대한 이해를 증진하는 방안을 진행하겠다고 함.

3. 연호 분쟁해결 절차에 대한 서면제의는 GATTHARTRIDGE 국장의 제의대로 사무국을 통해 제출, 이를 협상참가국에 배포토록 조치 위계임.끝

(대사 박수길-국장)

6-72

특 허 청

국협 28140- 2142 (568-6077) 1991. 7. 3.

수신 수신처참조

제목 '91 제1차 UR/TRIPs 회의결과 보고서 송부

1. 통기 20644-28919 (91.6.25) 관련입니다.

2. '91.6.27(목) - 28(금)간 제네바에서 개최된 표제회의 결과보고서를 별첨과 같이 송부하오니 업무에 참고하시기 바라며, 향후 협상에 대비하여 계속 소관사항 대책수립에 만전을 기해 주시기 바랍니다.

첨부 표제회의 결과보고서 1부. 끝.

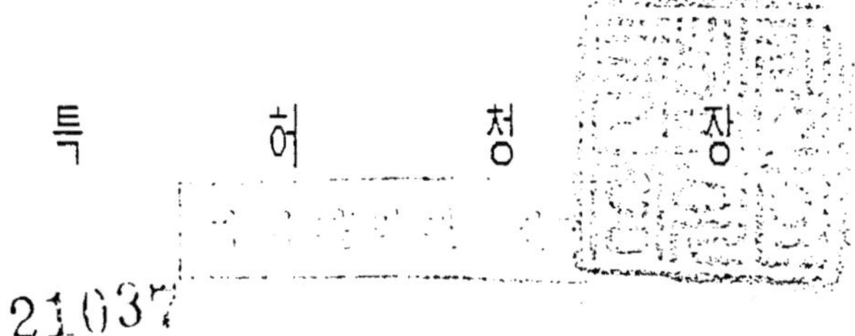

특 허 청 장

21037

수신처 : 경제기획원장관(대외경제조정실장), 외무부장관(통상국장), 상공부장관(전자전기공업국장), 보사부장관(약정국장), 문화부장관(어문출판국장), 과학기술처장관(기술정책관).

0151

'91 第1次 UR/TRIPs 會議 參加 結 果 報 告

1991. 7. 2

報 告 者 : 企劃管理官 盧 泳 旭

0152

Ⅰ. 出張者

o 特 許 廳 企劃管理官 盧 泳 旭

o " 주재관 김 준 규

o " 국제협력담당관실 사무관 이 잔 우

o 經濟企劃院 통상조정 3과 사무관 이 승 길

Ⅱ. 出張 期間

o 91. 6. 25 - 7. 1

Ⅲ. 出張 目的

o '91 第1次 UR/TRIPs 會議 參加

Ⅳ. 代表團 主要活動 內容

o TRIPs 協商의 公式會議 및 非公式會議에 參加, 我國의 立場 發表

o 主要國 代表와 非公式 接觸을 통해 各國立場 확인

o GATT 事務局의 貿易政策局長 Mr. Hartridge 를 訪問, 協商의 展望과 各國의 立場에 대해 事前 意見 交換

o 박수길 대사 예방 및 협상대책 보고

V. UR/TRIPs 會議內容 및 結果

1. 會議議題

o TRIPs 協商의 現狀況 (state) 점검

o 向後 協商計劃 (Organization of Further Work)

o 其他 (Other Business)

2. 會議進行 方式

o 公式會議 : 6.27 오전 및 6.28 오후

o 非公式會議 : 6.27 오후 및 6.28 오전

3. 會議內容

가. TRIPs 協商의 現狀況 점검 (Review of the State of the Negotiations)

o Anell 議長은 구체적이고 세부적인 사항은 9월로 예정된 회의에서 논의하고, 금번 회의에서는 브랏셀 각료회의 이후 6개월이 지난 현 싯점에서 각국의 입장에 대한 의견을 개진토록 함.

1) 開途國

- Egypt

. Brussels 회의에 제출된 議長報告書 (7次 議長報告書)에 아직 현저한(outstanding) 문제점이 많이 잔존함.

. 특히, 開途國의 利益이 반영되어 있지 않으므로 協商을 통해 TRIPs 協定이 開途國의 利益을 充分히 考慮한 유연한(flexible) 협정이 되어야 할것이라고 주장

. **印度**, 방글라데시, 브라질, 중국등 **多數 開途國**이 이에 **同調**

* Egypt 와의 **個別接觸時** Egypt 는 TRIPs 의 모든 규정이 문제가 있다고 **我國 代表**에게 설명함.

- 태국, 파키스탄, 방글라데시

. **美國**의 301조에 의한 **一方的**인 **制裁(報復)措置** (unilateral retaliatory pressure)가 그들의 **立場**을 **弱化**(weaken)시키고 있으며,

. 이는 '86, Punta del Este **宣言**에도 위배되는 것이라고 비난함.

- **印度(非公式會議**시 **發言)**

. 모든 국가가 good spirit 로 협상에 임해야 할것이라고 주장하고 **自國**의 **關心事項**이

① **特許對象** (Patentability)
② **基本原則** (Basic Principles)
③ **施行節次** (Enforcement)
④ **地理的表示** (Geographical Indications)
⑤ IC, **營業秘密** (Undisclosed Information)
⑥ **商標, 著作隣接權, 强制實施權**
⑦ **經過規程** (Transitional Arrangements)등

에 있다고 설명함.

※ **印度代表**와의 **非公式 接觸時** 인도대표는 지난 Brussels 회의에서 TRIPs 에 대한 108개의 **反對意見**을 제출한바 있다고 함.

2) 先進國 (EC)

- 議長報告書에 전반적으로 不滿足스러운 부분이 있음을 지적함.

- 협상의 진전이 적은 분야

① 컴퓨터 프로그램, 貸與權 (rental rights)

② 商標 (권리내용, 특히 유명상표 보호)

③ 地理的 表示: 제한적으로 반영

④ 特許의 强制實施權 : 충분한 논의가 없었음.

⑤ 施行節次

- 진전이 전혀 없었던 분야

① 著作隣接權 : 특히 音盤 (phonogram)의 보호

② 特許對象 (patentability)

③ 營業秘密

④ MFN (Most-Favoured-Nations)

- 특히, 매우 技術的인 分野인 73條 (經過規程)가 규정이 모호하므로 明確하게 redrafting 할것을 요구하고, 향후 협상은 상기 열거한 분야를 중심으로 논의할것을 주장함.

- EC 의 주장에 대한 開途國의 反應 (Egypt)

. 특히 施行節次에 대해 언급하면서 시행절차 규정이 各國의 司法 制度를 制約하는 과도한 것이라고 주장

3) 韓 國

- 兩者協商보다 GATT 내 多者間 協定 (multilateral agreement)에 의한 知的財産權 問題의 解決이 바람직함.

- 議長報告書에 아직 문제가 있는 내용이 많이 존재하고 있으므로 成功的인 協商妥結을 위해서는 立場이 對立되고 있는 分野에서 先.開途國간의 讓步가 있어야 할것이라고 촉구함.

- 妥結될 TRIPs 協定은 새로운 技術의 擴散과 權利者의 保護 양측면에 均衡을 유지해야 할것임을 지적함.

- 我國의 知的財産權 制度, 향후 발전방향에서 비추어 볼때 TRIPs 協定을 受容할 수 있지만 문제가 있는 규정들이 있다고 설명함.

  . 具體的인 규정에 대한 我國의 立場 表明은 一旦 留保함.

- 그리고 我國이 1990.11월에 제안한바 있는 (非公式 提案) 紛爭豫防節次 (pre-clearance system)에 대한 關心을 촉구함.

나. 向後 協商計劃 (Organization of Further Work) 論議

1) 協商의 基礎

o Anell 議長의 提議

- 지난 Brussels 회의에서 農産物, 서비스, 市場接近 (Market Access) 등 他協商그룹의 논의때문에 TRIPs 에 대한 논의에 진전이 없었다고 설명하고 協商의 出發點 (基礎, basis of negotiation) 을

  . 7次 議長報告書를 中心으로 하고,
  . 7次 議長報告書내에 있는 主要 issues 에 대해 論議하자고 함.
  . 이 논의를 통해 각국이 同意할수 있는 분야와 없는 분야에 대해 明確히 하자고 함.

- 새로운 element 의 도입에 대해서는 반대하지는 않으나, 7次 議長報告書를 中心으로 하는 것이 效率的이라고 함.

o 홍 콩

- 작년 12월이후 협상의 진전이 없었음에 비추어 7次 議長報告書가 9월 實質討議의 基礎로 되어야 할것임을 주장함.

o 말레이지아, 인도, 태국등 開途國

- 7次 議長報告書에 Brussels 會議에서 論議된 事項 (Work done in Brussels)을 追加해서 새로운 의장보고서 (revised text)를 만들어 토의하자고 함.

o 韓 國

- 7次 議長報告書의 내용중 bracket 으로 남아있는 사항을 중심으로 논의하고,

- GATTability 등 政治的인 問題 (political matters)는 高位級 會議로 미루는 것이 바람직하며,

- 協商妥結을 위해서는 Anell 議長이 各國의 讓步를 促求하는 노력이 있어야 할것이라고 주장함.

o Anell 議長

- 現 議長報告書 (7次 議長報告書)의 내용에도 美國, EC 등이 不滿足을 표시하고 있다고 설명하고, 이 상황에서 새로운 element 는 도입않는 것이 바람직 하다는 의견을 제시함.

2) 9月 會議議題 (agenda)

o Anell 議長의 提議

- 論議할 內容

. 7次 議長報告書를 中心으로 논의하되 입장이 대립되고 있는 분야, 同意할 수 있는 분야를 명확히 해나감.

. 政治的 問題 (political matters)는 技術的인 問題 (technical matters)에 대한 충분한 토의가 이루어지고 난 뒤 適正한 時間에 論議함.

. 政治的인 問題이면서도 技術的인 問題인 다음사항에 대해서도 논의함.

① 紛爭解決節次 (Dispute Settlement Procedure)

: GATTability 와 관련이 있는 문제로 政治的인 問題이나 현재까지 충분한 검토가 없었으므로 논의함.

* 議長報告書의 Annex 에 3가지 代案으로 포함되어 있음.

② 73條 (經過規程, Protection of Existing Intellectual Property)

: 매우 政治的인 問題이나 技術的인 내용이 포함되어 있으므로 논의를 하며, 쉽게 이해할수 있는 형태로 具體化 시키겠음.

. 具體的인 9月 會議 方向은 7月 TNC 會議 (7.29 주간으로 예정)와 他協商 그룹의 進展狀況에 따라 決定될것임.

- 會議日時 : 9.16 주간 (1주일 정도)를 제안하며 대부분의 기간이 非公式 會議로 進行될 것임을 언급함.

- 開途國이 요청한 Brussels 會議의 內容은 可能한한 書面 (written form)으로 配布하겠음.

o Egypt

- 技術的인 問題 (technical matters)중 해결된 것이 없으므로 의장 보고서의 全 條文을 論議하고 政治的인 問題 (political matters)는 나중에 논의함.

  * Egypt 와의 非公式 個別接觸時 Egypt 는 TRIPs 의 거의 모든 規程을 反對하며, 開途國도 그런 상황이므로 Anell 議長이 의도하는 特定 issues 만 論議하려는 것을 反對한다는 것을 알려옴.

- Brussels 會議內容에 대해 자세한 內容 및 分析 (assessment) 까지 알려줄것을 요구함.

o India

- Brussels 회의내용에 대한 分析 (assessment)까지 요구하는 것은 무리임.

- 그러나 Brussels 會議內容에 대해 議長이 書面(written form) 보다는 口頭(oral)로 알려줄것을 요구함. (Uruguay 도 동조)

  * 印度의 意圖를 個別的으로 探問

    . oral 로 요구하는 것은 會議內容이 書面으로 알려질 경우 具體事項 論議時 先進國이 書面에 명시되어 있다는 이유만으로 論議自體를 回避하는 것을 防止하기 위한 것이라고 함.

- 議長報告書가 basket 形式으로 되어야 함.

  . 즉, cover note 에 여러 異見이 있었다는 것만을 言及하지 말고, 各 條文에 具體的인 意見을 표시해 줄것을 요구

o Anell 의장

- 論議의 順序(order)를 정하는 것이므로 유연성(flexibility)를 확보할 필요 있음.

- Brussels 會議內容에 대해서는 단순히 information 形式으로 알리고 分析(assessment)까지는 않는 것이 現實的(practical way) 일것임.

- 9月 會議內容은 他協商그룹의 進展狀況에 영향을 많이 받을 것이나, 타협상 그룹보다 진전이 지연되어서는 안될 것이라고 언급함.

2. 會議 結果

o 6. 28일 오후 公式會議時 Anell 의장이 協議內容을 報告하고 이를 追認하는 形式으로 結論을 맺음.

가. 協商 全般

o TRIPs 協商이 農産物, 서비스, 市場接近(Market Access) 등 타 협상 그룹의 진전상황에 영향을 받는 것을 막을 수 없음.

- 협상그룹 간에 package 를 만들려 할 것임.
- 특히, 7月의 他 協商그룹 會議에 TRIPs 9月 會議가 영향을 받을 것임.

나. 協商의 基礎 (basis of work)

o Brussels 會議 內容을 充分히 考慮하되 7次 議長報告書가 協商의 基礎가 될 것임.

o Brussels 會議內容에 대해서는 동 회의에서 제출된 새로운 提案, 뉴스등을 모두 포함한 具體的인 ionformation 을 口頭(oral)로 알려줄 것임.
- 어느 정도의 分析(assessment) 도 포함될 것임.

다. 9月 會議 議題

o 타 협상그룹회의(7월 회의) 의 진전상황에 따라 변화될 수 있으나, 立場이 對立되고 있는 issue 중 技術的인 問題(technical matters) 를 중심으로 論議함.

o 다음 두 사항에 대한 논의를 포함

① 紛爭解決節次(Dispute settlement procedure)

- 協定의 國際履行(Int'l implementation) 및 GATTability 와 연관됨.

- 論議의 形式에 대한 印度의 질의에 대해 Anell 議長은 議長報告書 Annex 에 있는 세가지 代案에 대한 理解를 增進하는 方向으로 진행하겠다고 함.

② 經過規程 (第73條, Protection of Existing Intellectual Property)

- 明確하게 define 하겠음.

o 時間이 可能하면(available) 議長報告書의 全 條文 檢討

라. 會議 期間

o 9. 16 주간 (잠정적으로 1주) 으로 함.

Ⅵ. 其他 代表團 活動

1. Hartridge GATT 貿易政策局長 面談

가. 槪 要

o 日時 및 場所 : 6. 26(수) 15:00, GATT 사무실

o 面談者 : 企劃管理官 盧泳旭, 주재관 김준규, 사무관 이찬우

o 目 的 : 協商 展望 및 各國 立場의 事前 探問

나. 面談內容

1) 이번 會議 展望

o Agenda 가 low key 이며, Brussels 會議 以後 6개월 만에 開催되는 것이기 때문에 各國의 立場(position) 을 確認하고 爭點을 상기 (remind) 하기 위한 것임.

- 兩者(bilateral) 혹은 small group 會議를 組織하여 논의되도록 할것임.

2) TRIPs 向後 協商展望

o 私見임을 前提로 農産物等 他 協商그룹에 비해 obstacles 이 적기 때문에 금년내 타결되리라 봄.

o Brazil, Mexico, Argentina 등은 美國 綜合貿易法 301조에 의한 美國과의 兩者協商 結果 立場이 弱化되었으며, 美國은 業界의 壓力으로 立場이 强化되고 있음.

11

0163

- 아직 强傾한 立場을 취하고 있는 India, Egypt, Tanzania 등은 점점 孤立化 되어가고 있으며, 계속 강경한 입장을 취할 경우는 孤立化 시킬 수 밖에 없을 것임.

3) 我國提案(紛爭豫防節次)에 대한 意見 問議

o 9월에 紛爭解決節次에 대한 實質 討議가 이루어질 豫定인 바, 韓國이 이번 회의에 正式提案하는 것은 適切하다고 評價

- 事務局을 통해 提出해 줄것을 要請

4) 其 他

o Mr. Hartridge 局長이 我國의 關心事項에 대해 질의한 바, 貸與權, IC, 營業秘密, 國境措置, 經過規程에 대해 言及함.

2. 홍콩 Mission 主催 非公式 午餐

가. 概 要

o 日時 및 場所 : 6. 27(목) 주 제네바 홍콩 대표부

o 參加國 : 韓國, 호주, 뉴질랜드, 멕시코, 캐나다, 태국, 말레이지아, 홍콩 (8개국)

- 韓國 參加者 : 企劃管理官 盧泳旭, 주재관 김준규

나. 協議 內容

o 不特許對象, 商標, 地理的 表示, 컴퓨터 프로그램, 貸與權에 대해 의견을 모으고 특히, 태국은 經過規程에 대한 우리의 立場에 關心을 표하고 支持하는 입장을 보임.

o 오전에 발표한 我國의 基本 立場에 대해 특히 홍콩, 호주등이 支持하는 입장을 보임.

o 韓國은 紛爭豫防節次(pre-clearance system) 提案에 대한 支持를 要請함.

o 홍콩은 Anell 議長이 向後 協商日程에 대해 各國 代表와 充分히 協議하여야 할 것과 協商의 基礎로 7次 議長報告書가 되어야 할 것이라고 주장함.

※ 其他 反應

- 호 주 : 地理的 表示, 營業秘密, MFN 에 대하여 특히 우려를 표명하고 我國의 基本立場에 同調

- 태 국 : 거의 全條文에 問題가 있음을 指摘하고 今年 PFC 指定에 따른 태국 정부의 不滿表示와 함께 美國과 Pipeline product 協商이 進行中임을 설명하면서 특히 經過規程에 대해 우려 표명

- 브라질 : 그동안 美國과의 雙務協商을 否認하고, 종래 基本立場에 전혀 변화가 없음을 설명

13 0165

Ⅶ. 觀察 및 評價

o Brussels 閣僚會議 以後 6개월 만에 열리는 會議로 具體的인 內容보다 向後 協商의 framework 에 대한 論議를 중심으로 협의

o 各國이 그동안의 立場變化를 살피는 探索戰과 같은 성격

o 會議를 통해 先.開途國간 異見이 아직 크다는 것을 다시 確認하는 계기가 됨.

- 先進國도 7次 議長報告書에 대해 不滿足을 표시(EC)

- 開途國, 특히 印度, 이집트를 중심으로 한 强傾開途國은 TRIPs 協定 全 條文에 대해 反對하는 立場을 갖고 있음을 示唆

o 特記할 만한 것은 會議期間中 美國, 日本 代表의 發言이 전혀 없었다는 점임.

- Hartridge 局長에 探問한바, 美國은 業界의 강력한 로비로 議長報告書의 standard 를 높여야 할 입장이어서 各國의 反應만을 聽取하는것 같다는 評價를 함.

- 美國은 Brussels 각료회의 타결 실패후 多者보다는 兩者間 壓力에 중점을 두는 인상을 보여줌.

  * 開途國(태국, 이집트, 인도, 방글라데시, 파키스탄등) 의 美國의 一方的 制裁措置에 대한 公開的 非難

o TRIPs 協商이 農産物, 서비스, 市場接近(Market Access) 등 타 주요협상의 영향에서 벗어날 수 없다는 한계점을 다시 노출

Ⅷ. 向後 協商對策

o 9月 까지의 공백기간 동안 7次 議長報告書 全 條文 再檢討

- 특정 issues 뿐 아니라 거의 全 條文을 論議할 것으로 보임.

- 작년보다, 미국.EC등 선진국의 입장이 한층 강화될 것에 대비하여 我國의 關心事項에 대해 立場 再檢討, 調整 필요

o 특히, 論議가 적었던 紛爭解決節次에 대한 立場 마련

- 我國이 事務局을 통해 제출할 紛爭豫防節次에 대한 補充資料 및 說明資料 작성 준비

o 第73條(經過規程) 에 대한 內部立場 調整 및 EC등 對 先進國 對應方案 講究

- 73條를 redrafting 할 경우 同 情報를 입수하여 我國의 意見이 反映될 수 있도록 노력

o 協商에의 積極的 參與努力 必要

- 各國 代表들과의 事前 接觸, 個別接觸의 活性化

- GATT 事務局 職員과의 接觸 强化

정 리 보 존 문 서 목 록

기록물종류	일반공문서철	등록번호	2019090033	등록일자	2019-09-05
분류번호	764.51	국가코드		보존기간	영구
명 칭	UR(우루과이라운드) / TRIPs(지적재산권) 협상 그룹 회의, 1991. 전2권				
생 산 과	통상기구과	생산년도	1991~1991	담당그룹	다자통상
권 차 명	V.2 7-10월				
내용목차					

0001

분류기호 문서번호	기법02101-	협 조 문 용 지 (720-2946)	결재	담 당	담당관	조정관
시행일자	'91. 7. 2.					
수 신	통상국장	발 신	기획관리실장 (서명)			
제 목	부정경쟁방지법 개정안 의견조회					

특허청이 개정추진중인 별첨 부정경쟁방지법개정(안)에 대한 귀국의 검토의견을 '91.7.20.까지 당실로 회보하여 주시기 바랍니다.

첨 부 : 부정경쟁방지법개정초안 축조해설 1부. 끝.

0002

영업비밀보호를 위한 입법 초안

-부정경쟁방지법 개정초안 축조해설-

특 허 청

(영업비밀보호입법추진위원회)

0003

정 오 표

구 분	~를	~로
p 9 밑에서 첫째줄	밑출친	고딕체
p24 밑에서 첫째줄	p 11 p 16	p 10 p 15
p29 괄호안 위에서 네번째줄	임직원 또는 임직원이었던자	임・직원 또는 임・직원이었던자
p31 위에서 첫째줄	할 수	〈삭제〉
p40 위에서 두째줄	權源의	權原의

0004

目 次

1. 營業秘密의 定義

(부정경쟁방지법 개정초안 제2조 제2호)

2. "영업비밀"이라 함은 일반적으로 알려져 있지 아니하고 독립된 경제적 가치를 가지며, 상당한 노력에 의하여 비밀로 유지관리된 생산방법, 판매방법, 기타 영업활동에 유용한 기술상 또는 경영상의 정보를 말한다.

가. 취 지

영업비밀(註)의 개념을 명확히 정의하기 위하여 신설한 규정인 바, 비밀로 유지·관리된 생산방법등 **기술상의 정보** 뿐만 아니라 판매방법등 영업활동에 유용한 **경영상의 정보**도 포함됨을 명시하고 있다.

註) 미국의 32개 주에서 채택하고 있는 모델법인 통일영업비밀보호법 (Uniform Trade Secret Act)은 forumla (제법공식), pattern (정형, 양식, 무늬장식), compilation (편집물), program (프로그램), device (고안, 장치), method (방법), technique (기술), process (제조공정)를 영업비밀의 예로서 열거하고 있다.

- 3 -

0006

나. 해 설

(1) 영업비밀의 요건

영업비밀이 되려면 다음의 요건을 갖추어야 하는 바, 이들 요건은 상호 밀접 불가분한 관계에 있는 것으로서 개개로 분리될 수 있는 것이 아니다.

첫째, 그 자체가 일반적으로 알려져 있지 않은 정보일 것 (비공개성)

둘째, 독립적인 경제적 가치를 가지는 기술상 또는 경영상 유용한 정보일 것 (경제성)

세째, 상당한 노력에 의하여 비밀로서 계속 유지, 관리되고 있는 정보일 것 (비밀관리)

네째, 생산방법, 판매방법, 기타 영업활동에 이용될 수 있는 정보일 것 (이용성)

(2) 영업비밀의 實例

기술상의 영업비밀로는, 설계방법, 설계도(공장・기계장치・제품), 공정도, 실험데이타, 성분원료의 배합비, 강도계산의 운용방법등을 들 수 있고, 경영상의 영업비밀로는, 고객명부, 거래선명부, 신제품 제조・판매계획, 제품의 할인 시스템, 부기방법, 사무실 관리방법등을 들수 있을 것이다.

2. 영업비밀 침해행위의 유형

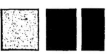

(부정경쟁방지법 개정초안 제11조 제1항 제1호 내지 제6호)

가. 규정의 체계

개정 초안에서는, 앞에서 본 바와 같이, 영업비밀 侵害行爲를 기본적으로 민법상 不法行爲의 특수형태인 不正競爭行爲의 일종으로 유형화하여 규정하고 있다.

침해행위의 유형은 6가지로 되어 있으나, 기본적으로는 不正取得行爲등(1호)과 秘密維持義務 違反行爲(4호)의 2가지 유형으로 구성되어 있으며, 이 2가지 유형의 기술적 침해행위에 따르는 사후적 관여행위를 각각 2가지씩 추가하여 규정하고 있다.

즉, 부정취득행위(1호)나 비밀유지의무위반행위(4호)가 있었다는 사실을 취득당시에 알거나 중대한 과실로 알지 못하고 당해 영업비밀을 취득·사용·공개하는 행위를 각각 2호, 5호에 규정하고 있으며, 부정취득행위(1호)나 비밀유지의무위반행위 (4호)를 취득당시에는 알지 못하였으나 취득 후 알게 되거나 중대한 과실로 알지 못하고 당해 영업비밀을 사용 또는 공개하는 행위를 각각 3호, 6호에 규정하고 있다.

- 5 -

0008

나. 침해 행위의 개별 유형

> 1. 절도, 횡령, 사기, 협박 기타 부정한 수단으로 영업비밀을 취득하는 행위 (이하 "부정취득행위"라고 한다.) 또는 그 취득한 영업비밀을 사용하거나 공개 (비밀을 유지하면서 특정인에게 알리는것을 포함한다. 이하 같다)하는 행위

(1) 취 지

형법상 범죄를 구성하는 행위 기타 社會常規에 어긋나는 수단에 의한 영업비밀의 취득행위를 금지하며, 또한 그렇게 취득한 영업비밀을 사용하거나 공개하는 행위도 불법행위의 産物을 사용하거나 공개하는 행위이므로 금지되어야 한다는 취지이다. 따라서, 불법적으로 취득한 영업비밀을 사용하거나 공개하는 행위는 각각 부정취득행위와는 별도로 침해행위를 구성한다.

(2) 해 설

침해행위의 態樣은 다음과 같이 나누어 볼 수 있다.

① 부정취득행위

가령, 乙이 甲의 사무실에 침입하여 영업비밀인 설계도면을 훔친 경우, 이는 영업비밀의 부정취득행위에 해당된다.

② 부정사용행위

부정취득자 乙이 당해 설계도면을 사용하여 상품을 제조·판매하는 경우, 이는 영업비밀의 부정사용행위에 해당된다.

③ 부정공개행위

부정취득자 乙이 위 설계도면을 제3자인 庚에게 매각, 라이센스등의 방법으로 공개하는경우, 이는 영업비밀의 부정공개행위에 해당된다.

"공개"의 개념에는 불특정 다수인에게 일반적으로 알리는 행위 뿐만 아니라 비밀을 유지하면서 소수의 특정인에게 알리는 행위까지를 포함한다. 예를들면, 부정취득자 乙이 제3자인 庚에게 비밀유지를 조건으로하여 라이센스 계약을 체결하는 경우이다.

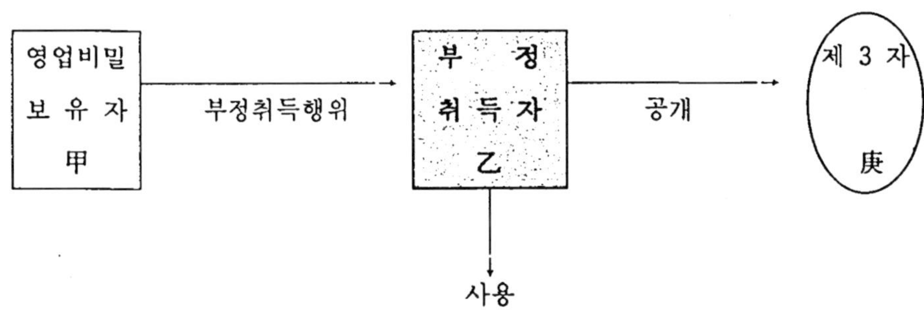

(3) 사 례

P제철의 『1984년도 실행 생산계획서』 유출사건 (1984년 1월)

J 국 M 상사 한국 주재원 B씨가, P제철에 업무차 방문중 책상위에 놓여있던 대외비 기밀문서인 "1984년도 실행 생산계획서"1권을 서류가방에 몰래 넣고 나와 복사한 다음 이를 J 국으로 보내려다가 K 공항에서 적발된 적이 있는바, 이경우 B씨의 절취행위는 이 호의 부정취득행위에 해당된다.

2. 영업비밀에 대하여 부정취득행위가 개입된 사실을 알거나 중대한 과실로 알지 못하고 그 영업비밀을 취득하는 행위 또는 그 취득한 영업비밀을 사용하거나 공개하는 행위

(1) 취 지

1호에 규정된 부정취득행위가 존재하는 것을 전제로 하여 부정취득된 영업비밀에 사후적으로 관여하는 것을 배제하기 위한 규정인 바, 이 호는 악의 또는 중과실이 있는 취득행위와, 악의 또는 중과실로 취득한 영업비밀을 사용하거나 공개하는 행위를 모두 금지하는 것이다.

(2) 해 설

(가) 例示

甲이 보유하고 있는 영업비밀을 乙이 절취하여 이를 丙에게 매각하였는데, 매수자 丙이 당해 영업비밀을 매수할때 그것이 乙이 절취한 것이라는 사실을 알았거나, 중대한 과실로 알지 못하였다면 丙의 취득행위는 영업비밀 침해행위를 구성하며, 丙이 그 영업비밀을 사용하거나 공개하는 행위도 영업비밀 침해행위가 된다.

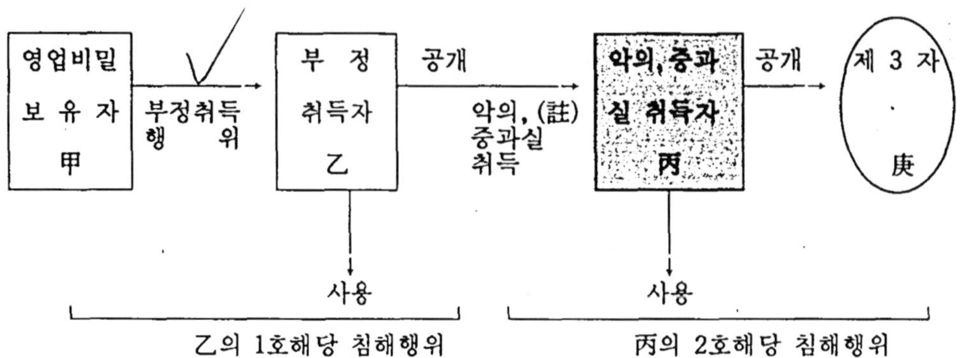

또한 丙이 부정취득· 공개한 乙로부터 직접 취득하지 아니하였어도, 즉, **甲과 丙사이에 어느 누구에 의해서든 부정취득행위 (및 공개행위)가 있었다는 사실**

(註)을 알면서 (또는 중대한 과실로 알지 못하고) 그 영업비밀을 취득하였다면, 丙의 취득행위 (또는 그영업비밀을 사용하거나 공개하는 행위)는 이 호의 침해행위에 해당된다.

(나) "중대한 과실로 알지 못하고"라 함은 매수자 丙이 부정취득자 乙로부터 영업비밀을 매수함에 있어서 사회적 지위, 종사하는 직업등에 따라 평균적으로 요구되는 주의를 현저하게 게을리 하였기 때문에 알지 못한 것을 말한다.

註) "惡意"라 함은 매수자 丙이 부정취득자 乙로부터 영업비밀을 매수함에 있어서 당해 영업비밀은 乙이 절취한 것이라는 사실, 즉 부정취득행위가 개입된 사실을 알고 있는 경우를 말한다.

註) 밑줄친 부분이 이 호의 "부정취득행위가 개입된 사실"에 해당한다.

3. 영업비밀을 취득한 후에 그 영업비밀에 대하여 부정취득행위가 개입된 사실을 알거나 중대한 과실로 알지 못하고 그 영업비밀을 사용하거나 공개하는 행위

(1) 취 지

2호와 같은 취지로, 부정취득한 영업비밀에 사후적으로 관여하는 것을 방지하기 위한 규정인 바, 이 호는 취득당시에는 그 영업비밀에 부정취득행위가 개입된 사실을 몰랐으나, 취득후 그 사실을 알았거나 중대한 과실로 알지못하고 그 영업비밀을 사용하거나 공개하는 행위를 금지하는 것이다.

(2) 해 설

(가) 例示

甲의 영업비밀을 乙이 절취등 부정한 수단으로 취득한 후, 이를 丙에게 자신의 영업비밀이라고 속여서 매각하였는 데, 매수자 丙은 취득당시 乙의 진술을 믿고 선의로 취득하였다. 선의의 매수자 丙이 그후 영업비밀보유자인 甲으로부터 경고를 받음으로써 그 영업비밀의 취득에 이와 같은 乙의 부정취득·공개행위가 개입된 것을 알았음에도 불구하고 (또는 중대한 과실로 알지 못하고) 이를 사용하거나 공개하는 경우, 매수자 丙의 사용 또는 공개는 이 호의 영업비밀 침해행위에 해당된다.

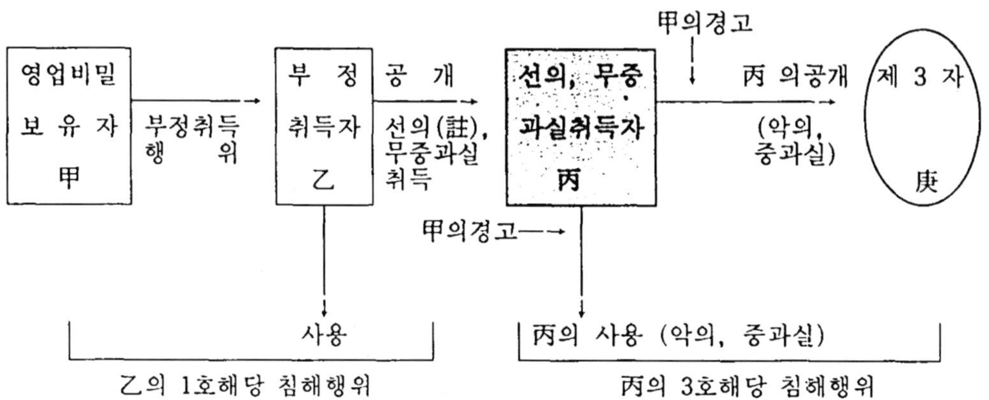

(나) 본호의 침해행위에 대하여는 제14조의 "善意者에 관한 특례" 규정이 적용된다. (P24 참조)

註) "善意"라 함은 매수자 丙이 부정취득자 乙로부터 영업비밀을 매수함에 있어서 乙이 절취한 것이라는 사실, 즉 부정취득행위가 개입된 사실을 알지못한 것을 말한다.

4. 계약관계등에 의하여 영업비밀을 비밀로서 유지하여야 할 의무가 있는 자가 부정한 이익을 얻거나 그 영업비밀의 보유자에게 손해를 가할 목적으로 그영업비밀을 사용하거나 공개하는 행위

(1) 취 지

계약관계등에 의하여 영업비밀을 비밀로 유지하여야 할 의무가 있는 자가 부정한 이익등을 목적으로 그 영업비밀을 사용하거나 공개하는 행위는 1호의 부정취득 행위와 마찬가지로 금지되어야 할 영업비밀 침해행위의 기본적 유형이라는 점에서 이를 규정하였다.

(2) 해 설

(가) 例示

영업비밀의 보유자인 甲의 회사에 근무하는 乙이, 또는 甲으로부터 그 영업비밀의 라이센스 계약을 체결한 丙이, 그 영업비밀을 비밀로서 유지하여야 할 의무가 있음에도 불구하고, 부정한 이익을 얻거나 甲에게 손해를 가할 목적으로, 그 영업비밀을 사용하거나 제3자 庚에게 공개하는 행위는 이 호의 침해행위에 해당된다.

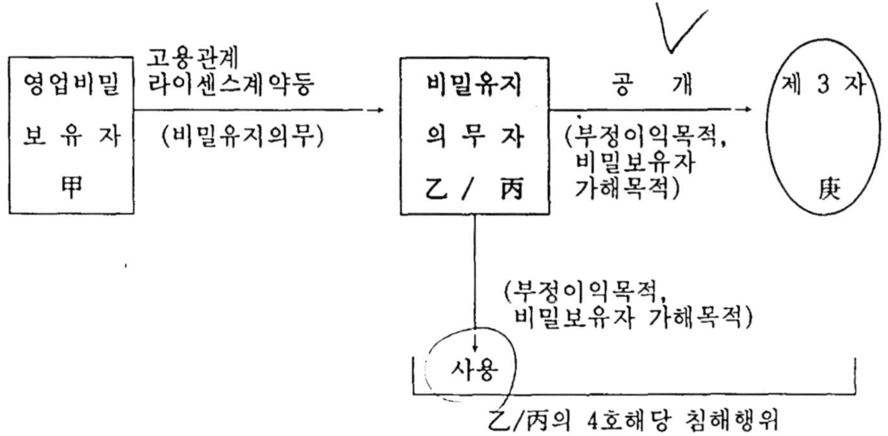

(나) 침해행위의 구성요건

① 계약관계등에 의하여 영업비밀을 비밀로 유지할 의무가 있는 자일 것

가령 고용관계, 라이센스계약등 여러가지 유형의 계약관계등에 의하여 영업비밀을 비밀로 유지할 의무가 있는 자라야 한다.

② 부정한 이익을 얻거나 그 영업비밀 보유자에게 손해를 가할 목적으로 공개할 것

따라서 부정한 이득을 얻거나 영업비밀 보유자에게 손해를 가할 목적이 아닌 다른 정당한 사유가 있는 경우에는 이 호의 규정에 의한 침해행위를 구성하지 아니한다.

③ 영업비밀 보유자의 영업비밀을 사용 또는 공개할 것

(다) 사 례

X선 촬영 조영제 제조기술 관련서류 유출사건 (1987년 4월)

T제약 회사가 10억원이 넘는 연구비를 들여 개발한 X선 촬영 조영제 『바리탑』의 제조기술 관련 서류 및 판매관계 영업장부를 이회사의 개발이사로

있던 K씨가 경쟁회사인 S제약회사로 이직하면서 S사에 유출한 사건이 있는 바, 이경우 K씨의 유출행위는 이 호의 침해행위에 해당된다.

5. 영업비밀이 제4호의 규정에 의하여 공개된 사실 또는 그러한 공개행위가 개입된 사실을 알거나 중대한 과실로 알지 못하고 그 영업비밀을 취득하는 행위 또는 그 취득한 영업비밀을 사용하거나 공개하는 행위

(1) 취 지

이 호는 4호의 부정하게 공개된 영업비밀에 대하여, 취득 당시 그러한 공개행위가 개입된 사실을 알거나 중대한 과실로 알지 못하고 그 영업비밀을 취득하는 행위 또는 그 취득한 영업비밀을 사용 또는 공개하는 행위를, 부정공개행위의 사후적 관여행위로서 금지하는 것이다.

(2) 해 설

영업비밀 보유자인 甲으로부터 그 영업비밀에 관하여 라이센스를 받은 丙이, 계약상의 비밀유지의무를 위반하여 부정한 이익등을 목적으로 丁에게 이를 매각하였는데, 매수자 丁이 악의 또는 중과실로 이를 취득하는 행위, 또는 그취득한 영업비밀을 사용 하거나 제3자인 庚에게 공개하는 행위는 이 호의 영업비밀 침해행위에 해당된다.

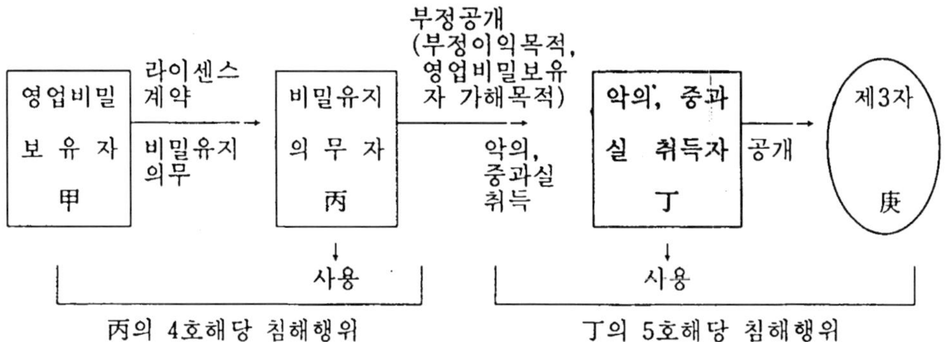

또한, 丁이 부정공개자 丙으로부터 직접 취득하지 아니하였더라도, 즉, 甲과 丁사이에 어느 누구에 의해서든 부정공개행위가 있었다는 사실을 알면서 (또는 중대한 과실로 알지 못하고) 그 영업비밀을 취득하였다면, 丁의 취득행위 (또는 그영업비밀을 사용하거나 공개하는 행위)는 이 호의 침해행위에 해당된다.

6. 영업비밀을 취득한후에 그 영업비밀이 제4호의 규정에 의하여 공개된 사실 또는 그러한 공개행위가 개입된 사실을 알거나 중대한 과실로 알지 못하고 그 영업비밀을 사용하거나 공개하는 행위

(1) 취 지

5호와 같은 취지로, 부정공개된 영업비밀에 사후적으로 관여하는 것을 방지하기 위한 규정인바, 이 호는 취득 당시에는 4호에 규정된 부정공개행위가 개입된 것을 몰랐으나, 취득후 이를 알았거나 중대한 과실로 알지 못하고 그 영업비밀을 공개하거나 사용하는 행위를 금지하는 것이다.

(2) 해 설

(가) 例示

영업비밀 보유자인 甲으로부터 당해 영업비밀에 관하여 라이센스를 받은 丙이, 계약상의 비밀유지의무를 위반하여 부정한 이익등을 목적으로 선의인 丁에게 이를 매각하였다. 丁은 취득당시에는 이러한 부정공개행위를 모르고 선의로 매수하였으나, 나중에 甲이 丁에게 경고를 하는 등의 이유로 丁이 이를 알게 되었음에도 불구하고 (또는 중대한과실로 알지 못하고) 丁이 당해 영업비밀을 사용하거나 제3자인 庚에게 공개한다면, 이들 사용 또는 공개행위는 이 호의 영업비밀 침해행위에 해당된다.

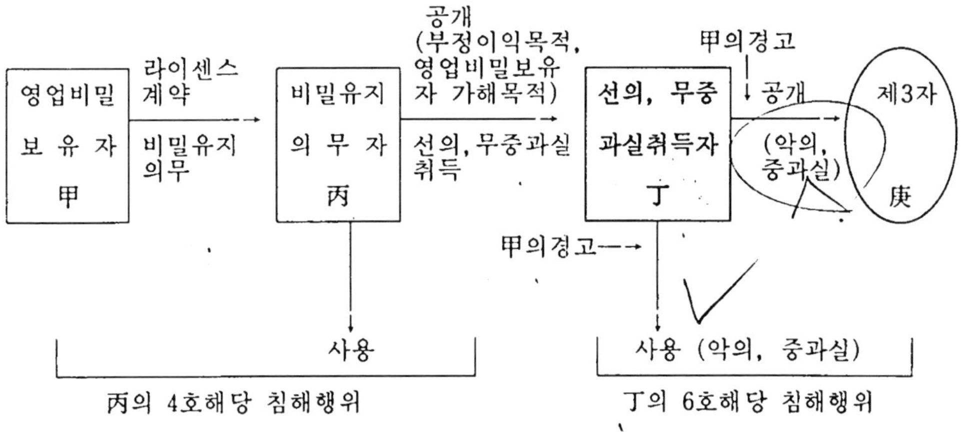

(나) 이 호의 침해행위에 대하여는 제14조의 "善意者에 관한 특례" 규정이 적용된다. (P24 참조)

3. 영업비밀 침해행위에 대한 민사적 구제수단

(부정경쟁방지법 개정초안 제11조 내지 제13조)

가. 침해행위에 대한 민사적 구제수단의 성격

현행 법체제 아래서는 개개의 구체적인 영업비밀 침해행위가 민사상 계약위반(채무불이행) 또는 불법행위등을 구성하는 경우에 한하여, 단지 이를 토대로 한 손해배상청구권등이 인정되고 있을 뿐이므로, 영업비밀 침해행위에 대한 민사적 구제수단이 극히 미흡하다고 볼 수 있다.

이에 본 개정초안에서는 앞에서 본 바와같이 제11조 제1항 제1호 내지 제6호에서 영업비밀 침해행위를 민법상 不法行爲의 특수한 형태인 不正競爭行爲의 유형으로 분류하여 명문으로 규정하였고, 이 조에서는 불법행위로서의 영업비밀 침해행위에 대한 民事的 救濟手段의 특칙으로서 침해행위 금지 또는 예방청구권, 침해행위로 만들어진 물건등의 폐기·제거청구권, 침해행위에 대한 손해배상 청구권, 영업비밀 보유자의 신용회복 청구권등을 규정하고 있다.

나. 금지 또는 예방 청구권

> **제11조 (영업비밀 침해행위에 대한 금지청구권등) ① 영업비밀의 보유자는 다음 각호의 1에 해당하는 행위 (이하 "영업비밀 침해행위"라한다)를 하거나 하려고 하는 자가 있는 경우에 그행위에 의하여 영업상의 이익이 침해되거나 침해될 우려가 있는 때에는 당해 행위의 금지 또는 예방을 청구할 수 있다.**

– 17 –

0020

(1) 취 지

영업비밀은 비밀성이 유지되는 동안 경제적 가치를 가지는 정보로서 일단 공개된 이후에는 그경제적 가치를 상실하게 된다. 따라서 영업비밀 보호 제도의 핵심은 바로 그 침해행위에 대한 금지 또는 예방 청구권에 있다.

(2) 해 설

(가) 본 규정에 따라 금지 또는 예방을 청구할 수 있는 자는, 침해행위에 의하여 영업상의 이익이 침해되거나 침해될 우려가 있는 영업비밀의 보유자이다.

영업비밀의 보유자는 영리를 목적으로 하는 기업에 한정되지 아니하므로, 영업비밀이 침해되지 않는데 대하여 영업상의 이익을 가지는 한, 비영리 단체 (가령 연구를 주목적으로 하는 연구소)등도 포함된다.

또한 영업비밀 보유자의 법인격의 유무도 불문하므로 예를들면 몇개의 기업이 공동 출자한 연구 목적의 조합등도 포함한다.

(나) 영업비밀의 보유자는 기술상, 경영상의 노우하우 (Know-how)를 최초로 생산-개발한자 (original developer)뿐만 아니라 그로부터 정당하게 양수받은 자등을 포함한다.

(다) "침해할 우려가 있는 때"라 함은 가령 사업계획서의 작성, 장비의 발주·구입, 전문인력채용등 객관적으로 침해의사가 표현된 것을 의미하는 바, 단순한 주관적인 우려만으로는 침해의 우려가 있다고 볼 수 없다.

(라) 영업상의 이익이 침해되거나 침해될 우려가 있으면 족하므로, 현실적으로 영업상의 이익이 침해되지 아니하여도 침해가 발생할 상당한 가능성이 있

으면, 본 규정의 금지 또는 예방 청구권이 인정된다. 즉, 영업비밀 침해 행위가 행하여지려는 경우에는 이에 대한 사전의 예방을, 영업비밀 침해 행위가 이미 행하여진 경우에는 이에 대한 장래의 금지를 청구할 수 있다. 다만, 영업비밀이 선의의 경쟁자에게 일반적으로 알려져 버렸거나 逆工程(reverse engineering)을 통해 알려졌다면 금지 또는 예방 청구권은 인정되지 못할 것이다.

(마) 금지 또는 예방 청구의 구체적 내용은, 침해행위의 구체적 態樣에 따라 결정될 것인 바, 장래 일정한 기간 (예를들면 영업비밀 침해행위로 인하여 침해자가 경쟁상의 우위를 지킬수 있는 선도기간, 註1) 동안, 일정한 부작위를 명하는 경우가 대부분 일것이다. 다만 이와 같은 법원의 명령을 어기는 경우에는 간접강제 (예를들면, 그 부작위 명령을 어긴자에 대하여 법원이 일정한 금액의 배상을 명령하는 등, 註2)의 수단에 의할 수 밖에 없다.

(3) 例

A 기업은 상당한 시간과 자금을 투자하여 일정한 물질을 배합하여 독특한 향이 있는 향료를 개발하였는 바, 그 개발이 완성될 무렵 개발작업에 참여한 연구반원 하나가 그 향료의 제법에 관한 연구자료를 경쟁사인 B 기업에 팔아넘긴 것을 발견한 경우, A 기업은 B 기업을 상대로 위 연구자료 자체의 반환을 청구하는 방법도 강구할 수 있겠지만 (註3),

---

註1) 先導期間 (leading period)

註2) 民事訴訟法 제693조 (간접강제) 참조

註3) 民法 第213條 (소유물 반환 청구권) 참조

더 나아가 B기업이 위 연구자료를 이미 복사하는 등의 방법으로 영업활동에 사용하고 있는 경우, 장래의 사용을 못하도록 하기 위하여 이 조에 규정된 침해행위 금지청구권을 행사할 수 있다.

다. 폐기·제거 청구권

제11조 ② 영업비밀 보유자가 제1항의 규정에 의한 청구를 할 때에는 침해행위에 의하여 만들어진 물건의 폐기, 침해행위에 제공된 설비의 제거 기타 침해행위의 예방에 필요한 행위를 청구할 수 있다.

(1) 취지 및 해설

초안 제11조제1항의 규정에 의한 영업비밀 침해행위의 금지 또는 예방청구뿐만 아니라, 장래의 침해행위를 방지하기 위하여 영업비밀을 사용하여 제작한 유체물 (예를들면, 설계도면 사본), 영업비밀을 사용하여 만들어진 제품 (예를들면, 생산제품) 또는 영업비밀의 사용 행위에 제공된 설비 (예를들면, 제조영업비밀의 경우 생산설비)의 제거를 청구할 수 있도록 하였다.

그러나, 이 항의 폐기·제거 청구권은, 영업비밀을 선의로 취득한 후 상당한 투자를 하여 실질적인 지위의 변경이 이루어진 경우, 또는 영업비밀의 사용이 전 제조공정이나 영업활동의 일체 불가분의 일부를 이루는 경우에는, 민법상 권리 남용으로 인정되지 않는 범위내에서 극히 제한적으로 인정될 것이다.

즉, 영업비밀 보유자가 제품·설비등의 폐기·제거 청구권의 행사로 인하여 얻게될 이익과 제품·설비등이 폐기·제거됨으로 인하여 영업비밀 침해자가 입게될 손실을 비교형량하여, 민법상 영업비밀 보유자의 권리 남용으로 되지 않는 범위까지만 제한적으로 인정될 것이다.

(2) 例

A 기업은 생명공학에 막대한 투자를 하여 특수한 효과를 가지는 미생물을 배양해 내었던 바, 경쟁사인 B 기업이 산업스파이를 동원하여 그 미생물의 시험종자를 절취하였다. 이 경우 위 미생물은 쉽게 배양 증식되는 것이므로, A 기업은 법원에 B 기업을 상대로 시험종자의 반환청구 및 그 배양설비등의 폐기를 청구할 수 있다.

라. 손해배상 청구권

제12조 (영업비밀 침해에 대한 손해배상 책임) 고의 또는 과실에 의한 영업비밀 침해행위로 영업비밀 보유자에게 손해를 가한 자는 그손해를 배상할 책임을 진다.

(1) 취 지

영업비밀 보호의 본질은 영업비밀 침해행위를 민법상 불법행위의 특수한 유형으로 보고 이를 규제하는 것이므로, 영업비밀 침해행위로 손해를 입은 자는 일반 민법상 불법행위의 경우와 같이 손해배상을 청구할 권리를 가진다.

(2) 해 설

영업비밀이 침해된 경우 그 손해액의 산정은 현실적으로 매우 어려운 것이 사실 이지만, 이는 결국 법원의 판례를 통하여 발전될 문제인 바, 특허권 침해 행위에 대한 손해배상에 준하여 (i) 현실적인 손해액, (ii) 침해행위자가 얻은 이익, (iii) 영업비밀을 사용하였더라면 얻을 수 있었던 실시료 상당액 등을 고려하여야 할 것이다.

(3) 例

A 기업은 병원에서 사용되는 주기억장치와 각 단말기 사이의 (자료의 저장. 송신 및 열람을 위한) 인터페이스 (interface)를 개발, 상품화에 성공하여 시장을 석권하던 중, A 기업에서 이 인터페이스를 개발하는 작업에 참석하였던 몇사람이 B기업을 설립한 다음, 위 인터페이스를 IBM 퍼스널 컴퓨터에 연결해서 사용할 수 있도록 개조하여 시장에 판매 함으로써, A기업의 시장 점유율이 대폭 떨어졌다. 이 경우 A 기업은 B 기업의 판매행위로 부터입게된 손해에 대하여 모 기업을 상대로 손해배상을 청구할 수 있다.

마. 신용회복 청구권

제13조 (영업비밀 보유자의 신용회복) 영업비밀보유자는 영업비밀 침해행위로 인하여 업무상의 신용을 실추하게 한 자에 대하여는 손해배상에 갈음하거나 손해배상과 함께 업무상의 신용회복을 위하여 필요한 조치를 법원에 청구할수 있다.

(1) 취 지

영업비밀 보유자는, 영업비밀 침해행위로 인하여 업무상의 신용이 실추된 경우, 신용회복을 위하여 필요한 조치 (예, 침해행위자로 부터 받은 사죄각서, 합의각서 등의 공개 또는 신문 광고, 註)를 청구할 수 있다.

註) 다만, 최근 헌법재판소는 사죄광고를 명하는 것은 헌법에 반한다고 판시한 만큼 법원의 판결로 사죄광고를 강제할 수 있는지의 여부에 대하여는 좀더 두고 보아야 할 것이다.

4. 선의자에 관한 특례

제14조 (선의자에 관한 특례) ① 거래에 의하여 영업비밀을 정당하게 취득한 자가 그 거래에 의해 얻은 權原의 범위내에서 그 영업비밀을 사용하거나 공개하는 행위에 대하여는 제11조 내지 제13조의 규정을 적용하지 아니한다.
② 제1항의 "영업비밀을 정당하게 취득한 자"라 함은 영업비밀을 취득할 당시에 그 영업비밀이 부정하게 공개된 사실 또는 영업비밀의 부정취득행위나 부정공개행위가 개입된 사실을 중대한 과실없이 알지 못하고 그영업비밀을 취득한 자를 말한다.

(1) 취 지

이 규정은 영업비밀에 관한 거래의 안정성을 확보하기 위하여 마련한 규정인 바, 제3자가 정상적인 거래에 의하여 영업비밀을 취득한 경우, 그 취득시점에는 고의 또는 중과실이 없었지만, 나중에 피해자인 영업비밀 보유자로 부터 경고장등을 받음으로써, 그후부터 영업비밀 침해행위의 존재에 대하여 알게 된 자(事後的 惡意者. 註)를 구제하기 위하여 마련한 특칙이다.

따라서 동 규정은 기본적으로 영업비밀 보유자의 이익과 선의취득자의 이익을 비교형량하여 조화를 도모하기 위한 것이라 할 수 있다.

註) P 11 의 제3호 해당 침해행위 및 P 16 의 제6호 해당 침해행위 참조

(2) 해 설

(가) 정당한 취득의 요건

①영업비밀의 취득자가 영업비밀을 취득할 당시에 善意라야 한다.

즉, 영업비밀을 취득할 당시에 그 영업비밀이 비밀보유자에 대한 의무를 위반하여 부정하게 공개된 사실 또는 영업비밀의 부정취득행위나 부정공개행위가 개입된 사실을 몰랐어야 한다.

②영업비밀 취득자에게 중대한 과실이 없어야 한다.

"중대한 과실"이라 함은, 거래에 있어서 평균적으로 요구되는 통상의 주의의무를 다하면 부정취득 또는 공개행위가 개입된 것을 쉽게 알수 있는데도 불구하고 그러한 주의를 현저히 게을리한 것을 말한다.

(나) "거래"라 함은 매매계약, 라이센스계약등 정형적인 거래 뿐만 아니라 비정형적인 사실상의 거래를 포함한다.

(다) "權原의 범위내에서"라 함은 거래의 내용 (예를들면, 매매계약, 라이센스 계약의 내용)에 따라 정당하게 취득한 권리의 범위내를 뜻한다.

(라) 이 규정은 法案 제11조 제1항 제3호 및 제6호의 침해행위에 대한 특칙이다.

(3) 본 규정 적용의 효과

영업비밀의 선의 취득자는 영업비밀 보유자가 그 침해자에 대하여 취할 수 있는 금지청구권, 손해배상청구권, 신용회복청구권등의 적용을 받지 않는다. 이 경우, 거래에 의하여 얻은 정당한 권원의 범위내에서 사용하거나 공개하는 것은 금지 청구의 대상이 되지 않으나, 정당한 권원의 범위를 넘어서 부당하게 이익을 꾀하거나 영업비밀 보유자에게 손해를 끼칠 의도를 갖고 사용 또는 공개하는 경우는 침해행위로 되어 금지청구권등의 대상이 된다.

5. 소 멸 시 효

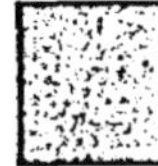

(부정경쟁방지법 개정초안 제15조)

제15조 (소멸시효) 제11조 제1항의 규정에 의하여 영업비밀 침해행위의 금지 또는 예방을 청구할 수 있는 권리는 영업비밀 침해행위가 계속되는 경우에 영업비밀 보유자가 그침해행위에 의하여 영업상의 이익이 침해되거나 침해될 우려가 있는 사실 및 침해행위자를 안 날로부터 3년간 이를 행사하지 아니하면 시효로 인하여 소멸한다. 그 침해행위가 시작된 날로부터 10년을 경과한 때에도 또한 같다.

가. 취 지

영업비밀 보유자가 침해행위 금지 또는 예방청구권을 오랫동안 행사하지 않고 있음에도 불구하고 그러한 권리를 기간 제한없이 계속적으로 인정하는 것은, 훗날 침해행위와 관련된 사업활동의 금지청구를 통하여 거래관계에 커다란 영향을 줄 우려가 있다. 따라서

① 영업비밀 침해에 관한 법률관계는 조기에 안정되는 것이 사회적으로 바람직하다는 점

② 침해행위가 장기간 계속되는 것을 그대로 방치하고 있는 영업비밀 보유자는 소위 권리위에 잠자는 자로서 법적보호를 받을 필요성이 감소된다는 점 등을 고려하여, 영업비밀 침해행위의 금지 또는 예방 청구권에 대한 소멸시효 규정을 둔 것이다.

나. 해 설

(1) 적 용 대 상

시효로 소멸하는 것은 영업비밀 침해금지 또는 예방청구권이고, 침해행위가 계속되는 경우에 한하여 이 규정의 적용을 받는다.

(2) 시효기간의 기산점

3년의 소멸시효는 영업비밀보유자가 『영업상의 이익이 침해되거나 침해될 우려가 있는 사실 및 침해행위자를 안 날』로 부터 진행하고, 10년의 소멸시효는 『영업비밀 침해행위가 시작된 날』로 부터 기산한다.

(3) 손해배상 청구권의 소멸시효

영업비밀 침해행위에 대한 손해배상 청구권은, 이 법안에는 규정되어 있지 아니하지만, 일반 불법행위에 대한 손해배상 청구권의 소멸시효 규정 (민법 제766조)에 의하여, 손해 및 영업비밀 침해행위자를 안 날로부터 3년간 이를 행사하지 아니하거나, 영업비밀 침해행위를 한 날로부터 10년을 경과하면, 시효로 인하여 소멸한다.

6. 영업비밀 침해행위에 대한 처벌

(부정경쟁방지법 개정초안 제16조)

제16조 ① 다음 각호의 1에 해당하는 자는 3년이하의 징역 또는 3천만원 이하의 벌금에 처한다.

1 ~ 2 (현행과 같음)

3. 기업의 임직원 또는 임직원이었던자가 정당한 이유없이 그기업의 생산방법 기타 기술에 관한 영업비밀을 제3자에게 누설한 때

② 제1항 제3호의 규정에 의한 죄는 영업비밀 보유자의 고소가 있어야 논한다.

가. 취 지

본조는 기업의 임직원 등이 영업비밀을 지킬 법률상 의무가 있음에도 불구하고 이를 위반하여 그 기업의 영업비밀을 누설하는 행위를 형사처벌하려는 조항이다.

영업비밀의 침해행위에 대한 형사처벌의 필요성은 일반적으로 인정되지만, 그 처벌범위를 지나치게 확대하는 경우에는, i) 법원 · 검찰등 사법기관에 의한 침해여부 판단의 곤란성, ii) 형사소추의 선호경향으로 인한 민사적 구제수단의 형식화 초래 우려, iii) 보호객체의 모호성으로 인한 죄형법정주의 위반가능성 등의 부작용이 예상되므로 그 형사처벌의 범위를 제한적으로 인정하였다.

나. 해 설

(1) 신설이유

본조를 신설하게 된 것은, 최근 경제사회에서 영업비밀의 중요성이 점차 증가하고 있으며, 그 침해사례도 늘어나고 있기 때문이다. 아울러, 이처럼 영업비밀 침해사례가 급증하고 있을 뿐만 아니라 그 수법도 한층 교묘해지고 있음에도 불구하고, 현행법 상으로는 그 서류·도면의 무단반출 등 유형적 위법행위를 수반하지 않는 경우에는 형사처벌할 적절한 규정이 없는 실정인바, 이와 같이 반도덕성이 현저한 영업비밀의 침해를 처벌할수 없다고 평가하는 것은, 건전한 거래질서의 확립에 반하는 것이기 때문이다.

(2) 행위주체

이 조는 기업의 내부자인 임직원 또는 임직원이었던 자의 누설행위에 국한하여 형사처벌대상으로 삼고 있다.

입법 정책적으로는 내부인의 누설행위 뿐만 아니라 외부인에 의한 일반적인 탐지행위까지도 형사처벌하는 것이 가능하지만, 이 법에서는 외부탐지행위는 형사처벌의 대상에서 제외하였다.

그 이유는, 내부의 누설행위는 자기가 속한 기업에 대한 배신행위라는 점에서 가벌성이 특히 높고, 그 행위형태도 전형적인 경우가 대부분인 반면, 외부탐지는 행위형태가 매우 다양하여 그 전부가 반 윤리적이라고 단정할 수 없을 뿐만 아니라, 일반적인 탐지행위 모두를 처벌대상으로 할 경우 형사처벌의 범위가 너무 광범위 해질 우려가 할 수 있기 때문이다 (註).

(3) 행위객체

누설의 대상은 모든 영업비밀이 아니라 '생산방법 기타 기술에 관한 영업비밀'에 국한하였다.

그 이유는 경영상의 영업비밀까지 형사 처벌에 있어서의 보호객체로 하게 되면, 그 비밀성 여부가 모호한 경우가 많고 영업비밀의 범위가 너무 광범위하게 되어, 형사처벌의 범위가 지나치게 확대될 우려가 있기 때문이다.

(4) 違法性 阻却事由

이 조에는 '정당한 이유없이'라는 제한을 두고 있다. 따라서 공해기업의 적발, 정당한 소비자 보호운동, 공익목적만을 위한 취재 보도등의 경우에는, 비록 그행위가 객관적으로 내부자에 의한 영업비밀 누설에 해당한다고 평가되더라도, 위법성은 阻却된다고 할 것이므로 형사처벌되지 아니한다.

註) 외부인이 영업비밀 침해행위는 다시 **내부자와 공모한 탐지행위와 순수한 외부탐지 행위**로 나누어 볼수 있을 것인 바,

① 내부자와 공모한 탐지행위에 대하여는 형법 제33조 (공범과 신분)의 규정에 의하여 외부탐지자도 영업비밀 누설죄의 공범으로 처벌할 수 있을 것이며,

② 순수한 외부탐지행위에 대하여는 탐지행위의 유형에 따라 절도죄, 주거침입죄, 공갈 협박죄등을 적용하여 처벌할 수 있을 것이다.

(5) 친고죄

이 조의 처벌에 있어서는, 그 처벌의 가능성 여부를 영업비밀 보유자의 고소유무에 의존케 하는 친고죄로 하여, 양 당사자가 영업비밀 침해여부에 관한 다툼을 민사적으로 해결하여 형사적 처벌을 바라지 않는 경우, 형사 소추를 할 수 없도록 하였다.

(6) 고소기간 및 공소 시효기간

형사소송법 제230조 (친고죄의 고소기간)의 규정에 의하여, 원칙적으로 영업비밀 보유자가 그 침해자를 알게된 날로부터 6월을 경과하면, 고소하지 못한다.

또한 형사소송법 제249조 (공소시효의 기간) 제1항 제5호의 규정에 의하여 영업비밀 침해행위가 있은 날로부터 3년이 경과하면 공소시효가 완성되어 검찰이 公訴를 제기할 수 없게 된다

다. 例

A 기업의 공장장 F가 A 기업이 개발·사용하던 기술상의 영업비밀을 불법으로 유출 하여, 이를 이용한 별개의 사업체를 시작한 경우, A 기업은 F를 상대로 이 규정에 의한 형사적 처벌을 요구하는 고소를 제기할 수 있다.

라. 외국의 입법례

독일은 부정경쟁방지법에서, 일본은 개정형법 초안에서, 각각 형사처벌 규정을 두고 있다.

7. 시행일 및 경과조치

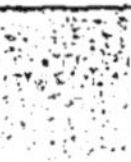

(부정경쟁방지법 개정초안 부칙)

가. 시 행 일

제1조(시행일) 이법은 공포한 날로부터 1년의 범위안에서 대통령령이 정한 날로부터 시행한다.

(1) 취 지

이는 이법 시행을 위한 시행령등의 개정기간이 필요하고, 또한 이법의 원활한 시행을 위해 이법의 취지 및 내용을 충분히 주지시키는데 필요한 시간적 여유를 둠으로써, 관련 기업들이 충분히 이에 대비하도록 하며, 이법의 급속한 시행으로 인한 충격을 완화하고자 함이다.

나. 경과조치

제2조(경과조치) 이법 시행전에 행하여진 제11조 제1항 각호에 해당하는 행위에 대하여는 제11조 내지 제13조 및 제16조 제1항 제3호의 규정은 이를 적용하지 아니한다. 이법 시행전에 영업비밀을 취득한 자 또는 사용한 자가 그 영업비밀을 이법 시행후 사용하는 경우에도 또한 같다.

- 33 -

0036

(1) 취지 및 해설

이법 시행에 있어서 기본적으로 이법 시행전의 행위자에게 손해를 주지 않아야 한다는 배려에서,

① 이법 시행전에 행하여진 영업비밀 침해행위

② 이법 시행전에 영업비밀을 취득한 자 또는 사용한 자가 이법 시행후 그 영업비밀을 사용하는 행위에 대하여는, 이법 제11조 (영업비밀 침해행위에 대한 금지청구권등), 제12조 (영업비밀 침해에 대한 손해배상책임), 제13조 (영업비밀 보유자의 신용회복), 제16조 제1항 제3호 (벌칙)를 적용하지 아니하도록 하고 있다.

위 ①의 경우는 이법 시행전의 행위에 까지 이법을 소급적용하지 않는다는 취지이며, 위 ②의 경우는 이법 시행전에 이미 영업비밀을 취득하거나 사용한 자가 단순히 자기 스스로 사용하는 행위에 그치는 경우, 이법을 적용하지 않는다는 취지이다.

《 부록 》

不正競爭防止法 改正草案

— 35 —

0038

第 1 章　總　則

第 1 條(目的) 이法은 부정한 手段에 의한 營業上의 競爭을 防止하여 건전한 去來秩序를 維持함을 目的으로 한다.

第 2 條(定義) 이法에서 使用하는 用語의 定義는 다음과 같다.

1. "不正競爭行爲"라 함은 다음 各目의 1에 해당하는 行爲를 말한다.

   가. ~ 마. (현행과 같음)

2. "營業秘密"이라 함은 일반적으로 알려져 있지 아니하고 獨立된 經濟的 價値를 가지며, 상당한 노력에 의하여 秘密로 유지관리된 生産方法, 販賣方法 기타 營業活動에 有用한 技術上 또는 經營上의 情報를 말한다.

第 2 章　不正競爭 行爲등의 防止

第3條 ~ 第8條 (현행과 같음)

第 9 條(다른法律과의 관계) 特許法, 實用新案法, 意匠法, 商標法, 獨占規制 및 公正去來에관한法律, 商法중 商號에 관한 規定 또는 刑法중 國旗.國章에 관

한 規定에 第2條 내지 第4條, 第16條 第1項 第1號 및 第2號의 規定과 다른 規定이 있는 경우에는 그 法에 의한다.

第 10 條(현행과 같음)

第 3 章　　營業秘密의 보호

第 11 條(營業秘密 침해행위에 대한 禁止請求權등) ① 營業秘密의 保有者는 다음 各號의 1에 해당하는 행위 (이하"營業秘密 침해행위"라 한다)를 하거나 하려고 하는 자가 있는 경우에 그 행위에 의하여 營業上의 이익이 침해되거나 침해될 우려가 있는 때에는 당해 행위의 禁止 또는 豫防을 請求 할 수 있다.

1. 竊盜, 橫領, 詐欺, 脅迫 기타 부정한 수단 으로 營業秘密을 취득하는 행위 (이하"不正取得行爲"라고 한다.) 또는 그 취득한 營業秘密을 사용 하거나 公開 (秘密을 유지하면서 特定人에게 알리는 것을 포함 한다. 이하 같다)하는 행위
2. 營業秘密에 대하여 不正取得行爲가 介入된 사실을 알거나 중대한 過失로 알지 못하고 그 營業秘密을 취득하는 행위 또는 그 취득한 營業秘密을 사용 하거나 公開하는 행위
3. 營業秘密을 취득한 후에 그 營業秘密에 대하여 不正取得行爲가 介入된 사실을 알거나 중대한 過失로 알지 못하고 그 營業秘密을 사용하거나 公開하는 행위

4. 계약관계등에 의하여 營業秘密을 비밀로서 유지하여야 할 의무가 있는 자가 부정한 이익을 얻거나 그 營業秘密의 保有者에게 손해를 가할 목적으로 그 營業秘密을 사용하거나 公開하는 행위

5. 營業秘密이 第4號의 規定에 의하여 公開된 사실 또는 그러한 公開行爲가 介入된 사실을 알거나 중대한 過失로 알지 못하고 그 營業秘密을 취득하는 행위 또는 그 취득한 營業秘密을 사용하거나 公開하는 행위

6. 營業秘密을 취득한후에 그 營業秘密이 第4號의 規定에 의하여 公開된 사실 또는 그러한 公開行爲가 介入된 사실을 알거나 중대한 過失로 알지 못하고 그 營業秘密을 사용하거나 公開하는 행위

② 營業秘密 保有者가 第1項의 規定에 의한 請求를 할 때에는 침해행위에 의하여 만들어진 물건의 廢棄, 침해행위에 提供된 設備의 除去 기타 침해행위 豫防에 필요한 행위를 請求할 수 있다.

第 12 條(營業秘密 침해에 대한 損害賠償 責任) 故意 또는 過失에 의한 營業秘密 침해행위로 營業秘密 保有者에게 損害를 가한 자는 그 損害를 賠償할 責任을 진다.

第 13 條(營業秘密 保有者의 信用回復) 營業秘密 保有者는 營業秘密 침해행위로 인하여 業務上의 信用을 失墜하게 한 자에 대하여는 損害賠償에 갈음하거나 損害賠償과 함께 業務上의 信用回復을 위하여 필요한 措置를 法院에 請求할 수 있다.

第 14 條(善意者에 관한 特例) ① 去來에 의하여 營業秘密을 정당하게 취득한 자가 그 去來에 의해 얻은 權源의 범위내에서 그 營業秘密을 사용하거나 公開하는 행위에 대하여는 第11條 내지 第13條의 規定을 適用하지 아니한다.

② 第1項의 "營業秘密을 정당하게 취득한 자"라 함은 營業秘密을 취득할 당시에 그 營業秘密이 부정하게 公開된 사실 또는 營業秘密의 不正取得行爲나 不正公開 行爲가 介入된 사실을 중대한 過失없이 알지 못하고 그 營業秘密을 취득한 자를 말한다.

第 15 條(消滅時效) 第11條 第1項의 規定에 의하여 營業秘密 침해행위의 禁止 또는 豫防을 請求할 수 있는 權利는 營業秘密 침해행위가 계속되는 경우에 營業秘密 保有者가 그 침해행위에 의하여 營業上의 이익이 침해되거나 침해될 우려가 있는 사실 및 침해행위자를 안 날로 부터 3년간 이를 행사하지 아니하면 時效로 인하여 消滅한다. 그 침해행위가 시작된 날로부터 10년을 經過한 때에도 또한 같다.

第 4 章 補 則

第 16 條(罰則) ① 다음 各號의 1에 해당하는 자는 3年이하의 懲役 또는 3千萬원 이하의 罰金에 처한다.

1. (현행과 같음)
2. (〃)
3. 企業의 任・職員 또는 任・職員이었던자가 正當한 理由없이 그企業의

生産方法 기타 技術에 관한 營業秘密을 第3者에게 漏泄한 때

② 第1項 第3號의 規定에 의한罪는 營業秘密 保有者의 告訴가 있어야 논한다.

第 17 條(兩罰規定) 法人의 代表者 또는 法人이나 個人의 代理人, 使用人 기타의 從業員이 그法人 또는 個人의 業務에 관하여 第16條 第1項 第1號 또는 第2號에 해당하는 違反行爲를 한때에는 行爲者를 罰하는 외에 그法人 또는 個人에 대하여도 第16條 第1項 第1號 또는 第2號의 規定에 의한 罰金刑을 科한다.

附　　　　則

第 1 條(施行日) 이法은 公布한날로부터 1년의 범위 안에서 대통령령이 정한 날로부터 施行한다.

第 2 條(經過措置) 이法 施行전에 행하여진 第11條 第1項 各號에 해당하는 행위에 대하여는 第11條 내지 第13條 및 第16條 第1項 第3號의 規定은 이를 適用하지 아니한다. 이法 施行전에 營業秘密을 취득한 자 또는 사용한자가 그營業秘密을 이法 施行후 사용하는 境遇에도 또한 같다.

0043

분류기호 문서번호	기법02101- 198	협 조 문 용 지 (720-2946)	결 재	담 당	담당관	조정관
시행일자	1991. 7. 12.					
수 신	통 상 국 장	발 신	기획관리실장 (서명)			
제 목	부정경쟁방지법 개정안 의견조회					

연 : 기법 02101-185(91. 7. 2)

연호와 관련, 부정경쟁방지법중개정법률안 및 신.구조문 대비표를 별첩과 같이 추가 송부하니 동 법률개정안 검토에 참고하시기 바랍니다.

첨 부 : 1. 부정경쟁방지법중개정법률(안) 1부.

2. 신.구조문 대비표 1부. 끝.

0044

不正競爭防止法中 改正法律案

1991. 6.

商 工 部

0045

1. 改正理由

가. 최근 기술혁신과 과학기술 투자의 확대에 따라 산출되는 기술상, 경영상 노우하우(영업비밀)의 중요성이 높아지고 있는 반면, 노우하우의 활발한 거래와 고용의 유동화등에 따라 영업비밀 침해를 둘러싼 분쟁은 증가하고 있음.

나. 이에 대하여 영업비밀의 도용등 침해행위를 방지하여, 기업간의 건전한 경쟁질서를 확립하고, 기업의 연구개발투자를 적극유인하기 위하여, 부정경쟁방지법을 개정하여 영업비밀 보호에 관한 규정을 신설하려는 것임.

다. 대외적으로도 영업비밀의 법적보호 문제가 연내 타결될것으로 전망되는 우루과이라운드 지적재산권 협상항목에 포함되어 있어 국제적인 통상마찰의 해소를 위해서도 이에 대한 적절한 보호제도 마련이 필요함

2. 主要骨子

가. 영업비밀에 대한 정의 규정을 둠
(案 第2條 第2項)

나. 영업비밀의 침해행위유형을 6가지로 규정함
(案 第11條 第1項)

다. 영업비밀 침해에 대하여 침해행위 금지.예방청구, 손해배상청구 및 신용회복조치 청구를 할 수 있도록 함
(案 第11條 第2項, 第12條 및 第13條)

라. 선의자에 대한 구제를 위하여 특례조항을 둠

(案 第14條)

마. 영업비밀 침해행위 금지 또는 예방청구권에 대하여 소멸시효 규정을 둠

(案 第15條)

바. 현행 벌칙을 상향조정하고, 기업체 임.직원등의 영업비밀 누설행위에 대하여 제한적인 벌칙을 두되, 친고죄로 함

(案 第16條 第3號)

사. 이법은 공포후 1년의 범위안에서 대통령령이 정한 날로부터 시행하도록 함

(案 附則 第1條)

아. 이법 시행전의 영업비밀 침해행위등에 대하여 경과조치 규정을 둠

(案 附則 第2條)

法律 第　　號

不正競爭防止法中改正法律案

不正競爭防止法중 다음과 같이 改正한다

第1條앞에 章名 "第1章 總則"을 新設한다.

第1條중 "商業上의"를 "營業上의"로 하고, "商去來의 秩序를"을 "去來秩序를"로 한다.

第2條 本文을 다음과 같이 한다.

이法에서 사용하는 用語의 定義는 다음과 같다.

第2條중 第1號 내지 第5號를 각각 가目 내지 마目으로 하고, 가目앞에 第1號本文을 다음과 같이 新設한다.

1. "不正競爭行爲"라 함은 다음 各目의 1에 해당하는 行爲를 말한다.

第2條에 第2號를 다음과 같이 新設한다.

2. "營業秘密"이라 함은 일반적으로 알려져 있지 아니하고 獨立된 經濟的 價値를 가지며, 상당한 노력에 의하여 秘密로 유지관리된 生産方法, 販賣方法 기타 營業活動에 有用한 技術上 또는 經營上의 情報를 말한다.

第3條앞에 章名 "第2章 不正競爭行爲등의 防止"를 新設한다.

第9條중 "第2條 내지 第4條 및 第11條의 規定"을 "第2條 내지 第4條, 第16條 第1項 第1號 및 第2號의 規定"으로 한다.

0048

第11條 및 第12條를 각각 第16條 및 第17條로 하고, 第10條 다음에 第3章을 다음과 같이 新設한다.

第 3 章　營業秘密의 보호

第 11 條 (營業秘密 침해행위에 대한 禁止請求權등) ① 營業秘密의 保有者는 다음 各號의 1에 해당하는 행위 (이하 "營業秘密 침해행위"라 한다)를 하거나 하려고 하는 자가 있는 경우에 그행위에 의하여 營業上의 이익이 침해되거나 침해될 우려가 있는 때에는 당해 행위의 禁止 또는 豫防을 請求할 수 있다.

1. 竊盜, 詐欺, 脅迫 기타 부정한 수단으로 營業秘密을 취득하는 행위 (이하 "不正取得行爲"라고 한다.) 또는 그 취득한 營業秘密을 사용하거나 公開 (秘密을 유지하면서 特定人에게 알리는 것을 포함한다. 이하 같다.) 하는 행위
2. 營業秘密에 대하여 不正取得行爲가 介入된 사실을 알거나 중대한 過失로 알지못하고 그營業秘密을 취득하는 행위 또는 그취득한 營業秘密을 사용하거나 公開하는 행위
3. 營業秘密을 취득한 후에 그營業秘密에 대하여 不正取得行爲가 介入된 사실 알거나 중대한 過失로 알지 못하고 그營業秘密을 사용하거나 公開하는 행위
4. 계약관계등에 의하여 營業秘密을 비밀로서 유지하여야 할 의무가 있는 자가 부정한 이익을 얻거나 그營業秘密의 保有者에게 손해를 가할 목적으로 그營業秘密을 사용하거나 公開하는 행위
5. 營業秘密이 第4號의 規定에 의하여 公開된 사실 또는 그러한 公開行爲가 介入된 사실을 알거나 중대한 過失로 알지 못하고 그營業秘密을 취득하는 행위 또는 그 취득한 營業秘密을 사용하거나 公開하는 행위
6. 營業秘密을 취득한후에 그營業秘密이 第4號의 規定에 의하여 公開된 사실 또는 그러한 公開行爲가 介入된 사실을 알거나 중대한 過失로 알지못하고 그營業秘密을 사용하거나 公開하는 행위

② 營業秘密 保有者가 第1項의 規定에 의한 請求를 할 때에는 침해행위에 의하여 만들어진 물건의 廢棄, 침해행위에 提供된 設備의 除去 기타 침해행위의 豫防에 필요한 행위를 請求할 수 있다.

0049

第 12 條 (營業秘密 침해에 대한 損害賠償 責任) 故意 또는 過失에 의한 營業秘密 침해행위로 營業秘密 保有者에게 損害를 가한 자는 그損害를 賠償할 責任을 진다.

第 13 條 (營業秘密 保有者의 信用回復) 營業秘密 保有者는 營業秘密 침해행위로 인하여 業務上의 信用을 失墜하게 한 자에 대하여는 損害賠償에 갈음하거나 損害賠償과 함께 業務上의 信用回復을 위하여 필요한 措置를 法院에 請求할 수 있다.

第 14 條 (善意者에 관한 特例) ① 法來에 의하여 營業秘密을 정당하게 취득한 자가 그法來에 의하여 얻은 權原의 범위내에서 그 營業秘密을 사용하거나 公開하는 행위에 대하여는 第11條 내지 第13條의 規定을 適用하지 아니한다.

② 第1項의 "營業秘密을 정당하게 취득한 자"라 함은 營業秘密을 취득할 당시에 그營業秘密이 부정하게 公開된 사실 또는 營業秘密의 不正取得行爲나 不正公開行爲가 介入된 사실을 중대한 過失없이 알지못하고 그營業秘密을 취득한 자를 말한다.

第 15 條 (消滅時效) 第11條 第1項의 規定에 의하여 營業秘密 침해행위의 禁止 또는 豫防을 請求할 수 있는 權利는 營業秘密 침해행위가 계속되는 경우에 營業秘密 保有者가 그 침해행위에 의하여 營業上의 이익이 침해되거나 침해될 우려가 있는 사실 및 침해행위자를 안날로부터 3년간 이를 행사하지 아니하면 時效로 인하여 消滅한다. 그침해행위가 시작된 날로부터 10년을 經過한 때에도 또한 같다.

제15조 다음에 장명 "제4장 보칙"을 다음과 같이 신설한다.

제16조 본문중 "2년 이하의 징역 또는 2천만원 이하의 벌금" 을 "3년 이하의 징역 또는 3천만원 이하의 벌금"으로 하고, 동조에 제3호를 다음과 같이 신설한다.

3. 企業의 任.職員 또는 任.職員이었던자가 正當한 理由없이 그企業의 生産方法 기타 技術에 관한 營業秘密을 第3者에게 漏泄한 때

0050

第16條에 第2項을 다음과 같이 新設한다.

② 第1項 第3號의 規定에 의한罪는 營業秘密 保有者의 告訴가 있어야 논한다.

第17條중 "第11條 각號의 1에"를 "第16條 第1項 第1號 또는 第2號에"로 하고, "第11條의"를 "第16條 第1項 第1號 또는 第2號의"로 한다.

附 則

第 1 條 (施行日) 이法은 公布한 날로부터 1年의 범위안에서 大統領令이 정한 날로부터 施行한다.

第 2 條 (經過措置) 이法 施行전에 행하여진 第11條 第1項 各號에 해당하는 행위에 대하여는 第11條 내지 第13條 및 第16條 第1項 第3號의 規定은 이를 適用하지 아니한다. 이法 施行전에 營業秘密을 取得한 자 또는 사용한 자가 그 營業秘密을 이法 施行후 사용하는 境遇에도 또한 같다.

0051

新·舊 條文 對比表

現 行	改 正 案	備 考
	第1章 總 則	<題名 新設>
第1條(目 的) 이 法은 부정한 수단에 의한 商業上의 競爭을 방지하여 건전한 商去來의 秩序를 유지함을 目的 한다.	第1條(目 的) 이 法은 부정한 手段에 의한 營業上의 競爭을 防止하여 건전한 去來秩序를 維持함을 目的으로 한다.	
第2條(定 義)이 法에서 사용되는 "不正競爭行爲"라 함은 그 目的의 여하를 불문하고 다음 各號의 1에 해당하는 행위를 말한다.	第2條(定 義)이 法에서 使用하는 用語의 定義는 다음과 같다. 1. "不正競爭行爲"라 함은 다음 各目의 1에 해당하는 行爲를 말한다.	
1. 國內에 널리 認識된 他人의 姓名·商號·商標·商品의 容器·包裝 기타 他人의 商品임을 표시한 標識와 동일 또는 유사한 것을 사용하거나 이러한 것을 사용한 商品을 販賣·頒布 또는 輸入·輸出하여 他人의 商品과 混同을 일으키게 하는 행위 2. 國內에 널리 認識된 他人의 姓名·商號·標章 기타 他人의 營業임을 표시하는 標識와 동일 또는 유사한 것을 용하여 他人의 營業上의 施設 또는 活動과 混同을 일으키게 하는 행위 3. 商品이나 그 廣告에 의하여 또는 公衆이 알 수 있는 방법으로 거래상의 書類 또는 通信에 허위의 原産地의 標識를 하거나 또는 이러한 標識를 한 商品을 販賣·頒布 또는 輸入·輸出하여 原産地의 誤認을 일으키게 하는 행위 4. 商品이나 그 廣告에 의하여 또는 公衆이 알 수 있는 방법으로 거래상의 書類 또는 通信에 그 商品이 生産·製造 또는 加工된 地域 이외의 곳에서 生産	가. ~ 마. (현행 1~5호와 같음)	

-1-

0052

現行	改正案	備考
또는 加工된 듯이 認識을 일으키게 하는 標識를 하거나 또는 이러한 標識를 한 商品을 販賣·頒布 또는 輸入·輸出하는 행위 5. 他人의 商品을 詐稱하거나 商品 또는 그 廣告에 商品의 品質·내용·製造方法·用途 또는 數量의 誤認을 일으키게 하는 宣傳 또는 標識를 하거나 이러한 방법이나 標識로써 商品을 販賣·頒布 또는 輸入·輸出하는 행위		
	2. "營業秘密"이라 함은 일반적으로 알려져 있지 아니하고 獨立된 經濟的 價値를 가지며, 상당한 노력에 의하여 秘密로 유지관리된 生産方法, 販賣方法 기타 營業活動에 有用한 技術上 또는 經營上의 情報를 말한다.	(新 設)
	第2章 不正競爭 行爲등의 防止	<章名 新設>
第3條(國旗·國章등의 사용금지) ①工業所有權의 보호를 위한 파리協約(이하 "파리條約"이라 한다) 當事國의 國旗·國章 기타의 徽章이나 國際機構의 標識와 동일 또는 유사한 것은 商標로 사용할 수 없다. 다만, 당해 國家 또는 國際機構의 許諾을 받은 경우에는 그러하지 아니하다. ②파리條約當事國의 政府의 監督用 또는 證明用 標識와 동일 또는 유사한 것은 商標로 사용할 수 없다. 다만, 當該國의 政府의 許諾을 받은 경우에는 그러하지 아니하다.	第3條 (현행과 같음)	

0053

現行	改正案	備考
第4條(不正競爭行爲의 中止請求등) ①第1條 各號의 1에 해당하는 행위로 인하여 자신의 營業上의 利益이 침해될 경우가 있다고 인정하는 자는 法院에 그 행위의 中止를 請求할 수 있다. ②第2條 各號의 1에 해당하는 행위로 인하여 자신의 營業上의 이익이 침해된 자는 法院에 損害賠償請求를 할 수 있다. ③第2條 各號의 1에 해당하는 행위로 인하여 자신의 營業上의 이익이 침해된 자는 第2項의 規定에 의한 損害賠償을 請求할 경우 損害賠償에 대신하여 또는 損害賠償과 함께 營業上의 信用을 회복하는데 필요한 措置를 法院에 請求할 수 있다.	第4條(현행과 같음)	
第5條(不正競爭審議委員會의 設置) ①이 法에 의한 不正競爭行爲의 방지등에 관한 사항에 대하여 特許廳長의 諮問에 응하게 하기 위하여 特許廳에 不正競爭審議委員會(이하 "委員會"라 한다)를 둔다. ②委員會의 組織 및 운영등에 관하여 필요한 사항은 大統領令으로 정한다.	第5條(현행과 같음)	
第6條(違反行爲의 是正勸告) 特許廳長은 第2條의 規定에 의한 不正競爭行爲 또는 第3條의 規定에 위반된 행위가 있다고 인정될 때에는 그 위반행위를 한 者에 대하여 30日내의 기간을 정하여 그 행위를 중지하거나 標識를 제거 또는 폐기할 것등 그 是正에 필요한 勸告를 할 수 있다.	第6條(현행과 같음)	
第7條(意見聽取) 特許廳長은 第6條의 規定에 의한 是正勸告를 하기 위하여 필요하다고 인정할 때에는 大統領令이 정하는 바에 의하여 當事者·利害關係人 또는 參考人	第7條(현행과 같음)	

-3-

0054

現行	改正案	備考
'의 의견을 들어야 한다.		
第 8 條 (外國人에 대한 適用의 예외) 外國人으로서 파리條約當事國안에 住所 또는 營業所가 있는 者외의 者는 第 4 條 規定에 의한 不正競爭行爲의 中止請求등을 할 수 없다.	第8條 (현행과 같음)	
第 9 條 (다른 法律과의 關係) 特許法, 實用新案法, 意匠法, 商標法, 獨占規制및公正去來에關한法律, 商法중 商號에 관한 規定 또는 刑法중 國旗·國章에 관한 規定에 第 2 條 내지 第 4 條 및 第 11 條의 規定과 다른 規定이 있는 경우에는 그 法에 의한다.	第 9 條 (다른法律과의 관계) 特許法, 實用新案法, 意匠法, 商標法, 獨占規制 및 公正去來에관한法律, 商法중 商號에 관한 規定 또는 刑法중 國旗·國章에 관한 規定에 第 2 條 내지 第 4 條, 第 16 條第 1 項第 1 號 및 第 2 號의 規定과 다른 規定이 있는 경우에는 그 法에 의한다.	
第 10 條 (權限의 委任) 이 法에 의한 特許廳長의 權限은 그 일부를 大統領令이 정하는 바에 의하여 서울特別市長·直轄市長 또는 道知事에게 委任할 수 있다.	第 10 條 (현행과 같음)	
	第3章 營業秘密의 보호	〈新設〉
	第 11 條 (營業秘密침해행위에 대한 禁止請求權등) ①營業秘密의 保有者는 다음 各號의 1 에 해당하는 행위 (이하 "營業秘密 침해행위"라 한다) 를 하거나 하려고 하는 자가 있는 경우에 그 행위에 의하여 營業上의 이익이 침해되거나 침해될 우려가 있는 때에는 당해 행위의 禁止 또는 豫防을 請求할 수 있다. 1. 竊盜· 詐欺·脅迫 기타 부정한 수단으로 營業秘密을 취득하는 행위 (이하 "不正取得行爲"라고 한다) 또는 그 취득한 營業秘密을	〈新 設〉

-4-

0055

現行	改正案	備考
	사용하거나 公開(秘密을 유지하면서 特定人에 알리는 것을 포함한다. 이하 같다)하는 행위 2. 營業秘密에 대하여 不正取得行爲가 介入된 사실을 알거나 중대한 過失로 알지 못하고 그 營業秘密을 취득하는 행위 또는 그 취득한 營業秘密을 사용하거나 公開하는 행위 3. 營業秘密을 취득한 후에 그 營業秘密에 대하여 不正取得行爲가 介入된 사실을 알거나 중대한 過失로 알지 못하고 그 營業秘密을 사용하거나 公開하는 행위 4. 계약관계등에 의하여 營業秘密을 비밀로서 유지하여야 할 의무가 있는 자가 부정한 이익을 얻거나 그 營業秘密의 保有者에게 손해를 가할 목적으로 그 營業秘密을 사용하거나 公開하는 행위 5. 營業秘密이 第4號의 規定에 의하여 公開된 사실 또는 그러한 公開行爲가 介入된 사실을 알거나 중대한 過失로 알지 못하고 그 營業秘密을 취득하는 행위 또는 그 취득한 營業秘密을 사용하거나 公開하는 행위 6. 營業秘密을 취득한 후에 그 營業秘密이 第4號의 規定에 의하여 公開된 사실 또는 그러한 公開行爲가 介入된 사실을 알거나 중대한 過失로 알지 못하고 그 營業秘密을 사용하거나 公開하는 행위 ②營業秘密 保有者가 第1項의 規定에 의한 請求를 할 때에는 침해행위에 의하여 만들어진 물건의 廢棄, 침해행위에 提供된 設備의 除去 기타 침해행위 豫防에 필요한 행위를 請求할 수 있다.	
	第12條(營業秘密 침해에 대한 損害賠償 責任) 故意 또는 過失에 의한 營業秘密 침해행위로 營業秘密 有保者에게 損害를 가한 자는 그 損害를 賠償할 責任을 진다.	(新設)

-5-

0056

現行	改正案	備考
	第13條(營業秘密 保有者의 信用回復) 營業秘密 保有者는 營業秘密 침해행위로 인하여 業務上의 信用을 失墜하게 한 자에 대하여는 損害賠償에 갈음하거나 損害賠償과 함께 業務上의 信用回復을 위하여 필요한 措置를 法院에 請求할 수 있다.	〈新設〉
	第14條(善意者에 관한 特例) ①去來에 의하여 營業秘密을 정당하게 취득한 자가 그 去來에 의해 얻은 權原의 범위내에서 그 營業秘密을 사용하거나 公開하는 행위에 대하여는 第11條 내지 第13條의 規定을 適用하지 아니한다. ②第1項의 "營業秘密을 정당하게 취득한 자"라 함은 營業秘密을 취득할 당시에 그 營業秘密이 부정하게 公開된 사실 또는 營業秘密의 不正取得行爲나 不正公開 行爲가 介入된 사실을 중대한 過失없이 알지 못하고 그 營業秘密을 취득한 자를 말한다.	〈新設〉
	第15條(消滅時效) 第11條 第1項의 規定에 의하여 營業秘密 침해행위의 禁止 또는 豫防을 請求할 수 있는 權利는 營業秘密 침해행위가 계속되는 경우에 營業秘密 保有者가 그 침해행위에 의하여 營業上의 이익이 침해되거나 침해될 우려가 있는 사실 및 침해행위자를 안 날로 부터 3년간 이를 행사하지 아니하면 時效로 인하여 消滅한다. 그 침해행위가 시작된 날로부터 10년을 經過할 때에도 또한 같다.	〈新設〉
	第4章 補則	〈章名 新設〉
第11條(罰則) 다음 各號의 1에 해당하는 者는 2年以下의 懲役 또는 2千萬원 이하의 罰金에 처한다. 1. 第2條의 規定에 의한 不正競爭行爲를 한 者	第16條(罰則) ①다음 各號의 1에 해당하는 자는 3年以下의 懲役 또는 3千萬원 이하의 罰金에 처한다. 1. (현행과 같음)	

-6-

0057

現行	改正案	備考
2. 第3條의 規定에 위반한 者	2. (현행과 같음)	
	3. 企業의 任·職員 또는 任·職員이었던 자가 正當한 理由없이 그 企業의 生産方法 기타 技術에 관한 營業秘密을 第3者에게 漏泄한 때	〈新 設〉
	③第1項 第3號의 規定에 의한 罪는 營業秘密 保有者의 告訴가 있어야 논한다.	〈新 設〉
第12條(兩罰規定) 法人의 代表者 또는 法人이나 개인의 代理人·使用人 기타의 從業員이 그 法人 또는 개인의 業務에 관하여 第11條 各號의 1에 해당하는 위반행위를 한 때에는 行爲者를 罰하는 외에 그 法人 또는 個人에 대하여도 第11條의 規定에 의한 罰金刑을 科한다.	第17條(兩罰規定) 法人의 代表者 또는 法人이나 個人의 代理人, 使用人 기타의 從業員이 그 法人 또는 個人의 業務에 관하여 第16條 第1項 第1號 또는 第2號에 해당하는 違反行爲를 한때에는 行爲者를 罰하는 외에 그 法人 또는 個人에 대하여도 第16條 第1項 第1號 또는 第2號의 規定에 의한 罰金刑을 科한다.	
附 則	附 則	
이 法은 1987年 1月1日부터 施行한다.	第1條(施行日) 이 法은 公布한 날로부터 1年의 범위안에서 大統領令이 정한 날로부터 施行한다.	
	第2條(經過措置) 이 法 施行前에 행하여진 第11條 第1項 各號에 해당하는 행위에 대하여는 第11條 내지 第13條 및 第16條 第1項 第3號의 規定은 이를 適用하지 아니한다. 이 法 施行前에 營業秘密을 취득한 자 또는 사용한자가 그 營業秘密을 이 法 施行後 사용하는 境遇에도 또한 같다.	

-7-

0058

MULTILATERAL TRADE NEGOTIATIONS
THE URUGUAY ROUND

RESTRICTED
MTN.GNG/TRIPS/W/1
12 July 1991
Special Distribution

Group of Negotiations on Goods (GATT)

Original: English

Negotiating Group on Trade-Related Aspects of Intellectual Property Rights, including Trade in Counterfeit Goods

PROPOSAL FOR THE ESTABLISHMENT OF DISPUTE PREVENTION SYSTEM IN RESPECT OF TRANSFER OF TECHNOLOGIES

Communication from the Republic of Korea

The following communication, dated 28 June 1991, has been received from the Permanent Mission of the Republic of Korea, with the request that it be circulated to members of the Negotiating Group.

The Delegation of the Republic of Korea hereby submits the following Proposal for the Establishment of Dispute Prevention System in Respect of Transfer of Technologies ("Proposal"), and respectfully requests that it be formally incorporated and reflected in the Chairman's new draft of the TRIPS Agreement for substantive discussion and possible adoption thereof.

I. PROPOSAL

It is proposed to add, under PART V: DISPUTE PREVENTION AND SETTLEMENT, the following provision.

Article 67 bis: Prevention of Disputes Between Undertakings

1. Private undertakings of different PARTIES engaged in the negotiation of a voluntary licence agreement involving patent and/or know-how* may, through their respective government, request the Committee on Trade-Related Aspects of Intellectual Property Rights for an advisory opinion with regard to whether such licence agreement, either in part or as a whole, constitutes an abuse of the patents and/or know-how or has an adverse effect on competition in international trades, subject to the following provisions.

---

*Know-how, for the purpose of this Article, shall mean a body of Undisclosed Information which has an industrial application.

GATT SECRETARIAT
UR-91-0075

0059

2. Within two years from its first meeting, the Committee shall, through consultations with PARTIES and in cooperation with bodies of the World Intellectual Property Organization as provided in Article 71, promulgate a Guideline for the Prevention of Abusive Practices in Licence Agreement Involving Patents and/or Know-how.

3. Immediately after the establishment of such Guideline and upon receipt of such request, the Committee shall establish and commission a Licence Review Board(s) comprising a panel of experts selected from the roster established by the Committee for the purpose of reviewing such request and rendering its advisory opinion based on the Guideline.

4. The Committee shall also be authorised to issue an Implementation Regulation relating to:

(i) organisation and other institutional arrangements for the Licence Review Board; and

(ii) procedures for filing and examination of the request.

5. The Licence Review Board shall issue within six months from the referral of the request a written opinion accompanied by the reasons therefor. The Committee shall publish the opinion unless either PARTY, at the time of filing the request, submits a written objection to the publication.

6. The opinion shall not be binding upon any PARTY; and shall not affect any PARTY in adopting its national legislation and carrying out such appropriate measures as referred to in Article 43, para. 2B.

7. Notwithstanding para. 6 above, PARTIES shall not prevent their undertakings from voluntarily agreeing to be bound by the result of the opinion.

II. EXPLANATION OF THE PROPOSAL

A. In General

It is truistic that disputes between the PARTIES involving a right-holder's abusive practices originate from a private contract between the right holder and another individual party. Accordingly, in order to minimise the occurrence of disputes between the PARTIES, it is only logical to control the occurrence at the origin: i.e., the private contracts. This obvious conclusion forms the very foundation of this Proposal, which is designed to prevent the disputes between private parties negotiating a licence agreement involving patent rights and/or know-how.

B. Related Provisions in the TRIPS Agreement

1. Article 8, Para. 2 recognises the need to employ "appropriate measures" in order "to prevent the abuse of intellectual property rights or

0060

the resort to practices which unreasonably restrain trade or adversely affect the international transfer of technology."

As one of such appropriate measures, this Proposal envisages a dispute prevention system by way of allowing PARTIES on behalf of their respective undertakings to seek an advisory opinion from the Licence Review Board established and supervised under the aegis of the TRIPS Committee.

2. Article 43.3B provides that:

> Each PARTY shall enter, upon request, into consultations with any other PARTY which has cause to believe that an intellectual property right owner that is a national or domiciliary of the PARTY to which the request for consultations has been addressed is undertaking practices in violation of the requesting PARTY's laws and regulations on the subject matter of this Section, and which wishes to secure compliance with such legislations, without prejudice to any action under the law and to the full freedom of an ultimate decision of either PARTY. The PARTY addressed shall accord full and sympathetic consideration to, and shall afford adequate opportunity for, consultations with the requesting PARTY, and shall cooperate through the supply of available information of relevance to the matter in question, subject to and dependent upon the assurances of confidentiality given by the requesting PARTY unless the party providing the information agrees to its disclosure or disclosure is compelled by law.

The above provision contemplates a situation wherein a right holder who is a national or domiciliary of PARTY A is engaged in abusive practices in the territory of PARTY B in violation of the national law of PARTY B.

The above geographical confinement is a built-in limitation for an effective operation of the consultative mechanism. For instance, an agreement for international transfer of technology may not even involve any patents registered in PARTY B or know-how that exists in PARTY B. In this instance, Article 43.3B may not apply.

Furthermore, it is not clear as to what the obligations of PARTY A are; and, in the absence of satisfactory response from PARTY A for whatever reasons, disputes between the PARTIES will likely occur. In short, the efficacy of this provision is highly uncertain, if any.

3. On the other hand, Article 67 authorises the TRIPS Committee to render recommendations and rulings for the settlement of disputes between the PARTIES by way of establishing a panel of experts drawn from an existing roster of experts.

Since the nature of disputes arising out of a particular clause in a patent/know-how licence agreement on the question of an abusive practice is bound to be highly technical, they can be an ideal task for the panel of experts. In other words, the panel of experts envisaged in Article 67 can also be called upon rendering an advisory opinion prior to the occurrence of disputes between the PARTIES.

4. The language contained in Article 71 is broad enough to include, within the scope of the Committee's responsibilities and activities, the assignment of establishing a Licence Review Board and having it issue an advisory opinion on the propriety of a patent/know-how licence agreement, in addition to the promulgation of a Guideline to be used by the Board. Specifically, Article 71, in relevant parts, reads:

> The Committee shall ... afford PARTIES the opportunity of consulting on matters relating to trade-related intellectual property rights. It shall carry out such other responsibilities as assigned to it by the PARTIES, and it shall, in particular, provide any assistance requested by them in the context of dispute settlement procedures. In carrying out its functions, the Committee may consult with and seek information from any source they deem appropriate.

In short, the proposed dispute prevention mechanism does not require any other additional personnel or resources than those already envisaged for the purpose of carrying out the dispute settlement.

III. EXPLANATION OF ARTICLE 67 bis

A. Para. 1: Scope of Request

(i) Para. 1. makes it clear that the subject matter for which an advisory opinion is sought is limited to contractual clauses contained in a licence agreement involving patents and/or know-how. In other words, the subject matter does not include a licence agreement of such other IPRs as trademark or copyrights, although they can be an ancillary part of a patent/know-how licence agreement. The provision also excludes non-voluntary licence agreements.

(ii) The request for an advisory opinion is submitted not by the private undertakings but by the PARTIES where the licensor and the licensee reside. This is consistent with the existing procedures for consultations and settlement of disputes under GATT.

This procedural requirement will accord the PARTIES an opportunity to consider the desirability and appropriateness of not only making the request under this Article but also carrying out consultations and cooperation as provided in Article 43.3B.

B. Para. 2: Establishment of Standards for Determination of Abusive Practices

The last sentence of Article 71 mandates the TRIPS Committee to establish, within one year from its first (organisation) meeting, appropriate arrangements for cooperation with WIPO. Para. 2, therefore, contemplates a period of two years as sufficient to formulate and promulgate the Guideline. There are a number of reasons for this relative optimism.

0062

First, in order for the Committee to effectively carry out the settlement of disputes under the mandate of Article 67, they need to employ, in consultation with the panel of experts, certain standards or norms. It is expected that large parts of such standards will be equally applicable to the dispute prevention procedure under Article 67 bis.

Secondly, the existing laws and regulations in various countries that govern the abusive or anti-competitive practices of IPRs are relatively uniform. Especially, the principles established in those countries which have historically administered strict controls over anti-competitive practices, notably the US and the European Community, are of high standards, developed over long periods of time through numerous court decisions applied and tested in a plethora of differing circumstances. It is believed that most, if not all, of these principles can serve as an excellent reference for the establishment of the Guideline.

C. Para. 5: Evolution and Refinement of Standards through Case Law Approach

1. Even though the formulation and "legislation" of legal norms, i.e., the Guideline, may be rather easily accomplished, the task of applying them to an international contract in the context of the TRIPS Agreement will be a totally different matter.

In this connection, the approach taken by the European Community is highly instructive: that is, they have accomplished the harmonisation of not only the IPR statutes but also their interpretation through the case law approach. This case law approach adopted by EC did not go unchallenged, however.

In fact, the fiscal senate of the German Supreme Court held that certain decisions of the European Court of Justice were not binding upon it because the European Court had reached its conclusions by relying on its earlier decisions. However, the German Constitutional Court held that:

> development of the law on a case law basis is fully in conformity with European legal traditions because not only had the common law development been in England in this way, but also had Roman Law, German Gemeines Recht and French Administrative Law.*

As can be seen above, there is nothing novel in employing a case law approach even in civil law countries: as a matter of fact, the dynamic nature of IPRs together with diverse differences in the culture,

---

*In re Frau Kloppenburg (1988) CMLR 1. See also John Richards, "10 Years of Substantive Law Development in the European Patent Office," JPTOS, PP320-342 (1989).

0063

philosophy, level of technology and economy of PARTIES makes it a compelling case where the case law approach can be best utilised for harmonising the "law" that will govern the control of abusive practices in international transfer of technologies and its interpretation.

To adopt the stare decisis method, however, publication of written decisions fully supported by reasons therefor is essential. PARTIES should be, therefore, encouraged not to object to the publication of the opinions for an effective development of international law governing anti-competitive practices in exercising industrial property rights.

2. Needless to say, there should be a time limitation for the issuance of the opinion by the Licence Review Board as the private undertakings cannot be kept inactive too long. The current clearance system practiced by EC has a six-month period.

D. Para. 6: National Regimes not Preempted

One possible concern that PARTIES may express might be the preemptive effect of this procedure on their national regime and procedures established for reviewing and approving a licence agreement. In response to such concern, the following comments may be offered.

First, inasmuch as the request to the TRIPS Committee is to be made through the government where the concerned individual undertaking resides, the PARTY has the control or opportunity to consider the desirability and possible consequences which may result from making the request.

Secondly, there are situations where an intervention by the government of the licensee will only produce negative effects on the transfer of technology.

Thirdly, as stated previously, if the patents to be licensed are foreign patents, there is not much that the licensee's government can do, especially when the licensor's government is reluctant to interfere with the licensor's affairs.

Fourthly, the advisory nature of the opinion does not affect in any way for each PARTY to apply its national law, where appropriate, in regulating the licensor's unlawful conduct.

E. Para. 7: Restriction on PARTY's Undue Influence

In order for the TRIPS Agreement to be viable and successful, it must be assumed that the advisory opinion rendered under the auspices of the TRIPS Committee is reasonable and proper. Therefore, it only behoves the PARTIES to encourage their respective undertakings to respect and accept the Committee opinion to the maximum extent possible. Should, however, PARTIES be allowed to stop their willing nationals from adhering to the opinion, the very integrity of the whole TRIPS Agreement may be in jeopardy.

0064

2

원 본

외 무 부

종 별 :

번 호 : GVW-1355 일 시 : 91 0719 1800

수 신 : 장관(통기,특허청)

발 신 : 주 제네바 대사

제 목 : UR/TRIPS 아국 문서 배포

UR/TRIPS 협상 그룹은 아국의 기술이전 관련분쟁 예방 제도 설립에 관한 제안을 UR문서(MTN.GNG/TRIPS/W/1, 91.7.12 자)로배포하였는바, 동 문서를 금 파편 송부함. 끝

(대사 박수길-국장)

통상국 특허청 우주국

PAGE 1

91.07.20 06:23 DF

외신 1과 통제관

0065

원 본

외 무 부

종 별 :

번 호 : USW-3680 일 시 : 91 0723 1950

수 신 : 장 관(통이,경기원,상공부,경제수석)주제네바대사-직송필

발 신 : 주 미 대사

제 목 : HILLS USTR 대표의 상공장관앞 서한

HILLS USTR 대표는 이봉서 상공부장관에게 UR 의 무관세화 협상 및 무역관련 지적소유권 (TRIP) 과 관련하여 한국이 미국의 주요입장을 지지해줄것을 요청하고 나아가 최근 한국내의 수입 반대적 경향에 대해 각별한 신경을 써줄것을 희망하는 별첨 서한을 송부해온바, 동서한 원본은 파편 송부 예정임.

(대사 현홍주-국장)

첨부: USW(F)-2929 (3 매)

통상국 2차보 청와대 경기원 상공부

PAGE 1 91.07.24 09:15 WG

외신 1과 통제관

0066

번호: USW(F) - 2929
수신: 장관 (통이, 경기원, 상공부, 경제수석) 사본: 주제네바 대사 - 중계필
발신: 주미 대사
제목: USW - 3680 의 원본 (3매)

THE UNITED STATES TRADE REPRESENTATIVE
Executive Office of the President
Washington, D.C. 20506

JUL 19 1991

Mr. Lee Bong-Suh
Minister of Trade and Industry
Ministry of Trade and Industry
Kwachon, Korea

Dear Minister Lee:

It was a great pleasure to talk with you on July 19. This letter is meant to follow up on that conversation.

As we discussed, to enhance market access in the Uruguay Round, we would hope that Korea could participate in our "zero-for-zero" initiative to eliminate tariffs in key sectors. Korean participation is especially important to the success of our initiative in the steel, electronics, and construction equipment sectors. Without a much improved market access package, I am convinced that it will be impossible to conclude this Round satisfactorily.

With respect to the protection of intellectual property, as I promised, I am enclosing a non-paper which outlines points we believe must be part of a GATT TRIPs agreement. Without the provisions outlined in this paper, we will be unable to forge the political coalition in the United States necessary to counterbalance opposition to our efforts to liberalize textiles, agriculture, and market access. In short, as I noted in our conversation, without a solid TRIPs agreement, our ability to sell the Round domestically will be seriously jeopardized.

Finally, with respect to what appears to be a continuing pattern of anti-import activities in Korea, I would hope you could give this issue your personal attention, and intervene publicly to curb such activity when it occurs.

With personal regards.

Sincerely,

Carla A. Hills

Enclosure

0067

KEY ELEMENTS OF A TRIPS AGREEMENT FOR THE UNITED STATES

PATENTS

- 20-year term from filing

- Non-discrimination in subject matter (e.g. product protection for pharmaceuticals and chemicals and inclusion of biotechnology)

- Inclusion of conditions, such as importation meeting local working requirements, that will limit compulsory licensing practices that might render otherwise adequate protection ineffective

- Transitional (pipeline) protection for pharmaceutical products previously patented in the United States but not yet marketed (since they are awaiting regulatory approval), provided they have also not yet been marketed in your country

- Omission of any reference to international exhaustion (i.e. no parallel importation)

COPYRIGHT

- Protection of computer programs as literary works

- Recognition of the U.S. "works for hire" regime that permits legal persons (e.g. companies) to be "authors" and to exercise their legal rights

- A 50-year term and the exclusive right to control the rental of sound recordings and computer programs

- A clear definition of public performance

- Exclusion of moral rights from the agreement

- Protection for data bases

TRADE SECRETS

- Protection for trade secrets that is subject to the enforcement provisions of the agreement

- A period of exclusive use for registration data provided to governments

2929-2

0068

SEMICONDUCTOR LAYOUT DESIGNS

- Protection equal to that found in current U.S. law, which goes well beyond that provided under the Washington Treaty

ENFORCEMENT

- Effective internal and border enforcement to stop both domestic and imported piracy, counterfeiting, and infringement

IMPLEMENTATION

- Countries should agree to implement the agreement within a period not to exceed two years

- The agreement should be implemented as part of the GATT system

2929-3 End

0069

특 허 청

국협 28140-3176 568-6077 1991. 8. 5.

수신 수신처참조

제목 UR/TRIPs 미국측 요청사항에 대한 검토의견 요청

1. 미국측(USTR) 은 UR/TRIPs 협상에서 한국의 관심과 지지를 요청하는 분야를 상공부를 통해 알려 왔습니다.

2. 동 요청분야에 대해 당청이 작성한 검토의견을 귀부(원)에 송부하오니 향후 협상에 대비하여 검토하시어 '91. 8. 7(수) 까지 송부하여 주시기 바랍니다.

첨부 1. 미국측 요청사항 1부.

2. 특허청 검토자료 1부. 끝.

특 허 청 장

수신처 경제기획원(대외경제조정실장), 외무부(통상국장), 상공부(전자전기공업국장), 보사부(약정국장), 문화부(어문출판국장), 과기처(기술개발국장).

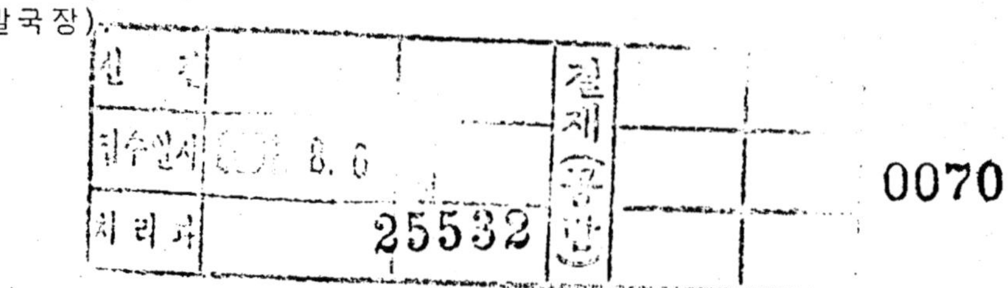

0070

UR/TRIPs 미국측 요청내용 검토

1. 경 위

o '91. 7.19 Ms. Carla A. Hills (미국 USTR) 우리 상공부장관과 전화 통화

- 구체사항은 Non-paper (7.19자)로 전달하여 미측입장에 대한 관심 표명과 지지 요청

- TRIPs에서 미측입장이 관철되지 않으면 농산물, Market Access에 대한 자유화를 자국 업계에 설득하기 힘듬.

o '91. 7.26 상공부, 특허청에 검토 요청 (비공식)

2. 미측입장에 대한 검토의견

가. 특허 (Patents)

1) 보호기간

o 미측입장 : 출원일로 부터 20년 (20-year term from filing)

o 검토의견

- 아국법은 '출원공고일 혹은 등록일로 부터 15년, 단, 출원일로 부터 20년 초과 불가'로 규정되어 있음.

- 출원일로 부터 출원공고일 까지의 보호는 보상금 청구권(민사) 임시 보호 권리(민.형사) 로 가능함.

. 구체적인 것은 관련법제의 비교검토가 필요함.

- 현재 법제로도 출원일로 부터 20년의 보호는 가능함.

0071

o 아측입장 : 미측 입장 수용가능

2) 특허대상 (Subject matter)

o 미측입장 : 대상에 따라 차별을 두지 않음 (의약, 화학, 생명공학 발명 포함등)

- Non-discrimination in subject matter(e.g. product protection for pharmaceutical and chemicals and inclusion of biotechnology)

o 검토의견

- 대상자체의 문제점, 기술경제 사정에 따라 불특허대상을 둘수 있어야 함.

. 미국에서도 보호요건(특히, 산업상 이용가능성) 과 윤리성을 이유로 일부 대상에 대해서는 특허권을 부여하지 않고 있음.

. 우리법상 동물특허(animal inventions and its varieties) 와 식물 특허 일부(유성생식 식물), 핵전환 제법에 의한 발명은 특허로 허여 하지 않고 있음.

o 아측입장

- 일부 대상에 대해서 불특허대상을 둘 수 있어야 함.

. 동물특허 (윤리성, 복제재현 가능성에 문제 있음)
. 식물특허 일부 즉, 유성생식 식물 (농업정책적 문제 있음)

- 핵전환 제법에 의한 발명은 양보 가능

3) 강제실시권의 범위 제한

o 미측주장 : 수입을 통해 국내수요를 충족하면 강제실시권을 허여하지 않아야 함.(강제실시권의 허여요건중 "불실시 또는 불충분한 실시"와 연관)

- Inclusion of conditions such as importation meeting local working requirements, that will limit compulsory licensing practices that might render otherwise adequate protection ineffective

o 검토의견

- 우리법에는 '실시(working)' 의 개념에 수입(importation) 이 포함되어 있음 (특허법 2조 3호)

- Paris 조약 제5조 A(1) : '수입'을 실시(working) 으로 보아야 함.

- 따라서, 수입을 통해 국내 수요를 충족할 경우 '불실시 또는 불충분한 실시' 가 되지 않는 것으로 해석할 수 있음.

o 아측입장 : 미측주장 수용 가능

- 수입을 통해 국내수요를 충족하면 강제실시권을 허여하지 않음.

4) Transitional Protection

o 미측입장 : 미국에서 특허를 받았으나 정부의 제조허가를 받기 위해 미국과 한국 양국에 시판되지 않는 물질 보호

- Transitional(pipeline) protection for pharmaceutical products previously patented in the United States but not yet marketed (since they are awaiting regulatory approval), provided they have also not yet been marketed in your country

o 검토의견

- 우리외 타국에 대해서는 타국이 미국에 대해, 한국이 미국에 대해 취해주고 있는 pipeline products 보호를 해줄 것을 요구하는 내용임.

- 우리에 대해서는 현재 취해주고 있는 pipeline products 보호를 확대해 달라는 주장임.

o 아측입장 : 당해국에 특허를 받지 않아도 보호해달라는 과도한 주장으로 수용 불가

- 소급보호의 확장임.

5) 권리소진 이론 (exhaustion)

o 미측입장 : 권리소진 이론에 대한 언급 삭제 (병렬 수입금지)

- Omission of any reference of international exhausion (i.e. parallel importation)

* 권리소진 이론 (exhaustion of rights)

- 권리자의 동의, 허가에 의해 판매, 배포된 제품에 대해서는 권리자의 권리가 소진된다는 이론

- 병렬수입 (parallel importation)과 연관이 있는 것으로 권리소진 이론이 부정되면 병렬수입이 금지됨.

* 병렬수입(parallel importation)의 예

- 외국의 A 라는 권리자가 우리나라의 甲에게, license 를 해준 경우, 甲이 license 를 통해 제조한 제품을 외국에 수출하는 것 (외국의 입장에서는 수입이 됨).

o 검토의견

- 현재 TRIPs 협정안(6조)에는 권리소진에 대해 각국이 결정할 수 있다고 되어 있음.

- 아국에 관련 규정 및 판례는 없으나 권리소진 이론의 규정을 지지하며, 이와 관련한 parallel importation이 허용되어야 한다는 입장임.

. 권리자의 동의에 의해 판매 되었으면 권리자가 그 판매행위를 통해 이익을 얻은 것임.

o 아측입장

- 권리소진 이론을 지지하며 parallel importation 는 허용되어야 함.

나. 저작권

1) 컴퓨터 프로그램 보호

o 미측주장

- 어문저작물(literary works)로 보호 (Protection of CP as literary works)

o 검토의견

- 어문저작물로 보호함으로써 보호기간을 연장 (50년) 하고

- 권리침해 판단시 판단범위를 넓혀 자국의 컴퓨터 프로그램의 보호를 강화하자는 의도

. 어문저작물로 보호할 경우 "복제" 의 문제가 되는 것이 아니라 "표절" 의 문제가 되기 때문

- 아국은 CP를 어문저작물(저작권법)이 아닌 특별법으로 보호하고 있음.

. 보호기간 : 50년

0075

- 어문저작물로 보호할 경우 침해판단의 범위가 넓어질 우려가 있으므로 원칙상으로는 반대하는 입장

. 기술성, 산업연관성등 차이가 있음.

o 아측입장

- CP 는 일반적 어문저작물로 라는 다른 성격이 있으므로 원칙적으로는 반대함.

2) 법인, 단체를 저작권자로 인정

o 미측주장

- 법인(legal person) 회사등을 저작권자(authors)로 인정
(Recognition of the U.S. "works for hire" require that permits legal persons(e.g. companies0 to be "authors" and to excercise their legal rights)

o 검토의견

- 연구단체가 개발한 저작물, 컴퓨터 프로그램에 대해 법인, 단체가 권리를 갖도록 하자는 것.

- 우리법 (저작권법) 에서 법인을 저작권자로 인정하고 있음.

o 아측입장 : 미측 입장 수용가능

3) 보호기간

o 미측입장 : 50년 (50-year term)

o 검토의견
- 우리법에서도 50년임.

o 아측입장 : 미측 입장 수용가능

4) 대여권 인정

o 미측입장 : 음반, 컴퓨터 프로그램에 대한 대여권 인정

- neighboring right to control the rental of sound recordings and computer programs

o 검토의견

- 권리소진이론에 의해 수용 불가

- 컴퓨터 프로그램 보호법에 의해 컴퓨터 프로그램에 대한 대여권은 인정되고 있음.

- 음반 대여권은 양보가능 (음반대여업은 미미함)

- 영상저작물(cinematographic works : 비디오등) 은 국내 대여업계의 붕괴 초래 우려가 있으므로 수용 불가

o 아측입장

- 음반, 컴퓨터 프로그램에 대한 대여권은 수용 가능하나 영상저작물에 대한 대여권은 수용 불가

5) 공공실연 (public performance)

o 미측입장 : 공공실연에 대한 명백한 정의 규정

- a clear definition of public performance

o 검토의견

- 'public' 의 개념 정의에 관한 내용임.

. TRIPs 협정안 14조와 관련하여 'public' 의 개념을 정의해 저작권의 제한을 축소하려는 의도

- 각국은 공공목적(public)의 개념을 도입해 저작권에 제한을 가하고 있음.

  ex) 학교교육을 위한 전재, 시사보도, 비영리목적의 방송등

o 아측입장

- 명백한 정의를 하는 것을 원칙적으로 지지하나 일정범위내에서 공공목적을 위한 사용은 허용되어야 함.

6) 저작인격권 (moral rights)

o 미측입장 : 저작인격권 제외

- Exclusion of moral rights

* 저작인격권 (moral rights)

- 저작권은 저작재산권(economic rights)과 저작인격권(moral rights)으로 구성
- 저작재산권은 복제, 판매, 배포, 수입권등을 말함.
- 저작인격권은 성명표시권, 공표권, 동일성 유지권을 말함.

o 검토의견

- 저작권중 저작인격권을 제외하고 저작재산권만 인정하는 것은 영미법계의 특징

  . 영국도 '88 저작권법에 의해 저작인격권을 인정함으로써 미국만 저작인격권을 도입않는 국가가 되었음.

  . 미국은 저작권 분야에서 유럽보다 후진국이기 때문

- 아국 저작권법에서는 저작인격권 인정

- TRIPs 의 저작권분야가 Berne plus Approach 를 채택하고 있으며, Berne 협약에도 저작인격권을 규정하고 있으므로 저작인격권이 인정 되어야 할 것임.

o 아측입장

- TRIPs 협정에 moral rights 를 제외한다 해도 아국에의 영향은 없음.
- 따라서, TRIPs 협상에서 미측입장에 대해 공개적인 반대 의사표시는 하지 않아도 될 것임. 그러나 공개적인 지지는 할 수 없음.

7) Data Base 보호

o 미측입장 : Data Base 보호

- Protection for data bases

o 검토의견

- 현재 보호 법률은 없으나 보호를 위한 입법 추진 예정

o 아측입장 : 수용 가능

다. 영업비밀 (Trade Secrets)

1) 시행절차(enforcement)의 대상

o 미측주장 : 영업비밀을 Enforcement 절차의 적용범위가 되도록 함.

- Protection for trade secrets that is subject to the enforcement provisions of the agreement

o 검토의견

- 국내 민형사 절차에서 영업비밀을 시행절차의 적용범위로 하는 것은 수용 가능

- 그러나 국경조치(border measures)에서는 문제 있음.

. 즉, 세관당국이 영업비밀, 특허등의 침해여부를 판단할 전문 능력이 없으므로 인정할 경우 부당한 절차 남발로 국제교역에 막대한 지장 초래

o 아측입장

- 영업비밀을 시행절차중 국내 민.형사 절차의 대상으로 하는 것은 인정할 수 있으나 국경절차의 대상으로 하는 것은 수용 불가

2) 정부제출 자료 보호

o 미측주장 : 정부에 제출한 자료를 일정기간 타인이 사용하는 것을 금지

- A period of exclusive use for registration data provided to governments

o 검토의견

- 정부에 제출한 자료(ex. 임상실험자료등)를 일정기간 보호하는 것은 특허기간외에 추가적인 독점권을 권리자에게 인정하는 것이 됨.

- 미국에서도 저약가 정책을 위해 특허기간이 만료된 물질에 대해서 타인이 제조허가 신청시 전 임상실험자료를 제출하지 않고 생물학적 동등성 실험자료만 제출하도록 하여 전 임상실험자료를 원용할 수 있도록 하고 있음 (Waxman-Hetch 법)

- 일본, EC도 동등한 취지 입법을 하고 있으므로 국제관례에 어긋난 것임.

o 아측입장

- 미측입장은 권리자를 추가적으로 보호하고 국제 관례에도 어긋난 것이기 때문에 수용 불가

라. 반도체 칩 배치설계

o 미측주장 : 미국법에 준한 보호 (Protection equal to that found in current U.S. law, which goes well beyond that provided under the Washington Treaty)

- 보호범위 (IC를 내장한 최종제품까지 보호)

o 검토의견

- 최종제품(final product)을 보호할 경우 컴퓨터, 항공기등 제품에 침해한 IC 하나만 들어 있어도 컴퓨터등 그 자체가 침해한 제품이 되므로 교역에 장애 초래 가능

- Royalty 청구시 IC chip 보다 IC를 내장한 제품에 대해 royalty를 청구하는 것이 합법화되어 royalty 부담 증가 초래

  . 국내 입법(안) 에도 최종제품은 제외

o 아측입장

- 미측 입장 수용 불가

마. 시행절차 (Enforcement)

o 미측주장 : 효과적인 국내, 국경절차 마련

- Effective internal and horder enforcement to stop both domestic and imported piracy, counterfeiting, and infringement

0081

o 검토의견

- 효과적인 국내, 국경절차를 마련하는 것이 필요함.

- 그러나, 국경조치 (border measures)의 경우 적용범위를 저작권, 상표권 침해에 한정되어야 함.

. 세관당국에 전문적 판단 능력이 없으므로 신뢰성 저하

o 아측입장

- 지적재산권 보호를 위해 효과적인 국내, 국경절차를 마련하는 것은 지지하나,

- 국경조치의 경우 적용범위를 저작권, 상표권 침해로 한정되어야 함.

바. 조약의 집행 (Implementation)

1) 경과기간 (Transitional period)

o 미측주장 : 2년

- Countries should agree to implement the agreement within a period not to exceed two years

o 검토의견 : 아직 경과기간에 대한 구체적인 논의가 이루어진 적이 없음.

o 아측입장

- 개도국의 기술.경제 사정을 고려하여 충분한 경과기간이 마련되어야 함.

- 구체기간은 정치적인 사항이므로 입장 미정립

2) GATTability

o 미측주장 : GATT 규정에 포함

- The agreement should be implemented as part of the GATT system

o 검토의견 : 아측입장 수용

Key Elements of a TRIPs Agreement for the United States

Patents

- 20-year term from filing

- Non-discrimination in subject matter (e.g. product protection for pharmaceuticals and chemicals and inclusion of biotechnology)

- Inclusion of conditions, such as importation meeting local working requirements, that will limit compulsory licensing practices that might render otherwise adequate protection ineffective

- Transitional (pipeline) protection for pharmaceutical products previously patented in the United States but not yet marketed(since they are awaiting regulatory approval), provided they have also not yet been marketed in your country

- Omission of any reference on international exhaustion (i.e., Parallel importation)

Copyright

- Protection of computer programs as literary works

- Recognition of the U.S. "Works for hire" regime that permits legal persons (e.g. companies) to be "authors" and to exercise their legal rights
- A 50-year term and the neighboring rights to control the rental of sound recordings and computer programs

- A clear definition of public performance

- Exclusion of moral rights

- Protection for data bases

Trade Secrets

- Protection for trade secrets that is subject to the enforcement provisions of the agreement

- A period of exclusive use for registration data provided to governments

0084

Semiconductor Layout Designs

- Protection equal to that found in current U.S. law, which goes well beyond that provided under the Washington Treaty

Enforcement

- Effective internal and border enforcement to stop both domestic and imported piracy, counterfeiting, and infringement

Implementation

- Countries should agree to implement the agreement within a period not to exceed two years

- The agreement should be implemented as part of the GATT system

0085

THE UNITED STATES TRADE REPRESENTATIVE
Executive Office of the President
Washington, D.C. 20506

JUL 19 1991

Mr. Lee Bong-Suh
Minister of Trade and Industry
Ministry of Trade and Industry
Kwachon, Korea

Dear Minister Lee:

It was a great pleasure to talk with you on July 19. This letter is meant to follow up on that conversation.

As we discussed, to enhance market access in the Uruguay Round, we would hope that Korea could participate in our "zero-for-zero" initiative to eliminate tariffs in key sectors. Korean participation is especially important to the success of our initiative in the steel, electronics, and construction equipment sectors. Without a much improved market access package, I am convinced that it will be impossible to conclude this Round satisfactorily.

With respect to the protection of intellectual property, as I promised, I am enclosing a non-paper which outlines points we believe must be part of a GATT TRIPs agreement. Without the provisions outlined in this paper, we will be unable to forge the political coalition in the United States necessary to counterbalance opposition to our efforts to liberalize textiles, agriculture, and market access. In short, as I noted in our conversation, without a solid TRIPs agreement, our ability to sell the Round domestically will be seriously jeopardized.

Finally, with respect to what appears to be a continuing pattern of anti-import activities in Korea, I would hope you could give this issue your personal attention, and intervene publicly to curb such activity when it occurs.

With personal regards.

Sincerely,

Carla A. Hills

Enclosure

0086

특　　　허　　　청

국협 28140-3708　　　568 6077　　　1991. 8. 6.

수신　수신처참조

제목　UR/TRIPs 협상 실무 소위원회 개최

1. UR/TRIPs 협상과 향후 예상되는 TRIPs 분야 한.미 양지협의에 대비키 위해 표제회의를 다음과 같이 개최함을 통보하오니 참석하여 주시기 바랍니다.

2. 아울러, 동 회의 결과를 토대로 대책을 마련하여 UR 대책 실무 위원회에 보고후 확정할 계획임을 통보합니다.

다　　　음

가. 일　　시 : 1991. 8. 13(화), 15:00 - 17:00

나. 장　　소 : 특허청 14층 회의실

다. 참석범위 : 특 허 청　기획관리관 (주재)

특 허 청　국제협력과장

경제기획원　통상조정 3 과장

외 무 부　통상기구과장

상 공 부　전자부품과장

보 사 부　약무과장

문 화 부　지작권과장

과 기 처　정보산업기술과장 (무순). 끝.

26068

0087

국협 28140-

1991. 8. 6.

특 허 청 장

수신처 경제기획원장관(대외경제조정실장), 외무부장관(통상국장), 상공부장관(전자전기국장), 보사부장관(약정국장), 문화부장관(어문출판국장), 과학기술처장관(기술개발국장).

0088

외무부

관리 번호	91-569

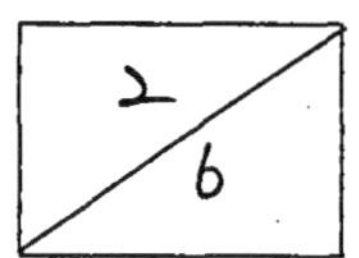

UR/TRIPs 협상전망 및 대책

1991. 8.

특 허 청

0089

I. UR/TRIPs 협상전망

1. 최근 동향

o '91.5.24 미 행정부의 신속승인권(fast-track authority) 연장을 의회에서 승인함으로써 본격적인 협상 개시

o '91.6.24 미국 USTR, 네덜란드 (EC 의장국) 무역장관 합의

- 주요 협상의제 : 농산물, 서비스, 시장접근, TRIPs
- UR 협상은 실패해도 주요협상 의제는 올해안 타결되어야 함.

o '91. 6.27-28 '91 1차 UR/TRIPs 회의 개최

- 합의사항

V ① 협상의 기초(basis of works): 7차 의장보고서

② 협상일정: '91.9.16 주간에 2차회의 개최

③ 협상방법: 기술적인 문제(technical matters)를 먼저 다루고 정치적인 문제(political matters)는 나중 논의

. Art.73(경과규정)과 분쟁해결절차에 대한 논의예정

o '91.7.17 G7 회의 금년내 UR의 성공적 타결을 위해 정상들이 직접 관여키로 합의

2. TRIPs 협상 전망

o 농산물, 서비스, 시장접근(Market Access) 협상의 진전과 밀접한 연관성을 갖고 진행될 예정

o 9월 회의에서는 7차 의장보고서의 협상쟁점을 중심으로 논의 예정

o 협상부진으로 미국등 선진국의 UR에 대한 관심이 떨어지고 있으나, 협상 부진이 초래하게 될 결과에 대한 우려가 오히려 각국의 양보를 촉구해 TRIPs 가 조속 타결될 전망도 있음.

1

0090

Ⅱ. '91 1차 UR/TRIPs 회의내용 및 결과

1. 회의 의제

o TRIPs 협상의 현상황(state) 점검

o 향후 협상 계획 (Organization of Further Work)

o 기타 (Other Business)

2. 회의 기간 : 1991. 6. 27 - 28

3. 회의 내용

가. TRIPs 협상의 현상황 점검 (Review of the State of the Negotiations)

o 선.개도국 모두 Brussels 회의에 제출된 의장보고서 (7차 의장보고서)에 불만족을 표시하고

- 개도국은 그들의 관심사항이
  . 기본원칙, 지작인접권, 상표, 지리적표시, 특허대상, 강제실시권, IC, 영업비밀
  . 시행절차
  . 경과규정

  에 있다고 설명함.

- 특히, 개도국은 미국의 301조에 의한 일방적 제재조치가 자국의 입장을 약화시키고 있다고 비난함.

- 선진국(EC)도 전반적으로
  . 컴퓨터 프로그램, 대여권, 저작인접권
  . 상표, 지리적 표시
  . 특허대상, 강제실시권, 영업비밀, 시행절차에 진전이 없었으며, 73조(경과규정)를 redraft 할것을 요구하였음.

*미·日 발언없었음

o 한국은 양자협상보다 다자간 협정에 의한 문제의 해결이 바람직 하다고 전제하고, 협상의 성공적 타결을 위해서는 선.개도국간 양보가 있어야 할 것으로 촉구함.

- 그리고 아국이 제안한 분쟁예방 절차에 대해 관심을 촉구하였음.

나. 향후 협상계획 (Organization of Further Work)

1) 협상의 기초 (basis of work)

o Anell 의장의 제의

- 7차 의장보고서를 중심으로 하고
- 주요 issues 에 대해 논의하는 방식으로 하자고 함.

o 개도국

- 7차 의장보고서에 Brussles 회의에서 논의된 사항을 추가해서 논의하자고 주장함.

o 한 국

- 7차 의장보고서의 내용중 bracket 으로 남아있는 사항을 중심으로 하고 정치적인 문제는 고위급 회의로 미루는 것이 바람직 할 것이라고 제안함.

o 결 론

- Brussels 회의내용을 충분히 고려하되 7차 의장보고서를 협상의 기초로 함.

2) 9월회의 의제

o 입장이 대립되고 있는 분야중 기술적인 문제 (technical matters)를 중심으로 함.

3

0092

o 다음 두사항 논의를 포함.

① 분쟁해결절차 (Dispute Settlement Procedure)

- GATTability 와 연관되이 정치적인· 문제이나 Annex 에 있는 세가지 대안에 대한 이해를 증진하는 방향으로 논의

② 경과규정 (73조, Protection of Existing Intellectual Property)

- 이해가 가능하도록 명확하게 define 할것임.

3) 9월 회의기간 : 9. 16 주간 (잠정적으로 1주)

4. 관찰 및 평가

o 구체적인 내용보다 향후 협상의 framework 에 대한 논의를 중심으로 협의하고 그 동안의 입장변화를 살피는 탐색전 성격

- 선.개도국의 이견이 아직 크다는 것을 다시 확인하는 계기

o 특기할만한 것은 회의기간중 미국, 일본 대표의 발언이 전혀 없었다는 점.

- 탐문한 비로는 미국이 업계의 강력한 로비로 의장보고서의 standard 를 높여야 할 입장이어서 각국의 반응만을 청취하는 것 같다는 평가

- 미국은 다자보다는 양자간 압력에 중점을 두는 인상을 보여줌.

Ⅲ. 협상대책(안)

분 야	대 응 논 리
<제 1 안> : 1 - 18	
1. Public 의 정의	
- "Public" 용어의 국내법 위임한계 설정 (정상 관행)	- 권리의 균형과 공공목적의 실현을 위한 각국의 노력에 부당한 압력을 가하므로 반대
2. 특허권의 보호기간	
- 출원일로부터 최소 20년	- 동일한 보호기간 설정위해 단일기간 20년
3. 입증책임의 전환	
- 입증책임 전환 요건을 다음과 같이 규정 . 신물질인 경우, 실질적 유사성이 있는 경우	- 입증책임의 전환규정은 특별한 예외 규정이므로 제한적으로 운용되어야 함.
4. 권리남용 및 반경쟁적 행위	
- 반경쟁적 행위에 대해 국내법상 조치 (계약실효등)	- 권리남용, 반경쟁적 행위는 규제 필요
5. 컴퓨터 프로그램 및 자료 편집물	
- 컴퓨터 프로그램을 어문저작물로 보호	- 컴퓨터 프로그램은 어문저작물과 다른 특성을 갖고 있음(기술성, 산업연관성)
<제 2 안> : 6 - 18	
6. 대여권 (보상청구권)	
- 최소한 음반, 컴퓨터 프로그램 및 영상저작물에 한해 보상청구권 인정	- 권리자의 동의에 의해 시판된 저작물에는 권리자의 권리가 소진되어 자유사용 가능

관 철 분 야	대 응 논 리
7. 외국유명상표 보호	
- 유명상표 판단기준은 관련업계에 알려진 정도, 국제교역증대에 따른 결과 반영	- 등록되지 않은 유명상표 보호는 예외적인 것으로 당해국내에서 유명한 것이어야 함.
8. 불특허대상	
- 동.식물 변종	- 경제, 기술수준, 대상자체의 문제점에 따라 불특허대상을 규정할수 있어야 함
9. 특허의 강제실시권 실시범위	
- 국내수요 충족만을 위해 실시	- 권리자가 국내에서 특허를 사용하지 않으면 적정한 조건하에 국가가 강제실시권을 부여할수 있어야 함. (이용발명에 대한 강제실시권의 경우 수출도 가능)
10. 분쟁예방 절차	
- 기술이전 검토위원회 설치 - 기술이전에 관한 지침 설정	- 권리자의 권리남용을 방지하기 위해 기술이전에 관한 지침설정과 검토를 통해 분쟁의 신속한 치리 및 해결
11. 분쟁해결절차	
- Text Ⅰ: 특별절차를 두되 cross-sectoral retaliation가능 - Text Ⅱ: 특별절차를 두고 보복조치 불인정 - Text Ⅲ: GATT 일반절차 적용(cross-sectoral retaliation 가능)	- 지적재산권 분야의 전문성을 감안할때 특별절차를 두는 Text Ⅰ 을 지지하되 보복은 지적재산권 범위내에 한정
------------------------------------	------------------------------------
<제 3 안> : 12 - 18	
12. 경과규정	
- TRIPs 발효시점에 존재하나 보호되지 않는 subject matter 는 TRIPs 규정 적용 제외	- 저작권등 지적재산권에 광범위하게 인정되고 있는 public domain (공중의 영역, Berne 조약 제7조)의 법리를 원용해서 지지 확보

관 철 분 야	대 응 논 리
13. 국경조치 적용범위	
- 위조상표 부착상품, 저작권 침해물품은 권리자의 청구에 의해 세관에서 통관 유예조치 발동 가능	- 특허, IC등 복잡한 기술분야에 피고(수출입업자)에게 항변할 기회도 부여않고 비전문인인 세관에서 침해여부를 판단하여 통관유예 조치를 발동하는 것은 새로운 무역장애를 초래하므로 위조상표, 저작권에 한정
14. IC 보호의 범위	
- IC 를 내장한 완제품도 보호 (권리를 침해한 IC가 계속 내장되어 있을 경우만)	- IC 가격과 IC를 내장한 제품과는 현격한 가격차이가 발생하므로 침해 IC 를 이유로 완제품을 유통정지하면 교역 증대에 장애 초래 - IC 만 제거하면 유통정지 하지 않아야 할것.
15. 정부제출 자료의 공개금지	
- 제약, 농약의 판매허가시 제출되는 기술자료 (ex. 임상실험자료)를 최소 5년간 타품목허가시 원용(rely on) 금지	- 저약가 정책을 위해 복사품목에 대해 품목허가를 신청하는 경우 기존자료를 원용하도록 하는 것이 국제관례이므로 반대 (미.일)
16. 음반소급 보호	
- TRIPs 발효당시 존재하고 있는 음반 보호	- 음반에 관해 규정하고 있는 Rome 협약(제20조), 음반협약(제7조 3항)에도 불소급효 규정
17. IC 선의의 구매자에 의한 행위	
- 선의로(침해한 IC 라는 것은 모르고) 구매한 IC 재고품을 사용한 제조행위에 대해 royalty 지급	- royalty 지급은 당연하나 IC 제조업자에게 직접 청구하는 것이 바람직하며, 최종제품 제조업자가 부담하는 것은 과부담이 됨.
18. 대여권 (대여금지권)	
- 최소한 음반, 컴퓨터 프로그램 및 영상저작물에 한해 대여금지권 인정	- 권리자의 동의에 의해 시판된 저작물에는 권리자의 권리가 소진되어 자유사용 가능 - 보상청구권은 인정 가능하나, 대여금지권은 불가

7

0096

Ⅳ. 기술이전에 관한 분쟁예방절차 마련을 위한 제안

1. 제안이유

o 지적재산권 보호체제 마련을 위한 TRIPs 협상에서는 보호수준의 향상으로 기술 공급자인 권리자의 이익을 보호하는데 중점을 두는 반면, 기술수요자의 측면 고려되지 않고 있음.

o 따라서, 기술이전 계약에 있어 반경쟁적 행위를 규제하고 발생가능한 분쟁을 사전에 예방하고자 함.

2. 제안 제출일지

o 1991. 7. 3 GATT 사무국에 제출

o 1991. 7.12 GATT 사무국 문서 (MTN. GNG/TRIPs/W/1)로 각국에 배포

3. 제안 내용

o 특히, know-how license 계약의 당사자는 자국의 정부를 통해 계약의 권리 남용 여부에 대한 판단을 TRIPs 위원회에 요청

o TRIPs 위원회는 기술이전 계약에 관한 Guideline 제정

o TRIPs 위원회는 위원회 산하 기술이전계약 검토위원회 (License Review Board)를 통해 심사

o 검토위원회가 서면 의견을 제시함.
- 체약국을 구속하지 않으나 계약당사자는 동 의견에 따를 수 있음.

4. 제안의 전망 및 효과

o 선진국 및 강경개도국의 반발이 예상되어 채택 가능성은 적음.

- 선진국의 반대이유

. 기본적으로 개도국이 제안한 반경쟁적 독점행위 규제 (Part Ⅱ, Section 8)과 맥을 같이 하고 있음.

. 권리자의 보호보다는 기술 사용자의 입장을 강조하고 있음.

- 강경개도국의 반대 이유

. License Review Board 의 의견이 체약국을 구속하지 않으므로 실효성이 없음.

. 분쟁당사자 일방이 동 절차로 가는 것을 기부할 경우 강제수단이 없음.

o 그러나, 어느정도 기술이용 능력을 갖고 있는 중도선진국 (호주, 캐나다) 및 온건개도국 (홍콩등)의 지지를 받고 있음.

- 기술 선진국과의 기술이전 계약시 권리자의 반경쟁적 행위를 규제하고 정당한 조건하에 기술이전을 할수 있기 때문

o 검토위원회의 서면의견이 구속력이 있는 것이 아니니 선언적인 효과를 갖는 것이며, 사전에 분쟁을 걸르는 효과가 있으며, TRIPs 협상에서 선.개도국간 조정자적 역할 강화 가능

외무부

관리번호	91-570

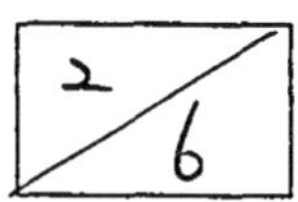

UR/TRIPs 한.미 양자협의 대책

1991. 8.

특 허 청

0099

8.16 → EPB 대외신장 주재
· (8.23) TRIPs 국장급 회의 예비

I . 미국의 양자협의 요청

o 1991. 7. 15 USTR 대표보 Ms. S. Kristoff, UR 협상진행과 관련하여 한.미 양자협의 개최를 요청

- 시 기 : 9월 중순 또는 10월경

- 주요관심분야 : 농산물, 시장접근(관세무세화), 서비스, 지적재산권, 통신, 섬유등 6개 분야

- 주요 양자협의 대상국은 불투명하나 소수의 주요 교역대상국 포함 예상

o 1991. 7. 19 미국 USTR 대표 Ms. Carla A. Hills, TRIPs 분야의 주요 미국 입장에 대한 한국의 관심 표명과 지지를 Non-paper 로 요청

√논리 : TRIPs 협상에서 미국 입장이 관철되지 않으면 농산물, 서비스, 시장 접근 분야에 대한 양보를 자국 업계에 설득하기 힘듬.

o 미국은 서비스, 시장접근 (관세무세화), 지적재산권 협상등에서 자국의 실리를 최대한 확보하면서 아울러 농산물 협상에서 대안을 검토하게 될 것으로 예상

II. 한.미 양자협의 대책

1. 양자협의 수용 여부

o 양자협의의 방식, 시기, 협의 level 에 대한 미국의 입장에 대한 탐색은 필요하되, 어떤 형식이든 TRIPs 분야에 대한 양자협의는 수용해야 할것으로 판단됨.

- 실무급 회의의 경우라면, 미국이 의도하는 입장 및 논리를 사전에 파악하고 분석할 수 있는 기회로 적극적인 방향으로 운영 가능

1

0100

- 고위급 회의의 경우라도 입장의 사전 노출 우려가 있으나, 적극적인 대처가 필요

. 협상의 현 단계에서는 이미 기술적 쟁점이 거의 노출된 상태

. 정치적 쟁점을 뒤로 미루는 것은 '90년 Brussels 회의 같은 실패를 초래할 우려가 있으므로 기술적 쟁점과 정치적인 쟁점을 함께 논의해야 할 때라는 합의가 이루어지고 있음 ('91. 7. 30, TNC 회의)

. 따라서, 고위급 한.미 양자협의를 통해 실무급에서 논의할 수 없는 정치적 쟁점에 대한 입장 교환도 바람직

2. 적극적 양자 협의대책

o 미국에서 요구하는 사항에 대한 검토 및 우리가 미국에 대해서 요구할 수 있는 사항 개발

o 우리의 요구할 수 있는 사항을 한.미 통상실무협의체 (TAG) 회의에서 논의하는 방안도 검토

、 능동적 자세에서 미측에 Non-paper 제출할수도.

Ⅲ. 미국 주요 관심사항 검토

1. 미국 주요 관심사항 검토

가. 특허청 소관사항

1) 특 허 (Patent)

① 보호기간

o 미측입장 : 20-year term form filing (출원일로 부터 20년)

o 검토의견

- 아국법은 '출원공고일 혹은 등록일로 부터 15년, 단, 출원일로 부터 20년 초과 불가'로 규정되어 있음.

- 출원공개일로 부터 출원공고일 까지의 보호는 보상금 청구권 (민사) 임시 보호 권리(민.형사) 로 가능함.
  . 출원일로 부터 보호하는 EC 도 출원일로 부터 출원공개일 까지의 보호에 대해서는 언급이 없음.

- 현재 심사기간이 3 - 5년 임과 심사청구제도를 고려할때 현 법제로도 출원일로 부터 20년 보호라는 요건 충족 가능

o 아측입장
- '출원일로 부터 20년 보호' 를 수용 가능

② 특허대상 (Subject Matter)

o 미측입장

- Non-discrimination in subject matter(e.g. product protection for pharmaceutical and chemicals and inclusion of biotechnology)
  (대상에 따라 차별을 두지 않음. 즉, 의약, 화학, 생명공학 발명 포함)

o 검토의견

- 미측입장은 특허대상을 전 기술분야로 확대하자는 의도임.

  . 그러나, 미국에서도 보호요건(특히, 산업상 이용가능성) 과 윤리성을 이유로 일부 대상에 대해서는 특허권을 부여하지 않고 있음.

3

0102

* 산업상 이용가능성

. 산업상 이용가능성(유용성)은 그 발명이 계속 재생산할 수 있어서 산업에 이용할 수 있어야 한다는 것

. 복제가능성과 밀접히 연관

- 우리법상 동물특허(animal inventions and its varieties) 와 식물 특허 일부(유성생식식물), 핵전환 제법에 의한 발명은 특허로 허여하지 않고 있음.

o 아측입장

- 연구자, 발명자의 노력에 대한 충분한 보상을 위해 특허대상을 확대하는 것을 지지함.

- 그러나, 대상 자체의 문제점, 개도국의 기술.경제적 사정을 고려하여 불특허대상을 규정할 수 있어야 함.

. 동물특허 : 윤리성, 복제재현 가능성에 문제 있음.

. 식물특허 일부 즉, 유성생식 식물의 경우는 특허보다는 특별법으로 보호하는 것이 바람직 (주로, 주곡에 해당되므로 특허권을 부여하는 것은 바람직하지 않으며 유성생식 식물을 특허로 보호하는 국가는 없음)

③ 강제실시권 범위의 제한

o 미측입장

- Inclusion of conditions such as importation meeting local working requirements, that will limit compulsory licensing practices that might render otherwise adequate protection ineffective

o 검토의견

- 우리법에는 '실시(working)' 의 개념에 수입(importation) 이 포함되어 있음 (특허법 2조 3호)

- Paris 조약 제5조 A(1):'수입'을 실시(working)으로 보아야 함.

- 따라서, 수입을 통해 국내 수요를 충족할 경우 '불실시 또는 불충분한 실시' 가 되지 않는 것으로 해석할 수 있음.

o 아측입장

- 수입을 통해 국내수요를 충족하면 강제실시권을 허여하지 않는다는 미국입장 수용

④ Transitional Protection

o 미측입장

- Transitional(pipeline) protection for pharmaceutical products previously patented in the United States but not yet marketed (since they are awaiting regulatory approval), provided they have also not yet been marketed in your country (미국에서 특허를 받았으나 정부의 제조허가를 받기 위해 미국과 한국 양국에 시판되지 않는 물질 보호)

o 검토의견

- 타국의 입장에서는, 한국이 미국에 대해 취해주고 있는 pipeline pipeline products 보호를 기간 제한 없이 미국에 대해 해 달라는 는 내용임.

- 우리의 입장에서는, 현재 미국에 대해 취해주고 있는 pipeline 를 products 보호조치를 타국에 확대하라는 주장임.

  *. 미국 주장대로 라면 현재의 pipeline products 보호를 EC, 일본등 모든 국가에 확대해야 함.

o 아측입장

- 국제관례에 어긋난 소급보호인 미국 입장을 한국이 지지해달라는 것은 무리한 주장임.

- 현재 국내 반발이 심한 pipeline products 보호조치를 타국도 미국에 대해서 취하라고 지지할 수도 없고 우리가 EC, 일본등 타국에 대해 확산 적용할수는 없음.

⑤ 권리소진이론 (exhaustion)

o 미측입장

- Omission of any reference of international exhausion (i.e. parallel importation) (권리소진 이론에 대한 언급 삭제(병렬 수입 금지))

* 권리소진 이론 (exhaustion of rights)

  - 권리자의 동의, 허가에 의해 판매, 배포된 제품에 대해서는 권리자의 권리가 소진된다는 이론
  - 병렬수입 (parallel importation)과 연관이 있는 것으로 권리 소진 이론이 부정되면 병렬수입이 금지됨.

* 병렬수입(parallel importation)의 예

  - 외국의 A 라는 권리자가 우리나라의 甲에게, license 를 해준 경우, 甲이 license 를 통해 제조한 제품을 외국에 수출하는 것 (외국의 입장에서는 수입이 됨).

o 검토의견

- 아국에 관련 규정 및 판례는 없으나 권리소진 이론의 규정을 지지하며, 이와 관련한 parallel importation이 허용되어야 한다는 입장임.

. 권리자의 동의에 의해 판매 되었으면 권리자가 그 판매행위를 통해 이익을 얻은 것임.

- 강제실시권을 통해 생산된 제품의 수출금지 규정과도 연관

. 즉, parallel importation 이 금지된다면, 강제실시권을 통해 생산된 제품을 수출할수 없게됨.

. 그러나, 진보된 발명(즉, 이용발명)을 이유로 한 강제실시권의 경우 후발명자가 강제실시권을 통해 생산한 제품을 수출할 수 있어야 한다는 입장이며, 그 이유는 이용발명을 이유로 한 강제실시권은 징벌적인(punitive) 성격인 불충분한 실시로 인한 강제실시권과 성격상 차이가 있고 점차 급증하고 있는 이용발명의 권리를 부당하게 제한할 수 없기 때문임.

o 아측입장

- 권리소진 이론을 지지하며 parallel importation은 허용되어야 함.

2) 영업비밀 (Trade Secrets)

① 시행절차의 대상

o 미측입장

- Protection for trade secrets that is subject to the enforcement provisions of the agreement (영업비밀을 Enforcement 절차의 적용범위가 되도록 함)

o 검토의견

- Enforcement 절차는 internal measures 와 border measures 로 구성되어 있음.

- 영업비밀을 침해했을 경우에, 영업비밀 보호를 위해 국내 민.형사 절차를 통해 적용하는 것은 수용할 수 있음.

- 그러나 국경조치(border measures) 의 경우에는 문제 있음.

. 즉, 세관당국이 영업비밀, 특허등의 침해여부를 판단할 전문 능력이 없으므로 인정할 경우 부당한 절차 남발로 국제교역에 막대한 지장 초래

o 아측입장

- 영업비밀을 시행절차의 대상으로 하여 효과적으로 보호하는 것은 찬성함.

- 그러나, 시행절차중 국경조치의 적용대상으로 할 경우 불확실한 조치의 남발로 정상적인 국제교역에 장애를 초래할 우려가 있으므로 반대함.

② 정부제출자료 보호

o 미측입장

- A period of exclusive use for registration data provided to governments (정부에 제출한 자료를 일정기간 타인이 사용하는 것을 금지)

o 검토의견

- 정부에 제출한 자료(ex. 임상실험자료등)를 일정기간 보호하는 것은 특허기간외에 추가적인 독점권을 권리자에게 인정하는 것이 됨.

- 미국에서도 저약가 정책을 위해 특허기간이 만료된 물질에 대해서 타인이 제조허가 신청시 전 임상실험자료를 제출하지 않고 생물학적 동등성 실험자료만 제출하도록 하여 전 임상실험 자료를 원용할 수 있도록 하고 있음 (Waxman-Hetch 법)

- 일본, EC 도 동등한 취지의 입법을 하고 있으므로 국제관례에 어긋난 것임.

o 이측입장

- 특허권 이외에 추가적으로 독점권을 부여하고 국제관례에도 어긋난 미국주장 수용 불가

3) 시행절차

o 미측입장

- Effective internal and border enforcement to stop both domestic and imported piracy, counterfeiting, and infringement (효과적인 국내, 국경절차 마련)

o 검토의견

- 효과적인 국내, 국경절차를 마련하는 것이 필요함.

- 그러나, 국경조치 (border measures)의 경우 적용범위를 저작권, 상표권 침해에 한정되어야 함.

. 세관당국에 전문적 판단 능력이 없으므로 신뢰성 저하

o 아측입장

- 지적재산권 보호를 위해 효과적인 국내, 국경절차를 마련하는 것은 지지하나,
- 국경조치의 경우 적용범위를 저작권, 상표권 침해로 한정되어야 함.

나. 문화부, 과기처 소관사항

① 컴퓨터 프로그램 보호

o 아측입장

- Protection of Computer Programs as literary works (어문저작물로 보호)

o 검토의견

- 어문저작물로 보호함으로써 보호기간을 연장 (50년) 하고
- 권리침해 판단시 판단범위를 넓혀 자국의 컴퓨터 프로그램의 보호를 강화하자는 의도
  . 어문저작물로 보호할 경우 "복제" 의 문제가 되는 것이 아니라 "표절" 의 문제가 되기 때문
- 아국은 CP를 어문저작물(저작권법)이 아닌 특별법으로 보호하고 있음.
  . 보호기간 : 50년
- 어문저작물로 보호할 경우 침해판단의 범위가 넓어질 우려가 있으므로 원칙상으로는 반대하는 입장
  . 기술성, 산업연관성등 차이가 있음.

o 아측입장

- CP 는 Berne 협약에서 규정하는 어문저작물과는 다른 성격이 있으므로 원칙적으로는 반대함.

② 법인, 단체를 저작권자로 인정

o 미측입장

- Recognition of the u.S. "works for hire" regime that permits legal persons (e.g. companies) to be "authors" and to excercise their legal rights (법인, 회사등을 저작자로 인정)

o 검토의견

- 연구단체가 개발한 저작물, 컴퓨터 프로그램에 대해 법인, 단체가 권리를 갖도록 하자는 것.

- 우리법 (저작권법) 에서 법인을 저작권자로 인정하고 있음.

o 아측입장 : 미측 입장 수용가능

③ 음반, 컴퓨터 프로그램의 보호기간

o 미측입장

- 50-year term (50년 보호)

o 검토의견

- 우리법에서는 보호기간이 음반의 경우 20년, 컴퓨터 프로그램의 경우 50년임.

√ - 저작인접권 보호에 관한 Rome 협약에서도 음반의 보호기간을 20년을 규정하고 있음.

~ 日本 [illegible]

o 아측입장

- 원 저작권에 파생된 권리인 음반등 저작인접권의 보호기간을 저작권과 동등하게 50년으로 하는 것은 무리이며 국제관례 (Rome 협약) 도 20년을 규정하고 있으므로

- 따라서, 음반의 경우는 50년을 주장하는 미측 주장을 받아들이기는 어려움.

④ 대여권 (유럽 : 비디오 대여권 인정 요구
미. 일 : 음반 ")

o 미측입장

- neighboring right to control the rental of sound recordings and computer programs(음반, 컴퓨터 프로그램에 대한 대여권 인정)

o 검토의견

- 권리소진이론에 의해 수용 불가

- 대여권은 대여금지권과 보상청구권으로 구분할 수 있음.
  . 대여금지권을 인정할 경우 국내 대여업계의 붕괴를 초래할 우려가 있으므로 수용불가하나 보상청구권으로는 수용 가능

ex) 국내 Video 업계 현황
  - VTR 보급대수 : 400만대 ('90) → 1,000만대 ('95)
  - Video shop : 25,000 여개소
  - 외국 Video 수입 : 약 4,000 종/년
    . 1종당 2,000 - 20,000회 복제
    . 편당 10 - 20회 대여

o 아측입장

- 대여권을 보상청구권으로는 수용 가능하나 대여금지권으로는 수용불가

⑤ 공공실연 (public performance)

o 미측입장 : 공공실연에 대한 명백한 정의 규정

- a clear definition of public performance

o 검토의견

- 'public' 의 개념 정의에 관한 내용임.

. TRIPs 협정안 14조와 관련하여 'public' 의 개념을 축소 정의해 저작권의 제한을 축소하려는 의도

- 각국은 공공목적(public)의 개념을 도입해 저작권에 제한을 기하고 있음.

ex) 학교교육을 위한 전재, 시사보도, 비영리목적의 방송등

o 이측입장

- 명백한 정의를 하는 것을 원칙적으로 지지하나 일정범위내에서 공공 목적을 위한 사용은 허용되이야 함.

- 현 TRIPs 협정안 (14조) 규정대로 라면 지지함.

* TRIPs 협정안

Article 14: Definition of Public
The term "public" shall not be defined in domestic law of PARTIES in a manner that conflicts with a normal commercial exploitation of a work and unreasonably prejudices the legitimate interests of right holders.

13

0112

⑥ 저작인격권 (moral rights)

o 미측입장

- Exclusion of moral rights (저작인격권 제외)

* 저작인격권 (moral rights)

- 저작권은 저작재산권(economic rights)과 저작인격권(moral rights) 으로 구성

- 저작재산권은 복제, 판매, 배포, 수입권등을 말함.

- 저작인격권은 성명표시권, 공표권, 동일성 유지권을 말함.

o 검토의견

√ - 저작권중 지작인격권을 제외하고 지작재산권만 인정하는 것은 영미법계의 특징

. 영국도 '88 저작권법에 의해 지작인격권을 인정함으로써 미국만 지작인격권을 도입않는 국가가 되었음.

. ~~미국은 저작권 분야에서 유럽보다 후진국이기 때문~~

이국 지작권법에서는 지작인격권 인정

- TRIPs 의 저작권분야가 Berne plus Approach 를 채택하고 있으며, Berne 협약에도 지작인격권을 규정하고 있으므로 지작인격권이 인정 되어야 할 것임.

o 아측입장

- 지적재산권 보호를 위해 국제적으로 인정 가능한 minimum standard 규정을 추구하고 있는 TRIPs 협정에서 Berne 협약에도 인정되고 있는 저작인격권을 제외하자는 것을 수용할 수 없음.

- 그러나, TRIPs 협정에 moral rights 를 제외한다 해도 아국에의 영향은 없음.

- 따라서, TRIPs 협상에서 미측입장에 대해 공개적인 반대 의사표시는 하지 않아도 될 것임. 그러나 공개적인 지지는 할 수 없음.

⑦ Data Base 보호

o 미측입장

- Protection for data bases (data base 보호)

o 검토의견

- 현재 보호 법률은 없으나 보호를 위한 입법 추진 예정

o 아측입장 : 수용 가능

다. 상공부 소관시항 (반도체칩 배치설계)

o 미측입장

Protection equal to that found in current U.S. law, which goes well beyond that provided under the Washington Treaty .
(미국법에 준한 보호)

o 검토의견

√- 최종제품(final product)을 보호할 경우 컴퓨터, 항공기등 제품에 침해한 IC 하나만 들어 있어도 컴퓨터등 그 자체가 침해한 제품이 되므로 교역에 장애 초래 가능

- Royalty 청구시 IC chip 보다 IC를 내장한 제품에 대해 royalty를 청구하는 것이 합법화되이 royalty 부담 증가 초래

. 국내 입법(안) 에도 최종제품은 제외

o 아측입장

- 미측 입장 수용 불가

라. 공통사항

1) 경과기간 (Transitional Period)

o 미측입장

- Countries should agree to implement the agreement within a period not to exceed two years (2년)

o 검토의견

- 아직 경과기간에 대한 구체적인 논의가 이루어진 적이 없음.

o 아측입장

- 개도국의 기술.경제 사정을 고려하여 충분한 경과기간이 마련되어야 함. 2년

- 구체기간은 정치적인 사항이므로 입장 미정립

2) GATTability

o 미측입장

- The agreement should be implemented as part of the GATT system (GATT 체제의 일부분으로 운영)

o 검토의견

- GATTability 지지

IV. 한국측 요청(안)

1. 필요성 및 제기방향

o 한.미 양자협의 개최를 전제로 할때 미국측 요청사항에 대해 수세적인 검토만 할 것이 아니라 우리의 관심사항중 미국의 지지를 요청할 사항에 대해 적극적으로 제기할 필요 있음.

o 우리측 제기사항은 협상안의 2안과 3안을 중심으로 작성

- 우리측 관심사항에 대해 명백히 하고 미국의 지지 요청

. 2안, 3안의 내용이 이미 협상에서 이측이 제기해 오던 사항이므로 협상안의 사전 노출이라는 우려는 없음.

2. 한국측 요청(안)

가. 저작권

① 음반, 영상저작물에 대한 대여권 인정 반대
② Rome 협약의 불소급보호 원칙에 부합하는 음반 보호

나. 특 허

① 국제적으로 채택하고 있는 선출원주의 채택
② 불특허대상으로 동.식물 변종 포함
③ 이용발명을 이유로 한 강제실시권을 통해 생산된 제품 수출 가능
④ 입증책임전환 요건 제한 (신물질의 경우만 적용)

다. 반도체칩 배치설계

① 보호범위를 배치설계, IC chip 으로 한정

② 선의 구매자의 보상책임 반대

라. 영업비밀

① 정부제출 자료를 일정기간 타인이 원용할 수 없다는 것 반대

마. 시행절차

① 국경조치의 적용범위 제한 (저작권, 상표권 침해에 한정)

바. 기 타

① 분쟁예방절차 제안 지지

② 경과규정 지지

UR/TRIPs 협상 실무 소위원회 회의 결과

1. 회의 목적 : 9월 중순경 개최 한.미 양자협의 대책 논의

2. 일시 및 장소 : '91. 8.13(화), 특허청

3. 참석자 : 특허청 기획관리관 회의 주재
관련부처 (외무, 경기원, 상공, 보사, 문화, 과기처) 담당 사무관 참석

4. 회의 내용

가. 한.미 양자협의 수용 여부

o 실무급 회의든, 고위급 회의든 TRIPs 한.미 양자협의 수용 거부할 이유없음.

o 양자협의시 미측 관심사항에 대한 아국 입장 제시뿐 아니라, 적극적 자세에서 미측에 Non Paper 형식으로 아국 관심사항 전달 검토중

나. 미측 관심사항 검토

o 주요 쟁점사항

- 컴퓨터 프로그램

. 미측 입장 : 어문 저작물로 보호

. 과기처 입장 : 어문 저작물로 보호할 경우 침해 판단의 범위가 넓어질 우려가 있으므로 미측 입장 수용 불가

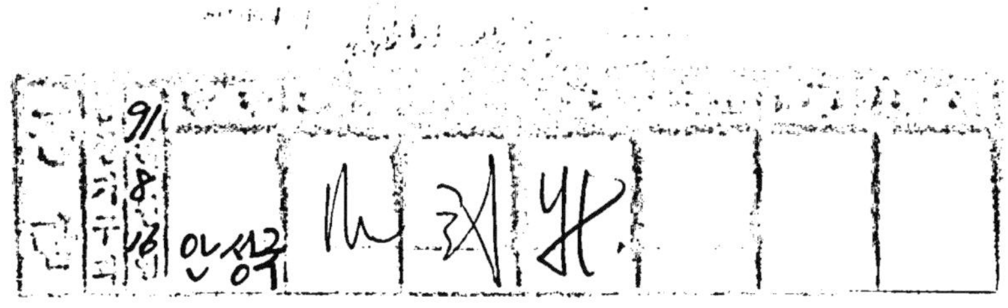

0118

. 특허청 입장 : 아국의 컴퓨터 프로그램 보호법에 의한 보호와 저작권법에서의 보호간 거의 차이가 없으므로 미측 입장 수용 가능

o 기타 상세사항 : 별첨 회의자료 참조

첨 부 : UR/TRIPs 한.미 양자협의 대책. 끝.

0119

원 본

외 무 부

종 별 :

번 호 : GVW-1540 일 시 : 91 0816 1830

수 신 : 장 관(통기,경기원,상공부,특허청)

발 신 : 주 제네바 대사

제 목 : UR/TRIPS 협상 그룹 의장 NOTE

8.13 자 배포된 UR/TRIPS 협상 그룹 의장 NOTE의 주요 내용을 하기 보고하니 9.16 부터 시작되는 동협상 그룹 회의 준비등 필요 조치 바람.

1. 회의기간

0 공식 회의: 9.16(월) 오후 개최

9.20(금) 오전 폐회(필요시 오후에 폐회)

0 비공식회의: 9.17(화)-19(목)

. 필요시 9.20(금) 오전까지 연장 가능

2. 공식 회의 의제

1) 위조 상품 교역을 포함한 무역 관련 지적재산권에 관한 협상 현황

(MFN.TNC/2/35/REV. 1 페이지 193-237)

2) 차기 협상 그룹 회의 준비 사항을 포함한 기타업무

3. 아국 서면 제안에 관한 토의

0 공식회의 의제 1항 토의시 아국이 제안한 '기술이전 관련 분쟁 예방 제도 설치'에 관해 아국 대표에게 제안 설명의 기회가 부여되고 이에대한 타국 대표들의 COMMENT 가 있을 것임.

4. 비공식 회의에서 토의 사항

1) 제 73조 (협정 발효시 기존재하는 지적 재산권보호)

2) 분쟁해결 절차

3) 브랏셀 회의시 제출된 의정 보고서 내용중주요 관심사항 (MTN.TNC/W/35/REV.1페이지 193-195)

5. 동 의장 NOTE 는 별첨 FAX 로 송부함. 끝

(GVW(F)-205) (대사-국장)

통상국 2차보 경기원 상공부 특허청

PAGE 1 91.08.17 09:45 WG

외신 1과 통제관

0120

Trade-Related Aspects of Intellectual Property Rights, including Trade in Counterfeit Goods

13 August 1991

GUW(Fi) - 205

ORGANISATION OF MEETING OF WEEK OF 16 SEPTEMBER 1991

Note from the Chairman

When the Group met on 27-28 June, it agreed to reserve the week of 16 September for its next meeting. At the end of the June meeting, I presented some ideas for the organisation of the Group's work in September but indicated that I would prefer to put them forward in more specific form after the July meeting of the TNC when a clearer picture of progress in the Uruguay Round as a whole would be available. The purpose of this note is thus to put to you such suggestions.

As indicated in June, I would envisage the September meeting as following broadly the same format as that in June, namely relatively brief formal opening and closing sessions with the time in-between devoted to informal consultations. My intention would be to call the opening formal session for the afternoon of Monday 16 September, and to hold the closing formal session on the morning of Friday 20 September, or in the afternoon of that day if further time is required.

The agenda I intend to propose for the formal meeting is as follows:

I. Status of the Negotiations on Trade-Related Aspects of Intellectual Property Rights, including Trade in Counterfeit Goods (MTN.TNC/W/35/Rev.1, pages 193-237).

II. Other Business, including Arrangements for the Next Meeting of the Negotiating Group.

Under agenda item I, an opportunity would be offered to the delegation of the Republic of Korea to introduce its proposal for the Establishment of a Dispute Prevention System in respect of the Transfer of Technologies (MTN.GNG/TRIPS/W/1) and for any comments that other delegations would wish to make or questions they would wish to put on the proposal.

Turning to the informal consultations, as indicated in June I would propose taking up: first, Article 73 of the draft Agreement on Trade-Related Aspects of Intellectual Property Rights, including Trade in Counterfeit Goods (MTN.TNC/W/35/Rev.1, page 228); then, dispute settlement (Annex to draft Agreement on Trade-Related Aspects of Intellectual Property Rights, including Trade in Counterfeit Goods, MTN.TNC/W/35/Rev.1, pages 229-231); and, finally, each of the other outstanding issues as listed in the commentary on TRIPS on pages 193-195 of MTN.TNC/W/35/Rev.1.

Of all the outstanding issues, Article 73, the Protection of Existing Intellectual Property, is the one where there appears to be the widest view that further technical work and some redrafting is necessary. While there are some issues of a more political nature that are closely related, I am confident that it is possible to do useful work on the technical aspects of

0121

Article 73 without necessarily attempting to deal with those more political issues as well. The annexed note is aimed at facilitating the work on Article 73. As indicated in my report to the GNG (MTN.GNG/W/28), this is intended as a checklist of decisions that have to be taken on Article 73. Given the stage reached in the work on TRIPS and in order to make the basic decisions required as clear as possible, it seemed best to place them in a draft text using square brackets. The text is a revised draft of Article 73 that aims to take account of the discussions on this provision in Brussels. For the sake of clarity, the square brackets reflect the range of the views presented without indicating the intermediate options that might be considered. For example, in previous discussions it has been suggested that some but not all of the provisions of Part II should apply to patents, designs etc. already under protection. It is my hope that the discussion in September on the basis of the Annex will enable the preparation of something close to the final draft of Article 73. Some explanatory notes have been added in the hope that they will assist participants in their preparations for that discussion.

As regards dispute settlement, the Annex to the draft Agreement on Trade-Related Aspects of Intellectual Property Rights, including Trade in Counterfeit Goods contains three draft texts indicating the range of options put before the Group. It will be recalled that the reason for this is that dispute settlement procedures are closely related to the question of the institutional arrangements for the international implementation of the results of the negotiations, on which there are different views and which question is specifically left for decision by Ministers when the results of the negotiations are established. Even if in September there continues to be a perception that the time is not yet ripe for attempting to move towards one text on dispute settlement, I believe that the Group would do valuable work in examining in detail the three proposals so as to maximise understanding of their respective provisions and implications. This part of the informal consultations would also provide an opportunity for any further discussion that delegations may wish on the Korean proposal on the Establishment of a Dispute Prevention System in respect of the Transfer of Technologies.

The third major item for informal discussion would be the remaining outstanding issues in the texts sent to Brussels as listed in the commentary on pages 193-195 of MTN.TNC/W/35/Rev.1. In introducing each of these points, it will be my intention to describe the work done at the Brussels Ministerial meeting, indicating the subjects discussed, any new ideas or proposals which emerged and, where possible, where there seemed to be some convergence of views. It is my hope that it will be possible for the work in September on these outstanding issues not only to take stock of the work done at Brussels and provide an opportunity for any further clarification of positions that participants feel necessary but also to aim at taking decisions. This will, of course, depend in large part on perceptions of delegations of the stage reached at that time in the Uruguay Round as a whole.

0122

In the closing formal session of the Negotiating Group, it would be my plan to make a detailed report on the informal consultations held, including on the description of the work undertaken at Brussels.

I should make it clear that it is not my intention to exclude, by this programme of work, further consideration of those points in MTN.TNC/W/35/Rev.1 which are not listed in the introductory commentary. However, I would expect that the work programme I have outlined would require the time available to this Group in the week of 16 September and that a final reading of the remaining parts of the text would have to be undertaken somewhat later.

Notes on paragraph 1

1. This provision would cover all subject matter created on or after the date of application.

2. It would also cover existing subject matter that might be or become capable of protection as a trademark or a geographical indication or as undisclosed information. Unlike subject matter protected under copyright and related rights, industrial design, patents and rights in layout-designs of integrated circuits, eligibility of existing subject matter for protection as a trademark or a geographical indication or as undisclosed information is not irredeemably lost because the subject matter is no longer new, or because procedures for acquisition or maintenance of protection have not been fulfilled within a certain period after its creation or becoming publicly known or used, or because it is subject to a finite term of protection which has expired.

3. It should be noted that the approach adopted in drafting the Sections of the Agreement on Trademarks and Geographical Indications has been to put within them rules aimed at protecting the interests of prior users of existing subject matter that might subsequently come under protection.

4. In previous discussions, a question was raised as to whether PARTIES should be obliged to apply the term of trademark protection provided under the Agreement to existing trademark registrations.

5. The opening phrase, "subject to the provisions of paragraph 2 below", is intended to take account of the possibility that paragraph 1 might otherwise be capable of being interpreted as obliging PARTIES to protect existing works, phonograms and broadcasts not older than the relevant term of protection laid down in the Agreement; and maybe also some existing industrial designs and integrated circuits not older than the relevant term of protection, particularly where a PARTY chooses to implement its TRIPS obligations through a form of protection that requires no formalities to be met. Such a rule would go beyond what is required by virtue of the reference to Article 18 of the Berne Convention in Article 15 of the TRIPS text as well as by virtue of the reference to Article 16(3) of the Treaty on the Protection of Intellectual Property in Respect of Integrated Circuits in Article 38 of the TRIPS text. It might also mean important differences in the treatment of existing industrial designs and layout-designs between countries requiring formalities to be met and those not doing so.

Notes on paragraph 2

1. This provision deals with existing subject matter in the areas of copyright and related rights, industrial designs, patents and the layout-design of integrated circuits. Newly created subject matter in these areas is covered by paragraph 1. It also raises the question as to whether any test data protection that might be agreed under Section 7 should be subject to the rules of this paragraph.

0124

2. The paragraph deals with four situations concerning subject matter existing as of the date of application of the Agreement:

First sentence:	Subject matter already under protection.
First part of second sentence	Subject matter in respect of which the decision on the grant of a title is pending.
Second part of second sentence	Subject matter in respect of which procedures for the acquisition of protection can still be validly initiated.
Third sentence	Other subject matter, i.e. not falling under sentences one or two. This would be subject matter often referred to as in the public domain.

3. In regard to the provisions of Article 11 on rental rights, it will be recalled that the scope of Article 15 is limited to the "rights secured under [the Berne] Convention" so as to ensure that it did not cover rental rights. Under the present draft of Article 73, the question of the application of rental rights to existing intellectual property is the same way as that of the application of patent, industrial design and layout-design rights to existing subject matter in these areas.

<u>Note on paragraph 3</u>

Paragraph 1 of Article 2 of Part I is dealt with in accordance with the rules in paragraphs 1 and 2 because, although it figures in Part I, it concerns minimum standards.

<u>Notes on paragraph 4</u>

1. The term "intellectual property" is defined in Article 1.2 of the Agreement.

2. The final phrase in square brackets is an invitation to consider whether there should be an obligation to apply Part IV to procedures and formalities already initiated at the time of application of the Agreement.

0125

ANNEX

Article 73: Protection of Existing Intellectual Property

1. Subject to the provisions of paragraph 2 below, each PARTY shall apply the provisions of Part II of this Agreement to subject matter which is protectable in its territory by virtue of the application of the criteria for protection, as laid down in this Agreement, as of or after the date of application of the provisions of this Agreement for that PARTY as defined in Part VI of the Agreement (referred to in this Article as "the date of application").

2. [No PARTY is obliged to] [Each PARTY shall] apply the provisions of Sections 1, 4, 5 and 6 [and of paragraph 4A of Section 7] of Part II to subject matter under protection in that PARTY as of the date of application, subject to the provisions of Article 15 [and of Article 16.6]. Where the acquisition of protection is subject to procedural requirements, a PARTY [is not obliged to] [shall] apply the provisions of these Sections to subject matter in respect of which procedures for the acquisition of protection have been initiated before, but not completed by, the date of application, [and] [but] shall apply these provisions to subject matter existing as of that date in respect of which procedures for the acquisition of protection can still be validly initiated in the sense that the criteria for protection can still be satisfied. Nothing in this Agreement shall oblige a PARTY to apply the provisions of Part II to other existing subject matter covered by these Sections, subject to the provisions of Article 15 [and of Article 16.6].

3. The application of paragraph 1 of Article 2 of Part I of this Agreement shall be governed by paragraphs 1 and 2 of this Article as appropriate to the intellectual property right in question.

4. With effect from the date of application, each PARTY shall apply the provisions of Articles 3, 4, 5 and 6 of Part I, Part III and Part IV with respect to all intellectual property. However, no PARTY is obliged to apply the provisions of Part III with respect to causes of action which occurred prior to the date of application [, or to apply the provisions of Part IV to procedures and formalities initiated prior to that date.]

0126

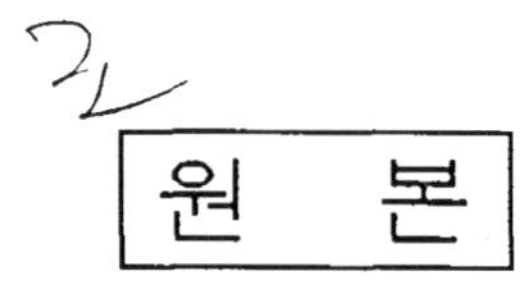

외 무 부

종 별 :

번 호 : GVW-1624 일 시 : 91 0830 1100

수 신 : 장 관(통기,경기원,특허청)

발 신 : 주 제네바 대사

제 목 : UR/TRIPS 회의 개최

1. GVW-1540 (91.8.16 자) 관련임.

2. 표제 회의가 아래와 같이 개최되는바 동회의에 참석할 아국 정부 대표단의 명단을 조속통보 바람.

0 회의기간: 9.16-20 (개회 9.16 오후 3시)

0 장소: 갓트 회의실

0 의제

- 위조 상품 교역을 포함한 무역 관련 지적재산권에 관한 협상 현황(MFN.TNC/W/35/REV.1.페이지 193-237)

- 차기 회의 준비 사항을 포함한 기타 업무

첨부: 표제회의 의제 1부. 끝(GVW(F)-317

(대사 박수길-국장)

통상국 구주국 경기원 특허청

PAGE 1 91.08.30 22:15 FL

외신 1과 통제관

0127

GVW(기)-0317 10830 1600

GVW-1624 관련

GATT/AIR/3226

28 AUGUST 1991

SUBJECT: URUGUAY ROUND NEGOTIATING GROUP ON THE TRADE-RELATED ASPECTS OF INTELLECTUAL PROPERTY RIGHTS, INCLUDING TRADE IN COUNTERFEIT GOODS

1. THE NEGOTIATING GROUP ON TRADE-RELATED ASPECTS OF INTELLECTUAL PROPERTY RIGHTS, INCLUDING TRADE IN COUNTERFEIT GOODS WILL MEET ON 16-20 SEPTEMBER, STARTING AT 3 P.M. ON 16 SEPTEMBER IN THE CENTRE WILLIAM RAPPARD.

2. THE FOLLOWING AGENDA IS PROPOSED FOR THE MEETING:

A. STATUS OF THE NEGOTIATIONS ON THE TRADE-RELATED ASPECTS OF INTELLECTUAL PROPERTY RIGHTS, INCLUDING TRADE IN COUNTERFEIT GOODS (MTN.TNC/W/35/REV.1, PAGES 193-237);

B. OTHER BUSINESS, INCLUDING ARRANGEMENTS FOR THE NEXT MEETING OF THE NEGOTIATING GROUP.

3. GOVERNMENTS PARTICIPATING IN THE MULTILATERAL TRADE NEGOTIATIONS, AND INTERNATIONAL ORGANIZATIONS WHICH HAVE PREVIOUSLY ATTENDED PROCEEDINGS OF THIS NEGOTIATING GROUP, WISHING TO BE REPRESENTED AT THIS MEETING ARE REQUESTED TO INFORM ME AS SOON AS POSSIBLE OF THE NAMES OF THEIR REPRESENTATIVES.

A. DUNKEL

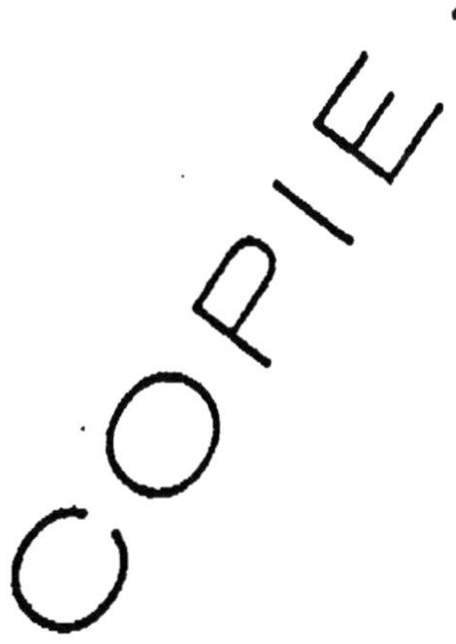

91-1194

0128

1-1

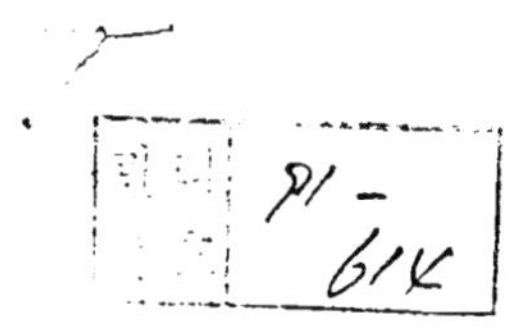

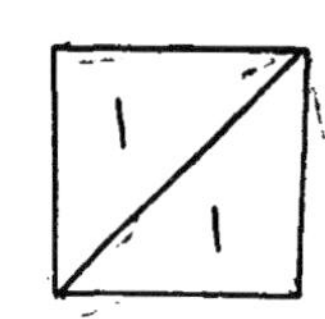

특 허 청

국협 28140-22　　568-6077　　1991. 9. 10.

수신 외무부장관

참조 통상국장

제목 '91 제2차 GATT/UR TRIPs 협상그룹회의 참가

'91.9.16 - 20간 스위스 제네바에서 개최되는 '91 제2차 GATT/UR TRIPs 협상그룹회의에 아래와 같이 참가하고자 하오니 정부대표 임명등 필요한 조치를 취해 주시기 바랍니다.

아 래

1. 회 의 명 : '91 제2차 GATT/UR TRIPs 협상그룹 회의
2. 기간 및 장소 : '91. 9.16 - 20, 스위스 제네바 GATT 본부
3. 참 가 자

소 속	직 위	성 명	비 고
특 허 청	국제협력담당관	권 영 수	수석대표
"	WIPO 주재관	김 준 규	대표(현지참석)
"	국제협력과 사무관	이 찬 우	대 표
	변 리 사	김 창 세	자문관

4. 출장기간 : 9.13(금) - 22(일) (9박 10일)

* 권영수 국제협력담당관은 연이어 개최되는 13차 WIPO 총회에 참가 (WIPO 총회 관련서류는 별도 송부할 계획임)

전 결		4856	결재(공람)		
접수일	1991 9.10	번호			
처리과					

0129

국협 28140-　　　　　　　　　　　　　　　　　　　　　　91.9.10.

5. 소요경비 : $ 7,068

6. 경비부담 : 특허청 소관예산

(단, 김창세 변리사 여비는 기획원에서 부담)

첨부 1. 회의의제 1부.

2. 대표별 업무분장 1부.

3. 세부여행일정 및 활동계획서 1부.

4. 국.영문 이력서 1부.

5. 경비내역 1부.

6. UR/TRIPs 협상전망및 대책

특　　허　　청

0130

1. 회의 의제

가. 분쟁해결절차

나. 경과규정

다. 기타 쟁점 의제

라. 차기 협상계획

0131

2. 대표별 업무분장

소 속	직 위	성 명	비 고
특 허 청	국제협력담당관	권 영 수	대 표 협상총괄 및 대표단 지휘
"	WIPO 주재관	김 준 규	대 표 협상지원 및 본부청훈 업무
"	국제협력담당관실 사무관	이 찬 우	대 표 대표단 실무담당
	변 리 사	김 창 세	자문관 대표단 활동에 대한 자문

0132

3. 세부여행 일정 및 활동계획서

일 자	활 동 계 획	비 고
9.13 (금)	서울 발 (KE 901), 파리경유 제네바 착 (SR 729)	
14 (토)	UR 협상대책 회의	
15 (일)	휴 일	
16 (월)	TRIPs 주요관계국 오찬 주최 오후: UR/TRIPs 회의	
17 (수) / 20 (금)	UR/TRIPs 회의	이찬우 사무관, 김창제 변리사
21 (토)	휴 일	제네바 발 (LH 1855) 프랑크푸르트 경유
22 (일)		서울 착 (KE 906)
23 (월)	WIPO 총회 참가	
24 (화)	제네바 발 (SR 836), 런던 경유	
25 (수)	서울 착 (KE 908)	

0133

4. 경비 내역

(단위 : $)

구 분	항공료	일 비	숙박비	식 비	판공비	계
4급 권영수	2,127	260	809	552	-	3,748
5급 이찬우	2,106	200	594	420		3,320
계	4,233	460	1,403	972		7,068

* 김창세 변리사 경비는 기획원에서 부담.

o 권영수 국제협력담당관 (12박 13일)

- 항공료 : $ 2,127
- 일 비 : $ 20 x 13일 = $ 260
- 숙박비 : $ 83 x 1박 = $ 83
  $ 66 x 11박 = $ 726
- 식 비 : $ 48 x 1일 = $ 48
  $ 42 x 12일 = $ 504

계 : $ 3,748

o 이찬우 사무관 (9박 10일)

- 항공료 : $ 2,106
- 일 비 : $ 20 x 10일 = $ 200
- 숙박비 : $ 66 x 9박 = $ 594
- 식 비 : $ 42 x 10일 = $ 420

계 : $ 3,320

0134

특 허 청

호 91- 1991. . .

본전을 수신자에게 전달하여 주시기 바랍니다.

수신 : 외무부. 통상기구과 안명수 사무관 귀하

(수신처 FAX No : 725-1737)

발신 : 특허청 국제협력담당관실

(FAX NO : 553-2641)

0135

훈 령 안

I. 기본입장

o '90 Brussels 회의 이후 실질적인 쟁점에 대한 토의가 이루어지는 만큼, 선.개도국의 입장 동향을 파악하고 지적재산권의 권리보호와 기술이전 확산의 균형을 도모한다는 차원에서 선.개도국 주장의 부당성을 지적하고 아국의 입장을 개진함.

o 협상 대응의 구체적인 방향을 9월 6일 UR/대책실무위원회에서 결정된 UR/TRIPs 협상전망 및 대책에 따라 대처함.

- 따라서, 공공목적의 사용, 특허권의 보호기간, 인증제인의 전환요건, 외국 유명상표 보호, 대여권 (보상청구권) 등 5개 분야의 경과기간, 특허의 강제실시권 실시범위, 분쟁예방절차, 경과규정, 음반소급보호, 권리소진 이론, 대여권 (대여금지권), 정부제출자료의 공개 금지, 선의의 IC 구매자, IC 보호, 국경조치 적용범위등 11개 분야에 대하여는 아국입장을 제시

- 저작인격권, 불특허대상, 분쟁해결절차등 3개 분야에 대하여는 협상 진행 대세를 존중하는 입장 제시

- 권리남용 및 반경쟁적 행위, 컴퓨터 프로그램 보호등 2개 분야에 대하여는 아국입장의 구체적 제시를 유보

o 기타 사항은 협상 동향에 따라 신축적으로 대응함.

0136

RECEIVED FROM 1991.09.12 09:22 P. 2

Ⅱ. 세부입장

1. 협상타결을 위해 선.개도국의 교량 역할을 한다는 견지에서 수용이 가능한 분야

o 공공목적의 사용 (Public 의 개념)

- 저작물의 권리자 동의 없이 공공목적을 위해 사용하는 범위 제한

o 특허권의 보호기간

- 권리자의 보호 강화, 국제적인 추세에 부합하기 위해 "출원일로 부터 최소 20년" 수용

o 입증책임의 전환요건

- 입증책임의 전환요건을

. 제법으로 만들어진 물질이 새로운 것인 경우
. 제법간에 실질적인 유사성이 있는 경우

중 하나만 인정해도 문제가 없는 것으로 해석 가능하므로 수용

o 외국 유명상표 보호

- 외국 상표의 유명성에 편승하려는 국내업자를 규제하고 아국 상표의 외국에서의 보호를 증진한다는 측면에서 선진국 입장 수용

o 대여권 (보상청구권)

- 저작물의 대여 행위에 대한 권리를 보상청구권 형식으로 인정

0137

2. 선.개도국간 혹은 선진국 간의 첨예한 이해가 대립되고 있으므로 적극적인 입장 표명을 유보해야할 분야

o 저작인격권

- 저작인격권은 제외하자는 것은 미국만의 주장으로 채택될 가능성이 없으므로 적극적인 입장을 유보

o 특허대상

- 선.개도국 간의 첨예한 이해가 대립되고 있는 정치적인 쟁점의 하나로 선진국 주장대로 채택될 가능성이 없으므로 일단 적극적인 입장 제시를 유보

o 분쟁해결절차

- GATTability 와 직접적으로 연관되는 문제로 cross-sectoral retaliation 과 관련하여 선.개도국 간에 의견이 첨예하게 대립될 것임.

- GATTability 를 지지하고 cross-sectoral retaliation 을 반대하기는 어려우므로 일단 선.개도국의 입장을 파악하고 우리 입장을 유보함.

o 권리남용 및 반경쟁적 행위

- 개도국의 주장으로 기술이전을 확보한다는 측면에서 장.단점이 있고 선.개도국간 이해가 대립되고 있는 분야이므로, 적극적인 입장 표명을 자제하고 아국이 제안한 "분쟁예방절차" 가 기술이전을 받기 위한 장치로 적절하다고 설득

0138

RECEIVED FROM 1991.09.12 09:24 P. 4

- 대상품목별 수출입자 지정

· 한국측 수출자 : 총 37 개업체 (종합상사 8개사, 제조업체등 29 개사)

. 수출자 지정은 우리측이 생산자단체를 통하여 자율적으로 조정한 결과에 따른 우리측안을 중심으로 이루어졌음

. 일부품목은 규격과 디자인이 다양한 품목의 특성과 소측의 요청을 고려하여 중소제조업체 및 관련 종합상사를 추가로 지정

. 소형전동기, 전화선 2 개품목 : 양측 의견차이로 수출자 지정을 보류

· 소련측 수입자 : 총 8 개 국영 수입기관

3. 수출절차 및 수출계약 현황

o 경협자금에 의한 대소 수출의 절차를 규정한 "대소련 원료 및 소비재차관 자금에 의한 수출요령" 을 제정, 시행 (상공부고시, '91.5.29)

- 수출절차

. 수출자는 수출계약 체결전에 상공부에 수출계획을 신고

. 지정된 수출입자간의 수출계약 체결

. 수출자는 수출계약 체결후 상공부에 보고

. 상공부는 차관자금에 의한 수출입을 확인하여 수출입은행에 통보

. 수출입은행의 융자승인 절차를 거쳐 수출품 선적 및 수출대금 지급

o 수출신고수리 및 수출계약체결 현황 ('91.8 말 현재)

- 수출신고수리 : 22 개업체 27 개품목 362백만불

- 수출계약체결 : 16 개업체 20 개품목 180백만불(냉연강판, 면도날, 축전지, 합성섬유사, 타이어코드지, 봉재제품 등)

3

0139

4. 향후 추진사항

o 상공부 및 소련 대외경제성간 실무회의시 ('91.5.20-24) 미합의 사항에 대한 협의

- 물량 미확정 품목에 대한 협의 : 스포츠신발, VCR 및 전자테인지부품, TDI (발포제) 등 3개 품목

- 수출자 미지정 품목에 대한 협의 : 소형전동기, 전화선등 2개 품목

- 소련측이 요청한 신규품목에 대한 협의 : LAB (합성세제원료), 섬유직물, 컨테이너 등

- '91 년 소비재차관 자금중 집행잔액 처리

0140

RECEIVED FROM 02 503 3142 1991.09.12 09:47 P. 4

기 안 용 지

분류기호 서번호	통기 20644-	(전화 : 720 - 2188)	시 행 상 특별취급	
보존기간	영구. 준영구 10. 5. 3. 1.	장 관		
수 신 처 보존기간				
시행일자	1991. 9.12.			

보조기관			협조기관		
	국 장	전 결			문 서 통 제
	심의관				
	과 장				
기안책임자		안 명 수			발 송 인

경 유 수 신 참 조	내부결재	발신명의		
제 목	UR/무역관련 지적재산권(TRIPs) 협상그룹 회의 정부대표 임명			

91.9.16-20간 스위스 제네바에서 개최되는 UR/무역관련

지적재산권 협상그룹 회의에 참가할 정부대표를 "정부대표 및 특별사절의

임명과 권한에 관한 법률"에 의거, 아래와 같이 임명할 것을 건의하니

재가하여 주시기 바랍니다.

- 아 래 -

0141

/뒷면 계속/

1. 회 의 명 : UR/무역관련 지적재산권 협상그룹 회의

2. 회의기간 및 장소 : 91.9.16-20, 스위스 제네바

3. 정부대표

o 특허청 국제협력담당관 권 영수

o 국제협력과 사무관 이찬우

o 변리사 김창세 (자문)

o 주제네바 대표부 관계관

4. 출장기간 : 91.9.13(금)-22(일)

5. 소요경비 : 소속부처 소관예산

6. 훈령(안) : 별도 건의 예정. 끝.

0142

45061

기 안 용 지

분류기호 서번호	통기 20644-	(전화 : 720 - 2188)	시 행 상 특별취급	
보존기간	영구. 준영구 10. 5. 3. 1.	장 관		
수 신 처 보존기간				
시행일자	1991. 9.12.			

보조기관		협조기관		문서통제
국 장	전 결			
심의관				
과 장				
기안책임자	안 명 수			발 송 인

경 유 수 신 참 조	특허청장	발신명의	
제 목	UR/무역관련 지적재산권 협상그룹 회의 정부대표 임명 통보		

91.9.16-20간 스위스 제네바에서 개최되는 UR/무역관련 지적재산권 협상그룹 회의에 참가할 정부대표가 "정부대표 및 특별사절의 임명과 권한에 관한 법률"에 의거 아래와 같이 임명 되었음을 알려 드립니다.

- 아 래 -

/뒷면 계속/

0143

1. 회 의 명 : UR/무역관련 지적재산권 협상그룹 회의

2. 회의기간 및 장소 : 91.9.16-20, 스위스 제네바

3. 정부대표

o 특허청 국제협력담당관 권 영수

o 국제협력과 사무관 이찬우

o 변리사 김창세 (자문)

o 주제네바 대표부 관계관

4. 출장기간 : 91.9.13(금)-22(일)

5. 소요경비 : 소속부처 소관예산

~~6. 훈령(안) : 별도 건의 예정.~~ 끝.

0144

지급

	분류번호	보존기간

발 신 전 보

번 호 : WGV-1223 910913 1945 FO 종별 : 암호송신

수 신 : 주 제네바 대사. 총영사

발 신 : 장 관 (통 기)

제 목 : UR/TRIPs 협상 그룹회의

대 : GVW-1624

1. 9.16-20간 개최되는 표제 회의에 참가할 정부대표를 아래 임명 하였으니 귀관 관계관과 함께 참석토록 조치바람.

(동 본부대표단 9.14(토) 17:20 AF-968 제네바 도착)

- 아 래 -

o 특허청 국제협력담당관 권영수

o 특허청 국제협력과 사무관 이찬우

o 변리사 (자문) 김창세

2. 훈 령

가. 90.12 브랏셀 각료회의후 2번째 공식 회의로서 실질적인 쟁점에 대한 토의가 이루어지는 만큼 각국 입장을 면밀히 파악함.

나. 지적재산권의 보호와 기술이전 확산간의 균형을 도모한다는 차원에서 아국 입장을 개진함.

다. 금번 회의시 의제별 논의시, 9.6 개최된 UR 대책 실무위원회 결과에 따라 대처함.

보안 통제	

앙 고 재	91년 9월 13일	통상기구과	기안자 성명		과 장	심의관	국 장		차 관	장 관
							전결			

외신과통제

0145

1) 아국 입장 제시 분야 :

o 공공목적의 사용, 특허권 보호기간, 입증 책임 전환요건, 유명상표 보호, 대여권(보상 청구권), 경과기간, 특허의 강제 실시범위, 분쟁예방 절차, 경과 규정, 음반 소급 보호, 권리조건, 대여권 (대여 금지권), 정부 제출 자료의 공개금지, 선의의 IC 구매, IC 보호, 국경조치 적용범위

2) 협상 대세 관망 분야

o 저작인격권, 불특허 대상, 분쟁해결 절차와 관련 협상 대세 관망

3) 아측 입장 제시 유보 분야

o 권리남용 및 반경쟁적 행위, 컴퓨터 프로그램 보호

라. 기술이전 관련 분쟁방지 체제 수립에 대한 아국 제안

금번 회의시 동 아국 제안(MTN.GNG/TRIPs/W/1)에 대한 공식 논의가 개시됨을 감안, 각국 입장을 면밀히 파악함. 끝.

(통상국장 김 용 규)

원 본

외 무 부

종 별 :

번 호 : GVW-1763 일 시 : 91 0917 1200

수 신 : 장 관(통기,경기원,상공부,보사부,문화부,과기처,특허청)

발 신 : 주 제네바 대사대리

제 목 : UR/TRIPS 협상(1)

9.16(월) 오후 개최된 표제회의 주요 내용을 하기보고함. (참석: 김 준규 주재관, 권영수 특허청국제 협력담당관, 김창세 변리사, 이찬우사무관)

1. 공식 회의

0 ANELL 의장은 회의 개최를 선포하고 이번회의가 TRIPS 협상의 성공적인 타결을 위해 실질적인 진전을 이룰수 있게 되기를 희망함.

0 금일과 9.20(금)에 공식 회의를 개최하고 9.17-19까지 비공식 회의를 개최할 것이라고 설명하고 아국이 제안한 '분쟁 예방 절차'에 대한 설명을 요청함.

0 아국 대표는 TRIPS 협상의 성공적인 타결과 집행을 위해서는 몇가지 요소가 고려되어야 하며 이중 중요한 요소가 국가간의 기술이전을 촉진 시킬수있는 국제적인 체제가 필요하다고 설명함.

- 이러한 관점에서 아국제안은 TRIPS 협정내에 분쟁예방 절차를 마련 함으로써 국가간 기술이전 계약에서 발생할수 있는 반경쟁적 행위를 규제하는 체제를 마련하고자 하는 것이라고 설명함.

0 콜롬비아는 TRIPS 협정내에 기술이전을 위한 체제를 마련하는 것이 필수불가결 하므로 아국제안을 지지한다고 하였으며, 베네주엘라도 이에 동조함.

- 이집트는 매우 흥미로운 제안이라고 하고 추후에 질문하겠다고 함.

0 미국은 아국제안에 대해 6 가지의 질문을 함.

- 분쟁 당사자 기업 일방이 분쟁예방 절차를 거부하면 어떻게 되는가

- LICENSE REVIEW BOARD 에서 심의하고 있는 동안라이센스 계약은 어떠한 상태에 있게되는가 (계약 체결이 중지 된다면 기술이전을 방해하는 것이 아닌가)

- 67. BIS 1항의 'HAS AN ADVERSE EFFECT' 는 TRIPS협정 8조 2항의 'UNREASONABLY RESTRAIN TRADE'과의차이는 무엇이며 이것은 너무 광범위하므로

통상국 2차보 보사부 문화부 경기원 상공부 과기처 특허청

PAGE 1 91.09.18 09:09 WG

외신 1과 통제관

0147

문제가있는 것이 아닌가

- 주석에 있는 KNOW-HOW 와 TRIPS 협정내에 비공개 정보와의 차이는 무엇인가

- GUIDELINE 설정시 WIPO 의 어느기구와 협의하여 결정한다는 것인가

- 제안이 채택될 경우 구체적인 절차는 어떻게할것인가

0 이에 대해 아국은 다음과 같이 답변함.

- 분쟁 당사자 기어중 어느하나라도 분쟁예방 절차를 거부하면 동 절차가 시작되지 않음.

- LICENSE REVIEW BOARD 가 계약을 심의하고 있는동안 라이센스 계약은 당사작인 기업에 의해 지연되거나 중시될수 있음. 그러나 계약 체결이 주이된다해도 라이센스 계약에 대한 분쟁해결이 이 시스템에 의해 해결된다면 중지기간이 최장 6개월이므로 기술이전을 저해하는 요소로 작용하는 문제는 발생하지 않을 것임.

- 표현의 차이는 구체적인 논의를 통해 TRIPS협정대로 바꿀수 있을 것임.

- KNOW-HOW 로 표현함으로서 TRIPS 협정의 비공개정보보다 범위를 줄이려고 하는것임.

- WIPO 어느기구와 협의할 것인가는 문제가 되지않음.

- 구체적인 절차는 TRIPS 위원회에서 결정될것임.

0 홍콩은 분쟁해결 절차와 분쟁예방 절차와의 상관관계에 대해 좀더 검토해야 할 것이라고 지적하였으며, 이에 대해 아국은 국가간 조약 의무위반으로 인한 분쟁과 기업간의 분쟁은 차이가있는 것이라고 함.

0 ANELL 의장은 구체적인 토의가 비공식회의에서 이루어질 것이라고 함.

2. 아국 주최 비공식 오찬 회의

0 아국은 12:00 호주, 스위스, 홍콩 등 7개국을 초청하여 아국제안에 대한 의견을 사전에 교환하였음.

0 스위스는 아국 제안의 기본적인 아이디어는 좋으나 실질적으로 TRIPS 위원회의 역할과 43조의 반경쟁적 행위에 대한 논의가 이루어지지 않은 상태이므로 차후에 논의 하는 것이 어떤가 하는 의견을 제시하였음.

0 홍콩은 기본적으로 좋으나 GATT 에서 국가간의 분쟁이 아닌 사기업간의 분쟁을 어떻게 해결할수 있는 가에 대해 의문을 제시하고 국가간의 분쟁해결 절차와 사기업간의 분쟁예방 절차와의 관계가 좀더 구체적으로 명백히 해야 할것이라고 함.

0 전반적으로 아국제안에 대해 동조하나 구체적인 절차, 내용에 대해 공식회의 비

공식 회의에서 좀더 명확히 해줄것을 대부분의 국가가 요구함.끝

(차석대사 김삼훈-국장)

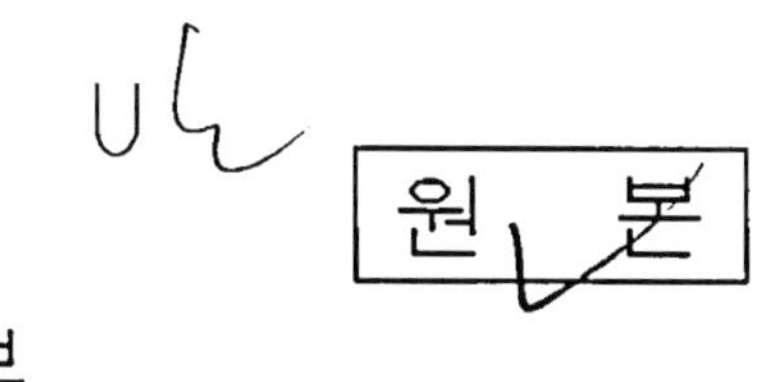

외 무 부

종 별 :

번 호 : GVW-1778 일 시 : 91 0919 1030

수 신 : 장관(통기,경기원,상공부,보사부,문화부,과기처,특허청)

발 신 : 주 제네바 대사대리

제 목 : UR/TRIPS 협상(2) [91V

9.17(화) 속개된 표제회의 주요 내용을 하기 보고함.

0 ANELL 의장은 회의 모두가 사무국에서 새로 작성한 ART. 73(경과규정)이 최종안이 아니라 토의를 위한 것이라는 것을 전제하고 73조의 전체적인 구조에 대해 설명함.

- EGYPT 동 문제가 매우 복잡하고 어려운 문제이므로 각국 법에 맡기자고 주장하고 인도와 중국은 사무국이 다시 작성한 배경 설명을 요청함.

- 이에 대해 ANELL 의장은 73조가 정치적인 문제와 기술적인 문제의 양면성을갖고 있다고 하고 이번에 새로이 작성한 이유는 73조의 기술적인 문제를 검토하기 ◦ 위한것이라고 함.

0 홍콩과 콜롬비아가 73조안에 PART I (기본원칙)의 적용에 대해서는 언급이 되어있지 않다고 주장하고 ANELL 의장은 73조가 MINIMUM STANDARD 로서 PART II (보호기준) 적용에관해서만 논의하는 것이므로 PART I 의 적용에관한것은 각국이 결정하면될 것이라고 설명함.

0 73조의 전체적인 접근 방식에 대해 홍콩은 ROME 협약처럼 불소급 보호원칙을천명하고 각개별 권리의 특수성을 고려하여 예외를 두는 방식으로 하자고 함.

- 칠레도 이에 동조하고 기본원칙부터 정하자고 주장함.

- EC 는 권리별로 차별하지 않고 전체에 대해 몇가지 기준을 정하자고 함.

0 이에 대해 ANELL 의장은 권리별로 구분하여규정하려고 하는 것이 아니라 각권리에 대한 이해를 증진하고 협상을 하기 위해서 현재대로 규정된것이라고 설명함.

- 그러나, 미국이 개별 권리별로 경과 규정에 따른 문제점을 검토할 것을 요청하고, 호주, 홍콩, EC등이 상표의 경우 선사용자 (PRIOR USER), 저작권의 경우

통상국 2차보 청와대 안기부 보사부 문화부 경기원 상공부 과기처
특허청

PAGE 1 91.09.20 03:46 DW

외신 1과 통제관

0150

새로운권리인 대여권의 적용문제에 대해 언급을 하게 되자, ANELL의장도 각 권리별로 문제점을 검토하자고 함.

0 각권리별로 논의된 사항은 다음과 같음.

- 저작권에 대해서는 대여권의 적용시점을 언제부터 할 것인가에 대해 카나다,홍콩등이 문제를 제기했으며, EC, 미국은 협정 적용일이후의 대여 행위에 대해서작용하면 될것이라고함.

. 일본은 베른 협약의 규정이 컴퓨터 프로그램과 데이타 베이스 보호에는 적용되지 않으며, 음반에대해서는 ROME 협약이 있으므로 저작권은 베른협약, 인접권에는ROME 협약, 새로운 권리는 TRIPS 협정 적용일에 의해 적용해야 한다고 주장하였음.이에 대해 아국도 동조함.

. 노르딕, 인도는 소급적용을 반대한다고 하였으며, 홍콩은 베른 협약의 소급적용에 관한 규정은 각 국가의 해석에 따르면 될것이라고 함.

. 스위스는 새로운 권리의 적용 시점에 대해 아국이 베른 협약 가입시에 적용한경과 조치를 기준으로 좀더 연구, 검토를 해야 할 것이라고 함.

- 상표에 대해서는 선 사용자 보호문제, 서비스표 도입시의 문제가 거론됨.

- 의장과 특허에 대해서는 일본과 아국이 현재 보호되고 있는 대상과 계류(PENDING)중인 대상에 대해 새협정을 적용할 경우에 자동적으로 보호기간이 연장되어 기술이전 계약시 기술 도입자가 불안정한 위치에 있게 되는등 문제가 있으므로 새 협정을적용해서는 안된다고 주장함.

. 미국, EC, 스위스는 이에 대해 반대하고 특히 스위스는 일반인이 기대가능(EXPECTATION)한 상태에 있으므로 문제가 없다고 주장하고 EC 도 이에 동조함.

0 ANELL 의장은 논의를 종합하면서 문제점들이 충분히 토의되었고 각국 입장이확인되었으므로 사무국과 협의하여 가능한 한 금주내에 좀더 나은 방법(BETTER WAY)으로 73조를 다시 작성하겠다고함.

- 그리고 잠정적으로 TRIPS 의 마지막 회의를 10.11-22 개최할 계획이라고 언급함.

끝

(차석대사 김삼훈-국장)

원 본

외 무 부

안

종 별 :

번 호 : GVW-1801 일 시 : 91 0920 1730

수 신 : 장 관(통기,경기원,상공부,보사부,문화부,과기처,특허청)

발 신 : 주 제네바 대사대리

제 목 : UR/TRIPS 협상(4)

9.19(목) 속개된 표제 회의 주요 내용을 하기보고함.

0 ANELL 의장은 주요 이슈에 대해 지난 브랏셀회의시 논의된 사항을 전체적으로설명함.

- 브랏셀 회의에 관한 정보를 공유함으로써 명료성을 높이기 위한 것이라고 함.

0 차기 회의 계획에 대해 ANELL 의장은 내일 (9.20) 오전 GREEN ROOM 회의가 개최될 것이며 이때 협상의 시한과 시한까지 협상의 운영방법을 논의할 것이라고 설명하고 이회의에서 각 협상 그룹의 보고서 제출 시한이 11.1 로 결정될것이라고 함.

- 따라서 10월에 약 2주간 (10.11-22)개최되는 TRIPS 회의가 마지막 회의가 될것이며, 이기간동안 협상 타결을 위해 실질적이고 적극적인 노력이 이루어져야 할것이라고 함.

- 동회의에서 협상을 통해 모든 문제에 대한 최종 PACKAGE 를 마련하게 될 것이라고 설명함.

- 10.11-16 까지는 제네바에서 개최되는 국제 통신연맹 회의 때문에 숙박시설에어려움이있으므로 제네바 이외의 곳에서 비공식 회의를 개최하고 10.17 이후 부터는 제네바에서 회의를 개최 (10.17 은 공식회의)하는 것을 검토 하겠다고함.

0 말레이지아, 인도등 개도국은 회의가 제네바 이외의 지역에서 개최될 경우 참가하기에 어려움이있다고 표시하고 브라질, 아르헨티나, 콜럼비아는 아직타협상 그룹에 진전이 없는 상황에서 TRIPS협상의 기술적, 정치적 쟁점에 대해 결론을 내리기 어렵다는 의견을 표명했음.

- ANELL 의장은 그 문제가 내일 GREEN ROOM회의에서 논의될 것이라고 답변함.

0 인도가 브랏셀 회의에서 논의된 사항에 대해 구체적인 정보를 요구하자 ANELL의장은 별도 NON-PAPERS 형식으로 지지정도를 구분해서 배포하겠다고 함.

통상국 2차보 보사부 문화부 경기원 상공부 과기처 특허청

PAGE 1 91.09.21 12:26 WF

외신 1과 통제관

0152

- 이에 대해 인도 이집트등은 어떤 기준으로 지지정도를 구분하는가에 대해 질문을 하였으며, ANELL 의장은 중립적인 방법 (NEUTRAL WAY)으로 제시하겠다고 함.

- 미국은 이러한 구분이 협상을 원활히 할수 있을것이라고 하였으며, 아국은 그구분이 단순히 국가수만 세어 결정하면 안될 것이라고 지적함.

0 홍콩은 의장이 제시하 자료를 미리 배포해 줄것을 요구했으며, 인도는 10월 회의시 수시로 새로운제안 (PIECEMEAL SUGGESTION)을 하는 것은 협상에 어려움을 주므로 자제해 줄것을 요구함.

- ANELL 의장은 자료를 가능한 한 빨리 배포하겠다고 함. 끝

(차석대사 김삼훈-국장)

원 본

외 무 부

안

종 별 :

번 호 : GVW-1808 일 시 : 91 0923 1000

수 신 : 장 관(통기,경기원,상공부,보사부,문화부,과기처,특허청)

발 신 : 주 제네바 대사

제 목 : UR / TRIPS 협상(5)

9.20(금) 개최된 UR/TRIPS 협상 공식회의 주요내용을 하기 보고 함

0 ANELL 의장은 9.17-19 간 개최된 비공식 회의 주요 내용을 보고하고 지난 브랏셀 회의시 논의사항과 제안들을 금일 오전중에 배포하겠다고함.

- 그리고, 브랏셀 회의 논의 사항을 포함한 FULLTEXT 는 가능한한 조속히 배포하겠다고 하고 각국의 새로운 제안을 하는 것을 배제하지 않을것이라고 설명함.

0 콜롬비아는 TRIPS 협정이 권리자와 이용자간의 균형, 기술이전을 촉진하는 내용이 되어야 함을 다시 주장하고

- 73조(경과 규정) 논의가 적용범주(SCOPE)에대한 이해를 증진하는 정도에 불과하고

- 분쟁해결 절차가 GATT 의 새로운 분쟁해결절차와 지적 재산권의 특수성을 고려한 내용이되어야 할 것이라고 함.

- 또한 다음 회의가 정치적인 사항에 대해서도 질적인 논의가 이루어지는 만큼타협상 그룹과 균형을 이룰수 있는 방안이 모색되어야 할것임을 주장함.

0 인도는 ANELL 의장의 보고가 자국이 제안한 분쟁해결 절차에 대해 언급이 없었고 브랏셀회의 내용에 대해서는 설명을 하는데 그치지 않았느냐고 지적하였으며

- 이에, ANELL 의장은 인도의 지적을 받아 들이고 분쟁해결 절차에 대해서는 각국이 주장한 내용을 포함해서 작성하겠다고 함.

0 다음 회의 계획에 대해서 ANELL 의장은 아직 TNC 회의의 결정이 없기 때문에 확신을 못하나 10.11-22 간 회의를 개최하고 10.17 혹은 18에 공식 회의를 개최할 것이라고 함.

- 타협상 그룹의 영향을 받을 것이나 잠정적으로 10월 회의에서 FINAL TEXT 를 만들기 위한 실질적 노력을 할 것이라고 설명함.

통상국 2차보 보사부 문화부 경기원 상공부 과기처 특허청

PAGE 1 91.09.23 20:49 FO

외신 1과 통제관

0154

0 인도, 우루과이는 타협상의 균형, 정치적 쟁점의 조정을 위해 가능한 한 제네바 에서 회의가 개치되기를 희망하였으며,

- ANELL 의장은 가능한한 노력은 해볼 것이나 어려울 것 같다고 함

0 아국이 제안한 '분쟁해결 절차'에 대해 비공식적으로 사무국과 접촉한 결과 10월회의시 아국이 다시 제기해서 실질적인 토의가 이루어진후 TEXT 에 포함될 것인지 여부가 결정될 것이라고함.

(차석대사 김삼훈-국장)

국협 28140-75　　568-6077　　1991. 9. 26.

수신 수신처참조

제목 '91 제2차 UR/TRIPs 협상그룹회의 결과보고서 송부 및 검토의견 요청

일반문서로 재분류(1991.12.31.)

1. 통기 20644-45061 (91. 9.12) 관련입니다.

2. '91. 9.16 - 20간 스위스 제네바에서 개최된 표제회의 결과보고서를 별첨과 같이 송부하오니 업무에 참고하시기 바랍니다.

3. 아울러 브랏셀 회의시 논의되었던 사항을 송부하오니 10.16-22간 개최될 것으로 예정되어 있는 3차 회의에 대비하여 7차 의장보고서와 함께 검토하시어 검토의견을 충분한 대응논리와 함께 10.4(금)까지 송부하여 주시기 바라오며, 기송부한 협상대책안(국협 28140-23)중 Group B 에 대해서도 입장을 명백히 하여 주시기 바랍니다.

첨부 1. '91 제2차 UR/TRIPs 협상 참석결과 보고 1부.

2. 브랏셀 회의시 논의사항 (works done in Brussels) 부. 끝.

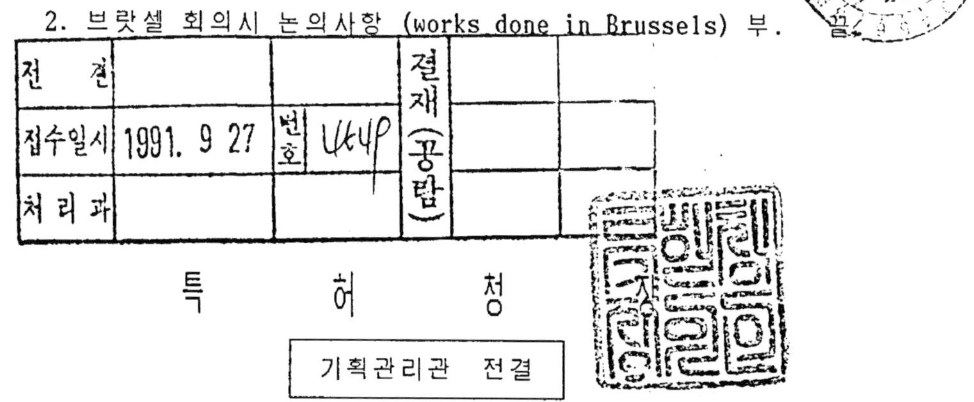

전 결			결재(공람)		
접수일시	1991. 9 27	번호 44440			
처리과					

특 허 청

기획관리관 전결

수신처 : 경제기획원장관(대외경제조정실장), 외무부장관(통상국장),
상공부장관(국제협력관, 전자전기공업국장),
보사부장관(약정국장), 문화부장관(어문출판국장),
과학기술처장관(기술개발국장).

0156

검토의견 작성 방향

1. 작성방향

o Brussels 회의시 논의사항을 7차 의장보고서와 비교 검토하여 의견 제시

'o 기송부한 협상대책안 (국협 28140-23)중 입장을 유보하기로 하였던 Group B에 대해 입장을 명백화

- 컴퓨터 프로그램의 보호방법(어문저작물로 보호): 과기처
- 저작인격권 : 문화부
- 권리남용 및 반경쟁적 행위 : 경제기획원
- 불특허대상 : 특허청
- 분쟁해결절차 : 경제기획원, 외무부, 상공부

o 기타 사항에도 발전된 입장이 있는 경우 제시

o 소관사항 이외에도 의견이 있는 경우 제시 요망

2. 작성양식

항 목	의장보고서 및 Brussels 회의시 논의사항	검토 의견	대응 논리	비 고

0157

Trade-Related Intellectual Property Rights, including Trade in Counterfeit Goods

20.9.1991

Section 1. COPYRIGHT AND RELATED RIGHTS: Work Done in Brussels

Articles 10 and 12: An attempt was made to see if agreement could be reached on the basis of the following approach:

- protection of computer programs as literary works under Berne;

- retention of a sentence clarifying what would not be considered as a form of expression and therefore not be protected;

- a sentence recognising the need to allow certain reproduction and adaptation of computer programs where necessary for their normal exploitation.

Article 11: In relation to the option between an exclusive rental right and the right to equitable remuneration, a suggestion was made that the latter should only be allowed to those countries which already have such a system in place. It was also suggested to replace the word "unauthorised" by "widespread". Another suggestion was to incorporate the notion that the rental right should be activated not only where material impairment of the reproduction right was shown to exist but also where such impairment was threatened or imminent. A fourth suggestion was to replace the phrase "to authorise or prohibit" in the first sentence by the phrase "in respect of", and to delete the language in the first set of square brackets.

Article 16: A suggestion was made with respect to paragraph 1 that the only act that performers should have the possibility of preventing should be that of the unauthorised fixation on phonograms of their performances. It was also suggested to replace the phrase "right holders in" by "producers of".

0158

Section 2. TRADEMARKS: Work Done in Brussels

Article 18.2: "Article 6*bis* of the Paris Convention shall apply, *mutatis mutandis*, to services. In determining whether a trademark is well-known, account shall be taken of the knowledge of the trademark in the relevant sector of the public, including knowledge in that PARTY obtained as a result of the promotion of the trademark."

Article 18.3: "Article 6*bis* of the Paris Convention shall apply, *mutatis mutandis*, to goods or services which are not similar to those in respect of which a trademark is registered, provided that use of that trademark in relation to those goods or services would indicate a connection between those goods or services and the owner of the registered trademark and provided that the interests of the owner of the registered trademark are likely to be damaged by such use."

Article 18.4: "The rights described in the foregoing paragraphs shall not prejudice any existing prior rights, nor shall they affect the possibility of PARTIES making rights available on the basis of use."

Article 18.3: It was suggested to insert after the word "connection" the phrase "in the course of trade".

0159

Trade-Related Intellectual Property Rights, including Trade in Counterfeit Goods

20.9.1991

Section 3. GEOGRAPHICAL INDICATIONS: Work Done in Brussels

Article 24.1: "Geographical indications are, for the purposes of this Agreement, indications which identify a good as originating in the territory of a PARTY, or a region or locality in that territory, where a given quality, [reputation] or other characteristic of the good is essentially attributable to its geographical origin."

Article 24.2: "In respect of geographical indications, PARTIES shall provide the legal means for interested parties to prevent:

(a) the use of any means in the designation or presentation of a good that indicates or suggests that the good in question originates in a geographical area other than the true place of origin in a manner which misleads the public as to the geographical origin of the good;

(b) any use which constitutes an act of unfair competition within the meaning of Article 10*bis* of the Paris Convention (1967)."

Article 24.3: "A PARTY shall, ex officio if its legislation so permits, or at the request of an interested party, refuse or invalidate the registration of a trademark which contains or consists of a geographical indication with respect to goods not originating in the territory indicated, if use of the indication in the trademark for such goods in that PARTY is of such a nature as to mislead the public as to the true place of origin."

0160

<u>Article 25.1</u>: "[Each PARTY shall provide the legal means for interested parties to prevent use of a geographical indication identifying wines for wines not originating in the place indicated by the geographical indication in question, even where the true origin of the goods is indicated or the geographical indication is used in translation or accompanied by expressions such as "kind", "type", "style", "imitation" or the like.]"

<u>Article 25.2</u>: "[The registration of a trademark for wines which contains or consists of a geographical indication identifying wines shall be refused or invalidated, <u>ex officio if domestic legislation so permits, or</u> at the request of an interested party, with respect to such wines not having this origin.]"

<u>Article 25.4</u>: "<u>In order to facilitate the protection of geographical indications for wine, negotiations shall be undertaken in the Committee concerning the establishment of a multilateral system of notification and registration of geographical indications eligible for protection in those PARTIES participating in the system</u>."

<u>Article 26.1</u>: "[Where a geographical indication of a PARTY has been used with regard to goods <u>or services</u> originating outside the territory of that PARTY in good faith and in a widespread and continuous manner by nationals or domiciliaries of another PARTY before the date of application of these provisions in the other PARTY as defined in Article 68 below <u>or prior to that geographical indication becoming eligible for protection under this Agreement</u>, nothing in this Agreement shall prevent such continued use of the geographical indication by those nationals or domiciliaries of the said other PARTY.]"

0161

Article 26.2: "[No PARTY shall [be required to] take action to refuse or invalidate the registration of a trademark applied for or registered in good faith, or to prevent the use of such a trademark or of a trademark for which rights have been acquired through use in good faith:

(a) before the date of application of these provisions in that PARTY as defined in Article 68 below;

(b) before the geographical indication became eligible for protection in its country of origin;

merely on the basis that the trademark is identical with, or similar to, a geographical indication.]"

Article 26.3: "No PARTY shall [be required to] apply the provisions of this Section in respect of a geographical indication of any other PARTY with respect to goods for which the relevant indication is identical with the term customary in common language as the common name for such goods in the territory of that PARTY. No PARTY shall [be required to] apply the provisions of this Section in respect of a geographical indication of any other PARTY with respect to products of the vine for which the relevant indication is identical with the customary name of a grape variety."

Article 27: It was suggested to delete this Article and add a new paragraph 4 to Article 25.

0162

Trade Related Aspects II Intellectual Property Rights, including Trade in Counterfeit Goods

20.9.1991 a.m.

Section 5. PATENTS: Work done in Brussels

Article 34(a): "Authorisation of such use shall be considered on its merits."

Article 34(b): "Such use may only be permitted if, prior to such use, the proposed user has made efforts to obtain authorisation from the right holder on reasonable commercial terms and conditions and that such efforts have not been successful within a reasonable period of time. This requirement may be waived by a PARTY in the case of a national emergency or other circumstances of extreme urgency or in cases of [public non-commercial use] [government use]. In such situations, the right holder shall, nevertheless, be notified whenever practicable and as soon as possible."

Article 34(g): "Authorisation for such use shall be liable to be terminated if and when the circumstances which led to it cease to exist and re unlikely to recur, subject to adequate protection of the legitimate interest of the persons so authorised ..."

Article 34(i): "The legal validity of any decision relating to the authorisation of such use shall be subject to judicial review or other independent review by a distinct higher authority in that PARTY."

Article 34(l): "PARTIES are not obliged to apply the conditions set forth in sub-paragraphs (b) and (f) above where such use is permitted to remedy a practice determined after judicial or administrative process to be anti-competitive. The need to correct anti-competitive practices may be taken into account in determining the amount of remuneration in such cases."

0163

<u>Article 30.1</u>: A suggestion was made to insert in the second sentence after the word "available" the phrase "and right holders shall be allowed to enjoy their rights".

<u>Article 30.2</u>: A suggestion was made to replace the word "or" in the second line by "and".

<u>Article 31</u>: A suggestion was made to insert at the beginning of the paragraph the phrase "where the subject matter of a patent is a product" and consequently to delete the phrase at the end "which is the subject matter of the patent".

<u>Article 34(g)</u>: A suggestion was made to redraft the last sentence to enable the competent authority to review, upon motivated request, the continuance of the authorisation if the person so authorised had failed without legitimate reasons to comply with the purposes for which the authorisation had been granted.

<u>Article 34(h)</u>: A suggestion was made to replace the two options by the phrase "adequate remuneration equitable in the circumstances of each case".

<u>Article 34(o)</u>: A suggestion was made to delete this sub-paragraph, in view of the changes made to sub-paragraphs (a) and (b). However, an alternative suggestion was made to retain this sub-paragraph in view of the difficulties with the application of one or more of the conditions to government use.

Section 6. LAY-OUT DESIGNS OF INTEGRATED CIRCUITS: Work Done in Brussels

Article 39: A suggestion was made to delete the square brackets and also the phrase "Rights extend to an article incorporating an integrated circuit". There was also a suggestion to make the exercise of rights in respect of such articles dependent on the exhaustion of other means of redress.

Article 40: Consideration was given to whether differences on the last sentence of paragraph 1 would be more easily settled if PARTIES were to be obliged rather than just permitted not to deem innocent infringement unlawful, by the deletion of the phrase "be obliged to" in the first line. It was also suggested that the liability to pay a reasonable royalty might be made dependent on the exhaustion of other means of redress.

Section 7. PROTECTION OF UNDISCLOSED INFORMATION: Work Done in Brussels

Article 42.2A: "Natural and legal persons shall have the possibility of preventing information lawfully within their control from being disclosed to, acquired by, or used by others without their consent in a manner contrary to honest commercial practices[1] so long as such information: ..."

Article 42.2A, footnote 1: "For the purpose of this provision, "a manner contrary to honest commercial practices" shall mean at least practices such as breach of contract, breach of confidence and inducement to breach, and includes the acquisition of undisclosed information by third parties who knew, or were grossly negligent in failing to know, that such practices were involved in the acquisition."

Article 42.4A: A suggestion was made to specify: that the provision should apply to pharmaceutical and agricultural chemical products utilising new chemical entities; the obligation to protect test data and the starting data for such protection where a country relies upon a marketing approval of other countries; the limits of obligations in respect of protecting test data against disclosure.

0166

Trade Related Aspects of Intellectual Property Rights, including Trade in Counterfeit Goods

20.9.1991

[Section 8, CONTROL OF ABUSIVE OR ANTI-COMPETITIVE PRACTICES IN CONTRACTUAL LICENCES]: Work Done in Brussels

Article 43.2B: Suggestions were made to replace this paragraph with the following: " Nothing in this Agreement shall prevent PARTIES from specifying in their national legislation licensing practices or conditions that may in particular cases constitute an abuse of intellectual property rights having an adverse effect on competition in the relevant market. They may adopt, consistently with the other provisions of this Agreement, appropriate measures to prevent or control such practices, for example exclusive grant back conditions, conditions preventing challenges to validity and tie-in conditions, where these are found to be abusive and anti-competitive in the light of the relevant laws and regulations governing competition and/or transfer of technology."

Article 43.3B: A suggestion was made to amend the second part of the last sentence to read as follows: "and shall be prepared to co-operate through the supply of available non-confidential information of relevance to the matter in question and of other information subject to the conclusion of mutually satisfactory assurances concerning the safeguarding of its confidentiality by the requesting PARTY."

0167

Trade Related Aspects of Intellectual Property Rights, including Trade in Counterfeit Goods

20.9.1991

Part III, Enforcement: Work Done in Brussels

Article 51: "In respect of the administration of any law pertaining to the enforcement of intellectual property rights, PARTIES shall only exempt both public authorities and officials from liability to appropriate remedial measures where actions are taken or intended in good faith in the course of the administration of such laws."

Article 54, footnote 3 and Article II of the Draft Agreement on Trade in Counterfeit and Pirated Goods, footnote 2, line 5: "... copy would have constituted an infringement of a copyright or a related right under the law of the country of importation."

Article 61(c): "PARTIES shall only exempt both public authorities and officials from liability to appropriate remedial measures where actions are taken or intended in good faith."

Article 44: A suggestion was made to insert in the second line of paragraph 1 after the word "permit" the following phrase: "within the limits of administrative and financial resources and capabilities". Alternative suggestions were made on paragraph 5. One would specify that there would be no obligation to allocate additional resources to the enforcement of IPRs. Another suggestion was made to add a sentence to the paragraph which would read as follows: "Nothing in this Part creates any obligation with respect to the distribution of resources as between the enforcement of intellectual property rights and the enforcement of laws in general."

0168

Part V, ACQUISITION AND MAINTENANCE OF INTELLECTUAL PROPERTY RIGHTS AND RELATED INTER-PARTES PROCEDURES: Work Done in Brussels

Article 65.4: "Procedures concerning the acquisition or maintenance of intellectual property rights and, where the national law provides for such procedures, administrative revocation and inter partes procedures such as opposition, revocation and cancellation, shall be governed by the general principles set out in paragraphs 2 and 3 of Article 44."

관리 번호

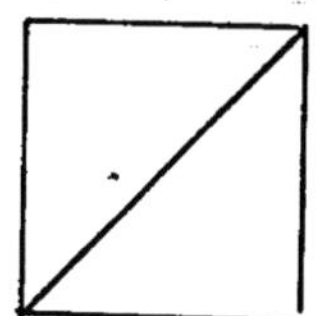

'91 제2차 UR/TRIPs 회의참석 결과 보고

1991. 9.

국제협력담당관실

0170

I. 회의개요

1. 회의명

o '91 제2차 GATT/UR TRIPs 협상그룹 회의

2. 기간 및 장소

o '91. 9.16(월) - 20(금), 스위스 제네바 GATT 본부

3. 참가자

o 특허청 국제협력담당관 권 영 수
o WIPO 주재관 김 준 규
o 특허청 국제협력담당관실 사무관 이 찬 우
o 변리사 김 창 세

4. 회의의제

o 협정안 73조(경과규정)에 대한 토의
o 분쟁해결절차에 대한 논의
o Brussels 회의시 논의되었던 주요 이슈에 대한 검토
o 차기회의 계획

5. 회의 진행방식

o 9. 16(월) 및 20(금) : 공식회의
o 9.17(화) - 19(목) : 비공식회의

6. 대표단 주요활동

o 아국이 제안한 "기술이전계약에 있어서의 분쟁예방절차"를 공식회의에서 제안설명을 하는 한편, 주요관심국의 지지를 확보하기 위해 오찬회의 개최

o 73조(경과규정), 분쟁해결절차등에 대한 논의에 참가

o 미국 USTR 주최 비공식 오찬에 참가하여 미국 및 각국의 주요 관심사항 파악

Ⅱ. 회의내용 및 결과

1. 분쟁예방절차

가. 개 요

o 정식명칭 : 국가간 기술이전과 관련한 분쟁예방절차 설치를 위한 제안 (Proposal for the Establishment of a Dispute Prevention System in Respect of Technology)

o '91. 7.12 아국이 공식 제안 (서면제출)

- 특허, know-how에 관한 licence 계약시, 계약의 전체 혹은 부분에 권리남용 혹은 반경쟁적 행위가 있을 경우 각 당사자는 자국정부를 통해 TRIPs 위원회에 계약 내용에 대한 심의를 요청할 수 있음.

- TRIPs 위원회는 전문가로 구성된 기술이전검토위원회(Licence Review Board)를 구성하고 TRIPs 위원회가 설정한 guideline에 의해 심의함.

- Licence Review Board는 6개월내 자문의견(advisory opinion)을 냄.

- 자문의견은 각 국가를 구속하지는 않으나 계약당사자가 동 의견에 따르는 것을 막지 않음.

o '91 제2차 GATT/UR TRIPs 협상그룹회의의 공식회의(9.16 오후)에서 제안설명을 할 기회가 부여됨.

나. 제안설명 및 각국의 논평

1) 제안설명

o TRIPs 협정이 성공적으로 타결되고 집행되기 위해서는 협정내에 여러가지 요소가 마련되어야 하나, 그중의 하나가 국가간 기술이전을 촉진시킬 수 있는 다자간 체제를 마련하는 것이 필요함.

o 아국의 이러한 제안은 현재 TRIPs 협정안 8조 2항의 "부당하게 무역을 제한하거나 국가간 기술이전을 저해하는 행위를 규제하기 위해 적절한 조치(appropriate measures)를 취할 수 있다" 라는 규정과는 부합되는 것임.

o 아국제안은 TRIPs 협정내에 분쟁예방절차를 마련하여 기술이전 계약에서 발생가능한 반경쟁적 행위를 규제함으로써 TRIPs 협정이 권리자 보호 강화와 기술이전 촉진이라는 두 목표의 균형을 이루게 하는데 목적이 있음.

2) 각국의 논평 및 답변

o 개도국

- 콜럼비아, 베네수엘라는 TRIPs 협정의 중요한 목적의 하나가 기술이전 촉진이라는 관점에서 기술이전을 위한 국내 그리고 국가간 체제를 만드는데 찬성하고, 분쟁예방절차 제안은 협정안 43조(반경쟁적 행위 규제), 31조(특허권자의 의무)와 관련이 있으며 좀더 연구 검토하겠다고 함.

- 이집트는 아국제안이 매우 흥미로운 것이며, 추후 검토후 질문하겠다고 함.

o 선진국 (미국)

- 아국제안에 대한 이해를 하기 위해 6가지의 질문을 제시함.

① 분쟁당사자 기업 일방이 분쟁예방절차를 거부하면 어떻게 되는가.

② License Review Board 에서 기술이전 계약을 심의하고 있는 동안 그 계약은 어떠한 상태에 있게 되는가, 만약 계약체결이 정지(suspend)되면 오히려 기술이전을 방해하는 것이 아닌가.

③ 아국제안 67bis 1항의 "has an adverse effect" 은 TRIPs 협정 8조 2항의 "unreasonably restrain trade"와 어떤 차이가 있으며 이것은 8조 2항의 적용범위보다 넓은 것이 아닌가.

④ 주석(footnote)에 있는 know-how와 TRIPs 협정내의 비공개정보 (Undisclosed Information)과의 차이는 무엇인가.

⑤ 기술이전계약에 관한 Guideline 설정시 협의토록 하고 있는 WIPO는 WIPO의 어느 기구를 말하는 것인가.

⑥ 제안이 채택될 경우 구체적인 절차는 어떻게 할 것인가.

o 미국의 질의에 대해 다음과 같이 답변함.

① 분쟁예방절차의 관계자라고 할수 있는 분쟁당사기업, 그 기업의 정부중 어느 하나라도 분쟁예방절차를 거부하면 동 절차는 시작되지 않음.

② License Review Board가 계약내용을 심의하고 있는 동안 그 계약 추진은 당사자인 기업에 의해 지연되거나 정지(suspend)될 수 있음. 그러나, 분쟁예방절차에 의한 심의기간이 6개월인데 비해 실제 기술이전 계약 실무상 기술이전 계약체결에 평균 1.5년 이상 소요 되므로 기술이전을 저해하는 요소로 작용하는 문제는 발생되지 않을 것임.

③ 아국제안 67bis 1항과 TRIPs 협정 8조 2항의 표현차이는 구체적인 논의를 통해 수정할 수 있을 것임.

④ 산업에의 적용가능성(industrial application)이 있는 know-how로 표현함으로써 TRIPs 협정의 비공개정보(undisclosed information)에 비해 범위를 한정하려고 한 것임.

⑤ WIPO 어느기구와 협의할 것인가에 대해서 아직 구체적인 idea는 없으나 TRIPs 협정이 체결된 후 WIPO와 협의할 수 있을 것임.

⑥ 구체적인 절차는 채택된 후 TRIPs 위원회에서 결정하면 될 것임.

o 중도국 (홍콩)

- 홍콩은 국가간 분쟁해결절차와 분쟁예방절차(아국제안)와의 상관 관계, 실제 분쟁예방절차가 어떻게 운영될 것인가에 대해 한국이 좀더 검토해야 할 것이라고 지적함.

o 홍콩의 지적에 대해 아국은 국가간 분쟁해결절차는 국가가 TRIPs 협정상의 의무를 위반했을 경우에 적용되는 절차이고 분쟁예방절차는 기업간의 기술이전계약 체결시 발생하는 분쟁을 사전에 예방하려는 것이므로 본질적인 차이가 있다고 답변함.

o Anell 의장은 아국제안에 대한 실질적인 토의를 비공식회의에서 하자고 제안함.

- 그러나 실제 비공식회의에서는 시간관계상 논의되지 않았음.

다. 회의결과

o 아국제안에 대한 향방에 대해 GATT 사무국에 탐문한바 아국제안이 이번 회의에서 실질적으로 논의되지 않았으므로 차기회의에 아국이 이 제안을 다시 제기하여 이루어지는 논의의 결과를 보아 TRIPs 협정안에 포함될지 여부가 결정될 것이라고 함.

2. 경과규정 (협정안 73조)

가. 개 요

o 정식명칭은 "존재하고 있는 지적재산권 보호 (Article 73: Protection of Eisting Intellectual Property Rights)" 임.

o 복잡한 기술적인 문제로 구체적인 토의가 이루어지지 않았기 때문에 '91.8 GATT 사무국이 다시 draft 해서 토의하게 된 것임.

o 주요내용

- 1항, 2항 : TRIPs 협정의 Part Ⅱ(보호기준) 적용에 관한 문제

① 새로이 보호대상이 될 수 있는 것(protectable)에 Part Ⅱ(보호기준 적용)

② 이미 보호되고 있는 대상(subject matter under protection)에 TRIPs 협정을 [적용한다] [적용하지 않는다]

. 출원 계류중인 대상에 대해 TRIPs 협정을 [적용한다] [적용하지 않는다]

. public domain에 있는 대상에 TRIPs 협정상 Part Ⅱ(보호기준)을 적용하지 않는다.

- 3항 : 1, 2항의 규정보다 Paris 협약등이 우선함.

- 4항 : Part Ⅰ(기본원칙), Ⅲ(시행절차), Ⅳ(권리획득절차)의 적용에 관한 규정

. TRIPs 협정 발효이후 모든 기존 지적재산권에 Part Ⅰ, Ⅲ, Ⅳ를 적용함.

나. 회의내용

1) Anell 의장의 제안 설명

o 경과규정(73조)는 복잡한 문제로 정치적인 성격과 기술적인 성격의 양면성이 있으므로 각국의 이해를 돕기 위해 사무국이 다시 draft 한 것이라고 설명함.

o 새롭게 draft 한 73조는 최종안이 아니라 논의를 위한 것 (framework for discussion) 이라고 함.

o 기술적인 문제를 중심으로 항(paragraph)별로 논의하기를 요청함.

o 73조의 전체구조에 대해 다음과 같이 설명함.

- 73조 1항 및 2항의 성격은 minimum standard 로서 이미 존재하고 있는 지적재산권에 대해 TRIPs 협정상의 Part Ⅱ(보호기준)를 적용할 것인가에 대해 규정하는 것이므로 동조에 규정되지 않은 사항은 각국의 자유로운 결정에 의하면 됨.

- 1항과 2항은 존재하고 있는 지적재산권에 대해 Part Ⅱ를 적용할 것인가를 규정하고 있으며 1항과 2항의 관계는 2항이 우선함.

- 3항은 기존 Paris 협약등에 본 협정상의 경과규정이 우선한다는 것을 규정한 것이고,

- 4항은 Part Ⅰ(기본원칙), Part Ⅱ(권리획득 및 유지절차)의 적용에 관한 규정임.

2) 논의내용

가) 전체적 접근방법

o Egypt 는 73조가 매우 복잡하고 어려운 문제이므로 협정에 규정하지 않고 각국법에 맡기자고 주장함.

o 홍콩은 73조에 Part I(기본원칙)의 적용에 관한 내용이 언급되어 있지 않으며,

- 전체적인 접근방식에 있어서 현재의 안 처럼 각 권리를 구분하여 규정할 것이 아니라 Rome 협약과 같이 "불소급보호 원칙"을 규정하고 각 개별권리의 특수성을 고려하여 예외를 두는 방식으로 하자고 함.

- 칠레도 홍콩의 주장에 동조함.

o EC도 권리별로 차별하지 않고 존재하고 있는 지적재산권 보호에 관한 몇가지 기준을 정하자고 주장함.

i) 본협정(TRIPs 협정)이 적용되는 activities 는 무엇인가.

- 본협정 발효이전 혹은 본협정 발효이후의 행위
- 본협정 발효이전의 activities에 적용하면 그 기준은 ?

ii) 체약국에 본 협정이 발효하는 시점에 존재하는 대상에 본 협정을 적용할 것인가.

iii) 본협정 발효시점에 계류중인 출원에 대해 본 협정을 적용할 것인가.

o EC의 주장에 대해 Anell 의장은 권리별로 구분하여 규정하고자 하는 것이 아니라 각 권리의 특성을 이해하고 협상추진을 위해 현재대로 규정한 것이라 설명

o EC의 주장에 대해 홍콩은 어떠한 기본원칙(basic principle)에서 부터 출발하는 가에 대해 언급이 없다고 지적함.

o 그러나, 미국이 개별권리별로 특성이 있으므로 권리별로 경과규정에 따른 문제점을 검토할 것을 요청하고 호주, 홍콩등도 실제 논의에 있어 상표의 경우 선사용자(prior user), 저작권의 경우 새로운 권리인 대여권의 적용문제에 대해 언급을 하게 되자,

- Anell 의장도 각 권리별로 문제점을 검토하자고 함.

나) 권리별 논의

① 저작권

o 대여권의 적용문제

- 캐나다.홍콩 : TRIPs 협정 적용시점에 존재하고 있는 저작물에 대해 새로운 권리인 대여권을 어떻게 적용할 것인가에 대해 문제 제기

. 홍콩 스위스는 말레이지아, 미국이 Berne 협약 가입시 제18조(소급보호규정) 적용을 배제한 예가 좋은 참고가 될 것이며, 이에 대한 연구. 검토가 필요하다고 주장함.

- 미국.EC : 이경우 진정한 public domain의 법리가 적용되는 것이며, 이에따라 이미 존재하고 있는 저작물의 경우에도 협정 적용시점 이후에 발생하는 대여행위에만 대여권이 적용되면 된다고 함.

o 일반 저작권의 소급적용 문제

- 일 본

. Berne 협약의 규정(소급보호규정 즉, 18조)이 저작권과 함께 Computer Program, Data Base 보호에 적용

. 음반등 저작인접권에 대한 권리는 Rome 협약이 있으므로 Rome 협약규정(불소급보호원칙 즉, 제7조)이 적용

. 대여권 같은 새로운 권리는 TRIPs 협정 적용시점 이후 부터 적용

- 한 국 : 저작인접권은 Rome 협약에 의해 새로운 권리는 TRIPs 협정 적용시점 이후부터 적용해야 한다고 주장함.

- 노르딕.인도 : 저작권에 관해 소급적용 규정을 반대함.

- 홍 콩 : Berne 협약의 소급적용에 관한 규정은 각 국가의 해석에 따르면 될 것이라고 주장함.

② 상 표

o 선사용자(prior users)의 문제

- 미국.호주등: TRIPs 협정 적용에 의해 보호가능한 대상 (protectable subject matter)이 되어 출원.등록된 상표를 보호하는 경우 등록이전의 선사용자(prior users) 보호문제가 발생함.

- EC : 선사용자 문제는 상표등록이 되었다고 해도 이미 그 상표를 사용하고 있는 제3자(earlier users)를 보호하는 법리를 적용하여 해결 가능함.

o 서비스표(service mark)의 문제

- 호주는 몇몇국가에 새로운 권리라고 할수 있는 서비스표 도입시 TRIPs 협정 적용문제가 발생할 수 있다는 것을 지적함.

③ 의장. 특허

o 한국, 일본

- TRIPs 협정 적용당시 이미 보호되고 있는 대상(subject matter under protection)과 출원 계류중인 대상에 새협정(TRIPs)을 적용하게 되면 자동적으로 보호기간이 연장되는 효과를 가져오게 됨.

- 따라서, 기술이전 계약시 기술도입자(licensee)가 불안정한 위치(unstable position)에 있게 되므로 새 협정을 적용하면 안될 것임. (∵ Royalty 지급기간이 연장됨)

o 미국, 스위스, EC

- 보호기간이 자동연장된다 해도 일반인이 기대가능(expectation)한 상태에 있으므로 이를 고려하여 기술이전계약을 해결하게 되어 문제가 없음.

다. 회의결과

o Anell 의장은 논의를 종합하면서 문제점들이 충분히 토의되었고 각국의 입장도 확인되었으므로 사무국이 좀더 나은 방법으로(better way) 73조를 재 작성하겠다고 밝힘.

3. 분쟁해결절차

가. 개 요

o GATTability 즉, TRIPs 협정이 GATT의 일부로 될 수 있는가의 문제와 의무 위반시 보복조치 (특히, 타상품교역에 대한 보복조치) 허용여부가 문제가 되어 구체적인 논의가 이루어지지 않았었음.

o 따라서, 다음 세가지 안이 병존해 있음.

- Text I : 뉴질랜드, 콜럼비아, 우루과이 제안

. GATT/UR 분쟁해결절차그룹의 결과를 가능한한 반영하되 다음의 절차를 둠.

① 협의(consultation), 중개(good offices), 화해(conciliation), 조정(mediation)

② 30일내 합의에 이르지 못한 경우 panel 설치를 요구할 수 있음.

③ panel에 지적재산권 전문가가 개입

④ 합리적 기간내 panel의 권고를 이행하지 않을 경우 본 협정의 적용 중지 혹은 상품관세 양허를 정지할 수 있음.

- Text Ⅱ : 인도 제안

① 협의, 중개, 화해, 조정

② 합리적 기간내 합의에 이르지 못할 경우 panel을 설치하고 panel이 심의함. panel은 분쟁당사국에 권고를 할 수 있음.

③ TRIPs 위원회가 panel 권고 이행여부를 감시

- Text Ⅲ : 미국 제안

. GATT/UR 분쟁해결절차그룹의 결과를 준용함.

나. 회의 내용

1) Anell 의장의 설명

o 분쟁해결절차가 정치적인 성격과 기술적인 성격을 모두 갖고 있으며, Brussels 각료회의에서 구체적인 논의가 이루어지지 못했음.

- 금일 논의에서는 정치적인 성격에 대해서는 논의하지 않고 기술적이고 실제적인 성격에 대해 논의함으로써 세가지 대안에 대한 이해를 높이는데 목적이 있음.

2) 회의 내용

가) Text I 에 대한 논의

o EC

- Text I 이 기본적으로는 TRIPs 협상의 목적에 배치되지 않으나, 구체적으로 살펴보면 TRIPs 협정이 GATT 의 일부로 되어야 한다는 정신에 위배됨.

- 따라서 GATT 분쟁해결절차 그룹의 결과를 준용하게 되어 있는 Text Ⅲ을 지지한다고 하고 Text I 의 문제점을 다음과 같이 지적함.

① 가능한한 (as far as possible) GATT 분쟁해결절차 그룹의 결과를 반영한다고 되어 있어 GATT 의 일부가 되지 않는 새로운 절차를 만드는 인상을 주고 있음.

② 기간제한이 명확하지 않고, 제소국의 panel 요청권 및 그 panel 의 권한이 명시되어 있지 않아 분쟁해결의 지연을 초래할 문제점이 있음.

③ paenl 에 무역, 경제전문가가 아닌 지적재산권 전문가만 참여 하게 되어 있음.

④ 불복의 정도에 대해 이견이 있을 경우 하게 되어있는 당사국간 중재에 대한 규정이 불명확

o 미국 : EC 의 의견에 동조하고 Text I 이 보조금 협상의 분쟁해결 절차와는 다르게 보복이 협정적용 중지와 양허정지등의 보복이 선택적으로 되어 있어 보복조치 내용이 약하다고 지적함.

o 노르딕 : EC 의 의견에 동조

o 일본 : GATT 분쟁해결절차그룹과 달리 중개(good offices), 화해 (conciliation), 조정(mediation)이 필수적인 절차로 되어 있는 것을 문제점으로 지적함.

- 분쟁해결의 지연을 초래할 가능성이 있음.

o 스위스 : EC 의 의견에 동조하나 지적재산권이 개인적 권리인 만큼 이에 대한 의무 위반으로 공공권리적인 성격을 갖고 있는 양허에 정지등의 교차보복(cross-retaliation)을 가할수 있느냐의 여부는 매우 흥미로운 연구의 대상이 될수 있다고 함.

o 콜롬비아: Text I 이 일반적인 GATT 분쟁해결절차와 지적재산권의 특수성을 고려한 합리적인 절차임.

o 싱가폴. 이집트: 지적재산권 문제가 무역과 관련이 없으므로 교차 보복은 허용되지 않아야 함.

o 칠레: 지적재산권의 특수성을 감안해서 현재 WIPO 에서 논의되고 있는 분쟁해결절차와 유사한 내용의 제안을 함.

- 칠레가 제안한 내용의 특징은

① 명시적인 단계별 기간제한 : GATT 분쟁해결절차보다 장기간
② TRIPs 위원회의 역할 명시 : 보복허용 및 보복에 대한 재심
③ 보복조치 허용 : cross-sectoral retaliation 허용
④ 보복조치에 대해 이견이 있을 경우 재심임.

- 태국이 지지를 표명하였으나, 말레이지아등은 교차보복은 허용 되지 않아야 할 것이라고 주장함.

- 홍콩은 보복조치의 의결정족수인 절대다수 (absolute majority)에 대해 질의
  . 단순 과반수보다 높은 것이라고 답변

- EC, 미국은 칠레 제안이 분쟁해결을 장기화하는 문제점이 있다고 지적함.

나) Text Ⅱ에 대한 논의

o 인도가 Text Ⅱ에 대한 제안설명을 다음과 같이 함.

- 분쟁해결절차는 협정의 이행(implementation)과 관련이 있는 것으로,

- Text Ⅱ의 특징은 보복조치가 없고, 절차의 각 단계별로 기간제한을 두지 않음으로써 신축성(flexibility)을 주고 있는 것이라고 함.
  . 단계별로 구체적인 절차는 TRIPs 위원회에서 결정할 것임.

- 국제사회에서 경제적 보복조치가 없이 도덕적인 제재만으로도 충분히 협정의 이행을 담보할 수 있으며, TRIPs 협정이 일반 GATT 규정과는 다른 특성이 있으므로 각 단계별로 신축성을 부여할 필요가 있기 때문이라고 설명함.

o 브라질, 중국: 인도의 주장에 동조

o 미국, EC, 스위스, 노르웨이, 일본등 대다수 국가

- 일반적인 GATT 절차와는 거리가 너무 멀고 협정이행에 필수적인 보복조치가 없어 실효성이 없으므로 반대함.

o 인도: 미국, EC 등 선진국의 논평에 대해 협정의 의무를 이행하지 않았을 경우, 국제적인 비난의 대상이 되는 것으로 충분하고 교차보복 반대는 GATTability 를 계속 반대해온 자국의 입장과 맥을 같이 하는 것이라고 함.

다. 회의 결과

o Anell 의장은 분쟁해결절차에 관한 두가지 접근방식과 각국의 입장을 충분히 이해했다고 밝히고 이를 정리해서 고위급 회의에서 결정하겠다고 함.

4. 브랏셀 회의시 논의사항 검토

o 브랏셀 회의시 논의된 사항과 새로운 제안에 대해 설명하고 확인하는데 그침.

5. 차기 회의 계획

가. Anell 의장의 제안

o TNC level 회의의 합의가 없으므로 확신은 할 수 없으나 9. 20(금) 11:00 Green Room 협의가 있을 예정이며,

- 동 회의에서 UR 협상의 시한 (deadline) 과 협상의 운영방법을 논의할 것이며,

- 각 협상그룹의 최종 보고서 제출시한이 11. 1 로 결정될 것임.

o 따라서, TRIPs 협상의 package 를 만들기 위한 실질적 노력이 이루어져야 할 것이며, 이를 위해 10. 11 - 22 간 (잠정적) 회의를 개최하고자 함.

- 10. 11 - 16 까지는 제네바에서 개최되는 국제 통신연맹회의 (Telecom Conference) 때문에 숙박에 어려움이 있을 것이므로 제네바 이외의 곳에서 비공식회의를 개최하고 10. 17 이후에는 제네바에서 회의를 개최함 (10. 17 혹은 18일에 공식회의 개최)

나. 논의내용

① 회의시기 및 장소

o 인도, 말레이지아등 개도국

- 타 협상그룹과의 균형, 정치적인 쟁점의 조정이 필요하므로 제네바 이외의 지역에서 개최될 경우 어려움이 있음.

o 브라질, 아르헨티나, 콜럼비아

- 아직 타협상그룹의 진전이 없는 상황에서 TRIPs 협상에서 협상의 package 작성을 위해 기술적, 정치적 쟁점에 대해 결론을 내리기 어려움.

o Anell 의장의 답변

- TNC 회의 혹은 9. 20(금) Green Room 협의에서 결정될 것임.

② 회의 방법

o 인도가 브랏셀 회의시 논의된 사항에 대해 구체적인 정보를 요구하자 Anell 의장은 별도 non-papers 형식으로 각 사항에 대한 지지 정도를 구분해서 배포하겠다고 함.

- 인도,이집트등: 어떠한 기준으로 지지정도를 구분하는가에 대해 질의

  . Anell 의장은 협상을 촉진하기 위해 neutral way 로 제시 하겠다고 답변함.

- 미국: 지지정도의 구분이 협상을 원활히 할수 있을 것이므로 환영

o 한국: 지지정도의 구분 혹은 차기 회의의 결정이 단순히 국가수만 세어 결정해서는 안될 것이라는 견해를 표명함.

o 홍콩: 의장이 제시한 자료를 미리 배포해 줄것을 요구함.

o 인도: 10월 회의에서 수시로 새로운 제안(piecemeal suggestion)을 하는 것은 협상에 어려움을 줄 것이라는 우려를 표시

다. 회의 결과

o 비공식회의에서 논의된 사항을 공식회의(9.20)에 보고하는 방법으로 결론을 내림.

o 차기회의 시기 : 10. 11 - 22 (잠정적)

o 회의 방법

- 10. 11 - 16 : 비공식회의, 제네바 이외 지역
- 10. 17 혹은 18 : 공식회의, 제네바
- 10. 19 - 22 : 비공식회의, 제네바

o 회의 자료

- 7차 의장보고서와 브랏셀 회의시 논의사항(9. 20 오전 배포)

* 10.16-22 스위스 제네바에서 개최하기로 결정

Ⅳ. 기타 대표단 활동

1. 아국 주최 비공식 오찬

가. 개 요

o 9. 16 공식회의에 앞서 아국이 제안한 분쟁예방 절차에 대해 사전 설명하고, 지지를 확보하기 위해 9. 16 12:00 주요 관심국가를 초청하여 오찬을 개최함.

o 참가국

- 한국, 홍콩, 태국, 말레이지아, 인도네시아, 스위스, 호주, 뉴질랜드 8개국 12명

나. 논의내용

o 아국이 제안한 분쟁예방절차에 대해 설명을 하고 각국의 의견을 들음.

o 스위스

- 아국 제안의 기본적인 idea 는 좋음.

- 그러나, 실질적으로 TRIPs 위원회의 역할과 43조의 반경쟁적 행위 규제에 대한 논의가 이루어지지 않은 상태이므로 차후에 논의하는 것이 바람직함.

- next round 에서는 중요한 issue 가 될수 있을 것임.

o 홍 콩

- 기본적으로 좋으나 GATT 의 기본내용과 거리가 있음.

. 즉, GATT 는 국가간의 분쟁을 해결하는 것이지 사기업 당사자간의 분쟁을 해결하는 것이 아님.

. 국가간의 분쟁해결절차와 아국제안인 사기업 당사자간의 분쟁해결 절차와의 관계를 명확히 할 필요가 있음.

- 실효성의 면에 있어서도 분쟁당사자 어느 일방이 분쟁예방 절차로 해결하는 것을 거부할 경우 동 절차가 발동되지 않으므로 문제가 있음.

- 국가가 분쟁예방절차에 구속되지 않는다고 했으나 사기업이 국가를 통해 분쟁예방절차를 요청하게 되어 있으므로 사실상 국가를 구속하는 효과가 있음.

- 따라서, 이러한 점을 좀더 깊이 연구 검토해 주기 바람.

o 태국, 말레이지아

- 기본적으로 좋으나 자국에는 아직 독점금지법이 없으며 선진국, 특히 미국, EC 등의 독점금지법 규정, 판례를 도입하기에는 아직 현실적으로 무리가 있음.

- 따라서, 반경쟁적 행위에 대한 국제적으로 인정된 규범을 설정할 수 있는가에 대해 의문이 있음.

2. 미국주최 비공식 오찬

가. 개 요

o 미국이 자국의 관심사항을 설명하기 위해 9. 17(화) 13:00 아국을 포함하여 홍콩, 태국등 10개국을 초청하여 오찬을 개최함.

o 아국은 권영수 국제협력담당관, 김준규 주재관 참석

나. 논의내용

o 미국이 각국 대표에게 현재 진행되고 있는 TRIPs 협상의 전망에 대해 질의하였는바, 각국의 답변은 다음과 같음.

- 태국, 싱가폴 : 낙관적임.

- 말레이지아 : 작년 브랏셀 회의 이후 자국의 기본입장에 변화가 없음.

- 한 국

. 작년 브랏셀 회의 이후 기본입장에는 큰 변화가 없었으나, 협상의 조속한 타결을 위해 유연성 (flexibility) 을 갖고 협상에 임할 것이며, 특히 이번 협상에 아국의 입장을 구체화할 것임.

. 아국이 제안한 "분쟁예방절차" 가 협정에 반영되기를 희망하며 이를 위해 공식회의에서 제기된 각국의 comment 를 참고하여 동 제안의 내용을 발전시키겠음.

o 미국의 관심사항을 미국대표 Mr. Michael Kirk (특허청 차장보) 가 다음과 같이 설명함.

- 자국업계의 압력이 강해지고 있어 미국의 주요 관심사항은

① 특허분야

. Pipeline products 를 10년간 보호
. 미국내 발명자 보호를 위해 선발명주의 유지

② 저작권분야

. Computer Program 을 저작권법에 의해 50년간 보호

③ 권리소진

. 국제적인 권리소진 (international exhaustion) 을 인정할 수 없으며, 이에 따라 병렬수입 (parallel importation) 금지

. 병렬수입을 인정할 경우 원권리자, 권리자로 부터 license 를 받은 업자보다 저렴한 가격으로 수입이 가능하게 되어 원권리자 등에게 피해를 주게됨.

. 원권리자등이 광고, 판매시장 확보등에 투자한 노력에 free-ride 하게 됨.

o 미국의 관심사항에 대해

- 홍콩, 아르헨티나, 싱가폴등 참가국 거의 대다수가 pipeline products 보호에 반대하였으며,

- 특히, 홍콩은 자유시장 원리에 의해 병렬수입이 인정되어야 한다고 강력히 주장함.

o 한 국

- Pipeline products 보호등 미국의 관심사항에 대해 구체적인 언급을 회피함.

V. 관찰 및 평가

o TRIPs 협상의 issues 에 대해 실질적인 토의가 이루어 지지 않고 각국도 입장 변화 내지 입장 표명을 유보하는 인상

- 명시적으로 금번 회기 의제에 포함되어 있는 73조 (경과규정) 와 분쟁해결 절차에 대해서만 실질적인 토의가 이루어짐.

- 당초 논의하고자 했던 outstanding issues 에 대해서는 Brussels 회의시 논의되었던 사항과 새로운 제안들에 대해서 확인하는 수준에 그침.

o 그러나, GATT 사무국과 선진국에서는 협상을 연내 혹은 늦어도 내년초까지 종결시키겠다는 목표를 갖고 추진해 나가는 인상을 줌.

- 지난 Brussels 회의시 논의를 토대로 널리 지지받았다 (widely support) 혹은 일반적인 지지를 받았다 (generally support) 등의 표현을 써서 밀고 나가려고 하는듯 함.

- 10월로 예정된 회의에서 최종 협상안 작성을 위해 각국이 자국입장의 관철을 위해 상당한 정도의 deal을 할 것으로 전망.

- 이는 지난 9월 개최된 4극 통상회의 (미국, EC, 일본, 캐나다) 의 합의와도 맥을 같이함.

  . Market Access 에서 EC 가 양보하는 자세를 보이고 IPR 분야에서 미국이 입장을 누그러뜨려 협상타결을 위한 통일안을 작성하고 개도국을 설득 하려고 함.

Ⅵ. 향후 협상대책

o 실질적인 논의가 예상되는 10월 회의에 대비하여 협상 대책안을 발전시켜 대응 논리를 보완

- Brussels 회의시 논의사항 (기입수)과 7차 의장보고서를 함께 검토

o 10월 회의에 선진국이 widely support 등으로 협상의 대세를 이끌어 나갈 것에 대비, 우리와 관심사항을 같이 하는 국가와 사전 개별 접촉을 통해 상호 협조

o 사무국과도 개별 접촉 강화

o 아국 제안인 분쟁예방절차를 계속 주장할 것인지, 협정안 8조 2항에 "분쟁예방절차 신설을 검토한다" 수준으로 주장할 것인지에 대해 정책적인 결정이 필요

관리번호 91-666

특 허 청

국협 28140-39　　568-6077　　1991. 10. 9.

수신 외무부장관

참조 통상국장

일반문서로 재분류 (1981 .12. 31.)

제목 '91 제3차 GATT/UR TRIPs 협상그룹회의 대표 추천

'91. 10.16 - 22간 스위스 제네바에서 개최되는 표제회의에 참가할 당청 대표를 아래와 같이 추천하오니 필요한 조치를 취해 주시기 바랍니다.

아 래

1. 회의명 : '91 제3차 GATT/UR TRIPs 협상그룹 회의
2. 일시 및 장소 : '91. 10.16 - 22, 스위스 제네바 GATT 본부
3. 참가자

소 속	직 위	성 명	비 고
특 허 청	기획관리관	노 영 욱	수석대표
"	국제협력담당관	권 영 수	대 표
"	WIPO 주재관	김 준 규	대표(현지참석)
"	사 무 관	이 찬 우	대 표

4. 출장기간 : '91. 10.14 - 24 (10박 11일)

　* 권영수 국제협력담당관 : '91. 10.14 - 23 (9박 10일)

5. 경비부담 : 특허청 소관예산.

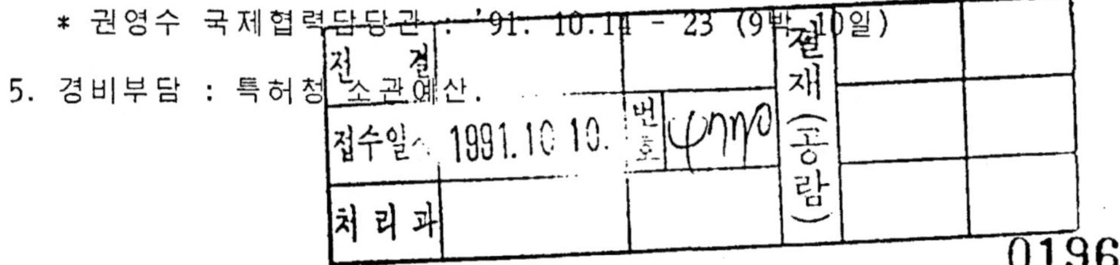
전결 / 결재(공람)
접수일시 1991.10.10. 번호 47710
처리과

0196

국협 28140-　　　　　　　　　　　　　　　　　　　1991.10.9.

첨부　1. 회의의제 1부.

2. 대표별 업무분장 1부.

3. 세부 여행일정 및 활동계획서 1부.

4. 경비내역 1부.

5. 훈령안 1부.　　　끝.

특　　　허　　　청

0197

1. 회의 의제

o TRIPs 협상현황 및 쟁점사항 논의

o 기타 업무, 차기회의 계획

0198

2. 대표별 업무분장

소 속	직 위	성 명	비 고
특 허 청	기획관리관	노 영 욱	수석대표 대표단 업무를 지휘 총괄
"	국제협력담당관	권 영 수	대 표 대표단 업무의 실무담당
"	WIPO 주재관	김 준 규	대 표 실무 및 본부청훈 및 보고 담당
"	사 무 관	이 찬 우	대 표 대표단 활동의 실무준비

0199

3. 세부여행일정 및 주요활동계획서

일 자	시 간	일 정	비 고
10.14 (월)	12 : 40	서울 발 (KE 901)	
	18 : 10	파리 착	
	20 : 45	파리 발 (SR 729)	
	21 : 45	제네바 착	
15 (화)		UR/TRIPs 대책회의	
16 (수) / 22 (화)		UR/TRIPs 회의	
23 (수)	18 : 05	제네바 발 (AF 969)	국장. 이찬우
	19 : 10	파리 착	
	20 : 30	파리 발 (KE 902)	
24 (목)	17 : 30	서울 착	
22 (화)	15 : 25	제네바 발 (BA 729)	권영수과장
	17 : 00	런던 착	
	20 : 30	런던 발 (KE 908)	
23 (수)	17 : 30	서울 착	

0200

4. 경비 내역

(단위 : $)

구 분	항공료	일 비	숙박비	식 비	판공비	계
국장 노영욱	2,099	275	790	506	1,000	4,670
4 급 권영수	2,127	200	594	420		3,341
5 급 이찬우	2,099	220	660	462		3,441
계	6,325	695	2,044	1,388	1,000	11,452

o 노영욱 기획관리관 (10박 11일)

- 항공료 : $ 2,099
- 일 비 : $ 25 x 11일 = $ 275
- 숙박비 : $ 79 x 10박 = $ 790
- 식 비 : $ 46 x 11일 = $ 506

계 : $ 3,670

o 권영수 국제협력담당관 (9박 10일)

- 항공료 : $ 2,127
- 일 비 : $ 20 x 10일 = $ 200
- 숙박비 : $ 66 x 9박 = $ 594
- 식 비 : $ 42 x 10일 = $ 420

계 : $ 3,341

0201

o 이찬우 사무관 (10박 11일)

- 항공료 : $ 2,099
- 일 비 : $ 20 x 11일 = $ 220
- 숙박비 : $ 66 x 10박 = $ 660
- 식 비 : $ 42 x 11일 = $ 462

계 : $ 3,441

※ 수석대표 활동을 위한 판공비 : $ 1,000

0202

훈 령 안

1. 기본입장

o 10월 회의는 11월에 제출될 최종보고서 작성을 위한 회의인 만큼 그 중요성을 인식하여 아국입장을 적극 주장하고, 선.개도국의 입장 및 동향을 파악하여 향후 협상대책 및 국내대책 마련에 참고가 되도록 함.

o 아국의 경제, 기술발전 수준에 부합되는 아국의 입장을 충분히 설명하고, 아국입장이 최종의장 보고서에 반영될 수 있도록 노력함.

o 구체적인 아국입장 제시 방향은 별첨 UR/TRIPs 협상전망 및 대책에 따름.

o 아국 관심사항외 기타사항은 협상 대세에 따라 신축적으로 대응함.

2. 세부입장

o UR/TRIPs 협상전망 및 대책 참조

0203

UR/TRIPs 협상전망 및 대책

1991. 10

특 허 청

0204

I. UR/TRIPs 협상전망

1. 최근 동향

o '91.5.24 미 행정부의 신속승인권(fast-track authority) 연장을 의회에서 승인함으로써 본격적인 협상 개시

o '91. 6.27-28 '91 1차 UR/TRIPs 회의 개최

- 합의사항
  ① 협상의 기초(basis of works): 7차 의장보고서
  ② 협상일정: '91.9.16 - 20, 2차회의 개최
  ③ 협상방법: 주요 issue 별로 논의
  . Art.73(경과규정)과 분쟁해결절차에 대해 논의

o '91.9.16-20 '91 제2차 UR/TRIPs 회의개최

- 미해결 쟁점사항중 정치적 결단이 필요한 쟁점(경과규정, 분쟁해결절차)을 보다 명확히 하는 방향으로 협의 추진

o '91.9.20 Green Room 회의

- 각 협상그룹의 협상을 가속화시켜 10월 중순 또는 11월초 까지 Brussels 회의에 제출한 Draft Final Act를 개선한 최종적인 종합초안을 마련

- 따라서 10월 회의에서는 협상그룹별로 집중적인 협상이 진행되고 이를 바탕으로 미해결 핵심쟁점사항에 대한 정치적 결단을 촉구하는 방향으로 협상이 진행될 것으로 예상

o '91.10.16-22 '91 제3차 UR/TRIPs 회의 개최 예정

2. TRIPs 협상 전망

o 10월 회의에서는 7차 의장보고서를 중심으로 세부쟁점사항에 대한 협상이 본격화되고 이를 토대로 일부 정치적 쟁점에 대해서도 협의를 촉구할 것으로 예상

o 아직, 농산물 협상등에서 선진국내의 합의가 이루어지지 않고 있으나, EC의 공동농업정책개혁안(CAP)이 확정될 경우 미국이 당초의 주장에서 다소 후퇴하여 이를 바탕으로 농산물협상을 타결할 것이라는 전망도 제시되고 있어, TRIPs 협상도 급진전할 가능성이 있음.

- '92년 예정되어 있는 미국대통령 선거등으로 92년에는 협상추진이 어렵게 되므로

. 선진국간의 극적 합의로 협상의 조기타결, 혹은

. '93년 이후까지 장기연장 되는 전망이 제시되고 있음.

- 그러나, 사무국의 조기타결 움직임이 역력함.

o 따라서 이번 10월 회의의 협상속도나 타결에 의해 TRIPs 협상뿐 아니라 모든 분야 협상의 장래가 결정될 것임.

0206

Ⅱ. '91 제2차 회의결과

1. 회의 의제

o 협정안 제73조(경과규정)에 대한 토의

o 분쟁해결절차에 대한 논의

o Brussels 회의시 논의되었던 주요 이슈에 대한 검토

o 차기회의 계획

2. 회의 결과

가. 협정안 제73조에 대한 토의

o 사무국이 좀더 나은 방법(better way)으로 73조를 재작성

나. 분쟁해결절차에 대한 논의

o 두가지 접근방식으로 다시 작성, 고위급 회의에서 결정할 계획

① GATT 분쟁해결절차 준용

- 교차보복 (cross-sectoral retaliation) 허용

② 특수절차 마련

- IP 전문가 개입
- 보복조치를 허용하지 않음.

다. Brussels 회의시 논의사항 검토

o 논의사항과 새로운 제안들에 대한 확인만 함.

라. 차기회의 계획

o 10.16 - 22 스위스 제네바에서 개최

3. 관찰 및 평가

o 협상쟁점에 대한 실질적인 토의가 이루어지지 않았음.

o GATT 사무국과 선진국에서는 협상을 연내 혹은 늦어도 내년초까지 종결 시키겠다는 목표를 갖고 추진해 나가는 인상을 줌.

- 최종 text 작성을 위해 10월 회의에서 집중적인 토의가 있을 것으로 예상

0208

Ⅲ. 협상대책안

1. 협상안의 구분

o Group A : 협상타결을 위해 선.개도국의 교량역할을 한다는 견지에서 수용이 가능한 분야

o Group B : 가능한한 우리의 입장을 표명하나 협상의 대세(타국의 지지정도)에 따라 신축적으로 대응할 분야

o Group C : 우리경제에 미치는 영향이 커서 적극적으로 우리의 입장을 주장할 분야

* 종래 Group B (입장유보)는 입장을 명확히 한다는 측면에서 조정

2. 협상대책(안)

《Group A》

GA-1. 저작물의 권리자 동의없이 공공목적이 사용하는 경우 (Public의 개념)

1) 협정안 내용

o [각국은 public 의 개념을 정상관행 (normal commercial exploitation), 권리자의 권리를 부당하게 침해않는 (unreasonably prejudices the legitimate interests of right holders) 범위내에서 국내법에 규정해야 함].

2) 협정안의 의미

o 동 조항은 각국 특히 개도국이 "공공목적(Public)" 의 개념을 이용해서 저작권자의 권리를 부당하게 제한하는 것을 가급적 축소하려는 선진국의 주장이 반영된 것임.

3) 검토의견 및 아국입장

o 우리 저작권법에서 "공공목적(Public)" 의 개념을 이용해 저작권에 제한을 두는 것은 다음과 같은 경우임.
 - 학교교육 목적을 위한 사용, 시사보도를 위한 이용, 비영리목적의 공연.방송, 시험문제로서 복제, 점자에 의한 복제등.

o 문제는 우리 저작권법에서 허용하고 있는 저작권의 제한이 협정안의 내용인 "정상관행등" 에 저촉 되는지의 여부임.

o 개도국은 자국의 사회 문화적 필요를 위해 공공목적의 사용범위를 넓히려고 하고 있으나, 우리로서는 우리 저작권법에서 인정하고 있는 공공목적 사용범위가 협정안의 "정상관행등" 에 저촉되지 않으므로 수용해도 문제가 없을 것임.

GA-2. 특허권의 보호기간

1) 협정안 내용

o [출원일로 부터 최소 20년]

2) 협정안의 의미

o 산업재산권 보호에 관해 규정하고 있는 Paris 협약처럼 보호기간에 관해 각국에 위임할 경우 각국, 특히 개도국이 자국법에 의해서특허 기간을 짧게 규정하는 것을 방지하기 위한 선진국 주장임.

3) 검토의견 및 아국입장

o 우리 특허법에 의하면, 특허권은 출원일로부터 최대 20년까지 보호 받을 수 있음.

o 그리고, WIPO 에서 추진하고 있는 특허법 Harmonization 회의에서도 추세가 "출원일로부터 최소 20년" 으로 되어가고 있음.

o 따라서, 개도국이 반대하고 있지만 개도국안 (각국에 위임)은 채택되지 않을 것으로 보며, 권리자의 보호를 통한 발명진작을 위하여 선진국안을 받아들여도 우리에게는 문제가 없음.

GA-3. 외국 유명상표 보호

1) 협정안 내용

o 유명상표는 보호되어야 하며, 유명성 여부의 판단은 관련업계에 알려진 정도, [국제교역 증대에 따라 알려진 정도]에 의해 해야 함.

2) 협정안의 의미

o 상표란, 보호받고자 하는 국가에 등록을 받아야 보호되는 것이나, 등록하지 않아도, 유명한 상표는 그 유명성에 편승하는 자를 막고 소비자의 혼동을 막기 위해 보호하는 것임.

o 동 조항은 이 유명성을 어떤 기준에 의해 판단할 것인가의 문제와 관련한 것임.

3) 검토의견 및 아국입장

o 산업재산권 보호를 위한 Paris 협약에는 유명상표로써 보호 받으려면 보호받고자 하는 국가내에서 유명해야 한다고 규정하고 있으나,

o 우리의 경우 '86년 한.미 양해각서에 의해 외국에서만 유명해도 유명상표로써 보호해 준다고 약속한 바 있으며, 이를 심사기준에 반영하여 실시해오고 있음.

o 따라서, 선진국의 주장에 대해 반대하기 어려운 입장이며 실질적으로 국제교역이 활발해 짐에 따라 외국의 유명상표가 우리 소비자에게 신속히 알려지고 있어서 이러한 유명성에 편승하려는 국내업자를 규제할 필요성이 있고, 외국에서 우리 상표의 보호를 증진한다는 점에서 선진국의 주장을 받아들여도 문제가 없을 것임.

GA-4. 입증책임의 전환 요건

1) 협정안 내용

o 제법특허 침해소송에 있어서 입증책임의 전환요건은 다음 두가지중 최소한 하나의 경우에 인정 [해야 한다 (shall)] [할수 있다 (may)]

- 제법으로 만들어진 물질이 새로운 (처음 시판된) 것인 경우;
- 제법간에 실질적 유사성 (substantial likelihood)이 있는 경우

2) 협정안의 의미

o 동 조항은 물질을 만드는 방법(제법)에 대한 특허에 관한 침해소송이 발생했을 경우, 권리자를 보호하기 위해 침해하지 않았다는 것을 피고가 입증하게 하는 내용과 관련된 것임.

3) 검토의견 및 아국입장

o 우리법에서는 제법으로 만들어진 물질이 새로운 것 (처음 시판된 것)에만 입증책임의 전환을 인정해 주고 있음.

o 미국.EC등 선진국은 두가지 경우 모두 인정하고 있고 TRIPs협정이 minimum standard 를 규정하고 있으므로 제법간에 실질적 유사성이 있는 경우가 삭제된다고 해도 미국.EC등 선진국의 법을 바꾸라고 주장할 수 없음.

- 따라서, 주장의 실익이 없음.

o 그리고, TRIPs 협정이 최소한 하나 이상의 경우에 (at least one of the following circumstances) 체약국이 입증책임의 전환을 인정해야 한다는 규정이므로, 우리가 새로운 것 (처음 시판된 것)인 경우에만 인정해도 협정상의 의무와 배치되지 않으므로 문제가 없음.

GA-5. 대여권 (보상청구권)

1) 협정안 내용

o 최소한 음반, 컴퓨터 프로그램, 영상저작물에 대해 대여행위에 대한 허가 금지권 [또는 보상청구권] 인정

* Brussels 회의시 제안

- 보상청구권은 자국내에서 보상청구권을 설정하고 있는 나라에 대하여 이를 인정

- 대여허가, 금지권 혹은 보상청구권으로 규정하는 대신에 "대여에 관한 권리"로 규정

2) 협정안의 의미

o 대여업의 성행으로 원 저작물의 판매가 축소되어 권리자의 권리가 사실상 제한되므로 대여권을 인정해서 권리자의 권리를 보호하고자 하는 선진국의 주장임.

3) 검토의견 및 아국입장

o 개도국과 함께 권리소진이론 (권리자의 의사에 의해 한번 판매된 이후에 그 물건에 대해서는 권리를 주장할 수 없음)에 의거해서 반대해 왔으나,

o 종전에 반대입장을 취하던 국가(일본, 맥시코등)가 지지로 입장을 바꾸고 있어 계속 반대하기는 어려움.

o 그리나 대여행위에 대한 허가금지권을 인정할 경우 권리자 (주로 외국 권리자)에 의한 대여업의 직접적인 franchising 이 가능하게 되어 우리의 대여업이 몰락할 우려가 있음.

o 따라서, 대여권을 인정하되 대여허가, 금지권이 아니라 대여행위에 대한 보상청구권으로 인정하는 방향으로 타협 모색

- 보상청구권을 인정한다 해도 큰 문제가 없을 것임.

0214

《Group B》

GB-1. 권리남용 및 반경쟁적 행위 (개도국 주장)

1) 협정안 내용

o [체약국이 국내법에 license 계약시 발생가능한 권리남용 및 반경쟁적 행위의 유형을 규정하고 이에 대해 계약실효등 적절한 규제조치를 취할 수 있음. 이러한 반경쟁적 행위의 유형으로는 price fixing, 특허기간 만료후 royalty 지급등 (14가지) 임.]

- Brussels 시 새로운 제안 (사무국안)

본 협정의 어느것도 특정한 경우에 권리남용 및 반경쟁적 행위를 구성하는 계약관행 및 조건을 국내법에 규정하는 것을 막을 수 없음. 각 체약국은 그러한 관행을 막거나 규제할 수 있는 적절한 조치를 취할 수 있으며, 그러한 관행으로는 grant-back, tie-in, 특허 유효성에 대한 도전 제한등임.

2) 협정안의 의미

o 개도국 (특히, 인도등 내수시장 기반이 큰 개도국)의 주장으로 조약에 반경쟁적 행위의 유형을 규정하고 이것이 반경쟁적 행위라는 이유로 규제조치를 취함으로써 선진국의 쌍무적 압력을 피하기 위한 주장임.

3) 검토의견 및 아국입장

o 현재 개도국이 제안하고 있는 내용중 국내 공정거래제도상 국제계약에 현재 적용되고 있는 부분이 있고, 또 그 존속이 필요한 사정이기 때문에 개도국 제안을 전면적으로 반대할 수는 없음.

o 그러므로, 동 항목에 대하여 적극적으로 개도국의 의견을 반대 또는 지지하는 입장을 표명하는 것은 유보하고 협상진행 상황을 계속 관찰하면서 아국입장을 표명함.

o 특히, 현행 협정안 보다 각 체약국에 유연성(flexibility)을 많이 주고 있는 Brussels 회의시의 제안에 대해서는 각국의 입장을 살피고 협상의 대세에 따라 지지하는 입장을 표명함.

GB-2. 분쟁예방절차 (아국제안)

1) 주요내용

o 특허, know-how licence 계약시 반경쟁적 행위가 있을 경우 계약당사자는 정부를 통해 TRIPs 위원회에 심의 요청

o TRIPs 위원회는 특허, know-how licence 계약에 대한 guideline 을 제정하고 위원회 산하에 Licence Review Board 를 설치

o Licence Review Board 는 guideline 에 의해 기술이전 계약 내용을 심의하고 advisory opinion 을 제시함.

o advisory opinion 은 체약국을 구속하지 않지만 계약당사자가 동 의견에 따르는 것은 자유임.

2) 의 미

o 특허등 기술이전 계약에 대해 심의할 수 있도록 함으로써 선진국의 기술을 합리적인 조건으로 이전 받을 수 있고,

o 발생 가능한 분쟁을 사전에 예방하고자 하는 내용임.

3) 검토의견 및 아국입장

o 9월 회의시 제안설명을 했으나 전반적인 분위기는 기본적인 idea 는 좋으나 실효성과 국가간 분쟁해결절차와의 관계에 대한 질의가 지배적이었음.

o 따라서, 10월 회의시 아국제안을 다시한번 제기하여 주장할 필요는 있으며, 각국의 동향(협사의 대세)에 따라 최소한 협정안 8조 2항에 사기업간의 분쟁예방절차 설치를 검토할 수 있음" 이 포함되도록 주장함.

12 0216

GB-3. 분쟁해결절차

1) 협정안 내용

o Text Ⅰ : GATT/UR 분쟁해결절차 그룹의 결과를 준용하되 IPR 의 전문성을 감안하여 TRIPs 위원회에 의해 선정된 IPR 전문가가 중개, 화해, 조정, panel 절차에 개입 (cross-sectoral retaliation 허용)

o Text Ⅱ : IPR 전문가가 분쟁해결 절차에 개입할 수 있는 특별절차 마련 sanction 은 허용 않음.

o Text Ⅲ : GATT/UR 분쟁해결절차 그룹의 결과를 그대로 준용 (cross-sectoral retaliation 허용)

2) 협정안의 의미

o Text I (콜럽비아.우루과이.뉴질랜드), Text Ⅱ (개도국), Text Ⅲ (미국) 의 주장으로 GATTability 문제와 직접 연관

3) 검토의견 및 아국입장

o GATTability 를 인정하면서 cross-sectoral retaliation 을 허용하지 않는다고 하는 것은 논리상 어려운 점이 있으나, cross-sectoral retaliation 을 인정할 경우 일반상품 교역에의 영향을 우려, cross-sectoral retaliation 인정을 반대

o 그러나, 선진국 및 개도국 일부 (콜롬비아, 우루과이등) 도 cross-sectoral retaliation 을 인정하자는 입장이므로 가능한한 협상의 동향에 따라 우리입장을 표명

GB-4. 권리소진 이론

1) 미측 주장

o 국제적인 권리소진 (병렬수입)에 관한 언급 삭제
(Omission of any reference of international exhaustion
(i.e. parallel importation))

2) 주장의 의미

o 권리소진 (exhaustion of rights)은 권리자가 일단 한번 판매하거나 license 한 그 지적재산권에는 권리자가 권리를 주장할 수 없다는 이론으로 이것은 병렬수입 (parallel importation) 허용여부와 밀접한 관련을 갖고 있음.

- 국제적인 권리소진이 인정되면 권리자가 일단 한번 판매하거나 license 한 지적재산권 관련 물품의 수출입에 권리를 주장할 수 없게 되므로, 병렬수입이 허용되고 권리소진이 부정되면 병렬수입이 금지되기 때문임.

- 병렬수입의 예를 크게 두가지로 나눌 수 있음.

① 미국의 특허권자(상표권자) A로 부터 license 를 받은 한국의 甲이 그 기술(상표)을 이용 생산한 제품을 미국에 역수출 혹은 제3국에 수출한 경우

② 벤츠자동차 상표의 license 를 받은 (주)한성이 벤츠자동차를 본사로 부터 수입하고 있는데 타업자가 외국의 자동차 dealer 로 부터 벤츠자동차를 직수입하는 경우

14

0218

3) 검토의견 및 아국입장

o 1국 1 특허의 원칙 (권리는 당해국가에 한정됨)에 따라 국내적인 권리 소진은 국제협약에 의해 인정되는 것임.

o 국제적 권리소진을 주장하는 국가는 수출에 중점을 두고 있는 국가 (홍콩, 싱가폴등) 임.

o 병렬수입의 사례중 ①의 경우는 실제 미국의 권리자가 한국의 甲에게 license 를 줄때 개별 licence 계약에 판매지역 제한등이 명시되므로, 국제협약에 규정하거나 일관된 원칙을 정할 수 는 없음.

- 따라서 이 경우는 개별 licence 계약에 의해 판단되어야 하며, 그 계약에 독점적인 내용이 있는 경우에는 규제되어야 함.

o ②의 경우는 다음 두측면이 있음.

- 병렬수입이 금지되었을 경우 독점이 발생하므로 소비자보호, 공정거래 차원에서 문제가 생길 수 있음.

- 병렬수입이 인정되었을 경우는 국내 licencee 보호의 차원에서 문제가 생길 수 있으며, 기술적용 수준 차이로 직수입품과 국내 생산품의 품질 차이가 발생하여 국내시장에 동일상표의 다른 품질의 상품이 혼재, 소비자 혼동을 불러 일으킬 수 있음.

o 따라서, 소비자의 편의도모, 상품종류의 다양화, 판매가격의 하락 등을 고려할때 국제적인 권리소진 원칙 (병렬수입)을 인정하는 것이 전체적으로 이익이 클 것임.

GB-5. 특허의 강제실시권 실시범위

1) 협정안 내용

o 국내수요 충족만을 위해 실시

2) 협정안의 의미

o 강제실시권 (Non-voluntary licence)은 일정한 요건(특허발명의 불실시 또는 불충분한 실시, 이용발명등)에 해당되어 필요한 경우에 권리자의 동의 없이 정부가 직접 혹은 제3자로 하여금 그 특허발명을 실시할 수 있도록 하는 제도임.

o 동 조항은 이런 이유로 강제실시권이 발동되었을 때 강제실시권에 의해 생산된 제품을 수출을 할수 있느냐의 문제와 관련된 것임.

3) 검토의견 및 아국입장

o '91.9.26 - 28 한.EC 협상시 '95년 부터 '신약재심사' 제도 도입키로 합의

- copy product에 대한 제조허가 신청시 full set of data를 제출하도록 되어 있음.

- 물론, 임상실험자료 전체를 제출하도록 하는 제도는 아니나, TRIPs 협정안에서도 제조허가를 위한 자료 (undisclosed test or other data)를 보호 해달라는 것이므로 실질적인 차이가 없음.

o '95년 부터 신약 재심사제도를 도입하게 되어 있으므로 TRIPs 협정이 아국에 적용되는 시점이 문제가 될수 있으나 최악의 경우 TRIPs 협정이 '92년 부터 발효하고 경과기간이 2년이라고 하면 1년의 차이 밖에 없음.

o 따라서, 경과기간을 최대한 확보하도록 노력하고 동 사항에 대해서는 협상의 대세에 따라 아국입장을 표명하도록 함.

16 0220

《Group C》

GC-1. 컴퓨터 프로그램 보호의 방법 (어문저작물로 보호 여부)

1) 협정안 내용

o 컴퓨터 프로그램을 베른협약하의 [어문(literary)] 저작물로 보호

2) 협정안의 의미

o 컴퓨터 프로그램을 어떠한 방법으로 보호할 것인가의 문제임.

3) 검토의견 및 아국입장

o 우리는 컴퓨터 프로그램을 저작권법이 아닌 특별법으로 보호하고 있음.

o 컴퓨터 프로그램을 어문저작물로 분류하여 저작권에 포함시킬 경우 현재 국내에서 컴퓨터 프로그램에 인정되는 대여권, 강제사용허락 제도와 상충되고 베른협약 가입시의 소급효 인정등 문제가 있다는 것이 과기처의 의견임.

o 따라서, 컴퓨터 프로그램과 어문저작물의 특성차이(기술성, 산업연관성등)를 이유로 반대입장을 표명.

GC-2. MFN 의 예외

1) 협정안 내용

o MFN 의 예외

(a) - (c)

(d) 한 체약국이 가입한 국제협정에 의해 TRIPs 협정보다 높은 대우를 하는 경우. 단, 그러한 협정은 모든 체약국에 개방되어 있거나 이익의 확대를 위해 선의의 협상을 개시할 준비가 되어 있어야 함.

2) 검토의견 및 아국입장

o (d) 항을 근거로 하여

- 미국은 TRIPs 협상이 미국이 요구하는 수준으로 타결되지 않을 경우, 양자협상을 통해 높은 수준의 지적재산권 보호규범을 제정하고자 하는 미국의 목표를 달성하려고 함.

- EC 도 EC 통합후 역내에서 높은 수준의 보호기준을 규정하는 협정을 체결하려고 있음.

o 따라서, 이 조항은 MFN 원칙에 정면으로 배치되고 지적재산권 문제를 다자간 차원에서 해결하려는 TRIPs 협상의 기본정신에 위배되며, 향후 예상되는 선진국의 양자간 압력을 정당화하는 문제점이 있으므로 반대

o 개도국을 중심으로 (d) 항을 반대하는 입장이 일고 있으므로 TRIPs 협상의 명분을 들어 충분히 반대 가능

GC-3. 정부제출자료의 공개금지

1) 협정안 내용

o [의약, 농약 제조허가시 제출된 기술자료를 최소 5년간 타 경쟁업자가 원용(rely on)할 수 없도록 함.]

2) 검토의견 및 아국입장

o '91.9.26 - 28 한.EC 협상시 '95년부터 "신약재심사 제도" 도입키로 합의

- 정부에 제출하는 자료는 pre-clinic test data와 clinic test data 로 구분할 수 있음.

- 신약 재심사제도에 의하면,

. 최초 제조허가 신청자는 pre-clinic과 clinic test data 를 모두 제출하고

. 후에 copy product에 대해 제조허가를 신청하는 업자는 clinic test data만 제출하게 되어 있음.

- 따라서, 신약재심사 제도에 의해서도 후신청 업자는 pre-clinic test data를 사실상 원용하게 되는 것임.

o 아국 제약업계의 현실상 copy product를 제조하는 것이 현실이며, 협정안에 의해 pre-clinic test data 까지 제출하게 한다면 아국업계에 타격이 클 것으로 예상

o 따라서, 협정안이 사실상 추가적인 독점권을 부여한다는 이유로 반대함.

GC-4. 경과규정

1) 협정안 내용

o TRIPs 협정 발효시점에 이미 존재하고 있는 대상 (public domain 에 있는 것) 은 TRIPs 협정상의 Part II(보호기준) 의 규정을 적용하지 않음.

2) 협정안의 의미

o 동 조항은, 우리가 미국에 대해 취해주고 있는 pipeline products 보호의 대 EC, 대일 동등대우 문제와 연관

- 대미조치(P.P) 가 TRIPs 의 MFN(최혜국대우) 원칙에 의해 자동확산 의무를 지게 되나,

- P.P 보호대상 품목은 public domain (공중의 영역 즉, 대상은 존재하나 아국에 물질특허 제도가 없어서 보호되지 않고 있었기 때문에 공중이 자유롭게 사용할 수 있는것) 에 해당되므로 public domain 에 있는 것은 TRIPs 협정의 일정 부분을 적용않는다고 함으로써 조약에 의한 확대적용 의무를 벗을 수도 있기 때문임.

3) 검토의견 및 아국입장

o 우리가 미국에 대해 취해주고 있는 pipeline products 보호조치의 대 EC, 대일 동등대우 문제와 연관됨.

o EC와 협상이 타결되었다 하더라도 일본, EFTA 국가에게 동 조치를 해줄수 없으므로 종전보다 주장의 실익이 감소했다 하더라도 MFN에 의해 타국에 자동 확산되는 것은 막아야 할 것임.

o 따라서, 우리의 입장을 표명하여 Part I의 규정도 적용하지 않는다고 주장해야 할 것임.

GC-5. 불특허대상

1) 협정안 내용

o 다음의 경우를 특허대상(patentability)에서 제외할 수 있음 (may)

- (a) 동물, 인간의 치료방법
- [(b)A 동물발명 및 변종은 불특허대상, 식물변종은 특별법 혹은 특허로 보호]
- [(b)B 동물, 식물, 미생물 발명]
- [(c)B 공서양속위반발명, 보건.국방등을 위한 발명]
- [(d)B 핵전환 제법에 의한 발명]

2) 협정안의 의미

o TRIPs 에서 가장 중요한 세가지 정치적 쟁점중의 하나 (patentability, 강제실시권, GATTability)로 아직 합의에 이르지 못하고 대안만 열거된 것임.

3) 검토의견 및 아국입장

o 우리법에서는 불특허대상으로 공서양속 위반 발명, 식물변종 일부(유성생식 식물), 핵전환 제법에 의한 발명, 동물발명 및 변종 (명문의 규정은 없음) 이며, TRIPs 협상에서도 입장은 동일함.

- 공서양속 위반발명은 선.개도국간에도 합의가 이루어지고 있고,

- 핵전환 제법에 의한 발명과 동물발명 및 변종에 대해서도 이를 인정하고 있는 국가가 적으며,

- 식물변종 일부 (유성생식 식물)은 주곡과 관계되기 때문에 인정하고 있는 국가도 적으며, 특허로 인정하기 위해서는 농업정책적 판단이 필요함.

  . 예를들어 씨(품종)의 경우 새로운 품종에 대해 특허로 보호할 경우 매년 농민이 영리목적으로 수확하여 판매한 것에 대해 royalty 를 지급해야 하는 문제가 발생

  . 따라서 이 가능성을 배제하기 위해 특별법 (식물품종보호법)으로 보호하는 방법이 UPOV (식물변종 보호에 관한 국제동맹)에서 추진되고 있으므로 이에 따르면 될 것임.

0226

GC-6. 대여권 (대여금지권)

1) 협정안 내용

o 최소한 음반, 컴퓨터 프로그램, 영상저작물에 대해 대여행위에 대한 허가 금지권 [또는 보상청구권] 인정

o Brussels 회의시 제안

- 보상청구권은 자국내에서 보상청구권을 설정하고 있는 나라에 대하여 인정

- 허가.금지권 혹은 보상청구권 대신에 "대여에 관한 권리" 로 규정

2) 협정안의 의미

o GA-5 와 동일

3) 검토의견 및 아국입장

o 대여행위에 대한 허가금지권까지 인정할 경우 권리자(주로 외국권리자)에 의한 대여업의 직접적인 franchising 이 가능하게 되어 우리의 대여업이 몰락할 우려가 있으므로 계속 반대.

o 다만, 보상청구권으로 타협 모색

o 아국주장이 관철되지 않을 경우 최소한 Brussles 회의시 제안된 바와 같이 허가, 금지권으로 규정하지 않고 "대여에 관한 권리" 로 규정

- 국내법에 유연성을 부여함.

GC-7. 컴퓨터 프로그램의 보호범위 (idea 등의 보호)

1) 협정안 내용

o [동 보호는 idea, 절차, 운영방법 혹은 수학적 관념에는 미치지 않음]

2) 협정안의 의미

o 컴퓨터 프로그램의 보호범위가 어디까지 미치느냐의 문제임.

3) 검토의견 및 아국입장

o CP 보호는 CP 의 표현만 보호하는 것이지 그 속의 idea 등을 보호하는 것이 아님.

o idea등 까지 보호 해준다면 현행법 및 국제관례에서 인정되고 있는 reverse engineering (역분해 or 역조작) 에 의한 새로운 프로그램 개발이 영원히 불가능 해지게 됨.

o 따라서, idea 등 까지 보호해주는 것은 계속 반대해야 할 것임.

GC-8. 음반소급보호

1) 협정안 내용

o [TRIPs 협정 발효시 존재하고 있는 음반 보호]

2) 협정안의 의미

o 음반을 TRIPs 협정에 의해 소급보호 하겠다는 의미

3) 검토의견 및 아국입장

o 음반에 관한 관련 국제협약에서 불소급보호 원칙을 천명하고 있고,

- 저작인접권 보호에 관한 Rome 협약 (20조)
- 음반협약 (7조 3항)

o 우리의 입장을 지지하는 국가가 많으므로 관철 가능

GC-9. IC 보호

1) 협정안 내용

o [IC chip 이 들어 있는 최종제품 까지 보호]

o [권리를 침해한 IC chip 인줄 모르고 (선의로) 구매한 업자는 royalty 지급 의무가 없음. 그러나 침해사실의 통고가 있고난 뒤 기존 재고품, 주문품의 사용에 대해서는 royalty 를 지급해야 함]

2) 협정안의 의미

o IC 배치설계권 (layout-design) 을 어디까지 확대할 것인가의 보호범위와

o 선의로 IC chip 을 구매한 사람의 royalty 지급 의무를 어디까지 면책할 것인가의 문제임.

3) 검토내용 및 아국입장

① 보호범위

o IC 보호를 최종제품 (end product or assembled product) 까지 확대하면 IC chip 이 들어있는 모든 공산품에 영향을 미침.

ex) 컴퓨터는 물론 자동차, 항공기 등에 IC 권리를 침해한 IC chip 하나만 들어 있어도 그 제품 전체가 침해물품으로 간주되어 유통정지, 통관(수출입) 정지가 가능하게 됨.

o 따라서, 최종제품 까지 확대하는 것은 계속 반대해야 하며 그 논리로서는 다음과 같음.

- IC 를 보호하고 있는 국가 18개국 중 최종제품을 보호하고 있는 나라는 미국, 일본 뿐이므로 TRIPs 에서 규정하고자 하는 minimum standard 가 아니라 maximum standard 임.

- IC chip 과 최종제품 과는 현격한 가격 차이가 나는데 IC chip 을 이유로 최종제품의 유통, 수출이 정지되면 GATT 의 목적인 자유교역 증진과도 배치됨.

- 침해한 IC chip 은 손쉽게 제거 가능함 등.

② 선의구매자

o 선의의 IC 구매자에 대한 보상책임을 인정하는 것은 다음과 같은 논리로 반대

- 권리침해자는 선의로 IC 를 구매해 최종제품을 만든 업자가 아니고 IC Chip 제조자임.

- IC chip 시장의 90% 이상을 차지하고 있는 memory chip 의 경우 정상제품과 권리를 침해한 IC 간의 가격 차이는 거의 없으므로 선의 IC 구매자는 권리침해의 직접적인 수혜자 (beneficiary) 가 아님.

- memory chip 생산 판매를 위해서는 막대한 설비 투자와 광고가 필요하므로 권리를 침해한 IC chip 제조자를 찾아내기 쉬움.

- 현재의 규정으로는 권리자가 IC chip 제조업자와 선의 구매자에게 royalty 를 이중청구할 수 있는 길이 열려 있어 문제임.
  . 보호범위와 연결하여 선의구매자가 제조한 제품을 유통, 수출입정지하고 난뒤 청구하면 선의구매자가 royalty 를 지급하지 않을수 없음.

o 따라서, 선의 구매자는 면책하고, 적어도 침해사실 통고 이후 기존 재고품, 주문품의 사용에 대해서 보상의무를 지지 않도록 해야 함.
- 그리고 침해사실 통고도 sufficient notice 가 되도록 해야 함.

GC-10. 경과기간

1) 미측주장

o 경과기간 2년 (Countries should agree to implement the agreement within a period not to exceed two years)

2) 주장의 의미

o TRIPs 협정을 체결후 2년내 국내에 적용해야 한다는 의미

3) 검토내용 및 아국입장

o 현행 TRIPs 협정에 경과기간은 X 년, X+Y 년(개도국), X+Y+Z 년(저개발국)으로 규정되어 있음.

- 미국의 주장은 X 를 2년으로 하자는 주장임.

o 우리가 개도국의 경과기간인 X+Y 년으로 적용될 수 있으면 문제가 없으나 실제 우리가 개도국으로 적용될 수 있느냐의 여부는 신중히 판단해야 할 문제임.

o 따라서 X 년을 2년이상 확보하는데 주력해야 할 것임.

GC-11. 국경조치 적용범위

1) 협정안 내용

o 위조상표 부착상품, 저작권 침해물품에 대해서는 세관에서 통관유예조치를 취한다 (shall)

o 기타 지적재산권 침해 물품에도 동 조치를 확대할 수 있다 (may)

2) 협정안의 의미

o 현재 미국 관세법 337조와 유사한 절차를 어느 범위까지 적용할 것인가의 문제임.

3) 검토의견 및 아국입장

o 상표권, 저작권 이외 다른 지적재산권 침해물품에도 적용할 경우 손쉬운 통관유예조치의 남발로 우리 수출에 막대한 지장 우려

o 따라서, 온건선진국, 개도국과 연계하여

- 특허권, IC 등 타 지적재산권의 경우 침해여부 판단이 어려운 것이며,

- 이를 비전문인인 세관이 판단하여 통관유예조치를 발동하는 것은 동 조치의 남발로 자유무역에 장애를 줄것이라는 이유로 계속 반대

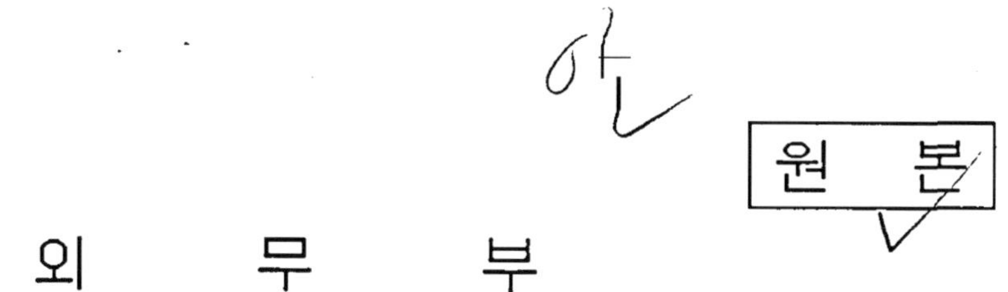

원 본

외 무 부

종 별 : 지 급

번 호 : GVW-2742 일 시 : 91 1219 1930

수 신 : 장 관 (통기,경기원,상공부,보사부,문화부,과기처, 특허청)

발 신 : 주 제네바 대사

제 목 : UR/TRIPS 10더하기 10 비공식 회의

0 12.18(수) 21:30 ANELL 의장 주재로 개최된 표제회의의 주요 내용을 하기 보고함.

0 ANELL 의장은 17(화), 18(수) 양일에 걸쳐 몇가지쟁점 (GATTABILITY, 지리적표시, 73 조)에 대한 PRIVATE CONSULTATION 이 개최되었음을 밝히고 현재까지의 협상결과를 반영하여 작성한 협정초안 DRAFT 를 제시 (저작권, 지리적 표시, 특허, 영업비밀, 반경쟁적 행위, 시행절차,분쟁해결 절차, 경과기간, 경과규정등)하고 이에대해 각국의 의견을 문의함.

- 이집트는 제시된 DRAFT 에 개도국에 대한 충분한 고려가 되어 있지 않다고 지적하였으며, 인도는 타협상분야와의 DEAL 을 위한 PACKAGE가 없다고 지적하였음.

- 싱가폴, 홍콩이 PRIVATE CONSULTATION 과 관련하여 협상의 PROCESS 에 대해 의문을 표시하자 ANELL의장은 PRIVATE CONSULTATION 에서 쟁점에 대한 합의가 이루어진바 없으며, 현재의 DRAFT 는 현재까지 이루어진 협상의 결과를 반영하여 의장의 분석 (ASSESSMENT)을 통해 본인의책임 (RESPONSIBILITY)하에 작성되었다고 언급함.

0 세부사항에 대한 각국의 논평과 찬반의사표명이 있었으나, 부분적인 수정외에는 변화가 이루어지지 않았음.

0 아국 관심사항에 대한 논의내용은 다음과같음.

- 저작권분야: 대여권이 허가, 금지권으로 규정되어 있는데 대해 아국 및 개도국이 보상 청구권으로 되어야 한다고 주장하였으나, ANELL 의장은 대여권의 요건인 침해 사실의 증명을 권리자가하도록 규정함으로써 권리의 균형을 이루었다고 언급하고 현재의 DRAFT 를 그대로 제시하겠다고함.

- 특허: 불특허 대상에 관한 DRAFT 가 수술 진단방법, 동.식물 발병으로 한정되어

통상국 2차보 보사부 문화부 경기원 상공부 과기처 특허청

PAGE 1 91.12.20 09:50 WG

외신 1과 통제관

0234

있는 것에대해 개도국은 의약등 물질 발명을 불특허대상으로 추가할 것으로 주장하고, 미국은 불특허대상을 더 축소할 것을 주장함.

. 이에 의장은 현재의 DRAFT 를 제시할 것임을 다시 언급함.

- 영업비밀 : 정부제출 임상실험 자료를 불공정관행 (UNFAIR COMMERCIAL USE) 으로 부터 보호한다는 DRAFT 에 대해 개도국이 기간 제한이 없는 (OPEN.ENDED) 보호라고 반발하자, 의장이 구체적인기간 명시에 대해 논평할 것을 요청함.

. 선진국은 최소 5년, 개도국은 최대 5년을 주장하였으며, 의장이 최소 5년으로 할 뜻을 비추자

. 개도국은 최소 5년 보다는 기간 제한을 명시않는것이 바람직하다고 주장하여, 현재의 DRAFT로 할것이 결정됨.

- 시행절차: 국경조치의 SAFEGUARD (공탁금을 예치하고 통관 정지 물품을 통관 가능)에 대해 일본의 반대가 있었으나, 현재의 DRAFT 대로 제시하기로 함.

- 분쟁해결 절차: UR 전체의 통일된 분쟁해결 절차가 마련되면 그 절차에 따르기로 함.

- 경과기간: 개도국은 자국의 경제, 사회적 상황, 급격한 지적재산권 보호제도 변화의 불가피성을 들어 최소 10년 이상의 경과기간 및 특허대상, 경제실시권의 규정은 몇년 (5년)간 적용하지 않을수 있도록 할 것을 주장하였으나, 미, EC,스위스는 TRIPS협정의 적용이 최소 5년 내에 이루어져야 함을 주장

. 의장이 개도국의 기준에 대해 질의하자 EC 가 WORLD BANK 의 LOW-INCOME 개도국 기준으로 할것을 주장하자, 아국 및 BRAZIL 등 개도국은 UR전체적인 차원에서 결정되어야 할 것임을 주장

. 이에 의장은 논의결과를 충분히 반영하여 결정하겠다고 함.

- 경과규정: QUAD GROUP 의 DRAFT 를 일부 수정한 내용을 의장이 채택하자, 인도, 브라질등은 동 규정이 전체적인 PACKAGE 에 관련 있음을 들어 입장을 유보함. 끝

(대사 박수길-국장)

외교문서 비밀해제: 우루과이라운드2 17
우루과이라운드 지적재산권 협상

초판인쇄 2024년 03월 15일
초판발행 2024년 03월 15일

지은이 한국학술정보(주)
펴낸이 채종준
펴낸곳 한국학술정보(주)
주 소 경기도 파주시 회동길 230(문발동)
전 화 031-908-3181(대표)
팩 스 031-908-3189
홈페이지 http://ebook.kstudy.com
E-mail 출판사업부 publish@kstudy.com
등 록 제일산-115호(2000. 6. 19)

ISBN 979-11-7217-119-3 94340
979-11-7217-102-5 94340 (set)

책에 대한 더 나은 생각, 끊임없는 고민, 독자를 생각하는 마음으로 보다 좋은 책을 만들어갑니다.